OECD Factbook 2005

ECONOMIC, ENVIRONMENTAL
AND SOCIAL STATISTICS

ORGANISATION FOR ECONOMIC CO-OPERATION AND DEVELOPMENT

ORGANISATION FOR ECONOMIC CO-OPERATION AND DEVELOPMENT

The OECD is a unique forum where the governments of 30 democracies work together to address the economic, social and environmental challenges of globalisation. The OECD is also at the forefront of efforts to understand and to help governments respond to new developments and concerns, such as corporate governance, the information economy and the challenges of an ageing population. The Organisation provides a setting where governments can compare policy experiences, seek answers to common problems, identify good practice and work to co-ordinate domestic and international policies.

The OECD member countries are: Australia, Austria, Belgium, Canada, the Czech Republic, Denmark, Finland, France, Germany, Greece, Hungary, Iceland, Ireland, Italy, Japan, Korea, Luxembourg, Mexico, the Netherlands, New Zealand, Norway, Poland, Portugal, the Slovak Republic, Spain, Sweden, Switzerland, Turkey, the United Kingdom and the United States. The Commission of the European Communities takes part in the work of the OECD.

OECD Publishing disseminates widely the results of the Organisation's statistics gathering and research on economic, social and environmental issues, as well as the conventions, guidelines and standards agreed by its members.

HULL LIBRARIES	
54072 01110537	
Bertrams	04.11.05
(31)	£35.00

This work is published on the responsibility of the Secretary-General of the OECD. The opinions expressed and arguments employed herein do not necessarily reflect the official views of the Organisation or of the governments of its member countries.

Also available in French under the title:
Les statistiques de l'OCDE 2005
ÉCONOMIE, ENVIRONNEMENT ET SOCIÉTÉ

© OECD 2005

No reproduction, copy, transmission or translation of this publication may be made without written permission. Applications should be sent to OECD Publishing: rights@oecd.org or by fax (33 1) 45 24 13 91. Permission to photocopy a portion of this work should be addressed to the Centre français d'exploitation du droit de copie, 20, rue des Grands-Augustins, 75006 Paris, France (contact@cfcopies.com).

OECD Factbook 2005

FOREWORD

This *OECD Factbook 2005* is the first truly horizontal statistiscal publication of the OECD. It draws on the full range of data available within the Organisation, including data from two agencies affiliated to the OECD: *the International Energy Agency (IEA)* and *the European Conference of Ministries of Transport (ECMT)*.

The great physicist Niels Bohr once declared "*Nothing exists until it is measured*". We would suggest that environmental, economic and social challenges exist, but they certainly cannot be managed unless they are measured.

Statistics represent critical information for policy-makers but, as Albert Einstein famously declared, "*Information is not knowledge*". However, statistics represent the raw material for the creation of knowledge, just as steel represents the raw material for the manufacture of automobiles. But it is also knowledge that takes steel and turns it into an automobile, and it is knowledge which takes the raw material of statistics and turns it into understanding and interpretation, and in a further stage into policy. Hence, the very apt title of the Palermo Conference that the OECD organised in November 2004, with the support of the Italian Government: "*Statistics, Knowledge and Policy*".

Why this *Factbook*? Because governments pursue different economic, social and environmental policies, and it is extremely valuable to policy-makers and to the general public to compare cross-country data which they know to be comparable and reliable. For these statistics to have a real value in an international context, they must be comparable. And one of the strengths of the OECD has been to put national statistics on an internationally comparable basis.

That is what the OECD *Factbook* aims to do. Specifically it is intended to:
- meet the needs of a wide range of users in the form of a one-stop resource containing broadly based, comparative, country-based, economic, social and environmental data;
- build a product that enhances the visibility of OECD statistical work for a global audience;
- help users to assess the position and the performance of a single country *vis-à-vis* a broader universe of countries with reference to different statistical series;
- highlight measurement issues, including areas where the comparability of statistics across countries remains weak.

The OECD Factbook will be an annual publication. Each year, it will include a section dedicated to a specific issue. Given the recent evolution of the oil market, the special section in the 2005 volume deals with energy statistics, and reports on long-term developments in energy prices, production, consumption, CO_2 emissions and renewable energy sources. This section has been provided by the *International Energy Agency*.

The tables of the OECD Factbook 2005 are available on line at *new.sourceoecd.org/factbook/*.

The *OECD Factbook* reflects the work of statistical staff throughout the Organisation and was developed in co-operation with the *Directorate for Public Affairs and Communications*. The *Statistics Directorate*, which has coordinated the project, is grateful for the co-operation of the many staff members involved, but of course, this publication would not have been possible without the concerted efforts of statisticians from all member countries who have worked, over many years, to develop the wide range of statistics shown here.

Derek Blades, formerly Head of Division at the Statistics Directorate, has co-ordinated the editorial work, co-operating with colleagues from various Directorates in designing the tables, helping to draft many of the texts, checking the quality of data and ensuring the overall coherence of the volume. Armel Le Jeune and Jérome Cukier had overall responsibility for technical work on the manuscript.

Donald Johnston
Secretary-General

Enrico Giovannini
Chief Statistician and
Director of the Statistics Directorate

TABLE OF CONTENTS

Population and migration

DEMOGRAPHIC TRENDS
Evolution of the population 10
Ageing societies 14

INTERNATIONAL MIGRATION
Foreign population 16
International migration 18

Macroeconomic trends

GROSS DOMESTIC PRODUCT (GDP)
Size of GDP 22
Value added by activity 26

ECONOMIC GROWTH
Evolution of GDP 30
Evolution of value added by activity 32
Household saving 36

PRODUCTIVITY
Labour productivity 38
Multi-factor productivity 40

COMMODITIES: PRODUCTION AND SUPPLY
Energy supply 42
Electricity generation 44
Steel production 46
Fisheries 48

Economic globalisation

TRADE
Share of trade in GDP 52
Trade in goods 54
Trade in services 58
Trading partners 62
Balance of payments 66

FOREIGN DIRECT INVESTMENT (FDI)
FDI flows and stocks 68
FDI and employment 72

Prices

CONSUMER AND PRODUCER PRICES
Consumer price indices (CPI) 76
Producer price indices (PPI) 80

PURCHASING POWER AND COMPETITIVENESS
Long-term interest rates 82
Rates of conversion 84
International competitiveness 88

Labour market

EMPLOYMENT
Employment rates by gender 94
Employment rates by age group 98
Part-time employment 102
Self-employment 104

UNEMPLOYMENT
Standardised unemployment rates 108
Long-term unemployment 112

Science and technology

RESEARCH AND DEVELOPMENT (R&D)
Expenditure on R&D 116
Investment in knowledge 118
Researchers 120
Patents 122

INFORMATION AND COMMUNICATIONS TECHNOLOGY (ICT)
Size of the ICT sector 124
Investment in ICT 126
Computer and Internet access by households 128
High-technology exports 130

Environment

AIR, WATER AND LAND
- Emissions of carbon dioxide (CO_2) — 134
- Water consumption — 136
- Municipal waste — 138
- Nutrient use in agriculture — 140

ENERGY USE
- Energy supply and economic growth — 142
- Energy supply per capita — 144
- Renewable energy — 146

Quality of life

HEALTH
- Life expectancy — 190
- Infant mortality — 194
- Obesity — 196
- Public and private health expenditure — 198

WORK AND LEISURE
- Hours worked — 200
- Tourism: hotel nights — 202

CRIME
- Prison population — 204
- Victimisation rates — 206

TRANSPORT
- Road motor vehicles and road fatalities — 208
- Passenger transport by road and rail — 212

Education

OUTCOMES
- International student assessment — 150
- Tertiary attainment — 152

EXPENDITURE ON EDUCATION
- Expenditure by level of education — 156
- Public and private education expenditure — 158

FOCUS ON:

Energy

In close co-operation with the International Energy Agency

- World energy supply — 214
- Regional energy supply — 215
- Regional oil production — 216
- Regional natural gas production — 217
- Regional hard coal production — 218
- Annual growth of renewables supply — 219
- World electricity generation — 220
- Final consumption by sector — 221
- Selected world energy indicators — 222
- Crude oil prices — 223
- IEA government budgets for energy R&D — 224
- Increase in world energy production and consumption — 225
- World primary energy demand outlook — 226
- Regional primary demand outlook — 227
- Global oil import dependency — 228
- CO_2 emissions outlook — 229

Public policies

GOVERNMENT DEFICITS AND DEBT
- Government deficits — 162
- Government debt — 164

PUBLIC EXPENDITURE AND AID
- Social expenditure — 166
- Health expenditure — 168
- Agricultural support estimates — 170
- Government support for fishing — 172
- Official development assistance — 174

TAXES
- Total tax revenue — 178
- Taxes on the average production worker — 182

REGIONAL DISPARITIES
- Regional GDP — 184
- Regional unemployment — 186

Reader's guide — 230

Analytical index — 233

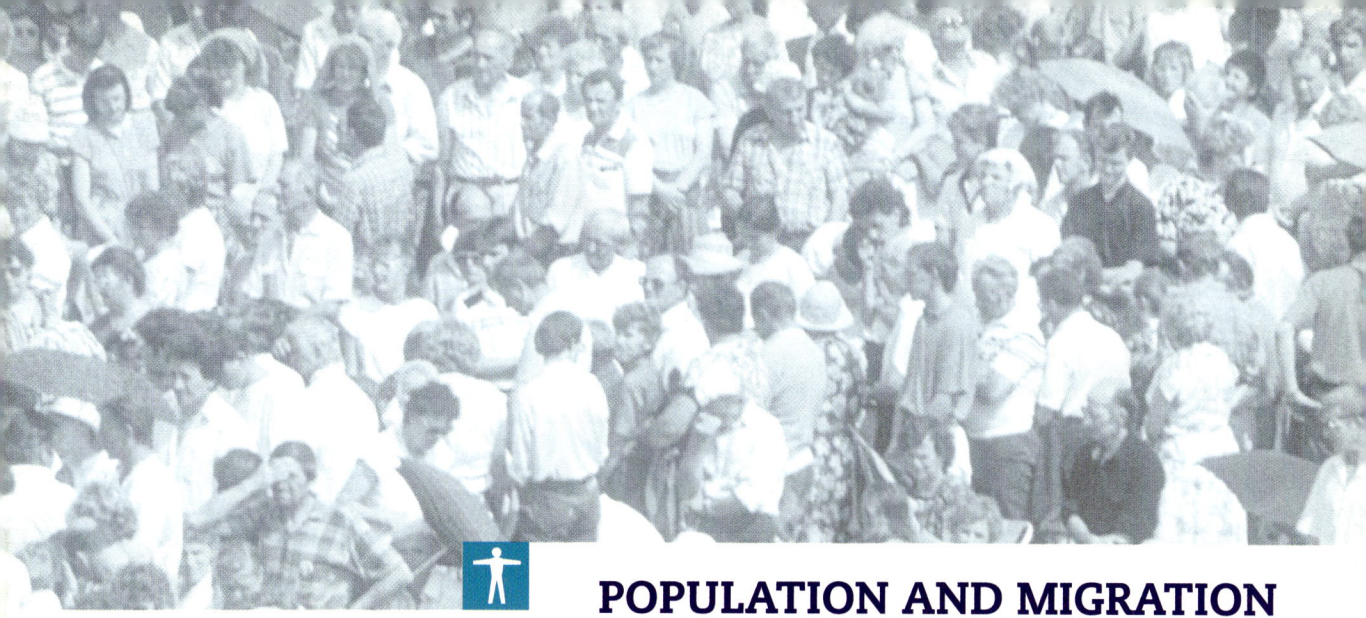

POPULATION AND MIGRATION

DEMOGRAPHIC TRENDS
EVOLUTION OF THE POPULATION
AGEING SOCIETIES

INTERNATIONAL MIGRATION
FOREIGN POPULATION
INTERNATIONAL MIGRATION

POPULATION AND MIGRATION • DEMOGRAPHIC TRENDS

EVOLUTION OF THE POPULATION

The size and growth of a country's population are both causes and effects of economic and social developments. The natural increase in population (births minus deaths) has slowed in all OECD countries, resulting in a rise in the average age of populations. In several countries, falling rates of natural increase have been partly offset by immigration.

Definition

The tables refer to the resident population. Growth rates are the annual changes in the population and are the net result of births, deaths and net immigration during the year. Birth rates are calculated as the number of live births per 1 000 population.

Long-term trends

In 2000, OECD countries accounted for just over 18% of the world's population of 6 billion. China accounted for 21% and India for just over 17%. The next two largest countries were Indonesia (3%) and the Russian Federation (2%). Within OECD, the United States accounted for nearly 25% of the OECD total, followed by Japan (11%), Mexico (9%), Germany (7%) and Turkey (6%).

Between 1990 and 2003, population growth rates for all OECD countries averaged 0.6% per annum. Growth rates much higher than this were recorded for Mexico and Turkey (high birth rate countries) and for Australia, Canada, Luxembourg and New Zealand (high net immigration). In the Czech Republic and Hungary populations declined from a combination of low birth rates and net emigration. Growth rates were very low, although still positive, in Italy, Poland, and the Slovak Republic.

From 1990 to 2000 average birth rates for all OECD countries fell from 14.3 per 1 000 population to 12.4. All OECD countries except Denmark and Luxembourg experienced falling birth rates over the period. Falls were small – less than 0.5 per 1 000 – in France, Greece, Japan, Netherlands, Portugal and Spain, but were very marked – 3.5 per 1 000 population or more – in Canada, Czech Republic, Iceland, Poland, Slovak Republic and Sweden. By the end of the period Iceland, Mexico, and Turkey had the highest birth-rates while the Czech Republic, Germany and Italy had the lowest.

Comparability

For most OECD countries, population data are based on regular, ten-yearly censuses, with estimates for intercensal years being derived from administrative data such as population registers, notified births and deaths and migration records. In some European countries, including Germany and the Netherlands, population censuses are no longer carried out and the estimates are based entirely on administrative records. In general, the population data for OECD countries are reliable, although, for some countries, there are breaks in the series as indicated by vertical lines in the tables.

There is a particularly important break in the series for the United States between 2000 and 2001.

Sources

For member countries: OECD (2004), *Labour Force Statistics*, OECD, Paris.

For non-OECD countries: Department of Economic and Social Affairs, United Nations.

Further information

• *Analytical publications*

OECD (2004), *OECD Employment Outlook*, OECD, Paris.

• *Statistical publications*

Maddison, Angus (2003), *The World Economy: Historical Statistics*, Development Centre Studies, OECD, Paris, also available on CD-ROM, www.theworldeconomy.org.

OECD (2004), *Quarterly Labour Force Statistics*, OECD, Paris.

• *Methodological publications*

OECD (2004), *Labour Force Statistics*, OECD, Paris.

• *Online databases*

SourceOECD Employment and Labour Markets.

• *Web sites*

World Population Prospects: The 2002 Revision Population Database: www.esa.un.org/unpp.

POPULATION AND MIGRATION • DEMOGRAPHIC TRENDS

EVOLUTION OF THE POPULATION

Total population
Thousands

	1990	1991	1992	1993	1994	1995	1996	1997	1998	1999	2000	2001	2002	2003
Australia	17 065	17 284	17 495	17 667	17 855	18 072	18 311	18 518	18 711	18 926	19 153	19 413	19 663	19 881
Austria	7 718	7 823	7 884	7 993	8 031	8 047	8 059	8 072	8 078	8 092	8 110	8 132	8 053	8 067
Belgium	9 967	10 004	10 045	10 084	10 116	10 137	10 157	10 181	10 203	10 226	10 251	10 287	10 333	10 372
Canada	27 698	28 031	28 367	28 682	28 999	29 302	29 611	29 907	30 157	30 404	30 689	31 021	31 362	31 630
Czech Republic	10 362	10 309	10 318	10 331	10 336	10 331	10 316	10 304	10 294	10 283	10 272	10 224	10 201	10 202
Denmark	5 141	5 154	5 171	5 189	5 206	5 233	5 263	5 285	5 304	5 322	5 340	5 359	5 374	5 387
Finland	4 986	5 014	5 042	5 066	5 088	5 108	5 125	5 140	5 153	5 165	5 176	5 188	5 201	5 213
France	56 709	56 976	57 240	57 467	57 659	57 844	58 026	58 207	58 398	58 623	58 896	59 193	59 489	59 768
Germany	..	79 984	80 595	81 179	81 422	81 661	81 895	82 052	82 029	82 024	82 160	82 277	82 456	82 502
Greece	10 089	10 200	10 322	10 380	10 426	10 454	10 475	10 498	10 516	10 721	10 937	10 971	11 003	11 036
Hungary	10 374	10 373	10 369	10 358	10 343	10 329	10 311	10 290	10 267	10 238	10 211	10 188	10 159	10 124
Iceland	255	258	261	264	266	267	269	271	274	277	281	285	288	289
Ireland	3 503	3 524	3 549	3 563	3 583	3 601	3 626	3 664	3 703	3 742	3 790	3 847	3 917	3 953
Italy	56 737	56 760	56 859	56 442	56 623	56 745	56 826	56 941	57 040	57 078	57 189	57 348	57 474	57 478
Japan	123 611	124 043	124 452	124 764	125 034	125 570	125 864	126 166	126 486	126 686	126 926	127 291	127 435	127 619
Korea	42 869	43 296	43 748	44 195	44 642	45 093	45 525	45 954	46 287	46 617	47 008	47 343	47 640	47 925
Luxembourg	384	390	395	401	407	413	416	421	427	433	439	443	444	452
Mexico	81 250	83 265	84 902	86 613	88 402	91 234	92 788	94 305	95 786	97 199	98 658	100 051	101 398	102 708
Netherlands	14 951	15 070	15 184	15 290	15 383	15 459	15 531	15 611	15 707	15 812	15 926	16 046	16 149	16 224
New Zealand	33 063	3 495	3 532	3 572	3 620	3 673	3 732	3 781	3 815	3 835	3 858	3 881	3 939	4 009
Norway	4 241	4 262	4 287	4 312	4 337	4 359	4 381	4 405	4 431	4 462	4 491	4 514	4 538	4 564
Poland	38 119	38 245	38 365	38 459	38 544	38 588	38 618	38 650	38 666	38 654	38 646	38 251	38 232	38 195
Portugal	9 877	9 961	9 965	9 983	10 013	10 041	10 070	10 108	10 129	10 171	10 229	10 305	10 380	10 449
Slovak Republic	5 298	5 283	5 307	5 325	5 347	5 364	5 374	5 383	5 391	5 395	5 401	5 379	5 379	5 380
Spain	38 851	38 935	39 054	39 167	39 264	39 345	39 427	39 520	39 648	39 844	40 171	40 615	41 200	41 874
Sweden	8 559	8 617	8 668	8 719	8 781	8 827	8 841	8 846	8 851	8 858	8 872	8 896	8 925	8 958
Switzerland	6 712	6 800	6 875	6 938	6 994	7 041	7 072	7 089	7 110	7 144	7 184	7 233	7 290	7 343
Turkey	56 154	57 262	58 374	59 491	60 612	61 737	62 873	64 015	65 157	66 293	67 420	68 529	69 626	70 712
United Kingdom	57 285	57 472	57 593	57 700	57 825	57 958	58 076	58 204	58 349	58 535	58 655	58 789	59 234	59 422
United States	249 973	252 665	255 410	258 119	260 637	263 082	265 502	268 048	270 509	272 945	275 372	285 321	288 205	291 049
EU15	..	365 884	367 566	368 623	369 827	370 873	371 812	372 751	373 535	374 644	376 140	377 695	379 631	381 155
OECD total	..	1 050 755	1 059 628	1 067 581	1 075 795	1 084 915	1 092 359	1 099 838	1 106 876	1 114 003	1 121 709	1 136 618	1 144 986	1 152 786

StatLink: *http://dx.doi.org/10.1787/846543818453*

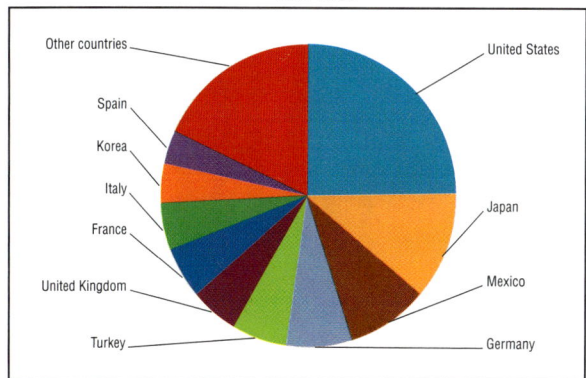

OECD population
Year 2000

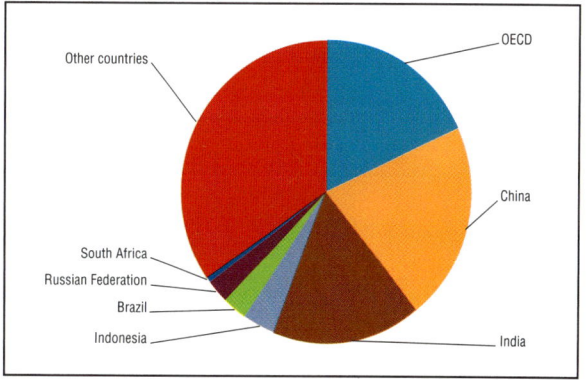

World population
Year 2000

StatLink: *http://dx.doi.org/10.1787/002318186276*

OECD FACTBOOK 2005 – ISBN 92-64-01869-7 – © OECD 2005

POPULATION AND MIGRATION • DEMOGRAPHIC TRENDS

EVOLUTION OF THE POPULATION

Population growth rates
Annual growth in percentage

	1990	1991	1992	1993	1994	1995	1996	1997	1998	1999	2000	2001	2002	2003
Australia	1.49	1.28	1.22	0.98	1.06	1.22	1.32	1.13	1.04	1.15	1.20	1.36	1.29	1.11
Austria	1.23	1.36	0.78	1.38	0.48	0.20	0.15	0.16	0.07	0.17	0.22	0.27	-0.97	0.17
Belgium	0.29	0.37	0.41	0.39	0.32	0.21	0.20	0.24	0.22	0.23	0.24	0.35	0.45	0.38
Canada	1.52	1.20	1.20	1.11	1.11	1.04	1.05	1.00	0.84	0.82	0.94	1.08	1.10	0.85
Czech Republic	0.00	-0.51	0.09	0.13	0.05	-0.05	-0.15	-0.12	-0.10	-0.11	-0.11	-0.47	-0.23	0.01
Denmark	0.16	0.25	0.33	0.35	0.33	0.52	0.57	0.42	0.36	0.34	0.34	0.36	0.28	0.24
Finland	0.44	0.56	0.56	0.48	0.43	0.39	0.33	0.29	0.25	0.23	0.21	0.23	0.25	0.23
France	0.51	0.47	0.46	0.40	0.33	0.32	0.31	0.31	0.33	0.39	0.47	0.50	0.50	0.47
Germany	..	..	0.76	0.72	0.30	0.29	0.29	0.19	-0.03	-0.01	0.17	0.14	0.22	0.06
Greece	0.51	1.10	1.20	0.56	0.44	0.27	0.20	0.22	0.17	1.95	2.01	0.31	0.29	0.30
Hungary	-1.93	-0.01	-0.04	-0.11	-0.14	-0.14	-0.17	-0.20	-0.22	-0.28	-0.26	-0.23	-0.28	-0.34
Iceland	0.83	1.26	1.20	1.03	0.83	0.53	0.56	0.74	1.07	1.24	1.44	1.39	0.88	0.59
Ireland	-0.34	0.60	0.71	0.39	0.56	0.50	0.69	1.05	1.06	1.05	1.28	1.50	1.82	0.92
Italy	-0.18	0.04	0.17	-0.73	0.32	0.22	0.14	0.20	0.17	0.07	0.19	0.28	0.22	0.01
Japan	0.29	0.35	0.33	0.25	0.22	0.43	0.23	0.24	0.25	0.16	0.19	0.29	0.11	0.14
Korea	0.99	1.00	1.04	1.02	1.01	1.01	0.96	0.94	0.72	0.71	0.84	0.71	0.63	0.60
Luxembourg	1.32	1.56	1.28	1.52	1.50	1.47	0.73	1.20	1.43	1.41	1.39	0.91	0.23	1.80
Mexico	..	2.48	1.97	2.02	2.07	3.20	1.70	1.64	1.57	1.48	1.50	1.41	1.35	1.29
Netherlands	0.69	0.80	0.76	0.70	0.61	0.49	0.47	0.52	0.62	0.67	0.72	0.75	0.64	0.46
New Zealand	0.99	3.93	1.06	1.13	1.34	1.46	1.61	1.31	0.90	0.52	0.60	0.60	1.49	1.78
Norway	0.33	0.50	0.59	0.58	0.58	0.51	0.50	0.55	0.59	0.70	0.65	0.51	0.53	0.57
Poland	0.41	0.33	0.31	0.25	0.22	0.11	0.08	0.08	0.04	-0.03	-0.02	-1.02	-0.05	-0.10
Portugal	-0.43	0.85	0.04	0.18	0.30	0.28	0.29	0.38	0.21	0.41	0.57	0.74	0.73	0.66
Slovak Republic	0.42	-0.28	0.45	0.34	0.41	0.32	0.19	0.17	0.15	0.07	0.11	-0.41	0.00	0.02
Spain	0.15	0.22	0.31	0.29	0.25	0.21	0.21	0.24	0.32	0.49	0.82	1.11	1.44	1.64
Sweden	0.78	0.68	0.59	0.59	0.71	0.52	0.16	0.06	0.06	0.08	0.16	0.27	0.33	0.37
Switzerland	0.98	1.31	1.10	0.92	0.81	0.67	0.44	0.24	0.30	0.48	0.56	0.68	0.79	0.73
Turkey	2.30	1.97	1.94	1.91	1.88	1.86	1.84	1.82	1.78	1.74	1.70	1.65	1.60	1.56
United Kingdom	0.27	0.33	0.21	0.19	0.22	0.23	0.20	0.22	0.25	0.32	0.21	0.23	0.76	0.32
United States	1.06	1.08	1.09	1.06	0.98	0.94	0.92	0.96	0.92	0.90	0.89	..	1.01	0.99
EU15	0.55	5.14	0.46	0.29	0.33	0.28	0.25	0.25	0.21	0.30	0.40	0.41	0.51	0.40
OECD total	..	..	0.84	0.75	0.77	0.85	0.69	0.68	0.64	0.64	0.69	1.33	0.74	0.68

StatLink: http://dx.doi.org/10.1787/242607112435

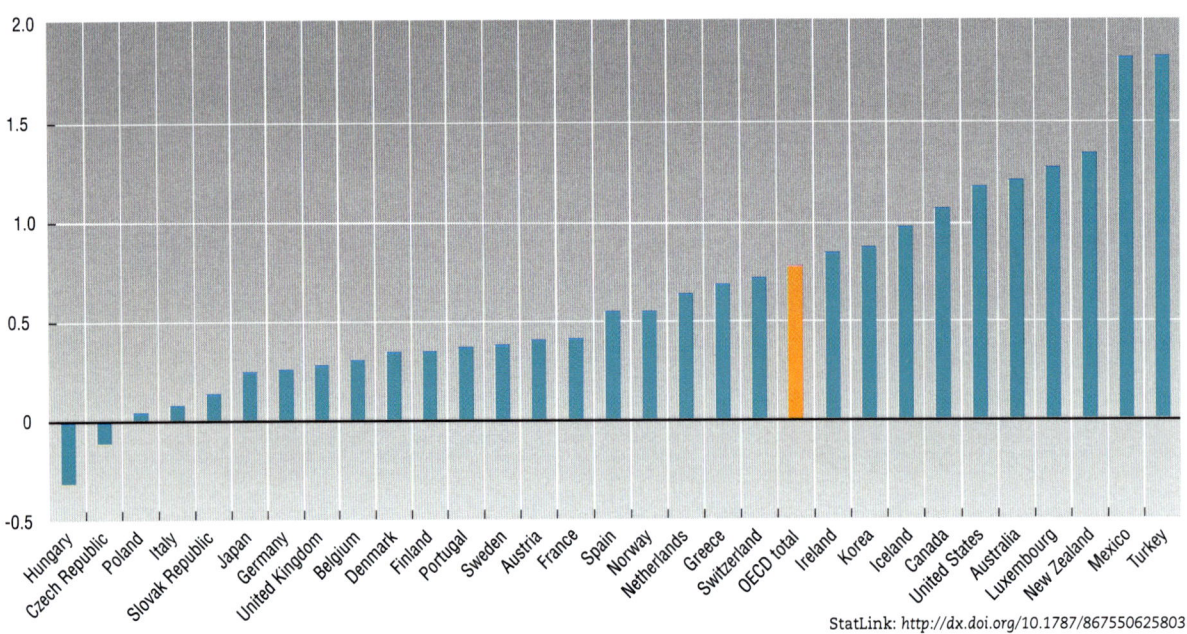

Population growth rates
Average growth rates in percentage, 1990-2003

StatLink: http://dx.doi.org/10.1787/867550625803

POPULATION AND MIGRATION • DEMOGRAPHIC TRENDS

EVOLUTION OF THE POPULATION

Birth rates
Number of live births per 1 000 population

	1990	1991	1992	1993	1994	1995	1996	1997	1998	1999	2000	2001	2002	2003
Australia	15.4	14.9	15.1	14.7	14.5	14.1	13.8	13.6	13.3	13.2	13.0	12.7	12.7	12.6
Austria	11.8	12.2	12.2	12.0	11.6	11.2	11.2	10.5	10.2	9.8	9.8	9.4	9.7	..
Belgium	12.4	12.6	12.4	12.0	11.5	11.4	11.5	11.4	11.2	11.1	11.3	11.1	10.8	..
Canada	14.6	14.4	14.1	13.5	13.3	12.9	12.4	11.7	11.3	11.1	10.7	10.8	10.6	..
Czech Republic	12.6	12.5	11.8	11.7	10.3	9.3	8.8	8.8	8.8	8.7	8.8	8.9	9.1	9.2
Denmark	12.3	12.4	13.1	12.9	13.4	13.4	12.9	12.8	12.5	12.4	12.5	12.1	11.9	12.1
France	13.4	13.3	13.0	12.4	12.3	12.6	12.7	12.5	12.6	12.7	13.2	13.0	12.8	12.7
Germany	11.5	10.4	10.0	9.8	9.5	9.4	9.7	9.9	9.6	9.4	9.3	8.9	8.7	..
Greece	10.1	10.0	10.1	9.8	10.0	9.7	9.7	9.7	9.6	9.5	..	..	..	..
Hungary	12.1	12.2	11.8	11.3	11.2	10.8	10.2	9.7	9.4	9.3	9.6	9.5	9.5	9.4
Iceland	18.8	17.5	17.6	17.4	16.5	17.2	16.0	15.3	15.3	14.8	15.3	14.4	14.1	14.3
Ireland	15.1	15.0	14.6	13.7	13.4	13.6	13.7	14.2	14.3	14.2	14.3	15.0	15.4	..
Italy	10.2	9.8	10.0	9.6	9.4	9.2	9.3	9.4	9.3	9.3	9.4	9.3	9.4	..
Japan	10.0	9.9	9.8	9.6	10.0	9.6	9.7	9.6	9.6	9.4	9.5	..	..	..
Luxembourg	12.8	12.9	13.0	13.6	13.6	13.2	13.7	13.1	12.7	12.9	13.1	12.2	12	11.8
Mexico	33.5	..	..	..	..	..	..	..	..	..	..	..	..	..
Netherlands	13.2	13.2	13.0	12.8	12.7	12.4	12.2	12.3	12.7	12.6	13.0	12.7	12.5	12.4
New Zealand	17.7	17.1	16.8	16.4	15.8	15.7	15.3	15.2	14.5	14.9	14.7	14.3	13.7	14
Norway	14.4	14.3	14.0	13.9	13.8	13.8	13.9	13.6	13.2	13.3	13.1	12.6	12.1	12.3
Poland	14.4	14.3	13.4	12.8	12.5	11.2	11.1	10.7	10.2	9.9	9.8	9.6	9.3	9.2
Portugal	11.7	11.8	11.7	11.5	11.0	10.8	11.1	11.4	11.4	..	..	..	..	..
Slovak Republic	15.2	14.9	14.1	13.8	12.5	11.5	11.2	11.0	10.7	10.5	10.2	9.5	9.5	9.7
Spain	10.3	10.2	10.2	9.9	9.4	9.2	9.2	9.3	9.2	9.5	9.9	10.0	10.1	..
Sweden	14.5	14.4	14.2	13.5	12.8	11.7	10.7	10.2	10.1	9.9	10.1	10.2	10.8	11.1
Switzerland	12.5	12.7	12.6	12.1	11.9	11.7	11.7	11.4	11.1	11.0	10.9	10.2	9.9	9.8
Turkey	24.9	24.6	24.4	24.1	23.9	23.8	23.6	23.4	23.1	22.6	22.2	21.7	21.3	20.9
United Kingdom	13.9	13.7	13.5	13.1	12.9	12.5	12.5	12.3	12.1	..	..	..	..	..
United States	16.6	16.3	15.9	15.5	15.2	14.8	14.7	14.5	14.6	14.4	14.3	14.1	13.9	13.9

StatLink: *http://dx.doi.org/10.1787/365321116443*

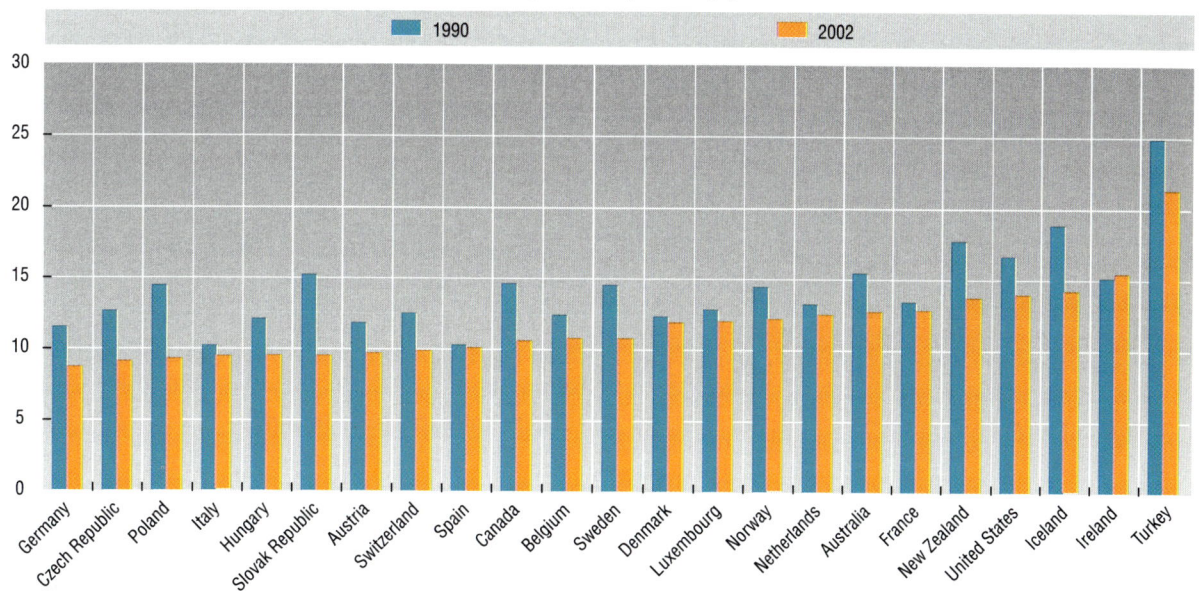

Birth rates
Number of live births per 1 000 population

StatLink: *http://dx.doi.org/10.1787/117884578382*

POPULATION AND MIGRATION • DEMOGRAPHIC TRENDS

AGEING SOCIETIES

The percentage of the population that is 65 years or older is rising in all OECD countries and is expected to continue doing so. Dependency ratios – the ratios of the number of persons 65 or older to the numbers in the labour force – are also increasing throughout OECD countries. These trends have a number of implications for government and private spending on pensions and health care and, more generally, for economic growth and welfare.

Definition

Populations are defined as the *de facto*, i.e. the resident, population. The labour force is defined according to the *ILO Guidelines* and consists of those in employment plus persons who are available for work and who are actively seeking employment. Population projections are taken from national sources where these are available, but for some countries they are based on Eurostat and UN projections.

Comparability

Almost all OECD countries now follow the *ILO Guidelines* for defining the labour force, so there is good comparability between countries.

All population projections require assumptions about future trends in life expectancy, fertility rates and net immigration. Often, a range of projections are produced using different assumptions about these future trends. The estimates shown here correspond to the medium or central variant.

The labour force projections start from the population projections described above but then require additional assumptions about the future propensities of men and women in different age groups to seek paid employment. For the projections shown here, particular care has been taken in modelling future trends in the labour force participation of women and of elderly persons. As with the population projections a range of estimates has been made for the labour force in each country and the medium or central variant is used here.

Sources

OECD (2004), *Labour Force Statistics*, OECD, Paris.

Eurostat, United Nations, national sources and OECD estimates.

Further information
• Analytical publications

Burniaux, J.-M., R. Duval and F. Jaumotte (2003), "Coping with Ageing: A Dynamic Approach to Quantify the Impact of Alternative Policy Options on Future Labour Supply in OECD Countries", *OECD Economics Department Working Paper*, No. 371, OECD, Paris, www.oecd.org/eco/working_papers.

OECD (2000), *Reforms for an Ageing Society*, OECD, Paris.

OECD (2001), *Ageing and Income: Financial Resources and Retirement in Nine OECD Countries*, OECD, Paris.

OECD (2001), *Ageing and Transport: Mobility Needs and Safety Issues*, OECD, Paris.

OECD (2003), *Ageing, Housing and Urban Development*, OECD, Paris.

OECD (2004), *Ageing and Employment Policies*, series, OECD, Paris.

OECD (2004), *OECD Employment Outlook*, OECD, Paris.

• Statistical publications

OECD (2004), *Main Economic Indicators*, OECD, Paris.

OECD (2004), *Quarterly Labour Force Statistics*, OECD, Paris.

• Methodological publications

OECD (1997), "Sources and Methods – Labour and Wage Statistics", *Main Economic Indicators*, Vol. 1997/4, OECD, Paris.

• Online databases

SourceOECD Main Economic Indicators.

SourceOECD Employment and Labour Markets.

Long-term trends

The youngest populations (low shares of population aged 65 or over) are either in countries with high birth rates such as Mexico, Iceland and Turkey or in countries with high immigration, such as Australia, Canada and New Zealand. All these countries will, however, experience significant ageing up to 2020.

The dependency ratio (right panel of the table) is projected to exceed 50% in Hungary, France, Italy and Japan by 2020. This means that for each elderly person there will be only two persons in the labour force. The lowest dependency ratios – under 30% – are projected for Mexico, Iceland, Turkey and Ireland.

Over the period from 2000 to 2020, dependency ratios are forecast to rise particularly sharply in the Czech Republic, Finland, Japan, Korea and Turkey; growth of dependency ratios will be lowest in Greece, Ireland, Portugal and Spain.

POPULATION AND MIGRATION • DEMOGRAPHIC TRENDS

AGEING SOCIETIES

Population aged 65 and over

	Ratio to the total population							Ratio to the total labour force						
	1990	1995	2000	2005	2010	2015	2020	1990	1995	2000	2005	2010	2015	2020
Australia	11.1	11.9	12.3	12.9	14.0	16.0	18.0	22.6	24.1	24.4	25.2	27.3	31.5	36.2
Austria	14.9	15.1	15.5	16.1	17.8	18.8	20.0	..	31.2	32.1	33.4	37.1	39.7	43.7
Belgium	14.9	15.9	16.8	17.3	17.5	18.9	20.4	38.1	38.5	39.1	39.2	39.7	43.1	47.2
Canada	11.3	12.0	12.5	13.2	14.2	16.2	18.4	21.9	23.8	24.1	24.9	26.7	30.7	35.8
Czech Republic	12.5	13.2	13.8	14.2	15.9	18.7	21.4	..	26.4	27.4	28.2	31.8	38.3	44.8
Denmark	15.6	15.2	14.8	14.9	16.2	18.4	19.7	27.7	28.5	27.8	28.4	31.5	36.1	39.3
Finland	13.4	14.2	14.9	15.7	16.7	19.8	22.1	25.8	29.3	29.8	31.2	33.9	41.6	48.1
France	14.0	15.2	16.1	16.5	16.9	18.7	20.6	32.4	35.0	36.6	37.6	39.2	44.5	50.5
Germany	14.9	15.5	16.4	18.3	19.9	20.4	21.7	30.3	32.1	33.2	36.7	39.9	41.0	44.5
Greece	13.8	15.6	17.4	18.6	19.3	20.2	21.3	35.1	38.8	41.4	42.7	43.5	45.2	47.2
Hungary	13.3	14.1	14.7	15.1	16.1	17.5	19.8	..	35.2	35.7	36.5	39.1	43.0	49.7
Iceland	10.6	11.2	11.6	11.7	12.4	13.9	15.8	..	20.2	20.3	20.1	20.9	23.2	26.6
Ireland	11.4	11.4	11.2	11.2	11.7	13.1	14.6	30.3	28.2	24.4	22.6	23.0	25.4	28.2
Italy	14.9	16.6	18.1	19.4	20.6	22.2	23.5	35.1	41.7	44.1	46.0	48.3	52.1	55.7
Japan	12.1	14.6	17.4	19.9	22.5	26.0	27.8	23.3	27.4	32.6	37.7	43.6	51.3	55.9
Korea	5.1	5.9	7.2	9.0	10.7	12.6	15.1	11.8	12.7	15.5	19.4	23.8	28.9	36.1
Luxembourg	13.4	14.2	14.3	14.9	15.7	17.0	18.5	32.1	34.9	33.8	34.6	36.5	39.8	44.2
Mexico	4.0	4.3	4.7	5.2	5.9	6.8	7.9	..	11.4	12.1	12.7	13.7	15.0	17.0
Netherlands	12.8	13.2	13.6	14.0	15.0	17.3	19.1	27.9	27.6	26.8	27.2	29.3	33.9	38.0
New Zealand	11.1	11.5	11.8	12.3	13.4	15.4	17.4	23.3	23.7	23.8	24.6	26.5	30.7	35.5
Norway	16.3	15.9	15.2	14.7	15.2	16.9	18.3	32.2	31.8	29.0	27.4	28.3	31.7	34.8
Poland	10.1	11.1	12.2	12.9	13.0	14.8	17.6	..	25.1	27.2	28.5	28.6	33.0	40.3
Portugal	13.4	14.6	15.5	16.0	16.3	17.1	18.1	28.0	29.9	30.9	31.1	31.5	33.2	35.2
Slovak Republic	10.3	10.9	11.4	11.8	12.4	13.8	16.3	..	23.6	23.9	23.6	24.7	28.0	34.0
Spain	13.6	15.3	16.9	17.3	17.8	18.7	19.7	33.7	36.7	37.5	37.0	38.2	40.4	43.1
Sweden	17.8	17.5	17.3	17.4	18.7	20.6	21.6	32.8	34.5	34.1	35.0	38.5	43.7	47.5
Switzerland	14.6	14.7	15.3	15.9	17.2	18.7	19.9	..	26.8	27.6	28.4	30.4	33.0	35.5
Turkey	4.3	4.7	5.4	5.9	6.2	6.9	7.9	11.9	13.4	16.5	18.6	20.0	22.6	26.7
United Kingdom	15.7	15.7	15.6	15.7	16.3	17.9	18.9	31.4	32.4	31.7	31.6	32.7	36.3	39.0
United States	12.5	12.8	12.6	12.6	13.2	14.7	16.5	24.8	25.4	24.7	24.7	26.1	29.4	33.8
EU15	14.6	15.5	16.3	17.2	18.1	19.4	20.7	..	34.3	35.1	36.4	38.3	41.5	45.1
OECD total	11.6	12.4	13.1	13.8	14.7	16.2	17.7	..	26.7	27.7	29.0	31.0	34.5	38.3

StatLink: http://dx.doi.org/10.1787/514333204602

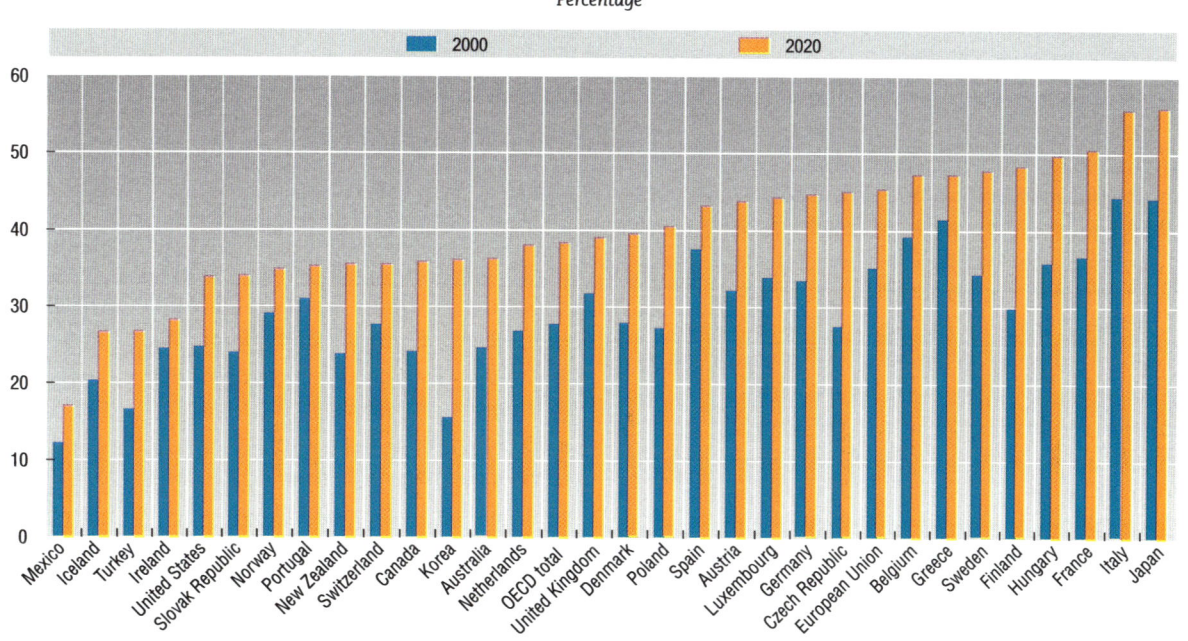

Ratio of the population aged 65 and over to the labour force
Percentage

StatLink: http://dx.doi.org/10.1787/866653733053

POPULATION AND MIGRATION • INTERNATIONAL MIGRATION

FOREIGN POPULATION

The size of a country's immigrant population is important for several reasons. Immigrants bring new ideas and enrich the cultures of their host nation, they may accept jobs that are no longer attractive to native workers, and in countries with low birth-rates immigrant workers can offset declining work forces and help to fund retirement pensions. At the same time, immigration on a large scale presents political and social challenges to government.

Definition

To measure the size of the immigrant population, OECD countries use two main approaches. Some countries record the number of residents who were born in a foreign country; others record the number of residents who have a foreign nationality.

Comparability

These two approaches give different results depending, in particular, on the rules governing the acquisition of citizenship in each country. For example, in some countries children born in the country automatically acquire the citizenship of their country of birth (countries of *jus solis*, the right of soil) while in other countries they retain the nationality of their parents (countries of *jus sanguinis*, the right of blood). Both measures are shown in the table for Denmark, Finland, the Netherlands and Sweden. It can be seen that for these countries the foreign-born criterion gives substantially higher percentages for the immigrant population than the approach based on nationality.

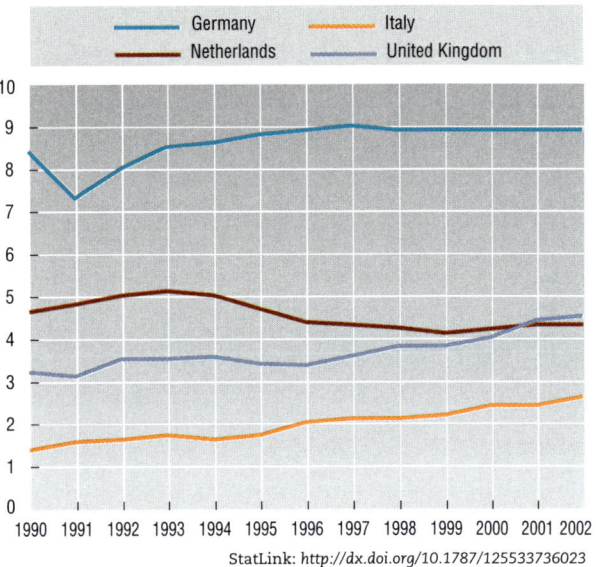

Foreign nationals in selected OECD countries
As a percentage of total population

Long-term trends

It is difficult to have a clear idea of the trend in the immigrant population from the statistics on the foreign population. This is because new additions to the foreign population due to immigration can be offset by the acquisition of nationality on the part of resident foreigners. The data on the foreign-born, however, are unambiguous: the percentage of the foreign-born has increased over the past decade in all countries for which data are available.

The countries with the largest share of the foreign population are Luxembourg and Switzerland. On the other hand, Australia, Canada and New Zealand have the highest proportion of foreign-born. Switzerland is certainly among those with high foreign-born populations, although no firm data on the foreign-born are as yet available.

Source
OECD (2005), *Trends In International Migration: SOPEMI*, OECD, Paris.

Further information
• *Analytical publications*

OECD (2000), *Globalisation, Migration and Development*, OECD, Paris.

OECD (2001), *Migration Policies and EU Enlargement: The Case of Central and Eastern Europe*, OECD, Paris.

OECD (2003), *Migration and the Labour Market in Asia: Recent Trends and Policies*, 2002 edition, OECD, Paris.

OECD (2004), *Migration for Employment: Bilateral Agreements at a Crossroads*, OECD, Paris.

OECD (2004), *OECD Employment Outlook*, OECD, Paris.

OECD (2004), *Trade and Migration: Building Bridges for Global Labour Mobility*, OECD, Paris.

• *Statistical publications*

OECD (2004), *Labour Force Statistics*, OECD, Paris.

• *Online databases*

SourceOECD International Migration Statistics.

POPULATION AND MIGRATION • INTERNATIONAL MIGRATION

FOREIGN POPULATION

Immigrant population in OECD countries
As a percentage of total population

	1990	1991	1992	1993	1994	1995	1996	1997	1998	1999	2000	2001	2002
Foreign-born													
Australia	22.8	22.9	23.0	22.9	22.9	23.0	23.3	23.3	23.2	23.1	23.0	23.1	23.2
Canada	..	16.1	..	..	..	..	17.4	..	..	..	..	18.2	..
Denmark	3.7	3.9	4.0	4.2	4.3	4.8	5.1	5.2	5.4	5.6	5.8	6.0	6.2
Finland	..	..	..	..	..	2.0	2.1	2.3	2.4	2.5	2.6	2.8	2.9
Netherlands	8.1	..	..	9.0	9.0	9.1	9.2	9.4	9.6	9.8	10.1	10.4	10.6
New Zealand	..	..	..	..	..	..	..	..	..	..	..	19.5	..
Sweden	..	..	9.6	9.9	10.5	10.5	11.0	11.0	10.8	11.8	11.3	11.5	11.8
United States	..	..	..	..	8.2	8.9	9.9	10.4	10.5	10.3	10.8	11.1	11.8
Foreign nationals													
Austria	5.9	6.8	7.9	8.6	8.9	8.5	8.6	8.6	8.6	8.7	8.8	8.8	8.8
Belgium	9.1	9.2	9.0	9.1	9.1	9.0	9.0	8.9	8.7	8.8	8.4	8.2	8.2
Czech Republic	..	..	0.4	0.8	1.0	1.5	1.9	2.0	2.1	2.2	1.9	2.0	2.3
Denmark	3.1	3.3	3.5	3.6	3.8	4.2	4.7	4.7	4.8	4.9	4.8	5.0	4.9
Finland	0.5	0.8	0.9	1.1	1.2	1.3	1.4	1.6	1.6	1.7	1.8	1.9	2.0
France	6.3	..	..	..	..	..	..	..	..	5.6	..	..	..
Germany	8.4	7.3	8.0	8.5	8.6	8.8	8.9	9.0	8.9	8.9	8.9	8.9	8.9
Greece	..	..	..	..	..	..	..	..	..	..	..	7.0	..
Hungary	..	..	..	..	1.3	1.4	1.4	1.4	1.4	1.5	1.1	1.1	1.1
Ireland	2.3	2.5	2.7	2.7	2.7	2.7	3.2	3.1	3.0	3.1	3.3	4.0	4.8
Italy	1.4	1.5	1.6	1.7	1.6	1.7	2.0	2.1	2.1	2.2	2.4	2.4	2.6
Japan	0.9	1.0	1.0	1.1	1.1	1.1	1.1	1.2	1.2	1.2	1.3	1.4	1.5
Korea	0.1	0.1	0.1	0.2	0.2	0.2	0.3	0.3	0.3	0.4	0.4	0.5	0.5
Luxembourg	29.4	30.2	31.0	31.8	32.6	33.4	34.1	34.9	35.6	36.0	37.3	37.5	38.1
Mexico	..	..	..	..	..	..	..	..	..	..	0.4	..	..
Netherlands	4.6	4.8	5.0	5.1	5.0	4.7	4.4	4.3	4.2	4.1	4.2	4.3	4.3
Norway	3.4	3.5	3.6	3.8	3.8	3.7	3.6	3.6	3.7	4.0	4.1	4.1	4.3
Poland	..	..	..	..	..	..	..	..	..	..	..	..	0.1
Portugal	1.1	1.2	1.3	1.3	1.6	1.7	1.7	1.8	1.8	1.9	2.1	3.4	4.0
Slovak Republic	..	..	..	0.2	0.3	0.4	0.5	0.5	0.5	0.5	0.5	0.5	0.5
Spain	0.7	0.9	1.0	1.1	1.2	1.3	1.4	1.6	1.8	2.0	2.2	2.7	3.1
Sweden	5.6	5.7	5.7	5.8	6.1	5.2	6.0	6.0	5.6	5.5	5.4	5.3	5.3
Switzerland	16.3	17.1	17.6	18.1	18.6	18.9	18.9	19.0	19.0	19.2	19.3	19.7	19.9
United Kingdom	3.2	3.1	3.5	3.5	3.6	3.4	3.4	3.6	3.8	3.8	4.0	4.4	4.5

StatLink: http://dx.doi.org/10.1787/586274682611

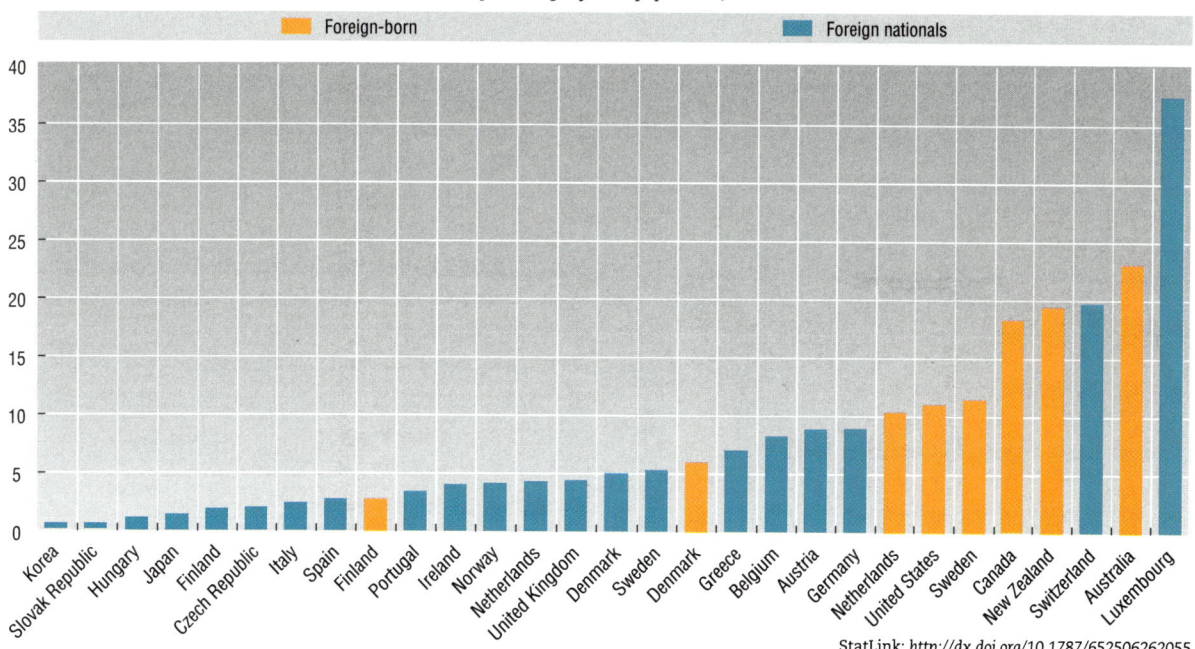

Immigrant population in OECD countries
As a percentage of total population, 2001

StatLink: http://dx.doi.org/10.1787/652506262055

OECD FACTBOOK 2005 – ISBN 92-64-01869-7 – © OECD 2005

INTERNATIONAL MIGRATION

The growth of a country's population depends on natural increase (births minus deaths) and net migration (immigrants minus emigrants). Rates of natural increase are declining in most OECD countries in Europe and net migration is becoming an important source of population growth.

Definition

Net migration is the total number of arrivals of foreigners and returning nationals minus departures of foreigners and nationals. Arrivals and departures of short duration, *e.g.* for tourism or business purposes, are excluded.

Comparability

The main sources of information on migration vary across countries, which poses difficulties for the comparability of available data on inflows and outflows. However, since the comparability problems generally concern the extent to which shorter-term movements are counted in the inflows and outflows, taking the difference between the two (net migration) tends to subtract out the movements that are the source of non-comparability. The net migration data are nonetheless subject to caution, firstly because irregular migration is not taken into account in the inflows and this is significant in some countries; secondly, because the data on outflows are of uneven quality, with departures being not well recorded in some countries or having to be estimated in others.

OECD activities in the field of international migration are aimed at improving the availability, comparability and reliability of data on international migration. These activities are based largely on a network of national correspondents in 30 countries and seek to enhance analysis and understanding of migration issues in the light of the socio-economic challenges facing OECD member countries.

Long-term trends

Positive net migration was very high in Luxembourg and Switzerland for most of the period since 1990. Australia, Canada, New Zealand, and the United States are often called "settlement countries" and positive net migration has remained substantial in all four for most of the period since 1990, although there was negative net migration from New Zealand for a short time in the late 1990s.

High rates of positive net migration were recorded for Austria and Germany in the years immediately following the fall of the Berlin Wall. Ireland, which has traditionally had net outflows towards the United Kingdom and the settlement countries has had substantial positive net migration since 1996 as high rates of economic growth have encouraged the return of former emigrants.

Netherlands and Sweden have had above average rates of positive net migration for most of the period covered, while positive net migration has been below average for the Czech Republic, Hungary and the Slovak Republic. Poland is the only country which has experienced net outflows throughout the period, although negative net migration was recorded in several years for Iceland and Japan.

Source

OECD (2004), *Labour Force Statistics*, OECD, Paris.

Further information

- **Analytical publications**

OECD (2000), *Globalisation, Migration and Development*, OECD, Paris.

OECD (2001), *Migration Policies and EU Enlargement: The Case of Central and Eastern Europe*, OECD, Paris.

OECD (2003), *Migration and the Labour Market in Asia: Recent Trends and Policies*, 2002 edition, OECD, Paris.

OECD (2004), *Migration for Employment: Bilateral Agreements at a Crossroads*, OECD, Paris.

OECD (2004), *OECD Employment Outlook*, OECD, Paris.

OECD (2004), *Trade and Migration: Building Bridges for Global Labour Mobility*, OECD, Paris.

- **Statistical publications**

OECD (2004), *Trends in International Migration: SOPEMI*, OECD, Paris.

- **Online databases**

SourceOECD International Migration Statistics.

POPULATION AND MIGRATION • INTERNATIONAL MIGRATION

INTERNATIONAL MIGRATION

Net migration
Per 1 000 population

	1990	1991	1992	1993	1994	1995	1996	1997	1998	1999	2000	2001	2002	2003
Australia	7.3	5.0	3.9	2.0	3.1	5.9	5.3	3.9	4.8	5.5	5.8	7.0	5.9	6.6
Austria	7.6	9.9	9.1	4.2	0.4	0.3	0.5	0.2	1.1	2.5	2.2	2.2	..	..
Belgium	2.0	1.4	2.5	1.9	1.8	1.3	1.3	0.6	0.7	1.7	1.4	..	..	..
Canada	6.5	4.3	6.1	5.0	5.3	5.5	5.6	5.2	3.9	5.2	6.5	7.6	6.2	..
Czech Republic	0.1	0.3	1.1	0.5	1.0	1.0	1.0	1.2	0.9	0.9	0.6	-0.8	1.2	2.5
Denmark	1.6	2.1	2.1	2.1	1.9	5.5	3.2	2.3	2.1	1.7	1.7	2.2	1.7	1.1
Finland	1.4	2.6	1.6	1.6	0.6	0.6	0.6	0.8	0.6	0.6	0.4	1.2	1.0	1.0
France	1.4	1.6	1.6	1.2	0.9	0.7	0.6	0.7	0.8	0.8	0.8	1.0	1.1	0.9
Germany	16.3	7.5	9.6	5.7	3.9	4.9	3.4	1.1	0.6	2.5	2.0	3.3	2.7	..
Greece	7.0	8.5	4.7	5.4	2.6	2.0	2.1	2.2	1.2	2.3	..	..	..	..
Hungary	1.7	1.7	1.7	1.7	1.7	1.7	1.7	1.7	1.7	1.7	1.7	1.0	0.4	..
Iceland	-3.9	4.3	-0.8	-0.4	-2.6	-2.6	-2.6	0.3	3.2	4.0	6.1	3.4	-1.0	-0.5
Ireland	-2.2	1.4	0.5	-0.9	-0.8	1.6	4.6	5.1	4.5	6.4	8.4	10.0	..	..
Italy	0.2	0.1	3.2	3.2	2.6	1.6	2.6	2.2	1.6	1.8	3.1	2.2	6.1	..
Japan	0.0	0.3	0.3	-0.1	-0.7	-0.4	-0.1	0.1	0.3	-0.1	0.3	..	..	..
Korea	..	..	..	..	..	..	..	..	..	..	..	..	..	..
Luxembourg	10.2	10.8	11.0	10.6	9.9	11.2	8.9	9.0	9.5	10.9	8.3	2.5	5.9	4.6
Mexico	-8.6	..	..	..	..	..	..	..	..	..	..	..	..	..
Netherlands	4.0	4.2	3.8	3.9	2.4	2.1	2.8	3.1	3.9	3.8	4.5	4.3	3.3	2.3
New Zealand	2.7	1.8	1.3	3.9	5.5	7.7	6.6	2.0	-1.7	-2.3	-2.9	2.5	9.7	8.7
Norway	0.5	1.9	2.3	3.0	1.6	1.4	1.4	2.5	3.2	4.3	2.0	1.8	3.7	2.4
Poland	-0.4	-0.4	-0.3	-0.4	-0.5	-0.5	-0.3	-0.3	-0.3	-0.4	-0.5	-0.4	-0.5	-0.4
Portugal	-5.6	-2.5	-1.0	1.5	1.0	0.5	1.0	1.5	1.5	..	..	..	..	..
Slovak Republic	0.4	0.2	0.4	0.3	0.9	0.5	0.4	0.3	0.2	0.3	0.3	0.2	0.2	0.2
Spain	0.9	0.9	0.9	0.9	0.9	0.9	1.3	1.6	3.1	4.9	9.0	10.2	16.1	14.3
Sweden	4.1	2.8	2.3	3.7	5.8	1.2	0.7	0.7	1.2	1.6	2.8	3.3	3.5	3.2
Switzerland	8.4	9.0	5.8	5.7	4.4	2.1	-0.8	-1.0	0.2	2.3	2.8	5.6	6.6	5.7
Turkey	5.1	1.7	1.7	1.7	1.6	1.6	1.6	1.6	1.5	1.5	1.5	1.5	1.4	1.4
United Kingdom	1.2	1.3	0.8	1.5	1.4	2.0	1.8	1.5	1.2	..	..	..	..	..
United States	2.2	3.8	3.9	3.4	3.1	3.3	3.5	3.6	3.2	3.1	3.1	4.5	4.5	4.4

StatLink: http://dx.doi.org/10.1787/414217837336

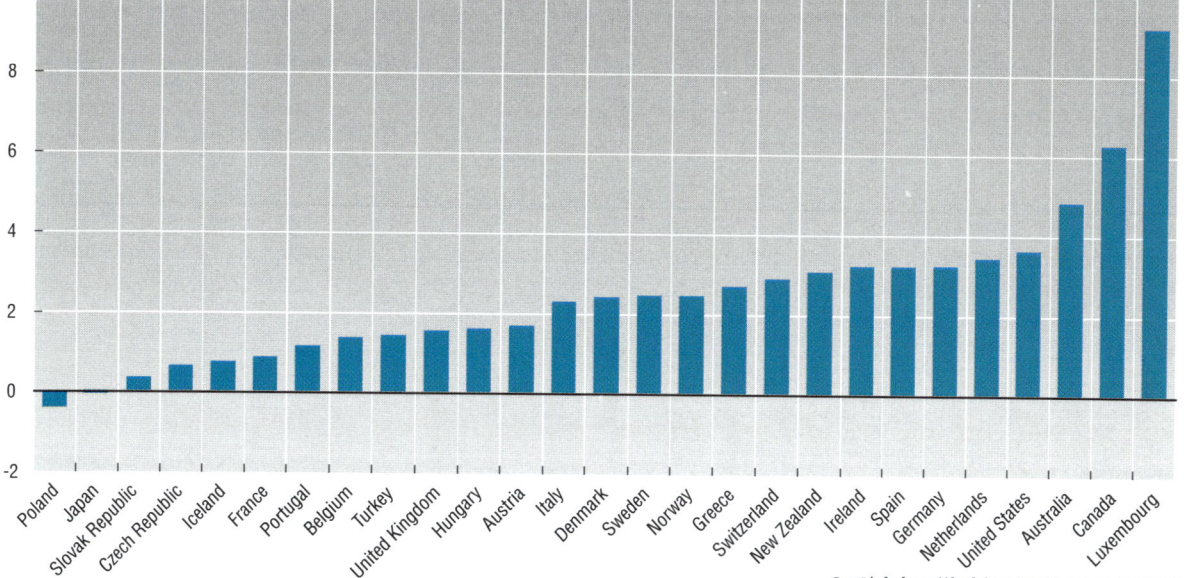

Net migration
Per 1 000 population, average 1990-2003

StatLink: http://dx.doi.org/10.1787/751148527455

MACROECONOMIC TRENDS

GROSS DOMESTIC PRODUCT (GDP)
SIZE OF GDP
VALUE ADDED BY ACTIVITY

ECONOMIC GROWTH
EVOLUTION OF GDP
EVOLUTION OF VALUE ADDED BY ACTIVITY
HOUSEHOLD SAVING

PRODUCTIVITY
LABOUR PRODUCTIVITY
MULTI-FACTOR PRODUCTIVITY

COMMODITIES: PRODUCTION AND SUPPLY
ENERGY SUPPLY
ELECTRICITY GENERATION
STEEL PRODUCTION
FISHERIES

MACROECONOMIC TRENDS • GROSS DOMESTIC PRODUCT (GDP)

SIZE OF GDP

Gross domestic product (GDP) is the standard measure of the incomes generated from productive activity. Total GDP is used as an indicator of the "size" of a country's economy and per capita GDP is a broad indicator of economic living standards.

Each country calculates GDP in its own currency and, in order to compare countries, these estimates have to be converted into a common currency. Often, the conversion is made using exchange rates, but these give a misleading comparison of the real volumes of goods and services in the GDP. Comparisons of real GDP between countries can only be made using purchasing power parities (PPPs) to convert each country's GDP into a common currency (see also page 84).

Long-term trends

In terms of total GDP, the United States is by far the largest member country. In 2002, its GDP of 10 429 billion US dollars exceeded even the combined GDP of the 15 members of the European Union (9 960 billion US dollars). Japan is the second largest economy followed, at some distance, by the four large EU members – Germany, France, United Kingdom and Italy. The next four largest are Canada, Mexico, Spain and Korea. These rankings have not changed significantly over the period shown, although, in 1990, the combined GDP of the EU15 was higher than that of the United States.

Per capita GDP for the OECD as a whole was just under 26 000 US dollars per head in 2002; this contrasts with a figure of 9 300 US dollars for the 150 countries generally defined as "developing". Six OECD countries had per capita GDP in excess of 30 000 US dollars – Luxembourg, United States, Norway, Ireland, Switzerland and Canada. Just under half of the 30 OECD members had per capita GDP between 25 000 and 30 000 US dollars, while 11 countries had per capita GDP below 25 000 US dollars. Turkey, Mexico and the four new member countries from central Europe had the lowest per capita GDP. Note that both GDP and PPPs contain statistical errors, and differences between countries in per capita GDP of 5% or less are not significant.

Note that for the last two tables, the OECD averages exclude the Czech Republic, Hungary, Poland, and the Slovak Republic.

Definition

Gross domestic product can be defined in three different ways: as the sum of labour incomes, net profits and depreciation; as the difference between gross output and intermediate consumption; or as the sum of consumption expenditures, fixed capital formation, changes in inventories and net exports.

PPPs are currency converters that equalise the purchasing power of the different currencies.

Gross Domestic product can be expressed in current prices (nominal GDP) or constant prices (real GDP). Real GDP is more appropriate for making comparison over time.

Comparability

Virtually all OECD countries now follow the 1993 System of National Accounts. However, since Luxembourg and, to a lesser extent, Switzerland, have a relatively large number of frontier workers, their GDP per capita is overstated compared with other countries. Such workers contribute to the GDP but are excluded from the population figures.

Source

OECD (2004), *National Accounts of OECD Countries*, OECD, Paris.

Further information

• *Analytical publications*

OECD (2003), *The Sources of Economic Growth in OECD Countries*, OECD, Paris.

OECD (2004), *OECD Economic Outlook*, No. 76, OECD, Paris.

• *Statistical publications*

Maddison, Angus (2003), *The World Economy: Historical Statistics*, Development Centre Studies, OECD, Paris, also available on CD-ROM, www.theworldeconomy.org.

• *Methodological publications*

OECD (2000), *System of National Accounts, 1993 – Glossary*, OECD, Paris.

UN, OECD, IMF, World Bank, Eurostat (eds.) (1993), *System of National Accounts 1993*, United Nations, Geneva, http://unstats.un.org/unsd/sna1993.

Online databases

SourceOECD Economic Outlook.

SourceOECD National Accounts.

Web sites

OECD Economic Outlook – Sources and Methods: www.oecd.org/eco/sources-and-methods.

MACROECONOMIC TRENDS • GROSS DOMESTIC PRODUCT (GDP)

SIZE OF GDP

Gross domestic product
Billion US dollars, current prices and PPPs

	1990	1991	1992	1993	1994	1995	1996	1997	1998	1999	2000	2001	2002	2003
Australia	288.9	298.7	316.2	335.1	357.6	383.4	402.4	426.2	453.0	482.7	507.1	534.7	557.3	..
Austria	145.0	155.0	162.3	166.7	174.6	182.1	189.8	194.9	202.8	211.7	223.3	228.1	233.4	239.1
Belgium	179.3	189.0	196.3	198.9	209.6	220.1	226.1	234.3	242.1	250.9	265.6	278.9	287.5	295.5
Canada	534.6	541.5	558.8	585.0	626.1	656.6	679.9	720.6	758.4	812.5	874.9	912.5	958.6	994.1
Czech Republic	113.9	104.2	106.1	108.6	113.3	123.1	131.8	131.8	131.9	133.4	136.4	147.1	155.6	164.6
Denmark	94.3	98.7	101.6	104.0	112.0	118.0	124.4	130.5	135.3	143.6	150.2	156.7	157.7	161.2
Finland	89.7	87.0	85.8	86.7	92.0	97.2	101.6	111.5	119.8	122.2	131.3	136.9	137.8	141.8
France	1 034.0	1 080.8	1 122.2	1 137.8	1 185.8	1 236.7	1 279.7	1 342.9	1 406.7	1 460.4	1 532.5	1 619.3	1 678.9	1 714.9
Germany	1 403.0	1 526.0	1 596.1	1 615.1	1 687.8	1 761.3	1 821.4	1 860.8	1 918.7	1 971.5	2 042.8	2 098.6	2 142.5	2 178.2
Greece	114.8	122.5	126.2	127.1	132.3	138.6	144.0	152.4	159.0	165.6	175.6	186.8	202.9	215.6
Hungary	..	84.7	84.0	85.5	89.9	93.5	97.3	102.5	108.7	114.0	121.2	133.2	141.6	148.2
Iceland	5.1	5.3	5.3	5.4	5.8	5.9	6.4	6.7	7.2	7.5	7.9	8.3	8.2	8.7
Ireland	45.3	47.8	50.6	53.1	57.4	64.5	70.3	80.7	88.8	97.1	106.7	115.7	126.7	134.9
Italy	988.3	1 037.0	1 069.0	1 083.9	1 131.2	1 194.3	1 239.4	1 272.1	1 338.2	1 369.2	1 425.9	1 469.5	1 491.6	1 520.4
Japan	2 323.4	2 485.2	2 567.2	2 632.6	2 717.7	2 826.7	2 979.0	3 084.9	3 084.0	3 130.3	3 289.6	3 382.5	3 422.4	3 571.9
Korea	357.6	404.2	436.0	470.5	520.1	578.0	630.2	670.5	631.5	701.4	777.5	826.6	897.8	940.8
Luxembourg	9.6	10.8	11.3	12.0	12.7	13.2	13.9	15.2	16.8	19.1	21.3	21.8	22.4	23.5
Mexico	515.8	556.2	589.8	615.1	655.8	627.9	672.9	730.4	775.7	815.4	887.9	909.0	929.1	..
Netherlands	267.0	283.0	293.8	302.6	317.8	335.9	351.2	370.0	389.1	404.2	429.6	461.4	470.7	475.1
New Zealand	49.0	50.0	51.8	56.4	60.6	64.4	67.9	70.1	71.1	75.7	79.4	83.9	89.0	..
Norway	76.2	81.7	86.4	90.7	97.5	104.4	115.3	122.5	121.1	133.9	161.0	165.3	161.6	165.0
Poland	227.5	219.0	229.6	243.7	262.0	287.4	312.7	336.5	356.6	373.8	392.8	406.3	415.8	438.6
Portugal	107.3	115.9	119.9	120.1	123.9	132.5	138.2	146.4	156.1	166.4	175.4	183.9	190.4	191.3
Slovak Republic	..	..	35.5	37.1	40.2	43.6	47.5	50.1	52.8	53.9	57.4	61.2	66.1	70.0
Spain	507.2	538.3	555.8	562.7	588.3	620.1	648.2	676.8	719.0	771.3	811.3	860.1	911.8	949.4
Sweden	160.3	164.1	165.7	166.1	176.7	188.6	195.6	201.5	208.2	222.3	235.8	239.6	244.3	252.3
Switzerland	164.2	168.6	172.5	176.0	181.7	187.1	187.1	197.6	205.2	206.4	216.3	219.9	228.2	230.5
Turkey	255.3	266.6	289.1	319.5	308.5	339.2	372.5	403.5	420.7	403.7	454.0	415.4	450.8	484.8
United Kingdom	944.3	964.0	988.1	1 034.4	1 102.9	1 157.3	1 219.3	1 300.9	1 356.5	1 403.6	1 485.1	1 573.5	1 661.5	1 726.6
United States	5 757.2	5 946.9	6 286.8	6 604.3	7 017.5	7 342.3	7 762.3	8 250.9	8 694.6	9 216.2	9 764.8	10 049.0	10 429.0	..
EU15	6 089.5	6 420.1	6 644.7	6 771.0	7 104.9	7 460.4	7 763.3	8 090.6	8 457.2	8 779.1	9 212.2	9 630.9	9 960.3	10 219.6
OECD total	16 879.2	17 669.2	18 459.6	19 136.6	20 159.0	21 124.1	22 228.5	23 395.5	24 329.7	25 439.9	26 940.3	27 885.7	28 871.5	..

StatLink: http://dx.doi.org/10.1787/603760283737

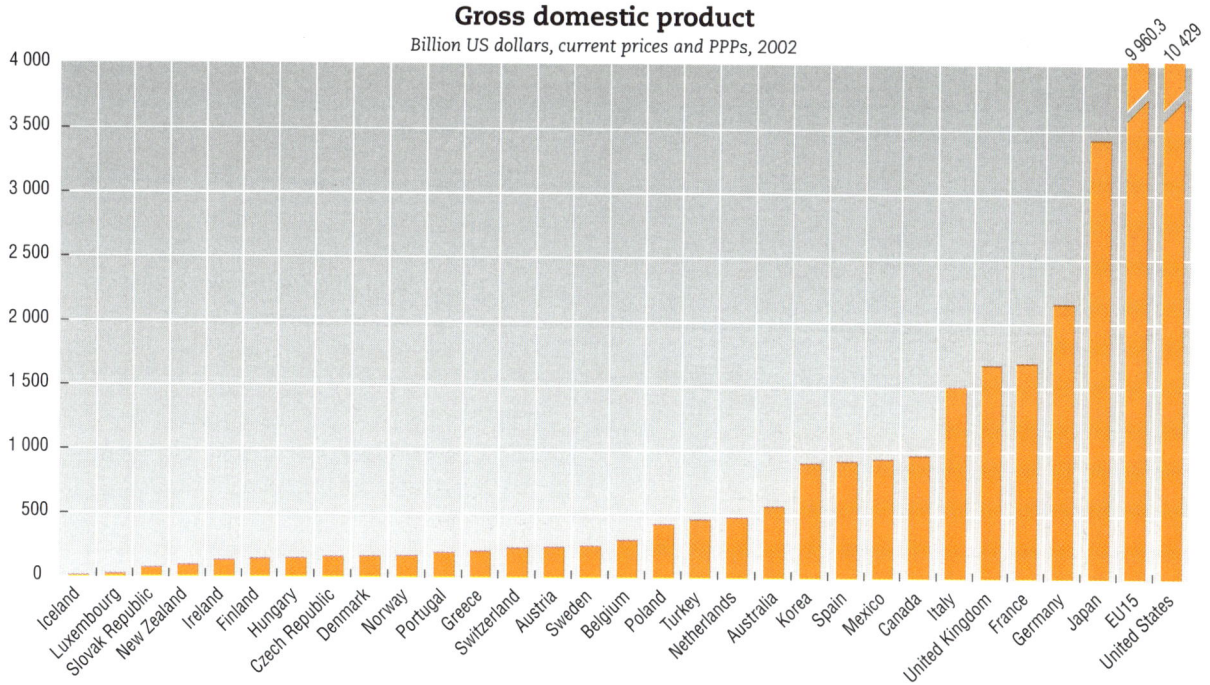

Gross domestic product
Billion US dollars, current prices and PPPs, 2002

StatLink: http://dx.doi.org/10.1787/454088531624

MACROECONOMIC TRENDS • GROSS DOMESTIC PRODUCT (GDP)

SIZE OF GDP

GDP per capita
US dollars, current prices and PPPs

	1990	1991	1992	1993	1994	1995	1996	1997	1998	1999	2000	2001	2002
Australia	16 663	17 039	17 862	18 758	19 790	20 973	21 755	22 853	24 048	25 448	26 224	27 332	28 068
Austria	18 698	19 809	20 496	20 869	21 752	22 818	23 764	24 438	25 434	26 504	27 865	28 373	28 872
Belgium	17 932	18 854	19 530	19 728	20 726	21 634	22 186	22 996	23 740	24 554	25 916	27 096	27 716
Canada	19 101	19 146	19 545	20 248	21 414	22 245	22 797	23 976	25 047	26 631	28 367	29 290	30 303
Czech Republic	11 087	10 209	10 397	10 640	11 098	12 020	12 882	12 933	12 970	13 133	13 669	14 860	15 102
Denmark	18 303	19 137	19 663	20 059	21 528	22 477	23 562	24 673	25 528	27 004	28 144	29 223	29 231
Finland	17 990	17 357	17 009	17 118	18 078	19 037	19 824	21 684	23 240	23 668	25 359	26 390	26 495
France	17 718	18 453	19 091	19 292	20 026	20 730	21 381	22 424	23 436	24 235	25 293	26 552	27 217
Germany	17 621	19 045	19 796	19 905	20 733	21 487	22 160	22 661	23 400	24 029	24 851	25 456	25 917
Greece	11 073	11 733	12 016	12 040	12 479	12 983	13 399	14 126	14 683	15 220	16 073	17 020	18 439
Hungary	..	8 176	8 137	8 307	8 758	9 022	9 400	9 954	10 592	11 146	11 879	13 043	13 894
Iceland	20 047	20 537	20 098	20 558	21 668	22 051	23 494	24 788	26 282	27 134	27 949	29 031	28 399
Ireland	12 891	13 541	14 219	14 872	16 000	17 885	19 390	22 064	23 923	25 922	28 035	29 822	32 646
Italy	17 368	18 241	18 793	19 009	19 778	20 764	21 515	22 100	23 248	23 766	24 682	25 377	25 568
Japan	18 715	19 968	20 593	21 089	21 694	22 484	23 652	24 499	24 462	24 801	25 984	26 636	26 954
Korea	7 416	8 313	8 886	9 502	10 394	11 451	12 344	13 093	12 281	13 718	15 186	15 916	17 016
Luxembourg	25 068	27 848	28 656	30 144	31 485	32 161	33 283	36 138	39 450	44 120	48 420	49 230	49 150
Mexico	6 289	6 519	6 795	6 967	7 296	6 932	7 270	7 765	8 107	8 356	9 110	9 148	9 215
Netherlands	17 808	18 749	19 347	19 798	20 664	21 643	22 540	23 685	24 790	25 578	26 982	28 711	29 009
New Zealand	13 982	13 943	14 385	15 298	16 330	17 018	17 508	18 233	18 278	19 378	20 412	21 230	21 783
Norway	17 908	19 137	20 139	21 054	22 490	23 865	26 228	27 778	27 326	30 002	35 816	36 587	35 482
Poland	6 038	5 800	6 072	6 434	6 899	7 529	8 180	8 813	9 329	9 742	10 174	10 496	10 846
Portugal	10 806	11 722	12 029	12 051	12 390	13 159	13 687	14 490	15 420	16 368	17 150	17 886	18 434
Slovak Republic	..	..	6 700	6 967	7 522	8 109	8 818	9 305	9 804	10 010	10 657	11 323	12 255
Spain	13 014	13 807	14 242	14 401	15 023	15 750	16 443	17 186	18 231	19 477	20 317	21 347	22 406
Sweden	18 666	19 008	19 109	19 064	20 126	21 286	22 040	22 762	23 530	25 106	26 576	26 902	27 209
Switzerland	24 300	24 592	24 833	25 131	25 721	26 143	26 073	27 583	28 593	28 542	29 759	30 036	30 455
Turkey	4 526	4 643	4 947	5 372	5 092	5 480	5 918	6 324	6 495	6 135	6 730	6 046	6 408
United Kingdom	16 359	16 664	17 068	17 850	18 984	19 903	20 930	22 347	23 276	24 014	25 322	26 627	27 948
United States	23 005	23 418	24 400	25 318	26 571	27 554	28 767	30 278	31 607	33 013	34 602	35 179	36 121
EU15	16 581	17 428	17 976	18 253	19 086	19 931	20 687	21 565	22 519	23 315	24 364	25 333	26 019
OECD total	16 667	17 294	17 914	18 415	19 223	19 973	20 824	21 799	22 535	23 364	24 573	25 174	25 810

StatLink: http://dx.doi.org/10.1787/107776373482

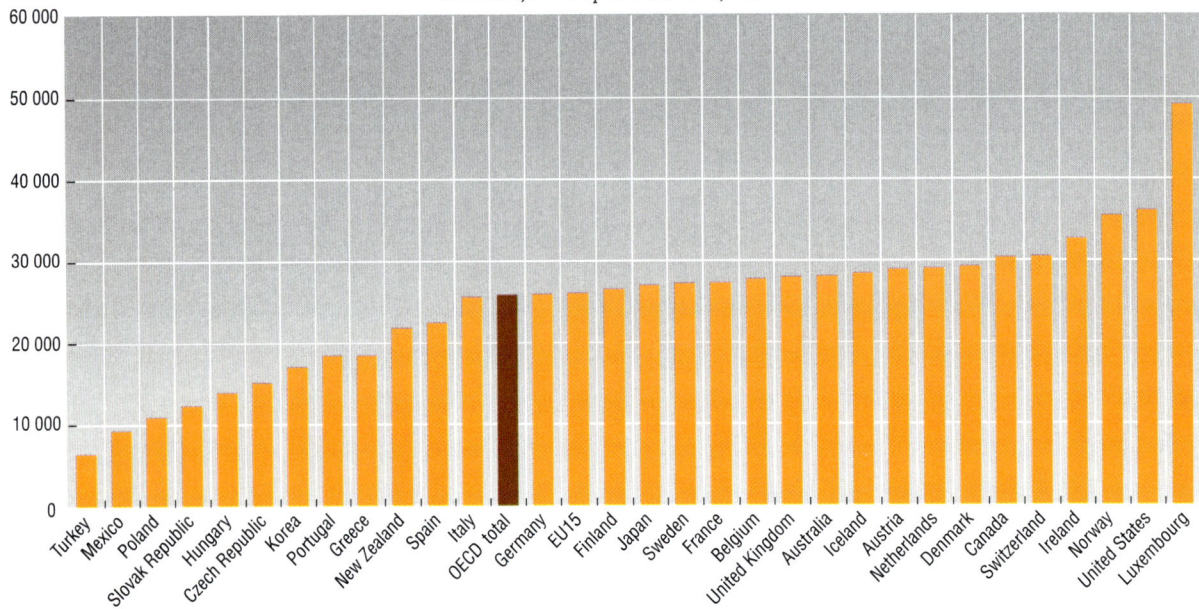

GDP per capita
US dollars, current prices and PPPs, 2002

StatLink: http://dx.doi.org/10.1787/850132735516

MACROECONOMIC TRENDS • GROSS DOMESTIC PRODUCT (GDP)

SIZE OF GDP

Volume index of GDP per capita
OECD = 100, at 1995 price levels and PPPs

	1990	1991	1992	1993	1994	1995	1996	1997	1998	1999	2000	2001	2002
Australia	100.2	99.1	100.5	102.9	103.8	105.0	105.4	106.0	108.2	108.8	106.0	108.8	109.1
Austria	112.2	114.5	114.4	113.3	113.1	114.2	113.9	112.6	114.6	114.7	114.7	115.2	115.2
Belgium	107.6	109.0	109.0	107.1	107.8	108.3	107.1	107.6	107.4	108.1	108.5	108.8	107.8
Canada	114.6	110.7	109.1	109.9	111.4	111.4	109.6	110.1	111.4	114.0	115.3	116.2	117.5
Czech Republic	66.5	59.0	58.0	57.8	57.7	60.2	61.5	59.5	57.8	56.8	56.9	58.9	59.5
Denmark	109.8	110.7	109.8	108.9	112.0	112.5	112.3	112.1	112.2	112.1	111.4	112.6	112.1
Finland	108.0	100.4	94.9	92.9	94.0	95.3	96.6	99.7	102.4	103.1	104.8	105.6	106.6
France	106.3	106.7	106.6	104.7	104.2	103.8	102.4	101.2	102.3	102.7	102.8	104.3	103.9
Germany	105.7	110.1	110.5	108.1	107.8	107.6	105.8	104.3	104.3	103.9	103.4	104.0	102.9
Greece	66.4	67.8	67.1	65.4	64.9	65.0	64.7	64.9	65.4	65.8	66.4	68.9	70.6
Hungary	..	47.3	45.4	45.1	45.6	45.2	44.9	45.8	47.2	48.2	49.2	51.2	52.6
Iceland	120.3	118.8	112.2	111.6	112.7	110.4	113.0	114.3	117.0	117.6	118.7	120.3	117.2
Ireland	77.4	78.3	79.4	80.7	83.2	89.5	94.1	100.8	105.9	113.8	120.0	125.6	130.9
Italy	104.2	105.5	104.9	103.2	102.9	104.0	102.7	101.8	101.5	100.7	100.5	101.9	101.0
Japan	112.3	115.5	115.0	114.5	112.8	112.6	113.7	112.5	108.8	106.2	105.6	105.7	104.5
Korea	44.5	48.1	49.6	51.6	54.1	57.3	59.4	60.1	54.6	58.7	61.7	63.1	66.0
Luxembourg	150.4	161.0	160.0	163.7	163.8	161.0	160.6	167.2	173.0	179.7	187.4	188.3	186.7
Mexico	37.7	37.7	37.9	37.8	38.0	34.7	35.0	35.7	36.1	35.8	37.0	36.3	35.7
Netherlands	106.9	108.4	108.0	107.5	107.5	108.4	108.9	109.5	111.3	112.4	111.8	112.3	110.6
New Zealand	84.1	80.4	79.5	83.2	84.5	85.2	85.1	83.1	81.3	82.9	82.0	84.0	85.3
Norway	107.5	110.7	112.4	114.3	117.0	119.5	122.5	124.8	124.8	123.7	122.4	124.1	123.2
Poland	36.2	33.5	33.9	34.9	35.9	37.7	39.1	40.6	41.7	42.5	42.8	43.2	43.8
Portugal	64.8	67.8	67.1	65.4	64.4	65.9	66.6	67.2	68.6	69.3	69.1	69.7	68.7
Slovak Republic	..	..	37.4	37.8	39.1	40.6	42.1	42.8	43.7	43.3	42.7	44.3	46.0
Spain	78.1	79.8	79.5	78.2	78.1	78.9	79.0	79.9	81.5	82.6	82.8	84.4	84.6
Sweden	112.0	109.9	106.7	103.5	104.7	106.6	105.5	105.2	106.8	109.1	110.1	110.7	111.3
Switzerland	143.6	140.5	137.7	135.9	133.4	130.9	128.4	127.3	127.9	126.0	125.8	126.1	123.5
Turkey	27.2	26.9	27.6	29.2	26.5	27.4	28.3	29.1	28.9	26.5	26.9	24.5	25.7
United Kingdom	98.2	96.4	95.3	96.9	98.7	99.7	100.0	100.4	101.2	101.3	101.6	103.0	103.3
United States	138.0	135.4	136.2	137.5	138.2	138.0	138.3	139.0	140.6	141.4	140.6	139.5	140.1
EU15	99.5	100.8	100.3	99.1	99.3	99.8	99.1	98.7	99.4	99.7	99.7	100.9	100.5
OECD total	100.0	100.0	100.0	100.0	100.0	100.0	100.0	100.0	100.0	100.0	100.0	100.0	100.0

StatLink: http://dx.doi.org/10.1787/650844670661

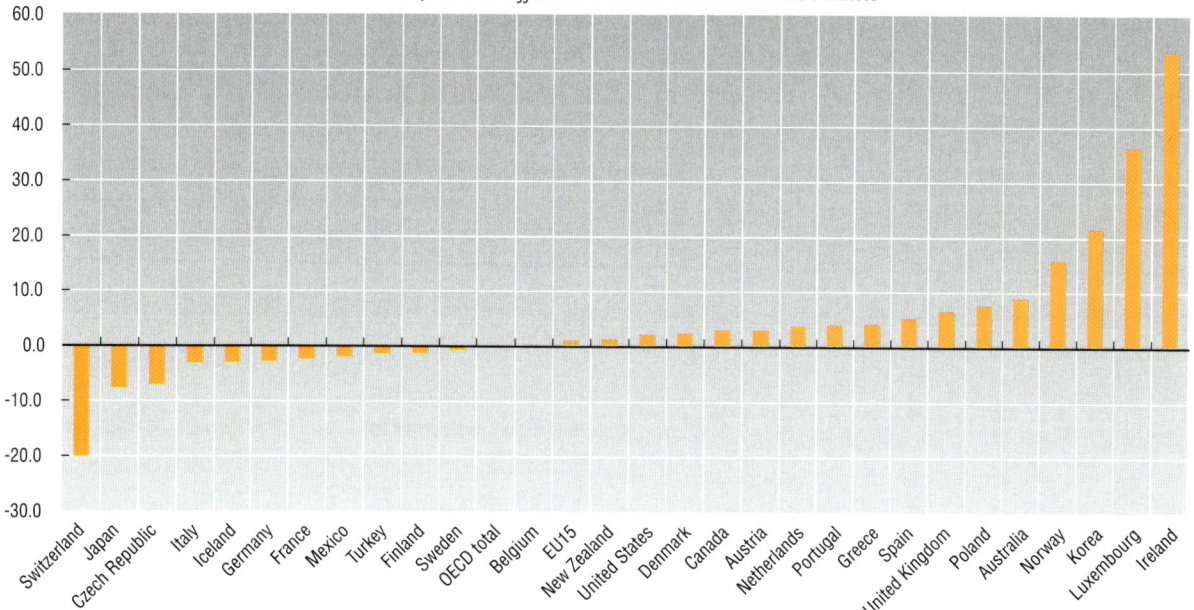

Change in volume indices of GDP per capita
OECD = 100, absolute differences between the 2002 and 1990 indices

StatLink: http://dx.doi.org/10.1787/568242257510

MACROECONOMIC TRENDS • GROSS DOMESTIC PRODUCT (GDP)

VALUE ADDED BY ACTIVITY

The contributions of primary, secondary and tertiary activities to total value added have changed sharply over recent decades. Agriculture, fishing and forestry are now relatively small in almost all OECD countries. The share of manufacturing has also fallen in most countries while services now account for well over 60% of total GDP in all OECD countries.

Definition

Value added is defined as gross output minus intermediate consumption and equals the sum of employee compensation, net operating surplus and depreciation of capital assets. The shares of each sector are calculated by dividing the value added in each sector by total value added. Total value added is less than GDP because it excludes value-added tax (VAT) and similar product taxes.

Industry consists of mining and quarrying, manufacturing, and production and distribution of electricity, gas and water; trade consists of retail and wholesale trade and repair services; real estate covers rents for dwellings including the imputed rents of owner-occupiers; government includes public administration, law and order and defense.

Comparability

Virtually all OECD member countries follow the international 1993 System of National Accounts so there is good comparability between countries as regards the definitions of value added and the coverage of the six sectors. However, the decline of industry and the rise of service activities are overstated to some extent because of the move in the last decade towards "outsourcing" by industrial enterprises of service activities that were previously carried out internally. For example, if cleaning and security services were earlier provided by employees of a manufacturing enterprise, their salaries would have formed part of value added by industry, but if these services are now purchased from specialised producers the salaries of the employees will form part of the value added of other business services. There will appear to have been a decline in the share of industry and a rise in the share of services although there may have been no change in the quantity of cleaning and security services actually produced.

Long-term trends

The share of agriculture has been declining throughout the period in almost all countries and towards the end of the period makes a significant contribution only in Greece, Iceland (fishing), New Zealand and Turkey. Shares in industry have also been falling throughout the period although for the OECD as a whole, industry still accounted for around 28% of GDP by 2000. Manufacturing is the most important activity within industry except in Norway where oil and gas production are more important.

All service activities account for around 70% of GDP for the OECD countries as a whole with very high shares in Denmark, Greece, Luxembourg, Netherlands and the United Kingdom and rather low shares in the Czech Republic, Korea, Norway and Turkey. It should be noted, however, that in most countries the largest part of service value added is "goods related" and consists of trade, transport and business services purchased by industry. A high share of service value added does not necessarily mean that a country has become a "service economy"; the production, transport and distribution of goods remains the predominant activity in most OECD countries in terms of employment and value added.

Source

OECD (2004), *National Accounts of OECD Countries*, OECD, Paris.

Further information

• *Analytical publications*

Lal, K. (2003), "Measurement of Ouput, Value Added, GDP in Canada and the United States: Similarities and Differences", *OECD Statistics Directorate Working Paper*, No. 2003/4, OECD, Paris, *www.oecd.org/std/workingpapers*.

OECD (1996), *Services: Measuring Real Value Added*, OECD, Paris.

OECD (2002), *Measuring the Non-Observed Economy: A Handbook*, OECD, Paris.

• *Online databases*

SourceOECD STructural ANalysis (STAN) Database.

• *Web sites*

OECD National Accounts: *www.oecd.org/std/national-accounts*.

OECD National Accounts Archive: *www.oecd.org/std/national-accounts/papers*.

MACROECONOMIC TRENDS • GROSS DOMESTIC PRODUCT (GDP)

VALUE ADDED BY ACTIVITY

Value added in agriculture and industry as a percentage of total value added

	Agriculture, hunting, forestry and fishing							Industry, including energy						
	1990	1995	1999	2000	2001	2002	2003	1990	1995	1999	2000	2001	2002	2003
Australia	3.8	3.7	3.2	3.7	4.2	2.9	..	22.4	21.7	19.5	20.0	19.4	19.3	..
Austria	3.6	2.5	2.4	2.3	2.3	2.3	2.2	25.5	23.0	23.3	23.4	23.1	23.1	22.8
Belgium	2.2	1.6	1.3	1.4	1.4	1.2	1.3	25.9	23.1	21.8	22.1	21.4	21.2	20.8
Canada	2.9	2.9	2.5	2.3	..	..	..	24.5	25.8	26.1	28.3	..	..	..
Czech Republic	8.2	4.7	4.2	4.3	4.3	3.7	3.4	36.6	33.3	31.8	32.3	32.7	31.9	31.5
Denmark	4.3	3.6	2.5	2.8	2.9	2.4	2.3	20.3	20.3	20.1	21.1	20.4	20.5	20.2
Finland	6.3	4.5	3.6	3.8	3.5	3.5	3.4	24.8	28.2	27.0	27.9	26.5	25.7	25.1
France	3.7	3.2	3.0	2.7	2.7	2.6	2.6	22.7	21.1	20.4	20.1	20.0	19.7	18.8
Germany	1.7	1.3	1.2	1.2	1.2	1.1	1.1	31.4	25.3	24.6	24.6	24.4	24.3	24.4
Greece	10.0	9.9	7.9	7.3	7.0	7.0	6.6	18.8	16.0	14.3	14.5	14.3	14.2	13.9
Hungary	..	6.8	4.8	4.3	4.3	3.7	..	..	26.3	27.7	27.8	26.1	24.9	..
Iceland	11.5	11.3	9.5	8.8	9.1	..	..	19.4	19.2	16.9	17.0	17.6	..	..
Ireland	9.2	7.5	4.0	3.8	3.5	3.3	..	30.0	33.0	35.3	34.3	33.4	34.1	..
Italy	3.4	3.2	3.0	2.8	2.7	2.6	2.5	26.1	24.9	23.4	23.1	22.7	22.1	21.6
Japan	2.4	1.8	1.4	1.3	1.3	1.3	..	28.6	25.0	23.9	24.0	23.0	22.5	..
Korea	8.8	6.3	5.2	4.9	4.5	4.1	3.6	30.4	30.3	31.1	32.4	30.6	29.9	29.6
Luxembourg	1.5	1.0	0.7	0.7	0.6	0.6	0.5	21.9	15.0	12.0	11.9	11.7	10.8	10.4
Mexico	7.8	5.2	4.5	4.0	4.0	3.8	..	24.2	22.6	23.5	22.6	21.8	21.0	..
Netherlands	4.4	3.5	2.8	2.8	2.7	2.5	..	24.0	22.4	19.8	20.1	19.8	18.9	..
New Zealand	6.7	7.2	7.1	8.7	..	..	..	22.7	21.9	20.0	20.2	..	..	..
Norway	3.4	3.0	2.4	2.1	1.8	1.6	1.4	29.3	29.6	29.9	37.7	35.6	32.3	31.8
Poland	..	6.5	3.8	3.5	3.7	3.1	3.0	..	29.7	25.7	25.3	23.7	23.6	24.8
Portugal	8.0	5.2	3.7	3.4	3.7	3.6	..	23.9	23.4	21.5	20.8	20.2	20.1	..
Slovak Republic	..	5.9	4.7	4.6	4.9	4.4	3.9	..	33.1	29.1	28.4	27.6	25.8	26.7
Spain	5.3	4.4	3.8	3.5	3.4	3.2	3.2	24.6	22.1	21.1	20.7	19.9	19.3	18.8
Sweden	3.3	2.7	2.1	1.9	1.9	1.8	1.8	23.9	25.7	24.8	24.7	23.5	23.1	22.9
Turkey	17.6	15.7	14.9	14.2	11.7	11.7	11.9	25.8	26.4	22.6	23.5	25.0	25.5	25.1
United Kingdom	1.8	1.8	1.1	1.0	0.9	0.9	0.9	27.3	25.9	22.5	22.1	20.8	19.9	19.5
United States	2.1	1.6	1.6	1.6	1.6	..	..	23.5	22.2	19.8	19.2	17.9	..	..

StatLink: http://dx.doi.org/10.1787/420835718563

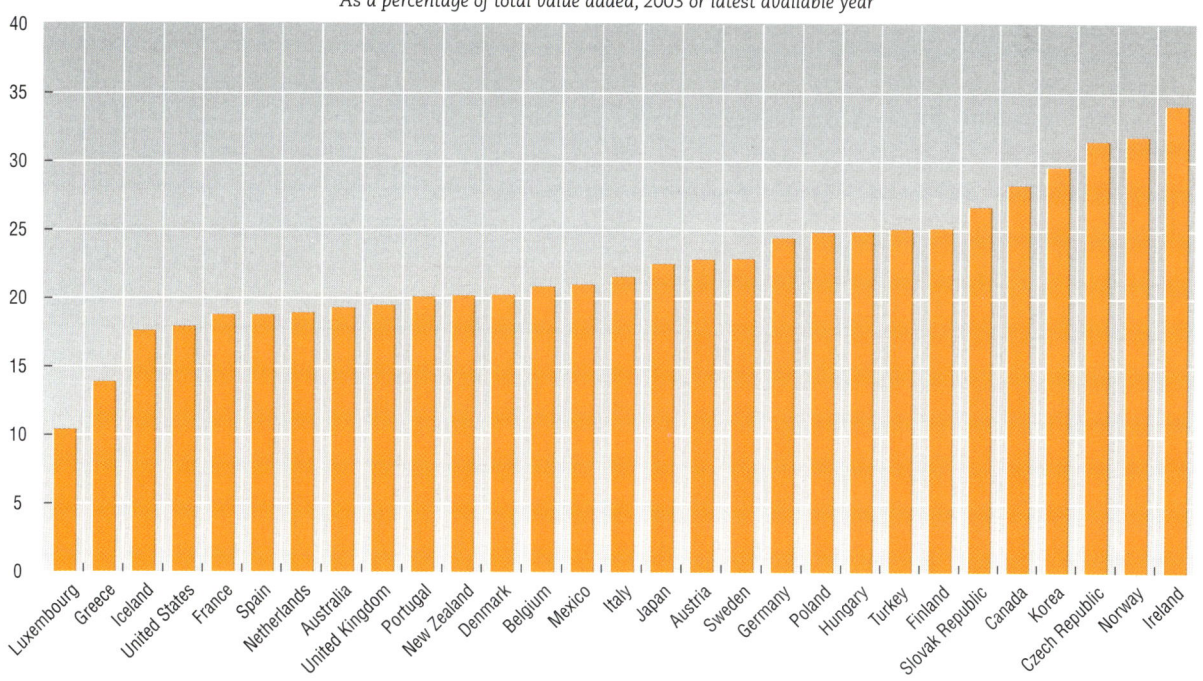

Value added in industry
As a percentage of total value added, 2003 or latest available year

StatLink: http://dx.doi.org/10.1787/065581213305

MACROECONOMIC TRENDS • GROSS DOMESTIC PRODUCT (GDP)

VALUE ADDED BY ACTIVITY

Value added in construction and in transport, trade, hotels and restaurants, as a percentage of total value added

	Construction							Transport, trade, hotels and restaurants						
	1990	1995	1999	2000	2001	2002	2003	1990	1995	1999	2000	2001	2002	2003
Australia	6.6	6.2	6.7	5.6	6.1	6.6	..	22.4	22.8	22.4	21.6	21.5	21.9	..
Austria	6.9	7.8	8.1	7.8	7.4	7.4	7.4	25.5	24.0	23.7	23.8	23.7	23.8	23.7
Belgium	5.5	5.2	5.0	5.0	4.9	4.9	4.8	20.9	20.7	19.9	19.9	20.3	20.2	19.9
Canada	6.8	4.9	5.1	5.0	..	..	..	21.7	20.7	21.0	20.3	..	..	..
Czech Republic	10.8	8.7	7.2	7.1	6.7	6.6	6.9	16.0	23.2	24.4	24.6	25.4	25.8	25.4
Denmark	5.0	4.5	5.3	5.2	5.0	5.0	5.0	21.7	22.4	22.1	21.8	21.6	21.2	21.3
Finland	8.3	4.5	5.8	5.5	5.6	5.4	5.3	21.8	21.0	22.2	21.6	22.1	22.3	22.6
France	5.7	5.2	4.4	4.6	4.8	4.9	5.0	20.0	19.3	19.3	19.1	19.3	19.0	18.6
Germany	6.1	6.7	5.5	5.2	4.8	4.5	4.2	17.4	17.7	17.5	17.7	18.1	18.0	18.0
Greece	7.6	6.4	7.3	7.5	8.3	8.1	9.0	25.6	26.8	28.8	29.1	29.1	28.2	28.2
Hungary	..	4.6	4.7	5.2	5.1	5.3	..	..	22.3	23.0	21.0	21.6	21.4	..
Iceland	9.1	7.5	8.1	8.6	9.0	..	..	22.7	23.4	22.1	22.0	20.0	..	..
Ireland	5.4	5.3	6.7	7.8	7.9	7.8	..	20.9	17.6	18.0	17.8	17.7	17.1	..
Italy	6.1	5.1	4.8	4.8	4.8	5.0	5.0	23.8	24.5	24.0	24.0	23.9	23.7	23.5
Japan	9.6	7.9	7.3	7.2	6.9	6.6	..	19.3	21.5	20.1	19.4	19.4	19.2	..
Korea	11.8	11.6	9.2	8.4	8.6	8.6	9.6	19.4	18.2	17.4	18.2	18.7	18.3	17.6
Luxembourg	6.8	6.2	5.5	5.5	5.9	6.0	5.9	23.1	20.9	21.3	22.4	21.8	20.7	20.4
Mexico	3.9	3.9	4.9	5.1	5.0	5.1	..	33.4	29.4	30.7	32.2	31.4	30.3	..
Netherlands	6.0	5.4	5.6	5.8	5.9	5.9	..	22.3	22.3	22.7	22.5	22.1	22.1	..
New Zealand	4.1	4.2	4.7	4.3	..	..	..	24.4	24.5	22.6	22.3	..	..	..
Norway	4.6	4.5	4.7	4.1	4.1	4.5	4.6	23.3	22.2	21.2	18.7	19.4	20.5	20.1
Poland	..	7.1	8.4	8.1	7.1	6.6	5.8	..	26.4	27.6	28.0	28.7	29.8	30.4
Portugal	5.9	6.6	7.5	7.7	7.8	7.4	..	24.4	23.8	23.6	23.6	23.9	23.9	..
Slovak Republic	..	5.1	5.5	5.4	5.1	5.3	5.3	..	24.7	26.8	27.0	27.4	26.2	24.2
Spain	8.6	7.5	7.9	8.4	8.7	9.2	9.7	25.0	26.7	27.6	27.5	27.7	27.9	27.8
Sweden	6.7	4.4	4.1	4.0	4.4	4.4	4.4	19.9	19.7	20.3	19.7	19.5	19.7	19.4
Turkey	6.4	5.5	5.5	5.2	5.0	4.1	3.6	31.2	33.2	32.3	34.4	35.8	35.5	35.4
United Kingdom	6.7	5.0	5.0	5.2	5.5	6.0	6.4	21.6	21.7	23.0	23.0	23.0	23.2	23.0
United States	4.6	4.2	4.8	4.9	5.0	..	..	21.9	22.3	22.7	22.8	22.6	..	..

StatLink: http://dx.doi.org/10.1787/346058855288

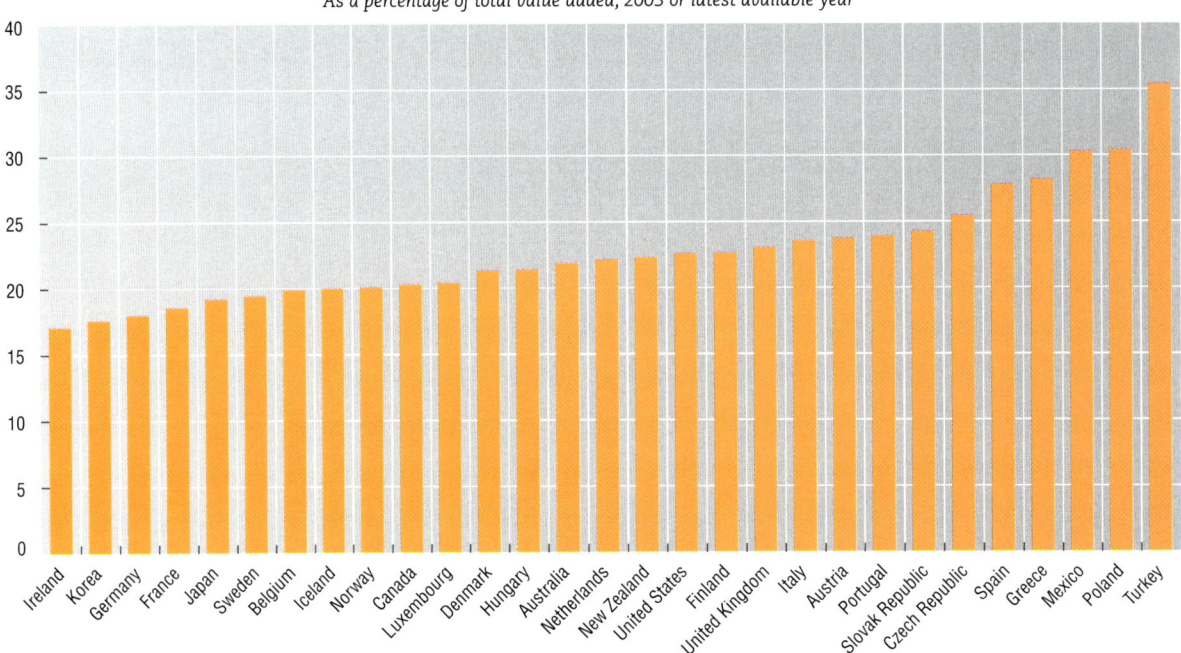

Value added in transport, trade, hotels and restaurants
As a percentage of total value added, 2003 or latest available year

StatLink: http://dx.doi.org/10.1787/105770577041

MACROECONOMIC TRENDS • GROSS DOMESTIC PRODUCT (GDP)

VALUE ADDED BY ACTIVITY

Value added in business services and in government and personal services as a percentage of total value added

	Banks, insurance, real estate and other business services							Government, health, education and other personal services						
	1990	1995	1999	2000	2001	2002	2003	1990	1995	1999	2000	2001	2002	2003
Australia	25.7	25.9	28.8	29.5	29.1	29.2	..	19.1	19.8	19.4	19.6	19.7	20.1	..
Austria	18.2	20.7	22.1	22.9	23.5	23.6	23.8	20.5	22.0	20.4	19.8	20.0	19.9	20.0
Belgium	23.0	25.9	28.2	28.0	28.0	27.9	28.5	22.6	23.9	23.7	23.7	24.1	24.6	24.7
Canada	22.7	24.2	25.6	24.9	..	..	..	21.4	21.4	19.7	19.2	..	..	..
Czech Republic	16.4	16.3	17.0	16.6	15.7	16.6	16.5	12.1	13.9	15.5	15.1	15.2	15.5	16.4
Denmark	22.9	22.5	23.2	23.4	24.1	24.3	24.4	25.9	26.6	26.7	25.7	26.1	26.6	26.8
Finland	16.8	19.1	19.9	20.4	21.1	21.5	21.4	22.0	22.7	21.6	20.7	21.2	21.6	22.1
France	26.8	27.7	29.2	29.9	29.6	29.9	31.0	21.2	23.5	23.7	23.5	23.5	24.0	24.0
Germany	23.2	27.3	29.7	29.8	29.9	30.2	30.5	20.4	21.6	21.5	21.5	21.5	21.8	21.7
Greece	17.5	21.2	21.4	21.5	21.2	21.3	21.3	18.7	19.7	20.3	20.1	20.2	21.1	21.0
Hungary	..	19.6	20.0	20.9	21.3	21.5	..	..	20.5	19.8	20.8	21.6	23.2	..
Iceland	16.7	16.3	19.3	19.6	20.6	..	..	20.6	22.4	24.1	23.9	23.7	..	..
Ireland	15.4	16.5	20.2	20.9	21.3	21.6	..	19.1	20.2	15.7	15.5	16.1	15.9	..
Italy	21.0	23.3	25.4	26.0	26.4	27.0	27.3	19.6	18.8	19.5	19.3	19.5	19.7	20.0
Japan	21.2	23.7	25.4	26.0	26.9	27.4	..	18.8	20.0	22.0	22.2	22.5	23.0	..
Korea	15.0	18.3	20.8	20.1	20.5	21.9	21.9	14.5	15.3	16.3	16.1	17.2	17.3	17.7
Luxembourg	29.2	40.2	44.8	44.4	44.2	46.1	47.2	17.4	16.7	15.7	15.1	15.7	15.8	15.7
Mexico	13.1	17.4	13.0	12.0	12.0	13.3	..	17.6	21.5	23.4	24.1	25.7	26.5	..
Netherlands	19.8	23.1	26.3	26.4	26.4	26.5	..	23.6	23.3	22.8	22.5	23.1	24.1	..
New Zealand	25.4	25.8	28.0	27.0	..	..	..	16.7	16.4	17.7	17.5	..	..	..
Norway	18.3	18.2	19.2	17.5	18.1	18.9	19.3	21.1	22.5	22.6	19.9	20.9	22.2	22.8
Poland	..	10.9	15.0	15.5	16.1	16.0	15.7	..	19.4	19.5	19.5	20.7	20.8	20.2
Portugal	18.6	18.2	19.2	18.9	18.9	18.4	..	19.2	23.0	24.6	25.5	25.6	26.7	..
Slovak Republic	..	17.5	18.0	18.3	17.8	20.7	21.9	..	13.7	15.9	16.3	17.2	17.6	17.9
Spain	17.9	18.6	19.0	19.3	20.0	19.9	20.1	18.6	20.7	20.7	20.6	20.2	20.4	20.5
Sweden	20.4	23.0	23.2	24.1	24.4	24.2	24.2	25.9	24.5	25.5	25.6	26.3	26.8	27.3
Turkey	6.6	7.4	9.7	8.5	8.3	8.9	9.2	12.4	11.9	15.0	14.2	14.2	14.3	14.9
United Kingdom	21.9	24.0	26.8	27.1	27.9	27.6	27.3	20.6	21.6	21.6	21.6	21.8	22.5	22.9
United States	24.8	26.3	29.0	29.7	30.3	..	..	23.2	23.4	22.1	21.9	22.7	..	..

StatLink: http://dx.doi.org/10.1787/262768236574

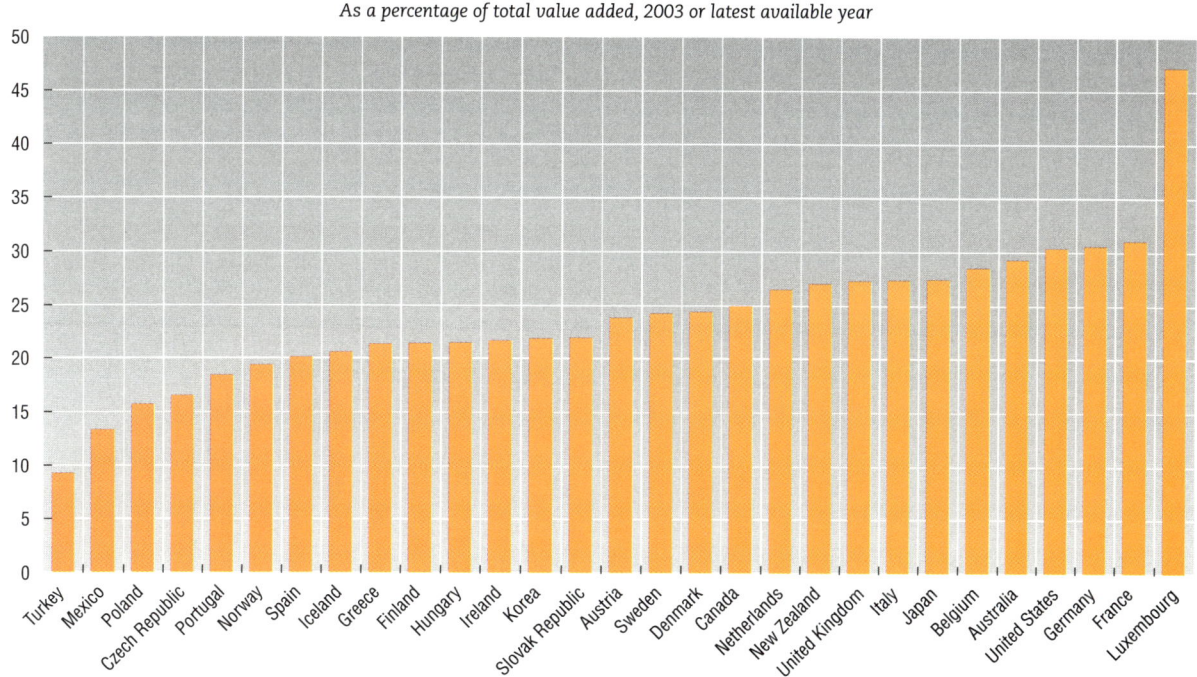

Value added in banks, insurance, real estate and other business services
As a percentage of total value added, 2003 or latest available year

StatLink: http://dx.doi.org/10.1787/432558880068

OECD FACTBOOK 2005 – ISBN 92-64-01869-7 – © OECD 2005

MACROECONOMIC TRENDS • ECONOMIC GROWTH

EVOLUTION OF GDP

Gross domestic product (GDP) is a broad measure of economic activity. Growth of "real" GDP, i.e. ignoring price changes, is widely used to assess governments' performance in managing their economies.

Real GDP growth is one of several macroeconomic indicators that are regularly forecast by the OECD secretariat. The table shows both actual estimates from 1990 to 2003 together with OECD projections for the following three years (2004-2006).

Definitions

Gross Domestic Product can be defined in three different ways: as the sum of labour incomes, net profits and depreciation; as the difference between gross output and intermediate consumption; or as the sum of consumption expenditures, fixed capital formation, changes in inventories and net exports. Real growth rates are obtained by converting GDP to constant prices and calculating the change from year to year.

Long-term trends

Annual growth for OECD total averaged 2.5% from 1991 to 2003. Ireland and Korea substantially outperformed the average with annual growth of over 5%. Growth rates in Ireland were particularly impressive between 1995 and 2000 – the *Celtic Tiger Period*. Korea's growth was badly affected by the financial crisis in Asia; real GDP fell by nearly 7% in 1998 but Korea has since returned to high rates of growth. Hungary, Luxembourg, Poland and the Slovak Republic all recorded growth of over 3.5% per year.

At the other end of the scale, four of the largest OECD economies – France, Germany, Italy and Japan – recorded average growth rates of less than 2% over the period. the United Kingdom was also at the lower end with average growth rates of 2.4%.

The Czech Republic, Hungary, Poland and the Slovak Republic all experienced substantial falls in real GDP in the early years of their transition to market-based economies but generally began to achieve positive rates of growth during the second half of the 1990s. Recent growth rates in Poland and the Slovak Republic are among the highest of all OECD countries and are forecast to remain above the OECD average through 2006.

The growth rates for OECD total and EU15 are averages of the growth rates of individual countries weighted by the relative size of each country's GDP in US dollars. Conversion to US dollars is done using purchasing power parities so that each country is weighted by the relative size of its real GDP. Note that OECD total GDP excludes the Czech Republic, Hungary, Poland and the Slovak Republic because growth rates for these countries are not available for the full period.

Comparability

The GDP statistics used for these growth rates have been compiled according to the 1993 System of National Accounts and GDP estimates at current prices are generally regarded as highly comparable between countries. However, there are no standard rules for converting current price GDP to constant prices and there are some differences between countries in the ways that they convert government consumption and some types of capital equipment to constant prices.

OECD projections

The OECD assessments of the future trends of key macroeconomic variables are best characterised as being conditional forecasts, since they depend on a set of technical assumptions about macroeconomic policies and international conditions such as nominal exchange rates, the paths of oil and non-oil commodity prices and other exogenous factors. Thus, the OECD projections provide answers to questions like: "What is likely to happen in country X if the government maintains the current set of macro policies and external/international conditions are broadly as assumed?" See Further information below for sources giving details on the methodology and underlying assumptions.

Sources

OECD (2004), *OECD Economic Outlook*, No. 76, OECD, Paris.

Further information

• **Statistical publications**

OECD (2004), *National Accounts of OECD Countries*, OECD, Paris.

• **Online databases**

SourceOECD Economic Outlook.

SourceOECD National Accounts.

• **Web sites**

OECD Economic Outlook – Sources and Methods: *www.oecd.org/eco/sources-and-methods*.

MACROECONOMIC TRENDS • ECONOMIC GROWTH

EVOLUTION OF GDP

Real GDP growth
Annual growth in percentage

	1991	1995	1996	1997	1998	1999	2000	2001	2002	2003	2004	2005	2006
Australia	-0.7	3.9	4.0	3.7	5.4	4.3	3.3	2.7	3.6	3.3	3.6	3.8	3.6
Austria	3.6	1.9	2.6	1.8	3.6	3.3	3.4	0.7	1.2	0.8	1.8	2.3	2.6
Belgium	1.8	2.3	0.8	3.8	2.1	3.2	3.7	0.9	0.9	1.3	2.7	2.4	2.7
Canada	-2.1	2.8	1.6	4.2	4.1	5.5	5.2	1.8	3.4	2.0	3.0	3.3	3.1
Czech Republic	..	5.9	4.3	-0.7	-1.1	1.2	3.9	2.6	1.5	3.1	3.9	4.2	4.1
Denmark	1.1	2.8	2.5	3.0	2.5	2.6	2.8	1.6	1.0	0.5	2.4	2.7	2.6
Finland	-6.4	3.5	3.7	6.5	4.9	3.2	5.4	1.0	2.3	2.1	3.1	2.8	3.1
France	1.0	1.8	1.0	1.9	3.6	3.2	4.2	2.1	1.1	0.5	2.1	2.0	2.3
Germany	5.1	1.8	0.8	1.5	1.7	1.9	3.1	1.0	0.1	-0.1	1.2	1.4	2.3
Greece	3.1	2.1	2.4	3.6	3.4	3.4	4.5	4.3	3.6	4.5	3.8	3.2	3.5
Hungary	..	1.5	1.3	4.6	4.9	4.2	5.2	3.9	3.5	2.9	3.9	3.6	3.5
Iceland	-0.2	0.1	5.2	4.7	5.5	4.1	5.7	2.2	-0.5	4.1	5.9	5.2	4.8
Ireland	1.9	9.8	8.1	10.8	8.7	11.1	9.9	6.0	6.1	3.6	4.9	5.5	4.9
Italy	1.4	3.0	1.0	2.0	1.7	1.7	3.2	1.7	0.4	0.4	1.3	1.7	2.1
Japan	3.4	1.9	3.4	1.9	-1.1	0.1	2.8	0.4	-0.3	2.5	4.0	2.1	2.3
Korea	9.2	9.0	7.0	4.7	-6.9	9.5	8.5	3.8	7.0	3.1	5.0	4.5	5.0
Luxembourg	8.6	1.4	3.3	8.3	6.9	7.8	9.0	1.5	2.5	2.9	4.2	4.5	4.3
Mexico	4.2	-6.2	5.1	6.8	4.9	3.7	6.6	-0.1	0.7	1.3	4.2	3.9	4.2
Netherlands	2.4	3.0	3.0	3.8	4.4	4.0	3.5	1.4	0.6	-0.9	1.2	1.2	2.4
New Zealand	-1.9	3.9	3.5	2.9	0.2	4.9	3.6	2.7	4.5	3.2	4.8	2.1	2.6
Norway	3.6	4.4	5.3	5.2	2.6	2.1	2.8	2.7	1.4	0.4	3.2	3.2	2.9
Poland	..	7.0	6.0	6.8	4.8	4.1	4.0	1.0	1.4	3.8	5.4	4.3	4.5
Portugal	4.4	4.3	3.5	4.0	4.6	3.8	3.4	1.6	0.4	-1.2	1.5	2.2	2.8
Slovak Republic	..	5.8	6.1	4.6	4.2	1.5	2.0	3.8	4.4	4.2	4.9	4.8	5.0
Spain	2.5	2.8	2.4	4.0	4.3	4.2	4.4	2.8	2.2	2.5	2.6	2.7	3.0
Sweden	-1.1	4.2	1.3	2.6	3.7	4.3	4.4	1.2	2.0	1.7	3.3	3.3	3.2
Switzerland	-0.8	0.4	0.5	1.9	2.8	1.3	3.6	1.0	0.3	-0.4	1.9	1.9	2.0
Turkey	0.9	7.2	7.0	7.5	3.1	-4.7	7.4	-7.5	7.9	5.8	9.8	6.4	5.8
United Kingdom	-1.4	2.9	2.8	3.3	3.1	2.9	3.9	2.3	1.8	2.2	3.2	2.6	2.4
United States	-0.2	2.5	3.7	4.5	4.2	4.5	3.7	0.8	1.9	3.0	4.4	3.3	3.6
OECD total	1.3	2.5	3.1	3.6	2.7	3.3	3.9	1.1	1.6	2.2	3.6	2.9	3.1

StatLink: http://dx.doi.org/10.1787/344630207118

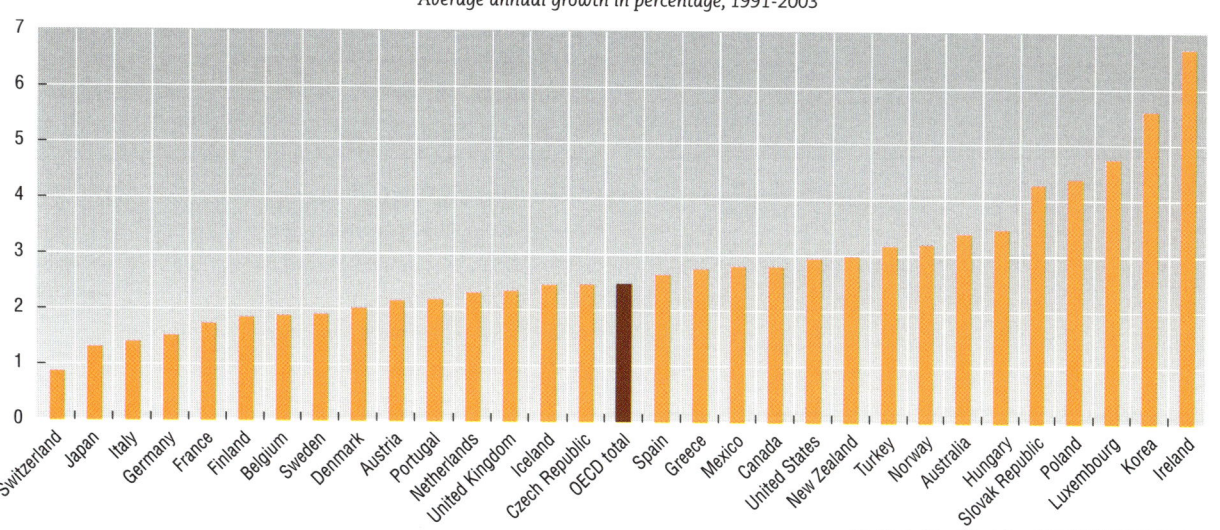

Real GDP growth
Average annual growth in percentage, 1991-2003

StatLink: http://dx.doi.org/10.1787/838512104052

OECD FACTBOOK 2005 – ISBN 92-64-01869-7 – © OECD 2005

MACROECONOMIC TRENDS • ECONOMIC GROWTH

EVOLUTION OF VALUE ADDED BY ACTIVITY

While total GDP has been growing in all OECD countries in most years since 1990, that growth is not evenly spread over all the different kinds of economic activities. Some economic activities have grown faster than others and some have tended to decline in importance. A convenient way to show how the patterns of growth are changing is to divide the economy into primary, secondary and tertiary sectors – agriculture, industry and services, respectively.

Definition

Value added is defined as gross output minus intermediate consumption and equals employee compensation, net operating surplus and depreciation of capital assets. The growth rates shown here refer to value added at constant prices.

Industry consists of mining and quarrying, manufacturing, and production and distribution of electricity, gas and water and construction. Services consists of retail and wholesale trade, transport and communications, real estate, finance, insurance and business services, education, health and other personal services, public administration and defence.

Long-term trends

For OECD countries as a whole, agriculture has been growing by about 1% per year since 1990, industry by just under 2.5% per year and services by 3% per year.

Annual growth in agriculture is generally very uneven, with changes from year to year of 10% or more being quite common. Growth in industry is somewhat smoother in most countries, while year-to-year growth in services tends to be very smooth in all countries, one reason being that services includes government services where value added – essentially compensation of employees – usually changes by only small amounts from year to year.

The graphs show growth rates averaged over the three latest years for which data are available. Over this recent period, agriculture declined in most OECD countries. Industry grew in most, although there were declines in the United Kingdom, Netherlands, Italy, Germany and Belgium. The service sector, however, grew in all countries with particularly sharp increases in New Zealand, United States, Canada, Greece, Korea and the Slovak Republic.

Comparability

Virtually all OECD member countries follow the international 1993 System of National Accounts, so there is good comparability between countries as regards the definitions and coverage. However, the decline of industry and the rise of service activities are overstated to some extent because of the move in the last decade towards "outsourcing" of service activities that were previously carried out internally within industrial enterprises. For example, if cleaning and security services were earlier provided by employees of a manufacturing enterprise, their salaries would have formed part of value added by industry but if these services are now purchased from specialised producers, the salaries of the employees will form part of the value added of the service sector. No change in the quantity of cleaning and security services produced may have occurred.

The OECD averages in these tables exclude the Czech Republic, Hungary, Ireland, Poland, Slovak Republic and Switzerland as data are not available for these countries for the full period. OECD averages for 2002 and 2003 include secretariat estimates and are provisional.

Source

OECD (2004), *National Accounts of OECD Countries*, OECD, Paris.

Further information

- *Analytical publications*

OECD (2004), *OECD Economic Outlook*, No. 76, OECD, Paris.

- *Statistical publications*

Maddison, Angus (2003), *The World Economy: Historical Statistics*, Development Centre Studies, OECD, Paris, also available on CD-ROM, *www.theworldeconomy.org*.

OECD (2005), *Quarterly National Accounts*, OECD, Paris.

- *Methodological publications*

OECD (2000), *System of National Accounts, 1993 – Glossary*, OECD, Paris.

UN, OECD, IMF, World Bank, Eurostat (eds.) (1993), *System of National Accounts 1993*, United Nations, Geneva, *http://unstats.un.org/unsd/sna1993*.

- *Online databases*

SourceOECD STructural ANalysis (STAN) Database.

- *Web sites*

OECD National Accounts: *www.oecd.std/national-accounts*.

MACROECONOMIC TRENDS • ECONOMIC GROWTH

EVOLUTION OF VALUE ADDED BY ACTIVITY

Real value added in agriculture, forestry and fishing
Annual growth in percentage

	1990	1991	1992	1993	1994	1995	1996	1997	1998	1999	2000	2001	2002	2003
Australia	6.57	-7.43	6.67	3.66	-17.17	23.49	8.19	-0.88	10.09	3.95	3.55	4.22	-26.96	..
Austria	4.08	-0.74	-0.83	-1.04	5.54	-1.08	-0.14	3.72	6.44	3.67	-3.01	0.58	-0.53	-1.31
Belgium	-7.47	8.16	16.35	6.16	-6.77	2.17	-0.24	2.86	3.39	5.09	1.00	-11.35	12.70	-3.22
Canada	3.06	-4.08	-6.06	6.74	1.32	1.41	0.09	-3.40	6.21	7.49	-1.39	-7.60	-5.18	..
Czech Republic	..	39.38	-21.00	51.69	-17.27	-4.87	-1.05	-3.01	11.76	4.09	5.67	-7.03	2.65	-0.96
Denmark	-1.18	-0.41	0.43	10.42	2.29	2.62	2.47	2.21	4.00	-2.03	6.35	-1.46	-4.33	3.27
Finland	-7.20	-12.85	3.95	4.81	9.43	-5.80	-0.77	12.47	-7.31	2.53	10.64	-4.77	3.63	0.60
France	4.35	-5.07	9.99	-4.73	1.49	3.58	5.10	1.75	1.67	3.71	-2.20	-3.96	4.75	-7.42
Germany	6.88	-7.99	5.93	2.11	-5.21	4.86	6.62	-0.35	2.31	5.50	-0.85	0.32	-1.79	-0.66
Greece	-15.29	17.49	-2.85	-1.41	5.85	-4.03	-3.33	0.41	2.30	3.50	-3.67	-3.76	-1.15	-3.98
Hungary	..	..	-16.54	-7.92	-0.45	2.65	4.15	-0.23	-1.36	0.92	-7.37	23.41	-12.08	-3.99
Iceland	2.16	-9.65	0.13	5.74	-4.78	-0.66	3.81	-1.75	0.33	-1.60	-0.64	1.19	2.73	..
Italy	-4.22	9.02	1.22	-0.42	0.72	1.42	1.93	1.12	1.18	5.77	-2.87	-0.50	-3.87	-5.66
Japan	-0.26	-11.23	2.73	-9.14	2.44	-5.98	2.38	-6.20	-3.09	-5.63	1.60	-4.09	2.45	..
Korea	-5.95	2.94	9.62	-4.55	0.23	6.63	2.30	4.62	-6.38	5.89	1.21	1.12	-3.50	-7.13
Luxembourg	-2.56	-10.53	38.24	2.84	-6.21	9.56	-4.03	-7.69	9.09	6.94	-7.14	-14.69	0.00	-2.46
Mexico	5.63	2.32	-0.97	3.08	0.18	1.83	3.80	0.16	3.03	1.50	0.38	5.94	-1.07	..
Netherlands	8.91	3.24	3.09	2.72	3.75	1.97	-1.95	-5.25	9.33	6.34	1.50	-4.33	-1.43	3.37
New Zealand	17.15	0.66	-11.96	16.86	0.58	7.33	7.68	0.73	-5.13	6.19	1.95	2.10	1.67	..
Norway	4.63	10.11	-4.97	14.62	2.81	6.53	-0.81	-1.42	2.33	-0.74	-1.71	-3.69	1.15	-2.85
Poland	..	..	..	6.00	-14.92	10.22	2.39	1.07	5.84	-0.23	-7.92	9.18	2.01	2.08
Portugal	-3.44	3.79	3.73	2.27	-2.11	-1.12	6.06	-8.08	-3.43	7.38	-4.02	-0.33	6.41	-3.40
Slovak Republic	..	..	..	..	..	8.13	-3.65	-2.35	10.03	5.43	0.27	1.86	4.89	-1.57	4.42
Spain	5.36	3.74	1.01	2.82	-4.74	-6.12	17.56	2.59	-0.62	-5.08	2.66	-2.95	1.68	-1.38
Sweden	8.20	-4.94	-1.63	2.13	-3.04	0.27	-0.81	1.51	-5.14	2.26	2.78	4.26	2.84	1.97
Turkey	6.82	-0.90	4.29	-1.28	-0.72	1.96	4.40	-2.34	8.37	-4.99	3.86	-6.51	6.87	-2.50
United Kingdom	1.52	4.99	4.12	-8.09	-1.21	-1.23	-2.23	2.28	2.77	3.36	-0.64	-9.09	11.91	-2.60
United States	4.03	1.68	8.45	-3.04	6.07	-10.06	5.85	10.28	4.66	13.28	8.68	-3.75	..	..
OECD unweighted average	1.74	-0.32	3.78	2.22	-0.39	1.65	2.66	0.39	1.93	3.09	0.75	-2.63	0.39	-1.61

StatLink: http://dx.doi.org/10.1787/806824527725

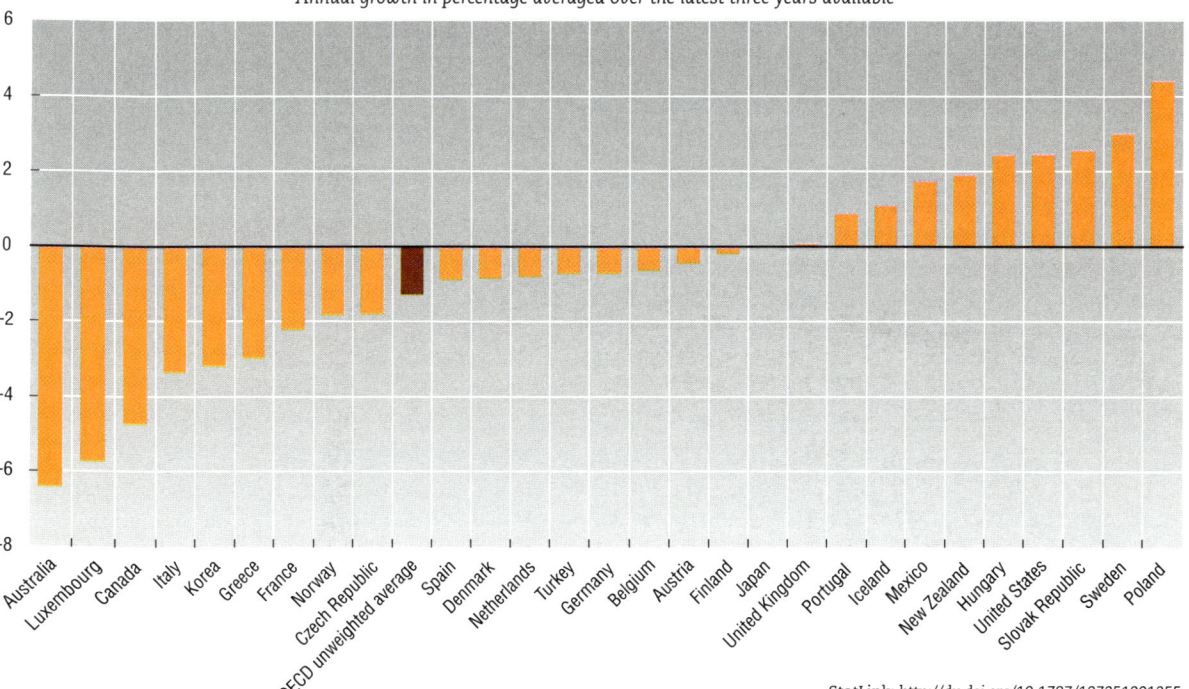

Real value added in agriculture, forestry and fishing
Annual growth in percentage averaged over the latest three years available

StatLink: http://dx.doi.org/10.1787/127351201355

OECD FACTBOOK 2005 – ISBN 92-64-01869-7 – © OECD 2005

MACROECONOMIC TRENDS • ECONOMIC GROWTH

EVOLUTION OF VALUE ADDED BY ACTIVITY

Real value added in industry
Annual growth in percentage

	1990	1991	1992	1993	1994	1995	1996	1997	1998	1999	2000	2001	2002	2003
Australia	0.26	-0.56	1.72	3.67	3.35	3.49	1.62	3.31	1.31	2.24	3.64	1.45	2.03	..
Austria	5.91	2.06	-0.31	-1.61	2.38	4.13	2.00	3.69	4.13	5.39	6.16	2.53	1.75	0.19
Belgium	2.67	-1.14	-1.86	-3.84	3.96	3.60	2.49	6.61	0.70	1.15	5.01	-0.30	-0.24	-0.26
Canada	-2.77	-3.85	0.89	4.63	6.16	4.53	1.19	5.00	3.43	5.64	8.15	-2.74	2.01	..
Czech Republic	..	-28.04	10.91	-14.91	8.55	7.45	13.17	-0.40	-10.19	8.77	7.10	-5.04	7.84	7.13
Denmark	-1.68	0.71	0.25	-4.49	8.93	6.29	-1.60	7.05	0.11	2.86	3.30	0.02	-0.44	0.35
Finland	-0.10	-10.73	0.22	4.95	11.54	6.46	3.25	8.68	6.71	5.26	11.00	0.28	2.14	0.94
France	1.86	1.26	0.75	-4.01	3.95	5.04	0.30	3.15	5.18	3.02	4.24	2.84	0.82	-0.10
Germany	4.28	3.28	-2.28	-6.86	2.58	0.53	-2.19	2.32	2.01	-1.54	4.62	-1.30	-0.37	0.46
Greece	-2.56	0.56	-0.20	-2.73	2.05	1.08	2.73	-2.79	5.85	2.25	5.30	2.98	2.60	2.04
Hungary	..	..	-6.67	2.96	5.95	6.88	2.97	11.25	7.73	7.08	6.35	0.43	1.26	5.37
Iceland	-2.42	1.62	-2.10	-0.92	2.41	1.23	6.68	4.45	2.50	4.70	5.62	2.63	1.14	..
Italy	1.25	-0.33	0.60	-3.37	6.18	4.57	-1.38	2.55	1.75	0.26	2.31	-0.25	-0.32	-0.98
Japan	7.56	4.91	-1.79	-3.56	-1.20	3.79	4.63	3.02	-4.99	1.60	6.71	-2.68	-1.69	..
Korea	9.34	9.46	5.24	5.76	10.89	10.81	6.55	5.16	-7.38	20.35	16.42	2.53	7.42	4.85
Luxembourg	1.95	1.91	2.95	3.60	4.63	1.68	2.70	6.03	0.70	1.90	6.90	0.99	2.00	2.61
Mexico	6.23	3.06	3.90	-0.29	4.03	-4.28	10.17	9.25	6.70	4.10	6.32	-2.97	-0.56	..
Netherlands	4.43	1.96	-0.53	-1.23	5.16	3.14	2.44	0.22	2.25	1.39	3.52	0.44	-0.32	-2.42
New Zealand	-1.61	-1.34	2.35	6.40	5.12	2.29	1.97	-0.58	-2.64	2.90	2.42	-0.02	5.82	..
Norway	1.87	5.16	6.48	2.18	7.53	6.24	5.43	5.07	-2.31	-0.38	3.81	1.85	0.62	-2.02
Poland	..	..	..	6.41	9.78	10.38	7.53	10.22	4.10	3.09	6.46	-0.34	-0.16	6.32
Portugal	5.93	-2.13	-2.67	-3.13	3.74	5.98	7.21	5.46	2.91	1.30	2.70	1.64	-0.93	-0.48
Slovak Republic	..	..	..	..	9.04	9.38	7.22	-7.44	3.24	5.09	-1.54	3.77	-0.33	9.53
Spain	2.20	1.96	-0.33	-3.50	1.87	3.44	2.01	5.37	4.67	3.88	3.95	2.46	0.67	1.27
Sweden	-0.33	-4.70	-3.61	1.40	12.05	11.63	2.43	6.73	6.73	7.98	8.23	-1.55	4.50	1.95
Turkey	8.64	2.72	5.94	8.21	-5.65	12.07	7.12	10.40	2.01	-5.02	6.05	-7.50	9.41	7.76
United Kingdom	-0.34	-3.36	0.35	2.19	5.42	1.72	1.37	1.35	1.03	1.22	1.91	-1.57	-2.50	-0.10
United States	-0.08	-3.01	0.79	3.17	6.80	6.34	2.09	4.46	3.19	4.60	3.32	-5.43	..	..
OECD unweighted average	2.19	0.39	0.70	0.28	4.74	4.41	2.97	4.41	1.94	3.21	5.48	-0.15	1.55	2.14

StatLink: http://dx.doi.org/10.1787/418578670180

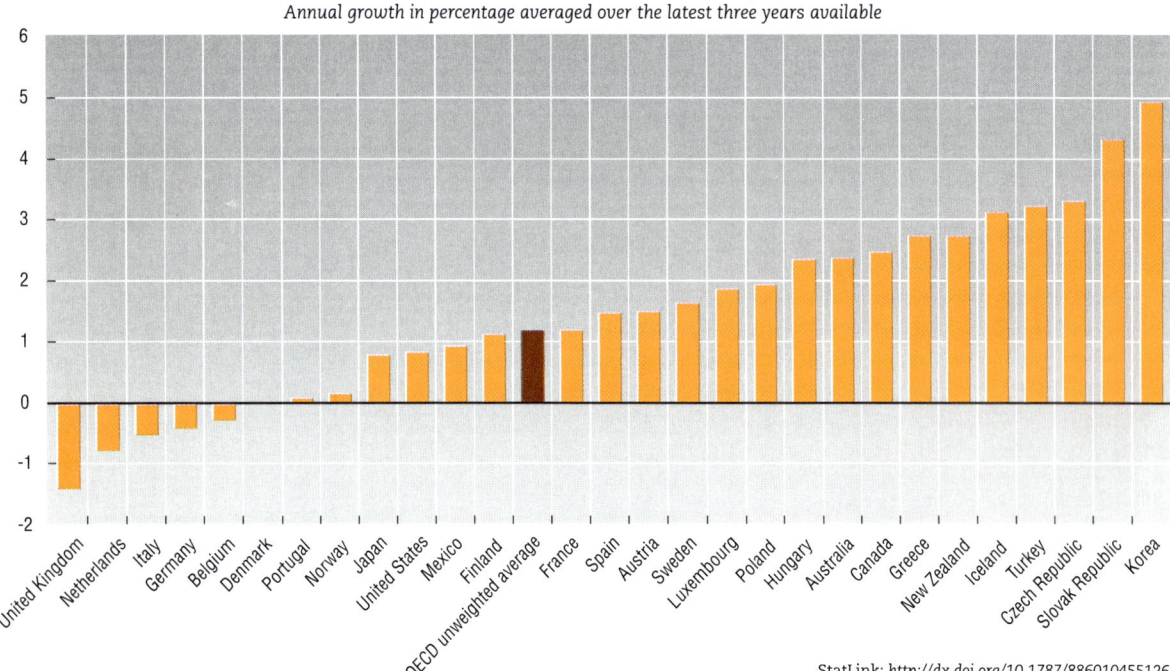

Real value added in industry
Annual growth in percentage averaged over the latest three years available

StatLink: http://dx.doi.org/10.1787/886010455126

MACROECONOMIC TRENDS • ECONOMIC GROWTH

EVOLUTION OF VALUE ADDED BY ACTIVITY

Real value added in services
Annual growth in percentage

	1990	1991	1992	1993	1994	1995	1996	1997	1998	1999	2000	2001	2002	2003
Australia	0.75	0.89	3.53	3.62	5.62	3.81	4.56	4.14	5.92	4.24	3.53	3.57	2.99	..
Austria	4.45	3.87	3.99	0.84	2.11	2.05	2.21	1.35	3.62	2.28	3.57	0.73	1.05	0.71
Belgium	3.90	3.13	1.88	-0.30	2.80	2.96	0.70	2.32	2.41	2.90	2.56	1.71	1.29	1.92
Canada	1.57	0.20	1.78	2.05	4.07	2.50	1.26	4.00	4.06	5.54	4.80	3.37	4.01	..
Czech Republic	..	9.67	-3.32	8.44	3.41	2.62	1.71	-0.53	3.30	0.63	3.15	7.85	-1.43	1.57
Denmark	2.81	0.81	-0.31	1.45	3.15	1.81	3.08	2.29	2.51	2.91	3.36	2.63	1.67	0.86
Finland	1.38	-4.83	-4.95	0.17	2.07	3.78	3.99	4.58	4.32	4.07	4.25	2.18	2.20	2.47
France	2.39	0.97	1.61	0.85	1.21	0.38	1.52	1.89	2.88	2.99	3.95	2.03	1.86	1.01
Germany	6.26	6.59	3.77	1.41	1.85	3.18	2.81	2.09	2.89	3.71	3.59	2.69	0.91	0.34
Greece	1.89	2.74	2.58	0.78	0.77	3.93	2.38	5.02	3.07	1.86	5.00	5.04	3.71	4.80
Hungary	..	..	-2.79	1.49	4.53	-3.30	2.44	2.40	3.86	3.16	4.04	4.25	4.43	2.00
Iceland	2.94	1.89	-0.82	0.49	3.81	2.65	5.58	5.18	6.29	7.25	5.81	3.42	1.01	..
Italy	2.35	1.06	1.13	0.98	1.67	1.97	1.88	1.99	1.93	1.63	4.12	2.82	0.98	0.65
Japan	3.95	4.41	3.12	2.51	2.57	3.16	3.05	2.65	1.08	0.42	1.39	2.12	1.20	..
Korea	8.07	8.64	7.12	6.85	7.85	8.13	6.19	5.07	-3.94	6.57	6.14	4.84	7.84	1.78
Luxembourg	7.56	9.98	4.43	5.67	4.93	2.48	3.39	7.93	7.67	6.80	8.15	2.30	2.43	2.54
Mexico	4.33	4.87	3.66	2.77	4.62	-6.40	2.94	6.45	4.56	3.54	7.11	0.95	1.28	
Netherlands	2.84	3.02	1.85	1.59	1.71	3.33	3.76	5.21	4.59	4.55	3.53	2.09	1.02	0.24
New Zealand	0.05	0.03	2.39	4.77	4.75	4.36	3.40	2.42	2.35	4.27	3.66	4.52	3.77	..
Norway	1.77	2.27	3.47	2.53	3.64	3.18	4.94	5.46	4.06	4.34	3.16	4.02	1.55	2.17
Poland	..	..	..	0.48	4.62	4.44	4.69	4.10	4.16	4.65	3.66	2.38	2.69	3.45
Portugal	6.92	7.22	3.53	-0.24	-2.04	2.39	1.68	4.55	5.52	5.04	4.66	3.36	1.03	-0.30
Slovak Republic	..	..	..	..	-1.24	6.33	0.79	12.96	5.42	1.60	2.88	8.10	8.13	3.42
Spain	3.61	2.30	0.89	-0.47	1.90	2.58	1.13	3.41	3.54	3.58	4.59	3.94	1.74	2.05
Sweden	2.52	0.78	-1.73	0.28	2.16	2.80	1.17	2.09	2.24	4.15	3.37	1.24	1.05	1.78
Turkey	8.26	0.56	5.25	7.49	-3.19	6.47	5.70	7.01	3.35	-2.43	6.46	-5.45	5.92	5.37
United Kingdom	1.28	-0.29	0.07	2.92	2.97	3.58	3.35	3.89	4.93	3.30	4.42	3.37	2.73	2.89
United States	2.08	0.65	2.41	1.82	2.67	2.82	4.12	5.05	5.42	4.40	5.34	2.24	..	..
OECD unweighted average	3.50	2.57	2.11	2.12	2.65	2.83	3.12	4.00	3.55	3.66	4.44	2.49	2.31	2.38

StatLink: http://dx.doi.org/10.1787/062764001686

Real value added in services
Annual growth in percentage averaged over the latest three years available

[Bar chart showing countries from lowest to highest: Austria, Netherlands, Germany, Sweden, Portugal, Italy, Japan, France, Belgium, Denmark, Turkey, Finland, OECD unweighted average, Luxembourg, Spain, Norway, Czech Republic, Poland, United Kingdom, Mexico, Australia, Iceland, Hungary, New Zealand, United States, Canada, Greece, Korea, Slovak Republic]

StatLink: http://dx.doi.org/10.1787/440400536536

MACROECONOMIC TRENDS • ECONOMIC GROWTH

HOUSEHOLD SAVING

Household saving is the main domestic source of funds to finance investment and, hence, to promote long-term economic growth.

Definition

In the national accounts, saving is estimated by subtracting household consumption expenditure from household disposable income.

The latter consists essentially of income from employment and from the operation of unincorporated enterprises, plus receipts of interest, dividends and social benefits minus payments of income taxes, interest and social security contributions. Note that enterprise income includes "imputed rents" paid by owner-occupiers.

Household consumption expenditure consists mainly of cash outlays for consumer goods and services but it also includes the "imputed expenditures" that owner occupiers pay, as occupiers, to themselves as owners of the dwelling.

Comparability

Saving rates may be measured on either a net or a gross basis. Net saving rates are measured after deducting consumption of fixed capital (depreciation) in respect of assets used in enterprises operated by households and in respect of owner-occupied dwellings. Consumption of fixed capital is deducted, as a production cost, from the disposable income of households so that both saving and disposable income are shown on a net basis. Several countries have difficulties in estimating consumption of fixed capital for the household sector and the international systems of accounts therefore provided for both disposable income and saving to be shown on a gross basis – i.e. with both aggregates including consumption of fixed capital.

There are two panels in the table so that countries that can estimate net saving rates are shown separately from those that can only calculate gross saving rates. Saving rates on a gross basis are higher than on a net basis, but both measures tend to follow similar trends.

Because saving is a residual between two large aggregates – disposable income and household consumption expenditure – both of which are subject to estimation errors, estimates of savings are subject to large relative errors and revisions over time.

Long-term trends

Household saving rates are very variable between countries. This is partly due to institutional differences between countries such as the extent to which old-age pensions are funded by government rather than through personal saving and the extent to which governments provide insurance against sickness and unemployment. The age composition of the population is also relevant because the elderly tend to run down financial assets acquired during their working life, so that a country with a high share of retired persons will usually have a low saving rate.

Over the period covered below, saving rates have been stable or rising in France, Ireland, Norway and Portugal but have been falling in the other countries in the table. Particularly sharp declines occurred in Australia, Canada, the United Kingdom, the United States, Finland and New Zealand. In Finland and New Zealand, negative rates – dis-saving – were recorded towards the end of the period.

Source

OECD (2004), *OECD Economic Outlook*, No. 76, OECD, Paris.

Further information

• **Analytical publications**

Cotis, J.P., J. Coppel and L. de Mello (2004), "Is the US Prone to Over-consumption?", paper presented at The Macroeconomics of Fiscal Policy Federal Reserve Bank of Boston Economic Conference, Cape Cod, 14-16 June, *www.oecd.org/eco/speeches*.

Harvey, R. (2004), "Comparison of Household Saving Ratios: Euro area/United States/Japan", *Statistics Brief*, No. 8, June, OECD, Paris, *www.oecd.org/std/statisticsbrief*.

Kohl, R. and P. O'Brien (1998), "The Macroeconomics of Ageing, Pensions and Savings – A Survey", *OECD Economics Department Working Paper*, No. 200, OECD, Paris, *www.oecd.org/eco/working_papers*.

de Serres, A. and F. Pelgrin (2003), "The Decline in Private Saving Rates in the 1990s in OECD Countries: How Much Can Be Explained by Non-wealth Determinants?", *OECD Economic Studies*, No. 36, 2003/1, OECD, Paris, *www.oecd.org/oecdeconomicstudies*.

• **Web sites**

OECD Economic Outlook – Sources and Methods: *www.oecd.org/eco/sources-and-methods*.

MACROECONOMIC TRENDS • ECONOMIC GROWTH

HOUSEHOLD SAVING

Household saving rates
As a percentage of disposable household income

	1990	1995	1996	1997	1998	1999	2000	2001	2002	2003	2004	2005	2006
Net saving													
Australia	9.3	4.9	5.8	3.9	1.9	1.5	2.9	2.5	-0.5	-2.2	-2.1	-1.8	-1.4
Austria	14.0	11.7	9.9	7.4	8.4	8.3	8.4	7.5	8.2	8.5	8.3	8.8	8.8
Canada	13.0	9.2	7.0	4.9	4.9	4.0	4.7	4.6	3.2	1.4	1.5	1.6	1.7
Czech Republic	..	..	..	..	..	..	..	..	..	..	..	..	..
Denmark	3.2	-0.1	-1.7	-4.5	-3.2	-8.0	-5.7	-1.2	0.1	0.3	-0.3	-1.6	-1.3
Finland	1.8	4.8	0.4	2.2	0.4	1.5	-1.4	-1.2	-0.2	0.4	1.6	1.1	0.8
France	7.8	11.2	10.0	11.3	10.8	10.4	11.0	11.5	12.1	11.1	10.2	9.9	9.6
Germany	13.9	11.2	10.8	10.4	10.3	9.8	9.7	10.2	10.5	10.7	11.1	11.1	10.8
Hungary	..	15.6	19.4	20.1	21.3	17.4	16.0	17.7	17.7	17.3	17.3	17.7	17.7
Ireland	7.9	11.3	9.7	10.6	13.3	12.2	9.9	10.4	10.3	8.3	8.2	8.2	8.2
Italy	24.0	18.0	18.9	15.4	12.2	9.8	9.2	10.3	10.6	10.5	11.3	10.9	10.3
Japan	13.9	11.9	9.8	10.0	11.0	10.7	9.5	6.6	6.4	6.3	5.1	5.0	5.0
Korea	22.0	18.0	17.1	16.3	23.7	16.2	10.5	6.0	1.5	2.5	3.4	3.7	5.1
Netherlands	17.5	14.4	13.0	13.4	12.9	9.6	6.8	9.5	10.0	10.1	10.7	10.7	9.9
New Zealand	0.7	-3.8	-2.5	-4.1	-4.2	-5.1	-4.1	-4.4	-5.2	-6.5	-8.1	-7.1	-6.3
Norway	2.2	4.6	2.2	2.8	5.8	5.5	5.2	4.1	9.2	7.6	7.5	7.7	7.8
Slovak Republic	..	..	..	..	..	..	..	..	..	..	..	..	..
United States	7.0	4.6	4.0	3.6	4.3	2.4	2.3	1.8	2.0	1.4	0.8	0.5	1.2
Gross saving													
Belgium	17.3	18.6	16.9	15.6	14.4	14.4	13.1	14.4	14.8	14.2	13.8	13.4	13.9
Portugal	..	13.6	11.8	10.3	9.9	8.6	10.9	11.9	12.7	13.0	12.8	12.8	12.4
Spain	12.3	16.2	14.2	13.4	12.2	11.1	10.7	10.3	10.6	10.6	10.7	11.0	11.0
Sweden	1.6	9.0	6.7	4.1	3.1	2.0	2.9	8.3	9.7	8.5	8.3	7.8	7.1
Switzerland	9.6	11.6	11.3	10.5	10.7	10.0	11.8	11.9	8.2	8.2	8.0	8.0	8.0
United Kingdom	8.0	10.0	9.4	9.4	6.1	4.9	5.0	6.5	5.3	5.5	6.4	7.4	7.9

StatLink: http://dx.doi.org/10.1787/466505330348

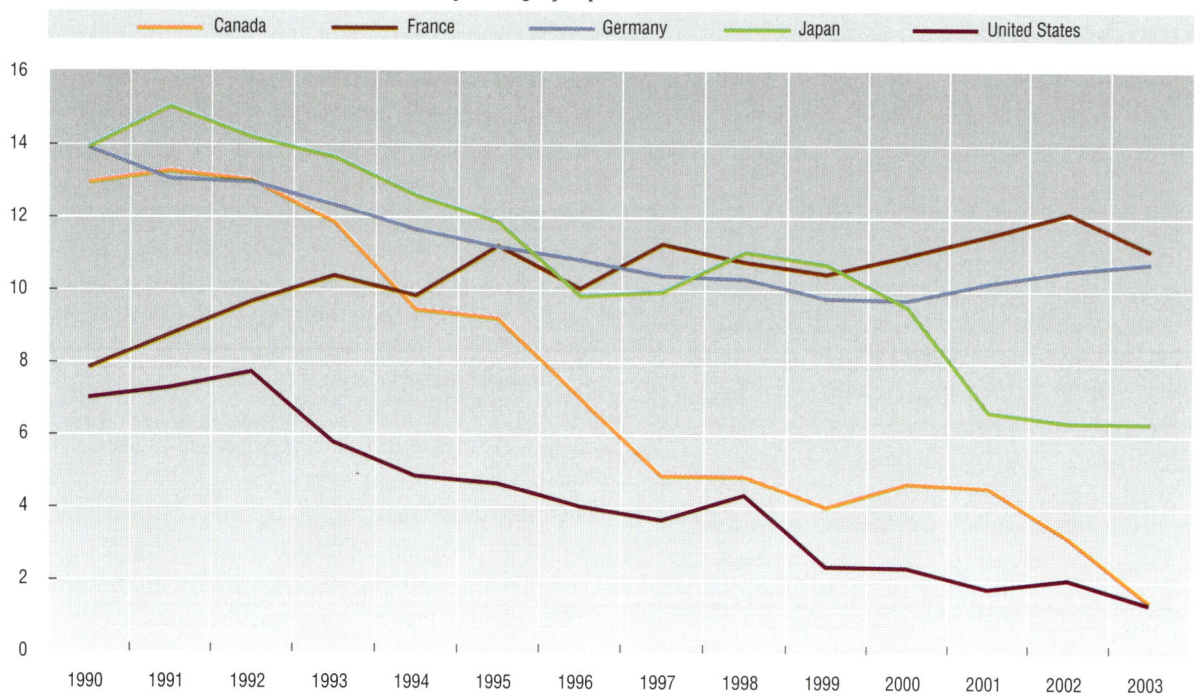

Household net saving rates
As a percentage of disposable household income

StatLink: http://dx.doi.org/10.1787/531165747267

MACROECONOMIC TRENDS • PRODUCTIVITY

LABOUR PRODUCTIVITY

The growth of labour productivity is one of the main sources of the growth of GDP and also provides a broad indication of the scope for non-inflationary increases in wages and salaries. The measurement is confined to the business sector because the conventions used by most countries to measure output in the government sector are based on the assumption that labour productivity is constant over time.

Definition

The growth of labour productivity shown in the table is obtained by dividing the growth of value added at constant prices by the growth of the labour force. Value added is measured after deducting government real consumption of fixed capital (*i.e.* at constant prices) and real indirect taxes less subsidies. It consists, therefore, of wages and salaries plus the net return to capital. The growth of the labour force is the change in the number of employees. The number of employees has not been adjusted for differences, over time and between countries, in the number of hours worked. The business sector is defined as the non-government part of the economy. Government value added and government employment have been deducted from total value added and total employment respectively.

Comparability

The definitions and methodologies underlying the estimates of nominal value added are generally comparable between countries but there are some differences between countries in the methods used to convert nominal values to real terms. These mainly concern the extent to which changes in the quality of goods and services are reflected in the price deflators.

The statistics on employment are comparable to the extent that all countries use the *ILO Guidelines* in defining the numbers employed. There are, however, differences between countries and over time in the numbers of hours worked.

Note that the growth rates of labour productivity are affected by structural shifts in employment. Growth rates will rise as labour moves from low productivity sectors, notably agriculture, into higher productivity sectors in manufacturing and some services.

Long-term trends

The growth in business sector labour productivity is quite variable from year to year, because employment generally moves more slowly than value added. Businesses do not immediately employ more staff when there is an upturn and they do not immediately lay off staff when there is a down turn.

Over the period covered in the table, labour productivity has grown in all countries although the chart shows that there have been considerable differences in growth rates between countries. From 1994 to 2003, the annual growth of labour productivity has averaged 1% or less in Mexico, Switzerland and the Netherlands, while in Ireland and Korea, the annual growth has averaged around 4%.

To preserve comparability, the chart is confined to countries for which data are available for the full period. This means that the Czech Republic, Hungary, Poland and the Slovak Republic are excluded, but, during the shorter periods for which data are available, all four countries have recorded average growth of labour productivity well above the OECD average.

Source

OECD (2004), *OECD Economic Outlook*, No. 76, OECD, Paris.

Further information

• *Analytical publications*

OECD (2004), *OECD Employment Outlook*, OECD, Paris.

• *Methodological publications*

Ahmad, N., *et al.* (2003), "Comparing Growth in GDP and Labour Productivity: Measurement Issues", *OECD Statistics Brief*, No. 7, December, OECD, Paris, *www.oecd.org/std/statisticsbrief*.

Ahmad, N., *et al.* (2003), "Comparing Labour Productivity Growth in the OECD Area: The Role of Measurement", *OECD Directorate for Science, Technology and Industry Working Paper*, No. 2003/14, OECD, Paris, *www.oecd.org/sti/working-papers*.

OECD (2001), *Measuring Productivity – OECD Manual*, OECD, Paris.

• *Online databases*

SourceOECD Economic Outlook.

OECD Productivity Database: *www.oecd.org/statistics/productivity*.

• *Web sites*

OECD Economic Outlook – Sources and Methods: *www.oecd.org/eco/sources-and-methods*.

MACROECONOMIC TRENDS • PRODUCTIVITY

LABOUR PRODUCTIVITY

Labour productivity in the business sector
Annual growth in percentage

	1994	1995	1996	1997	1998	1999	2000	2001	2002	2003	2004	2005	2006
Australia	1.6	-0.4	3.0	3.2	4.0	2.8	0.6	1.7	1.6	0.9	2.1	2.0	1.8
Austria	3.3	2.3	3.7	2.1	2.8	2.2	3.0	0.2	1.5	1.0	1.5	1.8	1.8
Belgium	3.8	1.8	0.4	3.2	0.4	2.1	1.9	-0.9	1.6	1.4	2.4	1.8	1.7
Canada	3.1	0.8	0.7	1.8	1.5	3.0	2.9	0.7	1.5	0.1	1.4	2.2	2.3
Czech Republic	..	..	4.3	-0.8	-0.2	3.7	5.3	2.8	0.4	3.4	4.9	4.7	4.4
Denmark	7.7	0.5	1.8	1.7	2.8	2.1	3.1	1.7	0.9	2.1	2.9	2.6	2.4
Finland	7.0	1.8	2.9	3.6	3.1	0.5	3.5	-0.6	1.8	2.6	3.8	2.7	2.7
France	2.1	1.1	0.6	1.5	2.2	1.2	1.5	0.2	0.4	0.8	2.8	1.8	1.6
Germany	2.8	1.6	1.1	1.6	0.8	0.8	1.0	0.3	0.7	0.9	1.0	1.1	1.3
Greece	0.1	1.4	3.1	4.8	-0.9	3.8	5.2	5.2	4.0	3.4	2.5	2.4	2.5
Hungary	..	-2.4	1.4	4.7	9.2	0.5	3.5	3.8	4.4	1.6	3.0	2.8	2.8
Iceland	3.8	-3.5	6.0	5.3	1.3	0.4	4.1	0.6	1.2	4.6	6.8	3.4	2.1
Ireland	2.7	5.2	4.4	7.6	0.2	5.1	5.4	3.2	4.8	2.1	3.5	4.1	3.7
Italy	3.9	3.3	0.7	1.7	0.7	1.1	1.5	0.1	-1.0	-0.2	0.3	0.6	1.4
Japan	1.1	1.7	2.9	0.9	-0.8	0.6	3.2	0.8	0.9	2.9	4.0	2.0	2.1
Korea	5.4	6.4	5.0	3.0	-1.1	8.3	4.4	1.9	4.2	3.3	3.3	3.1	3.3
Luxembourg	1.3	-1.4	0.5	5.5	2.7	3.0	3.4	-4.3	-0.8	1.0	2.1	2.1	2.0
Mexico	0.9	-8.1	1.3	0.3	2.2	2.7	4.8	-0.3	-2.0	0.1	2.6	1.3	1.7
Netherlands	2.6	0.8	0.8	0.7	1.9	1.5	1.4	-0.7	0.2	-0.6	2.6	0.7	1.1
New Zealand	1.5	-0.8	0.5	1.5	0.5	3.0	2.0	-0.1	1.9	1.3	2.5	1.3	1.9
Norway	2.3	1.1	1.7	2.0	2.3	3.3	2.2	2.3	1.7	1.8	4.3	2.6	2.3
Poland	..	..	5.6	6.4	4.1	9.6	6.4	3.7	5.2	5.6	5.4	3.9	4.1
Portugal	1.2	5.7	3.6	2.0	2.5	2.8	1.3	-0.4	-0.2	-1.2	1.6	1.5	1.5
Slovak Republic	..	-2.7	2.6	5.0	5.2	5.8	3.9	2.7	4.5	1.7	4.2	3.1	3.2
Spain	3.2	1.0	1.5	1.1	0.1	0.6	0.8	0.4	0.7	1.0	0.7	0.8	1.0
Sweden	6.1	2.8	2.5	4.7	2.4	2.4	1.2	-1.0	2.4	2.5	4.5	1.8	1.9
Switzerland	1.8	0.5	0.5	2.1	1.7	0.1	2.5	-0.7	-0.2	-0.3	1.8	1.1	0.9
United Kingdom	3.4	1.2	1.4	1.1	2.0	1.7	2.8	1.7	1.1	1.7	2.7	2.4	2.5
United States	1.3	0.3	2.0	2.3	2.1	2.8	2.3	1.0	3.7	3.4	3.7	2.0	2.2
OECD total	1.9	0.9	1.9	2.0	1.4	2.0	2.5	0.7	2.1	2.2	3.0	1.9	2.1

StatLink: http://dx.doi.org/10.1787/501424284350

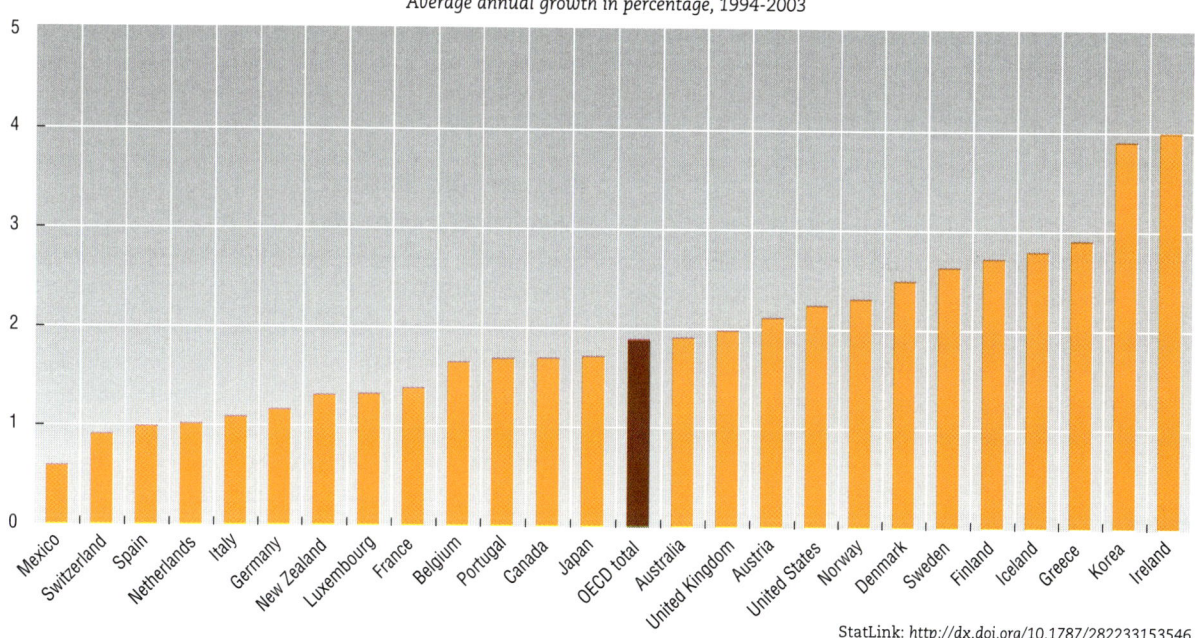

Labour productivity in the business sector
Average annual growth in percentage, 1994-2003

StatLink: http://dx.doi.org/10.1787/282233153546

OECD FACTBOOK 2005 – ISBN 92-64-01869-7 – © OECD 2005

MACROECONOMIC TRENDS • PRODUCTIVITY

MULTI-FACTOR PRODUCTIVITY

Growth accounting involves breaking down the growth of gross domestic product (GDP) into three components – the contribution of labour, the contribution of capital, and multi-factor productivity (MFP).

MFP is the change in GDP that cannot be explained by changes in the quantities of capital and labour that are made available to generate the GDP. MFP is sometimes described as "disembodied technological progress". It is the increase in GDP that is not "embodied" in either labour or capital and comes from more efficient management of the processes of production – through better ways of using labour and capital, through better ways of combining them, or through reducing the amount of intermediate goods and services needed to produce a given amount of output. Growth in MFP is a significant factor in explaining the long-term growth of real GDP.

Definition

The growth accounting framework, as applied here, decomposes annual growth in GDP into growth in labour and capital inputs and multi-factor productivity growth. The rate of growth of GDP is a weighted average of the rates of growth of capital and labour inputs. The weights attached to each input are the output elasticities for each factor of production. Since output elasticities cannot be directly observed, the factor shares of labour and capital are often used as weights. The rate of multi-factor productivity growth is the part of GDP growth which is not explained by the measured contribution of the factor inputs.

Long-term trends

Over the periods shown in the table, multifactor productivity was an important driver for growth in Portugal, Australia, Finland and, especially, Ireland. Annual growth in MFP exceeded 1% per year in France, in the United States and in the United Kingdom while MFP was between 0.5 and 1% per year for most other countries for which this indicator is available.

Comparability

The growth accounts for OECD countries are based on the OECD Productivity Database where the main problems of consistency of data sources and comparability across countries are addressed.

Output is measured as real GDP, compiled according to the 1993 System of National Accounts, although there may be some differences how countries convert current price GDP to real GDP. Labour input is measured as total hours actually worked and capital input is measured as the flow of capital services, based on an identical method for all countries.

Since MFP is obtained as a residual – i.e. that part of GDP growth that is left over when the growth of labour and capital inputs have been deducted – MFP necessarily contains any errors that may have been made in measuring GDP and labour and capital inputs. This is a particularly important issue as regards the measurement of capital inputs in the form of computers, software and communications equipment. To correct for differences in methods between countries, the OECD uses a standard method for these types of capital goods.

It must also be emphasised that the data used here relates to the total economy and therefore includes the government sector. Measuring output and productivity for the government sector is difficult and statistical practices as well as the size of the government sector may vary between countries. This should be kept in mind when interpreting the present series.

Source

OECD Productivity Database: *www.oecd.org/statistics/productivity*.

Further information

• *Analytical publications*

OECD (2003), *OECD Science, Technology and Industry Scoreboard*, OECD, Paris.

OECD (2003), *The Sources of Economic Growth in OECD Countries*, OECD, Paris.

OECD (2004), *Understanding Economic Growth*, OECD, Paris.

• *Methodological publications*

OECD (2001), *OECD Productivity Manual*, OECD, Paris.

Schreyer, P., P.E. Bignon and J. Dupont (2003), "OECD Capital Services Estimates: Methodology and a First Set of Results", *OECD Statistics Directorate Working Paper*, No. 2003/6, OECD, Paris, *www.oecd.org/std/workingpapers*.

MACROECONOMIC TRENDS • PRODUCTIVITY

MULTI-FACTOR PRODUCTIVITY

Multi-factor productivity

Annual growth in percentage   *Average annual growth rates in percentage*

	1990	1991	1992	1993	1994	1995	1996	1997	1998	1999	2000	2001	2002	1990-2001
Australia	-0.5	0.9	3.2	0.9	0.6	1.4	2.3	2.3	2.6	0.6	-0.5	2.7	0.7	1.55
Belgium	1.2	0.7	0.1	0.4	2.6	0.9	-0.2	0.6	-0.2	1.1	1.0	-1.6	..	0.50
Canada	-1.0	-1.1	0.6	-0.1	1.5	0.9	-0.9	1.8	0.7	1.6	2.3	0.1	1.5	0.68
Denmark	1.0	1.1	-0.7	2.1	0.0	2.5	0.8	0.3	-0.2	-1.8	2.3	-0.8	..	0.52
Finland	0.1	-2.6	1.1	2.9	3.5	1.6	2.4	4.5	2.9	0.4	3.8	-0.0	..	1.85
France	0.7	0.2	0.9	-0.2	1.5	1.4	0.0	1.2	2.1	1.1	3.0	0.9	1.8	1.11
Germany	..	..	1.6	-0.0	1.7	1.5	1.0	1.0	0.6	0.7	1.4	0.4	0.3	0.98
Greece	-1.7	3.9	-2.0	-3.6	1.0	0.9	0.8	3.4	-0.8	1.4	3.7	2.4	..	1.00
Ireland	4.4	3.0	4.5	1.7	2.5	4.8	3.6	8.3	2.2	5.5	4.1	2.8	..	3.91
Italy	-0.5	0.1	0.9	3.0	2.8	2.5	-0.3	0.7	0.1	-0.3	0.7	-0.3	..	0.90
Japan	3.8	1.5	-0.0	1.0	0.3	1.3	1.5	0.8	-1.1	0.6	1.4	0.4	0.5	0.70
Netherlands	1.6	0.9	-0.1	0.9	0.3	1.3	0.2	0.8	1.7	1.5	-0.3	1.2	..	0.77
Portugal	..	..	..	..	..	1.5	3.3	2.9	1.2	0.1	2.5	-1.3	..	1.46
Sweden	-0.8	-0.7	0.0	-0.3	2.1	1.5	0.2	1.8	1.0	0.8	1.8	-0.7	..	0.68
United Kingdom	-0.2	-0.6	1.7	2.1	2.2	0.7	0.9	0.7	0.8	0.8	2.0	0.4	..	1.06
United States	0.7	0.3	2.3	0.1	1.4	-0.1	1.7	1.2	1.0	1.3	1.2	0.7	2.0	1.01

StatLink: http://dx.doi.org/10.1787/533825424126

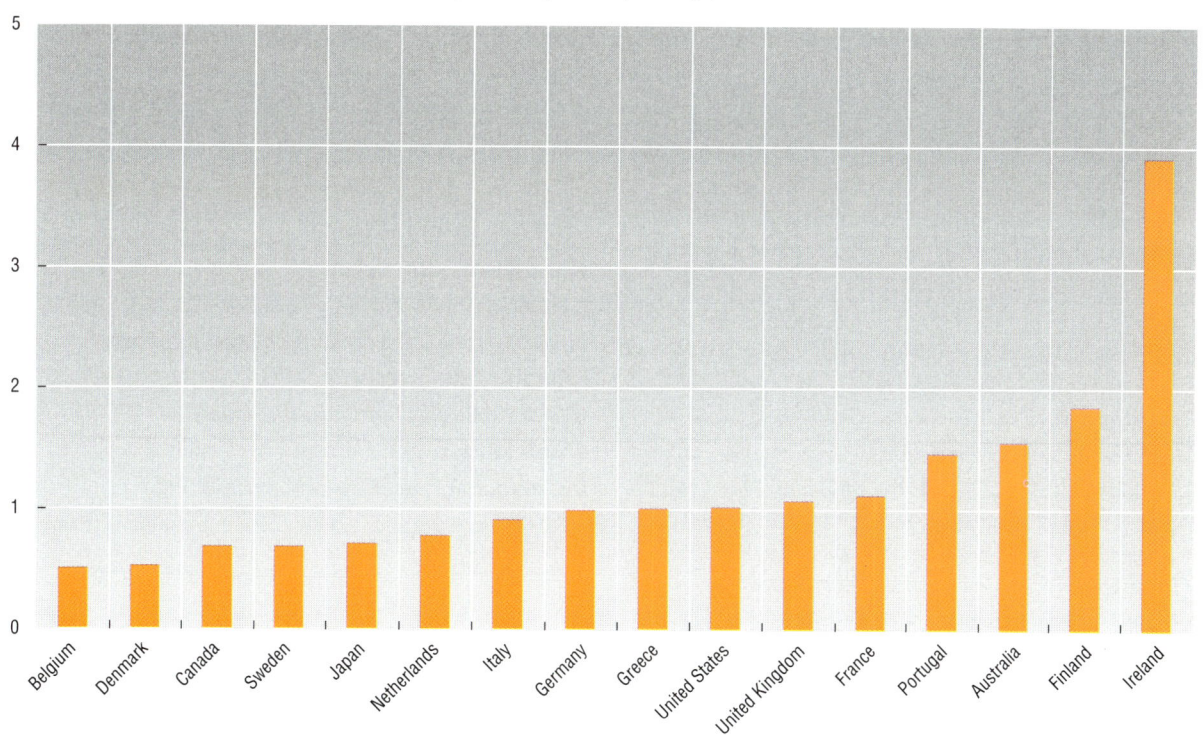

Multi-factor productivity
Average annual growth in percentage, 1990-2001

StatLink: http://dx.doi.org/10.1787/843224183438

ENERGY SUPPLY

An analysis of energy problems requires a comprehensive presentation of basic supply and demand data for all fuels in a manner which will allow the easy comparison of the contribution each fuel makes to the economy and their interrelationships through the conversion of one fuel into another. This type of presentation is suitable for the study of energy substitution, energy conservation and forecasting.

Definition

The table refers to total primary energy supply (TPES). TPES equals production plus imports minus exports minus international marine bunkers plus or minus stock changes. The IEA energy balance methodology is based on the calorific content of the energy commodities and a common unit of account. The unit of account adopted by the IEA is the tonne of oil equivalent (toe) which is defined as 10^7 kilocalories (41.868 gigajoules). This quantity of energy is, within a few per cent, equal to the net heat content of 1 tonne of crude oil. The difference between the "net" and the "gross" calorific value for each fuel is the latent heat of vaporisation of the water produced during combustion of the fuel. For coal and oil, net calorific value is about 5% less than gross, for most forms of natural and manufactured gas the difference is 9-10%, while for electricity there is no difference as the concept has no meaning in this case. The IEA balances are calculated using the physical energy content method to calculate the primary energy equivalent.

Comparability

While every effort is made to ensure the accuracy of the data, quality is not homogeneous for all countries/regions. In some countries data are based on secondary sources, and where incomplete or unavailable, the IEA has made estimates. In general, data are likely to be more accurate for production and trade than for international marine bunkers or stock changes. Moreover, statistics for combustible renewables and waste are less accurate than traditional commercial energy data in most countries.

Long-term trends

Over the 31-year period of 1971 to 2002, the world's total primary energy supply increased by 87%, reaching 10 230 Mtoe (million tonnes of oil equivalent). This equates to a compound growth rate of 2.0% per annum. By comparison, world population grew by 1.6% and gross domestic product by 2.9% per annum over the same period.

Energy supply growth was fairly constant over the period, except in 1974-1975 and in the early 1980s as a consequence of the first two oil shocks, and in the early 1990s following the dissolution of the Soviet Union.

Although the OECD is still the largest energy user, its share of total primary energy supply declined significantly from 62.1% in 1971 to 52.2% in 2002. Strong economic development in Asia led to a large increase in the share of Asia (including China) in world energy supply, from 13.5% in 1971 to 23.8% in 2002. By contrast, the combined share of the former USSR and non-OECD Europe decreased significantly in the late 1980s.

Sources

IEA (2004), *Energy Balances of OECD Countries*, IEA, Paris.
IEA (2004), *Energy Balances of Non-OECD Countries*, IEA, Paris.

Further information

• *Analytical publications*

IEA (2004), *Energy Policies of IEA Countries*, IEA, Paris.
IEA (2004), *World Energy Outlook 2004*, IEA, Paris.

• *Online databases*

IEA World Energy Statistics and Balances.

• *Web sites*

International Energy Agency: *www.iea.org*.
OECD Energy Statistics: *www.oecd.org/statistics/energy*.

MACROECONOMIC TRENDS • COMMODITIES: PRODUCTION AND SUPPLY

ENERGY SUPPLY

Total primary energy supply
Million tonnes of oil equivalent (Mtoe)

	1971	1990	1994	1995	1996	1997	1998	1999	2000	2001	2002	2003
Australia	52.2	87.5	92.9	94.4	100.9	102.2	103.9	107.5	109.8	108.3	112.7	115.8
Austria	19.0	25.3	25.9	27.1	28.6	28.7	29.2	28.9	28.8	30.9	30.4	31.8
Belgium	39.9	48.7	52.1	52.6	56.6	57.3	58.6	58.7	59.3	59.0	56.9	58.3
Canada	141.8	209.1	228.6	231.7	237.2	239.7	237.5	244.4	250.9	248.2	250.0	248.3
Czech Republic	45.6	47.4	40.4	41.0	42.2	42.5	41.1	38.2	40.4	41.4	41.7	43.7
Denmark	19.2	17.6	20.2	20.1	22.6	21.0	20.8	20.0	19.4	20.0	19.7	20.5
Finland	18.4	29.2	31.1	29.6	32.1	33.1	33.5	33.4	33.0	33.9	35.6	37.1
France	162.2	227.3	231.4	240.8	254.2	246.8	254.8	255.1	257.6	266.4	265.9	270.3
Germany	307.9	356.2	338.7	342.4	353.8	351.2	349.2	341.7	343.6	353.4	346.4	345.1
Greece	9.1	22.2	23.4	23.5	24.2	25.1	26.4	26.6	27.8	28.7	29.0	29.9
Hungary	19.1	28.6	25.0	25.7	26.1	25.6	25.4	25.3	25.0	25.6	25.4	26.1
Iceland	1.0	2.2	2.3	2.3	2.5	2.5	2.7	3.1	3.2	3.4	3.4	3.4
Ireland	7.1	10.6	11.3	11.4	11.9	12.5	13.3	13.9	14.3	15.1	15.3	14.6
Italy	114.5	152.6	152.8	160.9	160.4	162.8	167.4	170.5	171.7	172.6	172.7	180.7
Japan	269.5	445.9	490.3	500.1	513.3	518.9	513.6	516.4	521.6	517.0	516.9	514.5
Korea	17.0	92.6	134.6	147.7	163.1	176.4	162.2	178.5	190.9	193.9	203.5	208.7
Luxembourg	4.1	3.6	3.8	3.4	3.4	3.4	3.3	3.5	3.7	3.8	4.0	4.2
Mexico	43.5	124.1	136.8	132.7	136.8	141.5	148.0	149.9	150.6	152.1	157.3	166.1
Netherlands	51.3	66.5	70.8	72.1	75.2	74.0	74.3	73.5	75.5	77.3	77.9	80.1
New Zealand	7.2	13.9	15.5	16.0	16.9	17.5	17.2	17.9	17.9	18.1	18.0	18.1
Norway	13.6	21.5	23.5	23.9	23.2	24.6	25.5	26.8	25.8	26.4	26.5	23.8
Poland	86.3	99.8	96.7	99.9	107.5	103.5	97.1	93.2	89.5	90.0	89.2	92.4
Portugal	6.5	17.7	19.4	20.7	20.5	21.6	23.3	25.1	25.3	25.4	26.4	25.7
Slovak Republic	14.2	21.4	17.1	17.7	17.8	17.8	17.3	17.4	17.5	18.5	18.5	18.2
Spain	43.1	91.2	98.2	103.3	101.6	107.7	113.1	118.4	124.7	127.8	131.6	135.2
Sweden	36.5	46.7	49.4	50.0	51.1	49.8	50.7	50.4	47.5	51.2	51.0	50.0
Switzerland	17.1	25.1	25.6	25.3	25.7	26.3	26.7	26.7	26.5	28.0	27.1	27.0
Turkey	19.5	53.0	56.5	61.9	67.3	71.0	72.2	71.0	77.5	71.6	75.4	80.3
United Kingdom	211.0	212.2	227.6	223.2	233.2	227.2	230.3	231.7	231.1	234.4	226.5	229.5
United States	1 593.2	1 927.6	2 062.3	2 088.5	2 140.9	2 163.8	2 182.0	2 242.3	2 302.6	2 253.9	2 290.4	2 291.2
EU15	1 049.9	1 327.4	1 356.1	1 381.1	1 429.5	1 422.1	1 448.1	1 451.6	1 463.4	1 499.9	1 489.4	1 513.1
OECD total	3 390.7	4 527.1	4 804.2	4 889.8	5 051.0	5 096.0	5 120.6	5 210.2	5 313.1	5 296.3	5 345.7	5 390.8
Africa	198.0	394.9	429.4	446.6	458.9	472.0	483.4	494.6	507.7	521.9	539.8	..
Latin America	202.8	339.0	380.4	390.7	411.8	422.6	441.0	449.1	455.2	455.5	454.8	..
Asia excluding China	345.5	758.5	892.5	949.7	985.6	1 031.0	1 034.4	1 075.8	1 112.9	1 146.0	1 183.9	..
China	395.2	890.6	1 011.9	1 080.4	1 126.4	1 130.5	1 127.2	1 133.8	1 155.9	1 153.9	1 245.0	..
Former USSR	788.4	1 347.8	1 010.5	971.6	936.2	900.3	885.1	902.2	912.5	928.4	930.5	..
Non-OECD Europe	86.1	141.0	97.2	105.0	109.6	107.2	103.3	93.9	95.9	98.9	99.7	..
Middle East	51.7	229.0	310.2	320.6	337.3	347.4	369.9	378.8	397.8	409.9	431.3	..
Intl. marine bunkers	107.4	114.3	122.5	127.1	128.2	132.8	134.4	144.1	146.9	139.3	145.7	..
World	5 565.8	8 742.2	9 058.8	9 281.5	9 545.0	9 639.8	9 699.3	9 882.5	10 097.9	10 150.1	10 376.4	..

StatLink: http://dx.doi.org/10.1787/243357612260

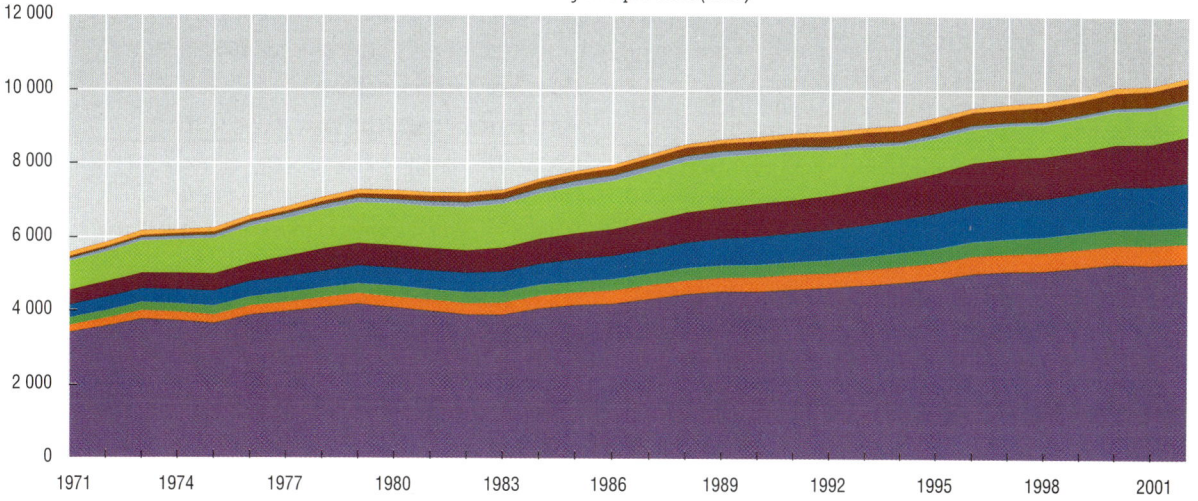

Total primary energy supply by region
Million tonnes of oil equivalent (Mtoe)

StatLink: http://dx.doi.org/10.1787/132766438830

OECD FACTBOOK 2005 – ISBN 92-64-01869-7 – © OECD 2005

ELECTRICITY GENERATION

The amount of electricity generated by a country and the breakdown of the production by fuel is a reflection of its natural resources, imported energy, national policies on security of energy supply, population, electrification rate and the development and growth of the economy in general.

Definition

The table refers to electricity generation from fossil fuels, nuclear, hydro (excluding pumped storage), geothermal, solar, biomass, etc. It includes electricity produced in electricity-only plants and in combined heat and power plants. Both public and autoproducer plants have been included, where data are available. Public supply undertakings generate electricity for sale to third parties as their primary activity. Autoproducer undertakings generate electricity wholly or partly for their own use as an activity which supports their primary activity. Both types of plants may be privately or publicly owned.

Long-term trends

World electricity generation rose at an average annual rate of 3.7% from 1971 to 2002, greater than the 2.0% growth in total primary energy supply. This increase was largely due to more electrical appliances, development of electrical heating in several developed countries and rural electrification programmes in developing countries.

The share of thermal electricity production has gradually fallen, from just under 75% in 1971 to 65% in 2002. This decrease was due to a progressive move away from oil, which fell from 20.9% to 7.2%.

Oil for power generation has been displaced in particular by dramatic growth in nuclear electricity generation, which rose from 2.1% in 1971 to just over 16.6% in 2002. The share of coal remained stable, near 38% while that of natural gas increased from 13.3% to 19.1%. The share of hydro-electricity decreased from 23% to 16%. Due to large programmes to develop wind and solar energy in several OECD countries, the share of new and renewable energies, such as solar, wind, geothermal, biomass and waste increased. However, these energy forms remain limited: in 2002, they accounted for only 1.9% of total electricity production.

Comparability

Some countries, both OECD and non-OECD, have trouble reporting electricity generation from autoproducer plants. It is also difficult to obtain information on electricity generated by combustible renewables and waste in some non-OECD countries. For example, electricity generated from waste biomass in sugar refining remains largely unreported.

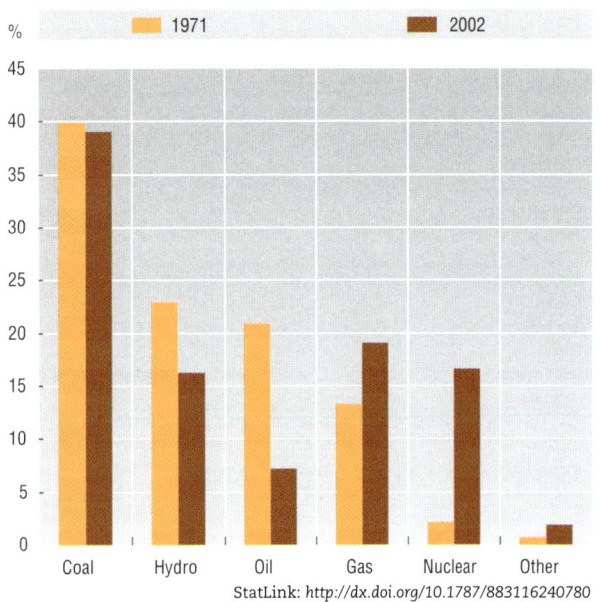

World electricity generation by fuel type

StatLink: http://dx.doi.org/10.1787/883116240780

Sources

IEA (2004), *Energy Balances of OECD Countries*, IEA, Paris.
IEA (2004), *Energy Balances of Non-OECD Countries*, IEA, Paris.

Further information

• *Analytical publications*

IEA (2003), *Energy to 2050 – Scenarios for a Sustainable Future*, IEA, Paris.
IEA (2004), *World Energy Outlook 2004*, IEA, Paris.

• *Statistical publications*

IEA (2004), *Electricity Information 2004*, IEA, Paris.
IEA (2004), *Energy Statistics of OECD Countries*, IEA, Paris.
IEA (2004), *Energy Statistics of Non-OECD Countries*, IEA, Paris.

• *Web sites*

International Energy Agency: *www.iea.org*.
OECD Energy Statistics: *www.oecd.org/statistics/energy*.

MACROECONOMIC TRENDS • COMMODITIES: PRODUCTION AND SUPPLY

ELECTRICITY GENERATION

Electricity generation
Terawatt hours (TWh)

	1971	1990	1994	1995	1996	1997	1998	1999	2000	2001	2002	2003
Australia	53.0	154.3	167.2	173.0	177.3	182.8	195.6	203.0	207.4	216.8	222.0	228.6
Austria	28.2	49.3	52.1	55.2	53.6	55.7	55.9	59.3	60.2	60.8	60.4	57.5
Belgium	33.2	70.3	71.3	73.5	75.1	77.9	82.1	83.4	82.8	78.6	80.9	83.3
Canada	221.8	481.9	555.5	559.9	572.8	573.5	561.5	578.8	605.5	589.6	601.4	583.7
Czech Republic	36.4	62.6	58.4	60.6	63.8	64.2	64.6	64.2	72.9	74.2	76.0	82.8
Denmark	18.6	26.0	40.2	36.7	53.6	44.3	41.1	38.9	36.0	37.7	39.2	46.0
Finland	21.7	54.4	65.6	63.2	69.4	69.2	70.2	69.5	70.0	74.5	74.9	83.8
France	155.8	416.7	474.7	490.9	508.0	500.8	507.1	519.3	536.0	546.4	554.8	563.3
Germany	327.2	547.7	525.2	532.8	550.7	548.0	552.4	550.3	567.1	581.8	566.9	590.5
Greece	11.6	34.8	40.4	41.3	42.4	43.3	46.2	49.4	53.4	53.1	53.9	57.8
Hungary	15.0	28.4	33.5	34.0	35.1	35.4	37.2	37.8	35.2	36.4	36.2	34.1
Iceland	1.6	4.5	4.8	5.0	5.1	5.6	6.3	7.2	7.7	8.0	8.4	8.5
Ireland	6.3	14.2	16.8	17.6	18.9	19.7	20.9	21.8	23.7	24.6	24.8	24.9
Italy	123.9	213.1	228.7	237.4	239.4	246.5	253.7	259.3	269.9	271.9	277.5	285.3
Japan	382.9	850.7	955.9	980.8	1 000.4	1 027.3	1 036.2	1 057.0	1 081.9	1 066.2	1 087.7	1 074.3
Korea	10.5	105.4	161.8	181.1	202.6	222.4	216.4	235.9	263.7	281.4	326.9	345.3
Luxembourg	1.3	0.6	0.6	0.5	0.4	0.4	0.4	0.4	0.4	0.5	2.8	3.0
Mexico	31.0	122.7	147.4	152.5	162.5	175.1	181.8	192.3	204.4	209.6	215.2	221.3
Netherlands	44.9	71.9	79.6	81.0	85.1	86.6	91.2	86.9	89.6	93.7	96.0	96.7
New Zealand	15.5	32.3	35.1	35.6	36.9	37.4	36.3	38.2	39.2	39.4	40.3	41.0
Norway	63.5	121.6	112.2	122.1	104.4	110.7	116.1	122.3	139.6	119.2	130.1	106.7
Poland	69.5	134.4	133.3	137.0	141.2	140.9	140.8	140.0	143.2	143.7	142.5	150.2
Portugal	7.9	28.4	31.3	33.2	34.4	34.1	38.9	42.9	43.4	46.2	45.7	46.3
Slovak Republic	10.9	23.4	25.0	26.0	25.0	24.5	25.2	27.4	30.3	31.9	32.2	31.4
Spain	61.6	151.2	160.8	165.6	173.4	189.2	193.4	205.9	222.2	233.2	242.7	260.1
Sweden	66.5	146.0	142.7	148.3	140.6	149.2	158.8	154.8	145.2	161.6	146.0	132.5
Switzerland	31.2	54.6	65.6	62.3	56.0	61.6	61.7	68.5	66.0	70.5	64.9	65.3
Turkey	9.8	57.5	78.3	86.2	94.9	103.3	111.0	116.4	124.9	122.7	129.4	140.3
United Kingdom	255.8	317.8	325.0	332.5	349.3	349.2	361.1	365.3	374.4	382.3	384.5	392.2
United States	1 703.4	3 202.8	3 451.8	3 558.4	3 651.2	3 672.2	3 804.5	3 873.5	4 025.7	3 838.6	3 992.7	3 984.9
EU15	1 164.6	2 142.3	2 255.3	2 309.6	2 394.5	2 414.1	2 473.2	2 507.2	2 574.4	2 646.9	2 651.1	2 723.1
OECD total	3 820.7	7 579.6	8 241.1	8 484.1	8 723.8	8 851.2	9 068.4	9 269.7	9 621.9	9 495.4	9 757.1	9 821.6
Africa	90.2	315.6	350.8	363.8	381.2	397.0	403.3	416.4	436.3	454.8	476.6	..
Latin America	134.7	491.3	585.0	620.3	653.3	693.1	719.4	741.1	778.4	763.1	784.5	..
Asia excluding China	129.7	619.1	842.7	919.9	977.6	1 048.1	1 098.4	1 165.0	1 243.5	1 298.7	1 357.8	..
China	144.0	650.1	954.8	1 035.6	1 108.5	1 163.4	1 197.6	1 268.8	1 386.9	1 504.1	1 674.8	..
Former USSR	800.4	1 727.0	1 329.4	1 291.8	1 261.1	1 234.7	1 220.9	1 235.8	1 270.6	1 291.9	1 301.1	..
Non-OECD Europe	92.2	195.7	164.3	175.1	185.6	185.2	183.9	175.5	176.2	182.1	183.7	..
Middle East	27.4	235.7	319.9	339.7	362.1	385.5	411.4	434.6	463.5	488.1	518.2	..
World	5 239.4	11 814.1	12 788.1	13 230.4	13 653.2	13 958.1	14 303.4	14 706.8	15 377.2	15 478.2	16 053.8	..

StatLink: http://dx.doi.org/10.1787/374463180133

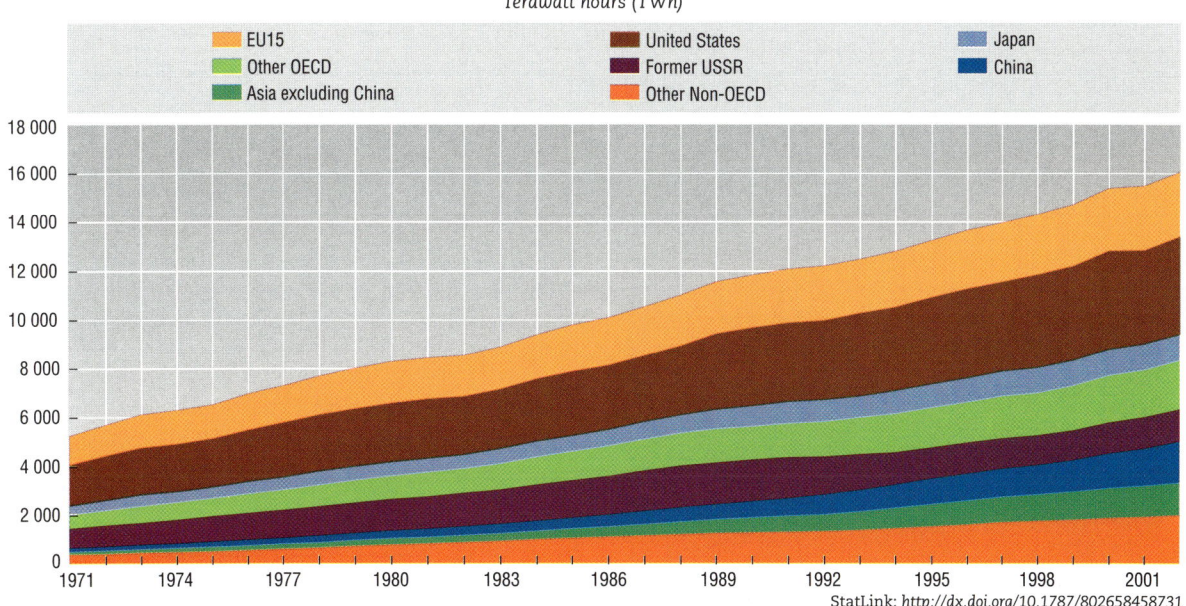

World electricity generation by region
Terawatt hours (TWh)

StatLink: http://dx.doi.org/10.1787/802658458731

STEEL PRODUCTION

Steel is a core commodity in industrial societies. The OECD regularly monitors capacity production, consumption, trade and employment in steel for its member countries as well as for all other major steel producing countries and areas.

The table omits production by minor steel producing countries (those with less than 2 million tonnes of production per year) in order to show production by major non-OECD producers.

Definition

Steel production is here measured in tonnes of "steel mill product equivalents". This is measured by crude steel production converted in ingot equivalent and then divided by a conversion factor (in most cases equal to 1.3) to account for losses between ingot production and steel mill production.

Comparability

The methodology and data sources are kept under continuous review by the OECD to ensure a high degree of comparability. However, the conversion from crude steel production to steel mill product equivalents uses standard conversion factors which, depending on the product mix, may not be accurate for all countries and at all periods. Small differences between countries may not be significant.

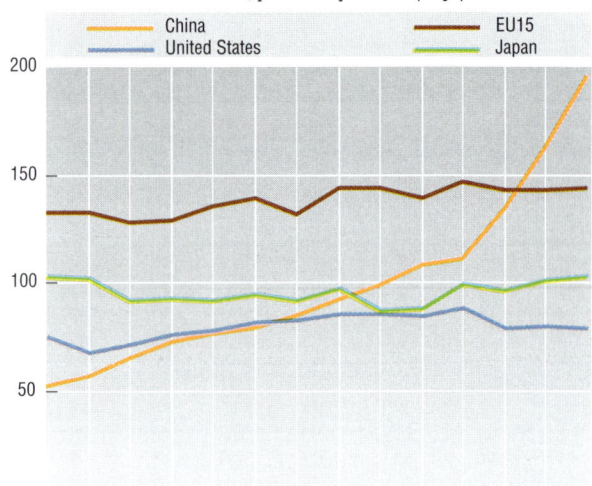

Steel production of selected countries
Million tonnes, product equivalent (Mtpe)

StatLink: http://dx.doi.org/10.1787/826544483884

Long-term trends

Over the period shown, world steel production has grown at just under 2% per year – more than twice the rate of growth for the OECD as a whole. Experience within the OECD has been mixed with falling production in several countries, especially the Czech Republic, Poland and the United Kingdom, and strong growth in Korea, Mexico and Turkey and, from a low base, in Austria and Finland.

Among the non-OECD countries, steel production in China has been growing at nearly 10% per year, at 6% in India and over 3% in Brazil. In Ukraine, however, steel production has fallen over the period and in Russia the annual growth has been less than 0.5%.

By the end of the period, China had become by far the largest steel producer. Its production in 2003 of just under 200 million tonnes was nearly twice that of the second country, Japan. The next largest producers were Korea, Germany and the United States.

Source

OECD (2004), *Iron and Steel Industry in 2002*, 2004 edition, OECD, Paris.

Further information

• *Analytical publications*

OECD (2005), *OECD Steel Outlook 2004-2005*, OECD, Paris.

• *Statistical publications*

OECD (2005), *Developments in Steelmaking Capacity of Non-OECD Countries*, 2003 edition, OECD, Paris.

MACROECONOMIC TRENDS • COMMODITIES: PRODUCTION AND SUPPLY

STEEL PRODUCTION

Steel production
Million tonnes, product equivalent (Mtpe)

	1990	1991	1992	1993	1994	1995	1996	1997	1998	1999	2000	2001	2002	2003
Australia	5.9	5.4	6.1	7.0	7.6	7.6	7.6	8.0	8.1	7.4	6.4	6.3	6.8	6.8
Austria	3.9	3.8	3.6	3.7	4.0	4.5	4.0	4.7	4.7	4.7	5.1	5.3	5.6	5.6
Belgium	10.2	10.1	9.3	9.1	10.2	10.4	9.7	9.7	10.3	9.9	10.5	9.7	10.3	10.0
Canada	10.2	10.9	11.8	12.3	11.9	12.4	12.6	13.3	13.6	13.9	14.2	13.1	13.7	13.6
Czech Republic	7.0	5.6	5.3	5.1	5.4	5.5	5.2	5.4	5.3	4.6	5.2	5.3	5.5	5.4
Finland	2.7	2.7	2.9	3.0	3.2	3.0	3.1	3.5	3.7	3.7	3.8	3.7	3.7	4.4
France	17.0	16.5	16.1	15.4	16.2	16.2	15.8	17.7	18.1	18.1	18.8	17.3	18.2	17.8
Germany	34.3	37.5	35.5	33.7	36.7	37.7	35.7	40.4	39.6	37.8	41.7	40.3	40.5	40.3
Italy	22.8	22.5	22.3	23.1	23.5	25.0	21.5	23.2	23.1	22.2	24.1	23.9	23.4	24.0
Japan	102.4	101.8	91.2	92.7	91.5	94.6	92.0	97.4	87.2	87.8	99.3	96.0	100.5	103.1
Korea	21.5	24.2	26.1	30.8	31.5	34.3	36.3	39.7	37.3	38.4	40.3	41.0	42.4	43.3
Luxembourg	2.9	2.8	2.5	2.7	2.5	2.2	2.1	2.3	2.2	2.3	2.3	2.5	2.5	2.4
Mexico	7.1	6.5	6.9	7.5	8.4	10.0	11.0	11.9	11.9	13.0	13.1	11.1	12.0	13.0
Netherlands	4.8	4.6	4.9	5.4	5.5	5.8	5.7	6.0	5.7	5.5	5.1	5.4	5.5	5.9
Poland	10.1	7.7	7.3	7.4	8.3	9.1	8.2	9.2	8.0	7.3	8.6	7.2	6.9	6.7
Slovak Republic	4.5	3.7	3.2	3.2	3.2	3.3	3.1	3.3	2.9	3.1	3.2	3.4	3.7	3.9
Spain	11.5	11.4	11.0	11.6	12.1	12.4	10.9	12.3	13.3	13.4	14.3	14.9	14.8	14.5
Sweden	4.0	3.8	3.9	4.1	4.5	4.5	4.4	4.6	4.6	4.6	4.7	5.0	5.2	5.2
Turkey	8.3	8.3	9.1	10.2	11.2	11.7	12.2	13.0	12.7	12.9	12.9	13.5	14.9	16.5
United Kingdom	15.7	14.6	14.3	14.7	15.3	15.6	16.0	16.5	15.5	14.6	13.6	12.2	10.4	11.7
United States	74.3	66.9	71.1	75.6	77.8	81.7	82.3	85.0	85.3	84.3	88.1	78.1	79.9	78.4
EU15	132.3	132.6	128.5	129.1	135.9	139.6	131.5	143.5	143.6	139.7	147.0	142.6	142.8	144.1
OECD total	387.9	377.4	370.2	384.7	396.5	413.5	405.6	433.3	419.7	416.0	442.3	421.7	433.3	439.0
China	52.3	57.2	65.5	73.0	76.2	79.3	85.1	92.7	98.8	108.3	111.1	134.3	162.4	196.7
India	11.8	13.5	14.3	15.0	15.9	18.2	19.9	20.4	19.7	20.4	22.6	22.9	24.1	26.6
Brazil	17.4	19.1	20.3	21.3	21.8	21.4	21.8	22.7	22.6	22.2	24.8	23.8	26.5	27.8
Russia	..	..	48.8	42.5	35.8	38.1	36.7	36.4	33.2	38.9	44.8	49.4	50.4	51.7
Ukraine	..	..	29.4	22.9	17.0	15.9	16.1	18.4	17.5	19.7	25.3	26.3	27.1	28.5
World	641.3	619.7	609.7	621.6	622.7	648.3	649.9	694.7	678.5	689.6	742.5	752.3	800.2	844.4

StatLink: http://dx.doi.org/10.1787/104728101880

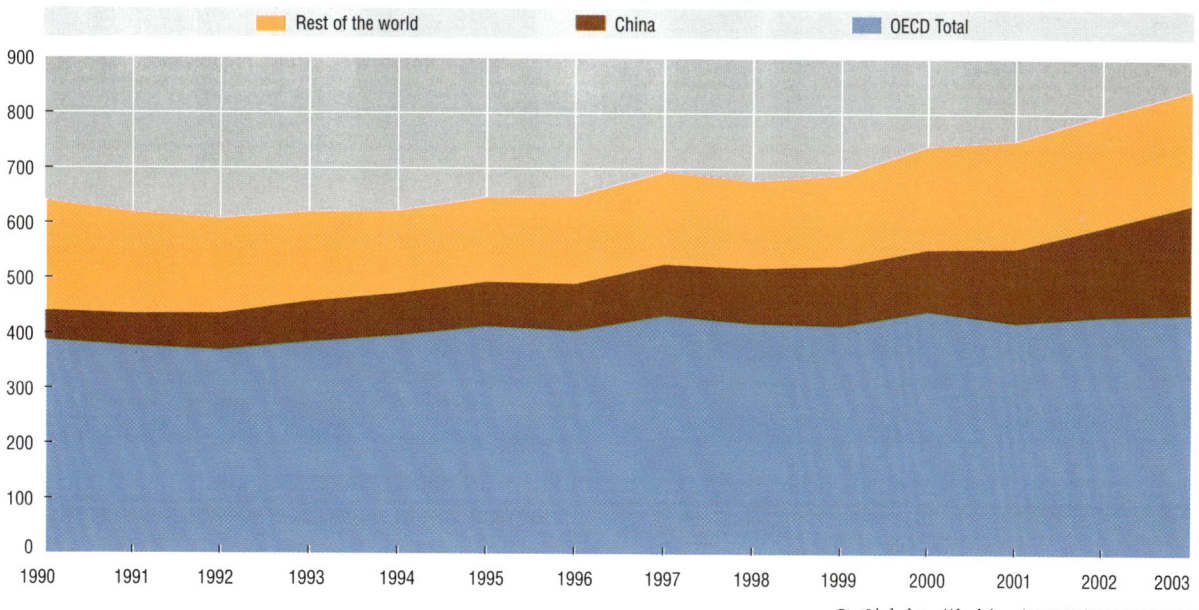

World steel production
Million tonnes, product equivalent (Mtpe)

StatLink: http://dx.doi.org/10.1787/512180745065

OECD FACTBOOK 2005 – ISBN 92-64-01869-7 – © OECD 2005

FISHERIES

Fisheries make an important contribution to sustainable income, employment opportunities and overall food protein intake. In certain countries, including at least two OECD countries – Iceland and Japan – fish is the main source of protein intake.

Definition

The figures refer to the tonnages of landed catches of marine fish, and to cultivated fish and crustacean taken from inland waters and sea tanks. Landed catches of marine fish for each country cover landings in both foreign and domestic ports. The table distinguishes between marine capture fisheries and aquaculture because of their different production systems and growth rates.

Comparability

The time series presented are relatively comprehensive and consistent across the years, but some of the variation over time may reflect changes in national reporting systems. In a few cases, the data shown are estimated by the OECD secretariat.

Long-term trends

The total production by OECD countries has decreased by more than 10% during the past decade. As the world fish production increased during the same period, the relative contribution of OECD countries dropped from 26% (in 1995) to 21% (in 2002). The decrease of the overall OECD production masks various tendencies. While aquaculture production increased by around 8% between 1995 and 2002, marine capture fisheries production dropped by 16%. This latter evolution mainly reflects both the worrying state of some major fish stocks, especially in the northern hemisphere, and changes in bilateral or international fishing arrangements regarding access to fish stocks in third countries' waters. Worldwide, it is estimated that around 25% of the stocks are overexploited, while around 50% of the stocks are fully exploited.

Marine captures fell particularly sharply in Japan, Denmark, Greece and Spain; in these countries, the annual decline exceeded 5%. A few countries did, however, increase captures – Norway, France, Canada and Iceland and all raised their tonnages by an average of 1% or more per year between 1995 and 2002. The 4% annual increase in tonnages landed by Iceland reflects good management of the cod and other fish stocks in its territorial waters but is also due to the exploitation of new species, such as blue whiting.

Most countries increased their aquaculture production, with annual growth of over 15% in Canada, Greece and Turkey. Aquaculture production fell rather sharply in Denmark and Mexico but, by 2002, aquaculture accounted for nearly 17% of total tonnages of fish production – up from 13% in 1995.

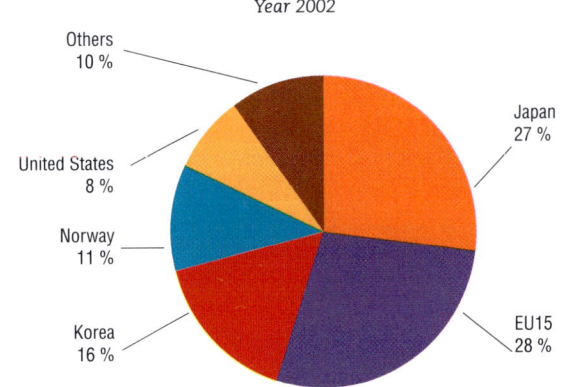

Aquaculture production for selected countries
Year 2002

- Others 10%
- Japan 27%
- United States 8%
- Norway 11%
- Korea 16%
- EU15 28%

StatLink: http://dx.doi.org/10.1787/264556561143

Source

OECD (2004), *Review of Fisheries in OECD Countries: Country Statistics 2002-2004*, Vol. 2, OECD, Paris.

Further information

• *Analytical publications*

OECD (2003), *The Cost of Managing Fisheries*, OECD, Paris.

OECD (2003), *Liberalising Fisheries Markets: Scope and Effects*, OECD, Paris.

OECD (2004), *Fish Piracy: Combating Illegal, Unreported and Unregulated Fishing*, OECD, Paris.

• *Statistical publications*

OECD (2003), *Review of Fisheries in OECD Countries: Policies and Summary Statistics*, Vol. 1, OECD, Paris.

• *Web sites*

OECD Fisheries: www.oecd.org/agr/fish.

MACROECONOMIC TRENDS • COMMODITIES: PRODUCTION AND SUPPLY

FISHERIES

Marine capture and aquaculture production
Thousand tonnes

	Fish landings in domestic and foreign ports							Aquaculture						
	1995	1997	1998	1999	2000	2001	2002	1995	1997	1998	1999	2000	2001	2002
Australia	201	194	210	210	185	189	190	24	27	28	34	37	40	44
Austria	..	..	..	..	..	..	..	4	..	..	..	..	..	..
Belgium	29	27	27	26	27	27	26	2	2	2	2	2	2	2
Canada	854	941	975	1 005	1 008	1 027	1 018	66	82	92	113	127	153	177
Czech Republic	..	..	..	..	..	..	..	19	17	18	19	19	20	19
Denmark	2 025	1 845	1 543	1 415	1 524	1 501	1 433	45	39	42	43	44	42	37
Finland	106	119	106	85	92	96	95	17	16	16	15	15	16	15
France	616	475	552	588	682	665	690	281	268	266	266	267	253	250
Germany	241	225	234	234	194	179	182	40	39	37	34	45	43	52
Greece	153	153	113	34	93	58	101	33	55	60	76	88	95	101
Hungary	..	..	..	..	..	..	..	9	15	..	..	..	..	..
Iceland	1 603	2 224	1 682	1 760	1 930	1 942	2 132	4	4	4	4	4	5	3
Ireland	379	308	337	269	291	305	281	27	39	42	44	41	54	53
Italy	301	301	292	265	387	339	304	225	191	217	217	228	264	260
Japan	7 450	6 071	5 394	5 311	5 092	4 814	4 465	1 390	1 340	1 291	1 315	1 292	1 311	1 363
Korea	2 322	2 423	2 247	2 306	2 090	2 142	1 987	1 017	336	797	777	667	668	794
Luxembourg	..	..	..	..	..	..	..	..	..	..	..	..	..	..
Mexico	1 222	1 222	954	1 096	1 193	1 251	1 284	158	169	160	48	46	75	71
Netherlands	463	329	342	404	404	404	467	84	100	92	92	92	92	92
New Zealand	567	653	577	544	536	501	..	69	75	83	83	87	76	76
Norway	2 701	2 856	2 851	2 627	2 894	2 862	2 928	278	368	413	476	492	511	554
Poland	241	381	287	235	200	207	204	25	29	31	33	32	34	33
Portugal	242	211	215	190	172	173	180	5	7	8	6	8	8	8
Spain	1 075	1 026	1 097	1 102	1 002	941	747	224	240	315	321	312	313	328
Slovak Republic	..	..	..	..	..	..	..	..	..	..	..	..	..	..
Sweden	379	350	401	329	341	308	284	8	7	6	6	6	8	8
Switzerland	..	..	..	..	..	..	..	1	..	..	..	..	..	..
Turkey	577	551	551	524	461	484	523	22	43	53	63	79	67	61
United Kingdom	912	888	898	835	748	738	685	92	127	138	144	144	150	150
United States	4 783	4 635	4 350	4 428	4 245	4 434	4 407	413	349	358	382	373	371	371
EU15	6 920	6 255	6 157	5 775	5 957	5 734	5 474	1 087	1 130	1 240	1 266	1 290	1 339	1 356
OECD total	29 442	28 405	26 233	25 820	25 791	25 587	24 612	4 567	3 970	4 566	4 612	4 544	4 671	4 922

StatLink: http://dx.doi.org/10.1787/852587355641

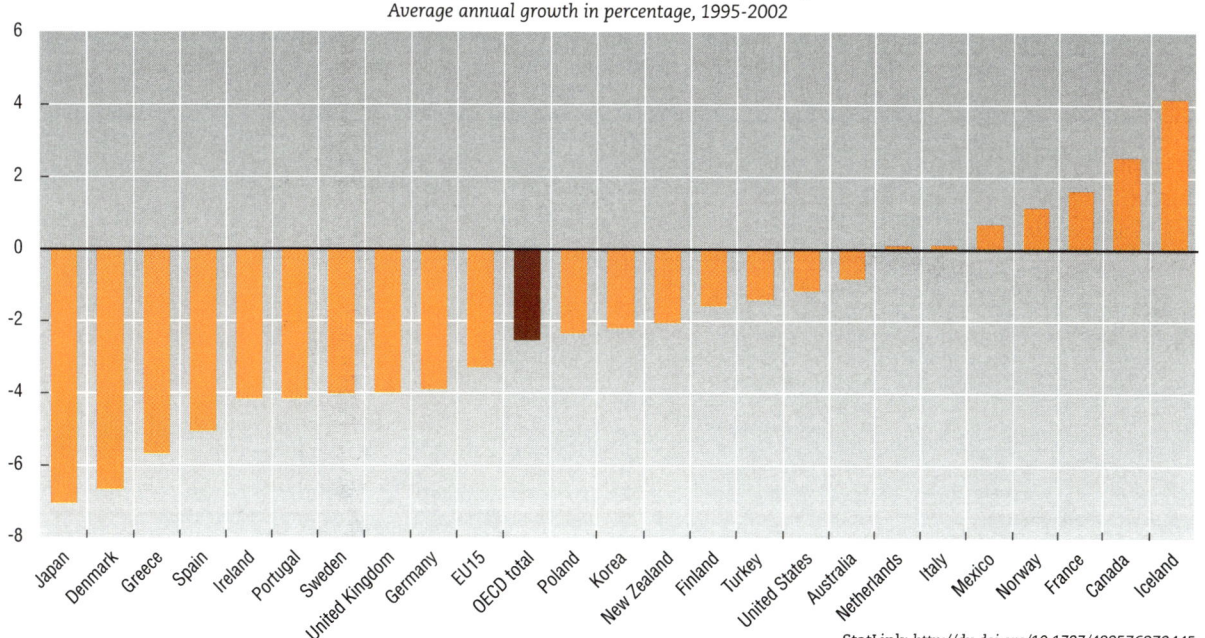

Fish landings in domestic and foreign ports
Average annual growth in percentage, 1995-2002

StatLink: http://dx.doi.org/10.1787/488576873445

ECONOMIC GLOBALISATION

TRADE
SHARE OF TRADE IN GDP
TRADE IN GOODS
TRADE IN SERVICES
TRADING PARTNERS
BALANCE OF PAYMENTS

FOREIGN DIRECT INVESTMENT (FDI)
FDI FLOWS AND STOCKS
FDI AND EMPLOYMENT

ECONOMIC GLOBALISATION • TRADE

SHARE OF TRADE IN GDP

International trade in goods and services is a principal channel of economic integration. A convenient way to measure the importance of international trade is to calculate the share of GDP in trade.

Definition

The rates shown in this table correspond to the average of imports and exports (of both goods and services) at current prices as a percentage of GDP. The data are taken from national accounts statistics compiled according to the System of National Accounts. Goods consist of merchandise imports and exports. Services cover transport, insurance, travel, banking and insurance, other business services, cultural and recreational services and government services.

Comparability

The ratios shown in this table are compiled using common standards and definitions and are highly comparable.

International trade tends to be more important for countries that are small (in terms of size or population) and surrounded by neighbouring countries with open trade regimes than for large, relatively self-sufficient countries or those that are geographically isolated and thus penalised by high transport costs. Other factors also play a role and help explain differences in trade-to-GDP ratios across countries, such as history, culture, trade policy, the structure of the economy (especially the weight of non-tradable services in GDP), re-exports and the presence of multinational firms which leads to much intra-firm trade.

The trade-to-GDP ratio is often called the trade openness ratio. However, the term openness may be somewhat misleading. In fact, a low ratio for a country does not necessarily imply high tariff or non-tariff obstacles to foreign trade, but may be due to the factors mentioned above, especially size and geographic remoteness from potential trading partners.

Long-term trends

Over the period shown, the unweighted average of the trade-to-GDP ratios for all OECD countries was 40%. For the reasons noted above, there were large differences in these ratios between countries. The ratios exceeded 50% for small countries – Belgium, Czech Republic, Hungary, Ireland, Luxembourg, Netherlands and the Slovak Republic – but were under 10% for the two largest OECD countries – Japan and the United States.

Between 1990 and 2002, trade-to-GDP ratios for the OECD as a whole, grew at about 2.5% per year. The ratios declined slightly in two countries – Norway and Portugal – and grew at less than 1% per year in Greece, Japan and the United Kingdom. On the other hand, substantial increases in trade-to-GDP ratios were recorded for Canada, the Czech Republic, Finland, Hungary, Ireland, Mexico, the Slovak Republic, Spain and Turkey.

As a share of GDP, trade in services rose faster than trade in goods in several OECD countries in the 1990s. Average annual growth in the trade-to-GDP ratio in services was over 6% for Greece, Hungary, Ireland and Turkey. It was negative for the Czech Republic, France, Mexico, Norway and the Slovak Republic.

Sources

OECD (2004), *National Accounts of OECD Countries*, OECD, Paris.

Further information

• **Statistical publications**

OECD (2004), *International Trade by Commodity Statistics*, OECD, Paris.

OECD (2004), *Main Economic Indicators*, OECD, Paris.

OECD (2004), *Monthly Statistics of International Trade*, OECD, Paris.

OECD (2004), *Statistics on International Trade in Services*, OECD, Paris.

• **Methodological publications**

Lindner, A., et al. (2001), "Trade in Goods and Services: Statistical Trends and Measurement Challenges", *OECD Statistics Brief*, No. 1, October, OECD, Paris, www.oecd.org/std/statisticsbrief.

UN, EC, IMF, OECD, UNCTAD and the WTO (2002), *Manual on Statistics of International Trade in Services*, United Nations, New York.

• **Web sites**

OECD International Trade Statistics: www.oecd.org/std/its.

ECONOMIC GLOBALISATION • TRADE

SHARE OF TRADE IN GDP

Trade in goods and services
Current prices, as a percentage of GDP

	1990	1991	1992	1993	1994	1995	1996	1997	1998	1999	2000	2001	2002	2003
Australia	16.7	17.1	18.3	18.8	19.7	19.9	19.7	20.7	20.1	21.3	22.9	21.6	20.9	..
Austria	39.0	38.8	37.2	35.7	36.7	37.2	38.4	42.6	43.7	45.9	50.6	52.4	51.7	51.0
Belgium	69.9	68.2	66.2	62.7	65.1	66.9	68.6	72.5	73.3	73.5	84.0	84.2	82.0	80.9
Canada	26.0	25.7	27.6	30.6	33.8	36.1	36.8	39.0	40.9	41.9	43.2	41.2	39.7	36.4
Czech Republic	43.9	49.3	54.3	54.4	51.8	56.0	55.7	59.5	59.4	61.2	71.5	72.1	66.3	67.2
Denmark	33.3	34.3	33.2	32.0	32.8	33.4	33.4	34.7	34.8	35.7	41.1	41.4	41.5	40.0
Finland	23.5	22.4	25.8	29.8	32.0	32.8	33.5	34.8	34.2	33.5	38.4	35.7	34.5	34.0
France	21.7	21.7	21.2	20.0	20.8	21.8	22.3	24.0	24.8	24.8	27.9	27.1	26.1	25.2
Germany	25.1	26.4	24.7	22.7	23.4	24.2	24.8	27.2	28.3	29.2	33.6	34.2	33.9	34.0
Greece	23.0	22.1	22.3	21.2	20.8	21.3	21.5	23.4	24.0	26.7	30.8	28.0	25.1	24.4
Hungary	..	41.8	39.7	38.2	40.3	44.6	48.2	54.6	62.6	65.7	75.9	73.5	65.1	63.9
Iceland	33.6	32.5	30.9	31.8	33.9	34.5	36.8	36.8	38.1	37.2	38.5	41.0	38.6	37.0
Ireland	54.7	55.4	57.0	60.7	65.8	70.7	71.7	73.5	80.7	81.6	91.1	90.9	85.2	76.0
Italy	19.7	18.6	19.1	20.6	22.1	25.0	23.4	24.4	24.6	24.5	27.8	27.7	26.5	25.1
Japan	9.9	9.2	8.8	8.0	8.0	8.4	9.5	10.2	9.8	9.3	10.1	10.1	10.6	11.0
Korea	28.2	27.4	27.0	26.1	27.0	29.4	29.6	32.7	39.7	35.7	39.2	36.7	34.6	36.9
Luxembourg	102.2	102.7	99.3	98.6	100.9	103.0	105.5	112.6	119.9	127.9	141.4	144.8	136.9	131.4
Mexico	19.2	17.8	17.8	17.2	19.2	29.1	31.1	30.4	31.8	31.6	32.0	28.6	27.8	..
Netherlands	52.6	52.7	50.8	49.7	51.9	54.5	55.0	58.1	58.2	58.1	64.9	62.7	60.1	..
New Zealand	26.9	27.9	30.3	29.3	29.9	28.9	28.0	28.1	29.6	31.3	35.1	33.7	31.5	..
Norway	37.2	36.0	34.5	34.8	35.1	34.9	36.3	37.3	36.8	35.7	38.0	37.2	34.3	34.5
Poland	23.4	22.9	21.4	21.0	21.1	22.6	23.5	25.9	28.9	27.6	31.1	29.5	31.3	35.7
Portugal	36.2	33.6	31.3	30.1	31.8	33.3	33.1	34.3	35.3	34.9	37.2	35.7	33.9	33.4
Slovak Republic	29.9	46.1	69.7	58.9	57.0	57.0	59.4	61.6	65.1	63.6	72.0	77.5	75.4	78.8
Spain	18.0	18.0	18.2	18.7	21.1	22.7	23.6	26.2	27.2	28.1	31.2	30.7	29.1	28.8
Sweden	29.4	26.6	26.4	30.1	33.2	35.9	34.6	37.8	39.4	39.6	43.2	42.7	40.7	40.4
Switzerland	35.1	33.6	33.5	33.0	32.9	32.9	33.7	37.1	37.8	38.9	42.8	42.6	40.5	..
Turkey	15.4	15.2	15.9	16.5	20.9	22.1	24.7	27.5	26.1	25.0	27.8	32.5	30.0	29.0
United Kingdom	25.3	23.7	24.2	26.0	26.8	28.5	29.6	28.7	27.3	27.3	29.1	28.7	27.7	26.6
United States	10.3	10.3	10.4	10.4	10.9	11.7	11.8	12.2	11.9	12.2	13.2	12.1	11.7	..
EU15	38.2	37.6	37.0	37.1	38.8	40.4	41.0	43.3	44.5	45.4	50.6	50.3	48.1	..
OECD total	32.0	32.6	33.2	32.9	34.2	36.0	36.8	38.9	40.5	41.0	45.5	45.2	43.1	..

StatLink: http://dx.doi.org/10.1787/151030611142

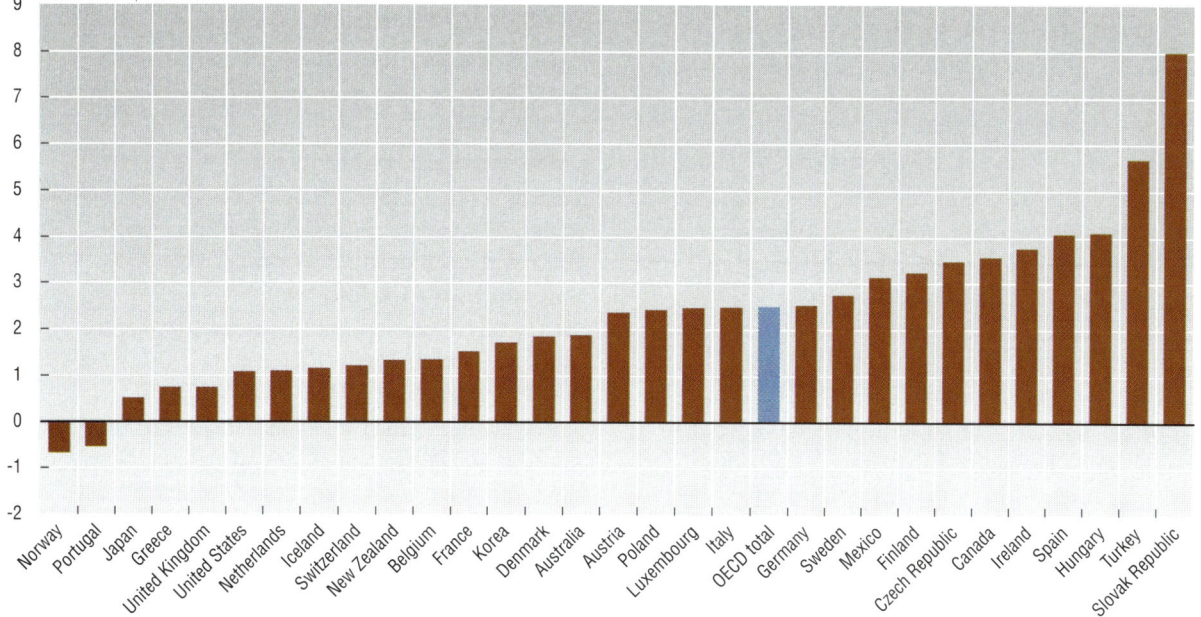

Trade to GDP ratios
Average annual growth in percentage, 1990-2003

StatLink: http://dx.doi.org/10.1787/420703251318

ECONOMIC GLOBALISATION • TRADE

TRADE IN GOODS

Since its creation, the OECD has sought to promote international trade considering it an effective way of enhancing economic growth and raising living standards. Member countries benefit from increased trade as do OECD's trade partners in the rest of the world.

Definition

According to United Nations guidelines, international merchandise trade statistics record all goods which add to or subtract from the stock of material resources of a country by entering (imports) or leaving (exports) its economic territory. Goods simply being transported through a country or goods temporarily admitted or withdrawn (except for goods for inward or outward processing) are not included in the international merchandise trade statistics.

Comparability

All OECD countries use the United Nations guidelines so far as their data sources allow. There are some, generally minor, differences between countries in the coverage of certain types of transactions such as postal trade, imports and exports of military equipment under defence agreements, sea products traded by domestic vessels on the high seas and goods entering or leaving bonded customs areas.

Exports are usually valued *free on board* (f.o.b.), with the exception of the United States which values exports *free alongside ship* (f.a.s.), which is lower than f.o.b. by the cost of loading the goods on board. Imports are valued by most countries at *cost, insurance and freight* (c.i.f.) i.e. the cost of the goods plus the costs of insurance and freight to bring the goods to the borders of the importing country. The following countries, however, report their imports at f.o.b. values: Australia, Canada, Czech Republic, Mexico, Slovak Republic and the United States. The trade balances shown in the table are, therefore, not strictly comparable because imports are not valued in the same way by all countries.

The introduction of the single market in 1993 resulted in some loss of accuracy for intra-EU trade because customs documents were no longer available to record all imports and exports. Note that while the OECD data mostly follow the UN recommendations, trade statistics reported by Eurostat follow the Community definitions. As a result, OECD trade statistics for European Union countries are not strictly comparable with those reported by Eurostat.

OECD total includes Hungary and Poland from 1992, the Czech Republic from 1993, Korea from 1994 and the Slovak Republic from 1997.

Long-term trends

Over the ten-year period from 1993 to 2002, relative import growth was low in Japan, Switzerland and Netherlands while relative import growth in some new member countries – Hungary, Poland and the Czech Republic – was particularly high.

Over the same period, relative growth rates of exports of goods were again high for Hungary, Poland and the Czech Republic but also for Ireland and Mexico. Japan, Greece, Spain and the Netherlands were among the countries with below average growth rates.

The United States' negative trade balance has been large throughout the period and growing in most years. Greece, Spain and the United Kingdom also recorded high negative trade balances for goods, while Germany and Japan both had large trade surpluses.

Source
OECD (2004), *Monthly Statistics of International Trade*, OECD, Paris.

Further information
• **Statistical publications**

OECD (2004), *International Trade by Commodity Statistics*, OECD, Paris.

• **Methodological publications**

Lindner, A., et al. (2001), "Trade in Goods and Services: Statistical Trends and Measurement Challenges", *OECD Statistics Brief*, No. 1, October, OECD, Paris, www.oecd.org/std/statisticsbrief.

OECD (2004), "International Trade by Commodity Statistics – Definitions", OECD, Paris, www.oecd.org/dataoecd/34/41/1906757.pdf.

United Nations (1998), *International Merchandise Trade Statistics: Compilers Manual*, United Nations, New York, http://unstats.un.org/unsd/trade/methodology.htm.

• **Online databases**

SourceOECD International Trade by Commodity Statistics.

SourceOECD Monthly Statistics of International Trade.

ECONOMIC GLOBALISATION • TRADE

TRADE IN GOODS

Trade balance: exports of goods minus imports of goods
Billion US dollars

	1990	1991	1992	1993	1994	1995	1996	1997	1998	1999	2000	2001	2002	2003
Australia	0.7	2.9	1.9	0.1	-2.7	-4.4	-1.2	1.0	-5.0	-9.5	-4.0	2.4	-4.5	-14.6
Austria	-8.1	-9.6	-9.7	-8.7	-10.2	-8.5	-10.1	-6.9	-6.2	-6.2	-5.2	-4.4	-0.1	-2.3
Belgium	..	..	..	11.4	13.3	15.4	11.4	12.3	14.4	14.3	13.5	11.6	17.7	19.9
Belgium/Luxembourg	-2.0	-2.8	-2.3	..	..	..	..	..	..	..	..	..	..	..
Canada	4.6	2.6	5.3	5.9	7.7	16.5	19.2	18.1	13.3	23.2	37.6	39.4	30.2	31.9
Czech Republic	..	..	..	0.2	-0.9	-3.9	-5.8	-4.4	-2.2	-2.0	-3.2	-3.1	-2.2	-2.5
Denmark	3.4	3.5	5.7	6.5	5.8	4.7	5.7	3.7	1.7	4.7	5.2	5.8	6.4	8.4
Finland	-0.4	1.4	2.8	5.5	6.4	10.9	9.7	10.0	10.8	10.2	11.7	10.7	11.0	10.9
France	-23.1	-17.4	-6.8	6.2	5.0	10.6	6.2	16.8	14.7	9.5	-8.5	-4.4	1.1	-4.5
Germany	57.1	13.6	22.0	37.4	45.6	59.6	68.3	67.1	72.3	69.3	54.8	85.7	125.6	146.8
Greece	-11.7	-13.0	-15.3	-14.0	-11.7	-15.0	-15.7	-15.8	-19.4	-18.8	-18.8	-17.9	-21.8	-31.2
Hungary	..	..	-0.4	-3.6	-4.2	-2.6	-3.1	-2.1	-2.7	-3.0	-4.0	-3.2	-3.3	-4.7
Iceland	-0.1	-0.2	-0.2	0.1	0.1	0.0	-0.1	-0.2	-0.6	-0.5	-0.7	-0.3	-0.0	-0.4
Ireland	3.0	3.3	6.1	7.2	8.2	11.5	12.4	14.4	19.9	24.0	25.6	26.4	36.0	..
Italy	-11.6	-13.0	-10.2	22.2	22.1	27.2	43.9	29.9	26.5	14.7	1.8	8.1	8.3	1.5
Japan	52.2	77.8	106.9	120.6	121.6	107.1	61.8	82.2	107.5	107.2	99.6	54.0	79.1	88.5
Korea	..	..	..	..	-6.5	-10.4	-19.6	-8.5	39.0	23.9	11.8	9.3	10.4	15.0
Luxembourg	..	..	..	..	..	..	..	..	..	-2.8	-2.8	-2.9	-2.9	-3.7
Mexico	-4.2	-11.5	-16.0	-13.6	-18.7	6.8	6.2	0.5	-8.0	-5.7	-5.8	-7.6	-5.7	-5.6
Netherlands	0.7	7.6	5.5	17.2	15.3	19.6	16.5	15.5	10.9	2.7	5.4	5.6	11.9	..
New Zealand	-0.4	0.8	0.2	0.6	-0.1	-0.7	-0.6	-0.8	-0.6	-2.4	-1.2	-0.0	-1.2	-2.0
Norway	6.8	8.5	9.1	7.9	7.3	9.0	14.0	12.8	2.9	11.3	25.5	26.0	24.7	28.1
Poland	..	..	-2.7	-4.7	-4.4	-6.1	-12.7	-16.5	-18.8	-18.5	-17.3	-14.2	-14.1	-14.4
Portugal	-9.0	-10.1	-12.0	-8.8	-9.1	-10.2	-10.6	-11.1	-12.8	-15.3	-15.6	-15.0	-13.5	..
Slovak Republic	..	..	..	..	..	..	..	-2.1	-2.4	-1.1	-0.9	-2.1	-2.2	-0.6
Spain	-32.0	-34.4	-34.9	-18.7	-19.0	-23.0	-21.0	-18.2	-25.8	-36.4	-39.5	-38.8	-40.0	..
Sweden	2.7	5.2	6.0	7.5	9.4	15.8	18.9	18.3	16.4	16.3	14.2	12.8	15.9	18.2
Switzerland	-5.9	-5.0	-0.0	2.5	2.4	1.5	1.5	0.3	-1.2	0.4	-2.0	-2.1	4.2	4.2
Turkey	-9.3	-7.5	-8.2	-14.1	-5.2	-14.1	-20.4	-22.3	-19.0	-14.1	-26.7	-10.1	-15.5	-22.1
United Kingdom	-39.9	-27.6	-35.3	-28.0	-31.3	-25.9	-28.7	-26.3	-46.9	-53.2	-55.7	-58.9	-63.1	-78.5
United States	-142.3	-65.4	-84.4	-115.4	-150.5	-158.6	-170.1	-180.3	-229.5	-328.5	-436.1	-411.8	-468.2	-581.4
EU15	-70.7	-93.2	-78.7	42.8	49.7	92.7	106.9	109.8	76.4	33.0	-13.9	24.3	92.4	85.4
OECD total	-168.6	-90.1	-67.1	29.2	-4.3	32.9	-23.9	-12.8	-50.7	-186.0	-341.3	-298.9	-276.0	-395.2

StatLink: http://dx.doi.org/10.1787/076740072546

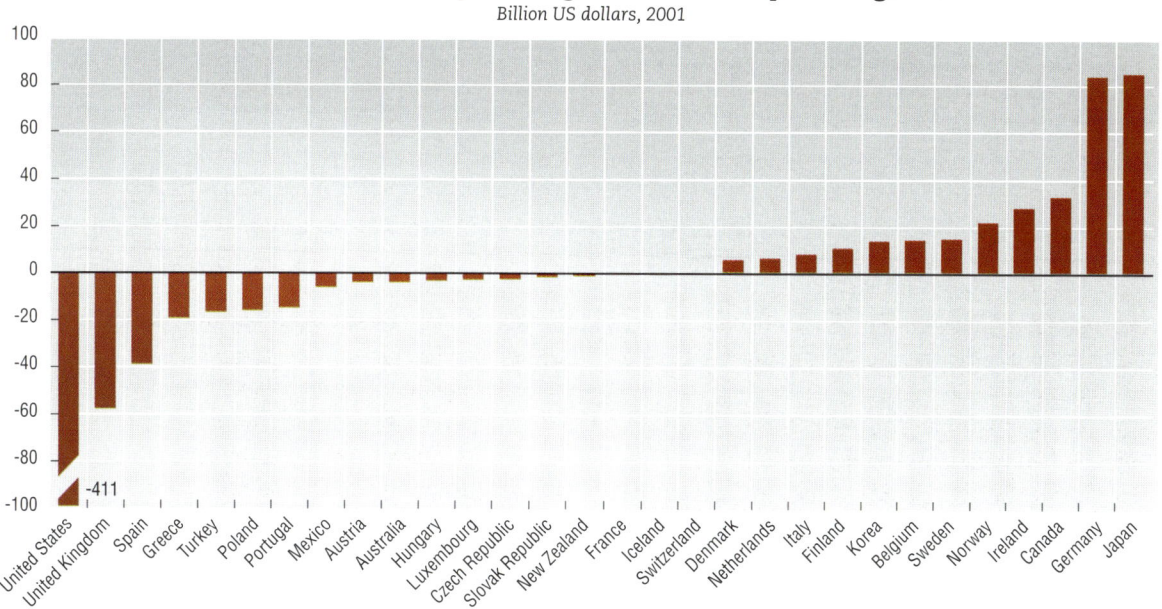

Trade balance: exports of goods minus imports of goods
Billion US dollars, 2001

StatLink: http://dx.doi.org/10.1787/280588430317

ECONOMIC GLOBALISATION • TRADE

TRADE IN GOODS

Imports of goods
Billion US dollars

	1990	1991	1992	1993	1994	1995	1996	1997	1998	1999	2000	2001	2002	2003
Australia	38.8	38.6	40.7	42.4	49.9	57.4	61.4	61.8	60.8	65.5	67.8	60.9	69.5	84.8
Austria	50.0	50.7	54.1	50.4	55.2	66.3	67.1	63.6	67.1	68.7	67.4	69.0	71.4	91.5
Belgium	..	..	..	114.8	127.6	152.4	159.4	158.3	164.9	164.6	171.7	178.7	198.1	235.5
Belgium/Luxembourg	120.3	121.2	125.0	..	..	..	..	..	..	..	..	..	..	..
Canada	116.7	118.2	122.6	131.7	148.4	164.5	171.0	197.1	201.3	215.6	240.0	221.6	222.2	236.9
Czech Republic	..	..	..	12.7	14.9	20.8	27.4	27.2	30.5	28.8	32.2	36.5	40.7	51.2
Denmark	33.5	34.3	35.7	31.0	36.5	45.6	45.0	44.5	46.2	44.3	44.4	44.3	49.3	56.2
Finland	27.1	21.7	20.7	18.0	23.3	29.5	30.9	31.0	32.4	31.6	34.1	32.2	33.6	41.6
France	233.2	230.8	238.9	210.1	228.3	273.5	277.7	266.6	285.8	292.8	304.0	304.2	303.8	362.4
Germany	349.3	389.1	408.2	342.6	381.7	464.3	444.4	445.3	471.6	473.5	495.4	486.3	490.1	601.8
Greece	19.7	21.7	25.2	22.8	20.9	25.9	27.0	27.0	30.3	29.5	29.8	28.2	32.5	44.9
Hungary	..	..	11.1	12.5	14.9	15.5	16.2	21.2	25.7	28.0	32.1	33.7	37.6	47.7
Iceland	1.7	1.7	1.7	1.4	1.5	1.8	2.0	2.0	2.5	2.5	2.6	2.3	2.3	2.8
Ireland	20.8	20.9	22.5	21.8	25.9	32.3	35.8	39.2	44.4	46.5	50.7	51.1	52.3	..
Italy	178.6	182.4	188.7	157.6	167.9	204.0	208.2	208.1	215.6	220.3	237.3	236.1	242.7	290.8
Japan	234.8	236.7	233.5	241.7	276.1	336.1	349.2	338.8	280.6	309.9	379.7	348.6	337.6	383.5
Korea	..	..	..	..	103.1	137.9	144.1	144.6	93.3	119.8	160.5	141.1	152.1	178.8
Luxembourg	..	..	..	..	..	..	..	..	..	10.6	10.6	11.2	11.5	13.6
Mexico	31.1	38.1	61.9	65.3	79.3	72.5	89.5	109.8	125.3	142.0	171.1	165.1	165.7	170.5
Netherlands	135.8	125.9	134.5	129.8	130.5	157.7	162.5	158.3	156.8	167.9	174.7	169.9	163.4	..
New Zealand	9.5	8.5	9.2	9.3	11.9	13.9	14.7	14.5	12.5	14.3	13.9	13.3	15.0	18.6
Norway	27.2	25.5	26.1	24.0	27.4	33.0	35.6	35.8	37.5	34.2	34.4	33.0	34.9	39.8
Poland	..	..	15.9	18.8	21.6	28.9	37.1	42.3	47.0	45.9	48.9	50.2	55.1	68.0
Portugal	25.4	26.4	30.6	24.2	27.1	33.6	35.2	35.1	37.0	39.8	39.9	39.4	40.0	..
Slovak Republic	..	..	..	..	..	..	..	11.7	13.1	11.1	12.7	14.7	16.6	22.6
Spain	87.6	93.0	99.7	79.7	91.0	116.5	123.6	124.4	137.2	147.9	152.9	155.0	165.9	..
Sweden	54.7	49.9	50.0	46.7	52.0	61.6	64.0	63.2	68.6	68.5	73.1	63.5	67.1	83.4
Switzerland	69.7	66.5	65.7	62.0	67.9	80.2	78.2	75.9	80.1	79.9	82.5	84.2	83.7	96.4
Turkey	22.3	21.0	22.9	29.4	23.3	35.7	43.6	48.6	45.9	40.7	54.5	41.4	51.3	69.3
United Kingdom	223.7	209.8	222.5	209.4	234.0	268.2	287.6	307.5	320.3	323.8	340.2	346.5	351.7	386.1
United States	516.7	486.9	532.4	580.4	663.1	743.3	795.1	869.4	911.6	1 024.3	1 217.9	1 140.9	1 161.2	1 305.1
EU15	1 559.7	1 577.8	1 656.4	1 458.8	1 601.7	1 931.3	1 968.4	1 972.0	2 078.1	2 130.3	2 226.4	2 215.6	2 273.5	2 207.8
OECD total	2 628.1	2 619.7	2 800.2	2 690.5	3 105.0	3 672.7	3 833.6	3 972.8	4 045.8	4 292.7	4 777.0	4 603.0	4 719.1	4 983.9

StatLink: http://dx.doi.org/10.1787/687272260670

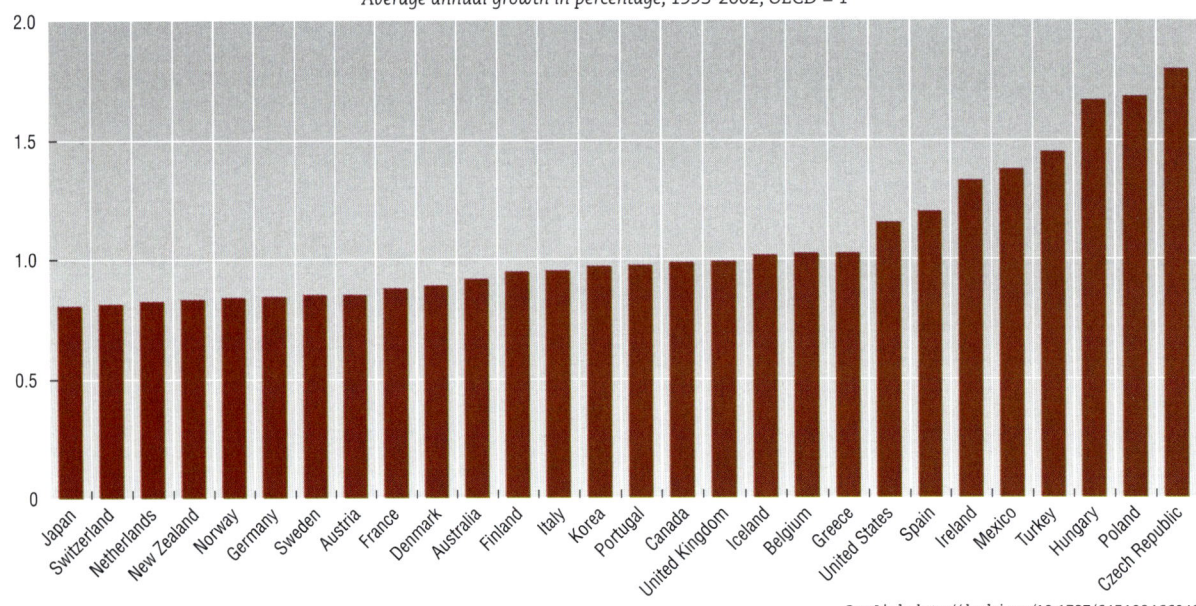

Relative growth of imports of goods
Average annual growth in percentage, 1993-2002, OECD = 1

StatLink: http://dx.doi.org/10.1787/645102466048

ECONOMIC GLOBALISATION • TRADE

TRADE IN GOODS

Exports of goods
Billion US dollars

	1990	1991	1992	1993	1994	1995	1996	1997	1998	1999	2000	2001	2002	2003
Australia	39.4	41.4	42.6	42.5	47.3	53.0	60.2	62.8	55.8	56.0	63.8	63.3	65.0	70.2
Austria	41.9	41.1	44.4	41.7	45.0	57.8	57.1	56.7	60.9	62.4	62.3	64.7	71.3	89.2
Belgium	..	..	..	126.1	140.9	167.7	170.8	170.7	179.4	178.9	185.2	190.3	215.8	255.3
Belgium/Luxembourg	118.3	118.4	122.7	..	..	..	..	..	..	..	..	..	..	..
Canada	121.4	120.9	127.9	137.6	156.1	181.0	190.2	215.1	214.6	238.9	277.6	261.0	252.4	268.8
Czech Republic	..	..	..	12.9	14.0	16.8	21.7	22.7	28.3	26.8	29.1	33.4	38.5	48.7
Denmark	36.9	37.7	41.4	37.5	42.3	50.3	50.7	48.2	47.9	49.0	49.6	50.1	55.7	64.6
Finland	26.7	23.1	23.5	23.5	29.8	40.4	40.6	41.0	43.2	41.8	45.8	42.8	44.7	52.5
France	210.2	213.4	232.1	216.2	233.3	284.1	283.9	283.4	300.5	302.3	295.6	299.8	304.9	357.9
Germany	406.4	402.7	430.2	380.0	427.3	523.9	512.7	512.4	543.8	542.8	550.2	572.0	615.6	748.5
Greece	8.1	8.7	9.8	8.8	9.2	11.0	11.3	11.2	10.9	10.7	11.0	10.3	10.8	13.7
Hungary	..	..	10.7	8.9	10.7	12.9	13.1	19.1	23.0	25.0	28.1	30.5	34.3	43.0
Iceland	1.6	1.6	1.5	1.5	1.6	1.8	1.9	1.9	1.9	2.0	1.9	2.0	2.2	2.4
Ireland	23.7	24.2	28.5	29.0	34.1	43.8	48.2	53.6	64.2	70.5	76.3	77.4	88.3	..
Italy	167.0	169.4	178.5	179.8	190.0	231.3	252.1	238.0	242.1	235.1	239.1	244.2	251.0	292.3
Japan	287.0	314.5	340.5	362.3	397.7	443.3	410.9	421.0	388.1	417.1	479.2	402.6	416.7	472.0
Korea	..	..	..	..	96.6	127.5	124.5	136.2	132.3	143.7	172.3	150.4	162.5	193.8
Luxembourg	..	..	..	..	..	..	..	..	..	..	7.8	7.9	8.3	8.6	10.0
Mexico	26.9	26.7	45.9	51.7	60.6	79.3	95.7	110.2	117.3	136.3	165.3	157.5	160.0	164.9
Netherlands	136.5	133.5	139.9	147.0	145.8	177.4	179.0	173.8	167.6	170.5	180.1	175.5	175.3	..
New Zealand	9.1	9.3	9.4	9.9	11.8	13.3	14.2	13.7	11.9	11.9	12.7	13.3	13.8	16.5
Norway	34.0	34.0	35.2	31.9	34.8	42.0	49.6	48.6	40.4	45.5	59.9	59.0	59.6	67.9
Poland	..	..	13.2	14.1	17.2	22.9	24.4	25.7	28.2	27.4	31.6	36.1	41.0	53.5
Portugal	16.5	16.4	18.6	15.4	18.0	23.4	24.6	24.0	24.2	24.5	24.4	24.4	26.5	..
Slovak Republic	..	..	..	..	..	..	..	9.6	10.7	10.1	11.8	12.6	14.5	22.0
Spain	55.5	58.6	64.8	61.1	71.9	93.5	102.6	106.2	111.4	111.5	113.3	116.1	125.9	..
Sweden	57.5	55.1	56.0	54.1	61.4	77.4	82.9	81.5	85.0	84.8	87.4	76.3	83.0	101.6
Switzerland	63.8	61.5	65.7	64.5	70.3	81.6	79.7	76.2	78.9	80.3	80.5	82.1	87.9	100.7
Turkey	13.0	13.6	14.7	15.3	18.1	21.6	23.2	26.2	27.0	26.6	27.8	31.3	35.8	47.3
United Kingdom	183.8	182.2	187.2	181.4	202.7	242.2	258.9	281.2	273.4	270.7	284.5	287.6	288.6	307.6
United States	374.5	421.6	448.0	465.0	512.5	584.7	625.0	689.1	682.1	695.8	781.8	729.1	693.1	723.7
EU15	1 489.0	1 484.5	1 577.7	1 501.6	1 651.4	2 024.0	2 075.2	2 081.8	2 154.5	2 163.4	2 212.5	2 239.9	2 365.9	2 293.3
OECD total	2 459.5	2 529.1	2 733.0	2 719.7	3 100.7	3 705.6	3 809.8	3 960.0	3 995.1	4 106.7	4 435.8	4 304.1	4 443.1	4 588.7

StatLink: http://dx.doi.org/10.1787/512072541065

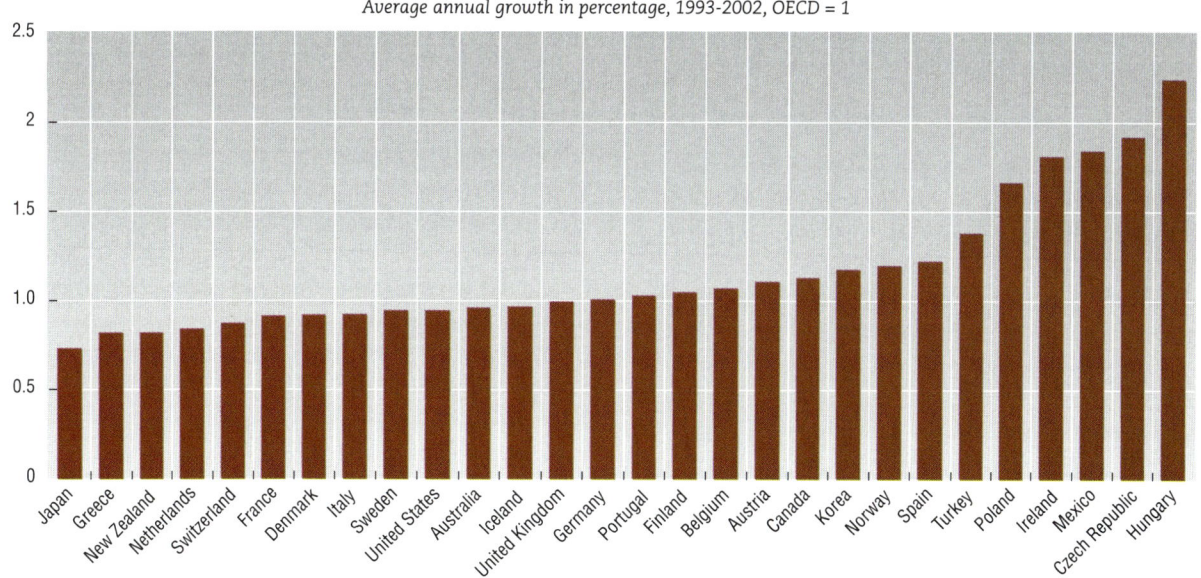

Relative growth of exports of goods
Average annual growth in percentage, 1993-2002, OECD = 1

StatLink: http://dx.doi.org/10.1787/561002747343

OECD FACTBOOK 2005 – ISBN 92-64-01869-7 – © OECD 2005

ECONOMIC GLOBALISATION • TRADE

TRADE IN SERVICES

International trade in services is growing in importance both among OECD countries and with the rest of the world. Traditional services – transport and insurance on merchandise trade as well as travel – account for about half of total international trade in services, but trade in newer types of services, particularly those that can be conducted via the Internet, are growing rapidly.

Definition

International trade in services is defined according to the 5th edition of the IMF Balance of Payments Manual (BPM5). Services include transport (both freight and passengers), travel (mainly expenditure on goods and services by tourists and business travellers), communications services (postal, telephone, satellite, etc.), construction services, insurance and financial services, computer and information services, royalties and licence fees, other business services (merchanting, operational leasing, technical and professional services, etc.), cultural and recreational services (rents for films, fees for actors and other performers, but excluding purchases of films, recorded music, books, etc.) and government services not included in the list above.

Comparability

BPM5 was issued in 1993 and countries began to implement it in the next two or three years. Prior to that, services were defined according to BPM4. The main difference between them is that BPM5 makes a clear distinction between transactions in services and payments of income. In the 4th edition, labour and non-financial property incomes were included with services. In BPM4, labour income included non-resident workers expenditures, in addition to the workers' earnings; in BPM5, workers' earnings are classified under compensation of employees in the income category and their expenditures are classified under travel services. Countries have tried to preserve continuity by revising earlier figures in line with BPM5 but this has not always been possible. For France and Portugal, for example, data prior to 1995 and 1996, respectively, are still mainly in line with BPM4.

Long-term trends

Between 1992 and 2003, growth of service imports in Ireland was about 3.5 times higher than the average and was also well above average in Hungary and Korea. Imports of services grew relatively slowly in France, Japan and Finland.

The growth rate of service exports in current US dollars for Ireland was again well above the average and relatively high growth was also recorded for New Zealand, Denmark, Luxembourg and Korea. Rather low relative growth occurred in France, Italy and Mexico.

Averaged over the last four years, trade in services was relatively balanced for most countries but large surpluses were recorded for Switzerland, France, the United Kingdom, Spain and the United States and substantial deficits occurred in Germany and Japan.

The fastest growing services – for both exports and imports – are now computer and information services and insurance. Imports of other business services are also growing strongly as are exports of personal cultural and recreational services. For both OECD exports and imports, construction services have been contracting in the recent period.

Sources

OECD (2004), *Main Economic Indicators*, OECD, Paris.

OECD (2004), *OECD Statistics on International Trade in Services: Volume I – Detailed Tables by Service Category – 1993-2002*, OECD, Paris.

Further information
• *Analytical publications*

OECD (2004), *Export Credit Financing Systems in OECD Member and Non-Member Countries*, OECD, Paris.

OECD (2004), *Promoting Trade in Services: The Experience of the Baltic States*, OECD, Paris.

• *Statistical publications*

OECD (2002), *Measuring Globalisation: The Role of Multinationals in OECD Economies, Volume II: Services*, OECD, Paris.

OECD (2004), *International Trade by Commodity Statistics*, OECD, Paris.

OECD (2004), *OECD Statistics on International Trade in Services: Volume II – Detailed Tables by Partner Country – 1999-2002*, OECD, Paris.

• *Methodological publications*

IMF (1993), *Balance of Payments Manual*, 5th edition, IMF, Washington, DC.

• *Web sites*

OECD International Trade in Services: *www.oecd.org/std/trade-services*.

ECONOMIC GLOBALISATION • TRADE

TRADE IN SERVICES

Services trade balance
Billion US dollars

	1990	1991	1992	1993	1994	1995	1996	1997	1998	1999	2000	2001	2002	2003
Australia	-3.6	-2.5	-2.6	-1.5	-1.3	-1.0	-0.0	-0.4	-1.1	-0.9	0.3	-0.3	-0.2	-0.2
Austria	..	..	9.4	7.5	7.4	4.6	4.6	1.0	2.4	1.8	1.6	1.8	0.6	0.9
Belgium	..	..	..	..	..	-0.1	0.2	1.3	0.8	1.4	2.1	1.8	1.9	1.8
Canada	-9.1	-10.0	-10.0	-10.5	-8.5	-7.4	-6.7	-6.4	-4.3	-4.5	-3.9	-4.7	-4.4	-7.8
Czech Republic	..	..	..	1.0	0.5	1.8	1.9	1.8	1.9	1.2	1.4	1.5	0.7	0.5
Denmark	1.8	2.8	2.3	1.6	0.5	0.7	1.3	0.1	-0.3	1.6	2.7	3.0	2.3	3.8
Finland	-3.2	-3.6	-2.9	-2.2	-1.8	-2.2	-1.7	-1.6	-1.1	-1.4	-2.3	-2.3	-1.5	-2.0
France	15.0	15.9	17.6	16.1	18.5	17.9	16.3	18.3	18.8	19.1	19.8	17.8	17.6	14.7
Germany	-22.5	-26.0	-36.1	-38.4	-46.2	-53.5	-51.7	-48.7	-52.2	-57.9	-55.0	-54.5	-43.9	-49.3
Greece	5.5	6.1	6.4	8.1	9.4	8.6	8.9	7.2	7.0	7.6	8.2	7.4	9.7	13.0
Hungary	0.5	0.5	0.8	0.2	0.2	0.6	1.5	2.3	1.8	1.4	1.1	1.5	0.6	-0.2
Iceland	0.0	-0.0	-0.0	0.0	0.0	0.0	0.0	0.0	-0.0	-0.1	-0.1	0.0	0.0	-0.1
Ireland	-1.7	-2.0	-3.0	-3.0	-4.1	-6.3	-7.7	-9.0	-9.9	-10.8	-12.8	-11.9	-13.4	-14.3
Italy	3.6	3.2	0.8	3.3	5.2	6.3	7.2	7.8	4.9	1.2	1.1	0.0	-2.9	-3.4
Japan	-42.8	-41.9	-44.0	-43.0	-47.9	-57.3	-62.3	-54.1	-49.3	-54.0	-47.6	-43.8	-42.0	-35.5
Korea	-0.6	-2.2	-2.9	-2.1	-1.8	-3.0	-6.2	-3.2	1.0	-0.7	-2.9	-3.9	-8.2	-7.6
Luxembourg	..	..	..	..	..	3.2	3.5	4.0	4.2	5.4	6.8	6.4	7.0	8.3
Mexico	-1.9	-1.8	-2.3	-2.1	-2.0	0.7	0.4	-0.7	-0.9	-1.8	-2.3	-3.6	-4.0	-4.5
Netherlands	-0.5	-0.8	-0.3	-0.1	0.1	1.1	2.0	3.3	2.4	2.6	-2.0	-2.5	-1.5	-1.2
New Zealand	-0.8	-0.8	-0.9	-0.6	-0.3	-0.2	-0.3	-0.7	-0.7	-0.2	-0.2	0.1	0.4	0.8
Norway	3.2	3.5	0.5	0.7	0.2	0.5	1.4	1.4	0.7	1.0	1.9	2.5	2.1	2.2
Poland	..	..	..	0.6	2.8	3.5	3.4	3.2	4.2	1.4	1.4	0.8	0.9	0.5
Portugal	1.2	1.2	1.1	1.4	1.3	1.6	1.4	1.5	1.9	1.9	1.9	2.5	2.9	3.9
Slovak Republic	..	..	..	0.3	0.8	0.7	0.2	0.2	0.2	0.2	0.4	0.5	0.5	0.2
Spain	11.8	12.1	12.4	11.7	14.8	18.6	20.4	20.0	21.8	23.0	22.4	24.3	24.9	30.7
Sweden	0.0	0.0	-2.3	0.1	0.2	-0.4	-0.9	-1.3	-1.6	-1.3	-1.5	-0.6	-0.8	-0.1
Switzerland	9.3	10.4	10.6	11.4	11.4	12.8	12.4	13.1	13.5	14.4	15.2	13.1	14.1	17.2
Turkey	4.9	5.2	5.8	6.7	7.0	9.6	6.6	10.9	13.5	7.5	11.4	9.1	7.9	10.5
United Kingdom	7.3	7.4	9.1	9.8	9.7	13.4	16.0	22.0	22.0	21.3	20.5	19.1	23.0	23.9
United States	30.2	45.8	57.8	62.3	67.5	77.9	87.1	89.9	81.8	82.8	74.1	64.5	61.2	51.0
Euro area	..	..	..	..	..	..	..	5.0	0.7	-7.9	-5.6	-0.2	12.6	19.4
EU15	24.5	22.8	18.0	15.1	14.1	15.7	17.2	20.0	13.3	7.9	6.8	9.0	22.9	..
OECD total	..	..	..	..	..	53.0	59.3	83.3	83.5	63.1	63.6	50.0	55.4	57.9

StatLink: http://dx.doi.org/10.1787/050017452836

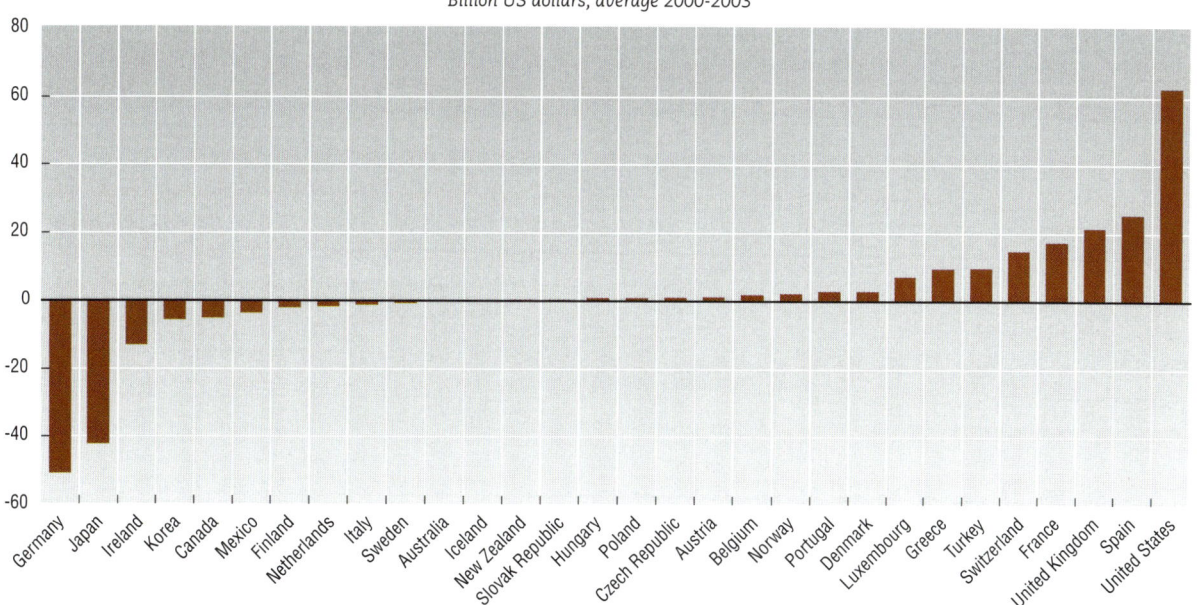

Services trade balance
Billion US dollars, average 2000-2003

StatLink: http://dx.doi.org/10.1787/487034083058

ECONOMIC GLOBALISATION • TRADE

TRADE IN SERVICES

Imports of services
Billion US dollars

	1990	1991	1992	1993	1994	1995	1996	1997	1998	1999	2000	2001	2002	2003
Australia	13.8	13.5	13.8	13.4	15.4	17.1	18.6	18.8	17.3	18.3	18.4	16.9	18.1	21.4
Austria	..	..	17.9	19.2	20.6	24.6	25.4	26.7	27.1	29.5	29.8	31.5	34.8	42.8
Belgium	..	..	..	..	..	29.7	29.0	27.8	30.0	31.2	32.3	33.6	35.8	42.9
Canada	28.3	30.3	30.8	32.4	32.5	33.5	35.9	38.0	38.1	40.6	44.1	43.9	45.1	50.6
Czech Republic	..	..	..	3.7	4.7	4.9	6.3	5.4	5.7	5.9	5.4	5.6	6.4	7.3
Denmark	10.1	10.3	10.9	10.6	11.8	13.2	13.9	14.2	15.5	18.4	21.1	22.1	24.3	28.6
Finland	7.7	7.7	7.5	6.6	7.3	9.6	8.8	8.2	7.8	7.9	8.4	8.1	8.0	9.7
France	60.2	61.4	73.0	68.9	70.4	66.1	67.3	63.4	67.1	64.3	60.8	62.3	68.2	84.3
Germany	87.7	93.0	106.4	104.7	114.0	137.5	138.8	134.3	139.2	144.0	140.5	145.0	149.7	174.4
Greece	5.0	4.6	5.3	3.4	3.8	4.1	4.2	4.1	4.5	9.7	11.5	10.6	9.6	11.2
Hungary	2.4	2.0	2.6	2.6	3.0	3.6	3.5	3.5	4.2	4.3	5.0	6.0	7.2	8.2
Iceland	0.6	0.6	0.6	0.6	0.6	0.6	0.7	0.8	1.0	1.0	1.2	1.1	1.1	1.5
Ireland	5.2	5.7	7.1	6.7	8.4	11.3	13.4	15.2	23.1	26.6	31.4	35.4	41.9	52.2
Italy	42.8	40.1	53.2	45.6	45.7	51.1	53.4	54.2	59.1	57.7	55.6	57.9	63.0	74.5
Japan	84.1	86.7	93.0	96.2	106.2	122.8	130.0	123.4	111.7	114.9	116.8	108.2	107.8	108.8
Korea	10.3	12.2	13.6	15.1	18.6	25.8	29.6	29.5	24.5	27.2	33.4	32.9	36.6	40.3
Luxembourg	..	..	..	..	..	7.5	8.5	8.7	9.9	11.5	13.2	13.3	13.2	16.5
Mexico	9.9	10.5	11.5	11.5	12.3	9.0	10.2	11.8	12.4	13.5	16.0	16.2	16.7	17.1
Netherlands	29.7	33.8	38.5	38.0	41.3	44.8	45.3	45.7	47.3	49.5	51.4	53.8	57.3	66.1
New Zealand	3.3	3.4	3.6	3.5	4.0	4.7	4.9	4.9	4.5	4.6	4.5	4.3	4.7	5.6
Norway	9.5	9.8	12.2	11.5	12.0	13.1	13.4	14.3	14.8	14.9	15.5	15.1	16.4	19.6
Poland	..	..	..	3.6	3.9	7.1	6.3	5.7	6.6	7.0	9.0	9.0	9.2	10.6
Portugal	3.8	4.2	4.5	5.5	5.4	6.6	6.5	6.2	6.9	6.8	6.6	6.3	6.8	7.9
Slovak Republic	..	..	..	1.7	1.6	1.8	2.0	2.1	2.3	1.8	1.8	2.0	2.3	3.0
Spain	16.0	17.2	21.3	18.9	18.9	21.5	24.0	24.3	27.4	30.7	31.4	34.0	37.4	46.0
Sweden	..	..	18.3	12.7	14.0	16.8	18.4	19.7	21.4	23.0	24.2	23.6	24.0	28.8
Switzerland	9.6	9.4	10.5	10.1	11.2	13.2	13.8	12.2	13.2	14.0	13.7	14.6	15.3	17.7
Turkey	3.1	3.2	3.6	3.9	3.8	5.0	6.4	8.5	9.9	9.4	9.1	6.9	6.9	8.5
United Kingdom	48.8	49.0	54.5	52.4	59.8	65.4	72.6	78.1	87.8	96.2	99.2	99.5	107.9	123.2
United States	117.7	118.5	119.5	123.7	132.9	141.3	152.4	166.4	181.3	199.7	224.9	223.5	233.0	256.3
Euro area	..	..	..	..	..	..	..	..	..	241.6	263.5	279.3	281.2	288.4	298.5	349.8
EU15	179.2	181.7	188.7	180.0	193.2	214.8	237.1	247.4	256.9	273.6	279.4	284.0	293.6	..
OECD total	..	..	..	..	..	913.3	963.8	976.0	1 021.5	1 084.1	1 136.1	1 143.2	1 208.4	1 385.6

StatLink: http://dx.doi.org/10.1787/727471765704

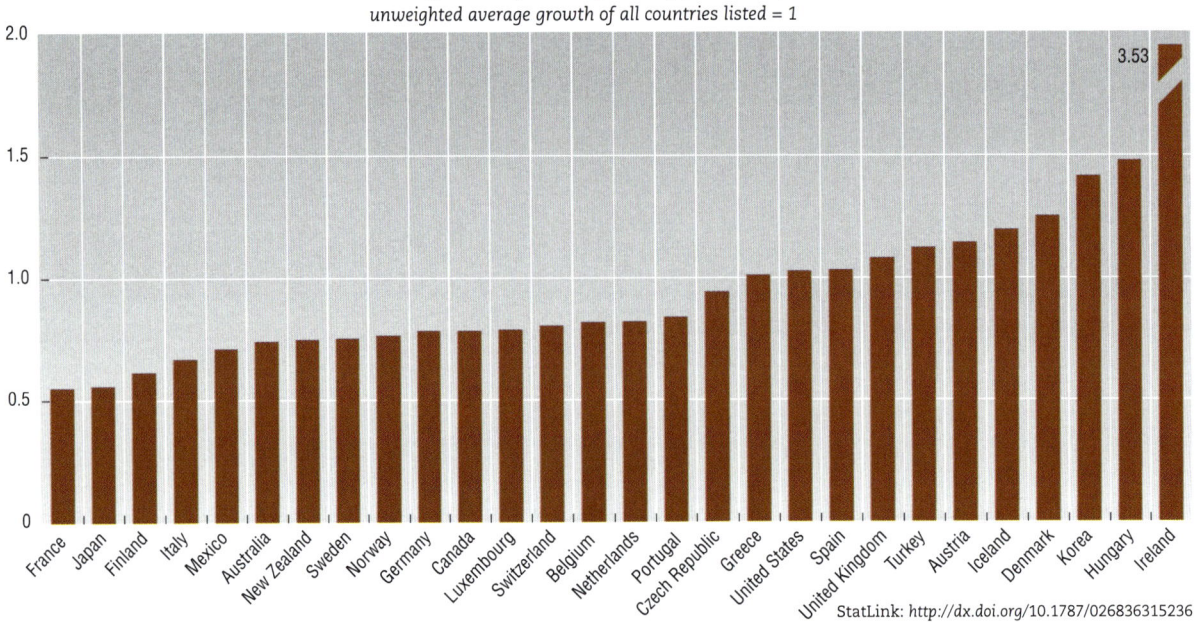

Relative growth in imports of services
Average annual growth in percentage, 1992-2003, unweighted average growth of all countries listed = 1

StatLink: http://dx.doi.org/10.1787/026836315236

ECONOMIC GLOBALISATION • TRADE

TRADE IN SERVICES

Exports of services
Billion US dollars

	1990	1991	1992	1993	1994	1995	1996	1997	1998	1999	2000	2001	2002	2003
Australia	10.2	11.0	11.2	11.9	14.2	16.1	18.6	18.4	16.1	17.4	18.6	16.7	17.9	21.1
Austria	..	..	27.2	26.7	28.0	29.2	30.0	27.7	29.5	31.3	31.4	33.3	35.4	43.7
Belgium	..	..	..	..	..	29.6	29.3	29.1	30.8	32.6	34.3	35.4	37.7	44.7
Canada	19.2	20.4	20.8	21.9	24.0	26.1	29.2	31.6	33.9	36.1	40.2	39.2	40.7	42.8
Czech Republic	..	..	..	4.7	5.2	6.7	8.2	7.2	7.6	7.1	6.9	7.1	7.1	7.8
Denmark	11.8	13.1	13.2	12.2	12.3	13.9	15.1	14.3	15.2	20.0	23.8	25.1	26.6	32.3
Finland	4.5	4.1	4.6	4.4	5.5	7.4	7.1	6.7	6.7	6.5	6.2	5.8	6.5	7.8
France	75.2	77.3	90.6	85.0	88.9	84.0	83.5	81.7	85.9	83.4	80.6	80.2	85.9	99.0
Germany	65.2	67.0	70.3	66.3	67.8	84.0	87.1	85.6	87.0	86.1	85.5	90.5	105.8	125.1
Greece	10.5	10.7	11.7	11.5	13.2	12.7	13.2	11.2	11.5	17.4	19.6	18.1	19.2	24.2
Hungary	2.9	2.5	3.4	2.8	3.1	4.3	5.0	5.7	5.9	5.6	6.1	7.5	7.8	8.0
Iceland	0.6	0.6	0.6	0.6	0.6	0.7	0.8	0.8	1.0	0.9	1.0	1.1	1.1	1.4
Ireland	3.4	3.7	4.0	3.8	4.3	5.0	5.7	6.2	13.3	15.7	18.6	23.5	28.5	37.9
Italy	46.4	43.4	54.0	48.9	50.9	57.5	60.6	62.0	64.0	58.9	56.7	57.9	60.1	71.1
Japan	41.3	44.9	49.0	53.2	58.3	65.5	67.7	69.3	62.4	60.9	69.2	64.5	65.7	73.3
Korea	9.6	10.0	10.7	13.0	16.8	22.8	23.4	26.3	25.6	26.5	30.5	29.1	28.4	32.7
Luxembourg	..	..	..	..	..	10.7	12.0	12.7	14.2	16.9	20.0	19.8	20.2	24.8
Mexico	8.0	8.8	9.2	9.4	10.3	9.7	10.6	11.1	11.5	11.7	13.7	12.7	12.7	12.6
Netherlands	29.2	33.0	38.2	37.9	41.4	45.9	47.2	49.0	49.7	52.1	49.3	51.3	55.8	64.9
New Zealand	2.5	2.6	2.6	2.9	3.7	4.5	4.7	4.2	3.8	4.4	4.4	4.4	5.2	6.4
Norway	12.7	13.3	12.7	12.2	12.2	13.7	14.8	15.7	15.5	15.9	17.4	17.6	18.5	21.8
Poland	..	..	..	4.2	6.7	10.7	9.7	8.9	10.8	8.4	10.4	9.8	10.0	11.2
Portugal	5.2	5.4	5.6	6.9	6.7	8.2	7.9	7.7	8.8	8.7	8.5	8.9	9.7	11.8
Slovak Republic	..	..	..	2.0	2.4	2.5	2.2	2.3	2.4	2.1	2.2	2.5	2.8	3.3
Spain	27.7	29.3	33.7	30.6	33.6	40.1	44.4	44.3	49.2	53.7	53.8	58.3	62.3	76.7
Sweden	..	..	15.9	12.8	14.2	16.4	17.5	18.4	19.7	21.7	22.7	23.0	23.3	28.7
Switzerland	18.9	19.8	21.1	21.5	22.6	26.0	26.2	25.3	26.7	28.4	28.9	27.7	29.4	34.9
Turkey	8.0	8.4	9.4	10.7	10.8	14.6	13.1	19.4	23.3	16.9	20.4	16.1	14.8	19.0
United Kingdom	56.1	56.5	63.6	62.2	69.4	78.8	88.6	100.1	109.8	117.5	119.7	118.6	130.8	147.0
United States	147.8	164.3	177.3	185.9	200.4	219.2	239.5	256.3	263.1	282.5	299.0	287.9	294.1	307.4
Euro area	..	..	..	..	..	..	..	..	246.5	264.2	271.4	275.6	288.2	311.1	369.2
EU15	203.7	204.6	206.6	195.1	207.3	230.5	254.3	267.4	270.3	281.5	286.2	293.0	316.5	..
OECD total	..	..	..	..	..	966.3	1 023.1	1 059.3	1 104.9	1 147.3	1 199.7	1 193.2	1 263.8	1 443.5

StatLink: http://dx.doi.org/10.1787/554328151426

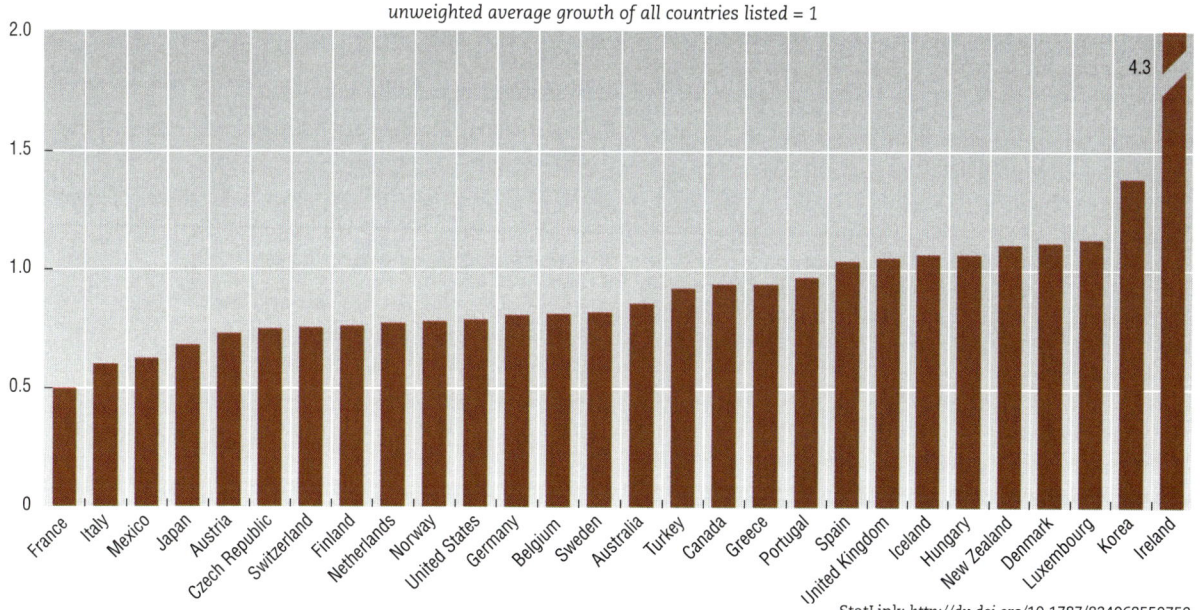

Relative growth in exports of services
Average annual growth in percentage, 1992-2003,
unweighted average growth of all countries listed = 1

StatLink: http://dx.doi.org/10.1787/834068552752

ECONOMIC GLOBALISATION • TRADE

TRADING PARTNERS

The pattern of OECD merchandise trade – where imports come from and where exports go to – has undergone significant shifts over the last decade. These are in response to changes in the distribution of global income and to globalisation – in particular, the outsourcing of manufacturing from OECD countries to the rest of the world.

These tables refer to total OECD imports and exports and show merchandise trade both among OECD itself and with countries in the rest of the world.

Definition

NAFTA is the North American Free Trade Area and consists of Canada, Mexico and the United States. OECD Asia and Pacific includes Australia and New Zealand as well as Japan and Korea. Non-OECD America covers the Caribbean, Latin America and Central America, except Mexico. Near and Middle East covers Israel, Jordan, Iran, Lebanon, Saudi Arabia, Yemen, Armenia, Azerbaijan, Georgia and the Gulf States.

The definitions of merchandise imports and exports are explained on page 54.

Comparability

OECD countries follow common definitions and procedures in compiling their merchandise trade statistics which are generally regarded as comparable and of good quality. The removal of customs frontiers following the creation of a common market in Europe required EU countries to adopt a system of recording trade flows through sample surveys of exporters and importers. This led to some fall in the reliability of merchandise trade statistics for trade between the EU countries. Statistics on trade between EU countries and non-EU countries, however, was not affected.

Source

OECD (2004), *International Trade by Commodity Statistics*, OECD, Paris.

Further information
• *Analytical publications*

OECD (2004), *Internationalisation and Trade in Higher Education: Opportunities and Challenges*, OECD, Paris.

OECD (2004), *The Dairy Sector*, Agriculture, Trade and the Environment, OECD, Paris.

OECD (2004), *The Impact of Regulations on Agro-Food Trade: The Technical Barriers to Trade (TBT) and Sanitary and Phytosanitary Measures (SPS) Agreements*, OECD, Paris.

OECD (2004), *Trade and Competitiveness in Argentina, Brazil and Chile: Not as Easy as A-B-C*, OECD, Paris.

OECD, IOM and the World Bank (eds.) (2004), *Trade and Migration: Building Bridges for Global Labour Mobility*, OECD, Paris.

• *Statistical publications*

OECD (2004), *Monthly Statistics on International Trade*, OECD, Paris.

OECD (2004), *Statistics on International Trade of Services*, OECD, Paris.

• *Methodological publications*

UN, EC, IMF, OECD, UNCTAD and the WTO (2002), *Manual on Statistics of International Trade in Services*, United Nations, New York.

• *Online databases*

SourceOECD International Trade by Commodity Statistics.

SourceOECD Monthly Statistics of International Trade.

• *Web sites*

OECD International Trade Statistics: *www.oecd.org/std/its*.

Long-term trends

Since 1990 there has been a steady decline in the share of OECD imports and exports among OECD member countries. In 1990, imports from OECD countries accounted for 78% of total OECD imports but by 2003 this had fallen to 71%. For exports the fall in intra-OECD trade was less marked – down from 81% in 1990 to 78% in 2003.

Outside the OECD area, the trade shares with Africa have fallen, and have remained virtually unchanged with non-OECD America and the Near and Middle East. Other (non-OECD) Asia covers the Indian sub-continent, China and South East Asia. OECD imports from these countries have risen from 9% to 16% over the period and exports to them from 8% to 11%. A large change occurred in trade between OECD and China. In 1990 China supplied nearly 2% of total OECD imports but by 2003 this had risen to nearly 8%. China's importance as a destination for OECD countries has increased less sharply, rising from 1% in 1990 to 3.5% in 2003.

ECONOMIC GLOBALISATION • TRADE

TRADING PARTNERS

Share of total OECD merchandise trade
Percentage, by partner country

	1990	1991	1992	1993	1994	1995	1996	1997	1998	1999	2000	2001	2002	2003
World	100.0	100.0	100.0	100.0	100.0	100.0	100.0	100.0	100.0	100.0	100.0	100.0	100.0	100.0
OECD	79.3	78.7	78.3	76.5	76.2	76.2	75.7	75.6	77.4	77.8	75.9	75.8	75.6	74.7
G7	51.8	51.3	51.0	50.5	50.4	49.6	49.0	49.1	50.1	50.4	49.2	48.7	47.8	46.2
NAFTA	17.5	17.6	17.9	19.7	20.3	19.1	19.7	21.2	21.7	22.8	23.9	23.1	22.3	20.0
Canada	4.3	4.3	4.3	4.7	4.8	4.5	4.6	4.8	4.9	5.1	5.2	5.1	4.8	4.5
Mexico	1.5	1.6	1.7	1.9	2.0	1.8	2.0	2.3	2.5	2.7	3.2	3.1	3.0	2.6
United States	11.8	11.6	11.9	13.1	13.5	12.8	13.1	14.0	14.3	14.9	15.5	14.9	14.5	12.9
OECD Asia and Pacific	8.7	8.6	8.2	8.6	9.1	8.9	8.4	8.1	7.3	7.7	7.9	7.2	7.1	6.8
Japan	5.6	5.6	5.3	5.6	5.9	5.6	5.3	5.1	4.7	4.8	4.9	4.4	4.2	3.9
Korea	1.7	1.8	1.6	1.7	1.8	2.0	1.9	1.7	1.4	1.7	1.9	1.7	1.7	1.7
OECD Europe	53.1	52.5	52.2	48.2	46.9	48.2	47.6	46.4	48.4	47.3	44.0	45.5	46.3	47.9
Switzerland	2.4	2.2	2.1	2.1	2.0	2.0	1.9	1.8	1.9	1.8	1.6	1.7	1.7	1.7
EU15	48.5	47.9	47.5	43.3	42.2	43.3	42.4	41.1	42.9	42.0	38.9	40.1	40.6	41.9
Sweden	1.9	1.7	1.6	1.5	1.5	1.6	1.6	1.5	1.6	1.5	1.4	1.4	1.4	1.5
United Kingdom	6.2	5.9	5.8	5.7	5.5	5.5	5.6	5.7	5.8	5.7	5.4	5.5	5.4	5.2
Austria	1.5	1.5	1.5	1.4	1.4	1.3	1.3	1.3	1.4	1.3	1.2	1.3	1.3	1.4
Belgium/Luxembourg	4.2	4.1	4.1	3.6	3.6	3.6	3.4	3.2	3.3	3.2	2.9	3.1	3.2	3.3
France	7.5	7.4	7.2	6.6	6.3	6.4	6.1	5.9	6.2	6.1	5.5	5.7	5.7	5.9
Germany	11.5	11.6	11.5	10.7	10.2	10.6	10.3	9.6	10.1	9.8	8.9	9.3	9.4	9.8
Italy	5.2	5.1	5.0	4.2	4.1	4.3	4.2	4.0	4.2	4.0	3.7	3.8	3.9	4.1
Netherlands	4.6	4.6	4.5	4.0	3.9	4.1	4.0	4.0	4.0	3.9	3.7	3.7	3.7	3.8
Spain	2.2	2.4	2.4	2.1	2.1	2.3	2.3	2.3	2.5	2.6	2.4	2.5	2.6	2.8
Non-OECD	19.2	19.7	20.2	22.0	22.3	22.4	22.8	23.4	21.6	21.2	23.0	23.0	23.3	24.2
Europe	2.0	1.8	1.8	1.9	2.0	2.1	2.2	2.3	2.2	1.9	2.1	2.4	2.5	2.8
Africa	3.1	2.9	2.8	2.7	2.4	2.3	2.4	2.3	2.2	2.1	2.2	2.2	2.2	2.3
America	2.8	2.8	2.9	3.0	3.1	3.1	3.1	3.3	3.2	3.0	3.0	3.0	2.8	2.7
South America	2.0	2.0	2.1	2.1	2.3	2.3	2.3	2.4	2.3	2.0	2.1	2.1	1.9	1.8
Near and Middle East	3.0	3.0	3.0	3.0	2.7	2.5	2.6	2.8	2.4	2.5	2.9	2.9	2.8	2.9
Other Asia	8.2	9.0	9.6	11.2	12.0	12.3	12.4	12.6	11.4	11.8	12.7	12.4	12.9	13.5
China	1.3	1.6	1.9	2.4	2.7	2.8	2.9	3.1	3.1	3.4	3.8	4.1	4.8	5.5
Chinese Taipei	1.7	1.8	1.9	2.0	1.9	1.9	1.8	1.8	1.8	1.8	2.0	1.7	1.6	1.5

StatLink: http://dx.doi.org/10.1787/107608222836

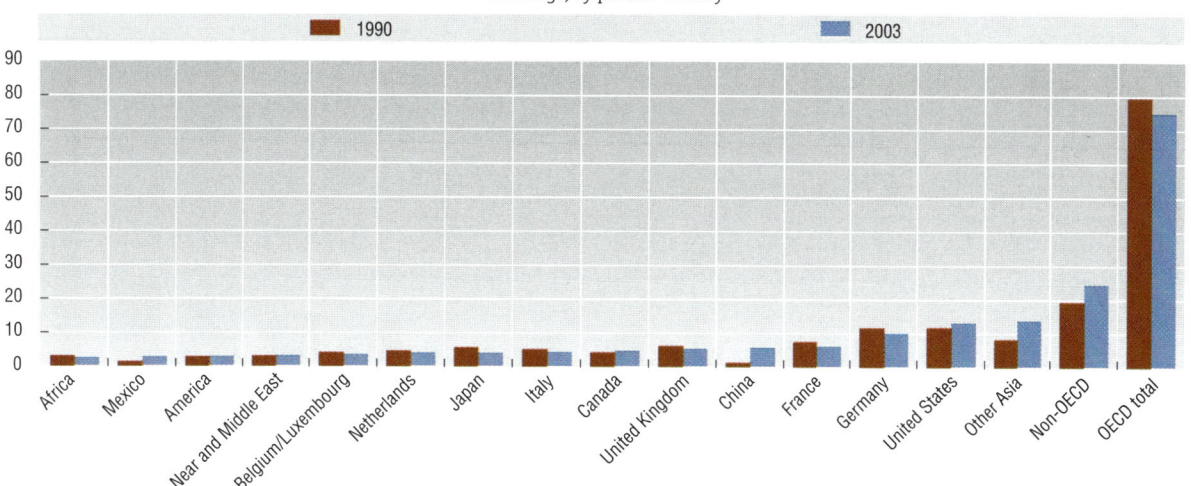

Share of total OECD merchandise trade
Percentage, by partner country

StatLink: http://dx.doi.org/10.1787/446613614127

ECONOMIC GLOBALISATION • TRADE

TRADING PARTNERS

Share of total OECD merchandise imports
Percentage, by country and region of origin

	1990	1991	1992	1993	1994	1995	1996	1997	1998	1999	2000	2001	2002	2003
World	100.0	100.0	100.0	100.0	100.0	100.0	100.0	100.0	100.0	100.0	100.0	100.0	100.0	100.0
OECD	78.0	78.1	78.1	76.3	76.1	76.5	75.7	75.4	76.8	75.9	73.0	73.1	72.9	71.6
G7	52.1	52.2	52.2	51.5	51.4	50.8	50.2	50.0	50.5	49.8	47.4	46.8	45.8	44.0
NAFTA	16.7	17.1	17.2	18.8	19.4	18.9	19.7	20.8	20.7	21.1	21.7	21.1	20.0	17.5
Canada	4.5	4.4	4.4	5.0	5.1	4.9	5.0	5.1	5.2	5.4	5.7	5.5	5.2	4.8
Mexico	1.5	1.5	1.5	1.7	1.9	2.0	2.2	2.5	2.6	2.9	3.3	3.3	3.3	2.9
United States	10.7	11.2	11.2	12.0	12.5	12.0	12.5	13.1	12.9	12.8	12.8	12.2	11.5	9.9
OECD Asia and Pacific	10.0	10.1	9.8	10.4	10.7	10.1	9.2	9.2	9.0	9.3	9.4	8.5	8.3	7.9
Japan	7.1	7.1	7.1	7.6	7.8	7.2	6.4	6.4	6.2	6.4	6.3	5.6	5.4	5.1
Korea	1.7	1.7	1.5	1.6	1.6	1.7	1.6	1.6	1.6	1.6	1.9	2.0	1.8	1.8
OECD Europe	51.3	51.0	51.2	47.1	46.0	47.5	46.9	45.5	47.1	45.6	41.9	43.5	44.7	46.1
Switzerland	2.1	2.0	2.0	2.0	1.9	1.9	1.9	1.7	1.8	1.7	1.5	1.6	1.6	1.6
EU15	46.8	46.5	46.6	42.5	41.5	42.7	42.0	40.6	42.1	40.6	36.9	38.2	39.1	40.2
Sweden	1.9	1.8	1.7	1.6	1.7	1.8	1.8	1.7	1.7	1.7	1.5	1.4	1.4	1.5
United Kingdom	5.3	5.4	5.3	5.2	5.1	5.1	5.2	5.2	5.2	5.1	4.8	4.7	4.5	4.3
Austria	1.3	1.3	1.4	1.3	1.3	1.2	1.1	1.1	1.2	1.2	1.0	1.1	1.2	1.2
Belgium/Luxembourg	3.9	3.9	3.9	3.4	3.3	3.4	3.2	3.0	3.0	2.9	2.6	2.8	2.9	3.0
France	6.9	7.0	7.0	6.3	6.1	6.1	5.9	5.8	6.1	5.8	5.1	5.3	5.3	5.4
Germany	12.4	11.9	12.0	10.9	10.4	11.0	10.6	10.0	10.5	10.2	9.1	9.6	10.1	10.5
Italy	5.2	5.2	5.1	4.5	4.5	4.6	4.6	4.3	4.5	4.2	3.7	3.8	3.9	4.0
Netherlands	4.5	4.5	4.5	3.9	3.8	4.0	3.9	3.9	4.0	3.8	3.5	3.5	3.5	3.7
Spain	1.8	1.9	1.9	1.8	1.9	2.0	2.1	2.1	2.2	2.1	1.9	2.0	2.1	2.3
Non-OECD	20.7	20.7	20.7	22.4	22.6	22.4	23.2	23.9	22.4	23.1	26.0	25.7	26.0	27.3
Europe	1.8	1.7	1.7	1.9	2.0	2.1	2.1	2.1	2.0	1.9	2.3	2.4	2.5	2.7
Africa	3.4	3.2	3.0	2.8	2.5	2.4	2.6	2.5	2.2	2.1	2.4	2.5	2.3	2.5
America	3.3	3.0	2.9	2.9	3.0	2.8	2.9	3.0	2.8	2.8	3.0	2.9	3.0	3.0
South America	2.7	2.4	2.3	2.3	2.4	2.2	2.2	2.3	2.1	2.1	2.2	2.2	2.3	2.3
Near and Middle East	3.5	3.2	2.9	3.0	2.7	2.6	2.8	2.9	2.3	2.5	3.6	3.3	3.0	3.2
Other Asia	8.7	9.5	10.1	11.7	12.2	12.3	12.7	13.2	13.1	13.7	14.6	14.5	15.2	15.8
China	1.8	2.2	2.5	3.2	3.6	3.7	3.9	4.4	4.5	4.9	5.3	5.8	6.7	7.5
Chinese Taipei	1.9	2.0	2.0	2.0	1.9	1.9	1.9	1.9	1.9	1.9	2.1	1.8	1.7	1.6

StatLink: http://dx.doi.org/10.1787/875272635684

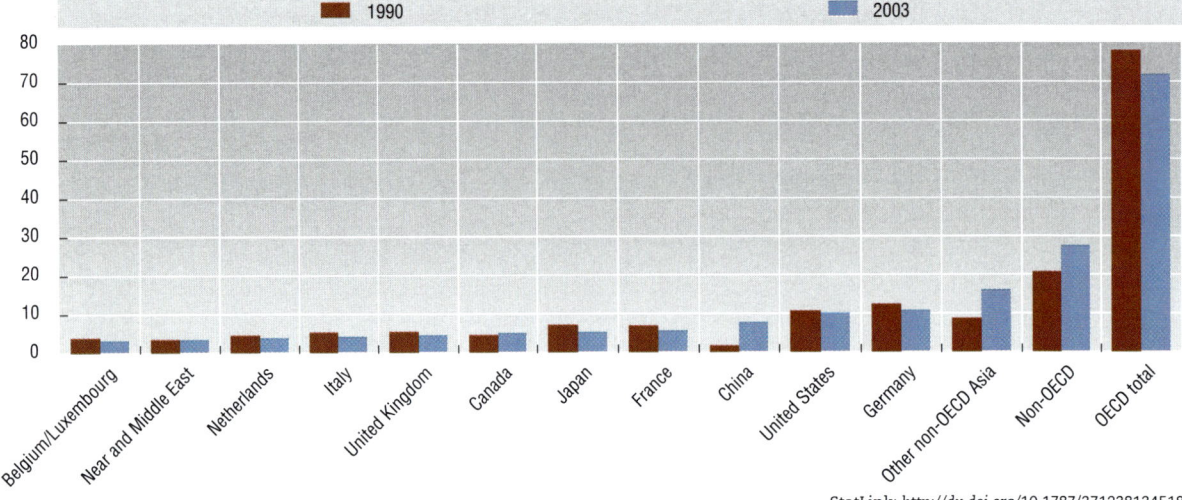

Share of total OECD merchandise imports
Percentage, by country and region of origin

StatLink: http://dx.doi.org/10.1787/371238134518

ECONOMIC GLOBALISATION • TRADE

TRADING PARTNERS

Share of total OECD merchandise exports
Percentage, by country and region of destination

	1990	1991	1992	1993	1994	1995	1996	1997	1998	1999	2000	2001	2002	2003
World	100.0	100.0	100.0	100.0	100.0	100.0	100.0	100.0	100.0	100.0	100.0	100.0	100.0	100.0
OECD	80.7	79.3	78.5	76.6	76.3	75.8	75.7	75.8	77.9	79.6	78.8	78.5	78.3	77.8
G7	51.6	50.4	49.8	49.5	49.3	48.4	47.9	48.2	49.7	51.1	50.9	50.6	49.8	48.5
NAFTA	18.4	18.1	18.7	20.6	21.2	19.2	19.7	21.6	22.6	24.5	26.1	25.1	24.6	22.4
Canada	4.1	4.3	4.1	4.5	4.5	4.1	4.2	4.5	4.6	4.8	4.8	4.6	4.5	4.1
Mexico	1.5	1.7	2.0	2.0	2.1	1.6	1.8	2.2	2.4	2.6	3.0	2.9	2.7	2.4
United States	12.8	12.1	12.6	14.1	14.6	13.5	13.7	14.8	15.6	17.1	18.3	17.6	17.4	15.9
OECD Asia and Pacific	7.3	7.2	6.5	6.7	7.5	7.6	7.6	7.0	5.7	6.1	6.5	5.9	5.9	5.7
Japan	4.1	4.0	3.6	3.6	4.1	4.1	4.1	3.8	3.2	3.3	3.4	3.2	2.9	2.7
Korea	1.8	2.0	1.7	1.8	2.0	2.2	2.2	1.9	1.2	1.6	1.8	1.6	1.7	1.7
OECD Europe	55.0	54.1	53.3	49.3	47.7	49.0	48.4	47.2	49.6	49.0	46.2	47.5	47.9	49.7
Switzerland	2.6	2.5	2.2	2.2	2.0	2.1	2.0	1.9	2.0	1.9	1.7	1.8	1.8	1.8
EU15	50.2	49.2	48.4	44.1	43.0	43.9	42.9	41.6	43.7	43.4	40.8	42.0	42.2	43.6
Sweden	1.8	1.6	1.5	1.3	1.3	1.5	1.5	1.4	1.5	1.4	1.4	1.3	1.3	1.4
United Kingdom	7.0	6.3	6.3	6.3	6.0	5.9	6.0	6.2	6.4	6.3	6.1	6.3	6.2	6.1
Austria	1.6	1.7	1.7	1.6	1.5	1.5	1.5	1.4	1.5	1.5	1.4	1.4	1.4	1.5
Belgium/Luxembourg	4.5	4.3	4.2	3.9	3.8	3.8	3.6	3.4	3.5	3.4	3.2	3.4	3.5	3.7
France	8.1	7.7	7.5	6.8	6.6	6.6	6.2	5.9	6.3	6.3	5.9	6.1	6.1	6.3
Germany	10.6	11.3	11.0	10.5	10.0	10.3	9.9	9.3	9.7	9.4	8.7	9.0	8.8	9.2
Italy	5.1	4.9	4.9	3.9	3.8	4.0	3.8	3.7	3.9	3.9	3.7	3.8	3.9	4.1
Netherlands	4.8	4.7	4.6	4.1	4.1	4.2	4.1	4.1	4.1	4.1	3.9	3.8	3.8	3.9
Spain	2.7	2.8	2.9	2.3	2.3	2.5	2.5	2.5	2.8	3.0	2.8	2.9	3.0	3.3
Non-OECD	17.6	18.8	19.7	21.5	22.0	22.5	22.4	23.0	20.8	19.3	20.0	20.3	20.6	21.1
Europe	2.1	1.9	1.8	1.9	1.9	2.0	2.3	2.5	2.3	1.8	1.9	2.3	2.6	2.9
Africa	2.8	2.6	2.6	2.5	2.3	2.2	2.2	2.1	2.3	2.0	1.9	2.0	2.0	2.0
America	2.3	2.6	2.8	3.0	3.2	3.3	3.3	3.7	3.7	3.1	3.0	3.1	2.7	2.4
South America	1.4	1.7	1.9	2.0	2.1	2.3	2.3	2.6	2.6	2.0	1.9	2.0	1.5	1.3
Near and Middle East	2.6	2.9	3.2	3.1	2.7	2.4	2.5	2.6	2.6	2.4	2.2	2.5	2.5	2.6
Other Asia	7.8	8.6	9.2	10.8	11.8	12.3	12.0	12.0	9.7	9.8	10.9	10.3	10.7	11.1
China	0.9	1.0	1.2	1.7	1.8	1.8	1.8	1.8	1.8	1.9	2.2	2.4	2.9	3.5
Chinese Taipei	1.5	1.7	1.8	1.9	1.9	1.9	1.9	1.7	1.8	1.7	1.7	2.0	1.5	1.5	1.4

StatLink: http://dx.doi.org/10.1787/867074860643

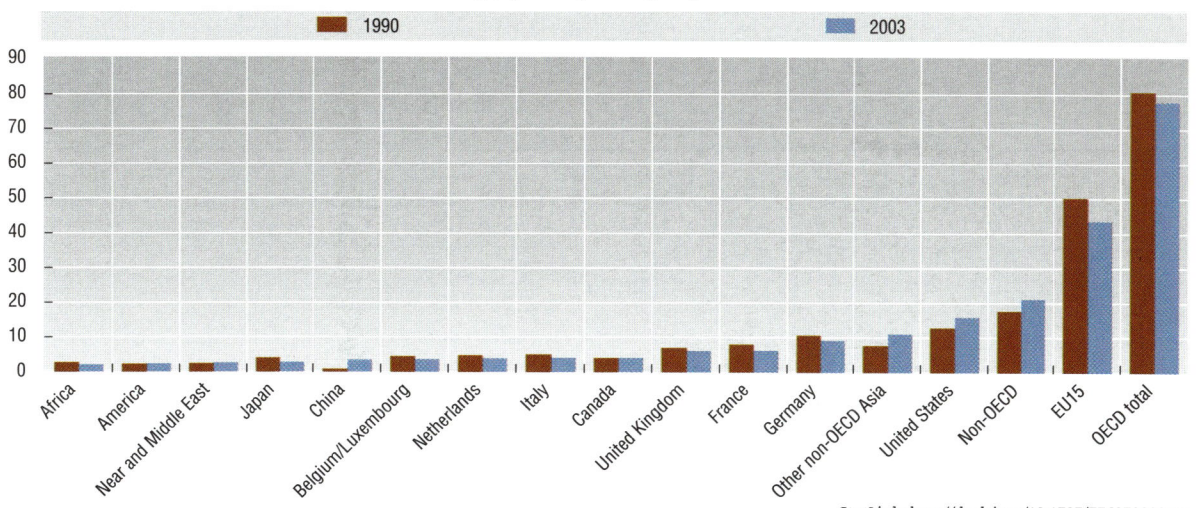

Share of total OECD merchandise exports
Percentage, by country and region of destination

StatLink: http://dx.doi.org/10.1787/776372338581

ECONOMIC GLOBALISATION • TRADE

BALANCE OF PAYMENTS

The current accounts balance is the difference between current receipts from abroad and current payments to abroad. When the current account balance is positive, the country can use the surplus to repay foreign debts or to lend to the rest of the world. When the balance is negative, the deficit will be financed by borrowing from abroad or by liquidating foreign assets acquired in earlier periods.

Definition

The current account balance is the difference between a country's current transactions with the rest of the world and its current payments to the rest of the world. Current transactions consist mainly of exports and imports of goods, exports and imports of services such as tourism, international freight and passenger transport, insurance and financial services, and income transfers consisting of wages and salaries, dividends, interest and other property income.

Note that property income includes retained earnings of foreign-owned subsidiaries. All earnings of foreign-owned subsidiaries are treated as if they were remitted abroad and the part which is actually retained in the country where the subsidiary is located is then shown as a re-investment flow in the capital account.

Comparability

The data in this table are taken from Balance of Payments statistics complied according to the International Monetary Fund (IMF) Balance of Payments Manual (BPM5). The IMF closely monitors balance of payments statistics reported by its member countries through regular meetings of balance of payments compilers. As a result there is good comparability across countries.

Because all earnings of foreign-owned subsidiaries are treated as though they are remitted even though a large part may in practice be retained by the subsidiaries in the countries where they are located, the existence of foreign-owned subsidiaries will tend to reduce the current account balance.

Long-term trends

Current account balances as a percentage of GDP have been negative throughout the period since 1990 in Australia, Mexico, New Zealand and the United Kingdom; this is partly due to the way in which earnings of foreign owned-subsidiaries are treated. Countries which have recorded current account surpluses throughout the period include Japan, Luxembourg, Netherlands, Norway and Switzerland.

Since 1990, current account balances have generally moved from deficit to surplus in Canada, Finland, Italy, Korea, and Sweden and have tended to move from surpluses to deficits in the Czech Republic, Portugal, the Slovak Republic, and the United States.

The chart shows current account balances averaged over the last three years. Deficits averaged 4% or more of GDP in Hungary, Greece, Portugal, Czech Republic, Slovak Republic, United States and Australia. Surpluses in excess of 4% were recorded by Belgium, Sweden, Finland, Luxembourg, Switzerland and Norway.

Source

OECD (2004), *OECD Economic Outlook*, No. 76, OECD, Paris.

Further information

• *Analytical publications*

OECD (2001-2004), *Export Credit Financing Systems in OECD Member Countries and Non-Member Countries*, OECD, Paris.

• *Statistical publications*

OECD (2004), *Main Economic Indicators*, OECD, Paris.

• *Methodological publications*

IMF (1993), *Balance of Payments Manual*, 5th edition, IMF, Washington, DC.

UN, EC, IMF, OECD, UNCTAD and the WTO (2002), *Manual on Statistics of International Trade in Services*, United Nations, New York.

• *Online databases*

SourceOECD Economic Outlook.

SourceOECD Main Economic Indicators.

• *Web sites*

OECD Economic Outlook – Sources and Methods: *www.oecd.org/eco/sources-and-methods*.

ECONOMIC GLOBALISATION • TRADE

BALANCE OF PAYMENTS

Current account balance of payments
As a percentage of GDP

	1990	1991	1992	1993	1994	1995	1996	1997	1998	1999	2000	2001	2002	2003
Australia	-5.2	-3.5	-3.7	-3.3	-5.1	-5.4	-3.9	-3.1	-5.0	-5.7	-4.1	-2.4	-4.3	-6.0
Austria	0.7	0.0	-0.3	-0.8	-1.7	-2.6	-2.3	-3.1	-2.5	-3.1	-2.5	-1.9	0.4	-0.6
Belgium	3.1	3.6	4.4	6.0	6.0	5.6	5.1	5.6	5.3	5.1	3.9	3.7	5.3	3.1
Canada	-3.4	-3.7	-3.6	-3.9	-2.3	-0.8	0.6	-1.3	-1.2	0.3	2.9	2.4	2.0	2.1
Czech Republic	..	..	..	1.3	-1.9	-2.6	-7.1	-6.7	-2.2	-2.7	-5.3	-5.7	-6.5	-7.1
Denmark	0.4	0.9	2.2	2.8	1.5	0.7	1.5	0.4	-0.9	1.8	1.5	3.1	2.0	3.0
Finland	-5.0	-5.5	-4.8	-1.4	1.1	4.2	3.9	5.4	5.7	5.6	7.4	7.2	7.6	5.7
France	-0.8	-0.4	0.4	0.8	0.5	0.7	1.3	2.7	2.7	2.9	1.3	1.6	1.9	1.0
Germany	2.9	-1.2	-1.0	-0.7	-1.4	-1.1	-0.6	-0.4	-0.6	-1.0	-1.2	0.2	2.2	2.2
Greece	-5.6	-2.8	-3.6	-2.2	-1.4	-3.9	-5.2	-4.4	-3.1	-6.2	-8.7	-8.1	-7.6	-6.5
Hungary	..	..	..	-10.0	-10.9	-3.4	-3.9	-4.4	-7.2	-7.8	-8.7	-6.3	-7.1	-8.9
Iceland	-2.1	-4.1	-2.4	0.7	2.0	0.8	-1.8	-1.7	-6.9	-7.0	-10.2	-4.1	-0.3	-5.6
Ireland	-0.8	0.7	1.0	3.7	2.7	2.6	2.8	2.4	0.8	0.3	-0.4	-0.7	-0.7	-2.0
Italy	-1.5	-2.0	-2.3	0.8	1.2	2.3	3.2	2.9	1.9	0.7	-0.6	-0.1	-0.8	-1.5
Japan	1.5	2.0	3.0	3.0	2.7	2.1	1.4	2.3	3.0	2.6	2.5	2.1	2.8	3.1
Korea	-0.8	-2.7	-1.2	0.3	-0.9	-1.6	-4.1	-1.3	11.8	5.5	2.4	1.7	1.0	2.0
Luxembourg	..	..	..	..	..	13.9	12.7	11.0	9.4	8.9	13.7	9.0	8.2	9.9
Mexico	-2.9	-4.6	-6.7	-5.8	-7.0	-0.5	-0.8	-1.9	-3.8	-2.9	-3.1	-2.9	-2.2	-1.4
Netherlands	2.7	2.4	2.1	4.1	5.0	6.2	5.2	6.6	3.3	3.9	2.1	2.1	1.4	1.5
New Zealand	-3.1	-2.7	-4.1	-3.8	-3.9	-5.1	-5.9	-6.5	-4.0	-6.2	-4.8	-2.6	-3.7	-4.5
Norway	2.5	3.6	3.3	2.9	3.0	3.6	6.9	6.4	0.0	5.3	14.9	15.5	12.9	13.0
Poland	..	..	..	-4.9	0.9	0.6	-2.2	-3.8	-4.1	-7.6	-6.0	-2.9	-2.6	-2.0
Portugal	-0.3	-0.8	-0.2	0.4	-2.4	-0.1	-3.8	-5.7	-6.9	-8.5	-10.9	-9.5	-6.7	-5.1
Slovak Republic	..	..	..	-4.3	4.7	2.7	-9.4	-8.6	-9.0	-4.7	-3.4	-8.2	-7.9	-1.0
Spain	-3.5	-3.6	-3.6	-1.1	-1.3	0.1	0.1	0.5	-0.5	-2.3	-3.4	-2.8	-2.4	-3.0
Sweden	-2.6	-1.9	-2.8	-1.3	1.1	3.4	3.6	4.2	3.9	4.2	3.9	3.9	4.1	6.3
Switzerland	3.7	4.5	6.1	7.9	6.4	6.7	7.3	9.7	9.7	11.5	12.8	8.5	8.5	10.2
Turkey	-1.7	0.2	-0.6	-3.5	2.7	-1.6	-1.3	-1.3	1.2	-1.0	-4.9	2.5	-0.8	-2.9
United Kingdom	-4.0	-1.8	-2.1	-1.9	-1.0	-1.3	-0.9	-0.1	-0.5	-2.7	-2.5	-2.4	-1.7	-1.7
United States	-1.4	0.1	-0.8	-1.2	-1.7	-1.4	-1.5	-1.5	-2.3	-3.1	-4.2	-3.9	-4.6	-4.9

StatLink: http://dx.doi.org/10.1787/431225768004

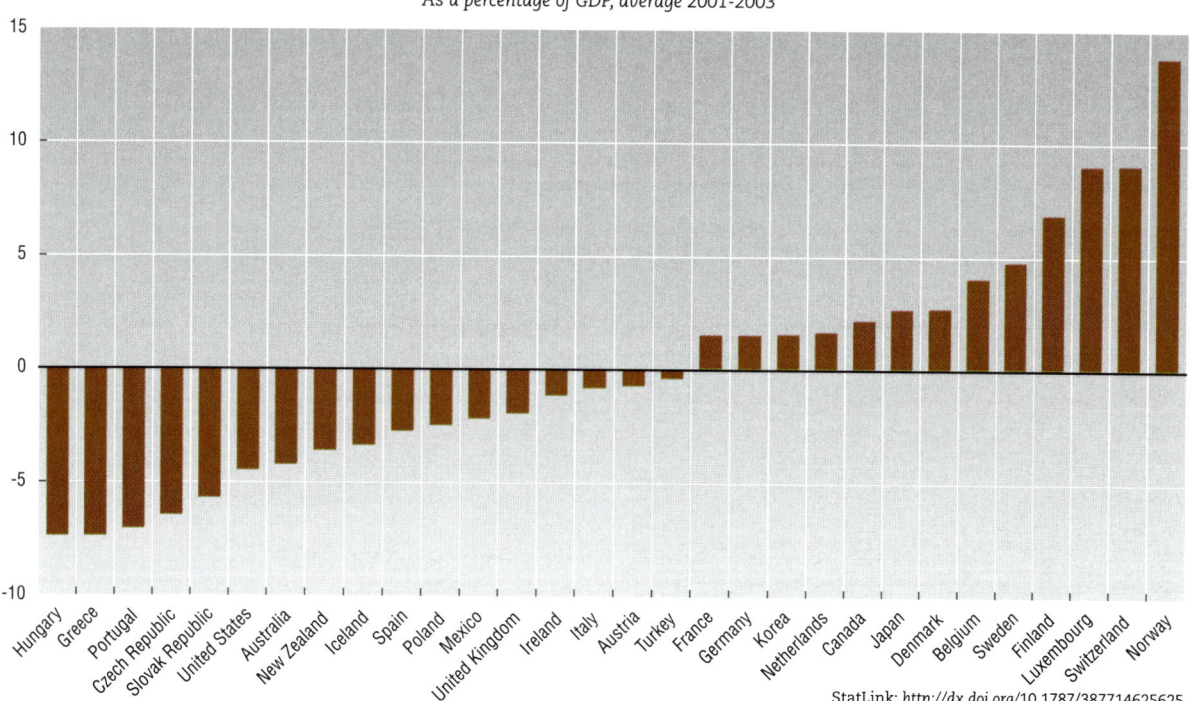

Current account balance of payments
As a percentage of GDP, average 2001-2003

StatLink: http://dx.doi.org/10.1787/387714625625

ECONOMIC GLOBALISATION • FOREIGN DIRECT INVESTMENT (FDI)

FDI FLOWS AND STOCKS

Foreign direct investment (FDI) is a key element in the rapidly evolving process of international economic integration. FDI creates direct, stable and long-lasting links between economies. It serves as an important vehicle for local enterprise development, and it may also help improve the competitive position of the recipient, or "host", economy. In particular, FDI encourages the transfer of technology and know-how between countries, and it allows the host economy to promote its products more widely in international markets. Finally, FDI is an additional source of funding for capital investment.

Definition

FDI is defined as investment by a resident entity in one economy with the objective of obtaining a lasting interest in an enterprise resident in another economy. The "lasting interest" means the existence of a long-term relationship between the direct investor and the enterprise and a significant degree of influence by the direct investor on the management of the direct investment enterprise. Direct investment involves both the initial transaction between the two entities and all subsequent transactions between them and among affiliated enterprises, both incorporated and unincorporated. Absolute control by the foreign investor is not required, and ownership of 10% of the ordinary shares or voting stock is the criterion for determining the existence of a direct investment relationship. An "effective voice in the management", as evidenced by an ownership of at least 10%, implies that the direct investor is able to influence, or participate in, the management of an enterprise.

Comparability

Despite improvements in the application of international standards in recent years, there are still methodological differences between countries.

A joint IMF/OECD survey analyses the extent of the application of international standards in OECD countries as well as in 30 non-OECD countries.

Totals for OECD and EU15 are only for the countries for which data are available. Data for 2002 and 2003 are provisional.

Long-term trends

Both inflows and outflows of FDI worldwide dropped drastically in 2001 following the spectacular investment boom of the late 1990s. FDI into to the OECD area continued to decline for the third consecutive year in 2003 when inflows dropped by 28 per cent, a trend which can be partially attributed to sluggish macroeconomic performance, weak economic recovery and the concerns about international security. FDI outflows from the OECD have, on the contrary, marked a slight recovery in 2003 allowing OECD countries to maintain a well established role as the world's foremost provider of direct investment funds.

Over the period, OECD countries were net exporters of FDI by 1.2 billion US dollars. Ireland and Poland were relatively the largest net recipients of FDI, followed by Australia, the Czech Republic and Hungary. Net outflows have been significantly high for the United Kingdom, representing half of the net outflows of EU15 countries, followed by France, Japan, Germany, Switzerland, the Netherlands, all ranging above 100 billion US dollars of net outflows. Among non-member countries, FDI inflows to China were particularly high.

Source

OECD (2004), *OECD International Direct Investment Statistics Yearbook*, OECD, Paris.

Further information

• *Analytical publications*

OECD (2001), *Measuring Globalisation: The Role of Multinationals in OECD Economies*, OECD, Paris.

OECD (2001), *Reviews of Foreign Direct Investment,* series, OECD, Paris.

OECD (2004), *International Investment Perspectives*, OECD, Paris.

• *Statistical publications*

OECD (2005), *Indicators of Economic Globalisation*, OECD, Paris.

• *Methodological publications*

OECD (1996) *OECD Benchmark Definition of Foreign Direct Investment*, Third edition, OECD, Paris.

IMF and OECD (2003), *Foreign Direct Investment Statistics: How Countries Measure FDI –2001*, IMF/OECD, Washington, DC, Paris, *www.imf.org/external/pubs/ft/fdis/2003*.

OECD (2004), *Handbook on Economic Globalisation Indicators*, OECD, Paris.

• *Web sites*

OECD International Investment:
www.oecd.org/daf/investment.

ECONOMIC GLOBALISATION • FOREIGN DIRECT INVESTMENT (FDI)

FDI FLOWS AND STOCKS

Cumulative FDI flows in OECD countries
Billion US dollars, 1990-2003

Inflows		Outflows		Net outflows	
Australia	104.6	Australia	66.7	Australia	-37.9
Austria	44.7	Austria	39.4	Austria	-5.4
Belgium/Luxembourg	800.6	Belgium/Luxembourg	793.8	Belgium/Luxembourg	-6.7
Canada	228.0	Canada	257.6	Canada	29.7
Czech Republic	38.6	Czech Republic	1.3	Czech Republic	-37.3
Denmark	97.0	Denmark	89.1	Denmark	-7.9
Finland	47.7	Finland	75.8	Finland	28.1
France	416.7	France	764.2	France	347.5
Germany	393.0	Germany	535.6	Germany	142.6
Hungary	38.1	Hungary	3.9	Hungary	-34.1
Iceland	1.0	Iceland	1.5	Iceland	0.5
Ireland	124.5	Ireland	27.7	Ireland	-96.8
Italy	102.3	Italy	140.5	Italy	38.2
Japan	56.5	Japan	381.7	Japan	325.2
Korea	44.2	Korea	42.6	Korea	-1.6
Netherlands	315.4	Netherlands	432.0	Netherlands	116.6
New Zealand	26.6	New Zealand	5.7	New Zealand	-20.9
Norway	38.9	Norway	42.3	Norway	3.4
Poland	54.8	Poland	1.1	Poland	-53.7
Portugal	33.7	Portugal	30.6	Portugal	-3.1
Slovak Republic	11.1	Slovak Republic	0.1	Slovak Republic	-11.0
Spain	232.7	Spain	243.4	Spain	10.7
Sweden	180.4	Sweden	173.8	Sweden	-6.6
Switzerland	90.4	Switzerland	218.9	Switzerland	128.6
Turkey	13.6	Turkey	3.7	Turkey	-9.9
United Kingdom	538.7	United Kingdom	956.8	United Kingdom	418.1
United States	1507.9	United States	1560.7	United States	52.7
EU15	3470.1	EU15	4309.2	EU15	839.2
OECD total	5751.1	OECD total	6899.8	OECD total	1148.7

StatLink: http://dx.doi.org/10.1787/225066564243

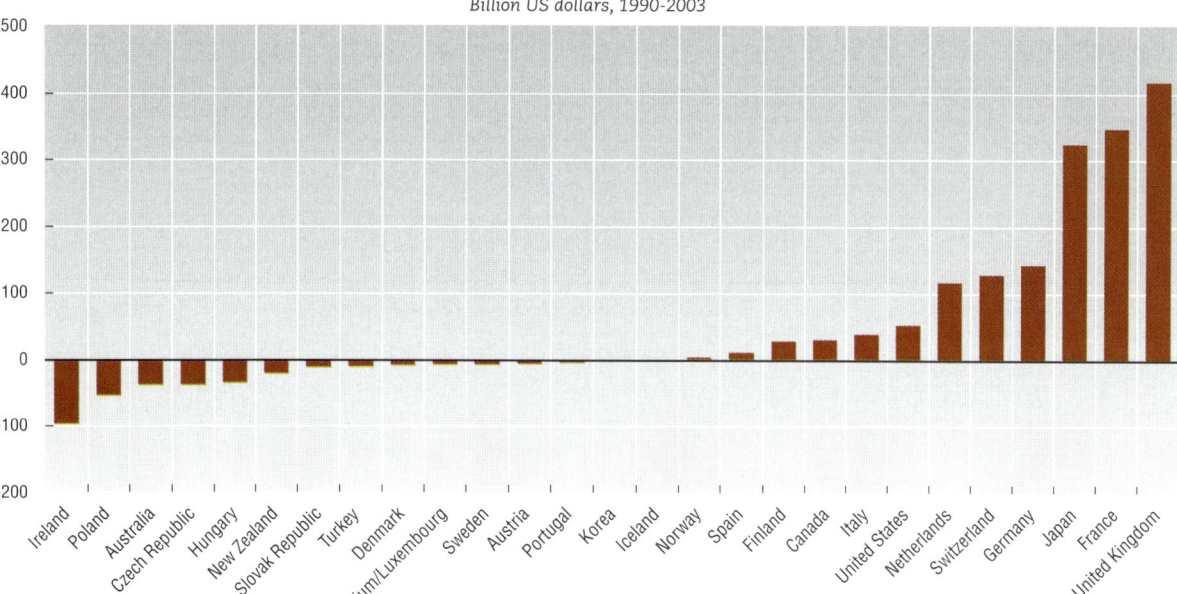

Net cumulative outflows
Billion US dollars, 1990-2003

StatLink: http://dx.doi.org/10.1787/000558777080

ECONOMIC GLOBALISATION • FOREIGN DIRECT INVESTMENT (FDI)

FDI FLOWS AND STOCKS

Inflows of foreign direct investment
Million US dollars

	1990	1991	1992	1993	1994	1995	1996	1997	1998	1999	2000	2001	2002	2003
Australia	8 116	4 302	5 720	4 282	5 025	11 963	6 111	7 633	6 003	3 268	13 199	4 679	16 457	7 848
Austria	651	351	1 433	1 137	2 103	1 904	4 429	2 656	4 534	2 975	8 842	5 921	953	6 862
Belgium/Luxembourg	7 516	8 919	10 957	10 468	8 313	10 894	13 924	16 510	30 147	142 512	220 988	84 718	..	..
Belgium	..	..	..	..	..	..	..	..	..	..	..	..	13 083	31 345
Canada	7 580	2 880	4 722	4 730	8 204	9 255	9 633	11 522	22 803	24 747	66 796	27 487	21 036	6 585
Czech Republic	..	..	..	653	868	2 562	1 428	1 301	3 716	6 326	4 980	5 645	8 483	2 592
Denmark	1 207	1 460	1 015	1 669	4 898	4 180	768	2 799	7 726	16 741	33 797	11 528	6 646	2 609
Finland	788	- 247	406	864	1 578	1 063	1 109	2 116	12 141	4 610	8 836	3 732	7 927	2 768
France	15 613	15 171	17 849	16 443	15 574	23 679	21 960	23 171	30 984	46 546	43 258	50 485	48 950	47 026
Germany	2 962	4 729	- 2 089	368	7 134	12 025	6 573	12 243	24 597	56 077	198 313	21 142	36 048	12 878
Greece	1 688	1 718	1 589	1 244	1 166	1 198	1 196	1 089	74	561	1 109	1 590	50	662
Hungary	312	1 474	1 477	2 446	1 144	5 102	3 300	4 171	3 337	3 313	2 763	3 936	2 845	2 470
Iceland	22	18	- 13	0	- 2	9	83	148	148	67	170	173	122	84
Ireland	623	1 361	1 458	1 068	856	1 442	2 616	2 710	8 856	18 210	25 783	9 653	24 392	25 463
Italy	6 343	2 481	3 211	3 751	2 236	4 816	3 535	4 962	4 280	6 911	13 377	14 873	14 558	16 979
Japan	1 809	1 286	2 755	207	890	43	230	3 223	3 194	12 740	8 319	6 248	9 243	6 322
Korea	789	1 180	728	588	809	1 776	2 325	2 844	5 412	9 333	9 283	3 528	2 392	3 222
Luxembourg	..	..	..	..	..	..	..	..	..	..	..	..	117 088	73 191
Mexico	2 633	4 761	4 393	4 389	10 973	9 647	9 943	14 160	12 170	13 166	16 449	26 569	14 435	10 731
Netherlands	10 516	5 779	6 169	6 443	7 158	12 307	16 660	11 137	36 925	41 206	63 866	51 937	25 593	19 693
New Zealand	1 683	1 696	1 089	2 212	2 616	2 850	3 922	1 917	1 826	940	1 344	4 198	- 556	836
Norway	1 177	- 49	810	1 461	2 778	2 408	3 168	3 946	4 354	7 062	6 908	2 009	679	2 190
Poland	88	359	678	1 715	1 875	3 659	4 498	4 908	6 365	7 270	9 341	5 713	4 131	4 225
Portugal	2 255	2 292	1 904	1 516	1 255	660	1 489	2 479	3 143	1 234	6 789	5 894	1 846	962
Slovak Republic	..	..	..	179	273	241	396	231	707	429	2 383	1 584	4 127	594
Spain	13 839	12 445	13 351	9 572	9 276	6 285	6 821	6 388	11 798	15 759	37 530	28 010	35 940	25 649
Sweden	1 971	6 356	41	3 845	6 350	14 447	5 437	10 967	19 843	60 929	23 245	11 900	11 644	3 436
Switzerland	5 485	2 643	411	- 83	3 368	2 223	3 078	6 642	8 942	11 714	19 266	8 859	5 656	12 162
Turkey	684	810	844	636	608	885	722	805	940	783	982	3 266	1 038	575
United Kingdom	30 471	14 849	15 475	14 821	9 255	19 968	24 441	33 245	74 349	87 973	118 824	52 650	27 802	14 574
United States	48 494	23 171	19 823	51 362	46 121	57 776	86 502	105 603	179 045	289 444	321 274	167 021	72 411	39 890
EU15	96 442	77 665	72 768	73 209	77 150	114 868	110 956	132 471	269 397	502 245	804 557	354 032	372 521	284 097
OECD total	175 314	122 196	116 206	147 987	162 700	225 268	246 296	301 526	528 357	892 847	1 288 014	624 946	535 019	384 424

StatLink: http://dx.doi.org/10.1787/630450014760

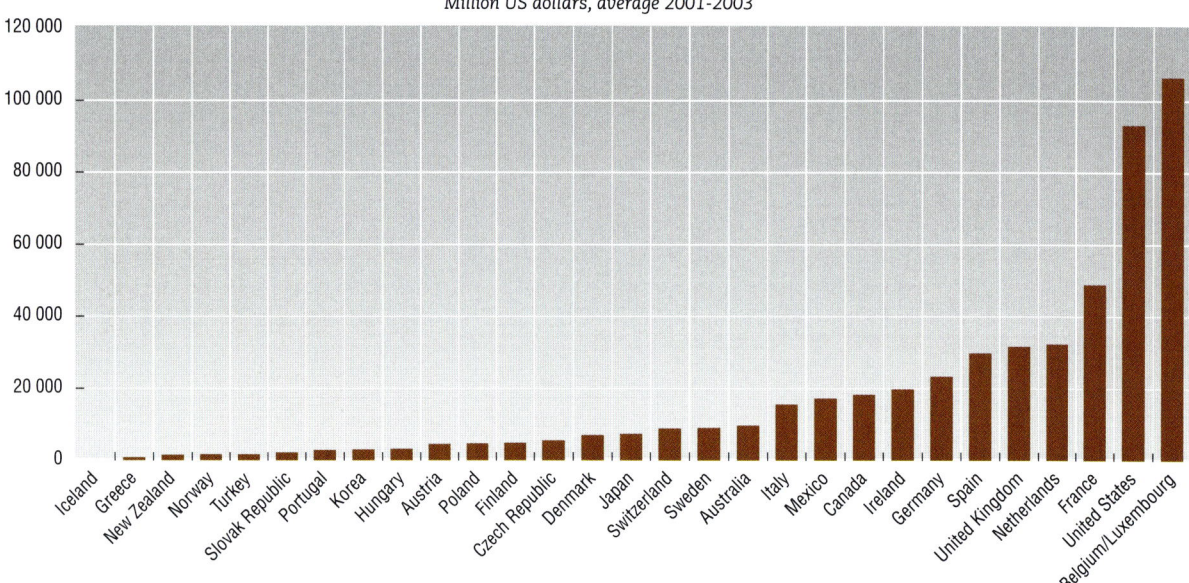

Inflows of foreign direct investment
Million US dollars, average 2001-2003

StatLink: http://dx.doi.org/10.1787/033006021104

ECONOMIC GLOBALISATION • FOREIGN DIRECT INVESTMENT (FDI)

FDI FLOWS AND STOCKS

Outflows of foreign direct investment
Million US dollars

	1990	1991	1992	1993	1994	1995	1996	1997	1998	1999	2000	2001	2002	2003
Australia	992	1 199	5 267	1 947	2 817	3 282	7 088	6 428	3 345	- 421	655	12 219	7 633	14 291
Austria	1 627	1 285	1 697	1 190	1 257	1 131	1 935	1 988	2 745	3 301	5 741	3 138	5 256	7 090
Belgium/Luxembourg	5 956	6 066	10 956	3 850	1 205	11 728	7 811	7 884	29 108	132 326	218 364	100 625	..	..
Belgium	..	..	..	..	..	..	..	..	..	..	..	..	10 952	38 960
Canada	5 235	5 832	3 589	5 700	9 294	11 462	13 094	23 059	34 349	17 250	44 678	36 113	26 415	21 559
Czech Republic	..	..	..	90	120	37	153	25	127	90	43	165	206	233
Denmark	1 618	2 052	2 236	1 261	3 955	3 063	2 519	4 207	4 477	16 988	26 542	13 377	5 694	1 159
Finland	2 709	- 124	- 752	1 407	4 298	1 497	3 597	5 292	18 642	6 616	24 035	8 372	7 629	- 7 381
France	36 228	25 138	30 407	19 736	24 372	15 758	30 419	35 581	48 613	126 859	177 482	86 783	49 478	57 333
Germany	24 232	22 947	18 595	17 196	18 858	39 052	50 806	41 794	88 837	108 692	56 567	36 861	8 630	2 562
Greece	..	..	..	..	..	..	..	..	- 284	552	2 137	617	656	47
Hungary	..	..	..	11	48	59	- 4	462	278	250	620	368	275	1 581
Iceland	12	29	6	14	24	25	63	56	74	123	393	342	215	165
Ireland	365	193	214	218	436	820	728	1 014	3 902	6 109	4 630	4 066	3 087	1 908
Italy	7 612	7 326	5 949	7 231	5 109	5 731	6 465	12 245	16 078	6 722	12 318	21 476	17 138	9 128
Japan	50 773	31 688	17 305	13 914	18 116	22 632	23 415	25 992	24 158	22 750	31 540	38 352	32 283	28 799
Korea	1 052	1 489	1 162	1 340	2 461	3 552	4 670	4 449	4 740	4 198	4 999	2 420	2 617	3 429
Luxembourg	..	..	..	..	..	..	..	..	..	..	..	..	126 229	81 813
Mexico	..	..	..	..	..	..	..	..	..	..	..	4 404	969	..
Netherlands	13 661	12 826	12 697	10 063	17 554	20 176	32 098	24 522	36 475	57 611	75 649	47 977	34 585	36 126
New Zealand	2 361	1 472	391	- 1 389	2 008	1 783	- 1 240	- 1 566	401	1 073	609	912	- 1 039	- 66
Norway	1 432	1 824	394	933	2 172	2 856	5 892	5 015	3 201	5 504	7 614	- 1 323	4 201	2 565
Poland	..	..	13	18	29	42	53	45	316	31	17	- 89	230	386
Portugal	165	474	684	107	283	685	785	1 926	3 846	3 168	7 514	7 566	3 291	96
Slovak Republic	..	..	..	13	18	43	63	95	147	- 377	29	65	11	13
Spain	3 442	4 424	2 171	3 174	4 111	4 158	5 590	12 547	18 938	42 085	54 685	33 100	31 540	23 395
Sweden	14 748	7 058	409	1 358	6 701	11 214	5 025	12 648	24 379	21 929	40 667	6 375	10 680	10 588
Switzerland	7 177	6 543	6 058	8 765	10 798	12 214	16 151	17 748	18 769	33 264	44 698	18 247	7 587	10 921
Turkey	- 16	27	65	14	49	113	110	251	367	645	870	497	175	499
United Kingdom	17 954	16 412	17 741	26 063	32 206	43 560	34 056	61 620	122 861	201 437	233 488	58 885	35 213	55 316
United States	37 183	37 889	48 266	83 950	80 167	98 750	91 885	104 803	142 644	224 934	159 212	142 349	134 835	173 799
EU15	130 316	106 076	103 005	92 854	120 345	158 573	181 835	223 267	418 616	734 393	939 818	429 217	350 058	318 139
OECD total	236 516	194 067	185 522	208 175	248 465	315 423	343 229	410 130	651 531	1 043 707	1 235 795	684 258	566 671	576 314

StatLink: http://dx.doi.org/10.1787/084732611753

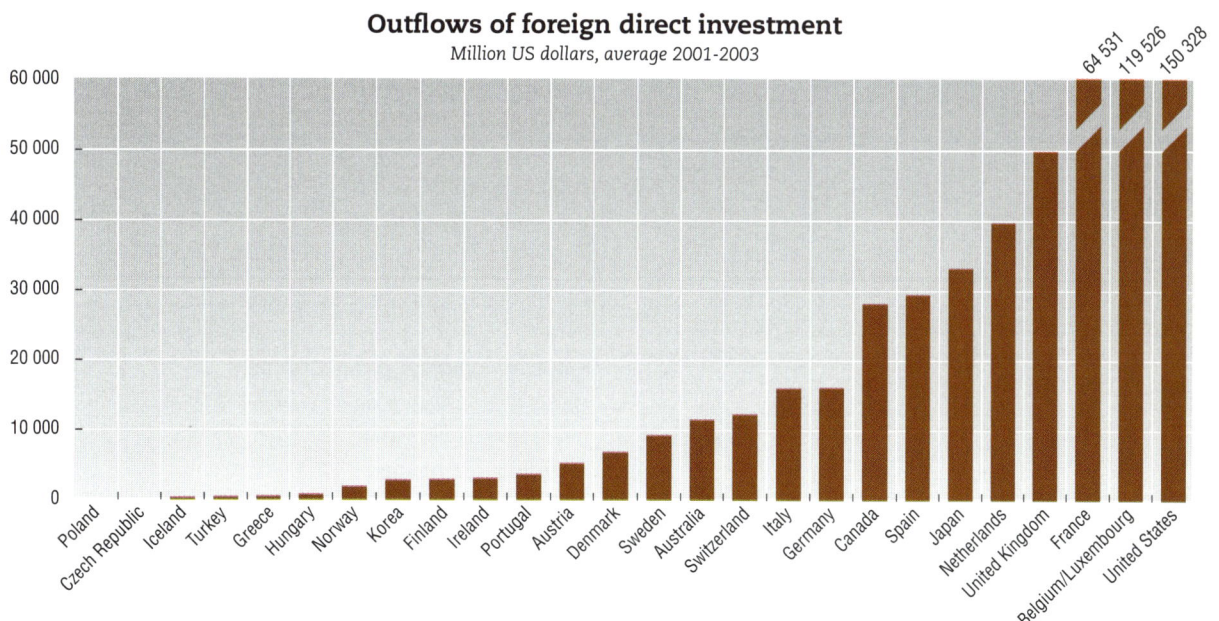

Outflows of foreign direct investment
Million US dollars, average 2001-2003

StatLink: http://dx.doi.org/10.1787/810383158565

FDI AND EMPLOYMENT

Firms in OECD countries increasingly adopt global strategies and establish overseas sales, marketing, production and research units to cope with new competitive pressures. Indicators on the activity of affiliates under foreign control are thus an important complement to information on FDI when analysing the weight and economic contribution of such firms in host countries.

While data on the manufacturing sector have been available since the beginning of the 1980s, the OECD did not start collecting data on the activity of affiliates under foreign control in services until the second half of the 1990s, and data are not yet available for all OECD countries.

Definition

An affiliate under foreign control is defined as one in which a single investor holds 50% or more of the shares with voting rights. The notion of control allows all of a company's activities to be attributed to the controlling investor. This means that variables such as a company's turnover, staff or exports are all attributed to the controlling investor and the country from which he or she comes. Control may be direct or indirect.

Comparability

Fewer countries are able to supply estimates of employment in service affiliates than manufacturing affiliates because collection of employment data on services began later. For employment in manufacturing, there are breaks in the series for the Czech Republic and France (1999/2000) and for the United States (1996/1997 and 2001/2002) because of changes to the data collection methods. For employment in services the main problem in comparability is that employment in financial intermediation is excluded by Belgium, Germany, Ireland, Netherlands, Portugal, Spain, Sweden, United Kingdom and the United States. Foreign controlled affiliates are common in banking and insurance in most of these countries.

Long-term trends

The shares of foreign affiliates in manufacturing employment show considerable variation across OECD countries going from under 10% in Germany, Turkey and Portugal to 30% or more in the Czech Republic, France, Belgium, Sweden, Hungary, Luxembourg and Ireland. Employment in service sector foreign affiliates is lower in all countries although as noted above, comparability is affected in several countries by the exclusion of employment in banking and insurance services. Shares of employment in services ranges from under 5% in Germany, Norway, Portugal and the United States to 15% or more in Belgium, Czech Republic, Ireland, Luxembourg and Poland.

In the period from 1996 to 2002, employment in foreign-controlled manufacturing affiliates grew in all countries for which data rare available except Germany, where the rate fell, and in Austria, Ireland, Spain and the United Kingdom where the shares have remained fairly stable. Particularly sharp increases were recorded by the Czech Republic, Finland, Norway, Poland and Sweden.

Data for employment in service activities are less complete and less comparable. Some growth appears to have occurred in Austria, the Czech Republic and Finland. In most other countries services employment appears to be rather stable.

Source

OECD (2003), *OECD Science, Technology and Industry Scoreboard*, OECD, Paris.

Further information

• *Analytical publications*

OECD (2002), *FDI from Developing Countries: A Vector for Trade and Development*, Development Centre Studies, OECD, Paris.

• *Statistical publications*

OECD (2001), *Measuring Globalisation*, OECD, Paris.

OECD (2005), *Economic Globalisation Indicators*, OECD, Paris.

• *Methodological publications*

OECD (2005), *Handbook on Economic Globalisation Indicators*, OECD, Paris.

• *Online databases*

SourceOECD Globalisation.

• *Web sites*

OECD Science, Technology and Industry: *www.oecd.org/sti*.

OECD Measuring Globalisation:
www.oecd.org/sti/measuringglobalisation.

ECONOMIC GLOBALISATION • FOREIGN DIRECT INVESTMENT (FDI)

FDI AND EMPLOYMENT

Share of employment of affiliates under foreign control
As a percentage of total employment

	Share of employment in manufacturing							Share of employment in services						
	1996	1997	1998	1999	2000	2001	2002	1996	1997	1998	1999	2000	2001	2002
Australia	..	..	..	..	22.67	..	..							
Austria	..	18.95	18.65	..	19.57	18.04	..	..	7.9	8.7	..	..	9.7	..
Belgium	..	19.07	..	..	..	..	32.34	22.5	24.4	..	..	..	..	17.2
Czech Republic	..	10.71	13.17	16.18	24.73	28.93	30.32	..	..	9.7	..	14.2	19.6	19.2
Denmark	..	..	..	10.17	..	..	..							
Finland	11.28	12.36	13.83	15.91	15.95	17.15	17.40	..	..	8.9	9.0	11.1	11.9	..
France	25.82	27.45	27.79	28.46	30.12	30.78	..	6.0	6.4	6.2	6.1	6.1	5.6	..
Germany	6.95	6.70	6.02	6.15	6.04	5.83	..	..	..	..	..	3.2	2.9	..
Hungary	35.61	41.17	45.01	46.49	44.48	45.20	43.62	..	..	14.6	..	15.2	15.1	14.8
Ireland	46.95	47.81	47.47	49.05	48.11	49.19	..	..	15.2	..	..	..	..	..
Italy	..	..	..	..	..	10.86	..	..	..	..	..	..	5.1	..
Luxembourg	41.81	42.75	46.30	41.35	45.92	..	..	..	..	16.3	..	..	..	..
Netherlands	19.03	19.71	21.89	18.87	18.25	21.01	..	..	8.8	..	..	8.7	..	..
Norway	14.31	14.23	17.42	19.92	21.44	23.13	..	..	3.5	..	..	..	..	..
Poland	..	12.52	14.76	18.62	20.95	21.92	24.08	..	..	7.4	..	..	13.4	15.3
Portugal	7.93	8.30	8.77	8.92	10.10	8.56	..	3.8	3.2	3.5	3.9	4.0	3.8	..
Spain	..	..	..	16.45	16.80	16.35	..	..	..	..	..	..	..	8.6
Sweden	19.90	19.04	21.07	24.14	29.10	32.71	..	..	11.4	11.8	14.0	14.5	..	..
Turkey	5.65	5.32	5.50	5.42	5.70	7.02	..							
United Kingdom	19.15	17.77	..	20.37	..	..	..	..	9.6	..	7.4	..	..	..
United States	11.69	11.17	12.08	12.13	12.57	12.05	12.77	..	3.2	..	..	..	..	4.1

StatLink: http://dx.doi.org/10.1787/746525865614

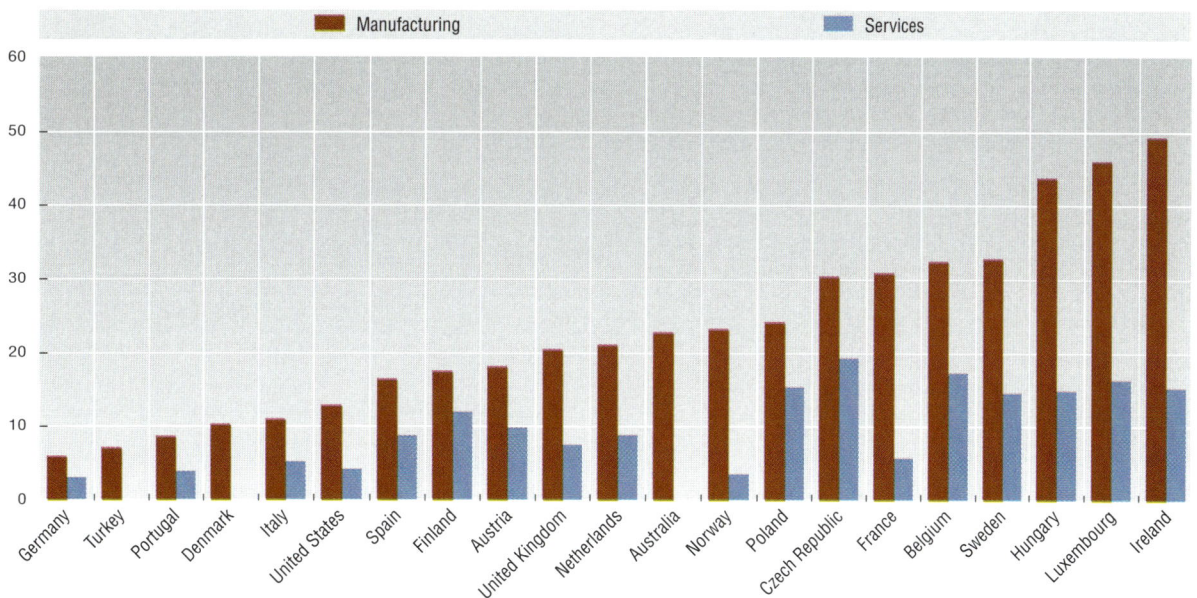

Share of employment in manufacturing and services of affiliates under foreign control
As a percentage of total employment, 2002 or latest available year

StatLink: http://dx.doi.org/10.1787/734817578056

```
            500,000 •  +
         15,579,200 •  −
         43,628,500 •  −
         36,286,400 •  +
     34,432,741,064 •  ◇

     34,432,741,064 •  ✳

        220,061,246 •  +
            242,765 •  +
         54,975,316 •  −
      3,458,295,462 •  −
      9,423,290,000 •  +
        527,646,320 •  −
        242,347,296 •  +
            312,759 •  +
         15,184,652,108 •  ◇
```

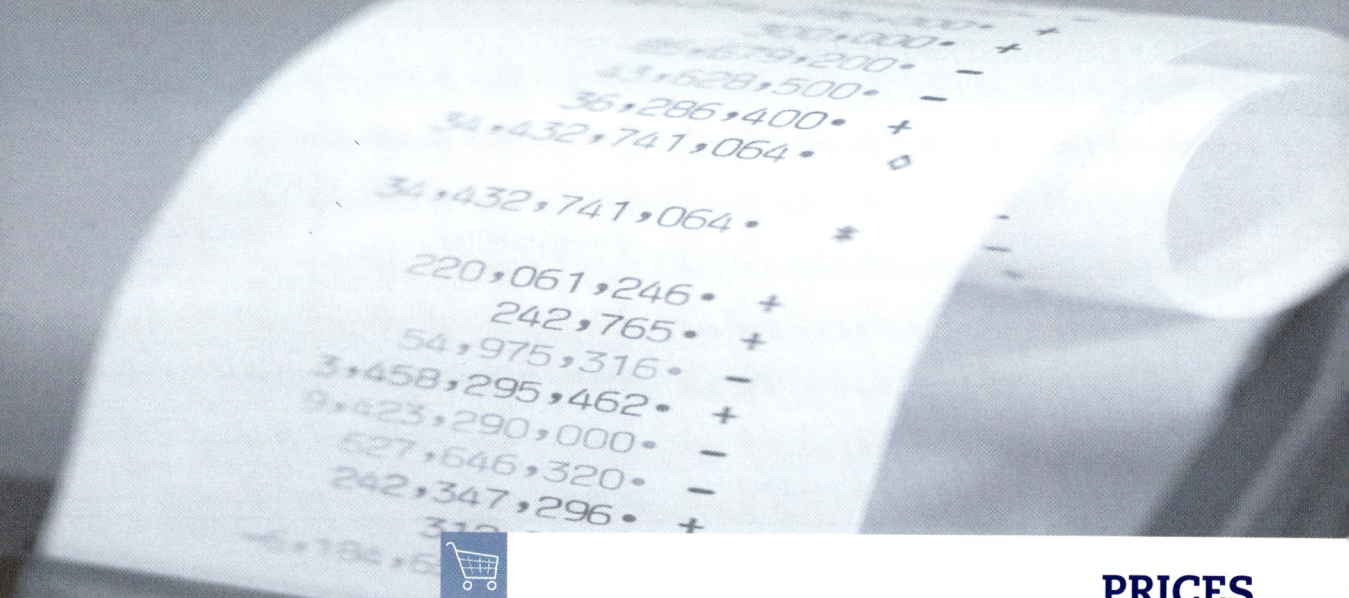

PRICES

CONSUMER AND PRODUCER PRICES
CONSUMER PRICE INDICES (CPI)
PRODUCER PRICE INDICES (PPI)

PURCHASING POWER AND COMPETITIVENESS
LONG-TERM INTEREST RATES
RATES OF CONVERSION
INTERNATIONAL COMPETITIVENESS

PRICES • CONSUMER AND PRODUCER PRICES

CONSUMER PRICE INDICES (CPI)

Consumer price indices have a long history in official statistics. They measure the erosion of living standards through price inflation and are probably the best known statistics among the media and general public.

Definition

Consumer price indices measure the change in the prices of a basket of goods and services that are typically purchased by specific groups of households. For the indices in these tables, the groups of households have been broadly defined and cover virtually all households except for "institutional" households – prisons, military barracks for example – and, in some countries, households in the highest income group.

The index for food is intended to cover food and non-alcoholic beverages but exclude purchases in restaurants. The index for energy is intended to cover all forms of energy including fuels for motor vehicles, heating and other household uses.

Comparability

There are a number of differences in the ways that these indices are calculated. The most important ones concern the treatment of dwelling costs, adjustments for changes in the quality of goods and services, the frequency with which the basket weights are updated and the index formulae used. In addition, there are practical difficulties in measuring consumer prices in countries experiencing very high inflation – such as Hungary, Mexico and Turkey during the period considered here.

For food, restaurant meals are included for Austria and Hungary, alcoholic beverages are included for France, and non-alcoholic beverages are excluded for Turkey. For energy, gasoline is excluded for Austria, Turkey and New Zealand.

Long-term trends

For most OECD countries, consumer price indices have grown only moderately since 1990, with inflation lower in the latter part of the period compared with the years up to 1995. Over the period as a whole, inflation has been exceptionally low in Japan, averaging less than 1% per year but quite substantial in Greece, Mexico, Turkey and the four recent member countries in central Europe – Czech Republic, Hungary, Poland and Slovak Republic.

Food and energy are shown separately because they are important items in the consumer price indices of all countries and because their price movements tend to be more volatile than other goods and services. Food prices have risen over the period by less than total consumer prices and increases have been moderate in most of the European Union countries. However, substantial increases occurred in 1991 and 2001 and, except in Europe, between 1996 and 1998. Energy prices have been rather volatile; for example they rose over 10% in 2000 but actually fell in 1998 and 2002. Over the period as whole, energy prices have risen faster that the total consumer price indices.

Source

OECD (2004), *Main Economic Indicators*, OECD, Paris.

Further information
• *Analytical publications*

Brook, A.M. et al. (2004), "Oil Price Developments: Drivers, Economic Consequences and Policy Responses", *OECD Economics Department Working Paper*, No. 412, OECD, Paris, www.oecd.org/eco/working_papers.

OECD (2004), *OECD Economic Outlook*, OECD, Paris.

• *Methodological publications*

ILO, IMF, OECD, Eurostat, World Bank (2004), *Consumer Price Index Manual: Theory and Practice*, ILO, Geneva.

OECD (1999), *Main Economic Indicators*, Vol. 1999/7, OECD, Paris.

OECD (2002), "Comparative Methodological Analysis: Consumer and Producer Price Indices", *Main Economic Indicators*, Vol. 2002, Supplement 2, OECD, Paris.

• *Web sites*

OECD Main Economic Indicators: www.oecd.org/std/mei.

PRICES • CONSUMER AND PRODUCER PRICES

CONSUMER PRICE INDICES (CPI)

CPI: all items
Year 2000 = 100

	1990	1991	1992	1993	1994	1995	1996	1997	1998	1999	2000	2001	2002	2003
Australia	80.4	82.9	83.8	85.3	86.9	90.9	93.3	93.5	94.3	95.7	100.0	104.4	107.5	110.5
Austria	79.6	82.2	85.5	88.6	91.2	93.3	95.0	96.3	97.2	97.7	100.0	102.7	104.5	105.9
Belgium	81.6	84.2	86.3	88.7	90.8	92.1	94.0	95.5	96.4	97.5	100.0	102.5	104.2	105.8
Canada	82.1	86.8	88.1	89.7	89.8	91.8	93.2	94.7	95.7	97.3	100.0	102.5	104.8	107.7
Czech Republic	-	44.8	49.8	60.1	66.2	72.2	78.5	85.2	94.3	96.2	100.0	104.7	106.6	106.8
Denmark	80.9	82.9	84.6	85.7	87.4	89.2	91.1	93.1	94.8	97.2	100.0	102.4	104.8	107.0
Finland	83.1	86.7	89.2	91.2	92.2	92.9	93.5	94.6	95.9	97.0	100.0	102.6	104.2	105.1
France	84.3	87.0	89.1	91.0	92.5	94.2	96.0	97.2	97.8	98.3	100.0	101.6	103.6	105.8
Germany	78.7	81.9	86.1	89.9	92.3	93.9	95.3	97.1	98.0	98.6	100.0	102.0	103.4	104.5
Greece	41.3	49.3	57.1	65.4	72.5	79.0	85.4	90.2	94.5	96.9	100.0	103.4	107.1	110.9
Hungary	15.9	21.5	26.6	32.6	38.7	49.7	61.3	72.5	82.8	91.1	100.0	109.1	114.9	120.2
Iceland	73.0	78.0	81.0	84.3	85.6	87.0	89.0	90.6	92.1	95.1	100.0	106.4	111.9	114.2
Ireland	77.8	80.3	82.8	84.0	85.9	88.1	89.6	91.0	93.2	94.7	100.0	104.9	109.7	113.6
Italy	69.2	73.5	77.4	81.0	84.2	88.7	92.2	94.1	95.9	97.5	100.0	102.8	105.3	108.1
Japan	92.1	95.1	96.7	97.9	98.6	98.5	98.6	100.4	101.0	100.7	100.0	99.3	98.4	98.1
Korea	60.9	66.6	70.8	74.2	78.8	82.3	86.4	90.2	97.0	97.8	100.0	104.1	106.9	110.7
Luxembourg	80.7	83.2	85.8	88.9	90.9	92.6	93.8	95.1	96.0	96.9	100.0	102.7	104.8	106.9
Mexico	18.6	22.8	26.3	28.9	30.9	41.7	56.0	67.6	78.3	91.3	100.0	106.4	111.7	116.8
Netherlands	78.6	81.1	83.7	85.8	88.2	89.9	91.7	93.7	95.6	97.7	100.0	104.2	107.6	109.9
New Zealand	84.0	86.2	87.1	88.2	89.7	93.1	95.2	96.3	97.6	97.5	100.0	102.6	105.4	107.2
Norway	79.4	82.1	84.0	85.9	87.1	89.2	90.4	92.7	94.8	97.0	100.0	103.0	104.3	106.9
Poland	9.2	16.2	23.7	32.5	43.2	55.3	66.2	76.1	84.9	91.0	100.0	105.4	107.4	108.2
Portugal	61.8	68.3	74.8	79.8	84.1	87.6	90.3	92.4	95.0	97.2	100.0	104.4	108.1	111.6
Slovak Republic	-	39.9	43.9	54.1	61.4	67.4	71.3	75.7	80.7	89.3	100.0	107.3	110.7	120.2
Spain	68.3	72.4	76.7	80.2	84.0	87.9	91.0	92.8	94.5	96.7	100.0	103.6	106.8	110.0
Sweden	77.6	85.2	87.4	91.5	93.7	96.4	97.2	98.0	98.4	98.7	100.0	102.6	105.1	107.3
Switzerland	82.5	87.4	90.9	93.9	94.7	96.4	97.2	97.7	97.7	98.5	100.0	101.0	101.6	102.3
Turkey	0.0	1.0	1.0	2.0	3.0	6.0	11.0	21.0	39.0	65.0	100.0	154.0	224.0	280.0
United Kingdom	74.1	78.4	81.3	82.6	84.7	87.6	89.7	92.5	95.7	97.2	100.0	101.8	103.5	106.5
United States	75.9	79.1	81.5	83.9	86.1	88.5	91.1	93.2	94.7	96.7	100.0	102.8	104.5	106.8
EU15	74.7	78.6	82.2	85.3	87.9	90.6	92.9	94.8	96.5	97.7	100.0	102.4	104.6	106.9
OECD total	63.1	67.0	70.4	73.5	76.8	81.2	85.6	89.5	93.0	96.2	100.0	103.5	106.2	108.9

StatLink: http://dx.doi.org/10.1787/201033151352

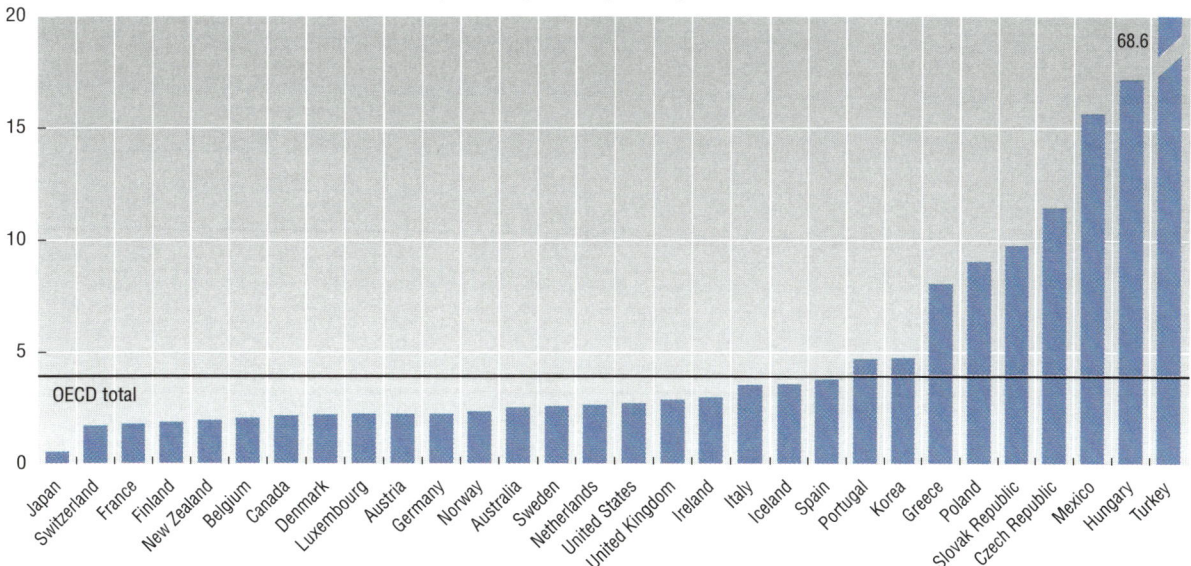

CPI: all items
Average annual growth in percentage, 1990-2003

StatLink: http://dx.doi.org/10.1787/767346722151

PRICES • CONSUMER AND PRODUCER PRICES

CONSUMER PRICE INDICES (CPI)

CPI: food
Year 2000 = 100

	1990	1991	1992	1993	1994	1995	1996	1997	1998	1999	2000	2001	2002	2003
Australia	77.6	79.7	80.2	82.1	84.0	88.1	90.7	93.2	96.0	99.4	100.0	106.2	110.2	114.3
Austria	87.7	91.3	94.7	96.8	98.2	96.5	96.6	98.1	100.0	99.4	100.0	103.6	105.1	106.9
Belgium	90.8	92.3	92.1	91.6	93.4	94.6	95.2	97.1	99.1	99.1	100.0	104.6	107.1	109.3
Canada	88.9	91.1	89.9	91.6	91.6	94.0	95.1	96.5	97.9	99.0	100.0	104.9	107.5	109.0
Czech Republic	-	-	-	-	79.6	89.0	96.1	100.3	104.7	98.9	100.0	105.0	103.0	100.7
Denmark	83.3	83.8	85.3	85.0	87.5	90.2	91.7	94.9	96.9	97.5	100.0	103.9	106.1	107.7
Finland	104.1	107.1	107.0	106.3	106.5	98.1	96.7	97.1	99.0	98.9	100.0	104.4	107.4	108.1
France	88.5	91.0	91.4	91.2	92.0	93.1	94.1	95.8	97.4	97.8	100.0	105.5	108.4	110.9
Germany	91.5	94.0	95.9	96.4	98.0	99.0	99.6	101.0	102.0	100.7	100.0	104.5	105.3	105.2
Greece	46.4	54.6	61.0	67.1	76.0	82.4	88.2	91.8	95.9	98.1	100.0	105.1	110.7	116.2
Hungary	18.6	22.5	27.1	35.0	43.3	56.6	66.4	78.0	89.0	91.6	100.0	113.7	118.6	120.3
Iceland	79.4	81.4	82.5	84.5	82.6	84.9	87.6	90.5	93.0	96.0	100.0	106.9	111.4	108.5
Ireland	81.2	81.6	82.6	82.4	85.1	87.6	89.1	90.4	94.1	97.0	100.0	106.5	110.2	111.8
Italy	74.3	79.0	82.9	84.6	87.7	93.0	96.7	96.6	97.6	98.5	100.0	104.1	107.9	111.3
Japan	94.7	99.9	99.9	100.8	101.5	99.9	99.8	101.4	103.2	102.4	100.0	99.3	98.2	98.1
Korea	59.9	65.8	68.6	70.5	78.2	80.2	82.5	86.0	94.7	99.1	100.0	105.0	110.0	115.1
Luxembourg	85.8	88.5	89.1	88.9	90.4	92.6	93.3	94.3	96.8	98.0	100.0	104.8	108.9	111.0
Mexico	20.5	24.5	27.1	28.6	29.9	41.7	59.3	70.7	82.0	94.9	100.0	105.1	109.1	115.1
Netherlands	88.4	91.4	93.0	92.7	94.5	94.8	94.8	96.4	98.6	99.7	100.0	107.0	110.5	111.7
New Zealand	89.9	90.1	90.0	91.1	90.4	91.4	92.6	94.7	98.1	99.0	100.0	106.7	109.8	109.3
Norway	82.1	83.7	85.0	84.2	85.4	86.7	88.1	91.1	95.4	98.1	100.0	98.1	96.4	99.7
Poland	-	-	-	-	-	63.3	74.5	83.7	89.6	91.2	100.0	104.6	104.0	102.7
Portugal	72.6	79.4	84.2	85.0	88.1	90.5	92.3	92.6	95.9	97.9	100.0	106.5	108.6	111.4
Slovak Republic	30.6	46.5	50.0	60.3	70.6	79.4	82.7	87.4	92.5	95.0	100.0	106.1	107.6	111.3
Spain	-	-	-	84.3	88.8	93.2	96.3	95.6	96.7	98.0	100.0	105.9	111.2	115.7
Sweden	101.2	105.8	100.4	101.1	102.8	104.3	97.1	97.4	98.5	100.0	100.0	102.9	106.2	106.5
Switzerland	92.6	96.7	96.7	96.5	97.0	97.6	97.1	97.8	98.6	98.5	100.0	102.2	104.6	105.9
Turkey	0.0	1.0	1.0	2.0	4.0	8.0	13.0	25.0	46.0	68.0	100.0	149.0	223.0	283.0
United Kingdom	83.3	87.6	89.5	91.1	92.0	95.5	98.6	98.7	100.0	100.3	100.0	103.3	104.1	105.4
United States	78.8	80.9	81.5	83.4	85.8	88.6	91.9	94.2	96.0	97.8	100.0	103.3	104.6	106.9
EU15	83.6	87.2	89.4	90.5	92.7	95.2	96.9	97.6	99.0	99.3	100.0	104.5	106.8	108.5
OECD total	67.6	71.2	73.2	75.4	78.7	83.3	87.8	91.5	95.4	97.8	100.0	104.4	107.1	109.5

StatLink: http://dx.doi.org/10.1787/540045148611

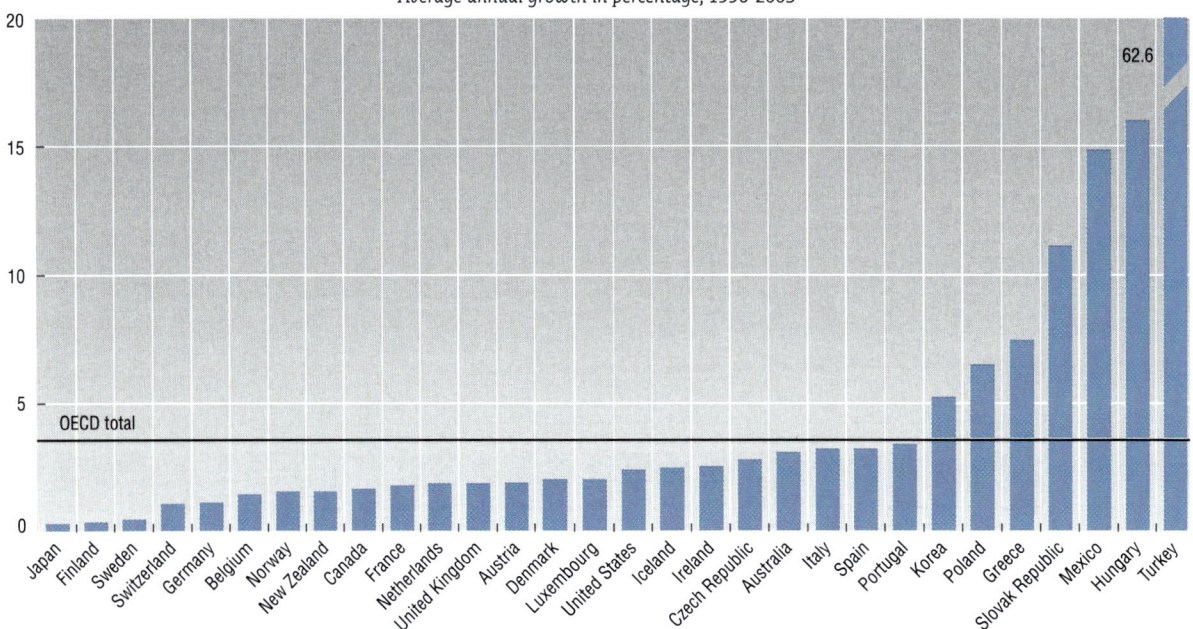

CPI: food
Average annual growth in percentage, 1990-2003

StatLink: http://dx.doi.org/10.1787/586602733817

PRICES • CONSUMER AND PRODUCER PRICES

CONSUMER PRICE INDICES (CPI)

CPI: energy
Year 2000 = 100

	1990	1991	1992	1993	1994	1995	1996	1997	1998	1999	2000	2001	2002	2003
Australia	77.3	78.2	80.3	81.5	81.7	84.2	85.8	87.3	84.3	85.8	100.0	102.5	103.3	108.6
Austria	78.9	78.9	81.3	80.7	81.9	84.9	90.3	93.0	90.0	90.3	100.0	100.5	98.1	99.1
Belgium	77.2	79.1	78.3	81.0	81.8	81.2	86.0	89.4	85.6	87.3	100.0	100.5	97.4	97.3
Canada	74.2	77.9	78.1	79.0	79.5	80.5	82.9	84.9	81.4	86.1	100.0	103.2	101.2	109.2
Czech Republic	-	-	-	-	-	-	58.6	67.3	83.6	88.8	100.0	106.1	108.5	109.5
Denmark	75.5	75.7	74.4	73.8	73.8	75.2	80.1	82.6	83.7	89.2	100.0	101.5	103.7	104.6
Finland	71.8	73.8	76.4	85.0	83.2	77.3	85.2	86.7	85.6	88.8	100.0	98.2	97.3	102.0
France	80.2	82.1	81.2	82.8	83.9	85.5	89.6	91.4	88.8	89.2	100.0	98.4	96.9	99.2
Germany	70.4	77.2	80.7	81.7	84.5	83.8	84.6	87.0	84.2	87.7	100.0	105.7	106.0	110.2
Greece	50.0	62.6	73.5	81.5	84.5	88.3	95.6	91.8	88.8	85.4	100.0	98.3	98.1	102.0
Hungary	10.0	17.4	22.7	26.8	29.9	41.4	53.5	67.3	77.4	86.8	100.0	105.5	108.7	115.6
Iceland	-	-	-	80.6	80.9	81.4	85.0	88.9	86.9	89.4	100.0	104.1	101.9	103.9
Ireland	79.9	81.0	79.7	80.0	80.5	80.9	84.0	86.9	86.4	88.0	100.0	97.4	100.7	104.8
Italy	77.2	85.7	87.1	90.9	94.5	99.0	88.6	90.2	89.0	89.6	100.0	101.8	99.0	102.2
Japan	104.5	106.9	105.9	106.1	104.2	102.4	100.0	103.1	98.8	97.2	100.0	100.5	98.1	98.0
Korea	40.6	45.9	50.8	53.7	53.7	54.7	60.2	70.5	90.9	91.3	100.0	107.0	103.6	107.4
Luxembourg	82.6	82.5	78.2	81.8	79.5	78.4	83.0	86.0	81.6	83.6	100.0	98.5	94.5	96.8
Mexico	12.5	16.1	20.7	23.3	26.0	37.2	50.5	62.4	71.9	84.9	100.0	108.6	117.4	128.4
Netherlands	69.1	74.7	74.4	71.1	73.8	74.2	79.0	85.2	85.1	87.1	100.0	107.0	109.5	114.5
New Zealand	76.7	79.7	81.6	83.1	83.1	84.9	87.2	89.2	87.7	88.8	100.0	99.2	100.7	104.9
Norway	69.4	75.0	76.2	79.2	79.2	83.7	86.7	91.1	87.5	89.7	100.0	108.4	105.9	126.8
Poland	-	-	-	-	-	50.5	60.1	70.5	81.2	88.1	100.0	107.0	112.2	116.9
Portugal	-	78.4	81.7	86.2	88.8	89.8	91.8	95.5	96.1	94.3	100.0	105.1	106.2	111.3
Slovak Republic	-	-	-	-	-	43.2	45.7	47.3	49.0	69.9	100.0	113.9	127.7	153.0
Spain	63.2	68.0	72.6	78.1	80.9	83.7	86.8	88.9	85.5	88.2	100.0	99.0	98.2	99.6
Sweden	66.6	71.8	71.6	81.3	81.7	83.1	88.5	92.9	92.9	92.7	100.0	107.1	108.6	121.8
Switzerland	76.6	77.9	75.8	80.2	79.3	81.5	84.8	87.5	82.4	85.0	100.0	98.7	93.8	95.0
Turkey	-	-	-	-	3.0	6.0	12.0	22.0	37.0	64.0	100.0	192.0	280.0	337.0
United Kingdom	69.3	74.6	76.5	78.5	82.0	84.8	86.9	89.5	89.8	93.5	100.0	97.4	97.0	99.8
United States	81.9	82.2	82.7	83.6	84.0	84.5	88.4	89.5	82.6	85.6	100.0	103.8	97.6	109.5
EU15	71.6	77.2	79.3	81.7	84.2	85.9	86.9	89.2	87.5	89.5	100.0	101.1	100.3	103.5
OECD total	68.9	71.5	72.2	73.3	74.1	76.1	80.6	84.8	83.5	87.4	100.0	104.4	103.0	110.6

StatLink: http://dx.doi.org/10.1787/150272675841

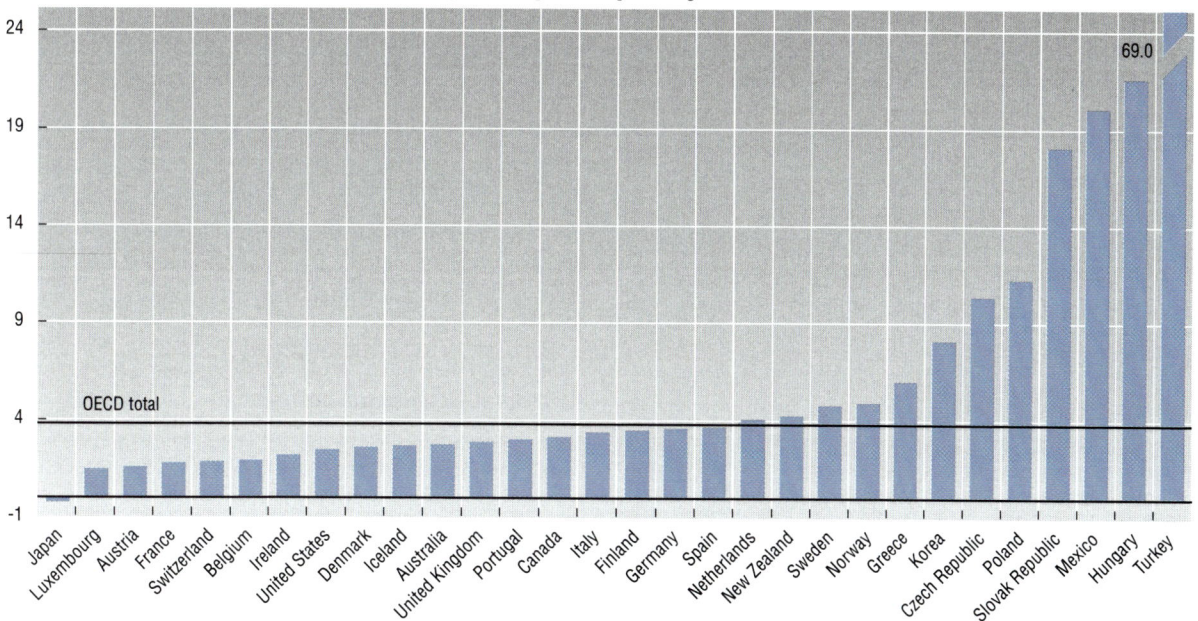

CPI: energy
Average annual growth in percentage, 1990-2003

StatLink: http://dx.doi.org/10.1787/527817211771

PRODUCER PRICE INDICES (PPI)

A variety of tools are used to measure price changes taking place in an economy. These include consumer price indices (CPI), price indices relating to specific goods and/or services, GDP deflators and producer price indices (PPI). Whereas CPIs are designed to measure changes over time in average retail prices of a fixed basket of goods and services taken as representing the consumption habits of households, the purpose of PPIs is to provide measures of average movements of prices received by the producers of commodities.

Producer price indices measure changes in prices at an early stage in the production process. Because of this, they are often seen as advance indicators of price changes throughout the economy, including changes in the prices of consumer goods and services.

Definition

Producer prices are defined as "ex-factory prices" and exclude any taxes, transport and trade margins that the purchaser may have to pay. Manufacturing covers the production of semi-processed goods and other intermediate goods as well as final products such as consumer goods and capital equipment.

Comparability

The price indices shown here are intended to be producer price indices for manufacturing. In practice many countries do not calculate such indices for the manufacturing sector alone. The indices for Austria, Greece, Italy, Luxembourg, Mexico, Spain, Switzerland and Turkey all have broader coverage, usually including (in addition to manufacturing) mining, electricity, gas and water and, in some countries, agriculture.

An additional problem is that Austria and Turkey calculate only wholesale price indices rather than producer price indices. Wholesale prices include taxes and transport and trade margins in addition to the ex-factory cost of the goods.

There are also differences between countries in the ways in which they adjust prices for quality changes, in the frequency with which the weights are updated, and in the price index formulae used.

Long-term trends

Compared with consumer prices, producer prices have risen more slowly throughout the period. More than half of OECD countries recorded average annual increases of under 2% and in four countries – Japan, Luxembourg, Switzerland and France – producer prices were actually lower at the end of the period than in 1990. All countries recorded unusually sharp rises in 1995 and 2000 due to sharp movements in world commodity prices, but for most of the period annual increases have been modest in the EU15 countries, in Australia, Canada, Japan, Korea, New Zealand and the United States. However PPIs rose sharply in both Mexico and Turkey, and the four new OECD member countries from central Europe also experienced above averaged increases in their PPIs; rises were particularly large in Hungary and Poland and more moderate in the Czech Republic and Slovak Republic.

Source
OECD (2004), *Main Economic Indicators*, OECD, Paris.

Further information
• *Analytical publications*

Brook, A.M. et al. (2004), "Oil Price Developments: Drivers, Economic Consequences and Policy Responses", *OECD Economics Department Working Paper*, No. 412, OECD, Paris, www.oecd.org/eco/working_papers.

IMF, ILO, OECD, Eurostat, UN, World Bank (2004), *Producer Price Index Manual: Theory and Practice*, IMF, Washington, DC.

OECD (2004), *OECD Economic Outlook*, OECD, Paris.

• *Methodological publications*

OECD (2002), "Comparative Methodological Analysis: Consumer and Producer Price Indices", *Main Economic Indicators*, Vol. 2002, Supplement 2, OECD, Paris.

• *Web sites*

OECD Main Economic Indicators: www.oecd.org/std/mei.

Technical Expert Group for Updating the Manual on PPI (TEGPPI): www.imf.org/np/sta/tegppi.

PRICES • CONSUMER AND PRODUCER PRICES

PRODUCER PRICE INDICES (PPI)

PPI: manufacturing
Year 2000 = 100

	1990	1991	1992	1993	1994	1995	1996	1997	1998	1999	2000	2001	2002	2003
Australia	82.2	83.4	84.7	86.4	87.0	90.2	91.0	92.1	92.7	93.3	100.0	103.1	103.3	103.8
Austria	95.9	96.7	96.5	96.1	97.4	97.7	97.7	98.1	97.6	96.7	100.0	101.5	101.1	102.8
Belgium	88.8	87.9	87.9	86.5	88.0	90.0	90.7	92.4	91.0	91.1	100.0	99.5	99.2	98.8
Canada	79.1	78.2	78.6	81.5	86.4	92.8	93.2	93.9	94.2	95.9	100.0	101.0	101.0	99.7
Czech Republic	-	60.1	65.8	72.0	75.9	82.3	86.3	90.4	94.6	94.6	100.0	102.7	101.3	101.0
Denmark	89.9	91.3	91.0	90.4	90.7	93.5	94.8	96.3	95.7	96.0	100.0	102.9	103.9	104.0
Finland	86.2	85.9	88.0	91.0	92.4	94.1	92.3	93.3	91.7	91.2	100.0	98.9	96.6	95.5
France	102.2	101.0	99.9	97.6	98.9	103.9	101.1	100.5	99.6	98.0	100.0	101.2	101.0	101.3
Germany	90.5	92.5	94.0	94.0	94.7	96.7	96.8	97.4	97.2	97.0	100.0	101.3	101.5	102.1
Greece	48.0	55.6	61.9	68.4	74.0	79.8	86.5	89.5	92.5	95.0	100.0	102.7	105.4	108.2
Hungary	-	-	-	-	-	53.0	64.5	77.3	85.4	89.3	100.0	104.3	101.7	103.2
Ireland	81.4	82.1	83.5	87.3	88.3	89.6	89.2	89.5	91.9	93.6	100.0	101.7	100.5	92.4
Italy	74.9	77.4	78.8	81.8	84.9	91.5	93.2	94.4	94.6	94.3	100.0	101.9	102.1	103.7
Japan	108.0	109.2	108.2	106.5	104.6	103.8	102.1	102.7	101.3	99.9	100.0	97.7	95.6	94.8
Korea	72.9	75.8	77.2	78.4	79.6	83.5	85.3	88.2	101.0	97.7	100.0	97.9	96.4	98.1
Luxembourg	103.5	100.9	98.8	97.1	97.3	100.7	96.5	98.1	99.8	95.0	100.0	99.8	99.0	100.2
Mexico	20.7	24.7	27.6	29.5	31.3	44.3	59.6	69.1	78.6	90.9	100.0	103.3	107.8	115.9
Netherlands	87.9	88.3	87.2	85.6	86.2	88.1	89.4	92.1	89.9	90.1	100.0	101.0	99.8	100.5
New Zealand	87.1	87.6	90.0	93.0	93.7	93.8	93.0	91.7	92.5	93.4	100.0	104.8	105.1	103.8
Norway	79.8	81.7	81.8	81.6	83.3	84.9	86.1	86.8	87.6	90.6	100.0	100.6	97.5	99.2
Poland	-	-	-	-	-	69.1	76.6	83.1	88.4	92.9	100.0	99.9	99.9	102.3
Portugal	71.4	73.0	73.1	74.5	76.9	80.8	85.5	88.1	83.9	86.9	100.0	102.7	103.1	103.5
Slovak Republic	-	-	-	-	-	78.2	81.9	86.0	88.6	91.6	100.0	105.9	106.7	109.4
Spain	79.0	80.2	81.3	83.2	86.8	92.3	93.9	94.8	94.2	94.8	100.0	101.7	102.4	103.9
Sweden	80.7	82.1	81.1	85.6	89.5	98.3	96.1	96.9	96.4	95.9	100.0	101.5	100.9	99.8
Switzerland	101.9	103.2	104.0	104.5	104.0	103.9	102.0	101.3	100.1	99.1	100.0	100.5	100.0	100.0
Turkey	1.0	1.0	1.0	2.0	4.0	8.0	14.0	25.0	43.0	66.0	100.0	162.0	243.0	305.0
United Kingdom	78.7	82.9	85.5	88.8	91.1	94.8	97.2	98.1	98.1	98.5	100.0	99.7	99.8	101.3
United States	85.7	86.8	87.9	89.2	90.4	93.1	95.2	95.5	94.5	96.1	100.0	100.8	100.1	102.7
EU15	84.7	86.6	87.7	88.9	90.8	94.9	95.5	96.4	96.0	95.8	100.0	101.2	101.2	102.0
OECD total	73.8	76.0	77.7	79.3	81.8	86.7	89.7	92.1	93.6	95.4	100.0	101.5	102.0	103.9

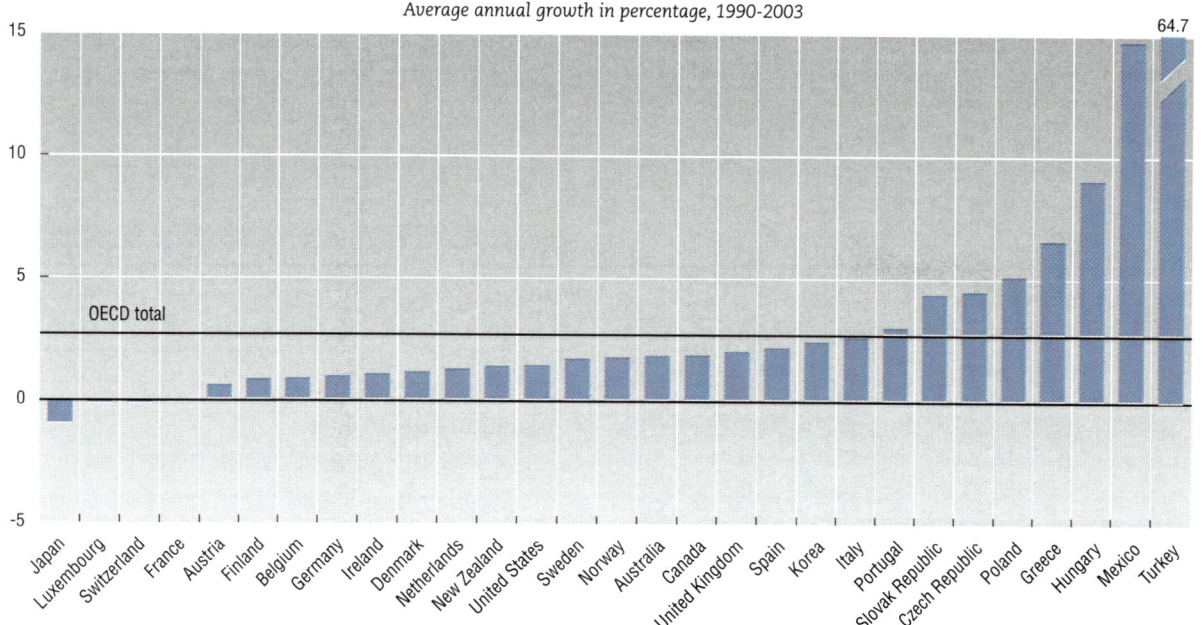

PPI: manufacturing
Average annual growth in percentage, 1990-2003

PRICES • PURCHASING POWER AND COMPETITIVENESS

LONG-TERM INTEREST RATES

Long-term interest rates are one of the determinants of business investment. Low interest rates encourage investment in new equipment and high interest rates discourage it. Investment is, in turn, a major source of economic growth.

Definition

These interest rates refer to government bonds with a residual maturity of about ten years. They are not the interest rates at which the loans were issued but the interest rates implied by the prices at which the bonds are traded on financial markets. For example if a bond was initially bought for 100 with an interest rate of 9%, but the bond is now trading at 90, the interest rate has risen to 10% ([9/90] x 100).

Comparability

The interest rates shown here are averages of daily rates for all countries except Japan, Australia, France, Iceland, Ireland, Switzerland and the United States. For these countries they are averages of rates recorded at the end of the month.

They are in all cases interest rates on bonds whose capital repayment is guaranteed by government.

Long-term trends

Interest rates are determined by three factors – the price that lenders charge for postponing consumption, the risk that the borrower may not repay the capital and the fall in the real value of the capital that the lender expects to occur because of inflation during the lifetime of the loan. The interest rates shown here refer to government borrowing and the risk factor is very low. To an important extent the interest rates in this table are driven by the expected rates of inflation.

From 1990, long-term interest rates fell for a few years but edged upwards again in 1994/1995. Since then they have been falling steadily in all countries, with particularly large declines, in relative terms, in Italy, Japan, Mexico, Spain and Sweden. For the 17 countries in the table for which data are a available for the full period from 1990 to 2003, long-term interest rates averaged 11% in 1990 but only just over 4% by 2003. For many countries the long-term interest rates recorded in 2003 were historic lows.

Another striking feature of long-term interest rates since 1990 is the reduction in the variance between countries. For the 17 countries, the variance (mean squared deviations around the mean) fell from 4.9 in 1990 to 1.1 in 2003. The convergence of interest rates is due to the increasing integration of financial markets – one aspect of globalisation – and was particularly pronounced among members of the Euro area. In the future, the differences in interest rates between these countries will mainly reflect differences in maturity dates.

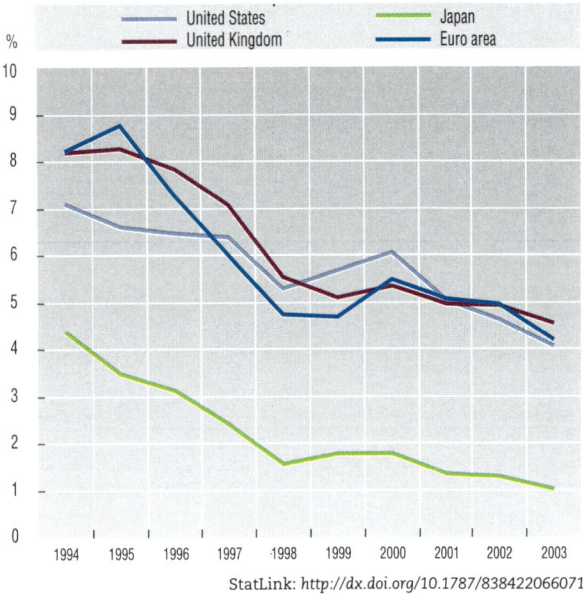

Evolution of long-term interest rates

StatLink: http://dx.doi.org/10.1787/838422066071

Source

OECD (2004), *Main Economic Indicators*, OECD, Paris.

Further information

• Analytical publications

OECD (2004), *OECD Economic Outlook*, OECD, Paris.

OECD (2004), *Financial Market Trends*, series, OECD, Paris.

• Methodological publications

OECD (2001), *Main Economic Indicators – Sources and Methods: Interest Rates and Share Price Indices*, OECD, Paris.

PRICES • PURCHASING POWER AND COMPETITIVENESS

LONG-TERM INTEREST RATES

Long-term interest rates
Percentage

	1990	1991	1992	1993	1994	1995	1996	1997	1998	1999	2000	2001	2002	2003
Australia	13.18	10.69	9.22	7.28	9.04	9.17	8.17	6.89	5.50	6.08	6.26	5.64	5.83	5.36
Austria	8.73	8.55	8.14	6.71	7.03	7.13	6.32	5.68	4.71	4.68	5.56	5.08	4.97	4.15
Belgium	10.06	9.31	8.66	7.22	7.70	7.38	6.30	5.59	4.70	4.71	5.57	5.06	4.89	4.15
Canada	10.73	9.46	8.06	7.24	8.36	8.16	7.24	6.14	5.28	5.54	5.93	5.48	5.30	4.80
Denmark	10.63	9.26	8.99	7.30	7.83	8.27	7.19	6.26	5.04	4.92	5.66	5.09	5.06	4.31
Finland	13.21	11.71	11.97	8.82	9.04	8.79	7.08	5.96	4.79	4.72	5.48	5.04	4.98	4.14
France	9.93	9.04	8.59	6.78	7.22	7.54	6.31	5.58	4.64	4.61	5.39	4.94	4.86	4.13
Greece	..	..	..	..	..	..	..	..	8.48	6.31	6.11	5.30	5.03	4.27
Iceland	..	..	..	..	6.98	9.65	9.24	8.71	7.66	8.47	11.20	10.36	7.96	6.65
Ireland	10.27	9.37	9.32	7.58	8.04	8.23	7.25	6.26	4.75	4.77	5.48	5.02	4.99	4.13
Italy	..	..	13.27	11.19	10.52	12.21	9.40	6.86	4.88	4.73	5.58	5.19	5.03	4.30
Japan	6.96	6.34	5.33	4.32	4.36	3.44	3.10	2.37	1.54	1.75	1.74	1.32	1.26	1.00
Luxembourg	..	..	..	..	7.15	7.23	6.30	5.60	4.73	4.67	5.52	4.86	4.68	3.32
Mexico	..	19.72	16.11	15.55	13.83	..	34.38	22.45	22.81	24.13	16.94	13.79	8.54	7.37
Netherlands	8.92	8.74	8.10	6.36	6.86	6.90	6.15	5.58	4.63	4.63	5.41	4.96	4.89	4.12
New Zealand	12.44	10.11	8.40	6.93	7.63	7.78	7.90	7.19	6.29	6.41	6.85	6.39	6.53	5.87
Norway	10.68	10.00	9.61	6.88	7.43	7.43	6.77	5.89	5.40	5.50	6.22	6.24	6.38	5.05
Portugal	..	..	..	..	10.48	11.47	8.56	6.36	4.88	4.78	5.60	5.16	5.02	4.19
Spain	14.68	12.43	12.17	10.16	9.69	11.04	8.18	5.84	4.55	4.30	5.36	4.87	4.62	3.52
Sweden	13.16	10.69	10.02	..	..	10.24	8.03	6.61	4.99	4.98	5.37	5.11	5.30	4.64
Switzerland	6.45	6.24	6.40	4.55	4.96	4.52	4.00	3.36	3.05	3.04	3.93	3.38	3.20	2.66
United Kingdom	11.80	10.11	9.06	7.47	8.17	8.24	7.82	7.05	5.52	5.08	5.31	4.94	4.91	4.52
United States	8.74	8.10	7.53	6.44	7.45	6.86	6.82	6.63	5.64	6.18	6.12	5.58	5.32	4.79
Euro area	..	..	..	..	8.18	8.73	7.23	5.96	4.70	4.66	5.44	5.03	4.92	4.16

StatLink: http://dx.doi.org/10.1787/852388073616

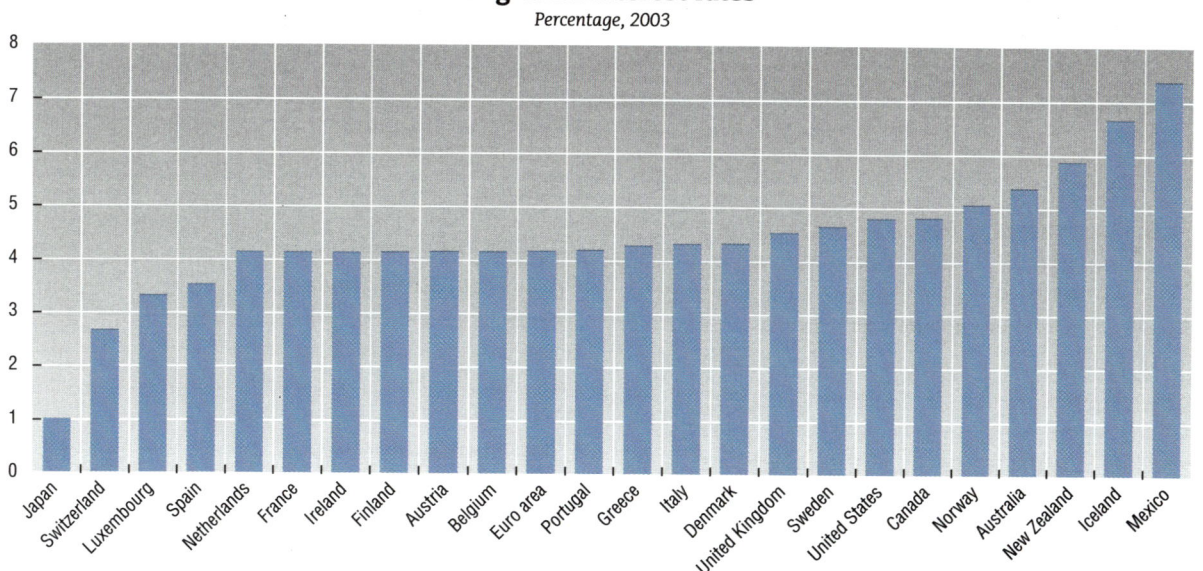

Long-term interest rates
Percentage, 2003

StatLink: http://dx.doi.org/10.1787/807135677813

PRICES • PURCHASING POWER AND COMPETITIVENESS

RATES OF CONVERSION

To compare a country's real GDP over a period of years, it is necessary to remove any movements that are due to price changes. In the same way, in order to compare the real GDPs of a group of countries at a single point in time, it is necessary to remove any differences in their GDPs that are due to differences in their price levels. Price indices are used to remove the effects of price changes in a single country over time; purchasing power parities (PPP) are used to remove the effects of the different levels of prices within a group of countries at a single point in time.

Long-term trends

Over the period 1990-2003, movements of PPPs and exchange rates were rarely similar and were often in opposite directions. In Australia, for example, the exchange rate rose indicating depreciation against the US dollar but the PPP declined indicating that the purchasing power of the Australian dollar (in Australia) was rising in relation to that of the US dollar (in the United States).

Exchange rates are sometimes used to convert the GDPs of different currencies to a common currency. However, comparisons of GDP based on exchange rates do not reflect the real volumes of goods and services in the GDPs of the countries being compared. For many of the low income countries, the differences between GDP converted using exchange rates and real GDP converted using PPPs are very considerable. The differences are illustrated by the graph on page 86.

For Poland, for example, the difference between exchange rate-converted and PPP-converted GDP is just over 100%, *i.e.* real GDP is twice the figure obtained using exchange rates. In general, the use of exchange rates understates the real GDP of low income countries and overstates the real GDP of high income countries.

The price level indices in the third table are the PPPs divided by exchange rates, with the OECD set to 100. In general, there is a positive correlation between income levels and price levels; Denmark, Norway and Switzerland, three high income countries, had the highest price levels in 2003 while the Czech Republic, Poland, the Slovak Republic and Turkey, four poorer OECD countries, had price levels 50% or less than that of the United States.

Definition

PPPs are currency converters that equalise price levels between countries. The PPPs shown here have been calculated by comparing the prices in OECD countries of a common basket of about 2 500 goods and services. Countries are not required to price all the items in the common basket because some of the items may be hard to find in certain countries, but the common basket has been drawn up in such a way that each country can find prices for a wide range of the goods and services that are representative of their markets.

The goods and services to be priced cover all those that enter into final expenditure – household consumption, government services, capital formation and net exports. Prices for the different items are weighted by their shares in total final expenditures to obtain the GDP PPPs shown here.

Comparability

The PPPs shown here have been calculated jointly by the OECD and Eurostat using standard procedures. In consultation with their member countries, OECD and Eurostat keep their methodology under review and improvements are made regularly. However, PPPs are statistical constructs rather than precise measures.

Source

OECD (2004), *Purchasing Power Parities and Real Expenditures: 2002 Benchmark Year*, OECD, Paris.

Further information

• *Analytical publications*

Schreyer, P. and F. Koechlin (2002), "Purchasing Power Parities – Measurement and Uses", *OECD Statistics Brief*, No. 3, March, OECD, Paris, www.oecd.org/std/statisticsbrief.

• *Statistical publications*

OECD (2004), *Main Economic Indicators*, OECD, Paris.

OECD (2004), "Comparative Tables", *National Accounts*, Vol. I, OECD, Paris.

• *Web sites*

OECD Purchasing Power Parities: www.oecd.org/std/ppp.

Joint World Bank-OECD Seminar on Purchasing Power Parities, 2001: www.oecd.org/std/ppp/seminar2001.

PRICES • PURCHASING POWER AND COMPETITIVENESS

RATES OF CONVERSION

Purchasing power parities (PPPs)
National currency units per US dollar

	1990	1991	1992	1993	1994	1995	1996	1997	1998	1999	2000	2001	2002	2003
Australia	1.38	1.36	1.35	1.33	1.32	1.31	1.32	1.32	1.31	1.30	1.32	1.34	1.35	1.36
Austria	0.921	0.924	0.936	0.942	0.947	0.946	0.938	0.936	0.940	0.931	0.926	0.932	0.935	0.938
Belgium	0.911	0.905	0.915	0.931	0.930	0.918	0.915	0.927	0.930	0.940	0.933	0.910	0.905	0.905
Canada	1.25	1.25	1.23	1.22	1.21	1.22	1.21	1.21	1.19	1.19	1.21	1.20	1.19	1.21
Czech Republic	5.50	7.23	7.94	9.40	10.4	11.2	11.9	12.7	13.9	14.3	14.5	14.8	14.6	14.6
Denmark	8.75	8.69	8.74	8.66	8.63	8.56	8.53	8.55	8.54	8.41	8.52	8.46	8.63	8.68
Finland	0.98	0.96	0.96	0.96	0.96	0.98	0.97	0.96	0.97	0.98	0.99	0.99	1.01	0.99
France	0.976	0.971	0.968	0.968	0.964	0.956	0.947	0.932	0.928	0.928	0.927	0.911	0.909	0.908
Germany	0.984	0.984	1.011	1.024	1.028	1.023	1.007	1.006	1.006	1.004	0.994	0.988	0.984	0.977
Greece	0.341	0.394	0.442	0.495	0.539	0.577	0.610	0.638	0.665	0.681	0.693	0.703	0.697	0.710
Hungary	..	29.8	35.3	41.9	49.0	60.0	70.9	83.3	92.8	100	109	112	118	125
Iceland	70.8	74.0	74.7	74.7	74.7	74.9	75.0	76.4	79.1	81.1	84.3	90.0	95.0	93.1
Ireland	0.801	0.788	0.792	0.814	0.811	0.814	0.823	0.830	0.873	0.921	0.966	1.00	1.01	1.00
Italy	0.690	0.717	0.733	0.745	0.755	0.773	0.793	0.807	0.802	0.809	0.818	0.829	0.845	0.856
Japan	189	188	187	184	180	176	171	169	167	162	155	150	146	140
Korea	529	566	596	623	657	690	712	732	767	755	744	753	762	767
Luxembourg	0.96	0.94	0.95	0.99	1.00	1.00	1.00	1.02	1.01	0.98	1.00	1.01	1.02	1.02
Mexico	1.43	1.71	1.91	2.04	2.17	2.93	3.75	4.35	4.96	5.63	6.18	6.39	6.73	7.05
Netherlands	0.912	0.906	0.907	0.903	0.905	0.900	0.897	0.902	0.910	0.926	0.936	0.931	0.946	0.956
New Zealand	1.49	1.46	1.45	1.45	1.44	1.44	1.43	1.44	1.44	1.43	1.45	1.47	1.46	1.46
Norway	9.54	9.42	9.15	9.15	8.96	8.98	8.90	9.07	9.35	9.21	9.13	9.23	9.42	9.48
Poland	0.26	0.40	0.54	0.68	0.92	1.15	1.33	1.50	1.65	1.75	1.84	1.87	1.88	1.86
Portugal	0.473	0.504	0.549	0.576	0.605	0.610	0.624	0.636	0.647	0.649	0.659	0.666	0.675	0.680
Slovak Republic	..	..	9.84	11.1	12.3	13.2	13.4	14.2	14.8	15.6	16.3	16.5	16.6	17.1
Spain	0.616	0.636	0.664	0.678	0.690	0.706	0.716	0.730	0.734	0.733	0.752	0.760	0.764	0.783
Sweden	8.87	9.34	9.23	9.29	9.31	9.39	9.28	9.37	9.47	9.34	9.31	9.46	9.61	9.67
Switzerland	1.99	2.04	2.03	2.04	2.02	1.99	2.00	1.93	1.90	1.93	1.92	1.92	1.89	1.88
Turkey	1540	2363	3782	6203	12541	22887	39661	71457	124133	191772	274409	429455	615791	742063
United Kingdom	0.590	0.608	0.618	0.621	0.618	0.621	0.626	0.623	0.634	0.644	0.641	0.632	0.628	0.637
United States	1.00	1.00	1.00	1.00	1.00	1.00	1.00	1.00	1.00	1.00	1.00	1.00	1.00	1.00

StatLink: http://dx.doi.org/10.1787/406082028347

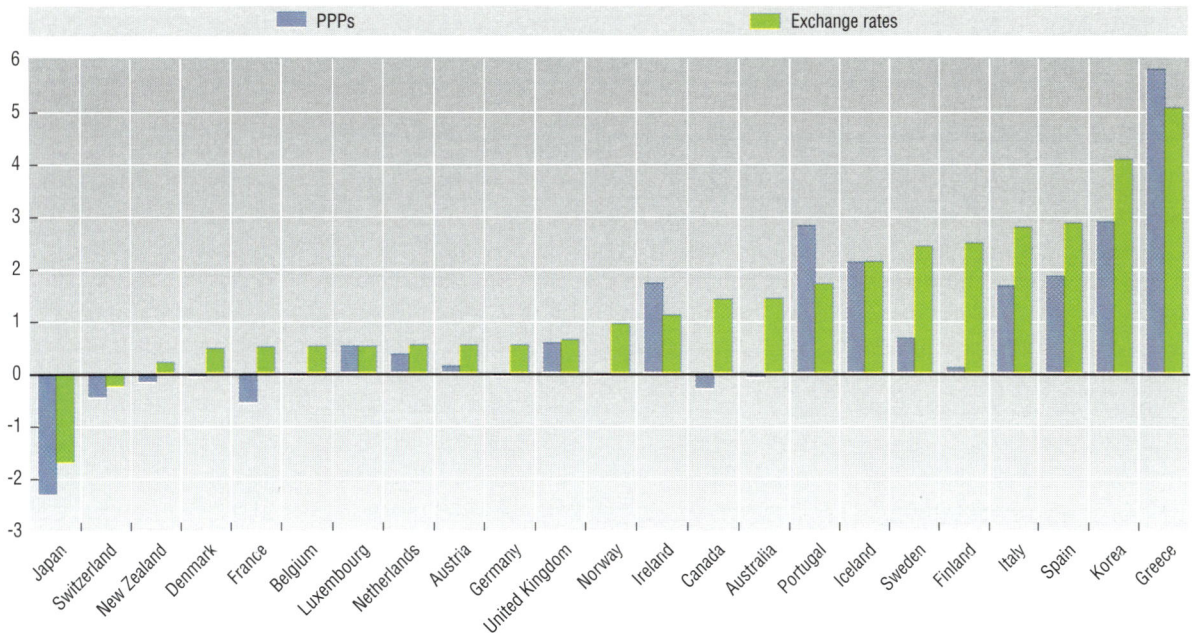

Changes in exchange rates and purchasing power parities
Average annual growth in percentage, 1990-2003

StatLink: http://dx.doi.org/10.1787/181328513670

OECD FACTBOOK 2005 – ISBN 92-64-01869-7 – © OECD 2005

PRICES • PURCHASING POWER AND COMPETITIVENESS

RATES OF CONVERSION

Exchange rates
National currency units per US dollar

	1990	1991	1992	1993	1994	1995	1996	1997	1998	1999	2000	2001	2002	2003
Australia	1.281	1.284	1.362	1.471	1.368	1.349	1.278	1.347	1.592	1.550	1.725	1.933	1.841	1.542
Austria	0.826	0.849	0.799	0.845	0.830	0.733	0.769	0.887	0.900	0.939	1.085	1.118	1.063	0.886
Belgium	0.828	0.847	0.797	0.858	0.829	0.731	0.768	0.887	0.900	0.939	1.085	1.118	1.063	0.886
Canada	1.167	1.146	1.209	1.290	1.366	1.372	1.363	1.385	1.483	1.486	1.485	1.549	1.569	1.401
Czech Republic	21.145	27.920	28.370	29.153	28.785	26.541	27.145	31.698	32.281	34.569	38.598	38.035	32.739	28.209
Denmark	6.189	6.396	6.036	6.484	6.361	5.602	5.799	6.604	6.701	6.976	8.083	8.323	7.895	6.588
Finland	0.643	0.680	0.753	0.961	0.879	0.734	0.773	0.873	0.899	0.939	1.085	1.118	1.063	0.886
France	0.830	0.860	0.807	0.863	0.846	0.761	0.780	0.890	0.899	0.939	1.085	1.118	1.063	0.886
Germany	0.826	0.849	0.798	0.845	0.830	0.733	0.769	0.887	0.900	0.939	1.085	1.118	1.063	0.886
Greece	0.465	0.535	0.559	0.673	0.712	0.680	0.706	0.801	0.867	0.897	1.072	1.118	1.063	0.886
Hungary	63.21	74.74	78.99	91.93	105.16	125.68	152.65	186.79	214.40	237.15	282.18	286.49	257.89	224.31
Iceland	58.28	59.00	57.55	67.60	69.94	64.69	66.50	70.90	70.96	72.34	78.62	97.42	91.66	76.71
Ireland	0.768	0.789	0.746	0.860	0.849	0.792	0.794	0.838	0.892	0.939	1.085	1.118	1.063	0.886
Italy	0.619	0.641	0.636	0.813	0.833	0.841	0.797	0.880	0.897	0.939	1.085	1.118	1.063	0.886
Japan	144.79	134.71	126.65	111.20	102.21	94.06	108.78	120.99	130.91	113.91	107.77	121.53	125.39	115.93
Korea	707.76	733.35	780.65	802.67	803.45	771.27	804.45	951.29	1401.44	1188.82	1130.96	1290.99	1251.09	1191.61
Luxembourg	0.828	0.847	0.797	0.858	0.829	0.731	0.768	0.887	0.900	0.939	1.085	1.118	1.063	0.886
Mexico	2.813	3.018	3.095	3.116	3.375	6.419	7.599	7.918	9.136	9.560	9.456	9.342	9.656	10.789
Netherlands	0.826	0.848	0.798	0.843	0.826	0.729	0.765	0.885	0.900	0.939	1.085	1.118	1.063	0.886
New Zealand	1.676	1.734	1.862	1.851	1.687	1.524	1.455	1.512	1.868	1.890	2.201	2.379	2.162	1.723
Norway	6.260	6.483	6.215	7.094	7.058	6.335	6.450	7.073	7.545	7.799	8.802	8.992	7.984	7.080
Poland	0.950	1.058	1.363	1.812	2.272	2.425	2.696	3.279	3.475	3.967	4.346	4.094	4.080	3.889
Portugal	0.711	0.721	0.673	0.802	0.828	0.754	0.769	0.874	0.898	0.939	1.085	1.118	1.063	0.886
Slovak Republic	..	..	..	30.770	32.045	29.713	30.654	33.616	35.233	41.363	46.035	48.355	45.327	36.773
Spain	0.613	0.625	0.615	0.765	0.805	0.749	0.761	0.880	0.898	0.939	1.085	1.118	1.063	0.886
Sweden	5.919	6.047	5.824	7.783	7.716	7.133	6.706	7.635	7.950	8.262	9.162	10.329	9.737	8.085
Switzerland	1.389	1.434	1.406	1.478	1.368	1.182	1.236	1.451	1.450	1.502	1.689	1.688	1.559	1.347
Turkey	2609	4172	6872	10985	29609	45845	81405	151865	260724	418783	625218	1225590	1507230	1500890
United Kingdom	0.563	0.567	0.570	0.667	0.653	0.634	0.641	0.611	0.604	0.618	0.661	0.695	0.667	0.612
United States	1.000	1.000	1.000	1.000	1.000	1.000	1.000	1.000	1.000	1.000	1.000	1.000	1.000	1.000

StatLink: http://dx.doi.org/10.1787/546085533180

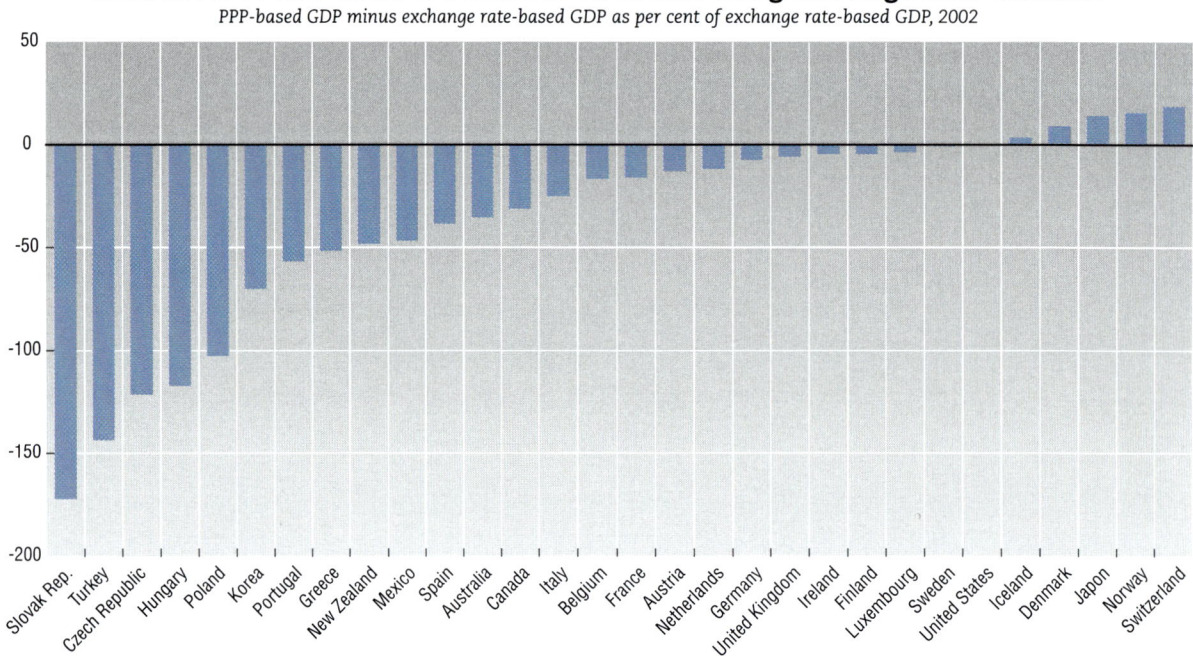

Differences in GDP when converted to US dollars using exchange rates and PPPs
PPP-based GDP minus exchange rate-based GDP as per cent of exchange rate-based GDP, 2002

StatLink: http://dx.doi.org/10.1787/857568152305

PRICES • PURCHASING POWER AND COMPETITIVENESS

RATES OF CONVERSION

Indices of price levels
OECD = 100

	1990	1991	1992	1993	1994	1995	1996	1997	1998	1999	2000	2001	2002	2003
Australia	100	98	89	84	87	84	93	95	82	83	80	75	79	88
Austria	104	100	105	103	104	112	111	102	105	99	89	91	95	106
Belgium	102	99	103	100	102	109	108	101	104	100	89	89	92	102
Canada	100	100	92	87	81	77	81	85	80	80	85	84	82	86
Czech Republic	24	24	25	30	33	37	40	39	43	41	39	42	48	52
Denmark	132	125	130	123	123	133	133	126	128	120	109	111	118	132
Finland	142	131	114	92	99	115	114	107	108	104	95	96	102	112
France	109	104	108	103	103	109	110	102	104	98	89	89	92	102
Germany	111	107	114	112	112	121	119	110	112	106	95	96	100	110
Greece	68	68	71	68	69	74	78	77	77	75	67	68	71	80
Hungary	..	37	40	42	42	41	42	43	43	42	40	42	49	56
Iceland	113	116	117	102	97	100	102	105	112	112	111	100	112	121
Ireland	97	92	95	87	87	89	94	96	98	98	92	97	102	113
Italy	104	103	103	84	82	80	90	89	90	86	78	81	86	96
Japan	122	129	133	152	160	162	143	135	128	142	150	134	125	120
Korea	70	71	69	72	74	78	80	75	55	63	68	63	66	64
Luxembourg	107	103	107	106	110	119	118	111	113	104	96	98	103	115
Mexico	47	52	55	60	58	40	45	53	54	59	68	74	75	65
Netherlands	103	99	102	99	99	107	106	99	101	98	90	91	96	108
New Zealand	83	78	70	72	78	82	89	92	77	76	68	67	73	85
Norway	142	134	132	119	115	123	125	125	124	117	108	112	127	134
Poland	26	34	35	35	37	41	45	44	48	44	44	50	50	48
Portugal	62	65	73	66	66	70	74	71	72	69	63	65	68	77
Slovak Republic	..	..	..	33	35	39	40	41	42	38	37	37	39	46
Spain	94	94	97	82	78	82	85	81	82	78	72	74	77	88
Sweden	140	143	142	110	110	114	125	119	120	112	105	100	106	119
Switzerland	134	131	130	127	134	146	147	129	132	128	118	124	130	139
Turkey	55	52	49	52	38	43	44	46	48	46	46	38	44	49
United Kingdom	98	99	97	86	86	85	89	99	105	104	101	99	101	104
United States	93	92	90	92	91	87	91	97	100	99	104	109	108	100
EU15	105	103	105	96	96	100	103	99	101	97	89	90	93	103
OECD total	100	100	100	100	100	100	100	100	100	100	100	100	100	100

StatLink: http://dx.doi.org/10.1787/257612671136

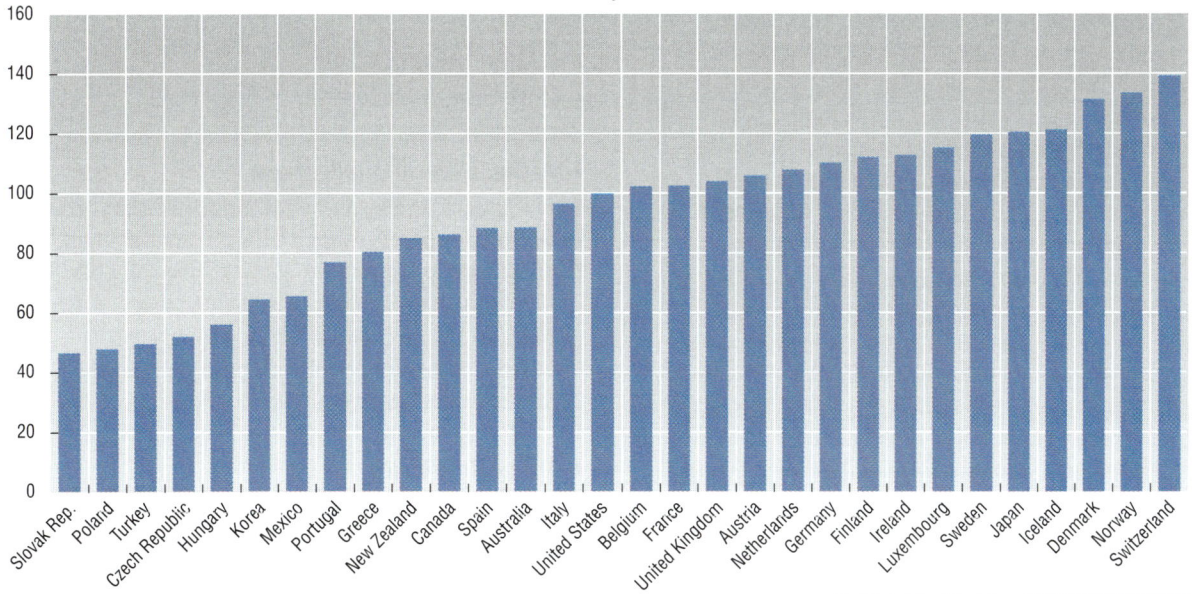

Comparative price levels
OECD = 100, year 2003

StatLink: http://dx.doi.org/10.1787/205571230564

OECD FACTBOOK 2005 – ISBN 92-64-01869-7 – © OECD 2005

PRICES • PURCHASING POWER AND COMPETITIVENESS

INTERNATIONAL COMPETITIVENESS

A broad interpretation of international competitiveness would involve comparison of the success of different countries in raising productivity, fostering innovation and improving living standards. The two competitiveness indicators shown here have a narrower objective – namely to measure changes in a country's price competitiveness in international markets based on changes in that country's exchange rate and price level (either consumer goods prices or unit labour costs in manufacturing) relative to those of its competitors. In addition, we present indices of nominal effective exchange rates. This indicator reflects only variations in market exchange rates, which is just one of the factors that enter the calculation of the two competitiveness indicators mentioned above.

Long-term trends

A rise in the indices represents an increase in the price of the country's exports relative to those of its competitors and thus indicates a deterioration in that country's competitiveness. Note that the indices only show changes in the international competitiveness of each country over time and that differences between countries in the levels of the indices have no significance.

All three indices are rather variable from year to year so that it is difficult to detect long-term movements. Between 2000 and 2003, Japan, Mexico and the United Kingdom have generally improved their international competitiveness as judged by both relative consumer price indices and unit labour costs in manufacturing, while the competitive positions of Australia, Canada and Italy has generally deteriorated. For both groups of countries, these changes reflected in large part movements in these countries' nominal effective exchange rates. By contrast, in the case of the United States, the improvement in competitiveness in terms of unit labour costs since 2000 has been significantly larger than the change in their nominal effective exchange rate, and therefore must have been due in part also to favourable developments in unit labour costs in manufacturing expressed in domestic currency, which in turn reflected trends in productivity and wage costs.

Definition

The nominal effective exchange rate indices are calculated by comparing, for each country, the change in its own exchange rate against the US dollar to a weighted average of changes in its competitors' exchange rates (also against the US dollar), using the weighting matrix for the current year.

The other two indicators, relative consumer price indices and relative unit labour costs in manufacturing, can also be called indices of real effective exchange rates. Unlike nominal effective exchange rates, they take into account not only changes in market exchange rates but also variations in relative price levels (using, respectively, consumer prices and unit labour costs in manufacturing) and therefore can be used as indicators of competitiveness. The change in a country's index of relative consumer prices between two years is obtained by comparing the change in the country's consumer price index (converted into US dollars at market exchange rates) to a weighted average of changes in its competitors' consumer price indices (also expressed in US dollars), using the weighting matrix for the current year. Changes in the index of relative unit labour costs in manufacturing are calculated in the same way.

Comparability

All three indices shown here are constructed using a common procedure.

Source

OECD (2004), *OECD Economic Outlook*, OECD, Paris.

Further information

• *Statistical publications*

OECD (2004), *Main Economic Indicators*, OECD, Paris.

• *Methodological publications*

Durand, M., C. Madaschi and F. Terribile (1998), "Trends in OECD Countries" International Competitiveness", *OECD Economics Department Working Paper*, No. 195, OECD, Paris, www.oecd.org/eco/working_papers.

Durand M., J. Simon and C. Webb (1992), "OECD's Indicators of International Trade and Competitiveness", *OECD Economics Department Working Paper*, No. 120, OECD, Paris, www.oecd.org/eco/working_papers.

• *Online databases*

SourceOECD Economic Outlook.

• *Web sites*

OECD Economic Outlook – Sources and Methods: www.oecd.org/eco/sources-and-methods.

PRICES • PURCHASING POWER AND COMPETITIVENESS

INTERNATIONAL COMPETITIVENESS

Relative consumer price indices
Year 1995 = 100

	1990	1991	1992	1993	1994	1995	1996	1997	1998	1999	2000	2001	2002	2003
Australia	118.6	116.2	105.0	96.9	101.7	100.0	109.4	108.4	99.1	99.4	94.6	91.0	96.0	108.6
Austria	96.2	94.6	96.0	97.1	97.3	100.0	97.4	94.1	94.3	93.4	90.9	91.0	91.2	93.5
Belgium	95.8	94.7	95.4	95.3	96.8	100.0	97.6	92.8	93.5	92.1	88.4	89.1	90.1	93.9
Canada	125.4	129.1	119.3	111.2	102.2	100.0	100.1	99.4	93.8	93.0	93.5	90.6	89.8	100.0
Czech Republic	..	..	..	92.1	96.7	100.0	106.6	108.4	118.7	117.0	119.3	127.2	141.1	137.4
Denmark	99.2	95.5	96.1	96.9	96.6	100.0	98.6	95.9	98.0	98.1	94.5	95.9	97.4	101.7
Finland	130.3	124.3	107.4	89.8	93.2	100.0	94.2	90.6	91.7	91.6	87.6	88.8	89.5	92.6
France	98.9	95.8	97.1	98.2	98.0	100.0	99.4	95.4	96.0	94.0	89.6	89.4	90.5	94.6
Germany	89.9	88.7	92.7	95.8	96.4	100.0	96.0	91.3	92.2	90.1	84.5	84.4	84.9	88.7
Hungary	..	..	..	107.9	105.3	100.0	101.1	107.2	108.0	111.2	112.7	121.9	134.3	136.2
Iceland	112.7	115.1	115.1	108.4	101.5	100.0	99.3	100.9	103.2	106.2	110.1	97.0	102.9	108.6
Ireland	107.5	104.0	107.2	99.4	99.1	100.0	101.6	100.4	97.3	94.2	89.9	93.5	98.5	109.3
Italy	132.8	133.5	131.3	110.9	107.8	100.0	110.7	111.2	112.7	111.6	107.2	108.4	110.6	116.3
Japan	70.8	76.3	78.5	91.1	98.3	100.0	83.6	78.9	79.7	89.4	94.7	84.8	79.3	80.1
Korea	107.5	107.0	100.6	97.8	98.9	100.0	103.6	97.7	74.5	84.6	90.9	86.0	90.5	91.5
Luxembourg	96.5	95.6	96.5	96.4	97.6	100.0	97.7	94.7	95.0	94.3	92.5	93.0	94.1	97.3
Mexico	120.4	133.3	144.5	154.4	147.6	100.0	111.7	129.2	130.5	142.7	154.9	165.0	165.1	147.6
Netherlands	96.2	94.3	95.9	96.3	96.4	100.0	97.3	92.1	94.6	94.0	89.0	91.5	94.7	100.7
New Zealand	100.7	95.5	86.6	88.6	93.3	100.0	106.0	108.0	96.5	91.8	83.2	82.5	89.9	101.7
Norway	108.0	104.3	104.2	100.3	97.7	100.0	98.8	100.0	97.4	97.8	96.5	100.2	107.9	106.0
Poland	..	..	..	92.3	93.4	100.0	107.4	111.1	117.9	114.9	126.9	143.4	136.9	121.5
Portugal	87.3	92.9	101.2	98.1	96.6	100.0	99.9	98.6	99.4	99.5	97.3	99.8	102.0	105.7
Slovak Republic	..	..	..	98.9	97.8	100.0	99.8	105.4	107.6	107.1	118.1	119.5	120.9	136.1
Spain	114.9	116.3	115.9	103.2	98.6	100.0	101.6	97.1	98.0	97.8	95.8	97.8	100.1	104.6
Sweden	118.8	124.5	124.5	102.3	100.9	100.0	107.7	102.3	99.3	97.4	95.8	87.8	89.9	94.9
Switzerland	90.4	90.2	88.6	90.2	94.3	100.0	96.4	89.0	90.5	89.4	86.8	88.6	91.7	91.8
Turkey	119.6	121.8	117.1	125.6	92.2	100.0	101.0	108.0	118.9	125.6	140.5	114.7	124.7	134.8
United Kingdom	117.9	120.4	116.0	103.4	103.8	100.0	101.7	119.1	128.0	127.8	131.5	128.8	129.6	126.0
United States	104.0	102.1	99.9	101.3	101.5	100.0	103.1	108.4	117.0	115.4	119.0	125.8	125.9	118.3

StatLink: http://dx.doi.org/10.1787/338377882758

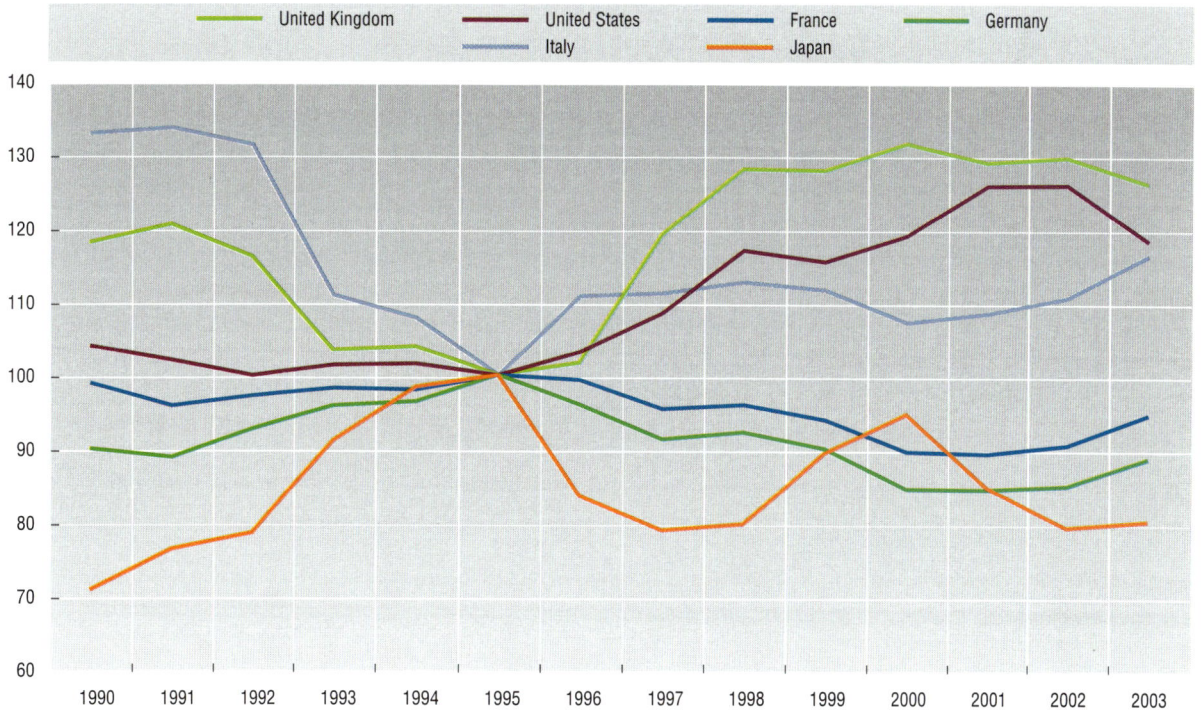

Relative consumer price indices
Year 1995 = 100

StatLink: http://dx.doi.org/10.1787/014800237184

PRICES • PURCHASING POWER AND COMPETITIVENESS

INTERNATIONAL COMPETITIVENESS

Relative unit labour costs in manufacturing
Year 1995 = 100

	1990	1991	1992	1993	1994	1995	1996	1997	1998	1999	2000	2001	2002	2003
Australia	149.7	132.9	115.6	101.5	102.9	100.0	103.6	104.6	93.2	91.4	87.0	81.6	87.0	99.7
Austria	105.8	103.7	105.2	107.5	100.4	100.0	102.1	92.0	82.1	79.4	72.4	70.4	71.9	74.2
Belgium	97.5	97.2	97.3	96.5	96.9	100.0	94.7	87.7	89.3	90.1	85.2	87.2	90.4	94.3
Canada	125.0	128.4	117.5	105.1	97.8	100.0	105.9	106.2	101.6	101.9	101.5	101.8	103.9	116.5
Czech Republic	..	..	..	90.2	96.7	100.0	106.9	105.4	116.1	118.0	117.9	121.2	128.5	124.4
Denmark	97.3	93.3	95.6	100.4	96.0	100.0	103.8	98.4	103.6	103.9	99.2	101.6	103.0	108.4
Finland	143.0	137.2	107.5	82.0	86.7	100.0	94.1	89.0	91.3	91.9	83.3	87.4	86.3	90.6
France	106.7	102.0	100.0	101.5	100.5	100.0	99.7	94.3	90.5	87.6	82.1	80.7	81.5	85.4
Germany	82.9	83.5	89.7	91.4	92.4	100.0	97.5	92.6	94.8	96.1	93.4	94.5	94.1	97.9
Greece	106.2	97.7	94.2	88.2	92.1	100.0	102.7	105.8	101.2	103.1	98.4	98.4	101.0	107.9
Hungary	..	..	..	122.5	121.7	100.0	92.4	92.7	85.6	85.9	78.6	86.2	98.3	102.4
Iceland	101.3	110.3	110.9	101.2	99.3	100.0	99.0	104.3	113.2	125.4	136.2	117.7	124.9	135.9
Ireland	132.9	126.7	122.8	113.0	109.0	100.0	99.1	91.6	81.7	81.8	74.4	71.7	71.4	76.8
Italy	129.8	133.0	131.1	119.9	114.0	100.0	111.9	113.3	119.5	121.2	113.7	115.1	123.5	135.6
Japan	61.9	67.6	74.5	89.2	98.5	100.0	84.8	80.3	87.6	99.2	102.3	96.1	88.5	86.9
Korea	96.4	98.1	90.3	87.3	89.8	100.0	107.1	93.5	64.8	67.5	70.8	68.7	76.4	80.9
Luxembourg	106.6	104.3	104.1	103.1	101.6	100.0	96.0	92.5	92.7	89.0	88.3	92.3	91.3	92.9
Mexico	122.9	137.3	152.8	164.7	160.6	100.0	101.8	111.8	108.3	112.8	122.1	129.5	133.3	120.0
Netherlands	99.1	97.5	100.4	99.8	96.3	100.0	96.7	93.6	97.6	95.4	93.5	93.1	97.9	106.9
New Zealand	92.8	91.8	82.2	85.4	93.3	100.0	111.2	116.6	107.8	108.1	97.4	95.2	104.5	119.4
Norway	94.7	93.2	91.9	89.9	94.5	100.0	99.5	107.3	112.0	115.1	118.2	122.1	137.1	136.4
Poland	..	..	..	89.9	95.8	100.0	102.0	102.4	108.0	101.5	100.9	104.9	94.5	77.0
Portugal	89.7	91.7	100.6	91.5	95.0	100.0	91.4	92.6	94.5	97.1	97.8	100.4	102.9	106.2
Slovak Republic	..	..	..	83.1	96.8	100.0	109.7	119.1	123.9	120.6	120.4	116.3	118.4	127.2
Spain	108.5	109.6	112.4	102.4	99.2	100.0	104.4	103.1	106.1	106.1	106.3	109.1	112.3	116.8
Sweden	148.9	151.4	148.4	105.9	100.1	100.0	111.7	105.1	101.2	95.8	89.7	82.1	84.4	89.4
Switzerland	85.8	86.1	83.8	83.3	91.4	100.0	95.9	91.2	94.0	95.3	94.5	99.1	106.6	109.7
Turkey	173.2	190.4	171.9	171.3	111.5	100.0	100.2	112.5	125.8	147.6	169.1	121.2	118.5	122.7
United Kingdom	116.7	120.0	111.2	98.3	100.5	100.0	103.4	125.2	138.5	141.2	145.8	143.2	146.9	138.5
United States	114.2	111.9	107.8	106.6	105.6	100.0	101.1	106.2	115.4	114.1	118.9	123.0	119.4	111.8

StatLink: http://dx.doi.org/10.1787/215764028230

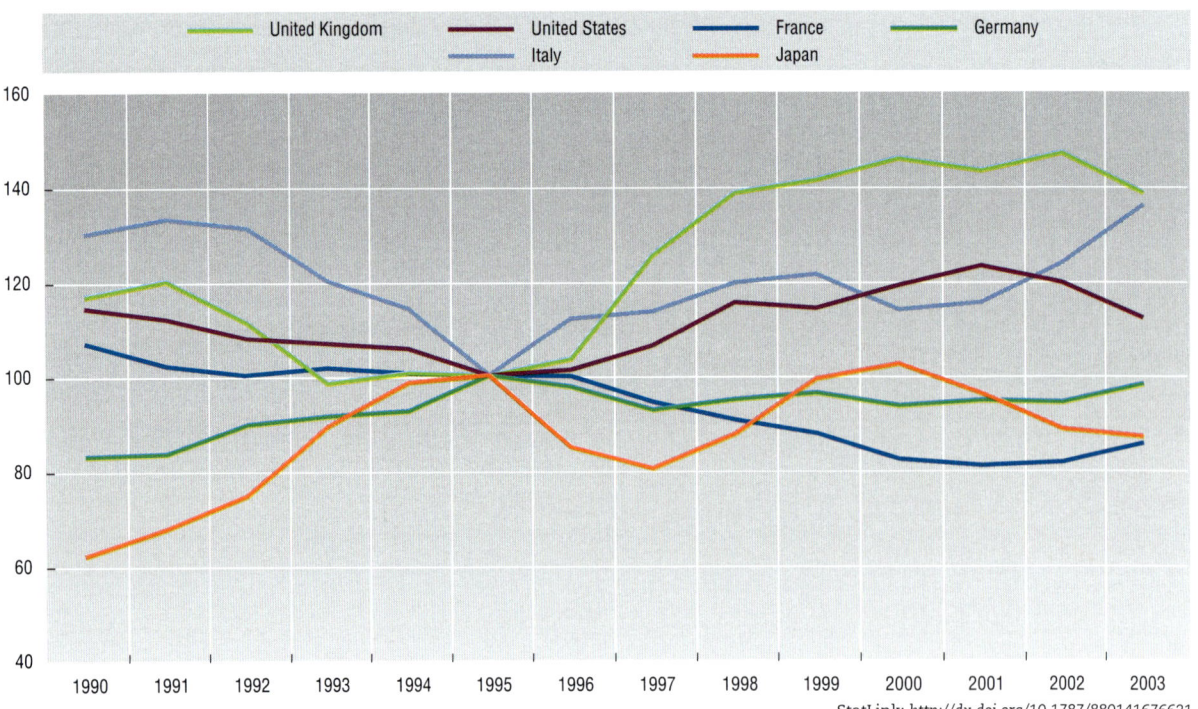

Relative unit labour costs in manufacturing
Year 1995 = 100

StatLink: http://dx.doi.org/10.1787/880141676621

PRICES • PURCHASING POWER AND COMPETITIVENESS

INTERNATIONAL COMPETITIVENESS

Real effective exchange rates
Year 1995 = 100

	1990	1991	1992	1993	1994	1995	1996	1997	1998	1999	2000	2001	2002	2003
Australia	107.0	107.7	100.9	95.7	103.1	100.0	109.7	111.0	103.5	103.6	96.3	90.3	93.6	104.5
Austria	87.9	88.1	90.2	93.2	95.4	100.0	99.1	97.2	99.2	99.9	97.7	98.1	98.6	101.7
Belgium	85.2	86.1	88.7	90.7	94.7	100.0	98.4	94.5	96.8	96.3	92.5	93.6	95.2	99.9
Canada	113.2	116.5	110.7	105.6	100.8	100.0	101.9	102.2	97.4	97.1	98.0	95.1	93.6	103.6
Czech Republic	..	..	..	95.9	99.3	100.0	101.6	98.6	100.3	99.9	101.2	106.2	118.2	117.5
Denmark	86.5	86.0	88.7	92.9	95.1	100.0	99.1	96.8	99.3	98.7	94.8	96.4	97.6	101.9
Finland	99.9	97.0	85.2	76.7	87.0	100.0	97.6	95.4	98.2	101.1	96.6	98.6	100.3	105.4
France	86.4	85.9	89.6	93.3	96.1	100.0	100.4	97.7	100.0	99.3	95.7	96.6	98.0	102.5
Germany	79.4	80.1	84.0	88.6	93.0	100.0	98.6	95.2	98.7	98.6	94.3	95.5	97.1	102.8
Greece	133.8	120.8	113.7	106.0	101.2	100.0	98.4	96.6	93.9	94.6	88.4	89.1	90.7	94.5
Hungary	..	..	..	140.1	126.0	100.0	85.2	78.9	71.5	69.0	65.5	66.7	71.2	70.4
Iceland	110.4	110.9	110.5	104.0	99.6	100.0	99.5	101.7	104.5	106.3	107.4	91.0	93.2	98.0
Ireland	98.6	97.5	101.7	96.6	98.2	100.0	102.6	102.4	99.4	96.5	89.5	90.7	92.8	101.7
Italy	126.1	127.3	126.2	108.7	108.6	100.0	110.0	111.5	113.9	113.5	109.4	110.7	112.7	118.1
Japan	53.2	59.9	65.0	80.4	93.4	100.0	87.2	83.3	86.6	99.3	108.1	99.7	95.5	98.6
Korea	111.3	107.4	100.1	98.6	99.7	100.0	101.6	94.1	68.1	77.9	83.4	77.1	79.7	79.0
Luxembourg	91.0	91.6	93.5	94.1	96.8	100.0	98.9	96.7	97.7	97.5	94.9	95.4	96.5	99.7
Mexico	193.5	186.9	187.1	196.5	190.3	100.0	84.9	83.3	74.0	70.6	72.1	74.1	71.8	62.8
Netherlands	81.4	82.0	85.2	89.3	93.6	100.0	98.6	93.9	97.2	97.1	92.2	93.5	95.6	101.7
New Zealand	92.0	89.5	83.3	87.3	93.6	100.0	106.3	108.9	97.8	94.4	85.6	84.7	91.5	103.6
Norway	95.8	95.0	96.7	95.7	96.4	100.0	100.1	101.1	98.0	97.9	95.8	99.0	107.3	104.9
Poland	..	..	..	139.0	113.5	100.0	93.2	86.6	84.8	79.2	81.6	90.0	86.1	77.4
Portugal	93.3	95.8	101.3	97.8	97.0	100.0	99.6	98.3	98.2	97.7	95.4	96.3	97.2	99.8
Slovak Republic	..	..	..	97.9	96.7	100.0	101.0	105.6	106.6	100.6	102.3	99.8	100.1	105.7
Spain	117.0	118.4	117.1	104.7	99.7	100.0	101.0	96.9	98.1	97.3	94.3	95.4	96.8	100.4
Sweden	115.7	116.7	119.6	98.4	99.6	100.0	110.1	106.6	106.3	106.1	106.3	97.8	100.2	105.9
Switzerland	80.5	80.2	79.7	83.5	91.9	100.0	98.7	93.1	97.2	97.8	96.1	100.0	105.1	106.8
Turkey	1 546.9	1 023.7	610.9	427.8	173.5	100.0	58.6	34.9	21.1	14.1	10.3	5.8	4.3	3.8
United Kingdom	109.0	111.1	108.4	100.2	103.4	100.0	102.3	119.2	127.0	127.5	130.9	129.6	131.1	126.4
United States	83.3	85.4	87.1	92.6	98.0	100.0	105.6	113.1	124.8	124.4	127.5	134.3	134.8	126.5

StatLink: http://dx.doi.org/10.1787/620632362218

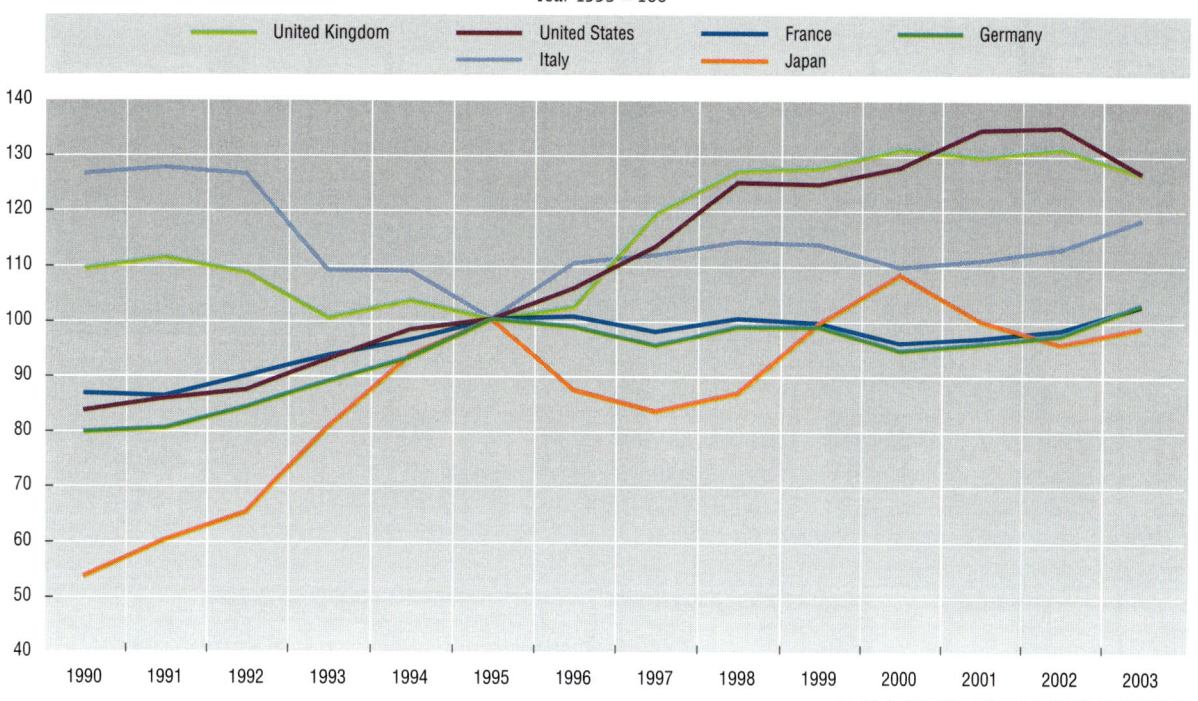

Real effective exchange rates
Year 1995 = 100

StatLink: http://dx.doi.org/10.1787/540132705512

LABOUR MARKET

EMPLOYMENT
EMPLOYMENT RATES BY GENDER
EMPLOYMENT RATES BY AGE GROUP
PART-TIME EMPLOYMENT
SELF-EMPLOYMENT

UNEMPLOYMENT
STANDARDISED UNEMPLOYMENT RATES
LONG-TERM UNEMPLOYMENT

LABOUR MARKET • EMPLOYMENT

EMPLOYMENT RATES BY GENDER

These rates show the percentage of persons of working age who are in employment. In the short term, these rates are sensitive to the economic cycle, but in the longer term they are significantly affected by government policies with regard to higher education and income support and by policies that facilitate employment of women.

Employment rates for men and women differ both between countries and over time in individual countries. Employment rates are here shown for total employment and for men and women separately.

Definition

Employment rates are calculated as the ratio of the employed to the working age population. To calculate this employment rate, the population of working age is divided into two groups – those who are employed and those who are not. Employment is generally measured through household labour force surveys and, according to the *ILO Guidelines*, employed persons are defined as those aged 15 or over who report that they have worked in gainful employment for at least one hour in the previous week. Those not in employment consist of persons who are out of work but seeking employment, students and all others who have excluded themselves from the labour force for one reason or another, such as incapacity or the need to look after young children or elderly relatives.

Working age is generally defined as persons in the 15 to 64 age bracket although in some countries working age is defined as 16 to 64.

Comparability

All OECD countries except Iceland, Mexico and Turkey use the *ILO Guidelines* for measuring employment. For the three countries that do not do so, employment rates are consistent over time but are not strictly comparable with the ratios for the other countries.

For the denominators – the population in each age group – the sources are a mixture of labour force surveys, administrative records and population censuses.

Source

OECD (2004), *OECD Employment Outlook*, OECD, Paris.

Further information

• *Analytical publications*

Evans, J. (2001), "Firms' Contribution to the Reconciliation Between Work and Family Life", *OECD Directorate for Employment, Labour and Social Affairs Working Paper*, No. 48, www.oecd.org/els/employment/workingpapers.

Jaumotte, F. (2003), "Female Labour Force Participation: Past Trends and Main Determinants in OECD Countries", *OECD Economics Department Working Paper*, No. 376, www.oecd.org/eco/working_papers.

OECD (2002-04), *Babies and Bosses – Reconciling Work and Family Life*, series, OECD, Paris. See Vol. I for Australia, Denmark and the Netherlands; Vol. II for Austria, Ireland and Japan; and Vol. III for New Zealand, Portugal and Switzerland.

OECD (n.d.), Putting More Women to Work: A Colloquium on Employment, Child Care and Taxes, www.oecd.org/employment/colloquium/women.

• *Statistical publications*

OECD (2004), *Labour Force Statistics*, OECD, Paris.
OECD (2004), *Quarterly Labour Force Statistics*, OECD, Paris.

• *Online databases*

SourceOECD Employment and Labour Markets.

• *Web sites*

Labour Force Statistics database: www.oecd.org/statistics/labour.

Long-term trends

Over the period shown in the tables, total employment rates (men and women) have fallen in 8 countries and risen in 22. Particularly large falls were recorded in Poland, Turkey, Sweden and Finland and particularly large increases occurred in Belgium, Spain, Netherlands and Ireland.

Growth in employment rates was very different for men and women. Employment rates for men decreased in 21 countries during the period with falls of 1% per year or more in Poland and Turkey. For women, on the other hand, employment rates grew in 23 countries with increases of 1% per year or more recorded for Belgium, Greece, Ireland, Italy, Luxembourg, Mexico, Netherlands and Spain.

Clearly, these differences in the growth of employment rates are leading to convergence in the rates for women and men although differences remain large in many countries.

LABOUR MARKET • EMPLOYMENT

EMPLOYMENT RATES BY GENDER

Employment rates: total
Share of persons of working age in employment

	1990	1991	1992	1993	1994	1995	1996	1997	1998	1999	2000	2001	2002	2003
Australia	67.9	65.5	64.7	64.1	65.7	67.5	67.3	66.3	67.4	67.8	69.2	68.7	69.2	69.3
Austria	..	..	..	..	68.3	68.6	67.7	67.7	67.7	68.2	68.2	68.1	65.8	68.7
Belgium	54.4	55.9	56.5	56.0	55.7	56.3	56.3	57.0	57.3	58.9	60.9	59.7	59.7	59.3
Canada	70.3	68.2	66.8	66.5	67.1	67.6	67.3	68.0	68.9	70.1	71.1	70.9	71.5	72.1
Czech Republic	..	..	..	69.0	69.2	69.4	69.3	68.7	67.5	65.9	65.2	65.3	65.7	64.9
Denmark	75.4	74.6	74.5	72.4	72.4	73.9	74.0	75.4	75.3	76.5	76.4	75.9	76.4	75.1
Finland	74.1	70.0	64.6	60.5	59.9	61.0	61.9	62.8	64.0	66.0	67.0	67.7	67.7	67.4
France	59.9	60.0	59.7	59.1	58.4	59.1	59.2	58.9	59.4	59.8	61.1	62.0	62.2	62.7
Germany	64.1	67.1	66.2	65.1	64.5	64.6	64.3	63.8	64.7	65.2	65.6	65.8	65.3	64.6
Greece	54.8	53.1	53.6	53.5	54.1	54.5	54.9	54.8	55.6	55.4	55.9	55.6	56.9	58.0
Hungary	..	..	58.0	54.5	53.5	52.9	52.7	52.8	53.8	55.7	56.0	56.2	56.2	57.0
Iceland	..	79.9	79.2	78.2	78.5	80.5	80.4	80.0	82.2	84.2	84.6	84.6	82.8	..
Ireland	52.1	51.2	50.7	50.9	51.9	54.1	55.0	56.3	59.6	62.5	64.5	65.0	65.0	65.0
Italy	52.6	52.6	52.3	52.5	51.5	51.2	51.4	51.6	52.2	52.9	53.9	54.9	55.6	56.2
Japan	68.6	69.2	69.6	69.5	69.3	69.2	69.5	70.0	69.5	68.9	68.9	68.8	68.2	68.4
Korea	61.2	61.7	61.9	61.8	62.8	63.5	63.7	63.7	59.2	59.6	61.5	62.1	63.3	63.0
Luxembourg	59.2	60.8	61.5	60.9	60.2	58.5	59.1	59.9	60.2	61.6	62.7	63.0	63.6	..
Mexico	..	58.0	58.7	59.3	58.7	58.2	59.1	61.0	61.3	61.2	60.9	60.1	60.1	59.6
Netherlands	61.8	62.9	63.8	63.8	63.9	65.1	66.2	68.1	69.8	71.3	72.1	72.8	73.2	72.7
New Zealand	67.3	65.5	65.3	66.0	67.8	70.0	71.1	70.5	69.5	70.0	70.7	71.8	72.4	72.5
Norway	73.0	72.1	71.6	71.3	72.2	73.5	75.3	77.0	78.3	78.0	77.9	77.5	77.1	75.9
Poland	..	..	59.9	58.9	58.3	58.1	58.4	58.8	58.9	57.5	55.0	53.5	51.7	51.4
Portugal	67.4	68.6	66.5	64.9	64.0	63.2	63.6	64.7	66.8	67.4	68.3	68.6	68.1	67.1
Slovak Republic	..	..	..	..	59.8	60.2	61.9	61.1	60.5	58.1	56.8	56.9	56.9	57.7
Spain	51.8	51.8	50.5	48.0	47.4	48.3	49.3	50.7	52.4	55.0	57.4	58.8	59.5	60.7
Sweden	83.1	81.0	77.3	72.6	71.5	72.2	71.6	70.7	71.5	72.9	74.2	75.3	74.9	74.3
Switzerland	..	78.2	78.0	77.3	76.1	76.7	77.0	76.9	78.0	78.4	78.3	79.1	78.9	77.8
Turkey	54.5	54.9	53.7	50.0	52.4	52.4	52.5	51.3	51.4	50.8	48.9	47.8	46.7	45.5
United Kingdom	72.5	70.9	69.1	68.3	68.8	69.3	69.9	70.8	71.2	71.7	72.4	72.8	72.7	72.9
United States	72.2	71.0	70.8	71.2	72.0	72.5	72.9	73.5	73.8	73.9	74.1	73.1	71.9	71.2
EU15	61.5	62.0	61.1	60.2	60.0	60.3	60.6	60.9	61.8	62.6	63.6	64.2	64.3	64.5
OECD total	65.6	65.0	64.3	63.9	64.1	64.3	64.6	65.0	65.2	65.4	65.7	65.5	65.1	64.9

StatLink: http://dx.doi.org/10.1787/885882710371

Employment rates: total
Average annual growth in percentage, 1990-2003

[Bar chart showing average annual growth from 1990-2003 by country, ordered from lowest to highest: Poland, Turkey, Sweden, Finland, Czech Republic, Slovak Republic, Hungary, United States, Portugal, Denmark, Japan, United Kingdom, Germany, Austria, Switzerland, Australia, Canada, Korea, Norway, Mexico, Iceland, France, Greece, Italy, New Zealand, Luxembourg, Belgium, Spain, Netherlands, Ireland]

StatLink: http://dx.doi.org/10.1787/465842176007

LABOUR MARKET • EMPLOYMENT

EMPLOYMENT RATES BY GENDER

Employment rates: men
Share of men of working age in employment

	1990	1991	1992	1993	1994	1995	1996	1997	1998	1999	2000	2001	2002	2003
Australia	78.5	74.8	73.7	73.1	74.8	76.1	75.9	74.7	75.3	76.2	76.6	75.9	76.4	76.4
Austria	..	..	..	..	77.5	78.1	77.0	76.8	76.6	77.0	76.8	76.2	72.8	76.0
Belgium	68.1	68.7	68.4	67.0	66.5	66.9	66.8	67.1	67.0	67.5	69.8	68.5	68.1	67.1
Canada	77.8	74.6	72.6	72.4	73.0	73.5	73.1	73.8	74.3	75.5	76.3	75.9	76.1	76.5
Czech Republic	..	..	..	77.6	77.5	77.9	78.1	77.4	76.3	74.3	73.6	73.6	74.2	73.4
Denmark	75.7	77.6	76.4	74.9	74.0	73.7	72.8	72.1	72.9	72.8	72.9	72.8	71.7	70.4
Finland	80.1	79.1	78.5	75.9	77.6	80.8	80.5	81.3	80.2	81.2	80.7	80.2	80.2	79.7
France	76.7	71.5	65.6	61.4	61.1	63.1	64.3	65.2	66.8	68.4	69.4	70.0	69.2	69.0
Germany	69.7	69.3	68.6	67.2	66.1	66.7	66.8	66.3	66.6	66.8	68.1	69.0	68.6	68.9
Greece	73.4	72.3	72.3	71.7	72.2	72.2	72.6	71.9	71.6	70.9	71.3	70.9	71.7	72.5
Hungary	..	..	64.0	60.0	59.6	60.2	60.2	60.3	60.6	62.6	62.7	63.0	62.9	63.4
Iceland	..	85.2	84.3	82.3	82.4	84.0	84.3	84.2	86.0	88.2	88.2	88.0	85.7	..
Ireland	67.5	66.0	64.2	63.5	64.8	66.7	66.6	67.8	71.0	73.5	75.6	76.0	74.7	74.5
Italy	69.2	68.9	68.3	69.3	67.8	67.0	66.9	66.8	67.1	67.6	68.2	68.7	69.2	69.7
Japan	81.3	81.6	82.2	82.3	81.9	81.9	82.1	82.4	81.7	81.0	80.9	80.5	79.9	79.8
Korea	73.9	75.0	75.5	75.2	76.3	76.8	76.7	76.2	71.3	71.3	73.1	73.5	74.9	75.0
Luxembourg	76.4	77.4	76.3	76.6	74.9	74.3	74.4	74.3	74.6	74.4	75.0	74.9	75.5	..
Mexico	..	84.1	84.2	84.3	82.9	81.0	82.7	84.4	84.7	84.6	84.0	83.4	82.6	82.0
Netherlands	75.7	76.0	76.3	75.2	74.9	76.0	76.9	78.4	79.9	80.8	81.4	81.6	81.5	80.2
New Zealand	76.1	73.7	73.3	74.3	76.1	78.5	79.0	78.5	77.1	77.3	78.0	78.9	79.6	79.3
Norway	78.6	77.1	76.4	75.8	76.8	78.1	80.0	81.7	82.8	82.1	81.7	81.1	80.2	78.8
Poland	..	..	66.9	65.9	64.9	64.7	65.2	66.1	65.8	63.6	61.2	59.2	57.0	56.7
Portugal	80.1	80.1	77.3	74.9	73.5	72.1	72.0	72.5	75.6	75.6	76.3	76.5	75.7	73.9
Slovak Republic	..	..	..	..	67.2	67.6	69.2	68.4	67.8	64.3	62.2	62.1	62.5	63.4
Spain	71.9	71.3	68.5	64.4	63.3	64.0	64.7	66.1	68.3	70.8	72.7	73.8	73.9	74.5
Sweden	85.2	82.7	78.3	73.1	72.3	73.5	73.2	72.4	73.5	74.8	76.1	77.0	76.3	75.6
Switzerland	..	90.0	88.9	88.2	86.6	87.4	86.8	85.9	87.2	87.2	87.3	87.6	86.1	84.9
Turkey	76.9	76.3	75.5	74.2	74.6	74.6	74.9	74.8	74.3	72.7	71.7	69.3	66.9	65.9
United Kingdom	82.1	79.6	76.3	74.8	75.3	76.1	76.4	77.5	78.1	78.4	79.1	79.3	78.9	79.3
United States	80.7	78.9	78.3	78.7	79.0	79.5	79.7	80.1	80.5	80.5	80.6	79.4	78.0	77.0
EU15	74.3	74.1	72.5	71.1	70.5	70.8	70.7	70.8	71.6	72.2	73.0	73.3	72.9	72.8
OECD total	77.5	77.4	76.1	75.6	75.4	75.5	75.7	76.0	76.1	76.1	76.3	75.8	75.1	74.7

StatLink: http://dx.doi.org/10.1787/704236721137

Employment rates: men
Average annual growth in percentage, 1990-2003

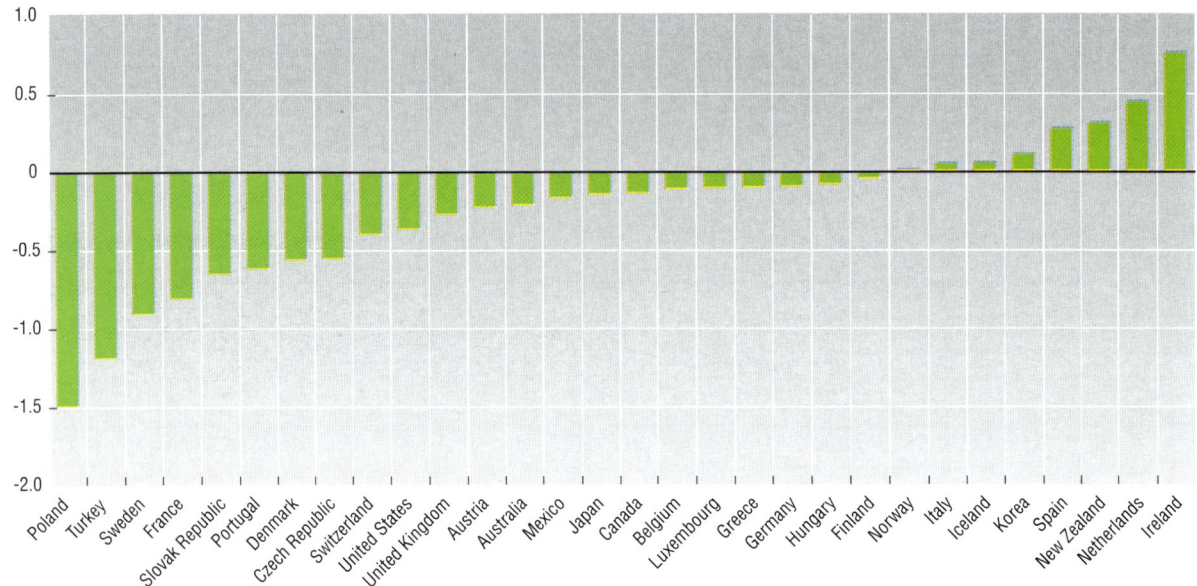

StatLink: http://dx.doi.org/10.1787/440202200150

LABOUR MARKET • EMPLOYMENT

EMPLOYMENT RATES BY GENDER

Employment rates: women
Share of women of working age in employment

	1990	1991	1992	1993	1994	1995	1996	1997	1998	1999	2000	2001	2002	2003
Australia	57.1	56.0	55.5	55.1	56.4	58.9	58.7	57.8	59.4	59.4	61.8	61.6	62.1	62.2
Austria	..	..	..	..	58.8	58.9	58.2	58.4	58.5	59.3	59.4	59.8	58.7	61.5
Belgium	40.8	43.0	44.6	44.9	44.8	45.4	45.6	46.7	47.5	50.2	51.9	50.7	51.1	51.4
Canada	62.7	61.8	61.0	60.6	61.1	61.7	61.5	62.2	63.6	64.7	65.8	66.0	66.8	67.7
Czech Republic	..	..	..	60.4	61.0	61.0	60.6	59.9	58.7	57.4	56.9	57.0	57.1	56.3
Denmark	70.6	70.1	70.4	68.7	67.1	67.0	67.4	69.4	70.3	71.6	72.1	71.4	72.6	70.5
Finland	71.5	68.4	63.7	59.6	58.8	58.9	59.4	60.4	61.2	63.5	64.5	65.4	66.1	65.7
France	50.3	50.8	50.8	51.1	50.8	51.6	51.8	51.7	52.4	53.0	54.3	55.2	55.8	56.7
Germany	52.2	56.3	55.7	55.1	54.7	55.3	55.5	55.3	56.3	57.4	58.1	58.7	58.8	58.7
Greece	37.5	34.9	36.2	36.4	37.1	38.0	38.5	39.1	40.3	40.7	41.3	41.2	42.7	44.0
Hungary	..	..	52.3	49.3	47.8	45.9	45.5	45.5	47.3	49.0	49.6	49.8	49.8	50.9
Iceland	..	74.5	74.0	74.0	74.6	76.8	76.5	75.6	78.3	80.2	81.0	81.1	79.8	..
Ireland	36.6	36.3	37.1	38.2	38.9	41.5	43.3	44.7	48.2	51.3	53.3	54.0	55.2	55.4
Italy	36.2	36.5	36.5	35.8	35.4	35.4	36.0	36.4	37.3	38.3	39.6	41.1	42.0	42.7
Japan	55.8	56.6	56.9	56.6	56.5	56.4	56.8	57.6	57.2	56.7	56.7	57.0	56.5	56.8
Korea	49.0	48.8	48.7	48.8	49.8	50.5	51.1	51.6	47.3	48.1	50.1	51.0	52.0	51.1
Luxembourg	41.4	43.6	46.2	44.8	44.9	42.2	43.6	45.4	45.6	48.5	50.0	50.8	51.5	..
Mexico	..	34.2	35.1	36.0	36.2	37.0	37.4	39.9	40.1	39.8	40.1	39.4	39.9	39.4
Netherlands	47.5	49.3	51.0	52.0	52.6	53.9	55.2	57.6	59.4	61.6	62.6	63.9	64.7	64.9
New Zealand	58.6	57.5	57.3	57.8	59.7	61.7	63.4	62.7	62.1	63.0	63.5	64.8	65.4	65.8
Norway	67.2	67.0	66.7	66.6	67.5	68.8	70.4	72.2	73.6	73.8	74.0	73.8	73.9	72.9
Poland	..	..	53.1	52.1	51.9	51.8	51.8	51.8	52.2	51.6	48.9	47.8	46.4	46.2
Portugal	55.4	57.6	56.1	55.3	55.0	54.8	55.6	57.2	58.3	59.5	60.5	61.0	60.8	60.6
Slovak Republic	..	..	..	..	52.6	53.0	54.6	54.0	53.5	52.1	51.5	51.8	52.1	52.2
Spain	31.8	32.5	32.5	31.5	31.5	32.5	33.8	35.2	36.5	39.1	42.0	43.8	44.9	46.8
Sweden	81.0	79.3	76.3	72.1	70.7	70.8	69.9	68.9	69.4	70.9	72.2	73.5	73.4	72.8
Switzerland	..	66.4	67.0	66.5	65.6	66.0	67.2	67.8	68.8	69.6	69.3	70.6	71.6	70.6
Turkey	32.9	33.7	31.9	25.8	30.4	30.2	30.3	28.0	28.5	28.9	26.2	26.3	26.6	25.2
United Kingdom	62.8	62.2	61.9	61.8	62.1	62.5	63.3	64.1	64.2	64.9	65.5	66.1	66.3	66.4
United States	64.0	63.3	63.6	64.0	65.2	65.8	66.3	67.1	67.4	67.6	67.8	67.1	66.1	65.7
EU15	48.7	49.9	49.7	49.3	49.4	49.9	50.4	50.9	51.8	53.0	54.2	55.1	55.6	56.1
OECD total	53.9	52.8	52.7	52.4	52.9	53.3	53.7	54.2	54.5	54.9	55.3	55.4	55.3	55.3

StatLink: http://dx.doi.org/10.1787/522260866753

Employment rates: women
Average annual growth in percentage, 1990-2003

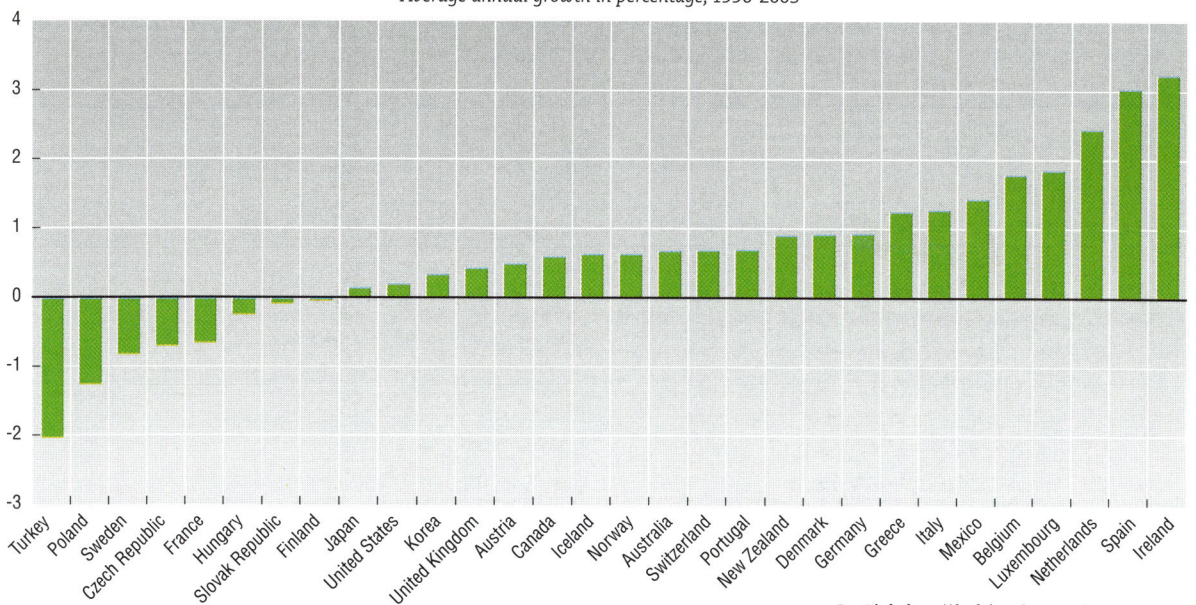

StatLink: http://dx.doi.org/10.1787/788314387318

LABOUR MARKET • EMPLOYMENT

EMPLOYMENT RATES BY AGE GROUP

These rates show the percentage of persons of working age who are in employment, broken down into three age groups. The youngest age group contains persons who are just entering the labour market, the second group those in their prime working lives, and the third group those who are approaching retirement.

Employment rates in these different age groups are significantly affected by government policies with regard to higher education, pensions and retirement age.

Definition

To calculate the employment rate for a given age group, the total population in that age group is divided between those in employment and those who are not. The numbers in employment are then expressed as a percentage of the total numbers in that age group.

Employment is generally measured through household labour force surveys and, according to the *ILO Guidelines*, employed persons are defined as those aged 15 or over who report that they have worked in gainful employment for at least one hour in the previous week. Those not in employment consist of persons who are out of work but seeking employment, students and all others who have excluded themselves from the labour force for one reason or another, such as incapacity or the need to look after young children or elderly relatives.

Comparability

All OECD countries except Iceland, Mexico and Turkey use the *ILO Guidelines* for measuring employment. For the three countries that do not do so, employment rates are consistent over time but are not strictly comparable with the ratios for the other countries.

For the denominators – the population in each age group – the sources are a mixture of labour force surveys, administrative records and population censuses.

Long-term trends

In general, employment rates for those in the prime age group – 25 to 54 – are very similar between countries with ratios for most countries over 70% in 2003. Rates are most variable between countries for those in the youngest age group where, in 2003, they ranged from under 30% in Poland, Italy, Greece, Hungary, Belgium and the Slovak Republic to over 60% in Switzerland and the Netherlands. Employment rates for the oldest age group also vary considerably between countries with nearly 70% of this age group in employment in 2003 in Norway and Sweden but less than 30% employed in the Slovak Republic, Belgium, Poland and Hungary.

Over the period shown in the tables, employment rates for the youngest age group have been falling for the OECD as a whole. This partly reflects government policies to encourage young people to enter tertiary education, but the falls have been most marked countries where total employment rates have been falling, such as the Czech Republic, Poland and Turkey; when the labour market is tight, young people have particular difficulties in finding employment. For those in the prime working age group – 25 to 54 – employment rates have remained stable for the OECD as a whole, but there were significant falls in the employment rates for Poland, Sweden and Turkey and large gains in Ireland, the Netherlands and Spain. Persons in the top age group have fared particularly well overall, with the largest increases in employment rates for Belgium, the Czech Republic, Netherlands and New Zealand.

Source

OECD (2004), *OECD Employment Outlook*, OECD, Paris.

Further information
• *Analytical publications*

Burniaux, J.-M., R. Duval and F. Jaumotte (2003), "Coping with Ageing: A Dynamic Approach to Quantify the Impact of Alternative Policy Options on Future Labour Supply in OECD Countries", *OECD Economics Department Working Paper*, No. 371 OECD, Paris, www.oecd.org/eco/working_papers.

OECD (2000), *From Initial Education to Working Life: Making Transitions Work*, OECD, Paris.

OECD (2004), *Ageing and Employment Policies*, series, OECD, Paris.

OECD (2004), NERO Meeting on Labour Market Issues, Paris, 25 June, www.oecd.org/eco/nero.

• *Statistical publications*

OECD (2004), *Labour Force Statistics*, OECD, Paris.

OECD (2004), *Quarterly Labour Force Statistics*, OECD, Paris.

• *Web sites*

OECD Ageing and Employment Policies: www.oecd.org/els/employment/olderworkers.

Youth Employment Summit: www.yesweb.org.

Labour Force Statistics database: www.oecd.org/statistics/labour.

LABOUR MARKET • EMPLOYMENT

EMPLOYMENT RATES BY AGE GROUP

Employment rates for age group 15-24
Persons in employment as a percentage of population in that age group

	1990	1991	1992	1993	1994	1995	1996	1997	1998	1999	2000	2001	2002	2003
Australia	61.1	56.0	55.0	54.4	57.3	59.5	59.7	56.2	58.0	59.3	60.4	60.1	59.6	59.9
Austria	..	..	..	..	59.5	57.3	55.7	54.8	54.1	54.0	53.1	52.0	48.7	51.5
Belgium	30.4	31.4	31.4	28.1	27.5	26.6	26.1	25.2	26.0	25.5	30.3	28.5	28.5	27.1
Canada	61.1	57.3	54.9	53.5	53.8	53.9	52.1	51.5	52.5	54.6	56.3	56.4	57.3	57.8
Czech Republic	..	..	..	46.9	47.5	46.6	45.8	44.2	43.0	40.1	38.3	36.1	33.7	31.4
Denmark	65.0	64.8	63.1	60.3	62.1	65.9	66.0	68.2	66.4	66.0	67.1	61.7	64.0	59.4
Finland	52.2	44.6	35.3	30.1	27.9	29.0	29.8	33.3	34.9	38.8	39.8	40.3	39.4	38.5
France	29.5	27.5	26.7	24.2	22.0	21.8	21.3	19.9	20.8	20.7	23.2	24.3	24.1	29.8
Germany	56.4	57.5	55.2	52.7	51.4	49.1	47.0	45.8	46.7	47.1	47.2	47.0	44.8	42.4
Greece	30.3	29.1	28.4	27.5	26.7	26.5	25.4	24.5	28.1	26.8	26.9	26.0	27.0	26.3
Hungary	..	..	35.4	31.5	30.8	31.3	30.4	31.4	35.3	35.7	32.5	30.7	28.5	26.7
Iceland	..	56.6	54.5	52.4	51.7	54.9	54.8	55.7	61.6	65.1	68.2	66.8	59.4	..
Ireland	41.4	38.1	35.9	34.4	33.6	37.3	36.4	38.3	43.0	46.4	48.2	47.0	45.3	45.8
Italy	29.8	29.2	27.8	30.0	28.3	27.3	26.9	27.0	27.2	27.3	27.8	27.4	26.7	26.0
Japan	42.2	43.4	44.6	44.8	45.0	44.7	45.0	45.3	44.6	42.9	42.7	42.0	41.0	40.3
Korea	32.5	34.6	34.6	33.6	34.5	34.6	33.7	32.2	27.1	27.6	29.4	30.1	31.5	30.8
Luxembourg	43.3	51.9	49.3	45.7	42.8	38.2	36.9	34.7	33.1	31.7	31.9	32.3	32.3	..
Mexico	..	49.3	50.5	51.6	50.3	48.6	48.9	49.7	50.9	50.5	49.6	47.7	46.0	44.7
Netherlands	54.5	55.6	56.9	55.5	55.4	56.3	58.3	61.1	62.4	66.0	66.5	67.0	66.9	65.4
New Zealand	58.3	54.3	53.1	53.4	56.2	59.4	59.4	58.1	55.7	54.6	54.7	56.0	56.8	56.6
Norway	53.4	50.3	48.9	47.8	48.4	49.2	52.3	55.1	57.9	57.8	58.1	56.5	56.9	55.3
Poland	..	..	32.3	29.5	28.0	27.3	27.9	28.8	28.7	24.3	24.5	22.1	20.0	19.6
Portugal	54.8	53.5	48.0	43.1	40.5	37.6	37.1	39.2	42.8	42.6	42.0	42.7	41.9	38.4
Slovak Republic	..	..	..	..	34.4	34.8	36.8	36.4	35.0	31.0	29.0	27.9	27.2	27.6
Spain	38.3	37.8	34.8	29.5	28.3	28.6	28.3	29.4	31.0	34.4	36.3	37.1	36.6	36.8
Sweden	66.0	60.6	52.1	42.5	41.4	42.3	40.3	39.6	41.6	43.8	46.1	47.9	46.5	45.1
Switzerland	..	69.3	67.5	67.9	63.9	62.6	63.3	62.9	63.3	64.7	65.0	64.0	65.3	63.2
Turkey	45.9	46.9	44.3	39.5	43.0	41.0	42.0	40.3	39.5	39.7	37.0	35.3	33.0	30.5
United Kingdom	70.1	66.0	61.5	58.9	58.9	59.0	60.2	60.9	60.8	60.7	61.5	61.1	61.0	59.8
United States	59.8	57.2	56.7	57.2	58.1	58.3	57.6	58.0	59.0	59.0	59.7	57.7	55.7	53.9
EU15	45.2	44.3	41.9	39.9	39.0	38.4	37.9	37.9	38.9	39.6	40.8	40.9	40.3	40.3
OECD total	48.8	48.1	46.6	45.7	45.7	45.2	45.0	45.0	45.4	45.4	45.7	44.8	43.7	42.9

StatLink: http://dx.doi.org/10.1787/273337273032

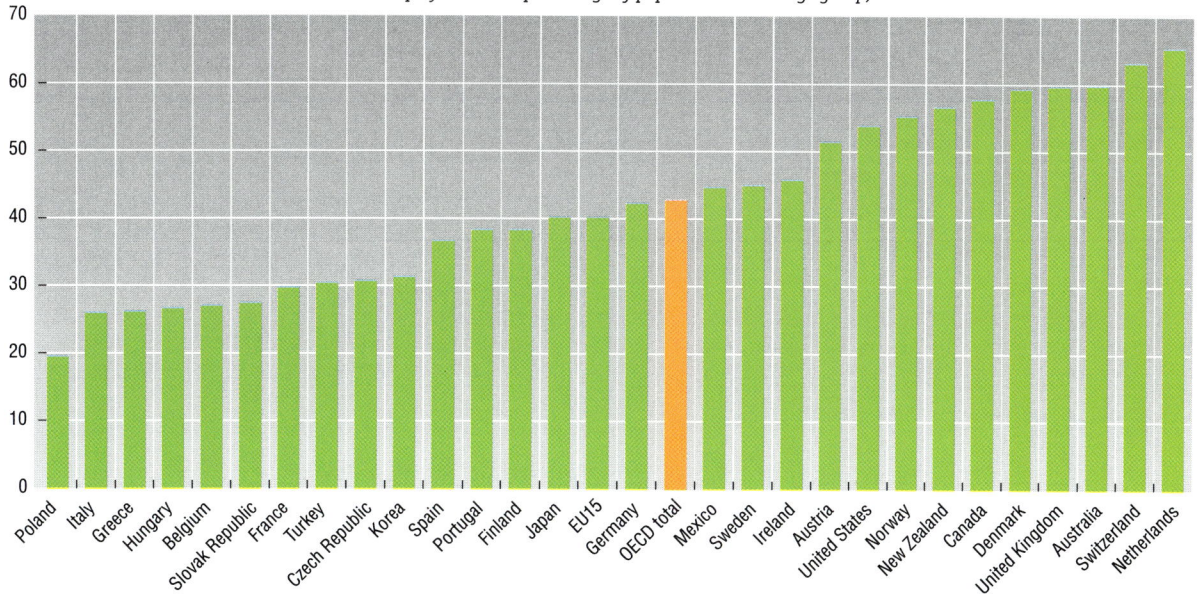

Employment rates for age group 15-24
Persons in employment as a percentage of population in that age group, 2003

StatLink: http://dx.doi.org/10.1787/821625416275

LABOUR MARKET • EMPLOYMENT

EMPLOYMENT RATES BY AGE GROUP

Employment rates for age group 25-54
Persons in employment as a percentage of population in that age group

	1990	1991	1992	1993	1994	1995	1996	1997	1998	1999	2000	2001	2002	2003
Australia	75.8	74.2	73.3	72.8	73.6	75.3	74.7	74.4	75.1	75.3	76.6	76.3	77.1	76.9
Austria	..	..	..	..	79.5	80.4	80.1	80.6	80.7	81.6	82.2	82.4	80.1	83.7
Belgium	71.7	73.2	73.6	73.6	73.1	73.7	73.9	74.6	74.4	76.4	77.9	77.6	76.6	76.1
Canada	78.0	76.3	74.9	74.9	75.5	76.3	76.1	77.3	78.3	79.2	79.9	79.8	80.2	80.6
Czech Republic	..	..	..	86.3	86.3	86.3	85.8	85.0	83.7	81.9	81.6	82.1	82.5	81.7
Denmark	84.0	83.1	83.1	80.8	80.5	81.7	82.2	82.8	83.4	84.4	84.3	84.5	84.8	83.5
Finland	87.9	84.0	79.2	74.9	74.9	76.0	76.8	77.5	78.9	80.3	80.9	81.5	81.6	81.1
France	77.4	77.9	77.4	77.0	76.3	77.0	76.9	76.4	76.8	77.0	78.3	79.3	79.4	79.3
Germany	73.6	78.8	77.7	76.8	76.2	76.8	76.8	76.7	78.0	78.7	79.3	79.3	78.8	78.2
Greece	68.5	66.6	67.6	67.8	68.6	68.8	69.5	69.7	69.9	70.0	70.2	70.4	71.5	72.6
Hungary	..	..	75.7	72.5	71.7	70.7	70.4	70.2	70.3	72.3	73.0	73.1	73.0	73.7
Iceland	..	88.1	88.0	87.0	87.5	89.1	89.3	88.2	88.9	90.9	90.6	90.7	90.0	..
Ireland	60.0	59.8	60.1	60.9	62.7	64.7	66.3	67.4	70.6	73.2	75.3	76.4	76.6	76.0
Italy	68.2	68.4	68.3	66.7	65.8	65.5	65.7	65.8	66.3	67.1	68.0	69.2	70.1	70.8
Japan	79.6	79.9	80.2	79.8	79.5	79.3	79.6	79.9	79.3	78.7	78.6	78.6	78.0	78.3
Korea	73.2	73.4	73.1	73.0	73.6	74.2	74.7	74.8	70.2	70.3	72.2	72.6	73.4	73.1
Luxembourg	71.8	72.9	74.1	73.3	73.5	71.9	73.2	74.4	74.7	76.7	78.2	78.7	79.1	..
Mexico	..	64.4	64.7	65.1	65.0	65.1	66.2	68.5	68.4	67.9	68.3	67.8	68.4	68.1
Netherlands	71.2	72.7	73.3	73.8	73.7	75.0	75.8	77.5	79.3	80.4	81.1	81.9	81.9	82.1
New Zealand	76.3	74.9	74.7	74.9	76.1	77.6	78.4	77.8	76.8	77.6	78.6	79.3	79.7	79.8
Norway	82.2	81.7	81.2	80.7	81.3	82.4	83.7	85.0	85.8	85.5	85.3	85.1	84.4	83.0
Poland	..	..	74.8	74.4	73.8	74.2	74.6	74.7	75.0	73.7	70.9	69.3	67.5	67.6
Portugal	78.4	80.2	79.6	79.5	78.7	78.7	78.7	79.3	80.1	80.6	81.8	82.2	81.6	81.0
Slovak Republic	..	..	..	..	78.4	78.7	80.3	79.3	78.5	76.1	74.7	74.8	75.1	76.0
Spain	61.4	61.7	60.5	58.7	58.4	59.5	60.6	62.0	63.6	66.1	68.4	69.5	70.1	71.3
Sweden	91.6	89.9	86.9	83.2	81.9	82.6	81.8	80.7	81.3	82.6	83.8	84.6	84.2	83.5
Switzerland	..	84.5	84.3	83.2	82.8	83.8	83.6	83.4	84.9	85.2	85.4	86.1	86.0	84.8
Turkey	61.6	61.5	61.0	58.0	59.8	60.5	60.1	59.0	59.2	58.2	56.7	55.5	54.6	54.0
United Kingdom	79.1	77.8	76.7	76.3	76.6	77.2	77.5	78.5	79.1	79.7	80.4	80.7	80.6	80.9
United States	79.7	78.6	78.3	78.5	79.2	79.8	80.2	80.9	81.1	81.4	81.5	80.5	79.3	78.8
EU15	73.4	74.6	73.9	73.0	72.7	73.2	73.5	73.8	74.6	75.5	76.5	77.0	77.0	77.2
OECD total	75.8	75.2	74.8	74.4	74.5	74.9	75.2	75.6	75.7	75.8	76.1	75.9	75.5	75.3

StatLink: http://dx.doi.org/10.1787/234218537843

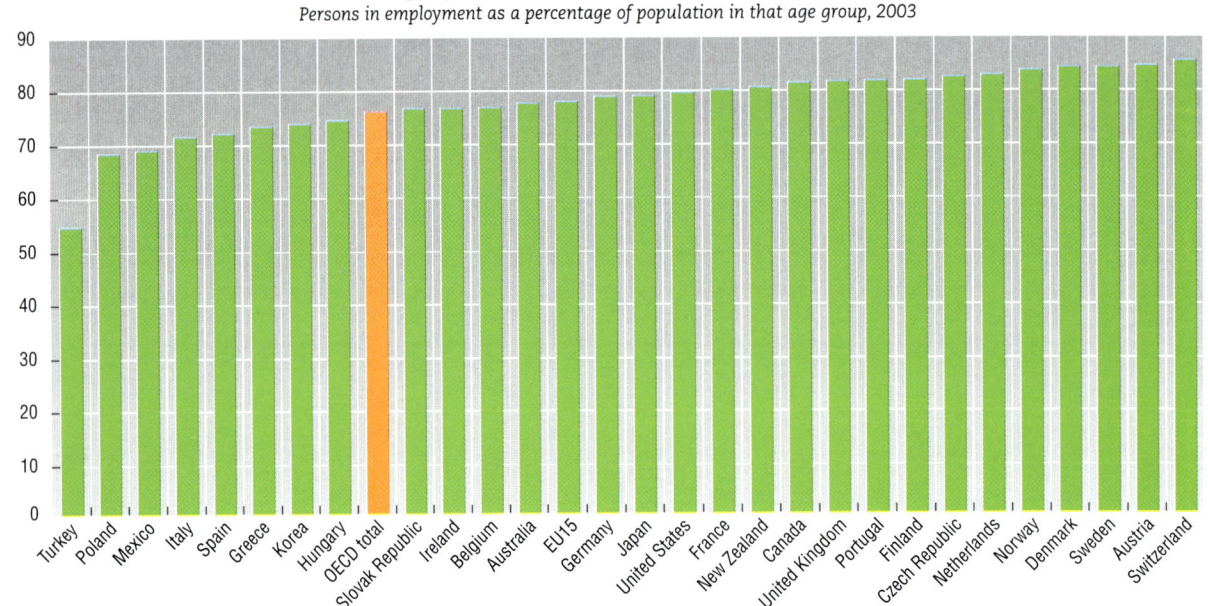

Employment rates for age group 25-54
Persons in employment as a percentage of population in that age group, 2003

StatLink: http://dx.doi.org/10.1787/002540880066

LABOUR MARKET • EMPLOYMENT

EMPLOYMENT RATES BY AGE GROUP

Employment rates for age group 55-64
Persons in employment as a percentage of population in that age group

	1990	1991	1992	1993	1994	1995	1996	1997	1998	1999	2000	2001	2002	2003
Australia	41.8	39.3	38.9	37.6	39.9	41.4	42.3	41.9	43.8	44.3	46.9	46.3	48.2	50.1
Austria	..	..	..	..	28.4	30.4	29.2	28.6	29.0	29.6	28.1	28.2	27.6	30.1
Belgium	21.4	21.6	22.4	21.9	22.4	23.3	21.8	22.0	22.5	24.7	25.0	25.2	25.8	28.1
Canada	46.3	44.5	43.9	43.2	43.8	43.4	43.5	44.5	45.3	46.9	48.4	48.3	50.4	53.0
Czech Republic	..	..	..	31.3	32.3	34.8	37.3	38.3	37.1	37.5	36.3	37.1	40.8	42.3
Denmark	53.6	51.7	52.3	51.3	50.2	49.3	47.5	51.4	50.4	54.2	54.6	56.5	57.3	60.7
Finland	42.8	40.6	37.3	34.8	33.5	34.4	35.6	35.7	36.2	39.2	42.3	45.9	47.8	49.9
France	35.6	34.8	33.9	33.9	33.4	33.5	33.5	33.6	33.0	34.2	34.3	36.5	39.3	36.8
Germany	36.8	35.9	35.9	35.9	35.9	37.4	38.0	38.3	38.4	37.8	37.6	37.9	38.6	39.0
Greece	40.8	39.0	39.4	38.8	39.5	40.5	40.7	40.7	39.1	38.4	39.0	38.0	39.2	41.9
Hungary	..	..	22.9	19.1	17.0	17.1	17.4	17.3	16.6	19.4	21.9	23.5	25.6	29.0
Iceland	..	85.4	83.0	83.2	84.7	85.1	83.8	83.7	86.7	85.9	84.2	85.6	87.2	..
Ireland	38.6	38.9	38.3	38.9	39.5	39.4	40.3	40.2	41.6	43.8	45.2	46.6	48.0	49.3
Italy	32.6	32.1	31.4	30.4	29.4	28.4	28.7	28.0	27.9	27.6	27.7	28.0	28.9	30.3
Japan	62.9	64.4	64.6	64.5	63.7	63.7	63.6	64.2	63.8	63.4	62.8	62.0	61.6	62.1
Korea	61.9	61.2	62.2	61.5	62.9	63.6	63.2	63.8	58.7	58.2	57.8	58.3	59.5	57.8
Luxembourg	28.2	23.2	24.7	26.1	23.2	24.0	22.6	23.7	25.0	26.3	27.2	24.8	27.9	..
Mexico	..	54.1	53.9	53.8	52.4	50.4	52.1	54.8	53.6	55.0	52.8	52.1	53.1	53.8
Netherlands	29.7	28.0	28.7	28.2	29.0	29.4	30.5	31.7	33.4	35.1	37.9	38.8	41.8	43.5
New Zealand	41.8	41.6	41.8	44.7	47.4	50.4	53.9	54.5	55.7	56.9	57.2	60.7	63.4	64.4
Norway	61.5	61.2	60.9	60.7	61.6	63.1	64.6	66.0	67.2	67.3	67.1	67.4	68.4	68.8
Poland	..	..	35.4	35.1	34.4	33.8	33.0	33.6	32.3	32.5	28.4	29.0	27.9	28.6
Portugal	47.0	49.3	47.2	44.9	45.9	44.6	46.2	47.1	49.7	50.4	50.8	50.0	50.9	51.1
Slovak Republic	..	..	..	..	21.3	21.7	22.8	21.4	22.8	22.3	21.3	22.3	22.9	24.6
Spain	36.9	36.4	36.1	34.5	32.7	32.4	33.2	34.1	35.1	35.1	37.0	39.2	39.7	40.8
Sweden	69.4	69.3	67.0	63.3	61.9	61.9	63.4	62.7	63.0	64.0	65.1	67.0	68.3	69.0
Switzerland	..	63.1	63.7	63.3	61.6	62.0	63.5	63.8	64.5	64.7	63.3	67.1	64.8	65.6
Turkey	42.8	43.4	42.4	37.7	40.8	41.7	41.6	40.5	41.1	39.3	36.4	35.9	35.3	32.7
United Kingdom	49.2	49.0	47.7	46.5	47.4	47.5	47.8	48.5	48.3	49.4	50.5	52.2	53.3	55.5
United States	54.0	53.2	53.4	53.8	54.4	55.1	55.9	57.2	57.7	57.7	57.8	58.6	59.5	59.9
EU15	38.5	37.8	37.2	36.5	36.1	36.4	36.8	37.1	37.3	37.7	38.3	39.3	40.6	41.5
OECD total	48.0	47.8	46.9	46.3	46.1	46.4	46.9	47.7	47.7	48.0	47.9	48.5	49.4	50.1

StatLink: http://dx.doi.org/10.1787/001772041701

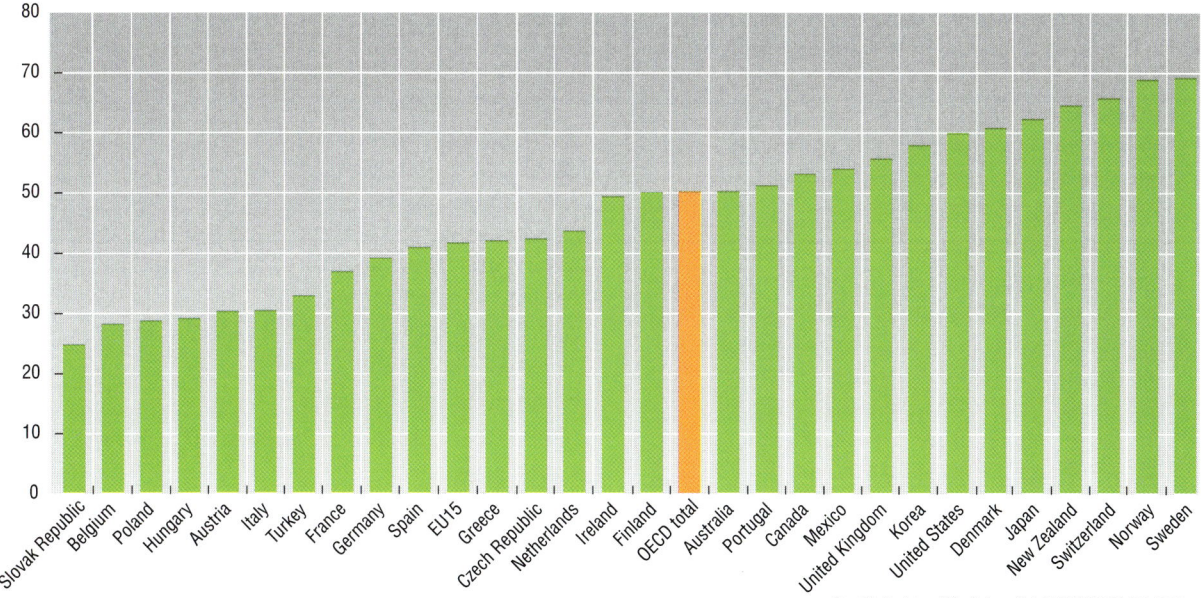

Employment rates for age group 55-64
Persons in employment as a percentage of population in that age group, 2003

StatLink: http://dx.doi.org/10.1787/173214111608

LABOUR MARKET • EMPLOYMENT

PART-TIME EMPLOYMENT

Part-time work accounted for a substantial share of overall employment growth in many OECD countries between 1990 and 2003. Part-time work has been an important factor behind employment growth of groups that are often under-represented in the labour force, such as women, youths and, to a lesser extent, older workers.

Recent surveys in a large number of OECD countries show that most people who work part-time do so from choice. This suggests that countries with little part-time employment could foster increased employment by policies that promote the availability of part-time positions. This would particularly benefit women with young children.

Definition

Part-time employment refers to persons who usually work less than 30 hours per week in their main job. Both employees and the self-employed may be part-time workers.

Employment is generally measured through household labour force surveys and, according to the *ILO Guidelines*, employed persons are defined as those aged 15 or over who report that they have worked in gainful employment for at least one hour in the previous week. The rates shown here refer to the numbers of persons who usually work less than 30 hours per week as a percentage of the total number of those in employment.

Comparability

All OECD countries except Iceland, Mexico and Turkey use the *ILO Guidelines* for measuring employment. For the three countries that do not do so, employment rates are consistent over time but are not strictly comparable with the ratios for the other countries. Information on the number of hours worked is collected in household labour force surveys and the rates shown here are considered to be of good comparability.

Long-term trends

For the OECD as a whole, part-time employment increased by about one third between 1990 and 2003. Part-time employment rates grew considerably in Finland, Ireland, Korea, Luxembourg and Spain but they also fell in several countries including Denmark, Greece, Mexico and, particularly, Turkey.

The chart shows great variation between countries in part-time employment in 2003. For Switzerland, Japan, Australia and Netherlands, over 25% of all those in employment were working part-time while part-time employment rates were under 10% in the Slovak Republic, Czech Republic, Hungary, Greece, Turkey, Korea and Spain. The average rate of part-time employment for the OECD as a whole was 15% in 2003 and was slightly higher in the countries of the European Union.

Source

OECD (2004), *OECD Employment Outlook*, OECD, Paris.

Further information

• **Analytical publications**

OECD (1999), *Implementing the OECD Jobs Strategy: Assessing Performance and Policy*, OECD, Paris.

OECD (2002-04), *Babies and Bosses – Reconciling Work and Family Life*, series, OECD, Paris. See Vol. I for Australia, Denmark and the Netherlands; Vol. II for Austria, Ireland and Japan; and Vol. III for New Zealand, Portugal and Switzerland.

OECD (2003), *The Sources of Economic Growth in OECD Countries*, OECD, Paris.

• **Statistical publications**

OECD (2004), *Labour Force Statistics*, OECD, Paris.

• **Web sites**

OECD Productivity Database: *www.oecd.org/statistics/productivity*.

Labour Force Statistics database: *www.oecd.org/statistics/labour*.

LABOUR MARKET • EMPLOYMENT

PART-TIME EMPLOYMENT

Part-time employment rates
As a percentage of total employment

	1990	1991	1992	1993	1994	1995	1996	1997	1998	1999	2000	2001	2002	2003
Australia	22.6	23.9	24.9	24.3	24.4	25.0	25.2	26.0	25.9	26.1	26.2	27.2	27.5	27.9
Austria	..	..	..	..	..	11.1	10.9	10.8	11.5	12.3	12.2	12.4	13.5	13.6
Belgium	13.5	14.6	14.3	14.7	14.6	14.6	14.8	15.0	15.6	19.9	19.0	17.0	17.2	17.7
Canada	17.1	18.3	18.7	19.3	19.0	18.9	19.2	19.1	18.9	18.5	18.1	18.1	18.1	18.8
Czech Republic	..	..	..	3.6	3.6	3.5	3.4	3.4	3.3	3.4	3.2	3.2	2.9	3.2
Denmark	19.2	18.7	18.9	19.0	17.3	16.9	16.6	17.2	17.1	15.3	16.1	14.7	16.2	15.8
Finland	7.6	7.9	8.2	8.9	8.9	8.7	8.5	9.3	9.7	9.9	10.4	10.5	11.0	11.3
France	12.2	12.0	12.6	13.2	13.8	14.2	14.0	14.8	14.7	14.6	14.2	13.8	13.7	12.9
Germany	13.4	11.8	12.3	12.8	13.5	14.2	14.9	15.8	16.6	17.1	17.6	18.3	18.8	19.6
Greece	6.7	6.9	7.2	7.1	7.8	7.8	8.0	8.3	9.1	8.0	5.5	4.9	5.6	5.6
Hungary	..	..	..	..	..	3.2	3.1	3.3	3.4	3.5	3.2	2.8	2.9	3.5
Iceland	..	22.2	22.1	22.4	22.6	22.5	20.9	22.4	23.2	21.2	20.4	20.4	20.1	..
Ireland	10.0	10.4	11.3	13.1	13.5	14.3	14.2	15.0	17.6	17.9	18.1	17.9	18.1	18.1
Italy	8.9	9.0	10.0	10.0	10.0	10.5	10.5	11.3	11.2	11.8	12.2	12.2	11.9	12.0
Japan	19.2	20.0	20.4	21.1	21.4	20.1	21.8	23.3	23.6	24.1	22.6	24.9	25.1	26.0
Korea	4.5	4.5	4.8	4.5	4.5	4.3	4.3	5.0	6.7	7.7	7.0	7.3	7.6	7.7
Luxembourg	7.6	8.8	9.5	9.9	10.7	11.3	10.4	11.0	12.6	12.1	12.4	13.3	12.6	..
Mexico	..	..	..	..	..	16.6	14.9	15.5	15.0	13.7	13.5	13.7	13.5	13.4
Netherlands	28.2	28.6	27.3	27.9	28.9	29.4	29.3	29.1	30.0	30.4	32.1	33.0	33.9	34.5
New Zealand	19.6	20.6	21.0	20.6	21.0	21.0	21.9	22.4	22.8	23.0	22.3	22.4	22.6	22.3
Norway	21.8	22.0	22.1	22.0	21.5	21.4	21.6	21.0	20.8	20.7	20.2	20.1	20.6	21.0
Poland	..	..	..	..	..	..	..	11.9	11.8	14.0	12.8	11.6	11.7	11.5
Portugal	7.6	8.8	8.8	8.8	9.5	8.6	9.2	10.2	10.0	9.4	9.4	9.2	9.6	10.0
Slovak Republic	..	..	..	..	2.7	2.3	2.1	2.0	2.0	1.8	1.9	1.9	1.6	2.3
Spain	4.6	4.4	5.3	6.0	6.4	7.0	7.5	7.9	7.7	7.8	7.7	7.8	7.6	7.8
Sweden	14.5	14.6	15.0	15.4	15.8	15.1	14.8	14.2	13.5	14.5	14.0	13.9	13.8	14.1
Switzerland	..	22.1	22.7	23.2	23.2	22.9	23.7	24.0	24.2	24.8	24.4	24.8	24.7	25.1
Turkey	9.2	11.2	11.6	8.9	8.8	6.4	5.4	6.1	6.0	7.7	9.4	6.2	6.6	6.0
United Kingdom	20.1	20.7	21.5	22.1	22.4	22.3	22.9	22.9	23.0	22.9	23.0	22.7	23.0	23.3
United States	14.1	14.7	14.7	14.8	14.2	14.0	13.9	13.5	13.4	13.3	12.6	12.8	13.1	13.2
EU15	13.3	13.1	13.6	14.1	14.6	14.8	15.1	15.6	15.9	16.1	16.2	16.2	16.4	16.6
OECD total	11.1	11.4	11.7	11.6	11.6	11.9	11.8	12.0	12.1	12.3	12.2	12.2	14.6	14.8

StatLink: http://dx.doi.org/10.1787/828714187326

Part-time employment rates
As a percentage of total employment, 2003

StatLink: http://dx.doi.org/10.1787/538827156348

LABOUR MARKET • EMPLOYMENT

SELF-EMPLOYMENT

Self-employment may be seen either as a survival strategy for those who cannot find any other means of earning an income or as evidence of entrepreneurial spirit and a desire to be one's own boss. The self employment rates shown in this section reflect these various motives.

Definition

Employment is generally measured through household labour force surveys and, according to the *ILO Guidelines*, employed persons are defined as those aged 15 or over who report that they have worked in gainful employment for at least one hour in the previous week.

Long-term trends

In 2003, the total self-employment rates (men and women together) ranged from under 8% in Luxembourg, Norway and the United States to over one third in Korea, Mexico and Turkey. In general, self-employment rates are highest in countries with low per capita income although Italy, with a self-employment rate of 27.5%, is a striking exception. Ireland and Spain are also countries with both high per capita incomes and high self-employment rates.

Over the period shown in the table, self-employment rates have been falling in most countries although there have been small increases in Canada, Germany, Iceland and Switzerland and much larger increases in the Czech Republic, Mexico, and Slovak Republic.

The levels and changes in total self-employment rates conceal significant differences between men and women. In more than half of the countries, over 15% of all men in employment were self-employed; the corresponding figure for women was under 10% (figures for 2003).

Growth rates have also differed. Self-employment rates for men rose in ten countries – by small amounts in Belgium, Canada, Italy, Mexico, Portugal, Sweden and Switzerland and by significant amounts in Czech Republic, Germany and the Slovak Republic. For women, self-employment grew only in five countries – marginally in Canada and Portugal and by larger amounts in the Czech Republic, Mexico and the Slovak Republic.

Self-employed persons include employers, own-account workers, members of producers' co-operatives, and unpaid family workers. The last of these are unpaid in the sense that they do not have a formal contract to receive a fixed amount of income at regular intervals but they share in the income generated by the enterprise; unpaid family workers are particularly important in farming and retail trade. Note that all persons who work in corporate enterprises, including company directors, are considered to be employees.

The rates shown here are the percentages of the self-employed in total civilian employment *i.e.*, total employment less military employees.

Comparability

All OECD countries except Iceland, Mexico and Turkey use the *ILO Guidelines* for measuring employment. For the three countries that do not do so, employment rates are consistent over time but are not strictly comparable with the ratios for the other countries.

For the denominators – the population in each age group – the sources are a mixture of labour force surveys, administrative records and population censuses.

Note that the composition of the self-employed with regard to the four categories listed above varies considerably between countries. In particular, countries with relatively large numbers of small farms, Mexico and Turkey for example, will have relatively large numbers of unpaid family workers.

Source

OECD (2004), *Labour Force Statistics*, OECD, Paris.

Further information

• *Analytical publications*

OECD (2000), "The Partial Renaissance of the Self-employed", *OECD Employment Outlook*, Chapter 5, OECD, Paris, pp. 155-199.

OECD (2004), *OECD Employment Outlook*, OECD, Paris.

• *Statistical publications*

OECD (2004), *Quarterly Labour Force Statistics*, OECD, Paris.

• *Online databases*

SourceOECD Employment and Labour Markets.

• *Web sites*

OECD Directorate for Employment, Labour and Social Affairs: *www.oecd.org/els*.

OECD Entrepreneurship at Local Level: *www.oecd.org/tds/leed/entrepreneurship*.

LABOUR MARKET • EMPLOYMENT

SELF-EMPLOYMENT

Self-employment rates: total
As a percentage of total civilian employment

	1990	1991	1992	1993	1994	1995	1996	1997	1998	1999	2000	2001	2002	2003
Australia	15.9	15.7	16.7	16.9	16.5	15.9	14.9	16.0	14.5	15.6	14.5	14.2	14.3	13.4
Austria	14.2	13.9	13.4	13.1	13.8	14.4	14.0	13.6	13.7	13.4	13.1	13.2	13.1	12.8
Belgium	18.1	18.3	18.4	18.9	18.9	18.8	18.8	18.6	18.2	17.8	..	..	..	..
Canada	9.5	9.8	10.1	10.7	10.8	10.6	11.0	11.4	11.7	11.3	10.7	9.9	9.8	9.7
Czech Republic	..	..	..	9.4	10.6	12.0	12.3	12.4	13.8	14.5	15.2	15.2	16.1	17.3
Denmark	11.7	10.9	10.8	10.8	10.0	9.6	9.5	9.1	9.4	9.1	8.7	8.9	9.0	8.8
Finland	15.6	15.3	15.7	16.0	16.3	15.6	15.3	14.9	14.3	14.0	13.7	13.0	12.9	12.9
France	13.2	12.7	12.2	11.7	11.3	10.8	10.4	10.1	9.8	9.5	9.2	8.9	8.7	8.8
Germany	10.9	9.8	10.1	10.4	10.6	10.7	10.8	10.9	11.0	10.8	11.0	11.1	11.2	11.4
Greece	47.7	46.8	47.4	46.7	46.7	46.1	45.7	45.2	43.4	41.7	41.6	39.8	39.8	..
Hungary	..	..	20.4	18.1	17.8	18.0	18.1	17.4	16.1	15.7	15.2	14.5	13.9	13.5
Iceland	15.1	20.3	19.3	18.0	18.4	19.6	18.2	17.7	17.9	17.7	18.0	16.8	16.6	..
Ireland	24.9	23.3	23.9	23.4	22.7	22.2	20.9	20.8	20.3	19.2	18.9	18.1	17.8	17.5
Italy	28.7	28.6	28.6	28.9	29.0	29.3	29.3	29.1	29.1	28.6	28.5	28.2	27.7	27.5
Japan	22.4	21.2	20.2	19.1	18.7	18.3	17.7	17.6	17.4	17.2	16.7	15.9	15.5	15.2
Korea	39.5	37.3	37.3	37.9	37.1	36.8	36.7	36.8	38.3	37.6	36.8	36.7	36.0	34.9
Luxembourg	9.4	8.5	8.2	8.0	7.8	7.6	7.5	7.4	7.1	6.8	7.3	7.0	6.9	6.8
Mexico	31.9	44.0	43.9	43.8	43.7	40.9	40.4	39.9	38.8	37.9	36.4	36.8	37.2	37.1
Netherlands	11.6	11.2	11.1	11.6	12.3	12.4	12.5	12.6	11.8	11.3	12.0	11.5	11.6	..
New Zealand	20.0	20.6	21.4	21.3	21.2	21.0	21.0	20.1	20.4	21.2	20.8	19.9	19.3	19.3
Norway	11.3	10.8	10.3	10.2	9.8	9.4	8.7	8.2	8.3	7.8	7.4	7.2	7.1	7.4
Poland	27.2	30.0	30.2	31.2	30.9	29.7	29.5	28.3	27.2	26.9	27.4	28.0	28.1	27.3
Portugal	29.4	30.6	25.7	26.3	27.7	27.9	28.6	28.9	28.3	27.2	26.5	27.0	26.7	26.8
Slovak Republic	..	..	..	..	6.3	6.5	6.4	6.3	6.8	7.7	8.0	8.4	8.6	9.8
Spain	25.9	25.2	25.7	26.0	25.9	25.2	24.7	23.5	22.7	21.2	20.1	19.8	19.2	18.6
Sweden	9.2	9.1	9.8	10.8	11.1	11.2	11.0	10.8	10.6	10.6	10.3	10.0	9.8	9.6
Switzerland	..	11.7	11.8	12.7	12.7	12.7	13.4	13.9	14.0	14.0	13.2	12.9	11.9	11.9
Turkey	61.0	62.0	60.3	57.8	59.1	58.5	57.2	55.4	55.4	55.0	51.4	52.8	50.2	49.4
United Kingdom	15.1	14.7	14.8	14.6	14.8	14.6	14.0	13.8	13.2	12.7	12.3	12.2	12.1	12.7
United States	8.8	9.0	8.7	8.8	8.8	8.5	8.4	8.2	7.9	7.7	7.4	7.4	7.2	7.6

StatLink: http://dx.doi.org/10.1787/571118072448

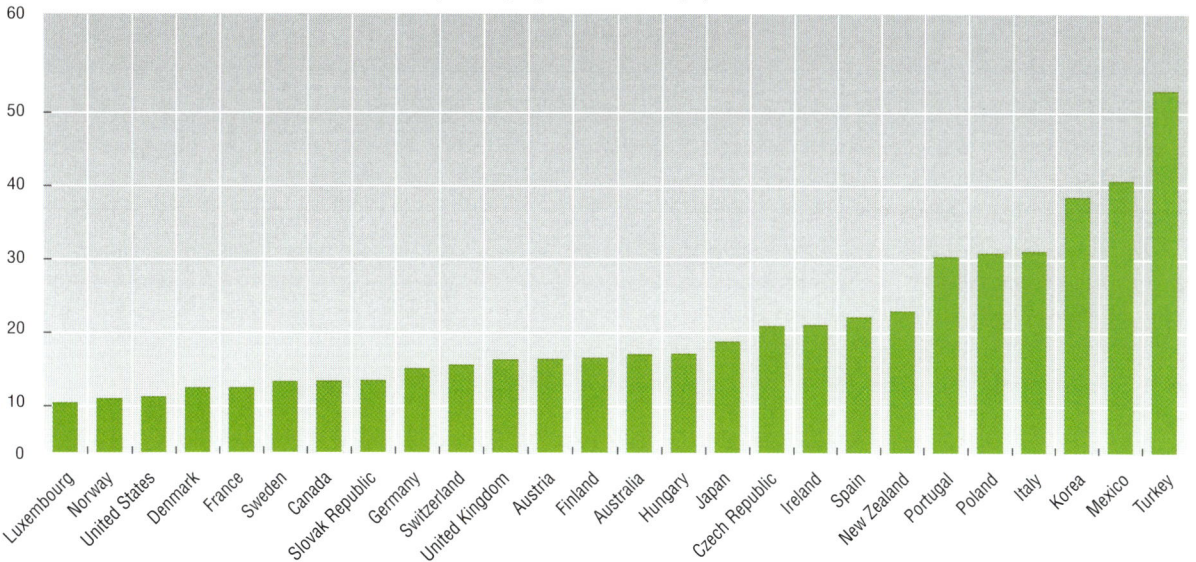

Self-employment rates: total
As a percentage of total civilian employment, 2003

StatLink: http://dx.doi.org/10.1787/825147537518

LABOUR MARKET • EMPLOYMENT

SELF-EMPLOYMENT

Self-employment rates: men
As a percentage of total male civilian employment

	1990	1991	1992	1993	1994	1995	1996	1997	1998	1999	2000	2001	2002	2003
Australia	18.1	18.0	19.2	19.6	19.1	18.8	17.2	18.4	17.0	18.4	17.3	17.0	17.1	16.1
Austria	..	..	..	..	..	..	14.1	14.0	14.2	13.9	13.9	14.1	14.2	14.0
Belgium	18.5	18.8	18.9	19.4	19.6	19.7	19.9	19.9	19.6	19.4	..	..	..	..
Canada	10.8	11.3	11.5	12.1	12.0	11.8	12.2	12.4	12.9	12.5	11.8	11.2	10.9	11.0
Czech Republic	..	..	..	12.0	13.7	15.1	15.7	15.9	17.3	18.4	19.1	19.1	20.3	21.7
Denmark	..	..	..	..	..	12.4	12.4	..	12.4	12.2	11.6	12.4	12.5	11.9
Finland	19.5	19.6	20.5	21.0	21.1	20.2	19.7	19.0	18.2	18.1	17.8	16.8	16.7	16.7
France	14.8	14.5	14.0	13.7	13.3	12.9	12.6	12.3	11.8	11.5	11.1	10.8	10.1	10.1
Germany	12.1	11.1	11.5	11.9	12.3	12.5	12.7	13.0	13.1	13.2	13.4	13.4	13.6	14.0
Greece	47.5	47.6	48.2	47.7	47.6	47.4	46.9	46.8	44.8	43.5	43.5	42.1	41.9	..
Hungary	..	..	23.9	21.9	21.9	22.1	22.6	21.5	19.9	19.5	19.2	18.1	17.3	17.1
Iceland	..	27.1	25.6	24.2	25.6	27.3	23.9	23.2	23.9	23.7	24.0	23.0	23.6	..
Ireland	32.3	30.4	31.5	30.9	30.3	29.9	28.1	28.1	27.4	26.1	25.8	25.2	25.2	24.7
Italy	31.1	31.2	31.3	31.4	31.6	32.3	32.5	32.4	32.5	32.1	32.3	32.2	31.7	31.5
Japan	18.9	18.1	17.4	16.6	16.4	16.2	15.9	15.9	15.7	15.8	15.5	15.0	14.9	14.7
Korea	36.9	34.7	34.9	35.4	34.7	34.3	34.4	34.7	36.3	36.1	35.7	36.0	35.7	35.3
Mexico	35.5	46.8	45.9	45.1	44.2	41.4	41.0	39.8	38.9	38.1	36.8	37.2	37.3	37.1
Netherlands	..	..	..	..	..	13.7	13.8	14.0	13.3	12.7	13.4	13.0	13.5	..
New Zealand	24.9	25.4	26.4	26.4	25.8	25.5	25.9	24.9	25.4	26.3	25.8	24.8	24.3	24.5
Norway	14.6	14.3	13.7	13.3	12.8	12.2	11.4	10.9	11.0	10.3	9.8	9.4	9.7	10.1
Poland	..	..	31.2	32.2	32.4	31.4	31.1	30.0	29.1	29.2	29.5	29.9	30.4	29.8
Portugal	..	..	26.8	27.4	29.0	29.9	30.3	30.0	29.5	28.4	27.8	28.5	28.3	28.4
Slovak Republic	..	..	..	..	8.6	8.7	8.7	8.4	9.1	10.4	10.8	11.4	11.9	13.0
Spain	25.9	25.4	26.2	26.9	27.0	26.3	26.1	25.3	24.4	23.2	22.2	22.0	21.6	21.0
Sweden	12.9	13.0	14.3	15.5	15.7	15.7	15.6	15.3	14.8	14.8	14.5	14.1	14.0	13.9
Switzerland	..	11.5	11.4	12.4	12.5	13.3	14.0	14.1	14.6	14.6	13.8	13.6	12.4	12.4
Turkey	53.5	54.2	53.3	52.8	52.7	52.1	50.5	49.8	49.8	48.9	46.5	47.5	45.1	44.5
United Kingdom	19.9	19.4	19.3	19.2	19.6	19.4	18.6	18.1	17.2	16.8	15.9	16.1	16.1	16.6
United States	10.5	10.8	10.6	10.9	10.3	9.9	9.8	9.5	9.2	8.9	8.6	8.5	8.4	8.8

StatLink: http://dx.doi.org/10.1787/465283244688

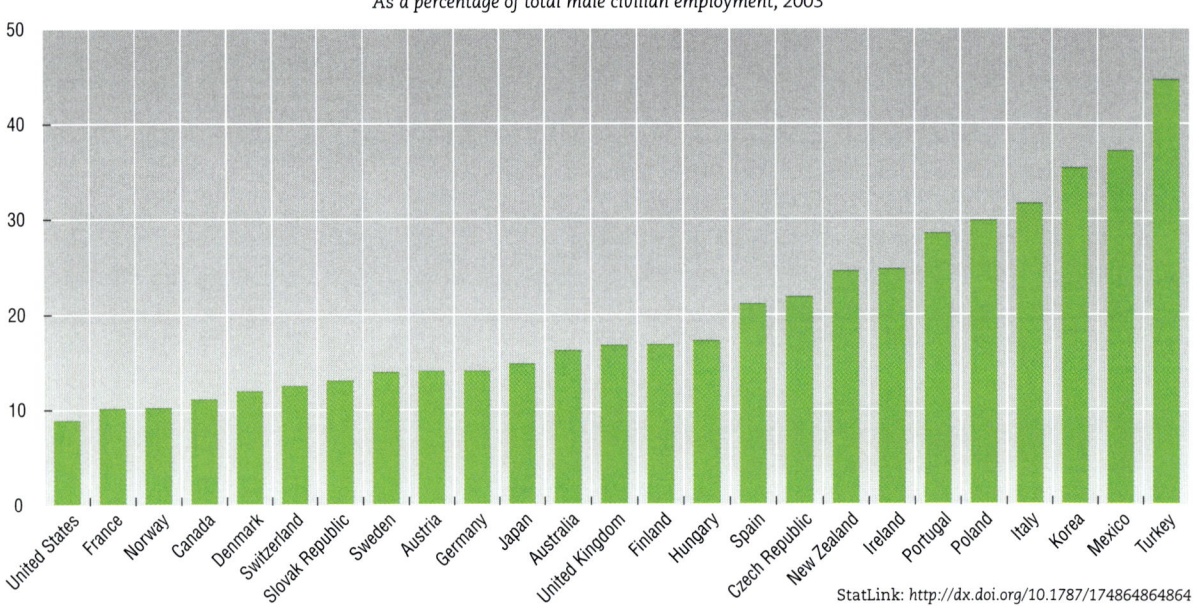

Self-employment rates: men
As a percentage of total male civilian employment, 2003

StatLink: http://dx.doi.org/10.1787/174864864864

LABOUR MARKET • EMPLOYMENT

SELF-EMPLOYMENT

Self-employment rates: women
As a percentage of total female civilian employment

	1990	1991	1992	1993	1994	1995	1996	1997	1998	1999	2000	2001	2002	2003
Australia	12.8	12.5	13.3	13.3	12.9	12.1	11.8	13.0	11.2	11.8	10.9	10.6	10.8	9.9
Austria	..	..	..	..	..	..	13.8	13.2	13.1	12.6	12.2	12.1	11.8	11.3
Belgium	17.5	17.7	17.7	18.1	17.7	17.6	17.4	16.9	16.2	15.7	..	..	..	..
Canada	7.9	7.9	8.3	9.0	9.2	9.1	9.7	10.2	10.4	9.9	9.3	8.4	8.5	8.3
Czech Republic	..	..	..	6.2	6.8	8.0	7.9	8.0	9.1	9.6	10.2	10.2	10.7	11.5
Denmark	..	..	..	..	..	6.3	6.1	..	5.8	5.6	5.5	4.9	5.2	5.3
Finland	11.3	10.9	10.7	10.8	11.1	10.5	10.5	10.2	10.0	9.5	9.2	8.9	8.8	8.8
France	11.0	10.3	9.8	9.2	8.8	8.3	7.9	7.5	7.3	7.1	6.9	6.7	7.1	7.4
Germany	9.2	8.0	8.1	8.2	8.3	8.3	8.1	8.1	8.2	7.8	7.9	8.4	8.2	8.4
Greece	48.1	45.4	45.9	44.9	45.2	43.8	43.7	42.4	41.1	38.7	38.5	36.0	36.5	..
Hungary	..	..	16.4	13.7	13.0	13.0	12.7	12.4	11.6	11.1	10.5	10.2	10.0	9.2
Iceland	..	12.0	11.8	10.7	10.4	10.6	11.6	11.4	11.1	10.8	11.0	9.8	8.7	..
Ireland	10.9	10.1	10.4	10.8	10.0	9.7	9.5	9.5	9.6	9.1	9.0	8.0	7.5	7.7
Italy	24.1	23.8	23.6	24.3	24.2	23.8	23.6	23.2	23.0	22.6	22.0	21.6	21.2	21.1
Japan	27.5	25.8	24.4	22.8	22.0	21.5	20.5	20.0	19.8	19.4	18.4	17.3	16.3	15.8
Korea	43.2	41.1	41.0	41.7	40.7	40.4	40.1	39.8	41.4	39.7	38.4	37.6	36.5	34.4
Mexico	20.4	37.8	39.3	41.0	42.6	39.8	39.1	40.1	38.6	37.6	35.7	36.0	37.1	37.2
Netherlands	..	..	..	..	..	10.7	10.6	10.7	9.8	9.4	10.2	9.5	9.1	..
New Zealand	13.7	14.6	15.0	14.8	15.3	15.4	14.9	14.1	14.3	15.0	14.7	14.0	13.3	13.2
Norway	7.4	6.8	6.5	6.6	5.8	6.1	5.7	5.1	5.3	5.0	4.8	4.7	4.2	4.3
Poland	..	..	29.0	29.9	29.3	27.7	27.5	26.3	25.0	24.1	24.8	25.7	25.4	24.3
Portugal	..	..	24.2	25.0	26.0	25.5	26.5	27.5	26.8	25.8	24.9	25.1	24.9	24.9
Slovak Republic	..	..	..	..	3.4	3.8	3.5	3.8	4.0	4.5	4.6	4.9	4.7	5.9
Spain	26.0	24.8	24.7	24.4	23.6	23.3	21.9	20.3	19.6	17.7	16.5	16.2	15.2	14.7
Sweden	5.2	5.1	5.1	5.8	6.3	6.4	6.0	5.9	6.0	6.1	5.7	5.6	5.3	5.1
Switzerland	..	12.0	12.4	13.1	13.0	11.9	12.6	13.6	13.2	13.2	12.3	12.0	11.3	11.4
Turkey	78.4	79.9	76.7	72.3	74.6	74.0	73.6	70.0	69.9	70.0	64.7	66.8	63.0	61.9
United Kingdom	8.9	8.7	9.1	9.0	9.0	8.7	8.5	8.6	8.3	7.7	7.8	7.4	7.4	7.8
United States	6.7	6.8	6.4	6.4	7.1	6.9	6.9	6.7	6.4	6.2	6.1	6.1	5.9	6.1

StatLink: http://dx.doi.org/10.1787/868738822446

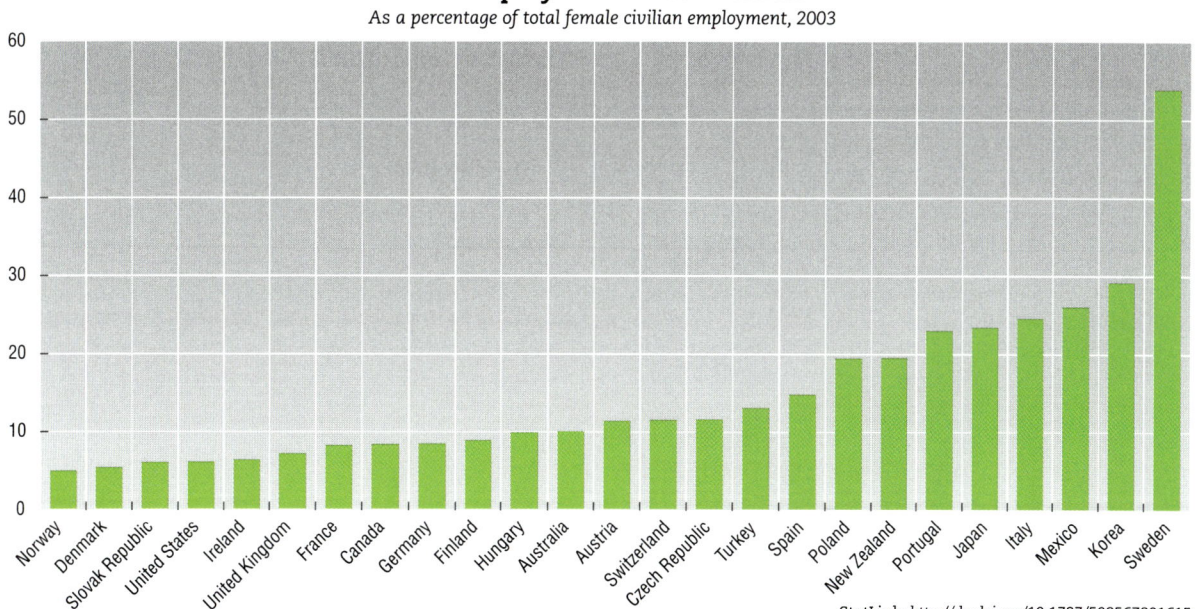

Self-employment rates: women
As a percentage of total female civilian employment, 2003

StatLink: http://dx.doi.org/10.1787/528567801615

LABOUR MARKET • UNEMPLOYMENT

STANDARDISED UNEMPLOYMENT RATES

Most OECD countries publish unemployment rates that are based on the numbers of persons who are registered as unemployed at government labour offices. Because they are available soon after the end of the month or quarter to which they refer, the numbers of registered unemployed are treated as the "headline" unemployment figures by many countries. However, the rules for registering at labour offices vary from country to country so that unemployment statistics based on this source are not comparable between countries. The unemployment rates shown here use *ILO Guidelines* that provide common definitions of unemployment and of the labour force.

Definition

Unemployed persons are defined as those who report that they are without work, that they are available for work and that they have taken active steps to find work in the last four weeks. The *ILO Guidelines* specify what actions count as active steps to find work and these include answering vacancy notices, visiting factories, construction sites and other places of work, and placing advertisements in the press as well registering with labour offices.

The unemployment rate is defined as the number of unemployed persons as a percentage of the civilian labour force, where the latter consists of the unemployed plus those in civilian employment. The latter are defined as persons who have worked for one hour or more in the last week.

When unemployment is high, some persons become discouraged and stop looking for work. They are then excluded from the unemployment rate which may fall, or stop rising, even though there has been no underlying improvement in the labour market.

Comparability

OECD countries follow the *ILO Guidelines* and there are regular meetings at OECD to review definitions and methodology. Despite this, changes over time and differences between countries need to be interpreted with caution.

Long-term trends

In almost all countries, unemployment rates rose in the early part of the 1990s but have been falling since then. Falls have been particularly marked in Finland, Ireland, Spain and Sweden.

There is no obvious pattern in the differences in unemployment rates for men and women. Unemployment rates for women are usually higher than for men, but in several countries unemployment rates for women are lower – Canada, Hungary, Korea, Sweden and the United Kingdom, for example. Part of the reason may be that women are more easily discouraged than men and so withdraw in larger numbers from the labour force when unemployment rises.

The charts shows unemployment rates averaged over the last decade. As regards total unemployment rates, countries can be divided into three groups: a low unemployment group with rates below 6% (Luxembourg to Portugal); a middle group with unemployment rates between 6% and 10% (Czech Republic to Greece); and a high unemployment group with average rates in excess of 10% (Italy to Spain).

Source

OECD (2004), *Quarterly Labour Force Statistics*, OECD, Paris.

Further information

• *Analytical publications*

OECD (2005), *Society at a Glance*, OECD, Paris.

• *Statistical publications*

OECD (2004), *Main Economic Indicators*, OECD, Paris.

OECD (2004), *OECD Employment Outlook*, OECD, Paris.

• *Online databases*

SourceOECD Employment and Labour Markets.

• *Web sites*

OECD Labour Force Statistics: *www.oecd.org/std/labour*.

OECD Employment Policy: *www.oecd.org/els/employment*.

LABOUR MARKET • UNEMPLOYMENT

STANDARDISED UNEMPLOYMENT RATES

Standardised unemployment rates: total
As a percentage of civilian labour force

	1991	1992	1993	1994	1995	1996	1997	1998	1999	2000	2001	2002	2003
Australia	9.3	10.5	10.6	9.5	8.2	8.2	8.3	7.7	6.9	6.3	6.8	6.4	6.1
Austria	-	-	4.0	3.8	3.9	4.4	4.4	4.5	4.0	3.7	3.6	4.2	4.3
Belgium	6.4	7.1	8.6	9.8	9.7	9.5	9.2	9.3	8.6	6.9	6.7	7.3	7.9
Canada	10.3	11.2	11.4	10.4	9.4	9.6	9.1	8.3	7.6	6.8	7.2	7.7	7.6
Czech Republic	-	-	4.4	4.3	4.1	3.9	4.8	6.3	8.6	8.6	8.0	7.3	7.8
Denmark	7.9	8.6	9.6	7.7	6.8	6.3	5.3	4.9	4.8	4.4	4.3	4.6	5.6
Finland	6.7	11.6	16.4	16.8	15.2	14.6	12.7	11.4	10.2	9.7	9.1	9.1	9.0
France	9.0	9.9	11.1	11.7	11.1	11.6	11.5	11.1	10.5	9.1	8.4	8.9	9.4
Germany	4.2	6.4	7.7	8.2	8.0	8.7	9.7	9.1	8.4	7.7	7.8	8.7	9.6
Greece	6.9	7.8	8.6	8.9	9.1	9.7	9.6	11.0	11.8	11.0	10.4	10.0	9.3
Hungary	-	9.9	12.1	11.0	10.4	9.6	9.0	8.4	6.9	6.3	5.6	5.6	5.7
Ireland	14.7	15.4	15.6	14.3	12.3	11.7	9.9	7.5	5.6	4.3	3.9	4.3	4.6
Italy	8.5	8.7	10.1	11.0	11.5	11.5	11.6	11.7	11.3	10.4	9.4	9.0	8.6
Japan	2.1	2.2	2.5	2.9	3.1	3.4	3.4	4.1	4.7	4.7	5.0	5.4	5.3
Korea	-	-	-	-	-	-	-	-	-	4.4	4.0	3.3	3.6
Luxembourg	1.6	2.1	2.6	3.2	2.9	2.9	2.7	2.7	2.4	2.3	2.1	2.8	3.7
Netherlands	5.5	5.3	6.2	6.8	6.6	6.0	4.9	3.8	3.2	2.9	2.5	2.7	3.8
New Zealand	10.3	10.4	9.5	8.1	6.3	6.1	6.6	7.4	6.8	6.0	5.3	5.2	4.6
Norway	6.0	6.6	6.6	6.0	5.5	4.8	4.0	3.2	3.2	3.4	3.6	3.9	4.5
Poland	-	-	14.0	14.4	13.3	12.3	10.9	10.2	13.4	16.4	18.5	19.8	19.2
Portugal	4.2	4.3	5.6	6.9	7.3	7.3	6.8	5.2	4.5	4.1	4.0	5.0	6.2
Slovak Republic	-	-	-	13.7	13.1	11.3	11.9	12.6	16.8	18.7	19.4	18.7	17.5
Spain	13.2	14.9	18.6	19.8	18.8	18.1	17.0	15.2	12.8	11.3	10.6	11.3	11.3
Sweden	3.1	5.6	9.0	9.4	8.8	9.6	9.9	8.2	6.7	5.6	4.9	4.9	5.6
Switzerland	1.9	3.0	3.9	3.9	3.5	3.9	4.2	3.6	3.0	2.7	2.6	3.2	4.2
United Kingdom	8.6	9.8	10.0	9.2	8.5	8.0	6.9	6.2	5.9	5.4	5.0	5.1	5.0
United States	6.8	7.5	6.9	6.1	5.6	5.4	4.9	4.5	4.2	4.0	4.7	5.8	6.0
EU15	7.9	8.7	10.1	10.5	10.1	10.2	10.0	9.4	8.7	7.8	7.4	7.7	8.1
OECD total	-	-	-	7.7	7.3	7.2	7.0	6.9	6.7	6.3	6.5	7.0	7.1

StatLink: http://dx.doi.org/10.1787/802452826444

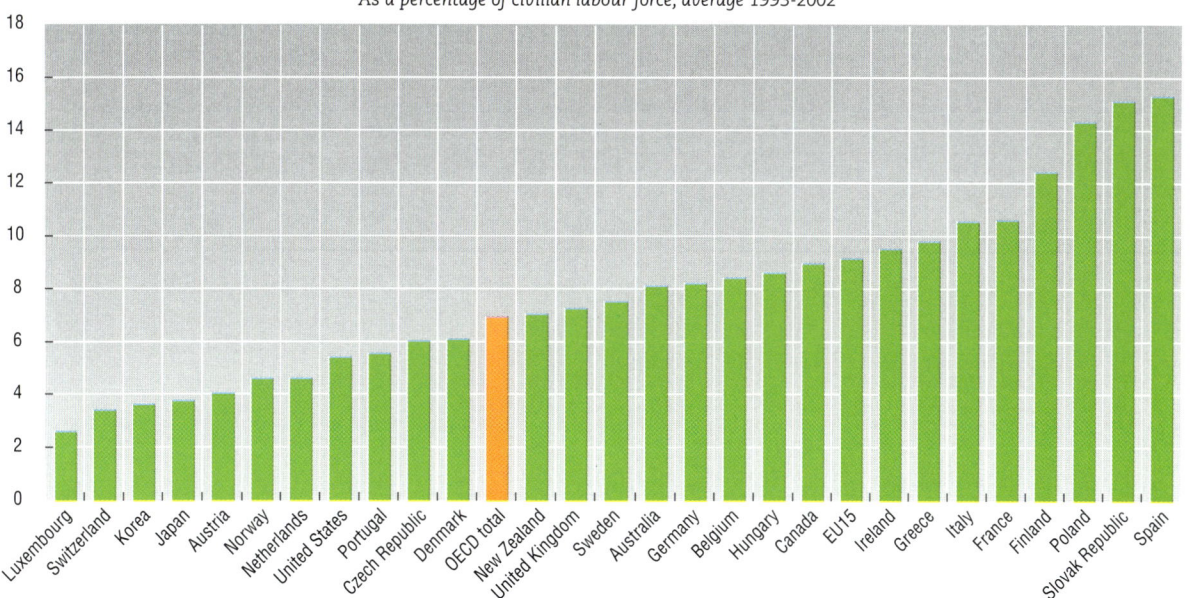

Standardised unemployment rates: total
As a percentage of civilian labour force, average 1993-2002

StatLink: http://dx.doi.org/10.1787/710343021336

LABOUR MARKET • UNEMPLOYMENT

STANDARDISED UNEMPLOYMENT RATES

Standardised unemployment rates: men
As a percentage of male civilian labour force

	1991	1992	1993	1994	1995	1996	1997	1998	1999	2000	2001	2002	2003
Australia	9.6	11.2	11.4	9.9	8.7	8.5	8.6	8.1	7.2	6.5	7.1	6.6	5.9
Austria	..	..	3.1	3.0	3.1	3.7	3.7	3.8	3.4	3.1	3.2	3.9	3.9
Belgium	4.2	5.1	6.7	7.7	7.6	7.4	7.3	7.6	7.3	5.6	6.0	6.7	7.6
Canada	10.9	12.0	12.0	10.9	9.8	9.9	9.3	8.6	7.8	6.9	7.5	8.1	8.0
Czech Republic	..	..	3.5	3.7	3.5	3.4	4.0	5.0	7.2	7.3	6.7	5.9	6.2
Denmark	7.3	8.0	9.3	7.1	5.7	5.3	4.5	3.9	4.4	4.1	3.9	4.4	5.3
Finland	8.0	13.6	18.1	18.6	15.4	14.4	12.3	10.8	9.7	9.0	8.6	9.1	9.1
France	7.0	8.0	9.6	10.1	9.4	10.0	10.1	9.5	9.0	7.6	7.0	7.9	8.5
Germany	..	5.1	6.5	7.1	7.0	8.1	9.1	8.6	8.1	7.5	7.8	8.9	10.0
Greece	4.3	4.9	5.7	6.0	6.2	6.0	6.2	7.2	7.8	7.2	6.9	6.6	5.9
Hungary	..	11.0	13.5	12.3	11.8	10.2	9.7	9.0	7.4	6.8	6.1	6.0	6.0
Ireland	14.2	15.1	15.4	14.2	12.2	11.5	9.9	7.7	5.7	4.3	4.0	4.6	4.9
Italy	6.0	6.3	7.5	8.5	8.8	8.9	8.9	9.0	8.6	8.0	7.3	7.0	6.7
Japan	2.0	2.1	2.4	2.8	3.1	3.3	3.4	4.2	4.8	4.9	5.2	5.5	5.5
Korea	..	..	..	..	..	..	..	..	..	5.0	4.5	3.7	3.8
Luxembourg	1.3	1.7	2.2	2.6	2.0	2.2	2.0	1.9	1.8	1.8	1.7	2.2	3.0
Netherlands	3.9	4.1	5.4	6.0	5.5	4.7	3.7	3.0	2.3	2.2	2.1	2.5	3.6
New Zealand	10.9	11.0	10.1	8.5	6.2	6.1	6.6	7.5	7.0	6.1	5.3	5.0	4.3
Norway	6.5	7.3	7.3	6.6	5.7	4.7	3.9	3.1	3.4	3.7	3.7	4.1	4.9
Poland	..	..	12.7	13.1	12.1	11.0	9.1	8.5	11.8	14.6	17.1	19.0	18.6
Portugal	2.9	3.6	4.8	6.1	6.5	6.4	6.0	4.1	3.9	3.3	3.2	4.1	5.4
Slovak Republic	..	..	..	13.3	12.6	10.2	11.1	12.2	16.7	18.9	19.8	18.6	17.2
Spain	9.9	11.7	15.5	16.2	14.9	14.4	13.1	11.2	9.1	7.9	7.5	8.0	8.2
Sweden	3.4	6.7	10.6	10.8	9.7	10.2	10.3	8.3	6.6	5.9	5.2	5.3	6.0
Switzerland	1.4	2.4	3.3	3.4	3.0	3.6	4.3	3.2	2.6	2.2	2.0	3.0	3.9
United Kingdom	9.6	11.6	11.9	10.9	9.9	9.3	7.7	6.9	6.5	5.9	5.5	5.6	5.5
United States	7.2	7.9	7.2	6.2	5.6	5.4	4.9	4.4	4.1	3.9	4.8	5.9	6.3
EU15	6.7	7.6	9.1	9.4	9.0	9.1	8.8	8.2	7.5	6.7	6.5	7.0	7.4
OECD total	..	..	..	7.3	6.8	6.8	6.5	6.4	6.3	5.8	6.1	6.7	6.9

StatLink: http://dx.doi.org/10.1787/406383255206

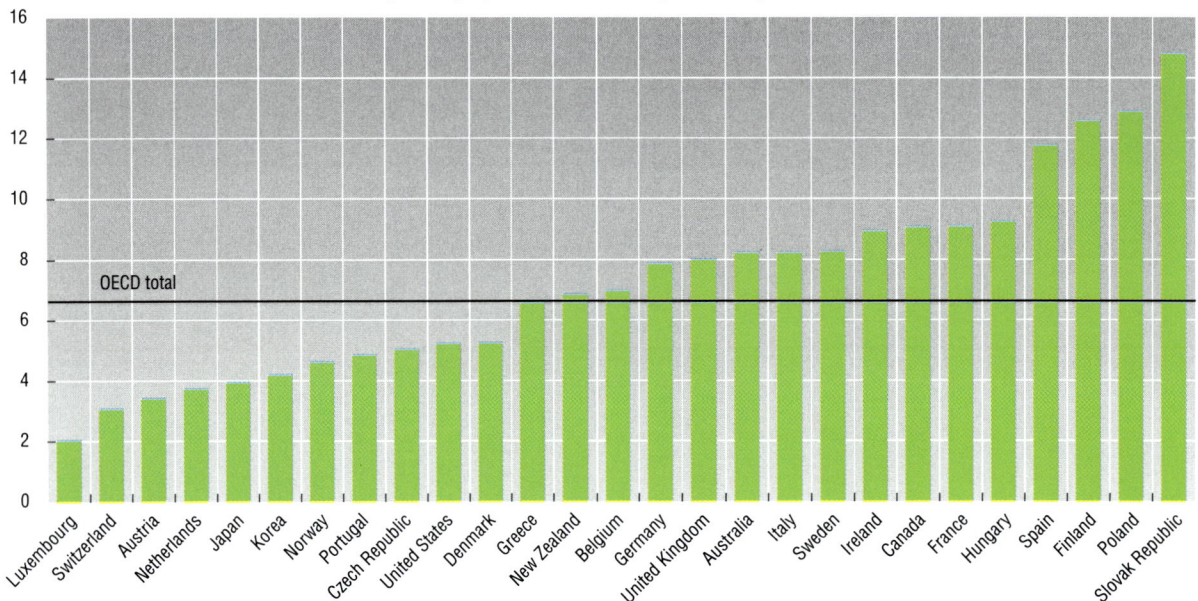

Standardised unemployment rates: men
As a percentage of male civilian labour force, average 1993-2002

StatLink: http://dx.doi.org/10.1787/635153302621

LABOUR MARKET • UNEMPLOYMENT

STANDARDISED UNEMPLOYMENT RATES

Standardised unemployment rates: women
As a percentage of female civilian labour force

	1991	1992	1993	1994	1995	1996	1997	1998	1999	2000	2001	2002	2003
Australia	8.7	9.5	9.8	9.0	7.9	7.9	8.1	7.5	6.8	6.2	6.6	6.2	6.2
Austria	-	-	5.0	4.9	5.0	5.2	5.4	5.4	4.7	4.3	4.2	4.4	4.6
Belgium	9.8	10.0	11.5	12.7	12.7	12.5	11.9	11.6	10.3	8.5	7.6	8.1	8.4
Canada	9.7	10.1	10.6	9.7	9.0	9.3	8.9	7.9	7.3	6.7	6.8	7.1	7.2
Czech Republic	-	-	5.4	5.2	4.8	4.7	5.9	8.0	10.2	10.3	9.6	9.0	9.8
Denmark	8.6	9.2	9.8	8.5	8.1	7.5	6.2	6.0	5.4	4.8	4.9	4.7	5.9
Finland	5.2	9.4	14.5	14.9	15.0	14.7	13.2	11.9	10.7	10.5	9.6	9.1	8.8
France	11.4	12.2	13.0	13.6	13.2	13.4	13.3	12.9	12.2	10.9	10.0	10.0	10.5
Germany	-	8.2	9.4	9.8	9.4	9.5	10.4	9.7	8.9	8.1	7.9	8.4	9.2
Greece	11.6	12.9	13.6	13.7	13.8	15.4	14.8	16.9	17.8	16.7	15.5	15.0	14.2
Hungary	-	8.7	10.4	9.4	8.7	8.8	8.1	7.7	6.3	5.6	4.9	5.1	5.5
Ireland	15.8	16.0	16.0	14.6	12.5	11.8	9.9	7.3	5.5	4.3	3.8	4.0	4.2
Italy	12.9	13.0	14.5	15.4	16.1	15.9	16.1	16.1	15.5	14.3	12.9	12.2	11.6
Japan	2.2	2.2	2.6	3.0	3.2	3.4	3.4	4.0	4.5	4.5	4.7	5.1	4.9
Korea	-	-	-	-	-	-	-	-	-	3.6	3.3	2.7	3.3
Luxembourg	2.3	2.8	3.3	4.1	4.3	4.2	3.9	4.0	3.3	3.1	2.7	3.8	4.6
Netherlands	7.9	7.2	7.4	7.9	8.1	7.7	6.6	5.0	4.4	3.8	3.1	3.0	4.0
New Zealand	9.6	9.5	8.8	7.6	6.3	6.1	6.6	7.4	6.5	5.8	5.3	5.3	5.0
Norway	5.5	5.7	5.7	5.3	5.1	4.8	4.2	3.2	3.0	3.2	3.4	3.6	4.0
Poland	-	-	15.6	16.0	14.7	13.9	13.0	12.2	15.3	18.6	20.2	20.7	20.0
Portugal	5.9	5.2	6.7	7.9	8.2	8.2	7.6	6.4	5.3	5.0	5.0	6.0	7.2
Slovak Republic	-	-	-	14.1	13.8	12.7	12.8	13.1	16.9	18.5	18.9	18.9	17.8
Spain	19.5	21.0	24.1	26.1	25.3	24.4	23.3	21.8	18.8	16.7	15.5	16.3	15.9
Sweden	2.8	4.4	7.3	7.8	7.9	9.0	9.5	8.0	6.8	5.3	4.5	4.6	5.2
Switzerland	2.6	3.7	4.7	4.5	4.1	4.2	4.1	4.0	3.5	3.2	3.4	3.4	4.5
United Kingdom	7.2	7.4	7.6	7.1	6.7	6.3	5.8	5.3	5.1	4.8	4.4	4.5	4.3
United States	6.4	7.0	6.6	6.0	5.6	5.4	5.0	4.6	4.3	4.1	4.7	5.6	5.7
EU15	9.7	10.3	11.4	11.9	11.7	11.7	11.6	11.0	10.2	9.2	8.5	8.7	9.0
OECD total	-	-	-	8.2	7.9	7.8	7.6	7.5	7.2	6.8	6.9	7.3	7.4

StatLink: http://dx.doi.org/10.1787/438684485073

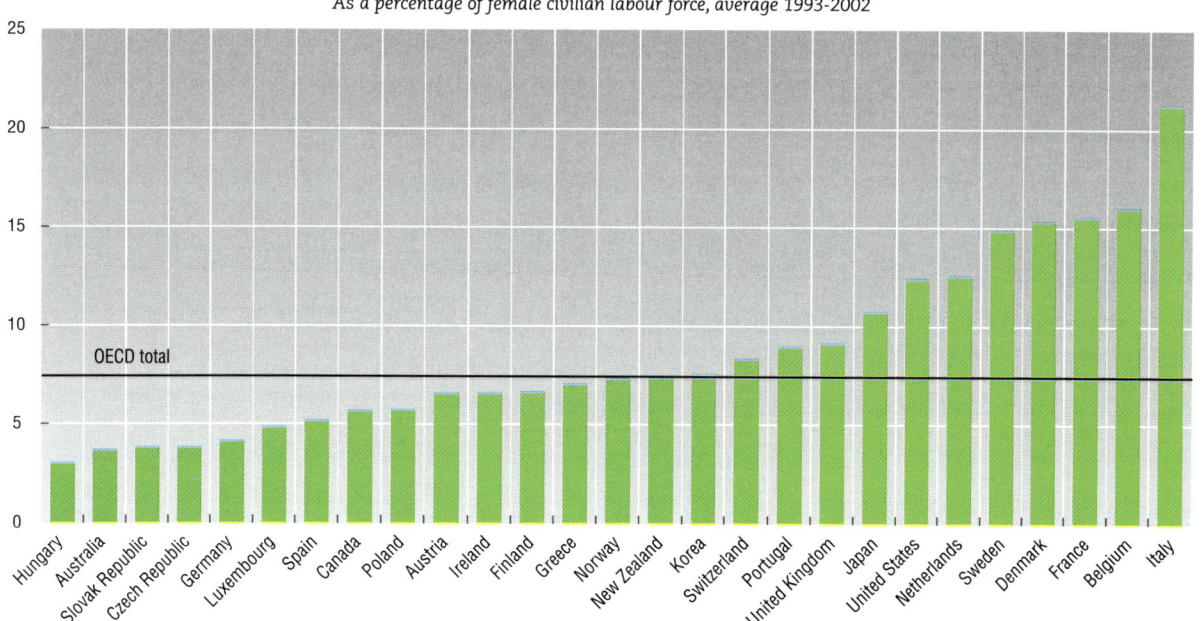

Standardised unemployment rates: women
As a percentage of female civilian labour force, average 1993-2002

StatLink: http://dx.doi.org/10.1787/767454531408

LABOUR MARKET • UNEMPLOYMENT

LONG-TERM UNEMPLOYMENT

Long-term unemployment is here measured as those who have been unemployed for 12 months or more as a percentage of the total number of persons unemployed. Clearly long-term unemployment is of particular concern to policy makers. Quite apart from the mental stress caused to the unemployed and their families, high rates of long-term unemployment indicate that labour markets are operating inefficiently and, in countries which pay generous unemployment benefits, the existence of long-term unemployment is a significant burden on government finances.

Definition

Long-term unemployment is conventionally defined either as those unemployed for 6 months or more or, as here, those unemployed for 12 months or more.

Unemployment is defined in most OECD countries according to the *ILO Guidelines*. Unemployment is usually measured by household labour force surveys and the unemployed are defined as those persons who report that they have worked in gainful employment for less than one hour in the previous week and who have taken actions to seek employment in the previous four weeks. The *ILO Guidelines* specify the kinds of actions that count as seeking work.

Comparability

Iceland, Mexico and Turkey do not fully observe the *ILO Guidelines* for measuring unemployment. Thus statistics for these countries will be comparable over time but less comparable with other countries.

In comparing rates of long-term unemployment it is important to bear in mind differences in institutional arrangements between countries. Rates of long-term unemployment will generally be higher in countries where unemployment benefits are relatively generous and are available for long periods of unemployment. In countries where the benefits are low and of limited duration, unemployed persons will more quickly lower their salary expectations or consider taking jobs that are in other ways less attractive than those which they formerly held.

Long-term trends

In 2003, rates of long-term unemployment varied from 10% or less in Korea, Mexico, Norway and Canada to 50% or more in Poland, the Czech Republic, Germany, Greece, Italy and the Slovak Republic. Lower rates of long-term unemployment are generally found in countries that have enjoyed relatively high rates of economic growth in recent years. There appears to be a two-way causal relationship here – on the one hand jobs are easier to find in a fast growing economy and, on the other, economies may grow faster by making unemployment an unattractive proposition.

Over the period shown in the table, long-term unemployment rates have been relatively stable for the OECD as a whole, but there have been some sharp rises in several countries and equally sharp falls in others. Rates of long-term unemployment have more than doubled in the Czech Republic, Hungary and the United States and have also risen sharply in Iceland, Japan and Switzerland. On the other hand, there have been large falls in the long-term unemployment rates in Ireland, Korea, Luxembourg, Norway and Turkey.

Source
OECD (2004), *Labour Force Statistics*, OECD, Paris.

Further information
• **Analytical publications**

OECD (2002), *OECD Employment Outlook: The Ins and Outs of Long-term Unemployment*, OECD, Paris.

OECD (2004), *OECD Employment Outlook*, OECD, Paris.

• **Statistical publications**

OECD (2004), *Quarterly Labour Force Statistics*, OECD, Paris.

• **Online databases**

SourceOECD Employment and Labour Markets.

• **Web sites**

OECD Employment Outlook:
www.oecd.org/els/employmentoutlook.

Labour Force Statistics database:
www.oecd.org/statistics/labour.

LABOUR MARKET • UNEMPLOYMENT

LONG-TERM UNEMPLOYMENT

Long-term unemployment

Persons unemployed for 12 months or more as a percentage of total unemployed

	1990	1991	1992	1993	1994	1995	1996	1997	1998	1999	2000	2001	2002	2003
Australia	21.6	24.9	34.5	36.5	36.3	30.8	28.4	30.7	34.5	30.2	29.1	21.2	22.1	22.5
Austria	..	..	..	..	18.4	29.1	24.9	27.5	30.3	29.2	25.8	23.3	19.2	24.5
Belgium	68.5	62.9	59.1	53.0	58.3	62.4	61.3	60.5	61.7	60.5	56.3	51.7	49.6	46.3
Canada	7.2	9.0	13.4	16.4	17.8	16.7	16.7	16.1	13.7	11.6	11.2	9.5	9.7	10.1
Czech Republic	..	..	..	18.5	22.3	31.2	31.3	30.5	31.2	37.1	48.8	52.7	50.7	49.9
Denmark	29.9	31.9	27.0	25.2	32.1	27.9	26.5	27.2	26.9	20.5	20.0	22.2	19.7	19.9
Finland	..	9.2	..	30.6	..	37.6	34.5	29.8	27.5	29.6	29.0	26.2	24.4	24.7
France	38.1	37.3	36.2	34.2	38.5	42.5	39.6	41.4	44.2	40.4	42.6	37.6	33.8	42.9
Germany	46.8	31.6	33.5	40.3	44.3	48.7	47.8	50.1	52.6	51.7	51.5	50.4	47.9	50.0
Greece	49.8	47.7	49.6	50.9	50.5	51.4	56.7	55.7	54.9	55.3	56.4	52.8	52.4	56.5
Hungary	..	..	20.4	33.5	41.3	50.6	54.4	51.3	49.8	49.5	49.0	46.6	44.8	42.2
Iceland	..	6.7	6.8	12.2	15.1	16.8	19.8	16.3	16.1	11.7	11.8	12.5	11.1	..
Ireland	66.0	61.6	58.8	59.1	64.3	61.6	59.5	57.0	..	55.3	..	33.1	29.3	35.4
Italy	69.8	68.1	58.2	57.7	61.5	63.6	65.6	66.3	59.6	61.4	61.3	63.4	59.2	58.2
Japan	19.1	17.9	15.9	15.6	17.5	18.1	19.3	21.8	20.3	22.4	25.5	26.6	30.8	33.5
Korea	2.6	4.2	3.8	2.6	5.4	4.4	3.8	2.6	1.5	3.8	2.3	2.3	2.5	0.6
Luxembourg	47.4	31.3	14.3	31.6	29.6	23.2	27.6	34.6	31.3	32.3	22.4	28.4	27.4	..
Mexico	..	..	..	..	..	1.3	2.2	1.4	0.8	1.7	1.1	1.1	0.9	1.0
Netherlands	49.3	46.1	43.9	52.4	49.4	46.8	50.0	49.1	47.9	43.5	..	..	26.7	29.2
New Zealand	20.9	23.8	32.0	33.2	32.3	25.5	20.9	19.4	19.5	20.9	19.2	16.8	14.4	13.3
Norway	20.4	20.2	23.5	27.2	28.8	24.2	14.2	12.4	8.3	7.1	5.4	5.5	6.4	6.4
Poland	..	..	34.7	39.1	40.4	40.0	39.0	38.0	37.4	34.8	37.9	43.1	48.4	49.7
Portugal	44.9	38.7	30.9	43.5	43.4	50.9	53.1	55.6	44.7	41.2	42.9	38.1	35.5	32.0
Slovak Republic	..	..	..	..	42.6	54.1	52.6	51.6	51.3	47.7	54.6	53.7	59.8	61.1
Spain	54.0	51.0	47.4	50.1	56.2	57.1	55.9	55.7	54.3	51.2	47.6	44.0	40.2	39.8
Sweden	12.1	11.2	13.5	15.8	25.7	27.8	30.1	33.4	33.5	30.1	26.4	22.3	21.0	17.8
Switzerland	..	17.0	20.0	20.3	29.0	33.6	25.6	28.2	34.8	39.6	29.0	29.9	21.8	27.0
Turkey	46.7	40.7	44.0	46.6	45.8	36.3	44.0	41.3	40.0	28.2	21.1	21.3	29.4	24.4
United Kingdom	34.4	28.8	35.4	42.5	45.4	43.6	39.8	38.7	32.7	29.6	28.0	27.8	23.1	23.0
United States	5.5	6.3	11.1	11.5	12.2	9.7	9.5	8.7	8.0	6.8	6.0	6.1	8.5	11.8
EU15	49.5	43.5	41.7	44.1	48.4	50.3	49.4	50.2	49.2	47.5	46.9	45.3	41.4	43.3
OECD total	31.2	27.6	28.8	31.9	35.5	34.2	34.4	35.1	33.3	31.8	31.6	29.7	29.6	31.0

StatLink: http://dx.doi.org/10.1787/767082433235

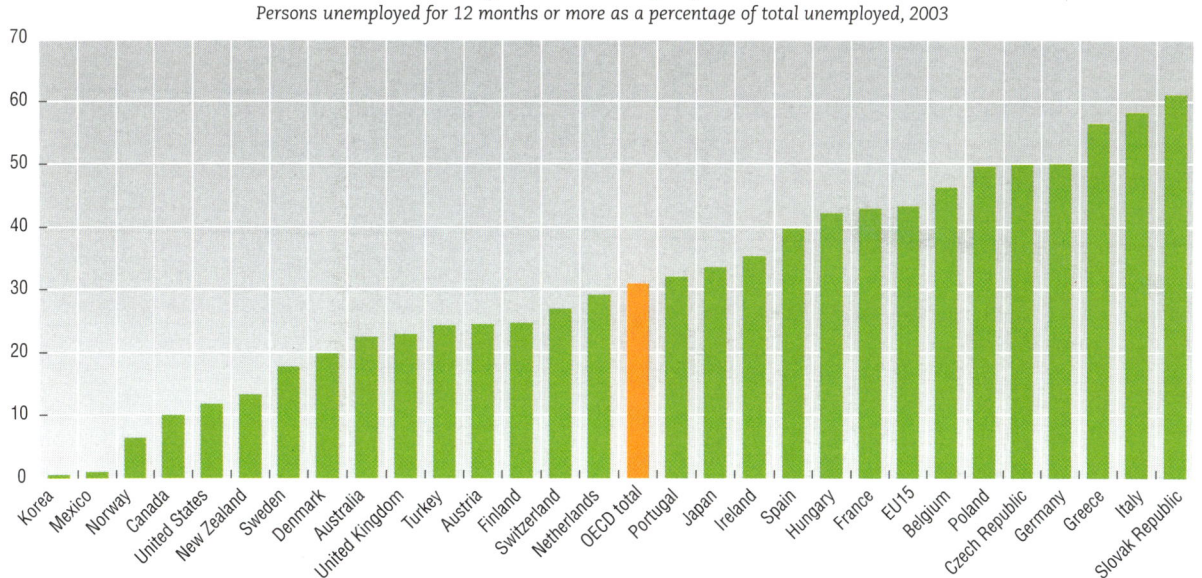

Long-term unemployment
Persons unemployed for 12 months or more as a percentage of total unemployed, 2003

StatLink: http://dx.doi.org/10.1787/016566618757

OECD FACTBOOK 2005 – ISBN 92-64-01869-7 – © OECD 2005   113

SCIENCE AND TECHNOLOGY

RESEARCH AND DEVELOPMENT (R&D)
EXPENDITURE ON R&D
INVESTMENT IN KNOWLEDGE
RESEARCHERS
PATENTS

INFORMATION AND COMMUNICATIONS TECHNOLOGY (ICT)
SIZE OF THE ICT SECTOR
INVESTMENT IN ICT
COMPUTER AND INTERNET ACCESS BY HOUSEHOLDS
HIGH-TECHNOLOGY EXPORTS

SCIENCE AND TECHNOLOGY • RESEARCH AND DEVELOPMENT (R&D)

EXPENDITURE ON R&D

Expenditure on research and development (R&D) is a key indicator of government and private sector efforts to obtain competitive advantage in science and technology. In 2001, research and development amounted to about 2.3% of GDP for the OECD as a whole.

Definition

Research and development (R&D) comprise creative work undertaken on a systematic basis in order to increase the stock of knowledge, including knowledge of man, culture and society, and the use of this stock of knowledge to devise new applications. R&D is a term covering three activities: basic research, applied research, and experimental development Basic research is experimental or theoretical work undertaken primarily to acquire new knowledge of the underlying foundation of phenomena and observable facts, without any particular application or use in view. Applied research is also original investigation undertaken in order to acquire new knowledge. It is, however, directed primarily towards a specific practical aim or objective. Experimental development is systematic work, drawing on existing knowledge gained from research and/or practical experience, that is directed to producing new materials, products or devices, to installing new processes, systems and services, or to improving substantially those already produced or installed.

The main aggregate used for international comparisons is gross domestic expenditure on R&D (GERD). This consists of the total expenditure on R&D by all resident companies, research institutes, university and government laboratories, etc. It excludes R&D expenditures financed by domestic firms but performed abroad.

Comparability

The R&D data shown here have been compiled according to the guidelines of the *Frascati Manual 2002*. It should however be noted that over the period shown, several countries have improved the coverage of their surveys of R&D activities in the services sector (Japan, Netherlands, Norway and United States) and in higher education (Finland, Greece, Japan, Netherlands, Spain and the United States). Other countries, including especially Italy, Japan and Sweden, have worked to improve the international comparability of their data. Some of the changes shown in the table reflect these methodological improvements as well as the underlying changes in R&D expenditures.

For Germany, data prior to 1991 refer only to West Germany. For Korea, social sciences and humanities are excluded from the R&D data. For the United States, capital expenditure is not covered.

Long-term trends

In the three main OECD regions, R&D expenditure relative to GDP (R&D intensity) has continued to increase steadily over the past three years. In Japan, this was due more to the stagnation in GDP since 1997 than to a significant increase in R&D expenditure. In the United States, however, the rise was mainly due to significant increases in R&D expenditure, as GDP also grew rapidly. In 2001, R&D intensity in the European Union exceeded 1.9% for the first time in a decade.

In 2001, Iceland, Japan, Finland and Sweden were the only four OECD countries in which the R&D-to-GDP ratio exceeded 3%, well above the OECD average of 2.3%. During the second half of the 1990s R&D expenditure grew fastest in Iceland, Greece, Mexico and Turkey all of which had average annual growth rates above 12%.

Source

OECD (2004), *Main Science and Technology Indicators*, OECD, Paris.

Further information

• **Statistical publications**

OECD (2004), *Research and Development Statistics*, OECD, Paris.

• **Analytical publications**

OECD (2000), "The Impact of Public R&D Expenditure on Business R&D", *OECD Directorate for Science, Technology and Industry Working Paper*, No. 2000/4, OECD, Paris, www.oecd.org/sti/working-papers.

• **Methodological publications**

OECD (2001), *Measuring Expenditure on Health-related R&D*, OECD, Paris.

OECD (2002), *Frascati Manual 2002: Proposed Standard Practice for Surveys on Research and Experimental Development*, OECD, Paris.

• **Online databases**

SourceOECD ANBERD: R&D Expenditure in Industry.

• **Web sites**

OECD Science, Technology and Industry: www.oecd.org/sti.

SCIENCE AND TECHNOLOGY • RESEARCH AND DEVELOPMENT (R&D)

EXPENDITURE ON R&D

Gross domestic expenditure on R&D
As a percentage of GDP

	1981	1985	1991	1995	1996	1997	1998	1999	2000	2001	2002
Australia	0.95	1.24	1.52	..	1.66	..	1.51	..	1.53	..	..
Austria	1.13	1.24	1.47	1.56	1.60	1.71	1.78	1.85	1.84	1.90	1.94
Belgium	..	1.62	1.62	1.72	1.80	1.87	1.90	1.96	..	..	..
Canada	1.24	1.44	1.60	1.72	1.68	1.68	1.79	1.81	1.87	1.94	1.85
Czech Republic	..	..	2.02	1.01	1.04	1.16	1.24	1.24	1.33	1.30	..
Denmark	1.06	1.21	1.64	1.84	1.85	1.94	2.06	2.19	..	..	..
Finland	1.17	1.55	2.03	2.28	2.54	2.71	2.88	3.23	3.40	3.40	..
France	1.93	2.22	2.37	2.31	2.30	2.22	2.17	2.18	2.18	2.20	..
Germany	2.43	2.68	2.53	2.26	2.26	2.29	2.31	2.44	..	2.49	2.50
Greece	0.17	0.27	0.36	0.49	..	0.51	..	0.67	..	..	..
Hungary	..	..	1.06	0.73	0.65	0.72	0.68	0.69	0.80	0.95	..
Iceland	0.64	0.74	1.18	1.57	..	1.88	2.07	2.39	2.77	3.06	3.04
Ireland	0.68	0.77	0.93	1.28	1.32	1.29	1.25	1.22	1.15	1.17	..
Italy	0.88	1.12	1.23	1.00	1.01	1.05	1.07	1.04	1.07	..	..
Japan	2.11	2.54	2.75	2.69	2.77	2.83	2.94	2.94	2.98	3.09	..
Korea	..	..	1.92	2.50	2.60	2.69	2.55	2.47	2.65	2.96	..
Mexico	..	..	0.22	0.31	0.31	0.34	0.38	0.43	..	..	..
Netherlands	1.79	1.99	1.97	1.99	2.01	2.04	1.94	2.02	1.94	..	..
New Zealand	0.99	..	0.98	0.96	..	1.11	..	1.03	..	..	..
Norway	1.17	1.48	1.64	1.70	..	1.64	..	1.65	..	1.62	..
Poland	..	..	..	0.69	0.71	0.71	0.72	0.75	0.70	0.67	..
Portugal	0.30	0.38	0.61	0.57	..	0.62	0.69	0.75	0.79	0.83	0.78
Slovak Republic	..	..	2.16	0.94	0.94	1.09	0.79	0.66	0.67	0.65	..
Spain	0.41	0.53	0.84	0.81	0.83	0.82	0.89	0.88	0.94	0.96	..
Sweden	2.17	2.71	2.70	3.35	..	3.54	..	3.65	..	4.27	..
Switzerland	2.18	2.82	2.66	..	2.73	..	..	..	2.63	..	..
Turkey	..	..	0.53	0.38	0.45	0.49	0.50	0.63	0.64	..	..
United Kingdom	2.38	2.24	2.07	1.95	1.88	1.81	1.80	1.88	1.85	1.90	..
United States	2.34	2.76	2.72	2.51	2.55	2.58	2.60	2.65	2.72	2.82	2.82
EU15	1.69	1.86	1.90	1.80	1.80	1.80	1.81	1.86	1.89	1.93	..
OECD total	1.95	2.26	2.23	2.10	2.13	2.15	2.17	2.20	2.25	2.33	..

StatLink: http://dx.doi.org/10.1787/740743821254

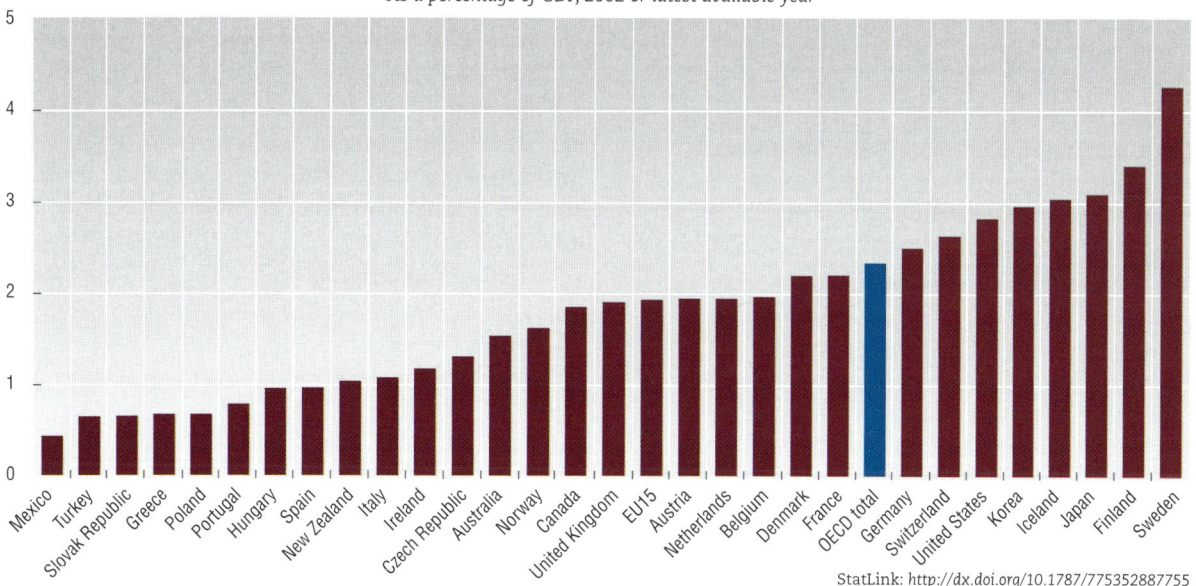

Gross domestic expenditure on R&D
As a percentage of GDP, 2002 or latest available year

StatLink: http://dx.doi.org/10.1787/775352887755

SCIENCE AND TECHNOLOGY • RESEARCH AND DEVELOPMENT (R&D)

INVESTMENT IN KNOWLEDGE

"Investment in knowledge" is a synthetic indicator designed to compare member countries' expenditures on their "knowledge base" which are aimed at bringing future returns.

Definition

Investment in knowledge is defined as the sum of expenditure on R&D, on total higher education (public and private) and on software. This sum is then divided by each country's GDP to produce a comparable indicator across countries. Simple summation of the three components would lead to overestimation of the investment in knowledge owing to overlaps (R&D and software, R&D and education, software and education). Therefore, data reported here have been adjusted to exclude the overlaps between components.

Note that as the term is used here, "investment" has a broader connotation than its usual meaning in economic statistics. It includes current expenditures, such as on education and R&D, as well as capital outlays, such as purchases of software and construction of school buildings.

Long-term trends

Most OECD countries are increasing investment in their knowledge base. During the 1990s, it increased by more than 7.5% annually in Denmark, Finland, Ireland and Sweden. The amount of investment in knowledge was still low in Greece, Ireland and Portugal, although growth of GDP was similar to that of the most knowledge-based economies (such as Finland and Sweden).

For most countries, increases in software expenditure were the major source of increased investment in knowledge. Notable exceptions are Finland (where R&D was the main source of increase) and Sweden (where all three components grew).

In 2000, investment in knowledge amounted to 4.8% of GDP in the OECD area. The ratio of investment in knowledge to GDP is 2.8 percentage points higher in the United States than in the European Union. In Sweden (7.2%), the United States (6.8%) and Finland (6.2%) investment in knowledge exceeds 6% of GDP. In contrast, it is less than 2.5% of GDP in southern and central European countries and in Mexico.

Comparability

The OECD is the source of the data on R&D and education. Because software investment data are only available for some OECD countries, this component was estimated using data from a private source. An OECD task force has developed a harmonised method for estimating software.

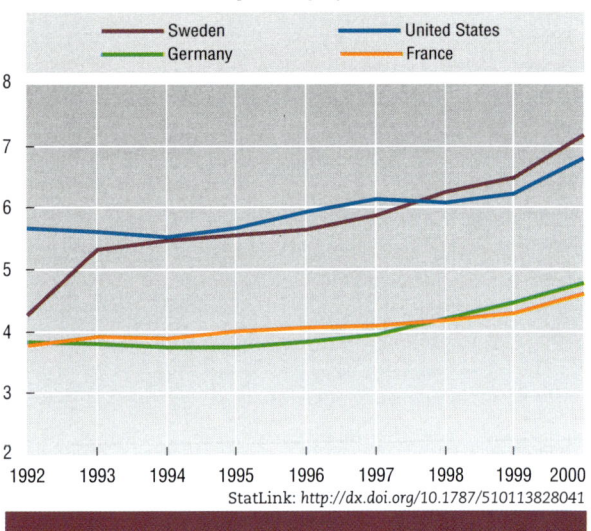

Investment in knowledge for selected countries
As a percentage of GDP

StatLink: http://dx.doi.org/10.1787/510113828041

Source

OECD (2003), *OECD Science, Technology and Industry Scoreboard*, OECD, Paris.

Further information

• **Analytical publications**

Ahmad, N. (2003), "Measuring Investment in Software", *OECD Directorate for Science, Technology and Industry Working Paper*, No. 2003/6, OECD, Paris, www.oecd.org/sti/working-papers.

• **Methodological publications**

Kahn, M. (2001), "Investment in Knowledge", *STI Review* No. 27, OECD, Paris.

• **Statistical publications**

OECD (2004), *Main Science and Technology Indicators*, OECD, Paris.

OECD (2004), *Research and Development Statistics*, OECD, Paris.

• **Web sites**

Measuring Science and Technology: www.oecd.org/sti/measuring-scitech.

OECD Science, Technology and Industry Scoreboard: www.oecd.org/sti/scoreboard.

SCIENCE AND TECHNOLOGY • RESEARCH AND DEVELOPMENT (R&D)

INVESTMENT IN KNOWLEDGE

Investment in knowledge
As a percentage of GDP

	1992	1993	1994	1995	1996	1997	1998	1999	2000
Australia	3.9	3.7	3.8	3.8	3.9	3.8	3.9	3.9	4.0
Austria	2.8	2.7	2.8	2.9	2.8	3.4	3.7	3.8	3.8
Belgium	..	..	..	..	..	..	..	4.3	..
Canada	5.3	5.0	4.9	4.9	4.7	4.5	4.7	5.4	5.4
Czech Republic	..	3.3	3.2	3.0	2.9	3.0	3.1	3.3	3.7
Denmark	3.6	3.8	3.8	3.8	3.9	3.9	4.8	5.0	..
Finland	4.3	4.4	4.1	4.3	4.7	4.8	5.2	5.8	6.2
France	3.8	3.9	3.9	4.0	4.0	4.1	4.2	4.3	4.6
Germany	3.8	3.8	3.7	3.7	3.8	3.9	4.2	4.4	4.8
Greece	1.1	1.2	1.3	1.2	1.4	1.6	1.8	1.6	..
Hungary	3.0	2.6	2.5	2.2	2.2	2.5	2.6	2.7	3.1
Ireland	2.6	2.8	2.9	2.8	2.9	2.8	2.9	2.9	3.1
Italy	2.3	2.2	2.0	2.0	2.0	2.0	2.1	2.1	2.3
Japan	4.0	3.9	4.0	4.1	4.2	4.4	4.5	4.6	4.7
Korea	..	..	..	4.5	4.8	5.1	5.2	5.0	5.4
Mexico	..	1.2	1.5	1.5	1.5	1.6	1.5	1.8	..
Netherlands	3.8	3.9	3.9	3.9	4.1	4.0	4.2	4.5	4.8
Norway	3.5	3.6	3.7	3.7	3.5	3.5	3.9	3.9	3.8
Poland	..	..	..	..	..	..	..	2.0	1.9
Portugal	1.4	1.6	1.5	1.6	1.7	1.7	1.9	1.9	2.2
Slovak Republic	..	..	..	..	..	..	..	2.4	..
Spain	1.9	1.9	1.9	1.9	2.0	2.1	2.2	2.2	2.5
Sweden	4.3	5.3	5.5	5.5	5.6	5.9	6.2	6.5	7.2
Switzerland	4.1	4.3	4.3	4.3	4.3	4.5	4.8	5.0	5.2
United Kingdom	3.7	3.7	3.6	3.7	3.8	3.7	3.9	4.1	4.3
United States	5.7	5.6	5.5	5.7	5.9	6.1	6.1	6.2	6.8

StatLink: http://dx.doi.org/10.1787/081167773644

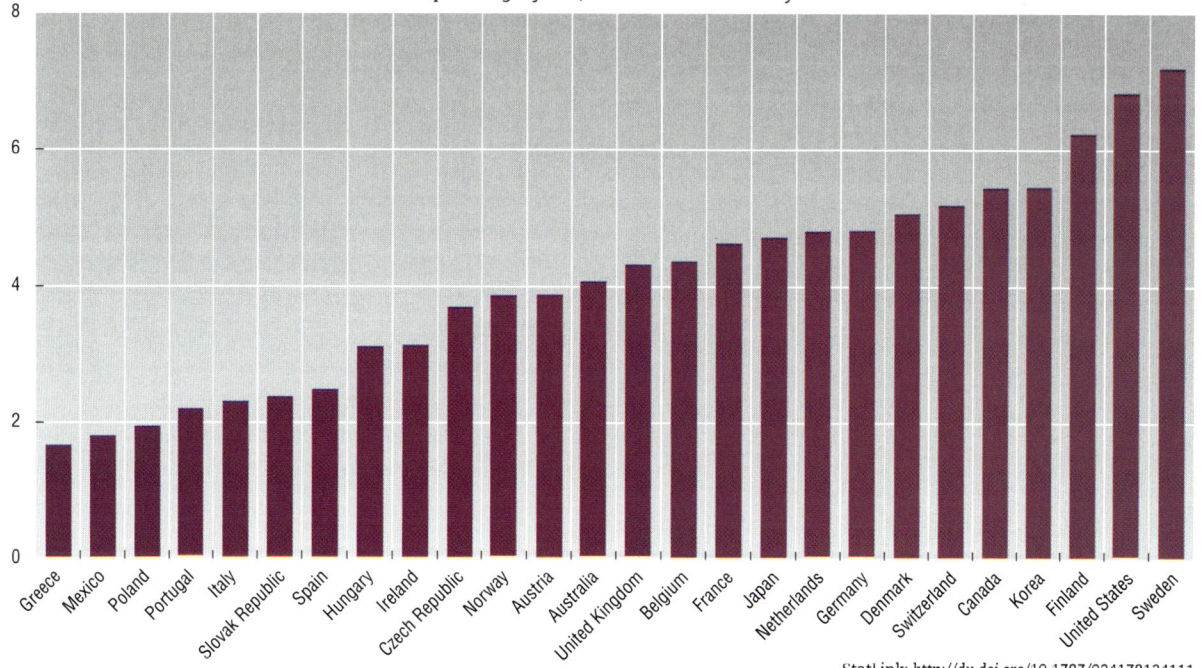

Investment in knowledge
As a percentage of GDP, 2000 or latest available year

StatLink: http://dx.doi.org/10.1787/024178124111

OECD FACTBOOK 2005 – ISBN 92-64-01869-7 – © OECD 2005

SCIENCE AND TECHNOLOGY • RESEARCH AND DEVELOPMENT (R&D)

RESEARCHERS

Researchers are the central element of the research and development system. In 2000, approximately 3.4 million persons in the OECD area were employed in research and development and approximately two-thirds of these were engaged in the business sector.

Definition

Researchers are defined as professionals engaged in the conception and creation of new knowledge, products, processes, methods and systems and are directly involved in the management of projects. They include researchers working in both civil and military research in government, universities, research institutes as well as in the business sector.

Comparability

The number of researchers is expressed in full-time equivalent (FTE) on R&D (*i.e.* a person working half-time on R&D is counted as 0.5 person-year) and includes staff engaged in R&D during the course of one year. The data have been compiled on the basis of the methodology of the *Frascati Manual* but comparability over time is affected to some extent by improvements in the coverage of national R&D surveys and efforts by countries to improve the international comparability of their data.

The figures for the United States exclude military personnel in the government sector.

Long-term trends

In 2000, there were about 6.5 researchers per thousand employees, a significant increase from the 1991 level of 5.6 researchers per thousand. The number of researchers has steadily increased over the last two decades. Japan has the highest number of researchers relative to total employment, followed by the United States and the European Union. The percentage of researchers in the United States, Japan, Sweden and Finland is substantially above the OECD average.

The number of researchers in the business sector is of particular interest because business sector research is more closely linked to the creation of new products and processes. Growth in the number of business researchers has been strong in smaller OECD countries such as Iceland, Mexico, Portugal and Turkey, where the number of business researchers increased by more than 12% annually over the last decade.

Countries in central and eastern Europe have been affected by the reduction in numbers of business researchers in the 1990s, although the trend has reversed in the Czech Republic and Hungary in the past few years. Italy is the only other OECD country where the number of business researchers has decreased.

Source

OECD (2003), *Main Science and Technology Indicators*, OECD, Paris.

Further information

• *Analytical publications*

OECD (2003), *OECD Science, Technology and Industry Scoreboard*, OECD, Paris.

• *Statistical publications*

OECD (2004), *Main Science and Technology Indicators*, OECD, Paris.

OECD (2004), *Research and Development Statistics*, OECD, Paris.

• *Methodological publications*

OECD (2002), *Frascati Manual: Proposed Standard Practice for Surveys on Research and Experimental Development*, OECD, Paris.

• *Web sites*

Measuring Science and Technology:
www.oecd.org/sti/measuring-scitech.

OECD Science, Technology and Industry:
www.oecd.org/sti.

SCIENCE AND TECHNOLOGY • RESEARCH AND DEVELOPMENT (R&D)

RESEARCHERS

Number of researchers
Per thousand employed

	1990	1991	1992	1993	1994	1995	1996	1997	1998	1999	2000	2001
Australia	5.5	..	6.8	..	7.0	..	7.2	..	7.2	..	7.2	..
Austria	..	..	..	3.3	..	..	..	..	4.7	..	..	..
Belgium	..	4.8	..	5.6	6.2	6.1	6.3	6.6	7.1	7.5	..	..
Canada	4.9	5.1	5.5	5.8	6.4	6.5	6.6	6.6	6.2	6.1	..	..
Czech Republic	..	..	..	..	..	..	..	..	..	..	..	..
Denmark	4.4	4.6	5.0	5.3	..	6.1	6.3	6.5	..	6.8	..	..
Finland	..	6.0	..	7.4	..	8.2	..	12.3	13.9	14.5	15.1	15.8
France	5.4	5.7	6.2	6.5	6.6	6.7	6.8	6.8	6.7	6.8	7.1	..
Germany	..	6.3	..	..	..	6.2	6.2	6.3	6.3	6.7	6.7	6.7
Greece	..	1.7	..	2.2	..	2.5	..	2.9	..	3.7	..	..
Hungary	3.9	3.2	3.0	3.1	3.1	2.9	2.9	3.1	3.2	3.3	3.8	3.8
Iceland	..	..	..	..	..	..	..	..	..	..	..	..
Ireland	4.0	4.4	4.8	4.1	4.3	4.5	4.8	5.0	5.1	4.9	5.0	..
Italy	3.4	3.3	3.3	3.3	3.4	3.4	3.5	3.0	2.9	2.9	2.9	..
Japan	7.4	7.5	7.7	7.9	8.1	8.3	9.2	9.2	9.7	9.9	9.7	10.2
Korea	..	..	..	..	..	4.9	4.8	4.9	4.6	5.0	5.2	6.4
Luxembourg	..	..	..	..	..	..	..	..	..	..	..	..
Mexico	..	..	..	0.4	0.5	0.6	0.6	0.6	0.5	0.6	..	..
Netherlands	..	..	..	4.6	4.9	4.8	4.7	5.0	5.1	5.1	5.2	..
New Zealand	5.1	5.0	6.1	6.3	..	5.7	..	7.5	..	7.6	..	..
Norway	..	6.6	..	7.2	..	7.5	..	7.9	..	8.0	..	8.5
Poland	..	..	..	..	3.3	3.4	3.5	3.6	3.6	3.7	3.7	3.8
Portugal	1.3	..	2.1	..	..	2.6	..	3.0	3.1	3.3	3.4	3.5
Slovak Republic	..	..	..	..	4.9	4.5	4.5	4.6	4.6	4.3	4.7	4.5
Spain	2.7	2.9	3.0	3.2	3.6	3.5	3.8	3.8	4.1	4.1	4.9	5.0
Sweden	..	5.9	..	7.2	..	8.2	..	9.2	..	9.6	..	10.6
Switzerland	..	..	..	..	..	..	..	..	..	..	..	..
Turkey	0.6	0.6	0.7	0.7	0.7	0.8	0.9	0.9	0.9	0.9	1.1	..
United Kingdom	4.6	4.6	4.8	4.9	5.0	5.3	5.2	5.2	5.5	..	..	..
United States	..	7.7	..	7.8	..	7.6	..	8.2	..	8.6	..	..
EU15	..	4.7	4.8	5.0	..	5.2	5.3	5.3	5.5	5.6	5.8	..
OECD total	5.8	5.6	5.7	5.8	5.9	5.8	6.1	6.1	6.3	6.4	6.5	..

StatLink: http://dx.doi.org/10.1787/858836037304

Number of researchers
Per thousand employed, 2001 or latest available year

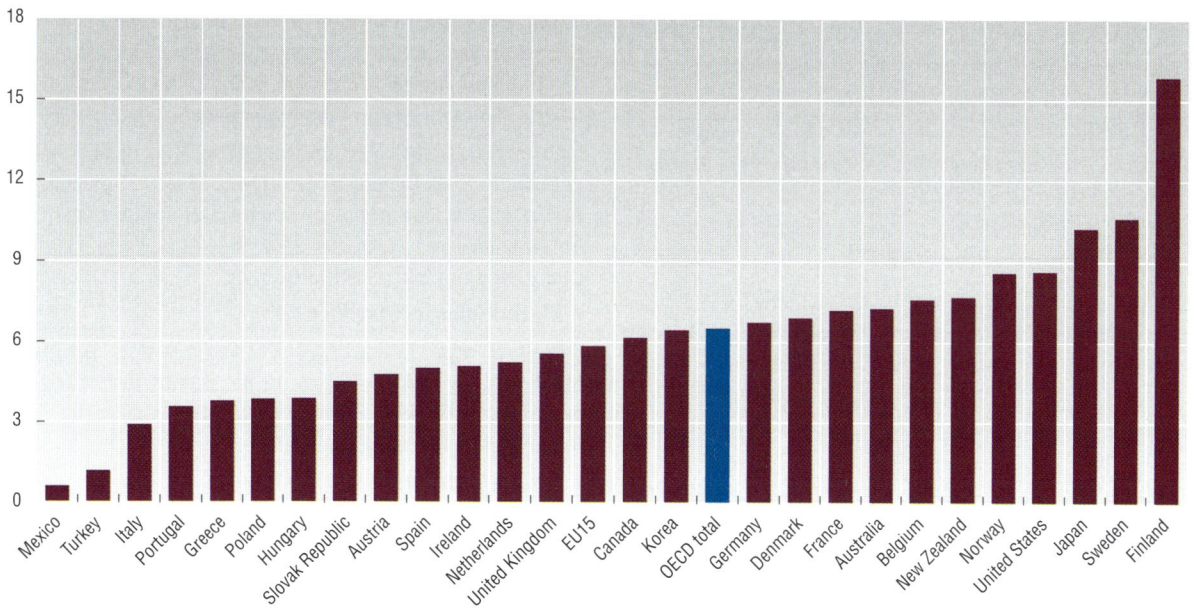

StatLink: http://dx.doi.org/10.1787/478586310848

SCIENCE AND TECHNOLOGY • RESEARCH AND DEVELOPMENT (R&D)

PATENTS

Patent-based indicators provide a measure of the output of a country's R&D: its inventions. However, the methodology used can influence the results. Simple counts of patents filed at an intellectual property office are affected by various sources of bias, such as weaknesses in international comparability (home advantage for patent applications) or highly heterogeneous patent values. The OECD has developed a patents indicator using what are here called triadic patent families. This indicator is designed to capture all important inventions and to be internationally comparable.

Definition

A patent family is defined as a set of patents taken in various countries (*i.e.* patent offices) to protect the same invention. A triadic patent family is a set of patents registered at all of the three largest patents offices, namely the European Patent Office (EPO), the Japanese Patent Office (JPO) and the US Patent and Trademark Office (USPTO).

Comparability

The concept of triadic patent families has been developed in order to improve the international comparability of patent-based indicators.

Long-term trends

In 1998, there were more than 40 000 patent families in the OECD area, a 32% increase from 1991. The United States accounted for around 36% of the OECD total, followed by the European Union (33%) and Japan (25%). Over the 1990s the European Union's share of patent families converged towards that of the United States, while that of Japan declined.

When population is taken into account, Switzerland and Sweden had the highest propensity to patent among OECD countries.

In 1998, Switzerland had 119 patent families per million population and Sweden had 107. Japan (81), Finland (75), Germany (70) and the United States (52) also had a high propensity to patent. In contrast, the Czech Republic, Mexico, Poland, Portugal, Slovak Republic and Turkey had a low propensity to patent.

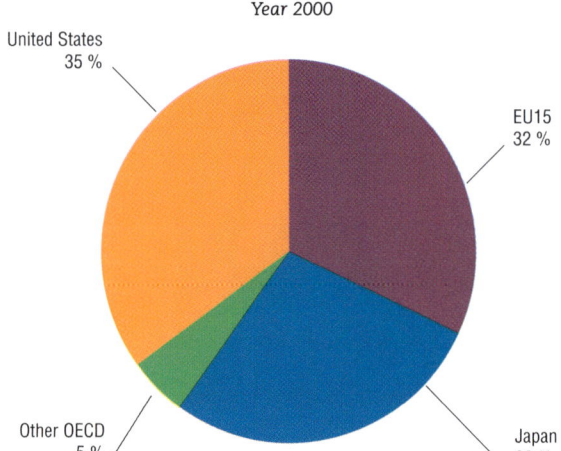

Share of triadic patent families
Year 2000

StatLink: http://dx.doi.org/10.1787/155726865671

Source

OECD (2003), *OECD Science, Technology and Industry Scoreboard*, OECD, Paris.

Further information

• *Analytical publications*

Dernis, H., D. Guellec and B. van Pottelsberghe (2001), "Using Patent Counts for Cross-country Comparisons of Technology Output", *STI Review*, No. 27, OECD, Paris.

Johnson, D. (2002), "The OECD Technology Concordance (OTC): Patents by Industry of Manufacture and Sector of Use", *OECD Directorate for Science, Technology and Industry Working Paper*, No. 2002/5, OECD, Paris, *www.oecd.org/sti/working-papers*.

Lichtenberg, F. and S. Virabhak (2002), "Using Patents to Map Technical Change in Health-Related Areas", *OECD Directorate for Science, Technology and Industry Working Paper*, No. 2002/16, OECD, Paris, *www.oecd.org/sti/working-papers*.

• *Methodological publications*

Dernis, H. and M. Khan (2004), "Triadic Patent Families Methodology", *OECD Directorate for Science, Technology and Industry Working Paper*, No. 2004/2, OECD, Paris, *www.oecd.org/sti/working-papers*.

• *Online databases*

OECD Patent Database: *www.oecd.org/sti/ipr-statistics*.

• *Web sites*

OECD Work on Patents: *www.oecd.org/sti/ipr-statistics*.
OECD Intellectual Property Rights: *www.oecd.org/sti/ipr*.

SCIENCE AND TECHNOLOGY • RESEARCH AND DEVELOPMENT (R&D)

PATENTS

Number of triadic patent families
According to the residence of the inventors

	1990	1991	1992	1993	1994	1995	1996	1997	1998	1999	2000
Australia	186	156	181	192	228	226	222	299	301	304	321
Austria	171	174	146	173	209	217	211	248	267	262	274
Belgium	223	239	291	329	346	369	351	395	387	366	359
Canada	285	275	269	300	353	382	420	525	557	539	519
Czech Republic	7	9	7	8	5	3	10	10	11	9	9
Denmark	127	105	135	159	174	188	216	221	227	250	254
Finland	149	161	222	245	336	312	342	416	426	419	489
France	1 919	1 783	1 646	1 695	1 865	1 905	2 103	2 200	2 276	2 081	2 127
Germany	4 112	3 676	3 865	3 989	4 346	4 815	5 473	5 634	5 988	5 867	5 777
Greece	4	5	6	3	4	1	12	9	10	4	6
Hungary	30	22	19	23	20	25	24	31	19	30	33
Iceland	1	3	0	1	3	6	7	4	4	5	4
Ireland	27	27	23	18	28	31	28	37	46	56	45
Italy	646	659	575	628	620	610	682	711	716	740	767
Japan	9 929	8 895	8 165	8 459	8 206	9 428	10 575	11 207	11 196	11 726	11 757
Korea	65	93	119	168	213	327	324	387	462	459	478
Luxembourg	17	9	9	14	7	13	15	16	19	19	17
Mexico	7	6	5	6	5	12	8	11	12	11	15
Netherlands	591	568	612	596	644	724	778	840	829	833	857
New Zealand	9	19	26	11	23	20	31	39	37	33	36
Norway	52	58	73	70	80	86	74	94	109	108	109
Poland	5	9	5	12	4	5	9	9	7	8	10
Portugal	1	3	4	4	2	2	3	6	8	5	8
Slovak Republic			1	1	1	2	1	4	3	3	4
Spain	73	70	65	73	84	87	87	108	111	120	113
Sweden	430	391	516	501	631	700	790	853	882	838	811
Switzerland	788	723	714	706	709	746	796	790	812	792	753
Turkey	1	0	0	2	2	2	2	3	6	5	6
United Kingdom	1 452	1 250	1 308	1 356	1 459	1 516	1 581	1 589	1 812	1 767	1 794
United States	11 165	10 217	10 568	10 531	11 095	12 312	14 726	14 763	14 810	15 079	14 985
EU15	9 942	9 122	9 423	9 784	10 754	11 489	12 672	13 283	14 004	13 627	13 699
OECD total	32 475	29 607	29 575	30 274	31 701	35 070	39 902	41 459	42 350	42 738	42 739

StatLink: http://dx.doi.org/10.1787/880053316378

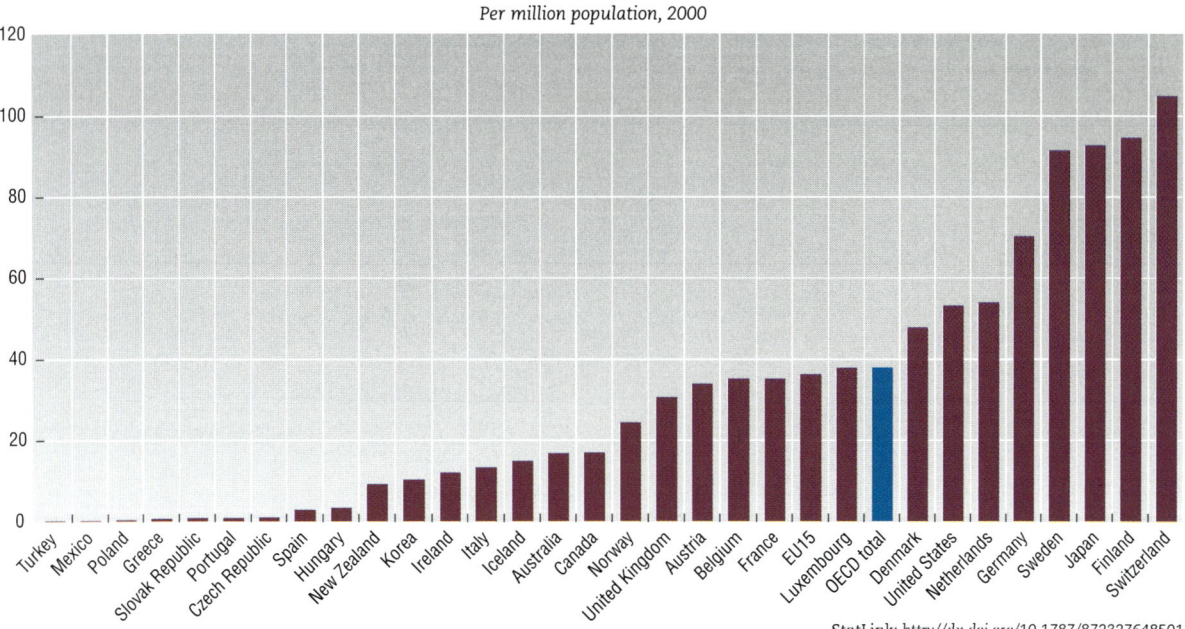

Number of triadic patent families
Per million population, 2000

StatLink: http://dx.doi.org/10.1787/872327648501

OECD FACTBOOK 2005 – ISBN 92-64-01869-7 – © OECD 2005

SCIENCE AND TECHNOLOGY • ICT

SIZE OF THE ICT SECTOR

Information and communication technologies (ICTs) have been at the heart of economic changes for more than a decade. ICT-producing sectors play an important role, notably by contributing to rapid technological progress and productivity growth.

Definition

In 1998, the OECD countries reached agreement on an industry-based definition of the ICT sector based on Revision 3 of the International Standard Industrial Classification (ISIC Rev. 3). The principles underlying the definition are the following.

For manufacturing industries, the products of a candidate industry must be intended to fulfil the function of information processing and communication including transmission and display, must use electronic processing to detect, measure and/or record physical phenomena or control a physical process.

For services industries, the products of a candidate industry must be intended to enable the function of information processing and communication by electronic means.

Comparability

The existence of a widely accepted definition of the ICT sector is the first step towards making comparisons across time and countries possible. However, the definition is not as yet consistently applied and data provided by member countries have been combined with different data sources to estimate ICT aggregates compatible with national accounts totals. For this reason, statistics presented here may differ from figures contained in national reports and in previous OECD publications.

Long-term trends

The ICT sector grew strongly in OECD countries over the 1990s. Rapid growth was especially apparent in Finland, Norway and Sweden. In Finland, the ICT sector's share of value added doubled over 1995-2001 and now represents over 16.4% of total business sector value added. In 2000, the ICT sector represented between 5% and 16.5% of total business sector value added in OECD countries. The average share in a group of 25 OECD countries was about 9.8%; it was 8.7% in the European Union.

In most OECD countries, ICT services have increased their relative share of the ICT sector, owing to the increasing importance of telecommunication services and software in OECD countries and, more broadly, a general shift towards a services economy.

Most OECD countries already have a well-developed telecommunication services sector, which makes a sizeable contribution to ICT sector value added. The Czech Republic and Hungary have the highest relative share of telecommunication services. At the same time, there is a noticeable increase in the contribution of computer and related services, mainly software services. The share of computer and related services in business services value added was highest in Ireland (7% in 1999), Sweden (5.7% in 2000), and the United Kingdom (5% in 2001). Software consultancy accounts for between 60% and 80% of computer services.

Source

OECD (2003), *OECD Science, Technology and Industry Scoreboard*, OECD, Paris.

Further information

• *Analytical publications*

OECD (2002), *Measuring the Information Economy*, OECD, Paris.

OECD (2003), *ICT and Economic Growth: Evidence from OECD Countries, Industries and Firms*, OECD, Paris.

OECD (2004), *Information and Communication Technology Outlook*, OECD, Paris.

OECD (2004), *Understanding Economic Growth*, OECD, Paris.

• *Statistical publications*

OECD (2003), *OECD Telecommunications Database*, OECD, Paris.

• *Web sites*

OECD Science, Technology and Industry: *www.oecd.org/sti*.

OECD Telecommunications and Internet Policy *www.oecd.org/sti/telecom*.

SCIENCE AND TECHNOLOGY • ICT

SIZE OF THE ICT SECTOR

Share of ICT in value added, 2000

	ICT services value added As a percentage of total business services value added					*ICT manufacturing value added* As a percentage of total manufacturing value added			
	Telecommunication services	Computer and related services	Other ICT services	Total	Change in the share 1995-2000, percentage	Computer & office equipment	Other ICT manufacturing	Total	Change in the share 1995-2000, percentage
Australia	4.9	2.4	2.0	9.3	..	0.6	2.7	3.3	..
Austria	2.8	1.8	4.0	8.6	..	0.4	6.9	7.3	0.1
Belgium	2.4	6.1	3.8	12.3	2.0	0.1	4.3	4.5	0.3
Canada	4.2	3.1	1.9	9.2	1.2	1.2	7.4	8.5	3.4
Czech Republic	9.0	2.8	0.0	11.8	6.2	0.3	4.0	4.2	1.5
Denmark	3.2	2.6	3.9	9.7	0.7	1.0	5.6	6.6	0.1
Finland	5.9	4.0	2.7	12.6	4.9	0.1	22.8	22.9	13.4
France	2.8	4.0	2.3	9.1	0.6	0.6	5.6	6.3	0.8
Germany	3.2	3.6	0.0	6.8	0.8	0.9	4.7	5.6	1.0
Hungary	6.8	2.6	1.1	10.5	3.0	1.6	6.9	8.4	..
Ireland	5.1	7.0	2.7	14.7	1.4	10.4	8.3	18.7	2.3
Italy	3.4	3.6	1.4	8.4	1.2	0.3	3.1	3.4	- 0.8
Japan	5.5	1.8	0.1	7.4	2.4	2.2	11.8	14.0	2.0
Korea	0.5	1.7	5.2	7.5	1.3	4.4	13.0	17.4	2.0
Mexico	3.1	0.2	1.0	4.3	0.3	3.1	5.0	8.1	2.9
Netherlands	2.2	3.9	5.5	11.5	1.8	0.6	6.3	6.8	- 0.3
Norway	3.2	3.5	2.6	9.3	1.4	0.9	4.1	5.0	0.4
Portugal	6.0	1.2	2.7	9.9	1.0	0.1	4.5	4.5	0.3
Slovak Republic	4.8	1.7	0.0	6.5	1.0	0.2	3.1	3.3	0.1
Spain	5.9	2.1	1.7	9.7	2.5	0.6	2.6	3.2	- 0.4
Sweden	4.5	5.7	2.5	12.6	3.6	0.4	6.5	7.0	- 1.4
United Kingdom	4.2	5.0	2.7	11.9	1.7	1.8	7.1	8.9	0.6
United States	4.4	4.4	1.8	10.6	1.6	2.6	10.2	12.8	2.0
EU15	..	..	..	6.8	..	..	..	1.9	..
OECD total	..	..	..	6.7	..	..	..	3.1	..

StatLink: http://dx.doi.org/10.1787/734333723707

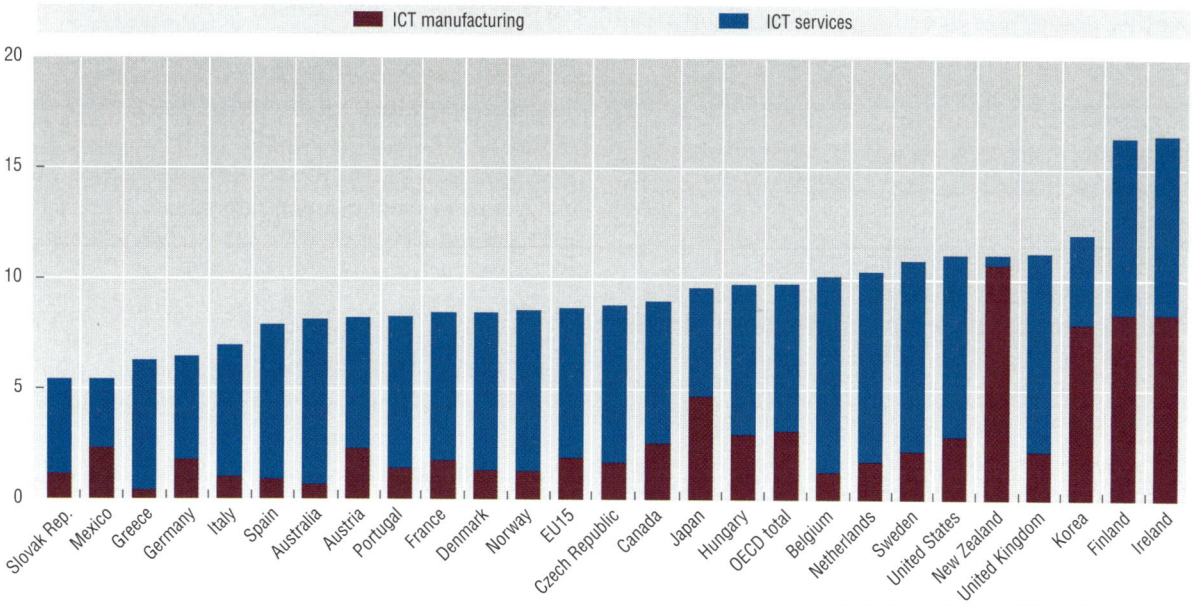

Share of ICT in value added
As a percentage of business sector value added, 2000

StatLink: http://dx.doi.org/10.1787/856481001740

SCIENCE AND TECHNOLOGY • ICT

INVESTMENT IN ICT

Investment in physical capital is important for growth. It is a way to expand and renew the capital stock and enable new technologies to enter the production process. Information and communication technology (ICT) has been the most dynamic component of investment in recent years.

Definition

Investment is defined in accordance with the 1993 System of National Accounts. It covers the acquisition of equipment and computer software that is used in production for more than one year. ICT has three components: information technology equipment (computers and related hardware), communications equipment and software. Software includes acquisition of pre-packaged software, customised software and software developed in house.

Comparability

Correct measurement of ICT investment in both nominal and volume terms is crucial for estimating the contribution of ICT to economic growth and performance. Data availability and measurement of ICT investment based on national accounts (SNA93) vary considerably across OECD countries, especially as regards the measurement of investment in software, the methods of deflation, the breakdown by institutional sector and the length of time series.

Expenditure on software has only recently been treated as investment in the national accounts, and methodologies vary greatly across countries. Only the United States produces estimates of expenditure on the three separate software components; other countries usually provide estimates for some software components only. To tackle the specific problems relating to software in the national accounts, a joint OECD-EU Task Force on the Measurement of Software in the National Accounts has developed recommendations concerning the capitalisation of software.

Note that ICT components that are incorporated in other products, such as motor vehicles or machine tools, are included in the value of those other products and are excluded from ICT investment as defined here.

Long-term trends

ICT's share in total non-residential investment doubled and in some cases even quadrupled between 1980 and 2000. In 2001/2002, ICT's share was particularly high in Sweden, the United Kingdom and the United States.

Software has been the fastest growing component of ICT investment. In many countries, its share in non-residential investment multiplied several times between 1980 and 2000. Software's share in total investment is highest in Denmark, Sweden and the United States.

Source

OECD Productivity Database:
www.oecd.org/statistics/productivity.

Further information

• *Analytical publications*

OECD (2003), *Communication Outlook*, OECD, Paris.

OECD (2003), *ICT and Economic Growth: Evidence from OECD Countries, Industries and Firms*, OECD, Paris.

OECD (2003), *OECD Science, Technology and Industry Scoreboard*, OECD, Paris.

OECD (2004), *Information Technology Outlook*, OECD, Paris.

• *Methodological publications*

Ahmad, N. (2003), "Measuring Investment in Software", *OECD Directorate for Science, Technology and Industry Working Paper*, No. 2003/6, OECD, Paris, *www.oecd.org/sti/working-papers*.

Lequiller, F. et al. (2003), "Report of the OECD Task Force on Software Measurement in the National Accounts", *OECD Statistics Directorate Working Paper*, No. 2003/1, OECD, Paris, *www.oecd.org/std/workingpapers*.

Schreyer, P., P.E. Bignon and J. Dupont (2003), "OECD Capital Services Estimates: Methodology and a First Set of Results", *OECD Statistics Directorate Working Paper*, No. 2003/6, OECD, Paris, *www.oecd.org/std/workingpapers*.

• *Statistical publications*

OECD (2003), *National Accounts of OECD Countries*, OECD, Paris.

OECD STructural ANalysis (STAN) on CD-ROM, 2003.

• *Online databases*

SourceOECD STructural ANalysis (STAN) Database.

SCIENCE AND TECHNOLOGY • ICT

INVESTMENT IN ICT

Share of ICT investment in non-residential fixed capital formation
As a percentage of total non-residential fixed capital formation, total economy

	1990	1991	1992	1993	1994	1995	1996	1997	1998	1999	2000	2001	2002
Australia	12.5	14.2	15.7	16.6	18.1	18.2	18.7	18.8	20.3	21.0	22.5	23.2	21.4
Austria	10.0	10.1	9.4	10.1	11.1	10.4	10.8	11.3	13.3	13.8	13.1	13.0	..
Belgium	16.2	16.5	17.5	15.2	16.0	16.5	17.3	18.1	20.0	20.8	23.7	21.9	..
Canada	13.2	14.2	16.1	16.9	16.4	16.8	18.0	17.5	18.8	19.9	20.5	20.3	19.8
Denmark	17.7	18.2	19.0	20.5	18.7	20.7	20.5	21.2	20.7	21.6	19.9	20.3	..
Finland	9.1	10.6	13.5	17.2	20.2	22.2	18.8	22.3	25.3	27.5	30.9	28.1	..
France	7.8	7.5	7.6	8.1	8.6	9.0	9.8	11.0	11.9	12.2	12.8	13.2	13.7
Germany	13.9	13.7	13.2	13.3	13.2	13.3	14.2	14.7	15.3	16.5	17.4	17.8	16.5
Greece	9.4	11.6	11.7	16.1	14.3	12.7	13.2	13.2	15.1	15.3	16.7	18.2	..
Ireland	8.3	9.7	9.5	10.2	11.7	15.6	14.4	14.7	13.4	12.4	14.4	12.8	..
Italy	14.2	14.2	14.2	14.3	15.1	14.8	15.1	16.3	15.9	16.1	16.1	15.5	..
Japan	8.0	8.5	8.6	8.9	9.0	10.3	12.5	12.3	12.6	13.8	14.4	14.2	13.1
Netherlands	14.0	13.6	14.3	14.8	14.6	14.1	14.8	16.2	17.8	18.3	18.5	18.0	..
New Zealand	12.3	12.9	12.9	11.4	11.4	10.8	10.9	11.3	13.6	12.7	15.5	14.4	13.6
Portugal	10.4	11.6	11.5	11.5	11.5	12.5	12.8	11.9	11.8	11.7	11.8	12.0	..
Spain	12.0	11.5	11.2	11.5	11.8	9.6	11.2	10.9	10.9	10.8	11.2	10.7	..
Sweden	15.0	16.4	19.0	24.3	23.8	23.5	22.7	24.2	26.3	27.9	30.0	29.5	..
United Kingdom	13.8	14.4	15.1	16.6	18.3	20.7	21.1	20.2	23.1	22.1	23.5	21.9	..
United States	24.6	26.3	27.7	26.8	26.3	27.3	27.9	28.8	28.9	31.3	33.4	32.1	32.6

StatLink: http://dx.doi.org/10.1787/877622703742

Share of ICT investment in non-residential fixed capital formation
As a percentage of total non-residential fixed capital formation, total economy, 2001

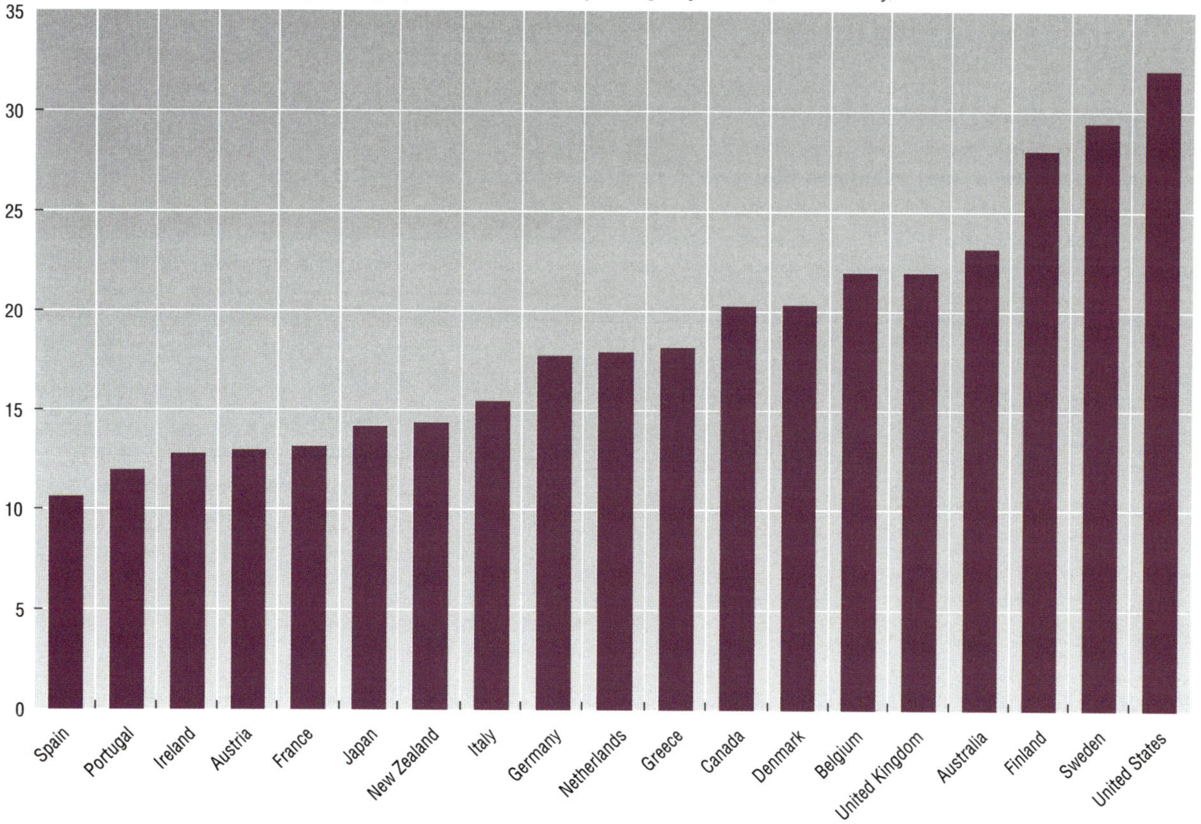

StatLink: http://dx.doi.org/10.1787/888803231626

SCIENCE AND TECHNOLOGY • ICT

COMPUTER AND INTERNET ACCESS BY HOUSEHOLDS

Computers are increasingly present in homes in OECD countries, both in countries that already have high penetration rates and in those where adoption has lagged.

Definition

The table shows the number of households that reported having at least one personal computer in working order in their household. The second part of the table shows the percentage of households who reported that they had access to the Internet. In almost all cases this access is via a personal computer either using a telephone modem or ADSL-type broadband access.

Comparability

Over a very short period, national statistical offices have made great progress in providing indicators of the use of information and communication technology. From an international perspective, the major drawback of official statistics on ICT use is that they remain based on different standards and measure rapidly changing behaviour at different points in time. Most countries use existing surveys, such as labour force, time use, household expenditure or general social surveys. Others rely on special surveys.

Another issue for international comparability is the choice between households and individuals as the survey unit. Household surveys generally provide information on both the household and the individuals in the household. Person-based data typically provide information on the number of individuals with access to a technology, those using the technology, the location at which they use it and the purpose of use.

Statistics on ICT use by households may run into problems of international comparability because of structural differences in the composition of households. On the other hand, statistics on individuals may use different age groups, and age is an important determinant of ICT use. Household- and person-based measures yield different figures in terms of levels and growth rates. Such differences complicate international comparisons and make benchmarking exercises based on a single indicator of Internet access or use misleading, since country rankings change according to the indicator used.

The OECD has addressed issues of international comparability by developing a model survey on ICT use in households/by individuals. The model survey is designed to be flexible; it uses modules addressing different topics so that additional components can be added as technologies reflecting usage practices and policy interests change.

Long-term trends

Penetration rates are high in Denmark, Korea, Norway, Sweden, Switzerland and Canada where approximately two-thirds of households had access to a home computer by 2003. On the other hand, shares in the Czech Republic, France, Ireland, Mexico and Portugal were below 50%. Between 2000 and 2003, the percentages of households with access to a home computer increased particularly sharply in Austria, France and Japan..

The picture with regard to Internet access is similar. In Canada, Denmark, Japan, Korea, Sweden and the United States, more than half of households had Internet access by 2003. In the Czech Republic, Mexico and Portugal, on the other hand, only about one-fifth or less had Internet access by 2003.

Data on Internet access by household composition are available for the United Kingdom, Finland, Austria and Germany. They show that more households with children have Internet access than households without children.

Source

OECD (2004), *Information Technology Outlook*, OECD, Paris.

Further information

• **Analytical publications**

OECD (2003), *Communications Outlook*, OECD, Paris.

OECD (2003), *OECD Science, Technology and Industry Scoreboard*, OECD, Paris.

OECD (2004), *Access Pricing in Telecommunications*, OECD, Paris.

• **Statistical publications**

OECD (2003), *OECD Telecommunications Database*, OECD, Paris.

• **Web sites**

OECD Science, Technology and Industry: *www.oecd.org/sti*.

OECD Telecommunications and Internet Policy *www.oecd.org/sti/telecom*.

SCIENCE AND TECHNOLOGY • ICT
COMPUTER AND INTERNET ACCESS BY HOUSEHOLDS

Households with access to home computers and the Internet

	Percentage of households with access to a home computer				Percentage of households with access to the Internet			
	2000	2001	2002	2003	2000	2001	2002	2003
Australia	53.0	58.0	61.0	..	32.0	42.0	46.0	..
Austria	34.0	..	45.4	49.3	32.0	42.0	46.0	..
Belgium	..	..	44.6	..	..	28.0	..	..
Canada	61.3	64.0	..	..	40.1	48.7	51.4	54.5
Czech Republic	..	..	24.6	..	..	..	16.4	..
Denmark	65.0	69.6	72.0	..	46.0	48.0	59.0	..
Finland	47.0	52.9	54.5	..	30.0	39.5	44.3	..
France	27.0	32.4	36.6	41.0	11.9	18.1	23.0	28.0
Germany	53.4	57.2	57.9	..	27.3	36.0	43.3	..
Ireland	32.4	..	..	42.3	20.4	..	..	33.6
Italy	29.4	..	..	..	18.8	..	..	..
Japan	38.6	50.1	57.2	63.3	34.0	35.1	48.8	52.0
Korea	71.0	76.9	78.6	77.9	..	39.9	51.3	..
Mexico	10.4	11.6	15.2	..	..	6.2	..	..
Netherlands	64.0	69.0	..	..	41.0	..	..	..
New Zealand	42.8	46.6	52.0	..	..	37.4	..	..
Norway	..	..	..	68.0	..	..	..	55.0
Portugal	29.4	39.0	..	38.3	9.0	13.0	..	21.7
Spain	30.4	..	..	..	..	..	..	..
Sweden	59.9	69.2	..	..	48.2	53.3	..	..
Switzerland	59.9	69.2	..	..	36.5	..	..	..
Turkey	12.3	..	..	..	6.9	..	..	..
United Kingdom	47.0	52.9	54.5	..	27.0	38.0	44.0	48.0
United States	51.0	56.5	..	..	41.5	50.5	..	..

StatLink: http://dx.doi.org/10.1787/331002074252

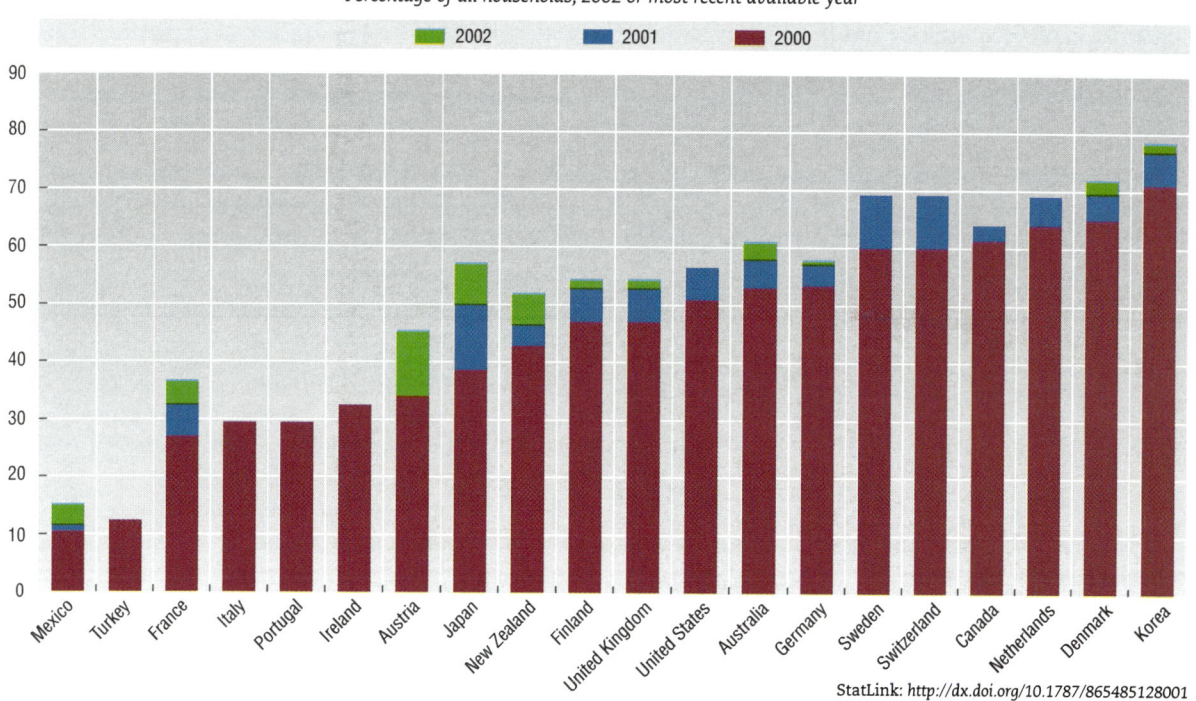

Households with access to home computer
Percentage of all households, 2002 or most recent available year

StatLink: http://dx.doi.org/10.1787/865485128001

SCIENCE AND TECHNOLOGY • ICT

HIGH-TECHNOLOGY EXPORTS

Technology-intensive exports accounted for much of the growth in trade over the past decade. In all OECD countries, they grew more rapidly than total manufacturing exports. This is especially the case for high-technology exports.

Definition
An industrial sector is defined as high-technology according to its overall R&D intensity (sum of direct and indirect). The direct intensity corresponds to the ratio of R&D expenditure to value added for each sector and country. For indirect intensity, embodied technology (R&D expenditure) in intermediate and capital goods purchased on the domestic market or imported was taken into account. To calculate indirect intensity, the technical coefficients of manufacturing industries extracted from input-output matrices were used.

Comparability
The methodology to define high, medium and low technology industries was developed by the OECD secretariat at the beginning of the 1980s and this methodology was adopted by member countries and other international organisations. For more details concerning definition and comparability see "Revision of the High-Technology Sector and Product Classification" below.

Long-term trends

Technology-intensive industries accounted for two-thirds of total OECD manufacturing exports in 2001. Differences among countries are substantial, however; the share of high and medium-high-technology industries ranges from over 80% in Japan and Ireland to less than 20% in New Zealand and Iceland.

Manufacturing exports are particularly technology-intensive in Ireland, Korea, United Kingdom and the United States, where high-technology industries account for a larger share of exports than medium high-technology industries.

Technology-intensive exports have grown very rapidly in Iceland, Turkey and the eastern European countries but still contribute little to international technology trade. The shares of Ireland, Korea and Mexico in total OECD technology exports have increased considerably at the expense of traditional European and Japanese technology suppliers.

With 20% of total OECD exports, the United States has the largest share of the technology market.

Export shares of high-technology industries in selected OECD countries

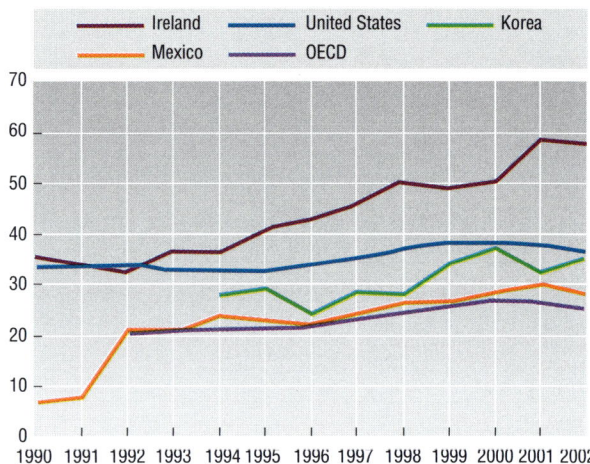

StatLink: http://dx.doi.org/10.1787/527822275287

Source
OECD (2003), *OECD Science, Technology and Industry Scoreboard*, OECD, Paris.

Further information
• *Analytical publications*

OECD (2002), *Non-tariff Measures in the ICT Sector: A Survey*, OECD, Paris.

OECD (2003), *Communications Outlook*, OECD, Paris.

OECD (2004), *Information Technology Outlook*, OECD, Paris.

• *Statistical publications*

OECD (2004), *International Trade by Commodity Statistics*, OECD, Paris.

• *Methodological publications*

Hatzichronoglou, T. (1997), "Revision of the High-Technology Sector and Product Classification", *OECD Directorate for Science, Technology and Industry Working Paper*, No. 1997/2, OECD, Paris, www.oecd.org/sti/working-papers.

• *Web sites*

OECD Science, Technology and Industry: www.oecd.org/sti.

International Trade Portal: www.oecd.org/std/trade.

SCIENCE AND TECHNOLOGY • ICT

HIGH-TECHNOLOGY EXPORTS

Export shares of high-technology industries in OECD countries
As a percentage of total manufacturing exports of goods

	1990	1991	1992	1993	1994	1995	1996	1997	1998	1999	2000	2001	2002
Australia	8.8	9.5	9.9	10.7	12.0	12.0	12.1	11.9	11.7	12.6	13.2	13.5	13.5
Austria	10.0	10.4	9.8	10.1	10.1	10.6	10.3	12.3	12.4	13.9	15.7	15.6	16.3
Belgium	7.7	8.1	8.4	9.6	9.3	9.8	10.6	11.0	12.0	12.9	14.0	15.3	19.4
Canada	11.3	12.5	11.3	10.2	10.3	10.9	11.4	12.7	13.3	13.0	16.1	14.3	12.2
Czech Republic	..	..	..	4.8	4.8	4.1	6.9	7.5	8.6	8.8	9.5	12.1	14.8
Denmark	13.2	13.1	13.4	13.6	14.7	15.1	15.9	17.1	18.1	19.0	20.7	20.7	22.1
Finland	8.8	8.5	9.7	11.5	13.3	15.0	16.3	18.7	21.9	24.1	27.3	24.4	24.6
France	16.3	18.3	18.3	18.8	18.8	19.4	20.2	21.7	23.2	24.0	25.6	25.5	24.1
Germany	13.9	15.0	14.8	15.3	15.4	15.2	15.3	16.5	17.3	18.7	20.2	20.6	19.3
Greece	2.1	2.5	2.0	3.2	3.7	4.4	3.4	4.3	6.7	7.6	9.7	9.0	10.4
Hungary	..	..	8.1	10.3	12.2	10.1	9.1	21.2	23.4	26.3	30.6	28.3	30.0
Iceland	1.0	0.1	0.3	0.4	2.1	2.6	2.8	2.9	2.3	2.6	2.7	3.4	5.0
Ireland	35.6	34.1	32.7	36.5	36.6	40.7	42.6	46.0	50.3	49.2	50.2	58.2	57.9
Italy	10.2	10.1	10.6	10.3	10.0	9.8	9.7	9.6	10.1	10.7	11.6	11.8	12.0
Japan	30.4	30.6	30.1	30.5	31.2	31.9	31.1	31.2	30.7	31.3	33.0	30.8	29.1
Korea	..	..	..	..	28.0	29.2	24.3	28.5	28.4	34.2	37.1	32.4	35.1
Mexico	7.0	8.3	21.2	21.2	24.0	23.2	22.5	24.5	26.4	26.9	28.7	29.9	28.4
Netherlands	16.1	15.7	16.6	19.7	19.9	21.3	22.8	25.1	27.5	30.3	32.6	29.8	28.6
New Zealand	1.5	1.8	2.1	2.2	2.3	2.6	4.0	3.2	4.7	3.1	3.0	3.0	3.3
Norway	7.9	7.5	8.6	8.7	8.4	8.4	8.6	9.4	10.1	10.0	10.3	12.0	13.9
Poland	..	..	3.7	4.0	4.1	4.2	5.0	6.0	6.5	6.4	6.4	6.8	7.0
Portugal	6.1	6.0	6.3	5.8	6.9	8.1	7.0	7.3	7.6	9.0	10.3	11.2	10.1
Slovak Republic	..	..	..	..	..	..	..	5.5	5.4	5.9	5.2	6.0	5.5
Spain	8.4	9.2	9.3	9.9	9.9	8.7	9.2	8.9	9.3	10.1	10.2	10.3	11.0
Sweden	16.0	17.1	17.6	18.4	18.9	21.5	23.7	25.6	26.2	27.9	28.8	23.4	21.9
Switzerland	26.3	26.9	28.3	28.3	28.2	28.6	30.0	30.2	31.5	34.6	33.8	37.1	37.7
Turkey	3.5	3.6	2.8	2.5	2.5	2.1	2.8	3.8	5.5	6.8	7.9	6.6	6.2
United Kingdom	26.3	26.4	25.7	27.6	27.7	28.5	29.7	29.7	32.4	33.8	37.4	40.3	38.5
United States	33.8	34.0	33.8	32.7	32.9	32.6	33.8	35.0	36.8	38.3	38.4	37.9	36.4
EU15	15.0	15.6	15.7	16.4	16.6	17.0	17.7	18.9	20.3	21.5	23.3	23.6	23.1
OECD total	..	..	20.5	21.0	21.2	21.3	21.7	23.0	24.0	25.2	26.9	26.4	25.4

StatLink: http://dx.doi.org/10.1787/041434262485

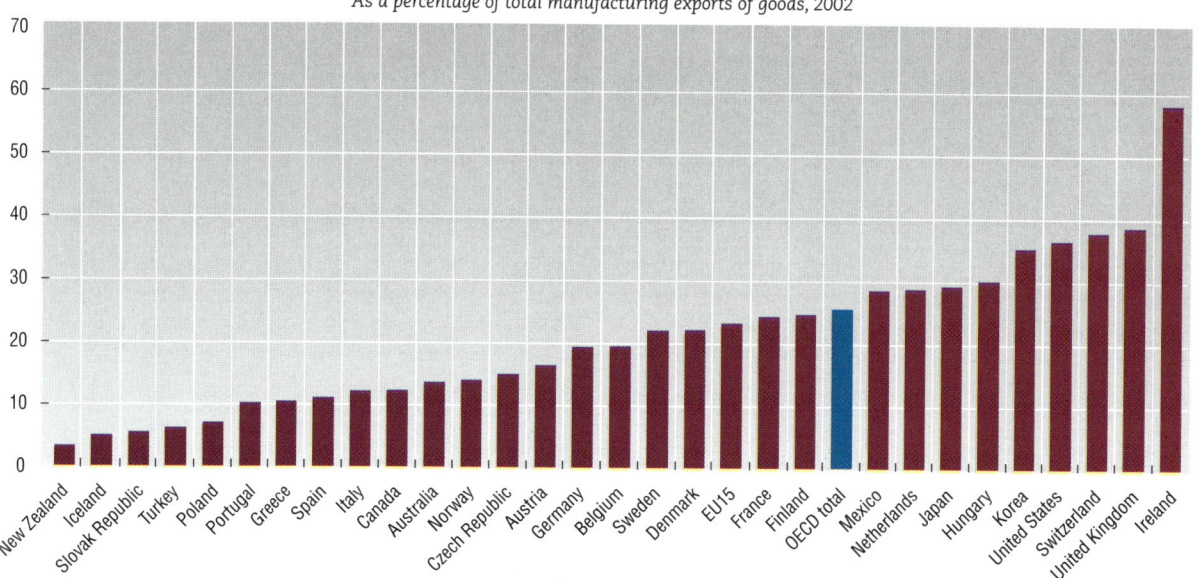

Export shares of high-technology industries in OECD countries
As a percentage of total manufacturing exports of goods, 2002

StatLink: http://dx.doi.org/10.1787/740658471240

ENVIRONMENT

AIR, WATER AND LAND
EMISSIONS OF CARBON DIOXIDE (CO_2)
WATER CONSUMPTION
MUNICIPAL WASTE
NUTRIENT USE IN AGRICULTURE

ENERGY USE
ENERGY SUPPLY AND ECONOMIC GROWTH
ENERGY SUPPLY PER CAPITA
RENEWABLE ENERGY

ENVIRONMENT • AIR, WATER AND LAND

EMISSIONS OF CARBON DIOXIDE (CO_2)

Carbon dioxide (CO_2) makes up the largest share of "greenhouse gases". The addition of man-made greenhouse gases to the atmosphere disturbs the earth's radiative balance. This may lead to an increase in the earth's surface temperature and to related effects on climate, sea level rise and world agriculture.

Definition
The table refers to emissions of CO_2 from burning oil, coal and gas for energy use. Carbon dioxide also enters the atmosphere from burning wood and waste materials and from some industrial processes such as cement production. Emissions of CO_2 from these sources are a relatively small part of global emissions and are not included in these statistics. The *Revised 1996 IPCC Guidelines for National Greenhouse Gas Inventories* provide a fuller, technical definition of how CO_2 emissions have been measured for this table.

Comparability
These emissions estimates are affected by the quality of the underlying energy data. For example, some countries, both OECD and non-OECD, have trouble reporting information on bunker fuels and incorrectly define bunkers as fuel used abroad by their own ships and planes. Since emissions from bunkers are excluded from the national totals, this affects the comparability between countries. On the other hand, since the estimates have been made using the same method and emission factors for all countries, in general, the comparability between countries is quite good.

Long-term trends

Global emissions of carbon dioxide have risen by 71% since 1971. At the beginning of this period, the current OECD countries were responsible for 66% of the total. As a consequence of rapidly increasing emissions in the developing world, the OECD contributed 52% to the total in 2002. By far the largest increases in non-OECD countries occurred in Asia, where emissions in China doubled over the period and emissions in the rest of Asia quadrupled. The use of coal in China increased levels of CO_2 by 1.9 billion tonnes over the 31-year period.

Two significant downturns can be seen in OECD CO_2 emissions, following the oil shocks of the mid-1970s and early 1980s. Emissions from the economies in transition declined over the last decade, helping to offset the OECD increases between 1990 and the present. This decline did not stabilise global emissions as emissions in developing countries grew.

Disaggregating the emissions data shows substantial variations within individual sectors. In the early part of the period, electricity generation accounted for the majority of the increase. More recently, transport has been the fastest growing sector in terms of emissions.

Fossil fuel shares in overall emissions changed slightly during the period. The relative weight of coal in global emissions has remained at approximately 40% since the early 1970s. The share of natural gas has increased from 14% in 1973 to 20% in 2002. Oil's share decreased from 51% to 42%. Fuel switching and the increasing use of non-fossil energy sources reduced the CO_2/total primary energy supply (TPES) ratio by more than 8% over the past 31 years.

Source
IEA (2004), CO_2 *Emissions from Fuel Combustion: 1971/2002*, IEA, Paris.

Further information
• *Analytical publications*

IEA (2001), *International Emission Trading – From Concept to Reality*, IEA, Paris.

IEA (2001), *Saving Oil and Reducing CO_2 Emissions in Transport: Options and Strategies*, IEA, Paris.

OECD (2004), *Can Cars Come Clean?: Strategies for Low-Emission Vehicles*, OECD, Paris.

• *Statistical publications*

IEA (2004), *Energy Statistics of OECD Countries*, IEA, Paris.

IEA (2004), *Energy Balances of OECD Countries*, IEA, Paris.

IEA (2004), *Energy Statistics of Non-OECD Countries*, IEA, Paris.

IEA (2004), *Energy Balances of Non-OECD Countries*, IEA, Paris.

• *Methodological publications*

WMO, UNEP, OECD, IEA (1996), *Revised 1996 IPCC Guidelines for National Greenhouse Gas Inventories*.

• *Online databases*

SourceOECD IEA CO_2 Emissions for Fuel Combustion.

SourceOECD IEA World Energy Statistics and Balances.

ENVIRONMENT • AIR, WATER AND LAND

EMISSIONS OF CARBON DIOXIDE (CO_2)

CO_2 emissions from energy use
Million tonnes

	1971	1990	1993	1994	1995	1996	1997	1998	1999	2000	2001	2002
Australia	143	260	269	272	280	296	303	319	324	329	342	343
Austria	49	57	57	57	60	64	64	64	63	63	67	66
Belgium	118	107	110	114	113	121	118	120	116	119	120	113
Canada	340	430	436	450	461	477	493	497	507	529	521	532
Czech Republic	156	154	125	118	121	125	120	113	109	118	119	115
Denmark	56	51	57	61	58	71	61	57	54	50	52	51
Finland	40	55	55	62	56	64	61	57	56	55	60	63
France	435	353	349	345	355	368	362	385	377	376	384	377
Germany	984	966	887	875	874	913	884	868	838	835	850	838
Greece	25	71	72	73	73	76	79	84	83	88	90	90
Hungary	62	71	60	59	59	59	57	57	61	55	56	55
Iceland	1	2	2	2	2	2	2	2	2	2	2	2
Ireland	22	30	31	32	33	34	36	38	40	41	43	42
Italy	295	400	394	391	413	409	414	424	423	425	426	433
Japan	743	1 015	1 040	1 105	1 112	1 139	1 150	1 107	1 153	1 178	1 165	1 207
Korea	51	226	299	332	362	392	418	363	397	428	442	452
Luxembourg	15	10	11	10	8	8	8	7	7	8	8	9
Mexico	97	292	307	327	313	319	332	352	344	362	360	365
Netherlands	130	157	169	169	171	178	175	174	169	173	178	178
New Zealand	14	22	24	25	26	27	30	29	31	31	33	34
Norway	24	29	32	33	33	34	36	37	39	34	34	33
Poland	298	350	338	331	333	348	339	316	305	293	292	283
Portugal	15	40	44	44	49	47	49	54	60	60	59	63
Slovak Republic	39	56	44	40	41	41	41	39	38	37	39	38
Spain	121	207	213	223	235	225	242	249	267	280	287	303
Sweden	83	51	52	54	53	59	52	53	51	51	48	50
Switzerland	39	42	42	41	42	43	42	44	44	43	44	43
Turkey	41	129	143	141	155	172	181	182	181	204	185	193
United Kingdom	627	560	538	531	533	547	524	532	527	525	542	529
United States	4 297	4 843	5 035	5 109	5 109	5 290	5 438	5 486	5 529	5 688	5 614	5 652
EU15	3 015	3 115	3 037	3 042	3 085	3 183	3 130	3 166	3 132	3 147	3 215	3 207
OECD total	9 362	11 034	11 233	11 427	11 532	11 948	12 109	12 109	12 197	12 480	12 462	12 554
Africa	266	547	572	572	603	624	650	671	673	695	718	743
Latin America	367	603	652	678	721	771	813	840	835	853	854	845
China	809	2 289	2 680	2 832	3 012	3 180	3 100	3 134	3 004	3 021	3 093	3 307
Other Asia	430	1 268	1 487	1 575	1 699	1 803	1 901	1 905	2 020	2 114	2 183	2 257
Former USSR	1 994	3 345	2 882	2 520	2 439	2 328	2 174	2 151	2 171	2 208	2 237	2 232
Non-OECD Europe	248	386	277	253	264	280	277	265	231	241	254	253
Middle East	127	590	735	792	814	852	891	928	963	1 005	1 035	1 093
International Marine Bunkers	342	363	385	389	404	407	422	427	458	467	442	463
International Civil Aviation	172	286	279	289	297	308	321	328	339	356	351	354
World	14 118	20 711	21 180	21 327	21 785	22 500	22 657	22 758	22 891	23 439	23 631	24 102

StatLink: http://dx.doi.org/10.1787/866344533771

World CO_2 emissions from energy use, by region
Million tonnes

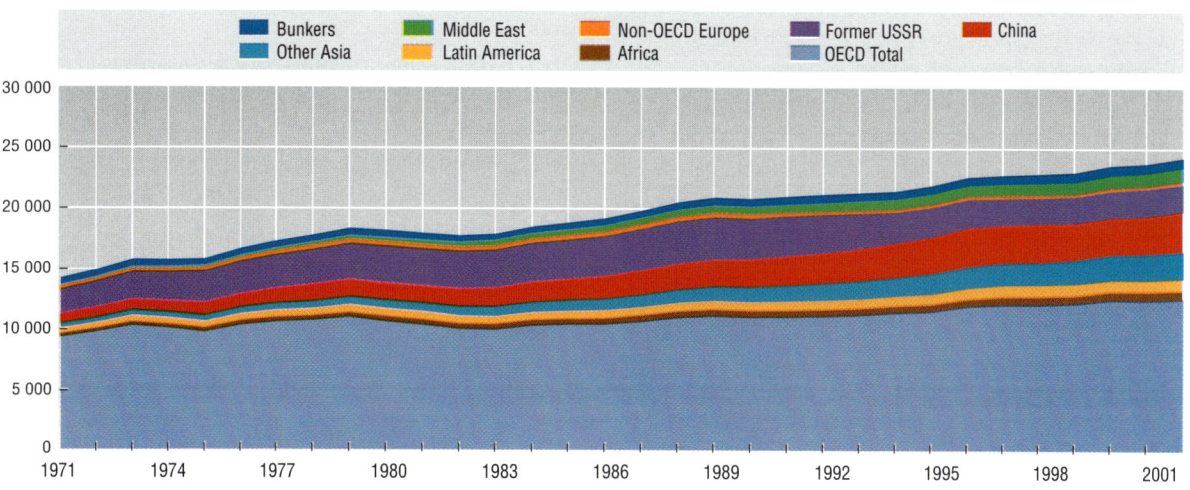

StatLink: http://dx.doi.org/10.1787/245427724220

ENVIRONMENT • AIR, WATER AND LAND

WATER CONSUMPTION

Freshwater resources are of major environmental and economic importance. Their distribution varies widely among and within countries. In arid regions, freshwater resources may at times be limited to the extent that demand for water can be met only by going beyond sustainable use in terms of quantity.

Freshwater abstractions particularly from public water supplies, irrigation, industrial processes and cooling of electric power plants exert a major pressure on water resources with significant implications for issues of quantity and quality of water resources. Main concerns relate to the inefficient use of water and to its environmental and socio-economic consequences: low river flows, water shortages, salinisation of freshwater bodies in coastal areas, human health problems, loss of wetlands, desertification and reduced food production.

Definition

Water abstractions refer to freshwater taken from ground or surface water sources, either permanently or temporarily, and conveyed to the place of use. If the water is returned to a surface water source, abstraction of the same water by the downstream user is counted again in compiling total abstractions.

Mine water and drainage water are included. Water used for hydroelectricity generation is an *in situ* use and is excluded.

Comparability

It should be borne in mind that the definitions and estimation methods employed by member countries may vary considerably and may have changed over time. In general, data availability and quality is best for abstractions for public supply, representing about 15% of the total water abstracted in OECD countries.

Vertical lines in the table indicate breaks in the series because of changes in the data sources or methods of calculation.

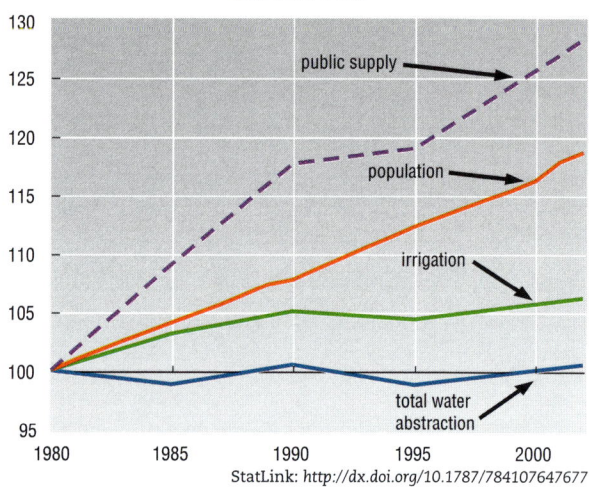

OECD water abstractions
Year 1980 = 100

StatLink: http://dx.doi.org/10.1787/784107647677

Source

OECD (2005), *OECD Environmental Data Compendium 2004*, OECD, Paris.

Further information

• *Analytical publications*

OECD (2003), *Improving Water Management: Recent OECD Experience*, OECD, Paris.

OECD (2003), *Social Issues in the Provision and Pricing of Water Services*, OECD, Paris.

OECD (2003), *Water: Performance and Challenges in OECD Countries*, OECD Environmental Performance Reviews, OECD, Paris.

OECD and WHO (2003), *Assessing Microbial Safety of Drinking Water: Improving Approaches and Methods*, OECD, Paris.

• *Statistical publications*

OECD (2005), *OECD Key Environmental Indicators 2004*, OECD, Paris.

• *Web sites*

OECD Environmental Indicators:
www.oecd.org/env/indicators.

Water Supply and Sanitation Sector Reform:
www.oecd.org/env/water.

Long-term trends

Most OECD countries increased their water abstractions over the 1960s and 1970s in response to demand by the agricultural and energy sectors. Since the 1980s, some countries have stabilised their abstractions through more efficient irrigation techniques, the decline of water-intensive industries (*e.g.* mining, steel), increased use of cleaner production technologies and reduced losses in pipe networks. However, the effects of population growth have led to increases in total abstractions, in particular for public supply.

At world level, it is estimated that water demand rose by more than double the rate of population growth in the last century, with agriculture being the largest user of water.

ENVIRONMENT • AIR, WATER AND LAND

WATER CONSUMPTION

Water abstractions

	Total gross abstractions (millions m³)					Per capita abstractions (m³/capita)
	1980	1985	1990	1995	2002 (or latest available year)	(Latest available year)
Australia	10 900	14 600	..	15 055	24 071	1 300
Austria	3 342	3 363	3 734	3 368	3 561	440
Belgium	..	..	..	8 149	7 442	730
Canada	37 594	42 383	45 096	..	42 214.	1 420
Czech Republic	3 622	3 679	3 623	2 743	1 908	190
Denmark	1 205	..	974	933	707	130
Finland	3 700	4 000	2 347	2 586	2 346	450
France	30 972	34 887	37 687	40 671	30 932	530
Germany	42 206	41 216	47 873	43 374	38 006	460
Greece	5 040	5 496	7 030	..	8 695	830
Hungary	4 805	6 267	6 293	5 976	5 591	550
Iceland	108	112	167	164	156	540
Ireland	1 070	..	..	1 176	..	330
Italy	..	..	..	..	56 200	980
Japan	86 000	86 357	88 009	88 202	86 104	680
Korea	12 800	..	21 300	23 700	26 000	560
Luxembourg	..	67	59	57	60	140
Mexico	56 003	..	..	73 672	72 564	730
Netherlands	9 198	9 349	7 984	7 919	8 889	560
New Zealand	1 200	1 900	..	2 000	..	560
Norway	..	2 025	..	2 420	..	550
Poland	15 131	16 409	15 164	12 924	11 728	300
Portugal	10 500	..	8 600	10 849	11 090	1 090
Slovak Republic	2 232	2 061	2 116	1 386	1 094	200
Spain	39 920	46 250	36 900	33 288	38 544	960
Sweden	4 106	2 970	2 968	2 725	2 689	300
Switzerland	2 589	2 646	2 665	2 571	2 539	350
Turkey	16 200	19 400	28 073	30 112	39 780	580
United Kingdom	13 514	11 533	12 052	9 547	12 375	230
United States	517 720	467 335	468 620	470 514	476 800	1 730
OECD total	1 006 500	994 300	1 011 400	994 000	1 017 700	920

StatLink: http://dx.doi.org/10.1787/213023756818

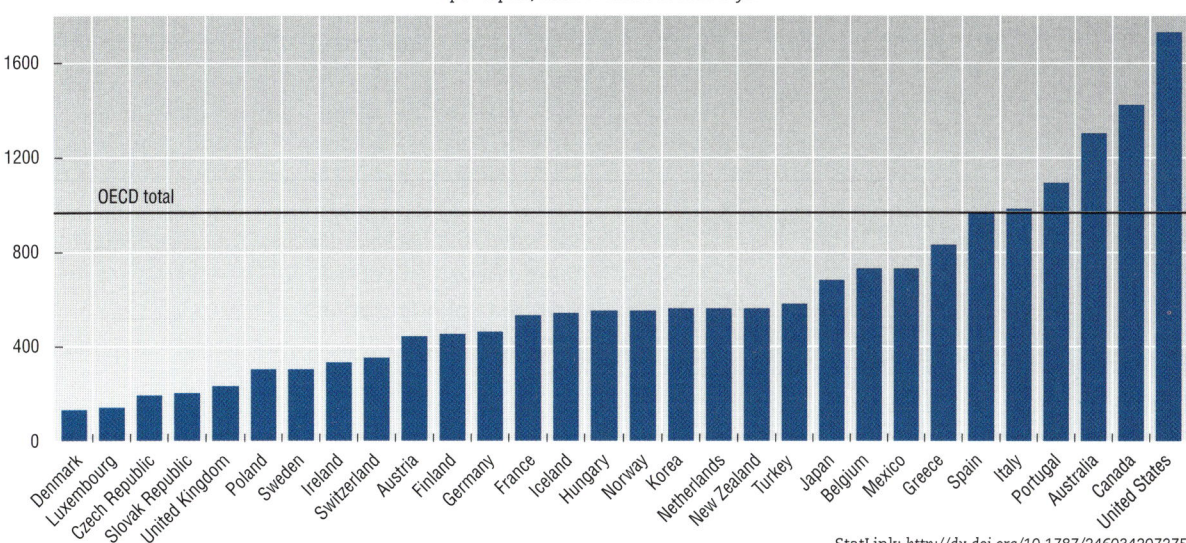

Water abstractions
m³ per capita, 2002 or latest available year

StatLink: http://dx.doi.org/10.1787/246034207275

137

ENVIRONMENT • AIR, WATER AND LAND

MUNICIPAL WASTE

The amount of municipal waste generated in a country is related to the rate of urbanisation, the types and patterns of consumption, household revenue and lifestyles. While municipal waste is only one part of total waste generated, its management and treatment often represents more than one third of the public sector's financial efforts to abate and control pollution.

The main environmental concerns relate to the potential impact from inappropriate waste management on human health and the environment (soil and water contamination, air quality, land use and landscape).

Kilogrammes of municipal waste per capita – or "waste generation intensities" – are broad indicators of potential environmental pressure. They should be complemented with information on waste management practices and costs, and on consumption levels and patterns.

Definition

Municipal waste is waste collected and treated by or for municipalities. It covers waste from households, including bulky waste, similar waste from commerce and trade, office buildings, institutions and small businesses, yard and garden waste, street sweepings, the contents of litter containers, and market cleansing waste. The definition excludes waste from municipal sewage networks and treatment, as well as municipal construction and demolition waste.

Comparability

The definition of municipal waste and the surveying methods used vary from country to country.

The main problems relate to the coverage of household-like waste from commerce and trade, and of separate waste collections, carried out by private companies.

Data for Canada and New Zealand refer to household waste only.

Vertical lines in the tables indicate a break in the series because of a change in data sources or methods of calculation.

OECD total does not include the Czech Republic, Hungary, Korea, Poland and the Slovak Republic.

Source

OECD (2005), *OECD Environmental Data Compendium 2004*, OECD, Paris.

Further information

• *Analytical publications*

OECD (2002), "OECD Workshop on Waste Prevention: Toward Waste Prevention Performance Indicators", proceedings, Paris, 8-10 October 2001, OECD, Paris, *www.oecd.org/document/52/0,2340,en_2649_34395_1954292_1_1_1_1,00.html*.

OECD (2004), *Addressing the Economics of Waste*, OECD, Paris.

OECD (2004), *Economic Aspects of Extended Producer Responsibility*, OECD, Paris.

• *Statistical publications*

OECD (2004), *Key Environmental Indicators 2004*, OECD, Paris.

• *Web sites*

OECD Environmental Indicators: *www.oecd.org/env/indicators*.

OECD Waste Prevention and Management: *www.oecd.org/env/waste*.

Long-term trends

The quantity of municipal waste generated in the OECD area has been rising since 1980 and reached 585 million tonnes in recent years (570 kg per capita). Generation intensity – i.e. kilogrammes per capita – has risen mostly in line with private final consumption expenditure and GDP, but there has been a slowdown in the rate of growth in recent years.

The amount of municipal waste also depends on national waste management practices. Only a few countries have succeeded in reducing the quantity of solid waste to be disposed of. In most countries for which data are available, increased affluence, associated with economic growth and changes in consumption patterns, tends to generate higher rates of waste per capita.

ENVIRONMENT • AIR, WATER AND LAND

MUNICIPAL WASTE

Municipal waste generation

	Total amounts generated (thousand tonnes)					Generation intensities (kg/capita)
	1980	1985	1990	1995	2002 or latest available year	Latest available year
Australia	10 000	..	12 000	..	13 200	690
Austria	..	..	3 204	3 476	4 111	510
Belgium	3 135	3 257	3 662	4 492	4 913	480
Canada	..	..	8 925	7 030	10 869	350
Czech Republic	..	2 600	..	3 200	2 845	280
Denmark	2 046	2 430	..	2 960	3 546	660
Finland	..	..	..	2 100	2 500	480
France	..	..	26 220	28 919	32 174	530
Germany	..	..	..	44 390	48 836	590
Greece	2 500	3 000	3 000	3 200	4 640	440
Hungary	..	..	5 500	4 752	4 646	460
Iceland	..	..	..	166	209	730
Ireland	640	1 100	..	1 848	2 704	700
Italy	14 041	15 000	20 000	25 780	29 788	510
Japan	43 995	43 450	50 441	50 694	52 362	410
Korea	..	20 994	30 646	17 438	18 214	380
Luxembourg	128	131	224	240	285	650
Mexico	..	..	21 062	30 510	32 174	320
Netherlands	7 050	6 933	7 430	8 469	9 953	620
New Zealand	880	..	1 140	1 431	1 541	400
Norway	1 700	1 968	2 000	2 722	2 755	620
Poland	10 055	11 087	11 098	10 985	10 509	270
Portugal	1 980	2 350	3 000	3 884	4 555	440
Slovak Republic	..	1 901	1 600	1 620	1 707	320
Spain	..	..	..	..	26 340	650
Sweden	2 510	2 650	3 200	3 555	4 172	470
Switzerland	2 790	3 398	4 101	4 200	4 743	660
Turkey	12 000	18 000	22 315	20 910	25 134	370
United Kingdom	..	..	27 100	28 900	34 851	580
United States	137 568	149 189	186 167	193 869	207 957	730
OECD total	369 000	399 000	481 000	523 000	585 000	570

StatLink: http://dx.doi.org/10.1787/280421883288

Municipal waste generation
kg per capita, 2002 or latest available year

StatLink: http://dx.doi.org/10.1787/544214425486

ENVIRONMENT • AIR, WATER AND LAND

NUTRIENT USE IN AGRICULTURE

Inputs of nutrients, such as nitrogen and phosphorus, are essential to agricultural production and integral to raising productivity. If soils are farmed and nutrients not replenished, this can lead to declining soil fertility and may impair agricultural sustainability through "soil mining" of nutrients. At the same time, a surplus of nutrients in excess of immediate crop needs can be a source of potential environmental damage to surface and ground water (eutrophication) and to air quality (acidification) and contribute to global warming (greenhouse effect). Many OECD countries have established goals to reduce nutrient emissions from agriculture. These are closely linked to the need for agriculture to comply with national standards for nitrate and phosphate emissions into aquatic environments. A number of international conventions and agreements also have the objective of limiting and reducing transboundary emissions into the environment, including nutrient emissions from agriculture into water and the atmosphere.

Definition

At the present time, the OECD Agricultural Nutrient Balance Indicator measures only the soil surface nitrogen balance. Work is currently underway to extend the indicator to cover phosphate balances and this broader indicator will be available early 2005.

The Agricultural Nutrient Balance Indicator measures the difference between the nitrogen available to an agricultural system (mainly from livestock manure and chemical fertilisers) and the uptake of nitrogen by agriculture (largely by crops and forage). A persistent surplus indicates potential environmental pollution, while a persistent deficit indicates potential agricultural sustainability problems. The nitrogen surplus is measured in kilograms per hectare of all land used for agriculture.

Comparability

The indicator provides information on the potential loss of nitrogen to the soil, the air, and to surface or groundwater, using a comparable and consistent methodology across OECD countries. However, nitrogen loss through the volatilisation of ammonia to the atmosphere from livestock housing and stored manure is excluded from the calculation.

While the indicator is derived by an internationally harmonised methodology, nitrogen conversion coefficients can differ between countries for a number of reasons, such as differing agro-ecological conditions, varying livestock weights yield, and differences in the methods used to estimate these coefficients. Also one part of the calculation is the atmospheric deposition of nitrogen which is mostly independent from agricultural activities.

Note that no data are available for Luxembourg and that the data shown for Iceland for the period 1995-97 actually refers to 1995.

Long-term trends

The trend with regard to surpluses in national nitrogen soil surface balances over the last decade is downward or constant for most OECD countries, which suggests that the potential environmental impact from agricultural nitrogen emissions is decreasing or stable. Some countries with a relatively high nitrogen surplus have reported significant reductions, although for a few countries surpluses have risen. The spatial variation of nitrogen surpluses within a country can be considerable. Regional data suggests that even in countries with a relatively low national nitrogen surplus, nitrate pollution is experienced in some localities, while soil nutrient deficits occur in others.

Source

OECD (2001), *OECD Environmental Indicators for Agriculture: Methods and Results*, Vol. 3, OECD, Paris.

Further information

• **Analytical publications**

OECD (1999), *OECD Environmental Indicators for Agriculture: Concepts and Framework*, Vol. 1, OECD, Paris.

OECD (1999), *OECD Environmental Indicators for Agriculture: Issues and Design – "The York Workshop"*, Vol. 2, OECD, Paris.

• **Online databases**

OECD Nitrogen Balance Database: *www.oecd.org/agr/env/nitrogen*.

• **Web sites**

OECD Agri-Environmental Indicators: *www.oecd.org/agr/env/indicators.htm*.

ENVIRONMENT • AIR, WATER AND LAND

NUTRIENT USE IN AGRICULTURE

Soil surface nitrogen balance estimates: 1985-87 to 1995-97

Nitrogen kg/ha of total agricultural land

	1985-87	1995-97	% change
Australia	6.54	7.11	8.75
Austria	34.88	27.42	-21.40
Belgium	189.18	181.00	-4.33
Canada	6.19	13.08	111.31
Czech Republic	98.96	54.47	-44.96
Denmark	154.06	118.10	-23.34
Finland	77.86	64.07	-17.71
France	59.23	53.03	-10.47
Germany	88.22	60.75	-31.14
Greece	57.88	38.17	-34.07
Hungary	47.04	-14.64	-131.12
Iceland	7.11	6.97	-1.99
Ireland	62.27	78.98	26.83
Italy	44.45	31.21	-29.78
Japan	144.68	134.89	-6.76
Korea	172.78	253.30	46.60
Mexico	27.77	20.05	-27.79
Netherlands	314.17	261.95	-16.62
New Zealand	4.67	6.13	31.47
Norway	72.44	73.02	0.80
Poland	47.51	28.80	-39.39
Portugal	62.25	66.44	6.74
Spain	40.19	40.59	1.00
Sweden	46.95	34.00	-27.58
Switzerland	80.17	60.82	-24.15
Turkey	17.20	12.23	-28.90
United Kingdom	107.25	86.44	-19.40
United States	25.28	31.16	23.24
EU15	68.76	58.39	-15.07
OECD total	23.41	23.27	-0.62

StatLink: http://dx.doi.org/10.1787/700842271423

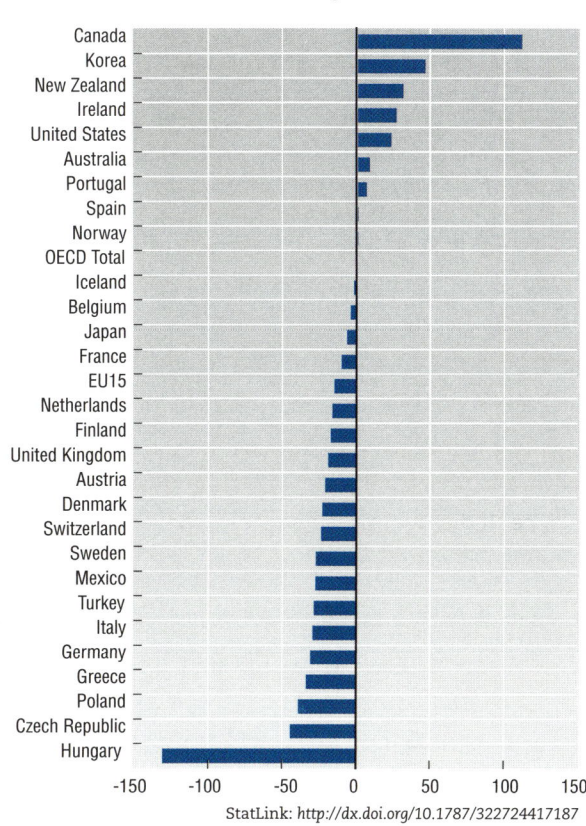

Change in the nitrogen balance between 1985-87 and 1995-97

Percentage

StatLink: http://dx.doi.org/10.1787/322724417187

ENVIRONMENT • ENERGY USE

ENERGY SUPPLY AND ECONOMIC GROWTH

It is not an easy task to monitor the overall trend in energy efficiency of a country, since there are numerous elements to consider such as climate change, outsourcing of goods produced by energy-intensive industries, etc. A common way to measure progress in energy intensity is to look at the changes in the ratio of energy use to GDP. Indeed, some experts look at energy intensity to derive trends of energy efficiency, but such an analysis has many limitations.

Definition

The table refers to total primary energy supply (TPES) per unit of GDP. The ratio is expressed in tonnes of oil equivalent (toe) per thousand 1995 US dollar of each country's GDP. GDP has been converted into US dollars using 1995 purchasing power parities (PPPs).

Comparability

Care should be taken when comparing energy intensities between countries and over time. Different national circumstances such as density of population, country size, average temperatures and economic structure will affect the ratios. A decrease in the TPES/GDP ratio may be partly attributable to a restructuring of the economy by transferring energy-intensive industries such as iron and steel out of the country – *i.e.* by purchasing energy-intensive products from abroad. The harmful effects of such outsourcing may actually increase the damage to the environment if the producers abroad use less energy efficient techniques.

Long-term trends

Sharp improvements in the efficiency of key end uses, shifts to electricity, and some changes in manufacturing output and consumer behaviour have occurred in many OECD countries since 1971. As a consequence, energy supply per unit of GDP fell significantly, particularly in the 1979-1990 period.

Contributing to the trend were higher fuel prices, long-term technological progress, government energy efficiency programmes and regulations. Overall growth in per capita GDP, combined with higher living standards and slow population growth, produced steadily rising demand after 1985.

The ratio of energy supply to economic growth (TPES/GDP) fell less than the ratio of energy consumption to economic growth (TFC/GDP), because of increased use of electricity. The main reason for this is that losses in electricity generating outweighed intensity improvements achieved in end uses such as household appliances.

Among OECD countries, the ratio of energy consumption to GDP varies considerably. Apart from energy prices, winter weather is a key element in these variations, as are raw materials processing techniques, the distance goods must be shipped, the size of dwellings, use of private rather than public transport and other lifestyle factors.

Source
IEA (2004), *Energy Balances of OECD Countries*, IEA, Paris.

Further information
• **Analytical publications**

IEA (2003), *World Energy Investment Outlook 2003*, IEA, Paris.

IEA (2004), *Energy Policies of IEA Countries: 2004 Review*, IEA, Paris.

IEA (2004), *World Energy Outlook 2004*, IEA, Paris.

• **Statistical publications**

IEA (2004), *Energy Balances of Non-OECD Countries*, IEA, Paris.

IEA (2004), *Energy Statistics of OECD Countries*, IEA, Paris.

IEA (2004), *Energy Statistics of Non-OECD Countries*, IEA, Paris.

• **Web sites**

OECD Energy Statistics: *www.oecd.org/statistics/energy*.
International Energy Agency: *www.iea.org*.

ENVIRONMENT • ENERGY USE

ENERGY SUPPLY AND ECONOMIC GROWTH

Total primary energy supply per unit of GDP
Tonnes of oil equivalent (toe) per thousand 1995 US dollar of GDP calculated using PPPs

	1971	1990	1994	1995	1996	1997	1998	1999	2000	2001	2002	2003
Australia	0.28	0.27	0.25	0.25	0.25	0.25	0.24	0.24	0.24	0.23	0.23	0.23
Austria	0.20	0.15	0.15	0.15	0.15	0.15	0.15	0.14	0.14	0.15	0.14	0.15
Belgium	0.32	0.24	0.24	0.24	0.26	0.25	0.25	0.24	0.24	0.23	0.22	0.23
Canada	0.44	0.35	0.36	0.35	0.36	0.35	0.33	0.32	0.31	0.30	0.30	0.29
Czech Republic	0.51	0.36	0.35	0.33	0.33	0.33	0.32	0.30	0.31	0.30	0.30	0.31
Denmark	0.25	0.16	0.18	0.17	0.19	0.17	0.16	0.15	0.14	0.15	0.14	0.15
Finland	0.34	0.29	0.33	0.30	0.32	0.31	0.30	0.29	0.27	0.27	0.28	0.29
France	0.23	0.19	0.19	0.20	0.20	0.19	0.19	0.19	0.18	0.19	0.18	0.19
Germany	0.31	0.22	0.20	0.20	0.20	0.20	0.19	0.18	0.18	0.18	0.18	0.18
Greece	0.11	0.17	0.17	0.17	0.17	0.17	0.17	0.17	0.17	0.17	0.16	0.16
Hungary	0.31	0.27	0.27	0.28	0.28	0.26	0.25	0.23	0.22	0.22	0.21	0.21
Iceland	0.36	0.37	0.38	0.39	0.40	0.39	0.39	0.43	0.43	0.43	0.44	0.43
Ireland	0.30	0.21	0.19	0.18	0.17	0.16	0.16	0.15	0.14	0.14	0.13	0.12
Italy	0.18	0.14	0.13	0.14	0.13	0.13	0.13	0.13	0.13	0.13	0.13	0.13
Japan	0.23	0.17	0.18	0.18	0.18	0.17	0.17	0.18	0.17	0.17	0.17	0.16
Korea	0.20	0.26	0.28	0.29	0.30	0.30	0.30	0.30	0.29	0.29	0.28	0.28
Luxembourg	0.77	0.33	0.29	0.26	0.25	0.23	0.21	0.21	0.20	0.20	0.21	0.22
Mexico	0.16	0.21	0.21	0.21	0.21	0.20	0.20	0.20	0.19	0.19	0.19	0.20
Netherlands	0.27	0.22	0.22	0.22	0.22	0.21	0.20	0.19	0.19	0.19	0.19	0.20
New Zealand	0.18	0.26	0.26	0.25	0.26	0.26	0.26	0.26	0.25	0.24	0.23	0.23
Norway	0.31	0.25	0.24	0.23	0.21	0.21	0.22	0.22	0.21	0.21	0.21	0.19
Poland	0.45	0.39	0.37	0.35	0.36	0.32	0.29	0.27	0.25	0.25	0.24	0.24
Portugal	0.11	0.15	0.15	0.16	0.15	0.15	0.16	0.16	0.16	0.16	0.16	0.16
Slovak Republic	0.44	0.45	0.42	0.41	0.39	0.37	0.34	0.34	0.34	0.34	0.33	0.31
Spain	0.14	0.16	0.16	0.17	0.16	0.16	0.16	0.17	0.17	0.17	0.17	0.17
Sweden	0.30	0.26	0.27	0.27	0.27	0.26	0.25	0.24	0.22	0.23	0.23	0.22
Switzerland	0.13	0.14	0.14	0.14	0.14	0.14	0.14	0.14	0.13	0.14	0.14	0.14
Turkey	0.16	0.18	0.18	0.18	0.19	0.18	0.18	0.19	0.19	0.19	0.18	0.19
United Kingdom	0.31	0.20	0.20	0.19	0.20	0.19	0.18	0.18	0.17	0.17	0.16	0.16
United States	0.44	0.30	0.29	0.28	0.28	0.27	0.26	0.26	0.26	0.25	0.25	0.24
EU15	0.25	0.19	0.19	0.19	0.19	0.18	0.18	0.18	0.17	0.17	0.17	0.17
OECD total	0.32	0.24	0.23	0.23	0.23	0.23	0.22	0.22	0.22	0.21	0.21	0.21

StatLink: http://dx.doi.org/10.1787/824576275421

Total primary energy supply per unit of GDP
Tonnes of oil equivalent (toe) per thousand 1995 US dollar of GDP calculated using PPPs, 2003

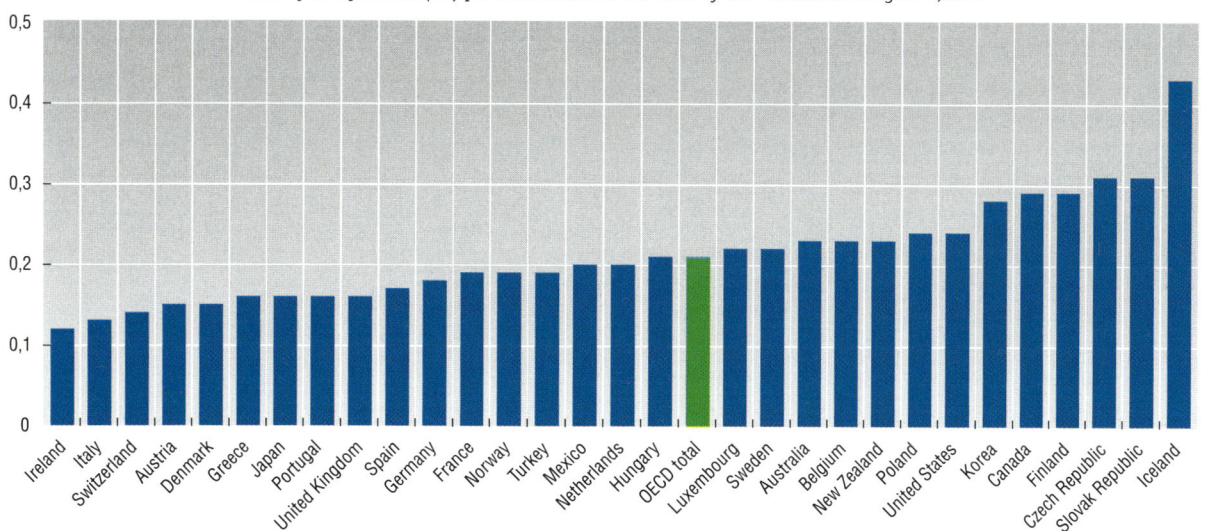

StatLink: http://dx.doi.org/10.1787/660641644443

ENVIRONMENT • ENERGY USE

ENERGY SUPPLY PER CAPITA

Total primary energy supply per capita is a common, albeit an imperfect measure of energy efficiency in a country. For instance, neither the impact of climate on energy use (heating, cooling) nor the size of the country and the density of the population are properly taken into account when comparing countries. Energy analysts usually prefer to compare energy use per unit of output or per unit of GDP. However, the ratio has been presented here since its use is widespread.

Definition

The table refers to total primary energy supply (TPES) per head of population. The ratio is expressed in tonnes of oil equivalent (toe) per person.

Comparability

Care should be taken when comparing energy supply per capita between countries and over time. Different national circumstances such as density of population, country size, temperatures, economic structure and domestic energy resources affect the ratios.

Long-term trends

The level of energy supply on a per capita basis varied significantly across OECD countries. The countries with the highest ratios were those countries with the smallest populations. In 2003, the energy supply per capita for Iceland was 11.7 toe/capita and for Luxembourg was 9.4 toe/capita. The high ratio for Iceland is explained partly by the climate but also be the availability of cheap – and non-polluting – thermal energy from hot springs. In the case of Luxembourg, the high ratio is partly due to low sales taxes on petroleum products; motorists and other consumers from neighbouring countries – Belgium, France and Germany – buy their supplies in Luxembourg.

The United States and Canada are also large consumers of energy per capita, with ratios of 7.9 toe/capita in 2003. On the other end of the scale, the countries with the lowest TPES/capita were Turkey (1.1 toe/capita) and Mexico (1.6 toe/capita).

Between 1971 and 2003, there are striking differences in the trends of the OECD countries. Compared to 1971, TPES/capita in 2003 was seven times higher in Korea and more than doubled in Greece, Iceland, Portugal and Spain. On the other hand, the ratio decreased in four OECD countries over this period: Luxembourg (–22%), Czech Republic (–7%), Poland (–7%) and Denmark (–2%).

Source

IEA (2004), *Energy Balances of OECD Countries*, IEA, Paris.

Further information

• **Statistical publications**

IEA (2004), *Energy Balances of Non-OECD Countries*, IEA, Paris.
IEA (2004), *Energy Statistics of OECD Countries*, IEA, Paris.
IEA (2004), *Energy Statistics of Non-OECD Countries*, IEA, Paris.

• **Web sites**

OECD Energy Statistics: *www.oecd.org/statistics/energy*.
International Energy Agency: *www.iea.org*.

ENVIRONMENT • ENERGY USE

ENERGY SUPPLY PER CAPITA

Total primary energy supply per capita
Tonnes of oil equivalent (toe) per capita

	1971	1990	1994	1995	1996	1997	1998	1999	2000	2001	2002	2003
Australia	3.96	5.10	5.17	5.19	5.48	5.49	5.52	5.64	5.70	5.55	5.71	5.81
Austria	2.53	3.27	3.23	3.42	3.59	3.61	3.66	3.62	3.60	3.84	3.78	3.94
Belgium	4.13	4.88	5.15	5.19	5.58	5.63	5.74	5.74	5.79	5.74	5.51	5.67
Canada	6.46	7.55	7.87	7.89	7.99	7.99	7.85	8.01	8.15	7.98	7.96	7.85
Czech Republic	4.64	4.57	3.91	3.97	4.09	4.12	3.99	3.72	3.93	4.05	4.09	4.29
Denmark	3.88	3.42	3.89	3.83	4.30	3.98	3.92	3.76	3.64	3.74	3.67	3.80
Finland	4.00	5.85	6.11	5.80	6.27	6.43	6.49	6.46	6.37	6.53	6.85	7.12
France	3.10	3.91	3.91	4.05	4.26	4.12	4.24	4.23	4.25	4.37	4.34	4.41
Germany	3.93	4.49	4.16	4.19	4.32	4.28	4.26	4.16	4.18	4.29	4.20	4.21
Greece	1.02	2.15	2.21	2.21	2.26	2.32	2.43	2.45	2.55	2.62	2.65	2.73
Hungary	1.84	2.75	2.43	2.49	2.53	2.49	2.47	2.47	2.45	2.51	2.51	2.57
Iceland	4.79	8.52	8.50	8.72	9.23	9.34	9.85	11.15	11.54	11.80	11.82	11.68
Ireland	2.37	3.02	3.15	3.15	3.29	3.41	3.57	3.71	3.77	3.93	3.91	3.70
Italy	2.12	2.69	2.67	2.81	2.79	2.83	2.91	2.96	2.97	2.98	2.98	3.11
Japan	2.57	3.61	3.92	3.98	4.08	4.11	4.06	4.08	4.11	4.06	4.06	4.03
Korea	0.52	2.16	3.01	3.27	3.58	3.84	3.51	3.83	4.06	4.10	4.27	4.35
Luxembourg	12.03	9.35	9.40	8.23	8.28	8.09	7.78	8.06	8.39	8.67	9.06	9.40
Mexico	0.87	1.53	1.53	1.47	1.48	1.51	1.55	1.54	1.55	1.53	1.57	1.63
Netherlands	3.89	4.45	4.60	4.67	4.84	4.74	4.73	4.65	4.74	4.82	4.83	4.96
New Zealand	2.51	4.08	4.26	4.33	4.49	4.61	4.49	4.65	4.63	4.62	4.53	4.48
Norway	3.49	5.07	5.42	5.48	5.30	5.58	5.76	6.02	5.74	5.86	5.84	5.22
Poland	2.63	2.62	2.51	2.59	2.78	2.68	2.51	2.41	2.32	2.33	2.33	2.44
Portugal	0.76	1.79	1.94	2.07	2.04	2.14	2.30	2.46	2.48	2.47	2.54	2.47
Slovak Republic	3.12	4.04	3.20	3.31	3.32	3.30	3.22	3.22	3.23	3.41	3.45	3.40
Spain	1.26	2.35	2.51	2.63	2.59	2.74	2.87	2.99	3.12	3.17	3.24	3.32
Sweden	4.51	5.45	5.63	5.66	5.78	5.62	5.73	5.69	5.35	5.75	5.72	5.59
Switzerland	2.69	3.74	3.66	3.59	3.64	3.71	3.75	3.74	3.69	3.87	3.72	3.70
Turkey	0.53	0.94	0.93	1.00	1.07	1.11	1.11	1.08	1.15	1.04	1.08	1.14
United Kingdom	3.77	3.69	3.90	3.81	3.96	3.85	3.89	3.89	3.87	3.98	3.83	3.86
United States	7.67	7.71	7.84	7.84	7.95	7.94	7.91	8.04	8.16	7.91	7.97	7.90
EU15	3.05	3.63	3.64	3.70	3.82	3.78	3.84	3.84	3.86	3.95	3.91	3.97
OECD total	3.84	4.34	4.44	4.49	4.60	4.60	4.59	4.64	4.70	4.65	4.67	4.69

StatLink: http://dx.doi.org/10.1787/477866446831

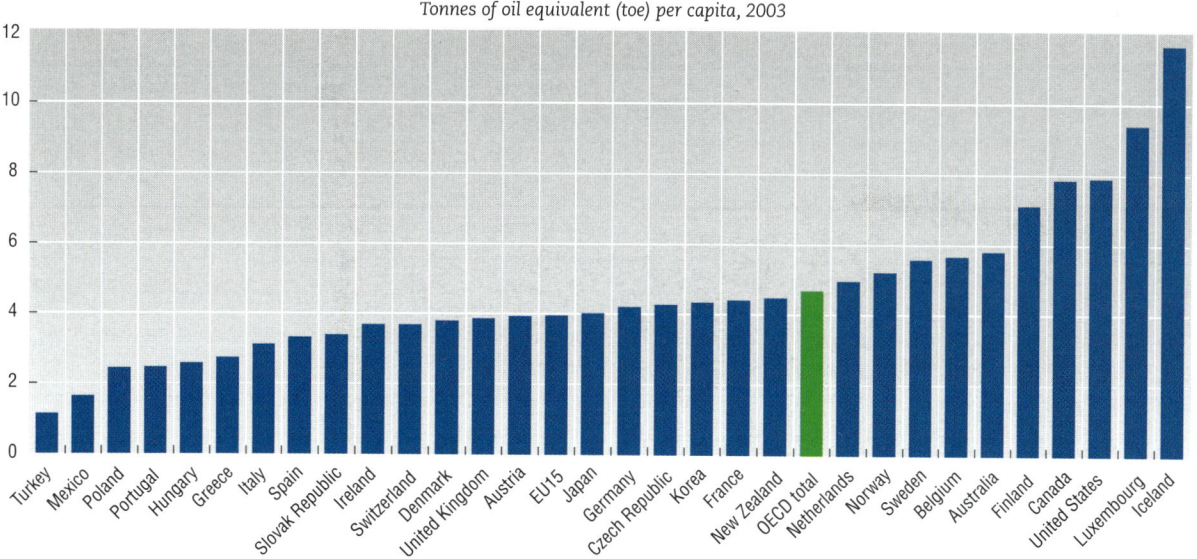

Energy supply per capita
Tonnes of oil equivalent (toe) per capita, 2003

StatLink: http://dx.doi.org/10.1787/585451025737

ENVIRONMENT • ENERGY USE

RENEWABLE ENERGY

More and more governments are recognising the importance of promoting sustainable development and combating climate change when setting out their energy policies. As energy use has increased, greenhouse gas emissions have spiralled up and their concentration in the atmosphere has increased. One way to reduce emissions is to replace energy from fossil fuels by energy from renewables.

Definition

The table refers to the contribution of renewables to total primary energy supply (TPES) in OECD countries. Renewables includes the primary energy equivalent of hydro (excluding pumped storage), geothermal, solar, wind, tide and wave. It also includes solid biomass, liquid biomass, biogas, industrial waste and municipal waste. Biomass is defined as any plant matter used directly as fuel or converted into fuels (*e.g.* charcoal) or electricity and/or heat. Included here are wood, vegetal waste (including wood waste and crops used for energy production), ethanol, animal materials/wastes and sulphite lyes. Municipal waste comprises wastes produced by the residential, commercial and public service sectors that are collected by local authorities for disposal in a central location for the production of heat and/or power.

Comparability

Biomass and waste data are often based on small sample surveys or other incomplete information. Thus, the data give only a broad impression of developments and are not strictly comparable between countries. In some cases, complete categories of vegetal fuel are omitted due to lack of information.

Long-term trends

In OECD countries, total renewables supply grew by 2.2% per annum between 1971 and 2003 as compared to 1.5% per annum for total primary energy supply. Annual growth for hydro (1.0%) was lower than for other renewables such as geothermal (5.9%), combustible renewables and waste (2.5%). Due to a very low base in 1971, solar and wind experienced the most rapid growth in OECD member countries, especially where government policies have stimulated expansion of these energy sources.

For total OECD, the contribution of renewables to energy supply increased from 4.7% in 1971 to 5.9% in 2003. The contribution of renewables varied greatly by country. On the high end, renewables represented 73% in Iceland and 44% in Norway. On the low end, renewables contributed only 1% to 2% of supply for Belgium, Czech Republic, Hungary, Ireland, Korea, Luxembourg, Netherlands and the United Kingdom.

Source
IEA (2004), *Renewable Information*, IEA, Paris.

Further information
• **Analytical publications**

IEA (2003), *Renewable Energy Policy … into the Mainstream*, IEA, Paris.

IEA (2003), *Renewables in Russia – From Opportunity to Reality*, IEA, Paris.

IEA (2004), *Biofuels for Transport – An International Perspective*, IEA, Paris.

IEA (2004), *Renewable Energy – Market and Policy Trends in IEA Countries*, IEA, Paris.

IEA (2004), *World Energy Outlook*, IEA, Paris.

• **Statistical publications**

IEA (2004), *Energy Balances of OECD Countries*, IEA, Paris.

IEA (2004), *Energy Balances of Non-OECD Countries*, IEA, Paris.

IEA (2004), *Energy Statistics of OECD Countries*, IEA, Paris.

IEA (2004), *Energy Statistics of Non-OECD Countries*, IEA, Paris.

IEA (2004), *Key World Energy Statistics*, IEA, Paris.

• **Web sites**

International Energy Agency: *www.iea.org*.

ENVIRONMENT • ENERGY USE

RENEWABLE ENERGY

Contribution of renewables to energy supply
As a percentage of total primary energy supply

	1971	1990	1994	1995	1996	1997	1998	1999	2000	2001	2002	2003
Australia	8.7	6.0	6.0	6.1	6.2	6.5	6.2	6.0	6.0	6.1	7.5	7.5
Austria	10.9	20.5	22.2	22.2	21.0	21.5	21.0	22.8	22.9	22.2	22.8	20.3
Belgium	0.0	1.5	1.3	1.5	1.4	1.4	1.4	1.5	1.5	1.7	1.7	1.8
Canada	15.2	16.1	16.6	16.7	17.0	16.7	16.3	16.7	16.7	15.8	16.6	16.3
Czech Republic	0.2	0.3	1.8	1.5	1.5	1.7	1.7	2.4	1.9	2.1	2.5	2.1
Denmark	1.7	6.8	7.5	8.0	7.6	8.7	9.2	10.1	11.3	11.9	13.1	13.2
Finland	26.9	18.8	18.7	20.7	19.7	20.9	22.2	22.2	24.3	23.0	22.5	21.5
France	8.4	7.0	7.8	7.4	7.1	6.9	6.8	7.1	6.7	6.9	6.2	6.4
Germany	1.2	1.8	2.1	2.2	2.2	2.5	2.8	2.8	3.1	3.4	3.7	3.9
Greece	7.4	5.0	5.4	5.6	5.9	5.5	5.2	5.6	5.3	4.7	4.9	5.4
Hungary	2.9	1.7	2.3	2.4	1.9	2.0	1.9	1.9	2.1	2.0	2.0	1.9
Iceland	42.9	64.5	65.5	67.2	65.1	66.5	67.2	70.9	71.1	72.9	72.3	73.4
Ireland	0.6	1.6	2.2	2.0	1.6	1.6	2.0	1.8	1.8	1.7	1.9	1.8
Italy	5.1	4.4	5.5	4.9	5.3	5.5	5.6	6.0	5.4	5.7	5.5	6.2
Japan	2.7	3.7	3.0	3.5	3.4	3.7	3.6	3.5	3.6	3.5	3.5	3.6
Korea	0.7	0.6	0.7	0.7	0.8	0.9	1.2	1.2	1.3	1.4	1.6	1.8
Luxembourg	0.1	0.9	1.3	1.4	1.1	1.4	1.5	1.3	1.5	1.6	1.4	1.3
Mexico	16.6	11.1	10.3	11.4	11.3	10.6	10.3	10.5	10.6	10.2	9.5	9.1
Netherlands	0.0	1.1	1.1	1.2	1.4	1.8	2.0	2.1	2.1	1.8	1.9	1.8
New Zealand	30.8	35.3	33.8	33.3	30.8	29.6	32.5	33.4	30.4	28.2	30.1	30.1
Norway	39.9	53.3	45.6	48.5	43.4	43.5	43.9	44.6	51.6	44.2	47.4	44.1
Poland	1.6	2.4	4.9	4.8	4.1	4.2	4.5	4.5	4.7	5.0	5.2	5.0
Portugal	18.9	18.5	17.6	16.0	18.5	17.4	16.0	13.4	15.2	16.1	13.8	16.7
Slovak Republic	2.3	1.5	3.2	2.8	2.5	2.4	2.5	2.6	2.8	4.4	4.3	3.4
Spain	6.4	6.9	6.2	5.5	7.1	6.4	6.2	5.3	5.7	6.5	5.4	6.7
Sweden	20.2	25.2	23.8	26.3	23.8	27.9	28.3	28.2	32.2	29.0	27.6	25.9
Switzerland	14.9	14.6	19.0	18.0	15.7	16.9	16.9	18.9	18.4	19.1	17.8	17.8
Turkey	31.1	18.2	18.4	17.4	16.7	15.8	15.9	15.1	13.1	13.2	13.4	12.4
United Kingdom	0.1	0.5	0.8	0.9	0.8	0.9	1.0	1.1	1.1	1.1	1.3	1.4
United States	3.7	5.2	5.2	5.3	5.4	5.2	5.1	4.9	4.8	4.1	4.3	4.4
EU15	4.1	5.0	5.4	5.4	5.4	5.6	5.8	5.8	6.0	6.1	5.9	6.2
OECD total	4.7	6.0	6.1	6.2	6.2	6.2	6.2	6.2	6.1	5.8	5.9	5.9

StatLink: http://dx.doi.org/10.1787/352031618170

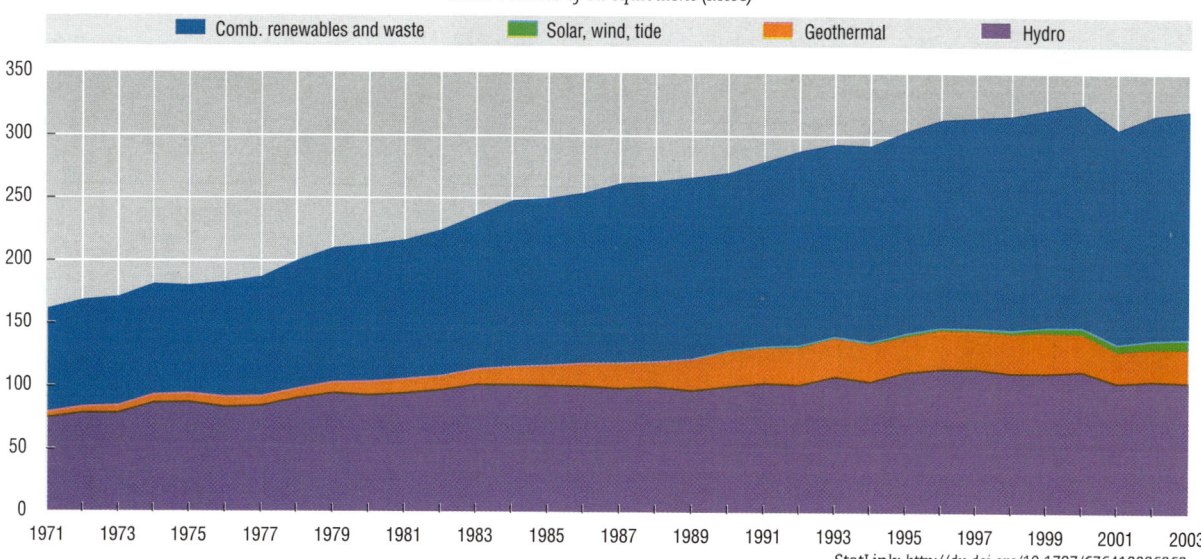

OECD renewable energy supply
Million tonnes of oil equivalent (Mtoe)

StatLink: http://dx.doi.org/10.1787/676412086363

EDUCATION

OUTCOMES
INTERNATIONAL STUDENT ASSESSMENT
TERTIARY ATTAINMENT

EXPENDITURE ON EDUCATION
EXPENDITURE BY LEVEL OF EDUCATION
PUBLIC AND PRIVATE EDUCATION EXPENDITURE

EDUCATION • OUTCOMES

INTERNATIONAL STUDENT ASSESSMENT

How effective are school systems at providing young people with a solid foundation of knowledge and skills that will equip them for life and learning beyond school? OECD's Programme for International Student Assessment (PISA) assesses student knowledge and skills in mathematics, science, reading and cross-curricular competencies at age 15, *i.e.* towards the end of compulsory education.

Definition

The PISA survey covers mathematics, reading, science and problem solving. PISA considers students' ability to reflect on their knowledge and experience in these areas and to apply them to real world issues. For the 2003 round of PISA, three and a half hours of testing time was in mathematics, plus one hour each for reading, science and problem solving. Each student spent two hours carrying out a combination of the assessment items.

Mathematical literacy is defined as students' capacity to identify, understand and engage in mathematics as well as to make well-founded judgements about the role that mathematics plays in an individual's current and future life as a constructive, concerned and reflective citizen.

Scientific literacy is defined as students' capacity to use scientific knowledge and to draw evidence-based conclusions in order to understand and help make decisions about the natural world and human interactions with it.

Reading literacy is defined as students' capacity to access, manage, interpret and reflect on written texts in order to achieve their goals, to develop their knowledge and potential, and to participate effectively in society.

Comparability

Decisions about the scope and nature of the assessments and the background information to be collected are made by leading experts in participating countries. Substantial efforts and resources are devoted to achieving cultural and linguistic breadth and balance in the assessment materials. Stringent quality assurance mechanisms are applied in translation, sampling and data collection.

Over a quarter of a million 15-year-old students in the 41 participating countries were assessed for PISA 2003. Because the results are based on probability samples it is possible to calculate the standard errors of the estimates and these are shown in the tables.

In Luxembourg, the assessment procedures were changed between the 2000 and 2003 rounds of PISA rounds and the results are not comparable.

Results

PISA results for 2000 (the first round of PISA) and for 2003 are shown in the table for mathematics, reading and science. Where no figures are shown for a country, either that country did not participate in the round or the response rates were too low to give reliable results. The graph shows the 2003 results for mathematics in terms of differences from the OECD average score (500). For Austria, Germany, Ireland and the Slovak Republic the mathematics scores are not significantly different from the OECD average.

Source

OECD (2001), *Knowledge and Skills for Life – First Results from PISA 2000*, OECD, Paris.

OECD (2004), *Learning for Tomorrow's World – First Results from PISA 2003*, OECD, Paris.

Further information

• *Analytical publications*

OECD (2001), *Literacy Skills for the World of Tomorrow – Further Results from PISA 2000*, OECD, Paris.

OECD (2004), *Problem Solving for Tomorrow's World: First Measures of Cross-curricular Competencies from PISA 2003*, OECD, Paris.

• *Online databases*

OECD PISA Database: *www.pisa.oecd.org*.

• *Web sites*

PISA Web site: *www.pisa.oecd.org*.

EDUCATION • OUTCOMES

INTERNATIONAL STUDENT ASSESSMENT

Mean scores on the reading and science scales in PISA 2000 and PISA 2003

	Reading scale				Science scale			
	PISA 2000		PISA 2003		PISA 2000		PISA 2003	
	Mean score	S.E.	Mean score	S.E.	Mean score	S.E.	Mean score	S.E.
Australia	528	(3.5)	525	(2.1)	528	(3.5)	525	(2.1)
Austria	507	(2.4)	491	(3.8)	519	(2.6)	491	(3.4)
Belgium	507	(3.6)	507	(2.6)	496	(4.3)	509	(2.4)
Canada	534	(1.6)	528	(1.7)	529	(1.6)	519	(2.0)
Czech Republic	492	(2.4)	489	(3.5)	511	(2.4)	523	(3.4)
Denmark	497	(2.4)	492	(2.8)	481	(2.8)	475	(3.0)
Finland	546	(2.6)	543	(1.6)	538	(2.5)	548	(1.9)
France	505	(2.7)	496	(2.7)	500	(3.2)	511	(3.0)
Germany	484	(2.5)	491	(3.4)	487	(2.4)	502	(3.6)
Greece	474	(5.0)	472	(4.1)	461	(4.9)	481	(3.8)
Hungary	480	(4.0)	482	(2.5)	496	(4.2)	503	(2.8)
Iceland	507	(1.5)	492	(1.6)	496	(2.2)	495	(1.5)
Ireland	527	(3.2)	515	(2.6)	513	(3.2)	505	(2.7)
Italy	487	(2.9)	476	(3.0)	478	(3.1)	486	(3.1)
Japan	522	(5.2)	498	(3.9)	550	(5.5)	548	(4.1)
Korea	525	(2.4)	534	(3.1)	552	(2.7)	538	(3.5)
Luxembourg	441	(1.6)	479	(1.5)	443	(2.3)	483	(1.5)
Mexico	422	(3.3)	400	(4.1)	422	(3.2)	405	(3.5)
Netherlands	..	..	513	(2.9)	..	..	524	(3.1)
New Zealand	529	(2.8)	522	(2.5)	528	(2.4)	521	(2.4)
Norway	505	(2.8)	500	(2.8)	500	(2.8)	484	(2.9)
Poland	479	(4.5)	497	(2.9)	483	(5.1)	498	(2.9)
Portugal	470	(4.5)	478	(3.7)	459	(4.0)	468	(3.5)
Slovak Republic	..	..	469	(3.1)	..	..	495	(3.7)
Spain	493	(2.7)	481	(2.6)	491	(3.0)	487	(2.6)
Sweden	516	(2.2)	514	(2.4)	512	(2.5)	506	(2.7)
Switzerland	494	(4.3)	499	(3.3)	496	(4.4)	513	(3.7)
Turkey	..	..	441	(5.8)	..	..	434	(5.9)
United Kingdom	523	(2.6)	..	..	532	(2.7)	..	..
United States	504	(7.1)	495	(3.2)	499	(7.3)	491	(3.1)
OECD total	499	(2.0)	488	(1.2)	502	(2.0)	496	(1.1)
OECD average	500	(0.6)	494	(0.6)	500	(0.7)	500	(0.6)

StatLink: http://dx.doi.org/10.1787/161240131183

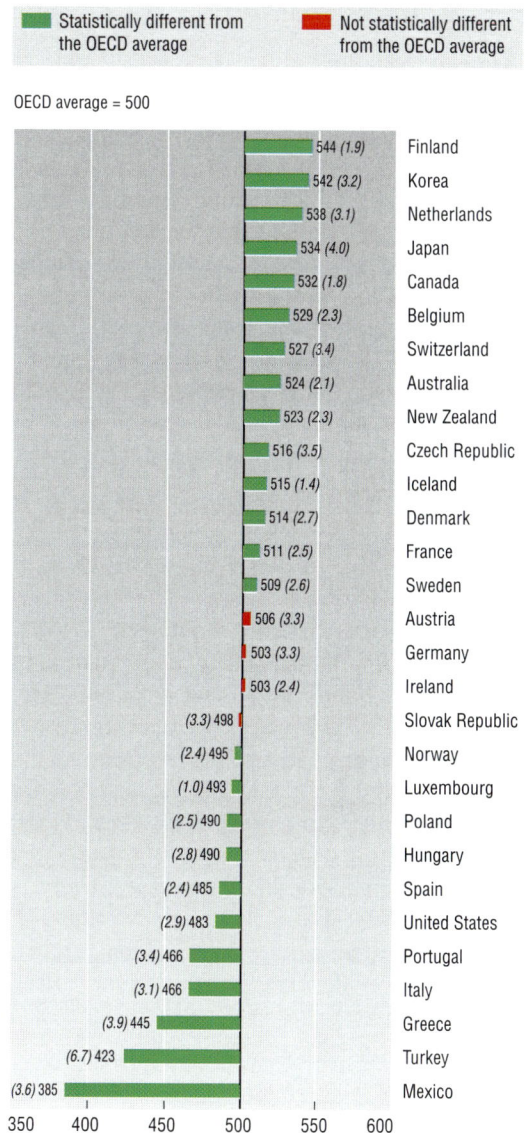

Performance on the mathematics scale in PISA 2003

151

EDUCATION • OUTCOMES

TERTIARY ATTAINMENT

The share of the population that has attained qualifications at the tertiary level is a key indicator of how well countries are placed to profit from technological and scientific progress. Differences between tertiary attainment of younger and older age groups is a measure of progress in the provision of higher education.

Definition

For each age group shown below, those who have completed tertiary education are shown as a percentage of all persons in that age group. Tertiary education includes both tertiary-type "A programmes", which are largely theoretically-based and designed to provide qualifications for entry to advanced research programmes and professions with high skill requirements, as well as tertiary-type "B programmes" which are classified at the same level of competencies as tertiary-type A programmes but are more occupationally-oriented and lead to direct labour market access. The tertiary attainment profiles are based on the percentage of the population aged 25 to 64 that has completed that specified level of education.

Comparability

The International Standard Classification of Education (ISCED-97) is used to define the levels of education. See the *OECD Handbook for Internationally Comparative Education Statistics* for a description of ISCED-97 education programmes and attainment levels and their mappings for each country.

Long-term trends

OECD countries have seen significant increases in the proportion of the adult population attaining tertiary education over the last decades. In 2002, for the 25-64 year-old population, 16 countries out of 30 are grouped together within a range of 10 points between 23 and 33% of the population having attained the tertiary level. Three of them are performing remarkably high: Canada, Japan and the United States. Conversely, two countries are significantly below this average percentage in tertiary attainment where less than 10% of the population attain tertiary qualifications: Portugal and Turkey.

In the youngest age group, 25 to 34 years old, tertiary attainment grew between 1991 and 2002 at rates from 20 to 28%. In three countries – Canada, Japan and Korea – over 40% of this age group has obtained a tertiary qualification. Korea shows a marked increase of 32 percentage points between the age groups 55-64 and 25-34 which is 20 percentage points higher than the OECD average increase between the two age groups. However, ten countries have experienced negative or slow (less than 2 percentage points) growth in tertiary attainment between these age groups.

Source

OECD (2004), *Education at a Glance*, OECD, Paris.

Further information

• *Analytical publications*

Blöndal, S., S. Field and N. Girouard (2002), "Investment in Human Capital through Upper-Secondary and Tertiary Education", *OECD Economic Studies*, No. 34, 2002/I, www.oecd.org/oecdeconomicstudies.

Vincent-Lancrin, S. (2004), "Building Capacity through Cross-Border Tertiary Education", paper prepared for the UNESCO/OECD Australia Forum on Trade in Educational Services, Sydney, 11-12 October, www.oecd.org/dataoecd/43/25/33784331.pdf.

• *Methodological publications*

OECD (2004), *OECD Handbook for Internationally Comparative Education Statistics*, OECD, Paris.

• *Web sites*

OECD Centre for Educational Research and Innovation (CERI): www.oecd.org/edu/ceri.

OECD *Education at a Glance*: www.oecd.org/edu/eag2004.

EDUCATION • OUTCOMES

TERTIARY ATTAINMENT

Tertiary attainment for age group 25-64
As a percentage of the population in that age group

	1991	1992	1993	1994	1995	1996	1997	1998	1999	2000	2001	2002
Australia	21.8	..	22.5	23.1	24.3	24.8	24.3	25.4	26.7	27.5	29.0	30.8
Austria	6.7	7.0	..	7.7	7.9	8.1	10.6	10.9	10.9	13.9	14.1	14.5
Belgium	19.6	20.2	..	22.3	24.6	23.9	25.1	25.3	26.7	27.1	27.6	28.1
Canada	29.9	30.8	..	34.2	34.9	35.6	37.3	38.1	39.2	40.0	41.6	42.6
Czech Republic	..	..	..	10.1	10.6	10.4	10.6	10.4	10.8	11.0	11.1	11.9
Denmark	18.3	19.2	..	19.6	20.4	20.9	..	25.4	26.5	25.8	26.5	27.4
Finland	25.0	25.9	..	26.8	27.7	28.4	29.4	30.2	31.3	32.0	32.3	32.6
France	15.2	16.0	17.1	17.8	18.6	19.2	20.0	20.6	21.5	22.0	23.0	24.0
Germany	20.5	20.1	..	20.4	22.2	21.8	22.6	23.0	22.9	23.5	23.2	23.4
Greece	..	..	..	17.9	17.4	18.9	15.5	16.8	17.5	17.6	17.8	18.3
Hungary	..	..	..			13.4	12.2	13.2	13.5	14.0	14.0	14.2
Iceland	..	..	..	..	..	20.8	20.9	21.0	22.4	23.2	24.6	26.3
Ireland	15.9	17.0	..	18.6	19.9	22.6	22.8	21.1	20.5	21.8	23.7	25.4
Italy	6.1	6.4	..	7.5	7.9	8.1	..	8.6	9.3	9.4	10.0	10.4
Japan	..	..	..	..	..	..	30.4	30.4	31.6	33.4	33.8	36.3
Korea	14.4	16.1	17.5	17.8	18.6	19.6	19.8	22.5	23.1	23.9	25.0	26.0
Luxembourg	..	..	..	..	18.1	19.0	..	..	18.3	18.3	18.1	18.6
Mexico	..	..	..	..	11.9	13.2	13.8	13.6	13.4	14.6	15.0	15.3
Netherlands	19.6	20.9	..	21.4	22.0	22.5	..	24.2	22.6	23.4	23.2	24.4
New Zealand	22.9	23.6	..	23.2	25.3	..	25.8	26.6	27.0	28.0	29.2	29.8
Norway	24.8	25.3	..	27.4	28.6	26.9	25.8	27.4	27.5	28.4	30.2	31.0
Poland	..	..	..	..	9.9	..	10.2	10.9	11.3	11.4	11.9	12.6
Portugal	6.7	..	..	10.7	11.0	10.9	..	8.3	8.7	8.9	9.1	9.3
Slovak Republic	..	..	..	11.3	11.1	11.5	10.5	10.3	10.1	10.4	10.9	11.0
Spain	9.9	13.1	..	15.0	16.1	17.5	18.6	19.7	21.0	22.6	23.6	24.4
Sweden	25.2	25.8	..	27.0	28.3	27.4	27.5	28.0	28.7	30.1	31.6	32.6
Switzerland	20.3	21.0	..	21.4	21.1	21.9	22.2	22.9	23.6	24.2	25.4	25.2
Turkey	6.3	4.8	..	7.0	8.4	..	7.6	7.5	8.1	8.3	8.4	9.1
United Kingdom	16.3	18.5	..	21.3	21.9	22.3	22.7	23.7	24.8	25.7	26.1	26.9
United States	30.1	30.2	..	32.2	33.3	33.9	34.1	34.9	35.8	36.5	37.3	38.1

StatLink: http://dx.doi.org/10.1787/427870181151

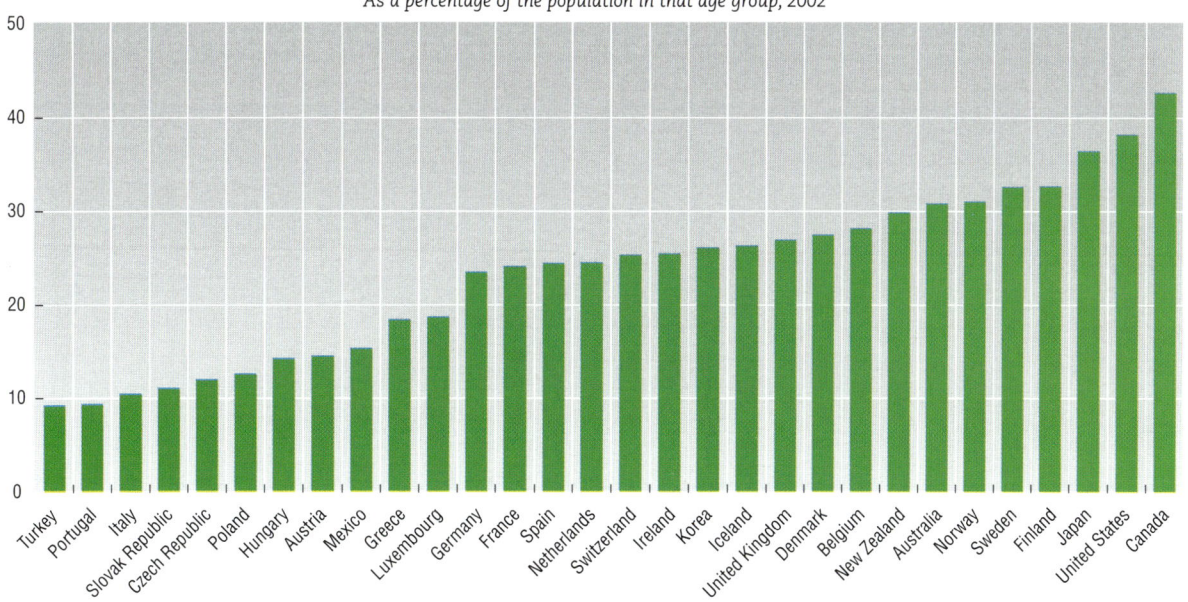

Tertiary attainment for age group 25-64
As a percentage of the population in that age group, 2002

StatLink: http://dx.doi.org/10.1787/155316687364

OECD FACTBOOK 2005 – ISBN 92-64-01869-7 – © OECD 2005

153

EDUCATION • OUTCOMES

TERTIARY ATTAINMENT

Tertiary attainment for age group 25-34
As a percentage of the population in that age group

	1991	1992	1993	1994	1995	1996	1997	1998	1999	2000	2001	2002
Australia	22.8	..	22.8	23.6	24.7	25.4	25.7	28.1	29.0	31.4	33.5	35.8
Austria	7.9	7.9	..	8.8	8.7	9.2	12.4	12.5	12.7	15.0	14.3	14.8
Belgium	26.8	27.2	..	30.0	32.9	32.2	33.1	33.8	34.4	36.0	37.5	37.6
Canada	32.9	34.2	..	37.8	39.3	40.6	44.1	45.5	46.8	48.3	50.5	51.2
Czech Republic	..	..	..	12.5	11.8	11.2	10.9	10.5	10.9	11.2	11.3	12.3
Denmark	18.7	19.5	..	19.7	20.3	20.7	..	26.8	28.6	29.3	29.1	30.6
Finland	33.3	33.5	..	34.1	35.0	35.2	36.4	36.0	37.5	37.6	38.2	39.2
France	20.1	21.6	23.1	24.3	25.4	26.0	27.8	29.6	30.9	32.4	34.2	36.1
Germany	19.6	18.8	..	18.7	20.8	20.3	21.0	21.5	21.5	22.3	21.8	21.7
Greece	..	..	..	25.0	26.0	28.2	22.3	24.3	24.6	24.3	24.0	24.1
Hungary	..	..	..	..	..	14.3	12.4	13.9	13.7	14.7	14.8	15.0
Iceland	..	..	..	..	..	23.7	23.0	24.2	27.6	27.8	26.5	29.1
Ireland	19.7	21.2	..	24.4	27.2	31.3	32.5	29.5	28.1	30.3	33.4	36.3
Italy	6.6	6.8	..	7.9	8.2	8.3	..	9.0	10.0	10.4	11.8	12.5
Japan	..	..	..	..	..	..	45.2	45.4	45.1	47.2	47.7	50.3
Korea	21.0	23.9	26.8	27.7	29.2	30.6	30.9	33.8	34.8	36.9	39.2	41.2
Luxembourg	..	..	..	..	..	..	..	..	21.2	22.9	23.4	22.6
Mexico	..	..	..	..	16.3	17.1	17.3	16.7	16.6	17.4	18.0	18.4
Netherlands	22.2	23.6	..	23.9	24.5	25.1	..	27.5	25.1	26.6	26.5	27.7
New Zealand	23.2	23.2	..	21.1	24.2	..	25.4	26.4	26.0	27.2	28.5	29.3
Norway	27.1	28.2	..	30.7	32.1	30.0	29.9	32.8	34.7	34.9	37.9	39.7
Poland	..	..	..	..	9.9	..	10.3	11.8	12.3	14.2	15.2	16.8
Portugal	8.5	..	..	13.2	13.5	14.4	..	11.5	12.2	13.0	14.0	15.0
Slovak Republic	..	..	..	12.5	11.6	12.4	10.4	11.3	11.1	11.2	11.9	11.9
Spain	16.3	22.5	..	25.2	26.6	28.6	30.3	32.0	33.5	34.1	35.5	36.7
Sweden	27.0	26.5	..	27.3	28.6	28.4	29.3	30.7	31.7	33.6	36.9	39.2
Switzerland	21.3	21.3	..	22.0	21.5	22.5	24.7	25.0	25.9	25.6	25.6	26.5
Turkey	6.1	5.6	..	6.6	7.5	..	7.3	7.8	8.7	8.9	9.1	10.5
United Kingdom	18.5	20.6	..	23.1	23.3	24.3	24.7	25.9	27.3	28.6	29.5	31.2
United States	30.2	30.2	..	32.0	33.6	35.2	35.7	36.2	37.4	38.1	39.1	39.3

StatLink: http://dx.doi.org/10.1787/030488655572

Tertiary attainment for age group 25-34
As a percentage of the population in that age group, 2002

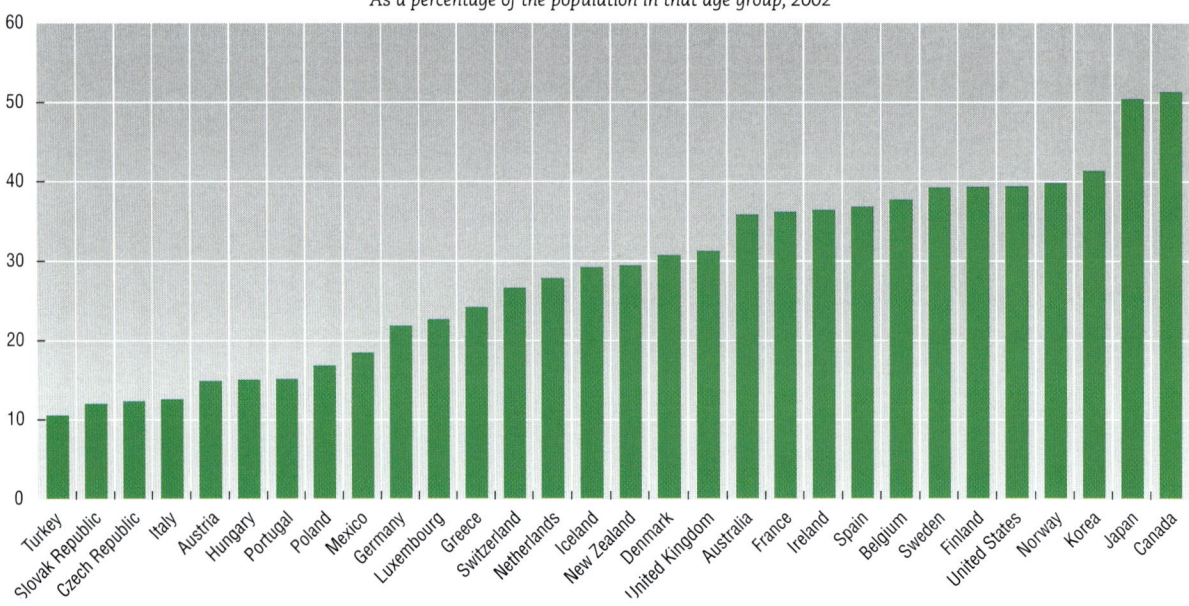

StatLink: http://dx.doi.org/10.1787/765748875407

EDUCATION • OUTCOMES

TERTIARY ATTAINMENT

Tertiary attainment for age group 55-64
As a percentage of the population in that age group

	1991	1992	1993	1994	1995	1996	1997	1998	1999	2000	2001	2002
Australia	13.4	..	13.5	14.7	17.2	16.9	17.1	17.0	17.5	19.1	21.1	22.5
Austria	3.8	3.3	..	3.6	4.2	4.7	6.3	6.5	6.5	9.9	10.6	11.0
Belgium	8.6	9.2	..	11.1	13.1	12.7	13.7	13.8	15.7	16.8	17.1	18.2
Canada	18.8	19.2	..	23.0	23.6	25.1	24.3	25.7	27.4	28.3	30.1	32.1
Czech Republic	..	..	..	7.6	8.3	7.5	7.9	8.5	9.4	9.1	9.3	10.6
Denmark	11.9	12.6	..	13.2	13.8	14.3	..	19.3	19.0	18.2	20.2	23.2
Finland	12.2	12.8	..	13.9	15.5	17.0	17.9	19.3	20.7	22.7	23.4	23.4
France	6.6	7.3	7.9	8.4	8.9	9.6	10.5	11.2	12.4	13.3	14.1	15.2
Germany	16.0	15.7	..	16.5	17.5	17.5	18.4	19.3	19.4	20.2	20.2	20.6
Greece	..	..	..	9.1	7.8	8.4	7.5	7.8	8.4	8.5	9.0	10.2
Hungary	..	..	..	..	..	8.9	8.5	10.2	11.2	11.8	11.5	12.6
Iceland	..	..	..	..	..	9.5	11.6	10.8	11.3	13.5	14.8	16.7
Ireland	9.6	10.4	..	11.3	11.0	12.6	12.5	11.4	12.6	13.3	13.5	14.5
Italy	3.3	3.5	..	4.2	4.4	4.6	..	4.8	5.5	5.5	6.2	6.7
Japan	..	..	..	..	..	..	13.7	13.2	14.3	15.1	15.1	18.0
Korea	5.8	6.0	6.7	6.7	6.8	6.8	6.5	8.3	8.5	8.6	8.9	9.1
Luxembourg	..	..	..	..	..	..	..	..	..	12.0	13.0	13.5	14.4
Mexico	..	..	..	..	4.4	4.6	5.7	4.9	5.7	7.0	7.2	7.2
Netherlands	12.2	13.2	..	14.4	14.2	15.6	..	16.9	16.9	17.7	17.4	18.8
New Zealand	..	17.1	..	17.9	21.1	..	21.2	23.1	23.1	24.2	24.1	26.2
Norway	14.0	14.2	..	17.7	18.0	16.9	17.5	18.9	18.8	20.4	21.5	21.7
Poland	..	..	..	..	8.2	..	9.1	9.9	10.4	9.9	10.2	10.5
Portugal	3.4	..	..	5.6	5.9	6.2	..	4.7	4.5	4.7	4.9	4.6
Slovak Republic	..	..	..	7.0	7.5	7.2	6.1	6.7	6.9	7.8	8.6	8.6
Spain	4.2	5.2	..	5.6	6.0	7.1	7.6	8.1	8.7	9.7	10.3	10.5
Sweden	15.5	16.5	..	19.4	20.2	18.5	19.3	19.9	21.3	23.0	24.4	25.2
Switzerland	15.5	17.0	..	16.9	17.4	16.8	16.5	18.0	17.8	18.3	20.2	21.3
Turkey	4.6	1.7	..	4.3	5.9	..	4.6	4.5	5.3	5.9	5.9	6.3
United Kingdom	10.9	13.6	..	15.5	16.2	16.9	16.3	17.2	18.5	18.9	19.1	19.8
United States	21.9	21.9	..	23.6	24.3	25.6	26.2	27.2	28.0	29.7	30.6	33.2

StatLink: http://dx.doi.org/10.1787/327150575508

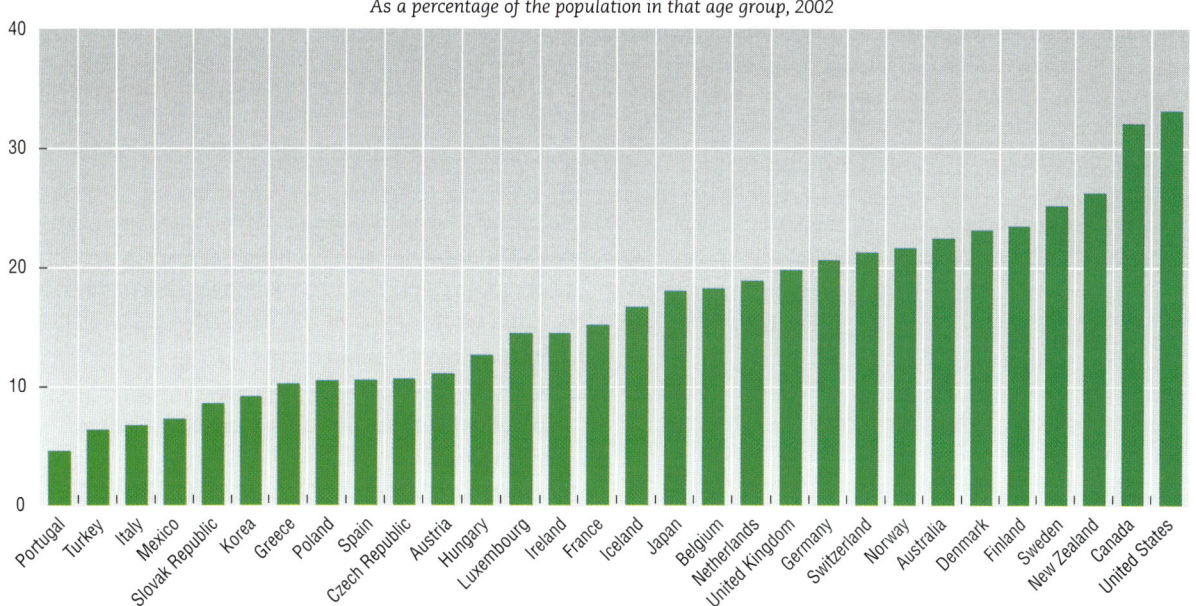

Tertiary attainment for age group 55-64
As a percentage of the population in that age group, 2002

StatLink: http://dx.doi.org/10.1787/642235012878

OECD FACTBOOK 2005 – ISBN 92-64-01869-7 – © OECD 2005

EDUCATION • EXPENDITURE ON EDUCATION

EXPENDITURE BY LEVEL OF EDUCATION

Expenditure per student is an indicator of the investment made by countries in each student at the different levels of education.

Definition

Expenditure on education per student at each level of education is obtained by dividing the total expenditure on educational institutions at that level by the number of full-time students (part-time students are converted to full-time equivalents). Only those educational institutions and programmes are taken into account for which both enrolment and expenditure data are available.

Expenditure in national currency is converted to US dollars by PPP exchange rates. The PPP exchange rate is used because the market exchange rate is affected by many factors (interest rates, trade policies, expectations of economic growth, etc.) that have little to do with relative purchasing power of currencies in different countries.

Comparability

The data on expenditure for 1995 were obtained by a special survey conducted in 2003. OECD countries were asked to collect the 1995 data according to the definitions and the coverage of a joint UNESCO-OECD-Eurostat data collection programme. All expenditure data have been adjusted to 2001 prices using the GDP price deflator.

Data for Hungary, Italy, Poland, Switzerland and Turkey are for public institutions only.

Long-term trends

Expenditure per primary, secondary and post-secondary non-tertiary student increased between 1995 and 2001 by over 25% in Australia, Greece, Ireland, Poland, Portugal, Spain and Turkey. Conversely, expenditure per student in the Czech Republic and Norway declined by over 5%. For Norway, the decline in expenditure by student between 1995 and 2001 is due to a substantial change in the GDP deflator caused primarily by an increase in oil prices. In 6 out of the 23 OECD countries, changes remained within plus or minus 6% compared with 1995.

At the tertiary level Denmark, Greece, Italy, Spain and Switzerland increased expenditure per tertiary student by over 20% per student in the period 1995-2001. In general however, there is a stronger trend towards decreased spending. In seven countries – Australia, Czech Republic, Hungary, Mexico, Norway, Poland and the United Kingdom – expenditure per tertiary student in real terms was lower in 2001 than in 1995.

Source

OECD (2004), *Education at a Glance*, OECD, Paris.

Further information

• *Analytical publications*

OECD (2003), *Education Policy Analysis*, OECD, Paris.

OECD (2004), *Higher Education Management and Policy*, OECD, Paris.

OECD (2004), *Internationalisation and Trade in Higher Education: Opportunities and Challenges*, OECD, Paris.

OECD (2004), *Reviews of National Policies for Education*, OECD, Paris.

OECD (2004), *Quality and Recognition in Higher Education: The Cross-border Challenge*, OECD, Paris.

• *Methodological publications*

OECD (2004), *OECD Handbook for Internationally Comparative Education Statistics: Concepts, Standards, Definitions and Classifications*, OECD, Paris.

UIS, OECD and Eurostat (2002), *UOE Data Collection – 2002 Data Collection on Education Systems: Definitions, Explanations and Instructions*, OECD, Paris.

• *Web sites*

OECD *Education at a Glance*: www.oecd.org/edu/eag2004.

EDUCATION • EXPENDITURE ON EDUCATION

EXPENDITURE BY LEVEL OF EDUCATION

Expenditure on education by level
US dollars, 2001 prices and PPPs

	1995			2001		
	Expenditure per student		GDP per capita	Expenditure per student		GDP per capita
	Primary, secondary and post-secondary non-tertiary education	Tertiary		Primary, secondary and post-secondary non-tertiary education	Tertiary	
Australia	4 846	13 897	23 135	6 063	12 688	26 685
Austria	..	10 341	24 889	7 852	11 274	28 372
Belgium	..	..	23 868	6 781	11 589	27 096
Canada	..	..	24 826	..	..	29 290
Czech Republic	2 927	8 785	13 426	2 819	5 555	14 861
Denmark	6 515	11 499	25 830	7 865	14 280	29 223
Finland	5 238	10 900	20 992	5 733	10 981	26 344
France	5 938	7 801	23 580	6 783	8 837	26 818
Germany	5 820	9 698	23 279	6 055	10 504	25 456
Greece	2 409	3 264	14 199	3 475	4 280	17 020
Hungary	2 335	7 767	10 171	2 677	7 122	13 043
Iceland	..	..	23 564	7 010	7 674	29 036
Ireland	3 042	7 223	18 802	4 397	10 003	29 821
Italy	6 577	5 621	22 889	7 714	8 347	25 377
Japan	5 134	9 691	25 092	6 179	11 164	26 636
Korea	..	...	12 780	4 406	6 618	15 916
Luxembourg	..	..	37 220	11 091	..	49 229
Mexico	1 263	4 821	7 737	1 575	4 341	9 148
Netherlands	4 548	12 311	24 503	5 654	12 974	28 711
New Zealand	..	..	19 053	..	..	21 230
Norway	8 425	14 087	31 146	8 109	13 189	36 587
Poland	1 528	4 023	7 682	2 396	3 579	10 360
Portugal	3 052	4 664	14 939	5 065	5 199	17 912
Slovak Republic	1 467	5 250	8 987	1 681	5 285	11 323
Spain	3 775	5 624	17 637	4 870	7 455	21 347
Sweden	6 180	..	22 846	6 372	15 188	26 902
Switzerland	8 844	15 802	27 537	8 844	20 230	30 036
Turkey	..	..	5 994	..	..	6 046
United Kingdom	4 941	10 981	23 006	5 324	10 753	26 715
United States	7 034	20 207	30 753	8 144	22 234	35 178

StatLink: http://dx.doi.org/10.1787/516503821100

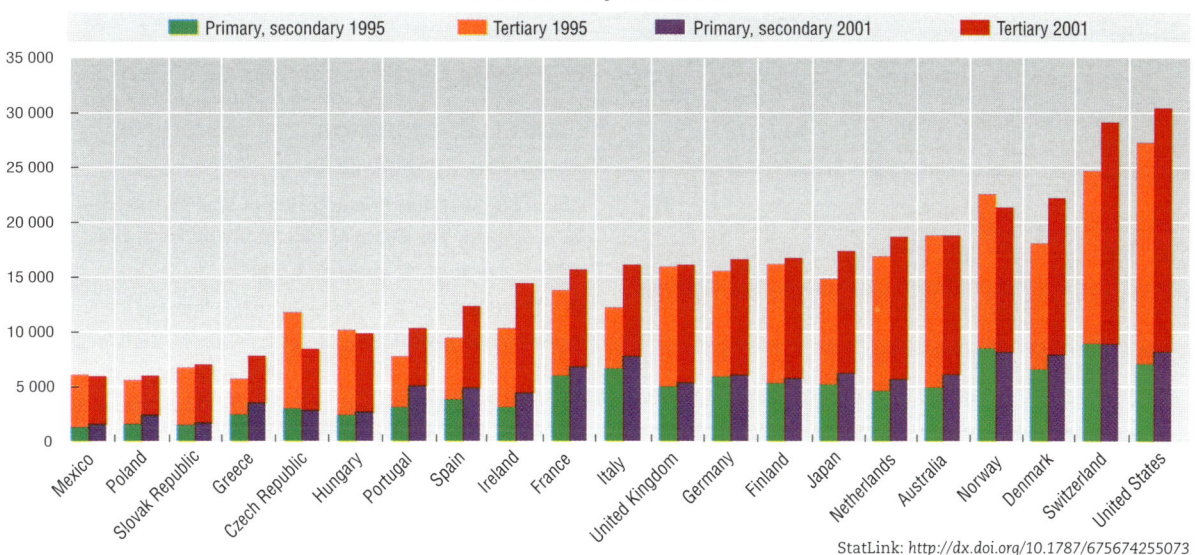

Expenditure on education by level
US dollars, 2001 prices and PPPs

StatLink: http://dx.doi.org/10.1787/675674255073

OECD FACTBOOK 2005 – ISBN 92-64-01869-7 – © OECD 2005

157

EDUCATION • EXPENDITURE ON EDUCATION

PUBLIC AND PRIVATE EDUCATION EXPENDITURE

Expenditure on education is an investment that can help to foster economic growth, enhance productivity, contribute to personal and social development, and reduce social inequality. The proportion of total financial resources devoted to education is one of the key choices made in each country by governments, enterprises and individual students and their families alike.

Definition

The expenditure data shown here includes expenditure on instructional/educational institutions as well as expenditure on non-instructional institutions that provide administrative, advisory or professional services to other educational institutions, although they do not enrol students themselves (*e.g.* national, state and provincial ministries or departments of education). Expenditure on institutions is not limited to expenditure on instructional services but also includes public and private expenditure on ancillary services for students and families, where these services are provided through educational institutions. At the tertiary level, spending on research and development can also be significant and is included in this indicator, to the extent that the research is performed by educational institutions. However, public subsidies for educational expenditure outside institutions even if it is subsidised, student living costs at tertiary level for example, are excluded.

In principle, public expenditure includes public subsidies to households attributable for educational institutions although several countries actually include them in private expenditure. Public expenditure also includes direct expenditure on educational institutions from international sources.

Comparability

The broad definition of institutions outlined above ensures that expenditure on services, which are provided in some OECD countries by schools and universities and in others by agencies other than schools, are covered on a comparable basis. Additionally, to ensure comparability over time the data on expenditure for 1995 were obtained by a special survey in 2003; expenditure for 1995 was adjusted to the methods and definitions used in the 2003 data collection.

Long-term trends

In 2001, OECD countries spent on average 5.6% of their GDP on education (from both public and private sources) ranging from the United States which spent 7.3% of GDP down to Turkey's 3.5%.

Of the 22 countries that provided comparable data for both 1995 and 2001, only 8 countries increased their spending on education relative to GDP (Australia, Denmark, Greece, Mexico, Sweden, Portugal, Turkey and the United States). Spending by Greece and Turkey increased the most significantly although this does not include data on private spending which was not available. However these countries still spend the least on education relative to GDP out of the OECD countries for which data are available. Eleven countries decreased their spending relative to GDP over the same period (Austria, Canada, Czech Republic, Finland, France, Germany, Hungary, Ireland, Norway, the Slovak Republic and Spain) and in five of these countries expenditure as a percentage of GDP decreased by more than 10% (Canada, the Czech Republic, Ireland, Norway and the Slovak Republic). In the remaining three countries (Japan, the Netherlands and the United Kingdom) there was little if any change.

It should be noted that strong growth in GDP (as for example in the case of Ireland) masks the fact that there was a significant increase in real terms in spending on educational institutions in almost all of the OECD countries from 1995 to 2001. In addition, the size of the school age population shapes the demand for education and training, and national levels of teachers' salaries also affect the share of expenditure on education.

Source

OECD (2004), *Education at a Glance*, OECD, Paris.

Further information

• *Analytical publications*

OECD (2002), *Education and Health Expenditure, and Development: The Cases of Indonesia and Peru*, OECD, Paris.

• *Methodological publications*

OECD (2004), *OECD Handbook for Internationally Comparative Education Statistics: Concepts, Standards, Definitions and Classifications*, OECD, Paris.

UIS, OECD and Eurostat (2002), *UOE Data Collection – 2002 Data Collection on Education Systems: Definitions, Explanations and Instructions*, OECD, Paris.

• *Web sites*

OECD *Education at a Glance: www.oecd.org/edu/eag2004*.

EDUCATION • EXPENDITURE ON EDUCATION

PUBLIC AND PRIVATE EDUCATION EXPENDITURE

Education expenditure
As a percentage of GDP

	1995			2001		
	Public	Private	Total	Public	Private	Total
Australia	4.5	1.2	5.7	4.5	1.4	6.0
Austria	5.9	0.3	6.2	5.6	0.2	5.8
Belgium	..	..	..	6.0	0.4	6.4
Canada	6.2	0.8	7.0	4.9	1.3	6.1
Czech Republic	4.7	0.7	5.4	4.2	0.4	4.6
Denmark	6.1	0.2	6.3	6.8	0.3	7.1
Finland	6.2	..	6.3	5.7	0.1	5.8
France	5.9	0.4	6.3	5.6	0.4	6.0
Germany	4.5	1.0	5.5	4.3	1.0	5.3
Greece	3.1	..	3.2	3.8	0.2	4.1
Hungary	4.9	0.6	5.5	4.6	0.6	5.2
Iceland	..	..	..	6.1	0.6	6.7
Ireland	4.7	0.5	5.3	4.1	0.3	4.5
Italy	4.7	..	..	4.9	0.4	5.3
Japan	3.5	1.1	4.6	3.5	1.2	4.6
Korea	..	..	..	4.8	3.4	8.2
Luxembourg	..	..	..	3.6	0.0	3.6
Mexico	4.6	1.0	5.6	5.1	0.8	5.9
Netherlands	4.5	0.4	4.9	4.5	0.4	4.9
New Zealand	4.8	..	..	5.5	..	..
Norway	6.8	0.4	7.1	6.1	0.2	6.4
Poland	5.7	..	..	5.6	..	..
Portugal	5.3	0.0	5.3	5.8	0.1	5.9
Slovak Republic	4.6	0.1	4.7	4.0	0.1	4.1
Spain	4.5	0.9	5.4	4.3	0.6	4.9
Sweden	6.1	0.1	6.2	6.3	0.2	6.5
Switzerland	5.4	..	..	5.4	..	..
Turkey	2.3	0.0	2.3	3.5	0.0	3.5
United Kingdom	4.8	0.7	5.5	4.7	0.8	5.5
United States	5.0	2.2	7.2	5.1	2.3	7.3
Country mean	..	..	..	5.0	0.7	5.6
OECD total	..	..	..	4.8	1.4	6.2

StatLink: http://dx.doi.org/10.1787/227034118233

Expenditure on educational institutions
As a percentage of GDP

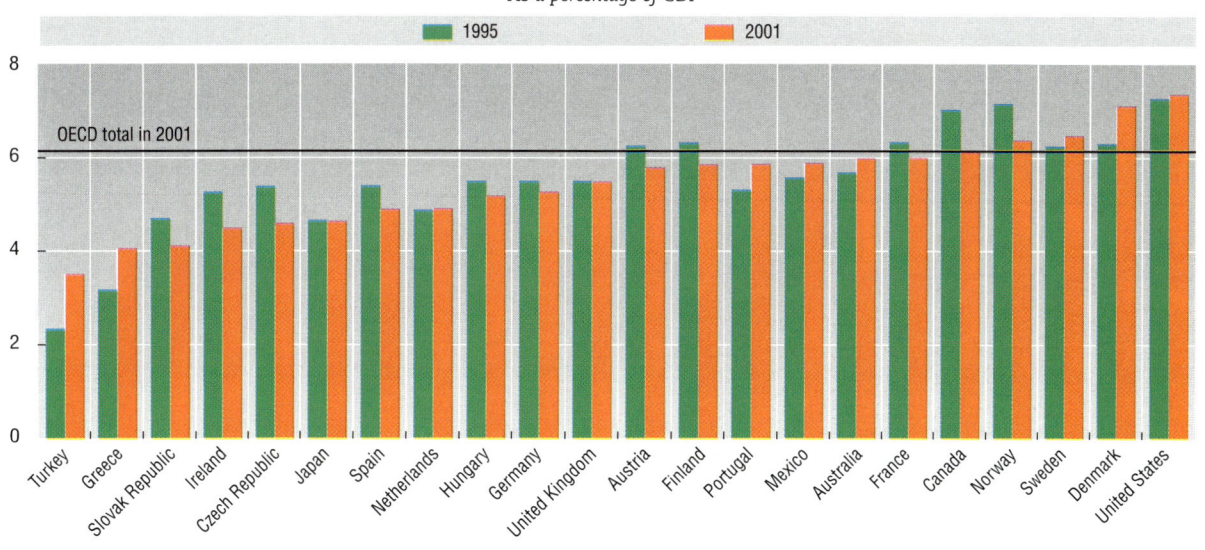

StatLink: http://dx.doi.org/10.1787/376301304120

PUBLIC POLICIES

GOVERNMENT DEFICITS AND DEBT
GOVERNMENT DEFICITS
GOVERNMENT DEBT

PUBLIC EXPENDITURE AND AID
SOCIAL EXPENDITURE
HEALTH EXPENDITURE
AGRICULTURAL SUPPORT ESTIMATES
GOVERNMENT SUPPORT FOR FISHING
OFFICIAL DEVELOPMENT ASSISTANCE

TAXES
TOTAL TAX REVENUE
TAXES ON THE AVERAGE PRODUCTION WORKER

REGIONAL DISPARITIES
REGIONAL GDP
REGIONAL UNEMPLOYMENT

PUBLIC POLICIES • GOVERNMENT DEFICITS AND DEBT

GOVERNMENT DEFICITS

Government deficits or surpluses are commonly assessed using the net borrowing (or net lending) figures of the general government sector of the national accounts. During the period since 1990, governments in most OECD countries had a net borrowing, which means a deficit. Government deficits have to be met, in general, by borrowing from residents or foreigners.

Definition

The net borrowing/net lending of the general government is the balancing item of the non-financial accounts (according to the System of National Accounts, SNA1993). It is also equal to the difference between total revenue and total expenditure, including the capital expenditure (in particular, the gross capital formation). The main revenue of general government consists in tax, social contributions, dividends and other property income. The main expenditure consists in the compensation of civil servants, social benefits, interest on the public debt, subsidies and gross fixed capital formation.

The data in the table are on a national accounts basis and may differ from the numbers reported to the European Commission under the excessive deficit procedure (EDP) for some EU countries and for some years

Comparability

Data in this table are based on the System of National Accounts so that all countries are using a common set of definitions. In several OECD countries, for years 2000 or 2001, the accounts have been affected by the sale of mobile telephone licences, recorded in national accounts as a negative expenditure (the sale of an asset).

The averages shown for both EU15 and OECD are unweighted averages. The OECD figures exclude the Czech Republic, Hungary, Poland and the Slovak Republic as data were not available for the whole period for these countries.

Long-term trends

Government deficits are sensitive to the economic cycle as well as to government taxation and spending policies. For the OECD as a whole, deficits as a percentage of GDP reached a peak in 1993 but then fell steadily over the next six years and had turned into surpluses (net lending) at the peak of the economic cycle in 2000. Since then deficits have been growing and the deficit to GDP ratio had become high in 2003 for most of the larger member countries including France, Germany, the United Kingdom, the United States and, especially, Japan. They are expected to remain high in 2004 and 2005.

In the run up of monetary union, EU countries that expected to adopt the euro followed fiscal policies aimed at reducing government deficits. Deficit reduction policies were successfully implemented in several other countries including New Zealand (since 1994), Australia (since 1997) and Sweden (since 1998). Korea is the only country which has recorded surpluses throughout the period, although Luxembourg and Norway had both surpluses in most years since 1990.

Source

OECD (2004), *OECD Economic Outlook, No. 76*, OECD, Paris.

Further information

• *Analytical publications*

OECD (2004), *National Accounts of OECD countries*, OECD, Paris.

OECD (2004), *OECD Economic Survey*, series, OECD, Paris. All OECD countries and a number of non-member economies are covered during each two-year cycle of publications.

• *Online databases*

SourceOECD Economic Outlook.

SourceOECD National Accounts.

• *Web sites*

OECD Economic Outlook – Sources and Methods: *www.oecd.org/eco/sources-and-methods*.

PUBLIC POLICIES • GOVERNMENT DEFICITS AND DEBT

GOVERNMENT DEFICITS

Government net borrowing/net lending[1]
As a percentage of GDP

	1990	1991	1992	1993	1994	1995	1996	1997	1998	1999	2000	2001	2002	2003
Australia	-1.74	-4.25	-6.37	-5.84	-4.83	-3.85	-2.18	-0.42	0.72	1.98	0.79	-0.80	0.29	0.78
Austria	-2.00	-2.29	-1.60	-3.93	-4.71	-5.75	-4.02	-1.96	-2.47	-2.35	-1.64	0.11	-0.41	-1.25
Belgium	-6.84	-7.46	-8.13	-7.39	-5.08	-4.38	-3.80	-1.96	-0.67	-0.40	0.15	0.57	0.07	0.31
Canada	-5.83	-8.35	-9.13	-8.71	-6.70	-5.33	-2.80	0.19	0.08	1.61	2.95	1.11	0.28	0.63
Czech Republic	..	..	..	..	..	-13.39	-3.08	-2.44	-5.02	-3.65	-3.65	-5.92	-6.75	-12.60
Denmark	-1.02	-2.40	-2.21	-2.86	-2.43	-2.26	-1.00	0.35	1.13	3.21	2.54	2.83	1.56	1.21
Finland	5.47	-0.99	-5.53	-7.24	-5.71	-3.87	-2.95	-1.25	1.64	2.17	7.09	5.20	4.25	2.11
France	-2.09	-2.45	-4.17	-5.98	-5.53	-5.50	-4.08	-3.04	-2.67	-1.77	-1.40	-1.53	-3.26	-4.14
Germany	-1.97	-2.95	-2.55	-3.11	-2.40	-3.32	-3.42	-2.72	-2.22	-1.49	1.33	-2.82	-3.68	-3.82
Greece	-15.72	-11.05	-12.24	-13.37	-9.25	-10.16	-7.44	-4.03	-2.46	-1.80	-4.18	-3.67	-3.80	-4.65
Hungary	..	-2.96	-7.09	-6.56	-11.02	-7.56	-5.87	-7.24	-8.04	-5.62	-3.01	-4.71	-9.34	-6.15
Iceland	-3.32	-2.95	-2.85	-4.54	-4.79	-3.02	-1.62	-0.02	0.50	2.40	2.50	0.17	-0.44	-1.65
Ireland	-2.80	-2.85	-2.95	-2.73	-1.96	-2.07	-0.12	1.46	2.27	2.47	4.41	0.97	-0.18	0.17
Italy	-11.77	-11.70	-10.67	-10.30	-9.29	-7.59	-7.10	-2.70	-3.10	-1.77	-0.67	-2.67	-2.41	-2.49
Japan	2.05	1.81	0.79	-2.38	-3.76	-4.71	-5.07	-3.79	-5.52	-7.23	-7.48	-6.13	-7.88	-7.67
Korea	3.20	1.64	1.28	2.22	2.80	3.80	3.39	3.29	1.72	2.88	5.42	4.62	5.46	4.15
Luxembourg	4.81	1.19	0.23	1.55	2.74	2.07	1.91	3.21	3.16	3.73	5.98	6.42	2.79	0.78
Netherlands	-5.32	-2.66	-4.21	-2.84	-3.45	-4.16	-1.82	-1.11	-0.76	0.66	2.20	-0.09	-1.94	-3.22
New Zealand	-4.34	-3.85	-3.27	-1.26	2.46	3.04	2.91	1.89	0.29	0.63	1.48	1.99	2.51	3.13
Norway	2.22	0.11	-1.87	-1.44	0.27	3.41	6.52	7.72	3.56	6.25	15.56	13.57	9.11	8.31
Poland	..	..	..	..	..	-3.88	-4.70	-4.52	-3.99	-3.19	-2.41	-3.84	-4.95	-3.84
Portugal	-6.62	-7.59	-4.76	-8.07	-7.72	-5.47	-4.77	-3.57	-3.17	-2.87	-2.90	-4.44	-2.73	-2.81
Slovak Republic	..	..	..	..	-6.13	-0.86	-7.40	-6.18	-3.77	-7.14	-12.31	-6.00	-5.72	-3.74
Spain	-3.89	-4.57	-3.67	-6.96	-6.49	-6.64	-4.95	-3.18	-3.03	-1.18	-0.90	-0.39	-0.14	0.41
Sweden	3.77	-1.91	-7.57	-11.41	-9.27	-6.93	-2.79	-1.02	1.92	2.35	5.07	2.85	-0.26	0.10
Switzerland	0.59	-1.14	-2.40	-2.68	-1.95	-1.24	-1.39	-2.40	-1.49	0.03	2.32	0.93	0.24	-0.80
United Kingdom	-1.59	-3.11	-6.46	-7.94	-6.78	-5.85	-4.21	-2.20	0.06	1.04	3.82	0.68	-1.73	-3.51
United States	-4.24	-4.92	-5.77	-4.94	-3.56	-3.14	-2.18	-0.79	0.43	0.85	1.62	-0.39	-3.79	-4.60
Euro area	-4.61	-5.00	-5.05	-5.76	-5.06	-5.05	-4.32	-2.64	-2.30	-1.33	0.07	-1.71	-2.42	-2.75
OECD total	-2.95	-3.73	-4.59	-4.96	-4.19	-3.96	-3.13	-1.68	-1.23	-0.77	0.27	-1.21	-3.17	-3.68

1. A negative figure indicates a deficit.

StatLink: http://dx.doi.org/10.1787/787757401550

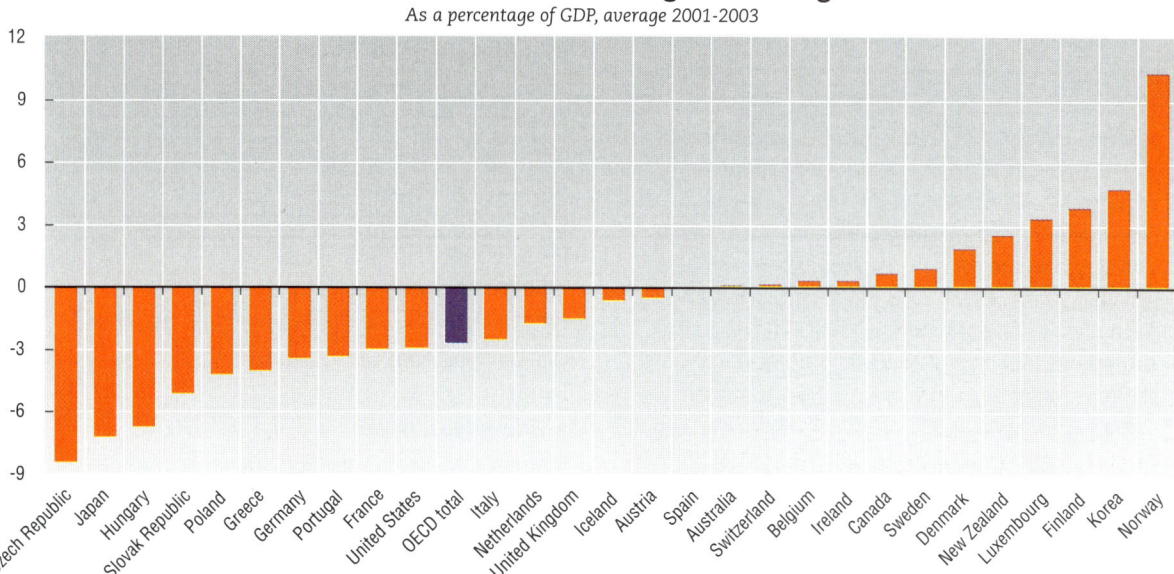

Government net borrowing/net lending
As a percentage of GDP, average 2001-2003

StatLink: http://dx.doi.org/10.1787/211816824512

GOVERNMENT DEBT

There are two standard ways to measure the extent of government debt – by reference to gross financial liabilities or by reference to net financial liabilities – the latter being measured as gross financial liabilities minus financial assets. Gross financial liabilities as a percentage of GDP is the most commonly used government debt ratio and is shown here.

Definition

For most countries, gross financial liabilities refer to the liabilities (short and long-term) of all the institutions in the general government sector, as defined in the 1993 System of National Accounts (SNA). However, for some EU countries (Czech Republic, Greece, Ireland, Luxembourg, Slovak Republic), the definition of debt applied under the Maastricht Treaty has been used. The Maastricht definition of debt essentially differs from the SNA definition in two respects. First, gross debt according to the Maastricht definition excludes trade credits and advances, as well as shares and insurance technical reserves. Second, government bonds are valued at nominal values instead of at market value or issue price plus accrued interest as required by the SNA rules.

In principle, debts within and between different levels of government are consolidated; a loan from one level of government to another represents both an asset and an equal liability for the government as a whole and so it cancels out (is "consolidated") for the general government sector.

Comparability

Comparability is affected to some extent by the use of Maastricht rules rather than SNA definitions as noted above. There are also difficulties for some countries in deciding on the scope of general government. For example, in Japan, government financial liabilities include the debt of the Japan Railway Settlement Corporation and the National Forest Special Account from 1998 onwards.

Because of the difficulties of compiling these figures, only 27 of the 30 member countries are currently publishing data on government gross financial liabilities.

Long-term trends

From 1990 to 1996 government gross financial liabilities were rising in most countries. Since then government debt has been decreasing as a percentage of GDP in many of the 27 countries in the table. For these countries, the peak was reached in 1995. There are, however, exceptions: government debt ratios continued to increase particularly fast in Japan and Korea and significantly in France, Germany and Greece. Korea's government debt ratio rose by over 7% per year from 1990 to 2003 but this is measured from a very low initial rate and by 2003, Korea's government debt ratio was still among the lowest in the OECD.

In 2003, government debt ratios exceeded 100% in Belgium, Greece, Italy and Japan. Most countries were in a band between 40% and 70%, with three countries reporting debt ratios of under 20% – Luxembourg, Korea and Australia.

Source

OECD (2004), *OECD Economic Outlook*, No. 76, OECD, Paris.

Further information

• *Analytical publications*

OECD (2002), *Debt Management and Government Securities Markets in the 21st Century*, OECD, Paris.

OECD (2004), *OECD Economic Surveys*, series, OECD, Paris. All OECD countries and a number of non-member economies are covered during each two-year cycle of publications.

• *Statistical publications*

OECD (2004), *Central Government Debt*, OECD, Paris.

OECD (2004), *National Accounts of OECD Countries*, OECD, Paris.

• *Online databases*

SourceOECD Economic Outlook.

SourceOECD National Accounts.

• *Web sites*

OECD Economic Outlook – Sources and Methods: www.oecd.org/eco/sources-and-methods.

PUBLIC POLICIES • GOVERNMENT DEFICITS AND DEBT

GOVERNMENT DEBT

General government gross financial liabilities
As a percentage of GDP

	1990	1991	1992	1993	1994	1995	1996	1997	1998	1999	2000	2001	2002	2003
Australia	23.1	23.9	28.7	32.2	42.6	44.6	41.4	39.6	34.1	28.4	25.2	22.1	20.7	19.6
Austria	57.6	57.6	57.3	62.1	65.0	69.7	69.9	69.9	67.4	69.8	69.4	70.2	71.9	69.7
Belgium	129.7	131.4	140.5	144.3	141.2	138.8	136.1	129.9	124.7	120.3	115.0	113.5	110.4	104.9
Canada	74.5	82.1	89.9	96.9	98.2	100.8	100.3	96.2	93.9	89.5	81.8	81.0	77.7	73.3
Czech Republic	..	..	..	..	..	..	..	12.2	12.9	13.4	18.2	25.3	28.8	37.8
Denmark	69.8	70.8	74.9	88.9	82.4	78.4	74.5	70.4	67.1	61.1	54.4	53.7	54.1	49.5
Finland	16.7	25.1	45.1	58.3	60.9	65.7	66.6	64.8	61.4	55.9	53.2	51.3	50.8	51.5
France	39.5	40.3	44.7	51.6	55.3	63.9	67.5	69.4	71.1	67.3	66.2	64.9	68.7	71.2
Germany	41.5	38.8	41.8	47.4	47.9	57.1	60.3	61.8	63.2	61.6	60.9	60.5	62.9	65.2
Greece	79.6	82.2	87.8	110.1	107.9	108.7	111.3	108.2	105.8	105.2	114.0	114.7	112.5	109.9
Hungary	..	..	..	..	..	..	..	67.3	64.9	66.4	60.2	60.1	61.1	60.3
Iceland	36.9	39.1	47.2	54.2	56.9	60.3	57.6	54.3	49.3	44.5	41.9	47.4	43.6	41.6
Ireland	94.0	95.4	92.4	95.0	89.5	81.9	73.4	64.6	53.7	48.7	38.3	35.9	32.7	32.1
Italy	112.5	116.5	126.0	127.9	134.4	133.5	135.7	133.0	133.4	128.4	124.5	122.0	121.5	120.9
Japan	68.6	64.8	68.7	74.9	79.7	87.1	93.9	100.3	112.2	125.7	134.1	142.3	149.3	157.5
Korea	7.7	6.7	6.3	5.6	5.2	5.5	5.9	7.5	13.1	15.6	16.3	17.4	16.6	18.7
Luxembourg	5.4	4.6	5.5	6.8	6.3	6.7	7.2	6.8	6.3	6.0	5.5	5.5	5.7	5.3
Netherlands	87.8	88.9	92.8	97.7	87.7	90.8	89.8	84.5	82.9	74.2	66.7	62.1	62.1	63.2
New Zealand	..	..	..	70.8	62.7	56.9	50.8	50.1	49.7	47.1	44.7	42.2	40.2	37.4
Norway	29.3	27.5	32.2	40.5	36.9	34.4	30.7	27.5	26.2	26.8	30.0	29.2	35.7	35.2
Poland	..	..	..	..	..	..	..	45.6	41.8	43.2	40.0	41.0	46.7	51.6
Portugal	..	..	..	..	..	72.5	71.8	68.0	64.2	62.8	61.4	65.1	68.1	70.3
Slovak Republic	..	..	..	..	..	..	30.6	33.1	34.0	47.2	49.9	48.7	43.4	42.8
Spain	48.8	50.7	53.0	66.8	65.4	70.3	77.1	76.0	76.1	70.3	67.3	63.5	61.3	59.4
Sweden	46.8	55.5	74.0	79.0	83.5	82.2	84.7	82.8	81.2	71.6	64.2	63.2	62.1	61.9
United Kingdom	33.0	33.6	39.8	49.6	47.8	52.7	52.6	53.2	53.8	48.8	45.9	41.2	41.5	42.0
United States	66.6	71.3	73.7	75.4	74.6	74.2	73.4	70.9	67.7	64.1	58.3	57.9	60.2	62.5

StatLink: http://dx.doi.org/10.1787/632323657872

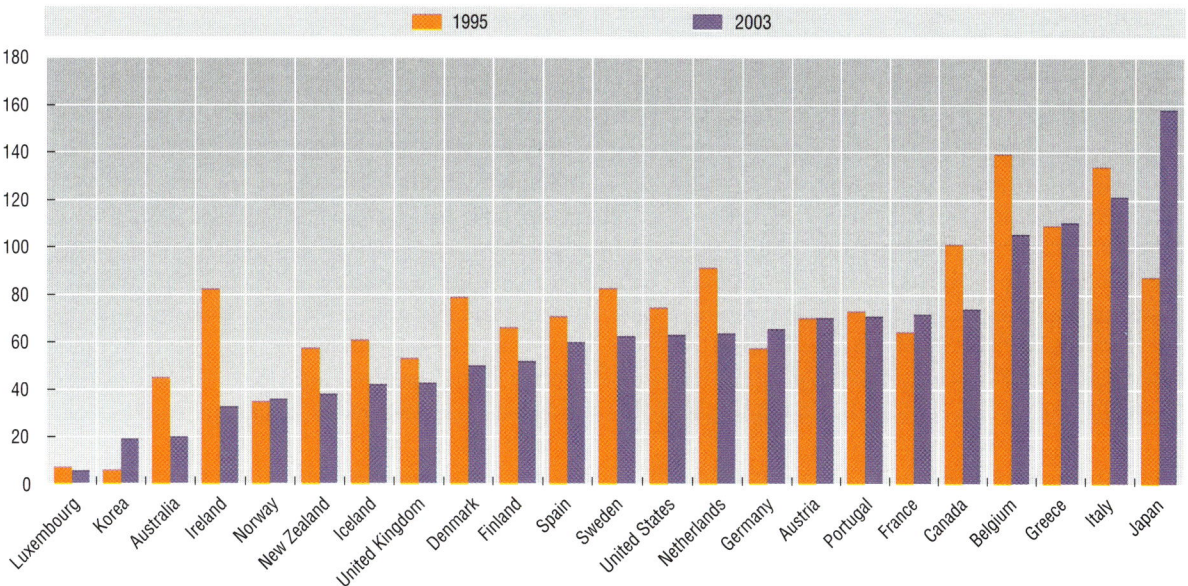

General government gross financial liabilities
As a percentage of GDP

StatLink: http://dx.doi.org/10.1787/187213041082

PUBLIC POLICIES • PUBLIC EXPENDITURE AND AID

SOCIAL EXPENDITURE

Social expenditures as a percentage of GDP are a measure of the extent to which governments assume responsibility for supporting the standard of living of disadvantaged or vulnerable groups.

Long-term trends

In 2001, on average, public social expenditure amounted to 21% of GDP, although there are significant cross-country variations. In Sweden and Denmark, public social spending is about 30% while it is 6% in Korea.

Changes in gross public social expenditures over time are also significant. After having almost doubled in the 20 years to 1980, the expansion of gross public expenditure continued at a reduced rate with the OECD average peaking at 23% in 1993. Since then, gross public social expenditure had declined – on average – by around 1.5 percentage points of GDP by 2001, with all the decline accounted for by non-health expenditures.

It is convenient to group expenditure along with their social purposes to better analyse policy focus and trends. Broadly speaking, the three biggest groups of social transfers are pensions (on average 8% of GDP), health (6%) and income transfers to the working-age population (5%). Public spending on other social services only exceeds 5% of GDP in the Nordic countries, where the public role in providing services to the elderly, the disabled and families is the most extensive.

Public support for families with children is nearly 2% of GDP on average, but this has increased in most countries since 1980. Family support exceeds 3% of GDP in the Nordic countries and Austria, as they have the most comprehensive public system of child allowances, paid leave arrangements and childcare. Moreover, governments also help families through the tax system; examples include the "quotient familial" in France and "income splitting" in Germany.

Social insurance spending related to work incapacity (disability, sickness and occupational injury benefits) has declined in as many countries as it has increased since 1980. Particularly large declines were found in Belgium, the Netherlands and Portugal. This mainly

Definition

Public social expenditure comprises cash benefits, direct "in-kind" provision of goods and services, and tax breaks with social purposes. To be considered "social", benefits have to address one or more social goals. Benefits may be targeted at low-income households, but they may also be for the elderly, disabled, sick, unemployed, or young persons. Programmes regulating the provision of social benefits have to involve: *a)* redistribution of resources across households, or *b)* compulsory participation. Social benefits are regarded as public when general government (that is central, state, and local governments, including social security funds) controls relevant financial flows.

Comparability

For cross-country comparisons, the most commonly used indicator of social support is gross (before tax) public social expenditure related to GDP. Measurement problems do exist, particularly with regard to spending by lower tiers of government, which may be underestimated in some countries.

Source

OECD Database on Social Expenditure: *www.oecd.org/els/social/expenditure*.

Further information
• *Analytical publications*

OECD (2002-04), *Babies and Bosses – Reconciling Work and Family Life*, series, OECD, Paris. See Vol. I for Australia, Denmark and the Netherlands; Vol. II for Austria, Ireland and Japan; and Vol. III for New Zealand, Portugal and Switzerland.

OECD (2003), *Transforming Disability into Ability. Policies to Promote Work and Income Security for Disabled People*, OECD, Paris.

OECD (2005), *Society at a Glance: OECD Social Indicators 2005*, OECD, Paris.

• *Web sites*

OECD Social and Welfare Statistics: *www.oecd.org/statistics/social*.

PUBLIC POLICIES • PUBLIC EXPENDITURE AND AID

SOCIAL EXPENDITURE

Social expenditure
As a percentage of GDP

	1990	1991	1992	1993	1994	1995	1996	1997	1998	1999	2000	2001
Australia	14.22	15.31	16.31	16.50	16.21	17.83	17.97	17.74	17.78	17.47	18.56	18.00
Austria	24.10	24.37	25.03	26.61	27.29	26.64	26.71	25.96	25.67	26.10	26.02	25.96
Belgium	26.92	27.65	28.43	29.93	29.17	28.07	28.55	27.47	27.45	27.21	26.71	27.23
Canada	18.61	21.13	21.78	21.61	20.55	19.62	18.81	18.29	18.36	17.44	17.33	17.81
Czech Republic	17.03	18.34	18.70	19.19	19.21	18.88	18.81	19.70	19.55	19.81	20.32	20.09
Denmark	29.32	30.17	30.72	32.35	33.06	32.41	31.69	30.66	30.17	29.85	28.89	29.22
Finland	24.75	29.89	33.88	33.89	33.05	31.10	30.91	28.66	26.47	26.09	24.50	24.80
France	26.61	27.23	28.03	29.48	29.27	29.24	29.38	29.42	28.96	28.91	28.34	28.45
Germany	22.80	24.87	26.37	26.94	26.91	27.46	28.09	27.62	27.37	27.37	27.17	27.39
Greece	20.90	20.07	20.20	21.14	21.16	21.38	22.07	22.09	22.79	23.57	23.58	24.34
Hungary	..	..	..	..	..	..	..	..	..	20.82	20.04	20.07
Iceland	16.45	17.14	17.77	18.21	18.42	18.98	18.78	18.53	18.72	19.64	19.69	19.83
Ireland	18.65	19.46	20.37	20.31	19.99	19.35	18.17	16.82	15.55	14.20	13.63	13.75
Italy	23.27	23.50	24.32	24.72	24.36	23.02	23.54	24.16	23.75	24.15	24.07	24.45
Japan	11.20	11.32	11.82	12.45	13.04	13.50	13.67	13.78	14.50	15.14	16.13	16.89
Korea	3.13	2.94	3.22	3.31	3.36	3.64	3.87	4.24	5.94	6.91	5.61	6.12
Luxembourg	21.86	22.38	22.77	23.13	22.98	23.81	23.86	22.61	21.72	21.55	20.03	20.84
Mexico	3.84	4.33	4.61	4.92	5.44	8.07	8.05	8.82	8.81	9.04	9.89	11.83
Netherlands	27.65	27.73	28.32	28.55	27.20	25.58	24.41	23.98	23.01	22.51	21.77	21.75
New Zealand	21.92	22.32	22.18	20.40	19.40	18.88	18.79	19.78	20.05	19.54	19.21	18.53
Norway	24.68	25.73	26.82	26.69	26.43	25.98	24.95	24.11	25.70	25.77	23.00	23.90
Poland	15.55	22.10	26.22	25.58	24.43	23.75	23.88	23.26	21.99	22.18	21.94	23.03
Portugal	13.90	14.91	15.63	17.18	17.30	18.03	19.10	18.88	19.15	19.84	20.50	21.10
Slovak Republic	..	..	..	..	..	19.23	19.13	18.67	18.97	18.93	18.26	17.90
Spain	19.55	20.33	21.44	22.47	21.99	21.39	21.57	20.94	20.29	19.93	19.91	19.57
Sweden	30.78	32.40	35.34	36.77	35.35	32.96	32.48	31.04	30.40	29.92	28.60	28.92
Switzerland	17.92	19.31	21.29	23.01	23.18	23.88	24.95	25.96	25.90	26.13	25.40	26.41
Turkey	7.64	8.16	8.53	8.28	7.89	7.52	9.67	10.80	11.12	13.20	..	..
United Kingdom	19.55	21.13	23.11	23.66	23.22	23.01	22.78	22.02	21.49	21.25	21.69	21.82
United States	13.43	14.48	15.18	15.42	15.41	15.45	15.27	14.91	14.49	14.24	14.24	14.78
EU15	23.37	24.41	25.60	26.47	26.15	25.56	25.55	24.82	24.28	24.16	23.69	23.97
OECD total	..	..	..	..	..	..	..	..	..	20.96	20.86	21.20

StatLink: http://dx.doi.org/10.1787/568011780445

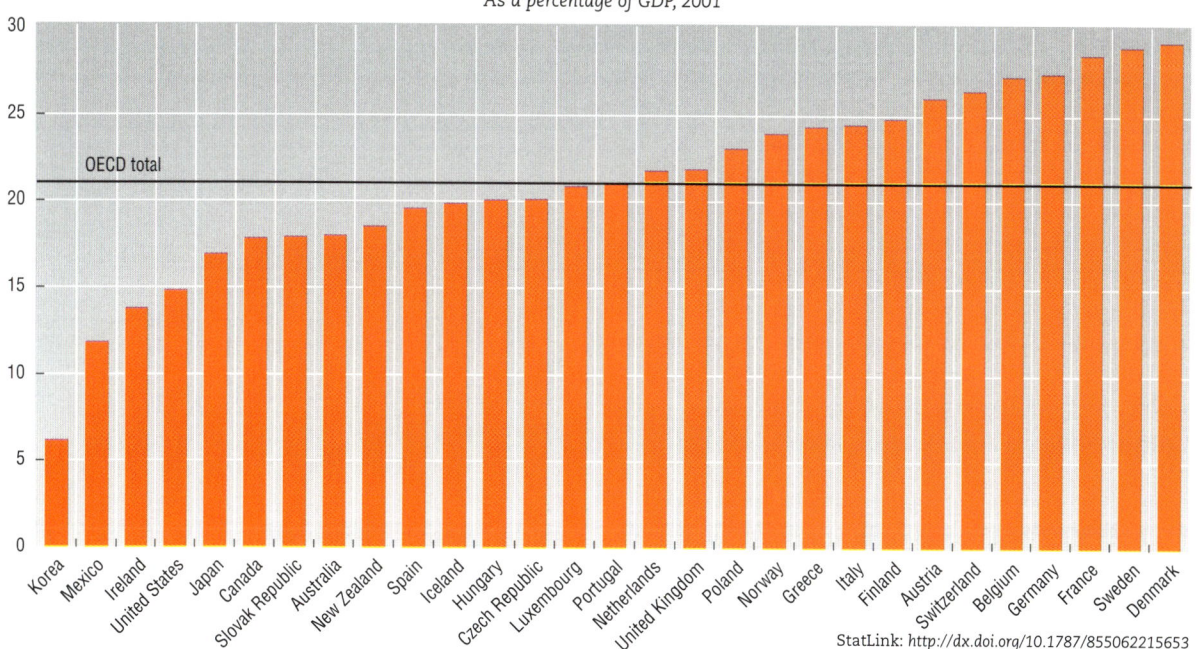

Total public social expenditure
As a percentage of GDP, 2001

StatLink: http://dx.doi.org/10.1787/855062215653

OECD FACTBOOK 2005 – ISBN 92-64-01869-7 – © OECD 2005

PUBLIC POLICIES • PUBLIC EXPENDITURE AND AID

HEALTH EXPENDITURE

The public sector is the main source of health funding in all OECD countries, apart from the United States and Mexico. Controlling the growth of health expenditure is seen as a key policy concern in many OECD countries, reflecting the pressure such growth places on public budgets.

Long-term trends

Among OECD countries, Norway has the highest public expenditure on health, reporting 2 845 US dollars per capita (calculated using PPPs) in 2002, followed by a group of countries, including the United States, Germany and several other Scandinavian countries. At the other end of the scale are Mexico and Turkey, which both have levels of public spending on health at around a tenth of the level of Norway.

In 2002, the public share of health spending stood at 73% on average across OECD countries. It accounted for more than 80% of total health expenditure in several countries, including the Czech Republic, Norway, Sweden and the United Kingdom. Mexico and The United States were the only two countries where government funding formed less than half the overall spending.

Generally, there has been a convergence in the share of public spending over the past three decades. Many countries which started out with a relatively high public share in 1970 had a lower public share by 2002 (e.g. the Czech Republic, Norway and the United Kingdom), while several countries which started with a low public share in 1970 have seen this share increase over time (e.g. Greece, Portugal and the United States).

Focusing on developments since 1990, the role of public funding has increased considerably in several lower-income countries which had seen a relatively low public share a decade or so ago (e.g. Korea and Portugal). In the United States, the increase in the public share of health spending during the 1990s reflects increases in the level and coverage of Medicare and Medicaid. While many higher-income OECD countries experienced a moderate decrease in the public share of health spending in the 1990s, there has been a more considerable decline in a few countries (e.g. Finland, Hungary, Italy and Sweden).

Definition

Expenditure on health measures the final consumption of health care goods and services (i.e. current health expenditure) plus capital investment in health care infrastructure. This covers spending on all personal medical services, pharmaceuticals and other medical goods, as well as public health and prevention programmes and administration. Excluded are health-related expenditure such as training, research and environmental health.

Comparability

The definition of health expenditure can vary between countries, in particular as regards the boundary between health and social care expenditure on long-term care.

Health expenditure per capita, converted to US dollars using purchasing power parities, can be used to compare the overall level of consumption of health goods and services across countries at a given point in time. The economy-wide (GDP) PPPs are used as the most available and reliable conversion rates.

The latest per capita expenditures available for Australia and Japan are for 2001 not 2002, and for 2000 in the case of Turkey.

Source

OECD (2004), *Health Data 2004*, OECD, Paris.

Further information
• *Analytical publications*

OECD (2002), *Measuring Up: Improving Health System Performance in OECD Countries*, OECD, Paris.

OECD (2003), *A Disease-based Comparison of Health Systems: What is Best and at What Cost?*, OECD, Paris.

OECD (2004), *The OECD Health Project: Private Health Insurance in OECD Countries*, OECD, Paris.

OECD (2004), *The OECD Health Project: Towards High-performing Health Systems*, OECD, Paris.

OECD (2005), *The OECD Health Project: Health Technology and Decision Making*, OECD, Paris.

OECD (2005), *Society at a Glance*, OECD, Paris.

• *Statistical publications*

OECD (2003), *Health at a Glance: OECD Indicators*, OECD, Paris.

• *Methodological publications*

OECD (2000), *A System of Health Accounts*, OECD, Paris.

• *Online databases*

SourceOECD OECD Health Data.

PUBLIC POLICIES • PUBLIC EXPENDITURE AND AID

HEALTH EXPENDITURE

Public expenditure on health

US dollars per capita, calculated using PPPs

Index with OECD average = 100

	1990	1991	1992	1993	1994	1995	1996	1997	1998	1999	2000	2001	2002	1990	2002
Australia	812	921	967	1 014	1 071	1 158	1 221	1 320	1 415	1 549	1 635	1 708	..	94	113
Austria	988	1 042	1 140	1 242	1 293	1 322	1 384	1 294	1 362	1 441	1 495	1 490	1 551	114	98
Belgium	..	..	..	..	..	1 308	1 408	1 374	1 433	1 510	1 613	1 743	1 790	..	113
Canada	1 277	1 384	1 452	1 456	1 469	1 459	1 445	1 494	1 617	1 688	1 788	1 922	2 048	148	129
Czech Republic	539	517	538	723	761	812	842	838	843	853	892	990	1 022	62	64
Denmark	1 286	1 339	1 382	1 453	1 508	1 521	1 607	1 669	1 755	1 888	1 940	2 083	2 142	149	135
Finland	1 144	1 254	1 227	1 081	1 049	1 079	1 150	1 202	1 226	1 235	1 276	1 389	1 470	132	93
France	1 191	1 273	1 355	1 427	1 471	1 546	1 592	1 649	1 696	1 754	1 832	1 964	2 080	138	131
Germany	1 318	..	1 588	1 595	1 690	1 822	1 941	1 912	1 942	2 015	2 080	2 151	2 212	152	139
Greece	450	466	530	595	614	660	697	723	743	810	872	887	960	52	60
Hungary	..	519	547	556	626	566	552	562	579	593	599	663	757	..	48
Iceland	1 384	1 461	1 420	1 447	1 495	1 555	1 637	1 686	1 870	2 130	2 140	2 230	2 357	160	149
Ireland	569	645	718	763	804	865	906	1 057	1 138	1 182	1 300	1 557	1 779	66	112
Italy	1 107	1 205	1 221	1 192	1 166	1 100	1 153	1 230	1 293	1 339	1 474	1 602	1 639	128	103
Japan	857	927	993	1 075	1 142	1 271	1 359	1 375	1 407	1 483	1 591	1 696	..	99	112
Korea	130	134	143	151	158	179	220	249	268	324	367	504	519	15	33
Luxembourg	1 427	1 524	1 645	1 743	1 759	1 898	1 974	1 978	2 117	2 455	2 406	2 603	2 618	165	165
Mexico	117	146	160	171	186	160	151	179	197	221	230	240	249	14	16
Netherlands	952	1 057	1 181	1 252	1 272	1 298	1 243	1 313	..	..	..	..	..	110	..
New Zealand	813	852	862	849	915	956	967	1 049	1 110	1 183	1 257	1 307	1 447	94	91
Norway	1 147	1 302	1 393	1 427	1 504	1 594	1 737	1 836	1 960	2 182	2 335	2 716	2 845	133	179
Poland	273	269	286	284	279	309	360	363	368	406	405	452	474	32	30
Portugal	433	503	499	550	580	676	748	801	866	962	1 091	1 173	1 201	50	76
Slovak Republic	..	..	..	..	..	..	..	498	512	518	528	565	621	..	39
Spain	681	733	801	830	843	863	905	932	990	1 056	1 069	1 118	1 176	79	74
Sweden	1 407	1 370	1 389	1 430	1 435	1 502	1 604	1 605	1 682	1 816	1 904	2 011	2 148	163	135
Switzerland	1 068	1 173	1 261	1 295	1 332	1 374	1 451	1 551	1 628	1 652	1 730	1 878	1 995	123	126
Turkey	100	112	125	132	127	130	159	190	224	240	281	..	..	12	21
United Kingdom	816	899	1 001	1 061	1 117	1 168	1 212	1 233	1 292	1 391	1 488	1 669	1 801	94	113
United States	1 085	1 217	1 344	1 447	1 568	1 656	1 731	1 784	1 823	1 905	2 017	2 185	2 364	125	149

StatLink: http://dx.doi.org/10.1787/874878133424

Public expenditure on health

US dollars per capita, calculated using PPPs, 2002 or latest available year

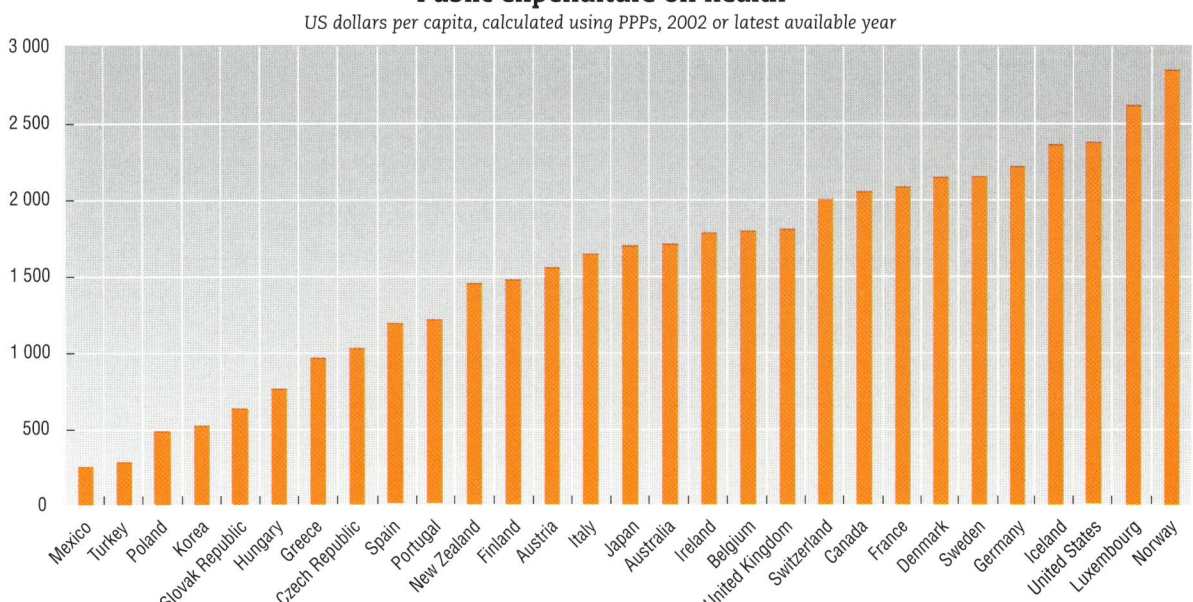

StatLink: http://dx.doi.org/10.1787/408352377263

OECD FACTBOOK 2005 – ISBN 92-64-01869-7 – © OECD 2005

PUBLIC POLICIES • PUBLIC EXPENDITURE AND AID

AGRICULTURAL SUPPORT ESTIMATES

During the mid-1980s when the Uruguay Round of agricultural trade negotiations was getting underway, OECD undertook to measure and codify support to the farm sector arising from agricultural policies. This led to the development of the producer support estimate (PSE), an indicator that is available on a timely and comprehensive basis for all 30 of the OECD's member countries (EU15 is treated as a single entity). The measure includes budgetary transfers financed by taxpayers but also includes the implicit tax on consumers that arises from policies – border protection, and administered pricing – that raise farm prices above the levels that would otherwise prevail. The measure is agreed by OECD member countries and is widely recognised as the only available internationally comparable indicator.

Definition

The OECD PSE is an indicator of the annual monetary value of gross transfers from consumers and taxpayers to agricultural producers, measured at the farm-gate level, arising from policy measures that support agriculture, regardless of their nature, objectives or impacts on farm production or income. It can be expressed as a total monetary amount, per hectare or per farmer but is more usually quoted as a percentage of gross farm receipts (%PSE).

Long-term trends

There are large and increasing differences in the levels of support among OECD countries. The %PSE currently ranges from 2% (New Zealand) to 74% (Switzerland). These differences reflect among other things, variations in policy objectives, different historical uses of policy instruments, and the varying pace and degrees of progress in agricultural policy reform. Over the longer term, the level of producer support has fallen in most OECD countries. The average %PSE in 2001-03 at 31% is lower than the 1986-88 average of 37% and has fallen in all countries, except Hungary, Japan, Mexico, Poland and Turkey. There has also been some change in the way support is delivered to the sector. Support known to be the most distorting in terms of production and trade is less dominant than in the past – 75% of total support during the 2001-2003 period compared to over 90% in 1986-1988.

Comparability

Continuous efforts are made to ensure consistency in the treatment and completeness of coverage of policies in all OECD countries through the annual preparation of the *Monitoring and Evaluation* report. Each year the provisional estimates are subject to review and approval by representatives of OECD's member countries, as are all methodological developments. The %PSE is the most appropriate and widely used measure to compare support across countries, commodities and time.

In the table, data for Austria, Finland and Sweden are available separately until 1994. These countries are included in EU15 from 1995 and in OECD total for the entire period. In the chart, data for the period 1986-88 correspond to 1991-93 for the Czech Republic, Hungary, Poland and the Slovak Republic.

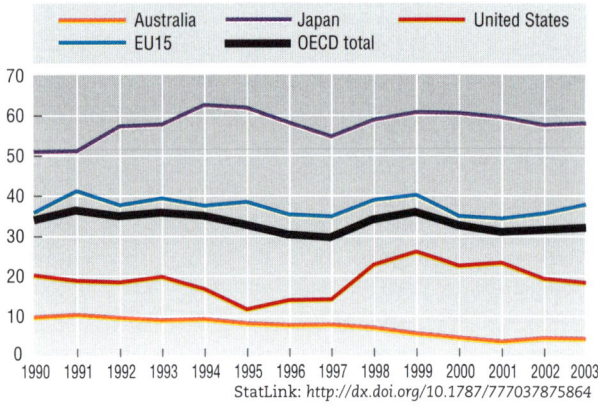

Producer support estimate for selected countries

Source

OECD (2004), *Agricultural Policies in OECD Countries: At a Glance – 2004*, OECD, Paris.

Further information

• *Analytical publications*

OECD (2001), *Market Effects of Crop Support Measures*, OECD, Paris.

OECD (2002), *Agricultural Policies in China after WTO Accession*, OECD, Paris.

OECD (2003), *Agricultural Policies in OECD Countries: Monitoring and Evaluation 2003*, OECD, Paris.

OECD (2004), *Analysis of the 2003 CAP Reform*, OECD, Paris.

• *Methodological publications*

OECD (2002), *Methodology for the Measurement of Support and Use in Policy Evaluation*, OECD, Paris

PUBLIC POLICIES • PUBLIC EXPENDITURE AND AID

AGRICULTURAL SUPPORT ESTIMATES

Producer support estimate by country
As a percentage of value of gross farm receipts

	1990	1991	1992	1993	1994	1995	1996	1997	1998	1999	2000	2001	2002	2003
Australia	9.51	10.10	9.31	8.73	8.97	7.85	7.45	7.54	6.75	5.35	4.33	3.41	4.21	4.07
Austria	50.19	53.59	57.39	58.55	60.65	..	..	..	..	..	..	..	..	..
Canada	35.69	34.97	28.89	24.76	18.53	19.02	16.41	14.42	17.07	17.90	18.61	17.11	19.57	21.27
Czech Republic	..	47.12	20.16	24.55	16.42	10.94	11.46	6.36	26.07	23.04	16.59	23.03	24.59	27.47
Finland	70.53	71.52	66.18	64.11	69.00	..	..	..	..	..	..	..	..	..
Hungary	..	10.77	17.98	20.46	21.94	13.19	10.61	10.95	24.62	23.74	22.33	22.13	33.03	26.60
Iceland	73.98	77.49	72.92	64.56	60.79	62.61	59.36	61.18	68.38	68.18	63.46	60.96	69.12	69.52
Japan	50.58	50.77	56.94	57.37	62.19	61.52	57.79	54.31	58.53	60.39	60.15	59.14	57.26	57.63
Korea	75.23	74.05	72.78	73.02	73.10	72.30	64.46	63.29	57.04	65.84	66.73	62.80	68.31	60.48
Mexico	17.74	27.30	30.28	30.20	22.69	-3.76	7.36	15.97	18.47	18.47	24.26	20.21	24.54	18.84
New Zealand	2.75	2.37	1.75	1.60	2.03	2.38	1.78	1.86	1.33	1.40	0.84	0.46	1.84	2.45
Norway	71.62	72.60	71.24	68.72	69.11	67.63	66.54	69.35	72.99	71.62	67.96	67.91	73.11	72.41
Poland	..	6.99	9.07	16.71	22.12	16.35	19.13	18.09	27.72	24.12	15.06	14.63	14.30	8.72
Slovak Republic	..	32.47	21.82	30.10	25.23	11.79	0.15	13.91	32.26	25.70	25.28	15.67	22.03	20.86
Sweden	58.23	63.30	58.49	53.67	51.00	..	..	..	..	..	..	..	..	..
Switzerland	74.21	75.69	71.00	73.30	75.05	71.99	69.44	70.28	72.10	74.69	72.38	71.97	73.69	74.07
Turkey	18.96	26.67	25.63	22.02	12.77	12.27	14.92	24.58	26.38	22.74	20.96	4.76	20.30	26.37
United States	19.93	18.56	18.14	19.47	16.44	11.34	13.61	13.83	22.45	25.62	22.16	22.95	18.94	17.98
EU15	35.38	40.82	37.22	38.92	37.09	38.01	34.85	34.39	38.47	39.67	34.44	33.86	35.16	37.36
OECD total	33.58	36.10	34.74	35.57	34.80	32.52	30.06	29.30	33.77	35.64	32.45	30.72	31.21	31.71

StatLink: http://dx.doi.org/10.1787/781002378040

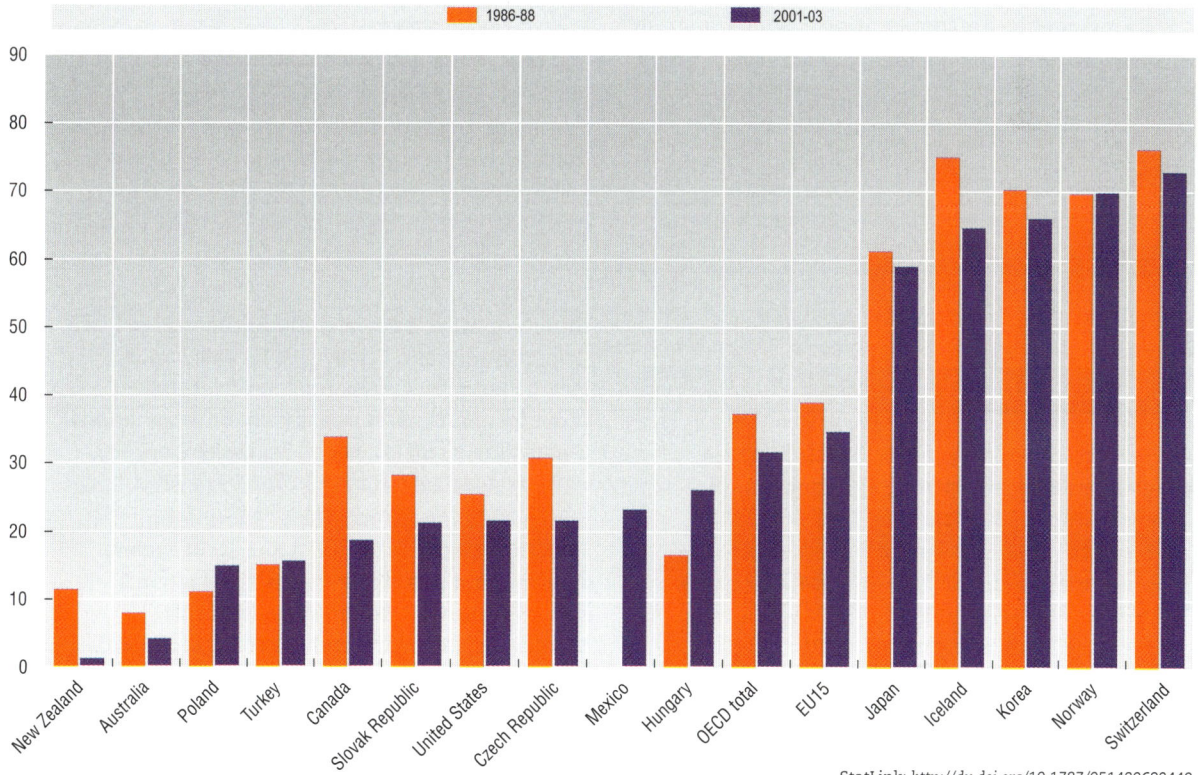

Producer support estimate by country
As a percentage of value of gross farm receipts

StatLink: http://dx.doi.org/10.1787/051420683442

PUBLIC POLICIES • PUBLIC EXPENDITURE AND AID

GOVERNMENT SUPPORT FOR FISHING

Catches from sea fishing have been declining both because of falling stocks due to over-fishing and because of national and international measures to preserve the remaining fish resources. This has been particularly marked in the Northern Hemisphere and has lead governments in many OECD countries to provide financial support to the fishing industry.

Definition

The time series "Government financial transfers (GFT)" provides an indicator of the financial support received by the fishery sector. GFTs consist of direct revenue enhancing transfers (direct payments), transfers that reduce the operating costs, and the costs of general services provided to the fishing industry. These general services consist mainly of fishery protection services but also include the costs of local area weather forecasting and the costs of navigation and satellite surveillance systems designed to assist fishing fleets.

Comparability

The data are relatively comprehensive and consistent across the years, but some year-to-year variations must be interpreted with caution, as they may reflect changes in national statistical systems. Note too that the general services provided by government may contain large and irregular capital investments. For example, the GFTs for Greece in 2001 and in particular for 2002 include the implementation cost of a satellite control system.

Long-term trends

Overall transfers to the fishing industry have been fluctuating at around USD 6 billion during the last decade. This represents around 15% of the value of the total catch from maritime capture. Most of the GFTs cover general services, which represent approximately 75% of the total GFTs. The remaining spending consists of direct payments (around 12% of total GFTs) and cost reducing transfers (around 13% of total GFTs).

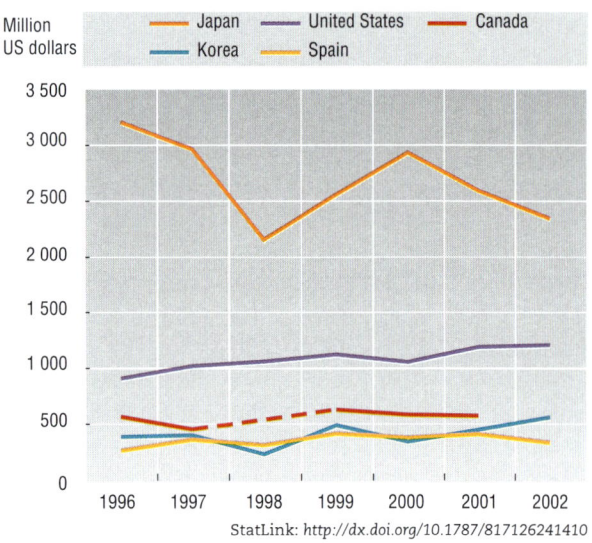

GFT for selected countries

StatLink: http://dx.doi.org/10.1787/817126241410

Source

OECD (2004), *Review of Fisheries in OECD Countries: Vol. 2 Country Statistics 2000-2002*, OECD, Paris.

Further information

• **Analytical publications**

Cox, A. (2003), "OECD Work on Defining and Measuring Subsidies in Fisheries", www.oecd.org/dataoecd/43/41/2507594.pdf.

Flatten, O. and P. Wallis (2000), "Government Financial Transfers to Fishing Industries in OECD Countries", www.oecd.org/dataoecd/2/32/1917911.pdf.

OECD (2000), *Transition to Responsible Fisheries: Economic and Policy Implications*, OECD, Paris.

Schmidt, C. (2004), "Globalisation, Industry Structure, Market Power and Impact on Fish Trade Opportunities and Challenges for Developed (OECD) Countries", paper prepared for the FAO Industry and Expert Consultation on International Trade, Rio de Janeiro, Brazil, 3-5 December 2003, www.oecd.org/dataoecd/8/12/25012071.PDF.

Schmidt, C. and A. Cox (2003), "Subsidies in the OECD Fisheries Sector: A Review of Recent Analysis and Future Directions", background paper for the FAO Expert Consultation on Identifying, Assessing and Reporting on Subsidies in the Fishing Industry, Rome, 3-6 December 2002, www.oecd.org/dataoecd/43/40/2507604.pdf.

• **Web sites**

OECD Fisheries: www.oecd.org/agr/fish.

PUBLIC POLICIES • PUBLIC EXPENDITURE AND AID

GOVERNMENT SUPPORT FOR FISHING

Government financial transfers for fishing
Thousand US dollars

	1996	1997	1998	1999	2000	2001	2002
Australia	37 391	41 230	..	..	82 272	75 902	..
Belgium	4 970	4 949	..	4 473	6 849	2 830	1 445
Canada	545 301	433 309	..	606 443	564 497	552 516	..
Czech Republic	..	..	..	269	241	223	235
Denmark	85 771	82 030	90 507	27 765	16 316	..	68 769
Finland	28 978	26 198	26 888	19 236	13 908	16 509	16 025
France	158 203	140 807	..	71 665	166 147	141 786	155 283
Germany	81 567	63 215	16 488	31 276	29 834	28 989	28 208
Greece	52 308	46 958	26 908	43 030	87 315	86 957	1 797 096
Iceland	43 770	38 678	36 954	39 763	41 978	37 576	41 151
Ireland	112 673	98 880	..	143 184	..	..	..
Italy	162 625	91 811	..	200 470	217 679	175 354	159 630
Japan	3 186 363	2 945 785	2 135 946	2 537 536	2 913 149	2 574 086	2 325 126
Korea	367 793	378 994	211 927	471 556	320 449	428 313	538 695
Mexico	14 201	16 808	..	..	..	..	..
Netherlands	39 927	35 849	..	..	1 389	12 779	12 443
New Zealand	37 241	40 397	29 412	29 630	27 273	27 311	33 333
Norway	65 279	65 290	41 192	64 744	19 545	11 346	11 389
Poland	8 148	7 927	..	..	..	..	..
Portugal	71 847	65 077	..	28 674	25 578	25 065	24 899
Spain	246 473	344 581	296 642	399 604	364 096	393 424	315 935
Sweden	62 320	53 452	26 960	31 053	25 186	22 505	24 753
Turkey	28 665	15 114	..	1 277	26 372	17 721	16 167
United Kingdom	115 359	128 066	90 833	75 968	81 394	73 738	..
United States	891 160	1 002 580	1 041 000	1 103 100	1 037 710	1 169 590	1 190 664

StatLink: http://dx.doi.org/10.1787/000305462471

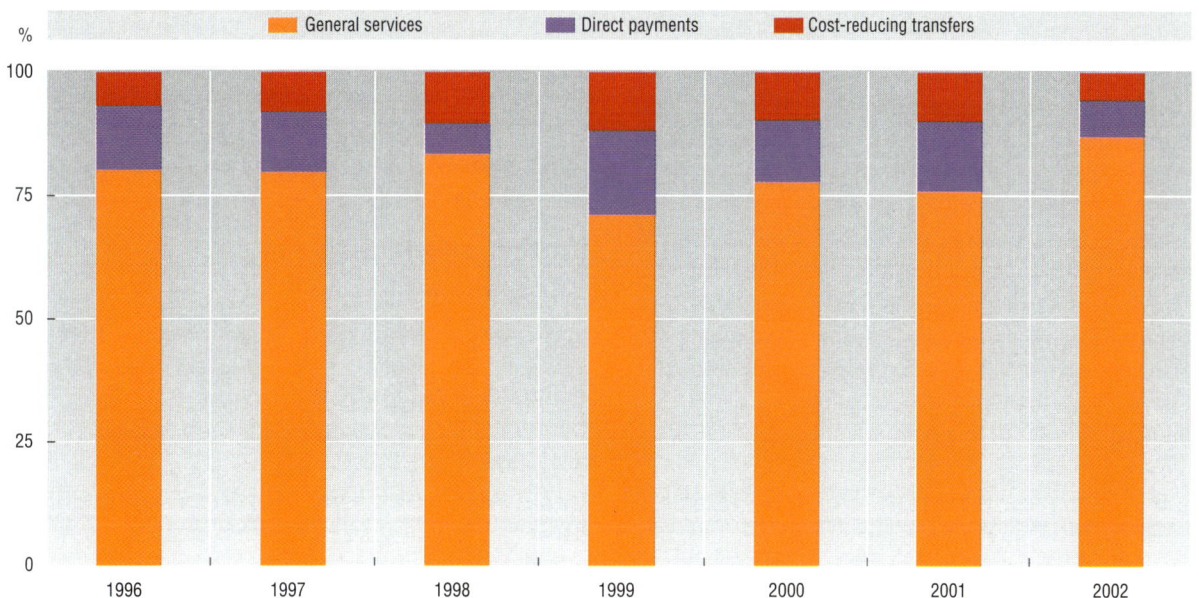

OECD total government financial transfers by category

StatLink: http://dx.doi.org/10.1787/037102561825

PUBLIC POLICIES • PUBLIC EXPENDITURE AND AID

OFFICIAL DEVELOPMENT ASSISTANCE

The promotion of economic and social development in non-member countries has been a principal objective of the OECD since its foundation. The share of national income devoted to official development assistance (ODA) is widely regarded as a test of a country's commitment to international development, and there is a long-standing United Nations target for developed countries to devote 0.7% of their gross national income (GNI) to ODA. The tables in this section show total ODA as shares of GNI as well as the geographical distribution of bilateral ODA.

Definition

Official development assistance is defined as government aid to developing countries designed to promote the economic development and welfare of recipient countries. Loans and credits for military purposes are excluded. The aid may be provided bilaterally, from donor to recipient, or it may be channelled through a multilateral development agency such as the United Nations or the World Bank.

Aid includes grants, "soft" loans, and the provision of technical assistance. Soft loans are those where the grant element is at least 25%. ODA is usually measured on a net basis, *i.e.* after subtracting loan repayments from the gross aid flows. Data on the geographical distribution of aid, however, is available only on a gross basis.

The OECD maintains a list of developing countries and territories, and only aid to these countries counts as ODA. The list is periodically updated and currently contains 150 countries or territories. All except Bahrain had per capita incomes of less than USD 9 206 in 2001 (by comparison, per capita income in OECD countries averaged over USD 25 000 in that year). Note that of the 30 member countries of the OECD, only the 22 shown in the table are members of the Development Assistance Committee (DAC), along with the European Commission.

Comparability

Statistics on ODA are compiled according to a set of directives drawn up by the DAC and each country's statistics are subject to regular peer reviews by other DAC members. Data for Greece are available only since 1996 as Greece joined the DAC in 1999.

Long-term trends

The weighted average shown in the graph is the total ODA provided by DAC members as a percentage of their total GNI. Over the period shown, this has fallen from 0.33% of GNI in 1990 to a 0.25% in 2003. The unweighted average measures "average country effort". This has also fallen over the period – from 0.45% in 1990 to 0.41% in 2003. The decline in both the weighted and unweighted averages has been halted and reversed in the last two or three years, as DAC members increase their aid following the commitments they made at the Monterrey 2002 Financing for Development Conference.

While aid as a share of GNI has declined over the period in most countries, and most notably in Canada, Finland, France, Germany, Italy, Japan and the United States, ODA shares have increased in Belgium, Luxembourg, Spain, Switzerland and the United Kingdom and, from low initial shares, Austria, Greece and Ireland. Only Denmark, Netherlands, Norway and Sweden have consistently met the United Nations 0.7% target over the whole period covered in the table, but Luxembourg has been meeting the target since 2000. Since ODA shares of GNI reached their low point in 1997, 15 of the 22 DAC members have increased their shares and 11 have committed to remain at or to attain the 0.7% target.

Sources

OECD (2004), *International Development Statistics on CD-Rom*, OECD, Paris.

Development Assistance Committee Aid Statistics: *www.oecd.org/dac/stats.*

Further information

• *Analytical publications*

OECD (2004), *Development Co-operation Report*, OECD, Paris.

• *Statistical publications*

OECD (2004), *Geographical Distribution of Financial Flows to Aid Recipients*, OECD, Paris.

OECD (2004), *Creditor Reporting System*, 6 volumes, OECD, Paris.

• *Web sites*

Calculation of the Grant Element of Loans: *www.oecd.org/dataoecd/15/0/31738575.pdf.*

PUBLIC POLICIES • PUBLIC EXPENDITURE AND AID

OFFICIAL DEVELOPMENT ASSISTANCE

Official development assistance

As a percentage of gross national income

	1990	1991	1992	1993	1994	1995	1996	1997	1998	1999	2000	2001	2002	2003
Australia	0.34	0.38	0.37	0.35	0.34	0.34	0.27	0.27	0.27	0.26	0.27	0.25	0.26	0.25
Austria	0.11	0.18	0.11	0.11	0.17	0.27	0.23	0.24	0.22	0.24	0.23	0.34	0.26	0.20
Belgium	0.46	0.41	0.39	0.39	0.32	0.38	0.34	0.31	0.35	0.30	0.36	0.37	0.43	0.60
Canada	0.44	0.45	0.46	0.45	0.43	0.38	0.32	0.34	0.30	0.28	0.25	0.22	0.28	0.24
Denmark	0.94	0.96	1.02	1.03	1.03	0.96	1.04	0.97	0.99	1.01	1.06	1.03	0.96	0.84
Finland	0.65	0.80	0.64	0.45	0.31	0.31	0.33	0.32	0.32	0.33	0.31	0.32	0.35	0.35
France	0.60	0.62	0.63	0.63	0.64	0.55	0.48	0.45	0.40	0.39	0.32	0.32	0.38	0.41
Germany	0.42	0.39	0.37	0.35	0.33	0.31	0.32	0.28	0.26	0.26	0.27	0.27	0.27	0.28
Greece	..	..	..	..	..	..	0.15	0.14	0.15	0.15	0.20	0.17	0.21	0.21
Ireland	0.16	0.19	0.16	0.20	0.25	0.29	0.31	0.31	0.30	0.31	0.30	0.33	0.40	0.39
Italy	0.31	0.30	0.34	0.31	0.27	0.15	0.20	0.11	0.20	0.15	0.13	0.15	0.20	0.17
Japan	0.31	0.32	0.30	0.27	0.29	0.27	0.20	0.21	0.27	0.27	0.28	0.23	0.23	0.20
Luxembourg	0.21	0.33	0.26	0.35	0.40	0.36	0.44	0.55	0.65	0.66	0.71	0.76	0.77	0.81
Netherlands	0.92	0.88	0.86	0.82	0.76	0.81	0.81	0.81	0.80	0.79	0.84	0.82	0.81	0.81
New Zealand	0.23	0.25	0.26	0.25	0.24	0.23	0.21	0.26	0.27	0.27	0.25	0.25	0.22	0.23
Norway	1.17	1.13	1.16	1.01	1.05	0.86	0.83	0.84	0.89	0.88	0.76	0.80	0.89	0.92
Portugal	0.24	0.30	0.35	0.28	0.34	0.25	0.21	0.25	0.24	0.26	0.26	0.25	0.27	0.22
Spain	0.20	0.24	0.27	0.28	0.28	0.24	0.22	0.24	0.24	0.23	0.22	0.30	0.26	0.23
Sweden	0.91	0.90	1.03	0.99	0.96	0.77	0.84	0.79	0.72	0.70	0.80	0.77	0.84	0.79
Switzerland	0.32	0.36	0.45	0.33	0.36	0.34	0.34	0.34	0.32	0.35	0.34	0.34	0.32	0.39
United Kingdom	0.27	0.32	0.31	0.31	0.31	0.29	0.27	0.26	0.27	0.24	0.32	0.32	0.31	0.34
United States	0.21	0.20	0.20	0.15	0.14	0.10	0.12	0.09	0.10	0.10	0.10	0.11	0.13	0.15
EU15	0.44	0.44	0.43	0.43	0.41	0.37	0.37	0.33	0.33	0.32	0.32	0.34	0.35	0.36
Total DAC	0.33	0.33	0.33	0.30	0.29	0.26	0.25	0.22	0.23	0.22	0.22	0.22	0.23	0.25

StatLink: http://dx.doi.org/10.1787/074470624621

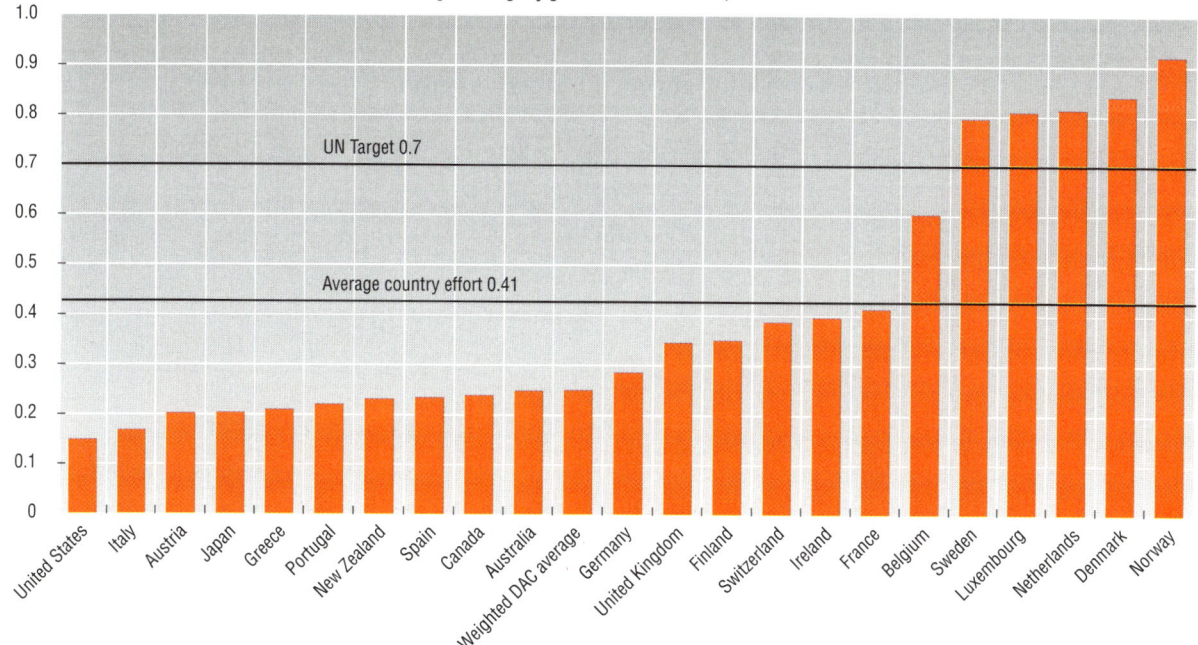

Net official development assistance
As a percentage of gross national income, 2003

StatLink: http://dx.doi.org/10.1787/548534858050

PUBLIC POLICIES • PUBLIC EXPENDITURE AND AID

OFFICIAL DEVELOPMENT ASSISTANCE

Major recipients by region of total bilateral gross ODA from DAC countries
Million US dollars, 3-year averages: 1989 to 2003

	Sub-Saharan Africa		South and Central Asia		Far-East Asia and Oceania	
1989-1991	Kenya	900	India	1 666	Indonesia	2 186
	Tanzania	826	Bangladesh	1 123	China	1 495
	Mozambique	775	Pakistan	850	Philippines	994
	Senegal	609	Sri Lanka	473	Thailand	794
	Congo, Democratic Republic	598	Nepal	261	Malaysia	404
	Zambia	589			Papua New Guinea	322
	Ghana	526			New Caledonia	308
	Côte d'Ivoire	490				
	Ethiopia	461				
	Total	**12 170**	**Total**	**4 624**	**Total**	**7 791**
1992-1994	Mozambique	908	India	1 696	Indonesia	2 439
	Tanzania	788	Bangladesh	919	China	2 414
	Côte d'Ivoire	759	Pakistan	800	Philippines	1 606
	Zambia	641	Sri Lanka	385	Thailand	778
	Cameroon	571	Nepal	270	Vietnam	487
	Somalia	543			New Caledonia	396
	Ethiopia	509			French Polynesia	360
	Kenya	482				
	Senegal	477				
	Total	**11 918**	**Total**	**4 622**	**Total**	**10 311**
1995-1997	Mozambique	706	India	1 656	China	2 107
	Côte d'Ivoire	626	Bangladesh	813	Indonesia	1 884
	Tanzania	597	Pakistan	661	Philippines	1 122
	Ethiopia	464	Sri Lanka	403	Thailand	970
	Senegal	428	Nepal	254	Vietnam	593
	Uganda	417			French Polynesia	437
	Cameroon	416			New Caledonia	416
	Kenya	415				
	Zambia	411				
	Total	**10 623**	**Total**	**4 597**	**Total**	**9 705**
1998-2000	Mozambique	748	India	1 483	Indonesia	2 203
	Tanzania	737	Bangladesh	813	China	2 105
	Côte d'Ivoire	483	Pakistan	586	Thailand	1 093
	Uganda	454	Sri Lanka	369	Vietnam	1 013
	Ghana	408	Nepal	232	Philippines	957
	Zambia	394			Papua New Guinea	277
	South Africa	390			French Polynesia	258
	Senegal	383				
	Cameroon	365				
	Total	**9 100**	**Total**	**4 489**	**Total**	**9 754**
2001-2003	Congo, Democratic Republic	1 889	India	1 639	China	1 920
	Mozambique	1 066	Pakistan	1 336	Indonesia	1 571
	Tanzania	962	Afghanistan	848	Philippines	1 014
	Ethiopia	641	Bangladesh	792	Vietnam	880
	Cameroon	632	Sri Lanka	396	Thailand	818
	Côte d'Ivoire	523			Cambodia	288
	Uganda	497			Papua New Guinea	226
	Ghana	448				
	Zambia	432				
	Total	**13 179**	**Total**	**6 636**	**Total**	**8 077**

StatLink: http://dx.doi.org/10.1787/321268846758

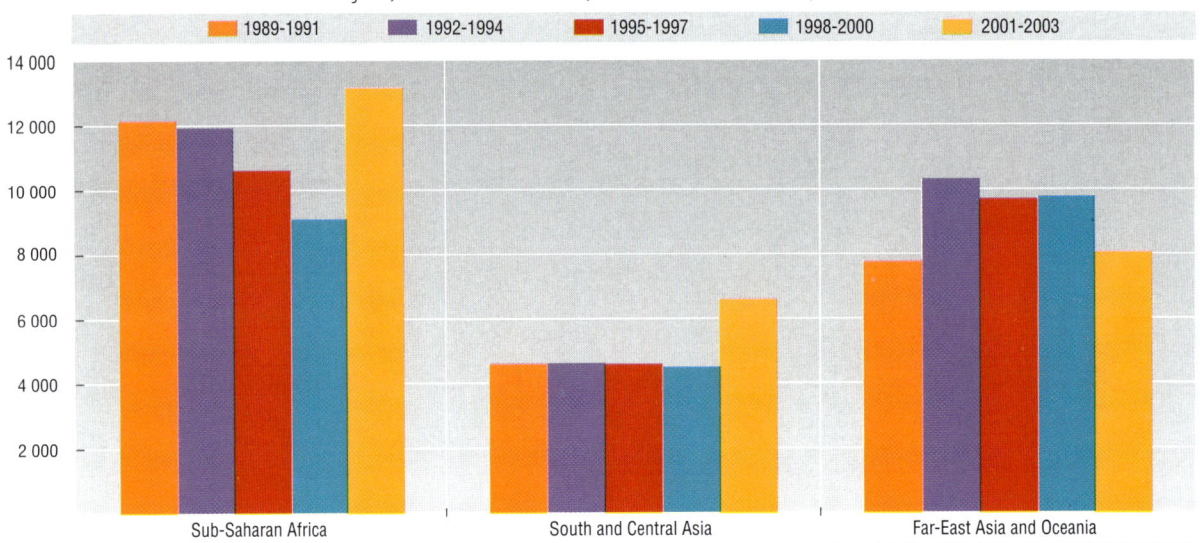

Major aid recipients by region
Sub-Saharan Africa, South and Central Asia, Far-East Asia and Oceania, million US dollars

StatLink: http://dx.doi.org/10.1787/257761305280

PUBLIC POLICIES • PUBLIC EXPENDITURE AND AID

OFFICIAL DEVELOPMENT ASSISTANCE

Major recipients by region of total bilateral gross ODA from DAC countries
Million US dollars, 3-year averages: 1989 to 2003

	Middle East and North Africa		Europe		Latin America and Caribbean	
1989-1991	Egypt	4 673	Turkey	902	Bolivia	499
	Israel	1 555	Albania	113	Nicaragua	480
	Morocco	600	States of the former Yugoslavia	85	Peru	427
	Jordan	446			Honduras	422
	Tunisia	332			Jamaica	401
	Total	**8 720**	**Total**	**1 264**	**Total**	**5 016**
1992-1994	Egypt	3 296	States of the former Yugoslavia	962	El Salvador	494
	Israel	1 691	Turkey	458	Bolivia	491
	Morocco	629	Albania	123	Peru	479
	Algeria	381			Mexico	415
	Jordan	329			Nicaragua	408
	Total	**7 608**	**Total**	**1 793**	**Total**	**5 501**
1995-1997	Egypt	1 826	Bosnia	618	Bolivia	547
	Israel	989	Turkey	408	Nicaragua	530
	Morocco	505	Albania	103	Peru	415
	Jordan	390			Brazil	329
	Algeria	261			Mexico	300
	Total	**5 318**	**Total**	**1 564**	**Total**	**4 938**
1998-2000	Egypt	1 503	Bosnia	584	Peru	481
	Morocco	489	Serbia and Montenegro	453	Bolivia	404
	Jordan	367	Turkey	305	Nicaragua	376
	Palestinian Administrative Areas	323			Brazil	361
	Tunisia	265			Honduras	306
	Total	**3 877**	**Total**	**2 264**	**Total**	**4 508**
2001-2003	Egypt	1 298	Serbia and Montenegro	1 135	Bolivia	679
	Iraq	760	Turkey	357	Colombia	587
	Jordan	687	Bosnia	337	Peru	582
	Morocco	476			Nicaragua	535
	Palestinian Administrative Areas	394			Brazil	369
	Total	**4 675**	**Total**	**2 813**	**Total**	**5 118**

StatLink: http://dx.doi.org/10.1787/147106332471

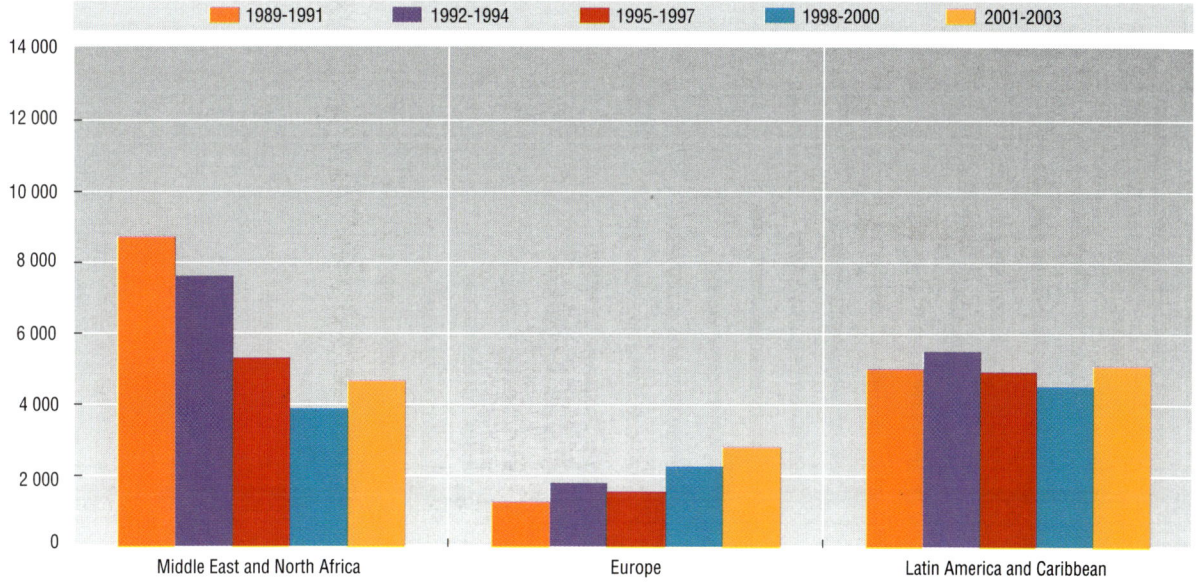

Major aid recipients by region
Middle East and North Africa, Europe, Latin America and Caribbean, million US dollars

StatLink: http://dx.doi.org/10.1787/028752325182

OECD FACTBOOK 2005 – ISBN 92-64-01869-7 – © OECD 2005

PUBLIC POLICIES • TAXES

TOTAL TAX REVENUE

Total tax revenue as a percentage of GDP indicates the share of a country's output that is collected by the government through taxes. It can thus be regarded as one measure of the degree to which the government controls the economy's resources. Taxes on incomes and profits as a percentage of GDP represents the amount of resources collected by government directly from the income of people and companies. Taxes on goods and services as a percentage of GDP represents the amount of resources the government collects from people as they spend their income on goods and services.

Definition

Taxes are defined as compulsory, unrequited payments to general government. They are unrequited in the sense that benefits provided by government to taxpayers are not normally in proportion to their payments.

Taxes on incomes and profits cover taxes levied on the net income or profits (gross income minus allowable tax reliefs) of individuals and enterprises. They include payments by employers and employees made under compulsory social security schemes. They also cover taxes levied on the capital gains of individuals and enterprises, and gains from gambling.

Taxes on goods and services covers all taxes levied on the production, extraction, sale, transfer, leasing or delivery of goods, and the rendering of services, or on the use of goods or permission to use goods or to perform activities. They consist mainly of value added and sales taxes.

> ### Long-term trends
> Total tax revenue as a percentage of GDP followed a slow upward trend in almost all OECD countries during the 1990s. However, in 2000, the upward trend stopped and, in 2001, tax revenues as a percentage of GDP fell in the majority of OECD countries.
>
> Taxes on income and profit as a percentage of GDP showed no overall trend in the first half of the 1990s. However, from 1996, there was an upward trend in most countries until 2000.
>
> Taxes on goods and services as a percentage of GDP have been remarkably stable over the 1990s, particularly in the European Union. There was a slight upward trend in the first half of the 1990s, followed by an even slower decline.

Comparability

The data are collected in a way that makes them as internationally comparable as possible. Country representatives have agreed on the definition of each type of tax and how they should be measured in all OECD countries, and they are then responsible for submitting data that conform to these rules. The rules are set out in "The OECD Interpretative Guide" at the end of each edition of *Revenue Statistics*.

Source

OECD (2003), *Revenue Statistics, 1965-2002*, OECD, Paris.

Further information

• *Analytical publications*

OECD (2004), *Recent Tax Policy Trends and Reforms in OECD Countries*, OECD Tax Policy Studies, No. 9, OECD, Paris.

OECD (2005), *Consumption Tax Trends: VAT/GST and Excise Rates, Trends and Administration Issues*, OECD, Paris.

• *Statistical publications*

OECD (2004), *Taxing Wages*, OECD, Paris.

• *Methodological publications*

OECD (1992-2004), *Model Tax Convention on Income and on Capital*, yearly updates, OECD, Paris.

OECD (2003), *Model Tax Convention on Income and on Capital*, condensed version, OECD, Paris.

• *Online databases*

SourceOECD Revenue Statistics.

SourceOECD Taxing Wages.

• *Web sites*

Tax Administration in OECD Countries: Comparative Information Series (2004): *www.oecd.org/ctp/ta*.

OECD Centre for Tax Policy and Administration: *www.oecd.org/ctp*.

PUBLIC POLICIES • TAXES

TOTAL TAX REVENUE

Total tax revenue
As a percentage of GDP

	1990	1991	1992	1993	1994	1995	1996	1997	1998	1999	2000	2001
Australia	29.3	27.7	27.2	27.6	28.9	29.7	30.3	30.0	30.0	30.8	31.5	30.1
Austria	40.4	40.9	42.4	42.7	42.6	41.6	43.5	44.4	44.1	44.0	43.3	45.4
Belgium	43.2	43.2	43.5	43.7	44.9	44.6	44.9	45.3	45.9	45.3	45.7	45.8
Canada	35.9	36.4	36.0	35.4	35.2	35.6	35.9	36.7	36.7	35.9	35.6	35.1
Czech Republic	..	..	..	42.9	41.3	40.1	39.3	38.6	37.9	38.9	38.9	38.4
Denmark	47.1	46.9	47.3	48.8	49.9	49.4	49.9	49.8	50.1	51.5	49.5	49.8
Finland	44.6	46.0	45.8	44.5	46.5	45.1	47.4	46.2	46.0	47.0	47.3	46.1
France	43.0	43.2	43.1	43.3	43.7	44.0	45.0	45.2	45.1	45.7	45.2	45.0
Germany	32.9	36.8	37.7	37.9	38.1	38.2	37.4	37.0	37.1	37.7	37.8	36.8
Greece	29.3	29.4	30.4	30.9	31.2	32.4	40.2	34.0	35.8	37.0	37.5	36.9
Hungary	..	45.9	45.7	46.5	44.0	42.4	40.7	39.0	38.8	39.1	39.0	39.0
Iceland	31.5	31.7	32.6	31.8	31.3	31.8	33.0	32.9	34.8	37.2	38.3	36.5
Ireland	33.5	34.1	34.4	34.4	35.5	32.8	32.8	32.2	31.5	31.0	31.2	29.9
Italy	38.9	39.3	41.7	43.4	41.4	41.2	42.7	44.2	42.5	43.3	41.9	42.0
Japan	30.0	29.6	28.1	28.0	27.1	27.6	27.5	27.9	26.8	26.4	27.5	27.3
Korea	19.1	18.7	19.4	19.9	20.4	20.5	21.4	22.7	22.9	23.6	26.1	27.2
Luxembourg	40.8	39.1	39.5	41.9	41.8	42.3	42.4	41.5	40.2	40.1	40.4	40.7
Mexico	17.3	17.3	17.7	17.7	17.2	16.7	16.7	17.5	16.6	17.3	18.5	18.9
Netherlands	43.0	45.3	45.1	45.3	43.3	41.9	41.5	41.9	40.0	41.2	41.1	39.5
New Zealand	37.6	35.8	36.1	36.0	36.5	37.0	34.9	35.5	34.1	33.9	33.8	33.8
Norway	41.5	41.4	40.7	39.8	41.0	41.1	41.1	41.8	42.7	40.4	39.0	43.3
Poland	..	37.2	38.2	42.4	40.4	39.6	39.4	38.8	37.6	35.0	34.3	33.6
Portugal	29.2	30.3	32.4	30.9	31.7	32.5	32.3	32.8	33.3	34.0	34.3	33.5
Slovak Republic	..	..	..	..	..	..	..	..	35.9	34.4	34.9	32.3
Spain	33.2	33.5	34.5	33.5	33.6	32.8	32.6	33.5	34.0	35.0	35.2	35.2
Sweden	51.9	50.3	48.0	46.9	47.2	48.5	50.4	51.6	52.0	52.3	54.0	51.4
Switzerland	26.9	26.5	26.8	27.3	27.9	28.5	29.0	28.5	29.7	29.8	31.2	30.6
Turkey	20.0	21.0	22.4	22.7	22.2	22.6	25.4	27.9	28.4	31.3	33.4	36.5
United Kingdom	36.8	35.1	34.6	33.1	33.7	34.8	34.8	34.9	36.7	36.1	37.2	37.3
United States	26.7	26.8	26.6	26.9	27.3	27.6	27.9	28.3	28.9	28.9	29.7	28.9
EU15	39.2	39.6	40.0	40.1	40.4	40.1	41.2	41.0	40.9	41.4	41.5	41.0
OECD total	34.8	35.3	35.6	36.1	36.1	36.0	36.6	36.6	36.5	36.8	37.1	36.9

StatLink: http://dx.doi.org/10.1787/486118320630

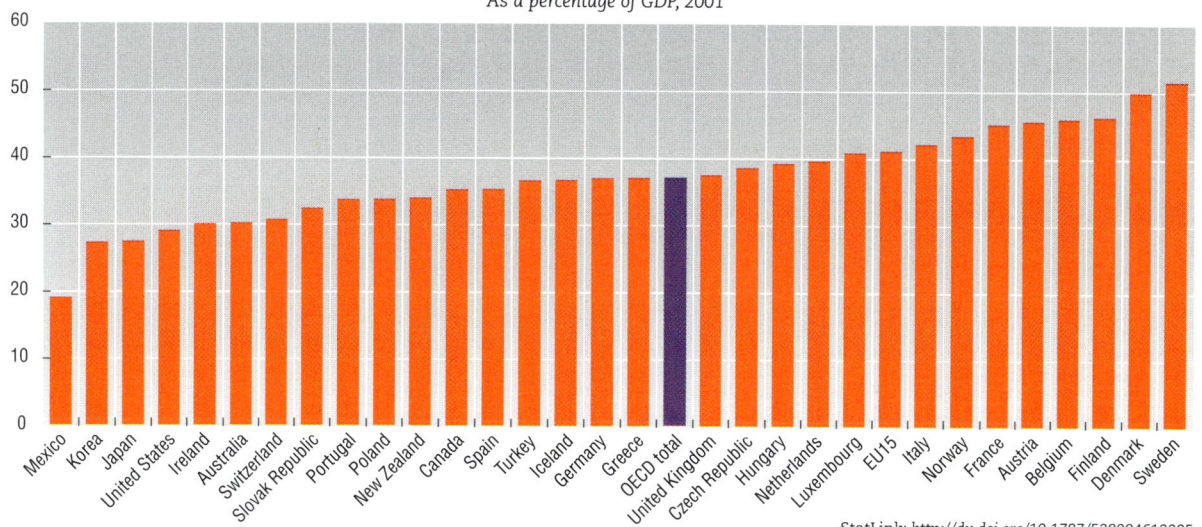

Total tax revenue
As a percentage of GDP, 2001

StatLink: http://dx.doi.org/10.1787/538284613325

OECD FACTBOOK 2005 – ISBN 92-64-01869-7 – © OECD 2005

PUBLIC POLICIES • TAXES

TOTAL TAX REVENUE

Taxes on income and profits
As a percentage of GDP

	1990	1991	1992	1993	1994	1995	1996	1997	1998	1999	2000	2001
Australia	16.7	15.5	15.1	14.9	15.7	16.4	17.1	17.0	17.3	18.2	18.1	16.7
Austria	10.3	10.9	11.4	11.5	10.5	11.1	12.1	12.8	12.9	12.6	12.3	14.3
Belgium	16.3	15.9	15.8	15.6	16.9	17.3	17.3	17.7	18.0	17.5	17.9	18.1
Canada	17.4	17.1	16.1	15.7	15.8	16.5	16.9	17.9	17.7	17.7	17.5	16.9
Czech Republic	..	..	..	10.9	10.3	9.9	9.2	8.5	8.8	8.7	8.8	9.0
Denmark	27.6	27.8	28.3	29.4	30.4	30.0	30.2	30.0	29.5	30.4	29.1	29.5
Finland	19.3	19.1	19.6	17.1	18.8	18.1	19.8	19.2	19.0	19.3	20.1	19.0
France	7.4	7.8	6.9	7.0	7.1	7.1	7.6	8.2	10.4	11.0	11.3	11.4
Germany	10.7	11.7	12.1	11.7	11.3	11.6	10.7	10.4	10.9	11.3	11.4	10.6
Greece	5.8	5.9	5.7	5.9	6.8	7.2	7.1	7.7	9.3	9.7	10.5	9.6
Hungary	..	12.7	10.0	9.6	9.2	8.9	9.0	8.5	8.7	9.1	9.5	10.0
Iceland	9.3	9.2	9.6	10.4	10.4	10.9	11.5	11.7	13.4	14.5	15.3	15.7
Ireland	12.4	13.0	13.4	13.8	14.3	12.8	13.3	13.3	13.1	13.3	13.4	12.5
Italy	14.2	14.2	15.7	16.0	14.4	14.5	14.8	15.6	13.9	14.7	13.9	14.4
Japan	14.5	13.9	12.0	11.4	10.2	10.1	10.1	9.9	8.8	8.3	9.2	8.9
Korea	6.2	5.4	6.1	5.9	6.2	6.5	6.5	5.9	7.0	5.8	7.5	7.2
Luxembourg	16.0	14.3	13.5	15.4	15.8	16.7	16.9	16.5	15.5	14.6	14.6	14.7
Mexico	4.7	4.7	5.2	5.5	5.2	4.1	4.0	4.6	4.7	5.0	5.0	5.3
Netherlands	13.9	15.1	14.1	14.8	12.1	11.1	11.2	10.9	10.5	10.5	10.3	10.6
New Zealand	21.8	20.2	20.6	21.3	21.9	22.4	20.5	20.9	19.6	19.4	20.0	19.8
Norway	14.6	14.9	13.3	13.4	14.3	14.4	14.9	15.8	15.8	14.5	15.9	19.9
Poland	..	8.3	12.3	13.5	12.4	12.1	11.6	11.3	11.1	10.7	10.5	9.9
Portugal	7.5	8.4	9.4	8.5	8.3	8.5	9.2	9.4	9.6	9.8	10.3	9.7
Slovak Republic	..	..	..	..	..	..	..	..	8.8	8.3	7.4	6.7
Spain	10.2	10.4	10.4	10.0	9.5	9.6	9.4	10.0	9.6	9.8	9.8	9.9
Sweden	21.6	18.6	18.3	19.2	20.0	19.0	19.7	20.3	20.3	20.9	22.3	19.3
Switzerland	12.5	12.3	12.7	12.3	12.9	12.3	12.7	12.3	13.0	12.5	13.7	12.9
Turkey	6.7	7.3	7.3	7.3	6.6	6.4	6.7	7.6	9.4	9.8	9.5	10.1
United Kingdom	14.1	13.3	12.3	11.5	11.9	12.7	12.7	12.9	14.1	14.1	14.5	14.8
United States	12.1	11.9	11.6	12.0	12.2	12.6	13.2	13.7	14.3	14.2	15.1	14.1
EU15	13.8	13.8	13.8	13.8	13.9	13.8	14.1	14.3	14.4	14.6	14.8	14.6
OECD total	13.2	12.9	12.8	12.8	12.8	12.8	13.0	13.1	13.2	13.2	13.5	13.4

StatLink: http://dx.doi.org/10.1787/452468433773

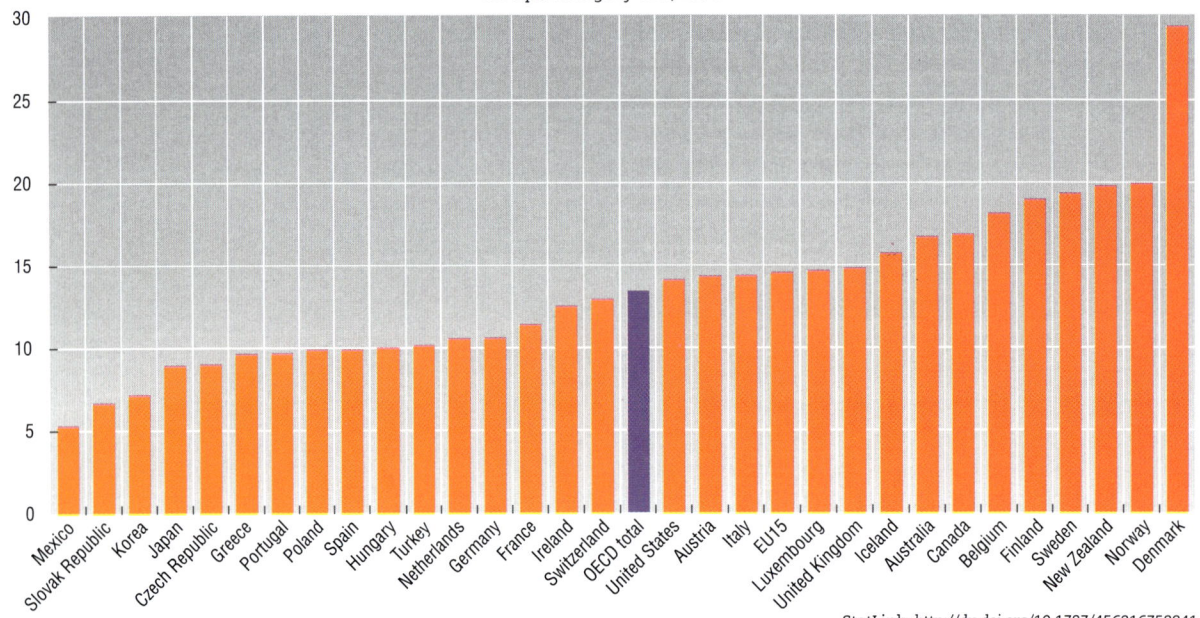

Taxes on income and profits
As a percentage of GDP, 2001

StatLink: http://dx.doi.org/10.1787/456216758841

PUBLIC POLICIES • TAXES

TOTAL TAX REVENUE

Taxes on goods and services
As a percentage of GDP

	1990	1991	1992	1993	1994	1995	1996	1997	1998	1999	2000	2001
Australia	8.1	7.7	7.7	8.2	8.5	8.6	8.5	8.3	7.9	7.7	8.7	8.7
Austria	12.7	12.5	12.8	12.5	13.2	11.5	12.4	12.5	12.3	12.4	12.3	12.3
Belgium	11.4	11.4	11.4	11.5	11.8	11.5	11.8	11.9	11.3	11.5	11.6	11.3
Canada	9.3	9.4	9.5	9.4	9.2	9.0	9.0	9.0	9.1	8.7	8.7	8.7
Czech Republic	..	..	..	14.3	13.8	13.2	13.0	12.6	11.8	12.6	12.5	11.7
Denmark	15.8	15.6	15.3	15.3	15.8	15.9	16.3	16.3	16.6	16.6	16.1	16.0
Finland	14.6	14.6	14.5	14.3	14.2	13.5	14.4	14.3	14.1	14.5	13.8	13.6
France	12.2	11.8	11.5	11.5	11.9	12.1	12.5	12.4	12.2	12.2	11.7	11.3
Germany	8.8	10.0	10.2	10.6	11.0	10.7	10.5	10.3	10.2	10.6	10.6	10.6
Greece	13.1	13.6	14.6	14.1	13.5	13.4	13.6	13.8	13.6	13.6	13.8	14.0
Hungary	..	15.2	16.4	17.3	16.3	17.2	16.6	15.3	15.1	15.8	15.8	15.1
Iceland	16.2	16.3	16.3	15.9	15.4	15.5	15.9	15.6	16.0	17.3	17.2	15.2
Ireland	14.2	13.9	13.8	13.2	13.9	13.4	13.2	12.8	12.2	11.6	11.6	11.2
Italy	10.9	11.0	11.3	11.3	11.7	11.2	11.0	11.4	11.7	11.9	11.9	10.8
Japan	4.0	4.0	4.0	4.0	4.2	4.2	4.2	4.6	5.2	5.3	5.1	5.2
Korea	9.2	8.6	8.9	8.7	8.8	8.8	9.5	9.7	8.7	9.5	10.0	10.8
Luxembourg	10.1	10.5	11.1	11.6	11.7	11.3	11.1	11.0	10.8	11.1	11.2	10.8
Mexico	9.6	9.3	8.9	8.3	8.1	9.0	9.3	9.4	8.3	8.6	9.8	9.7
Netherlands	11.3	11.5	11.6	11.1	11.4	11.4	11.8	11.6	11.6	11.9	12.0	12.1
New Zealand	12.6	12.7	12.9	12.3	12.3	12.3	12.0	12.3	12.3	12.3	11.7	12.0
Norway	14.8	14.5	15.2	15.3	15.8	15.9	15.6	15.5	16.0	15.1	13.4	13.6
Poland	..	9.8	11.6	14.5	14.4	14.0	14.1	13.5	12.9	13.1	12.5	12.0
Portugal	12.8	12.8	14.0	13.2	14.1	14.1	13.7	13.7	13.8	14.0	13.7	13.4
Slovak Republic	..	..	..	..	..	..	..	..	11.8	11.7	12.5	10.7
Spain	9.4	9.5	9.8	9.0	9.5	9.4	9.4	9.7	10.0	10.5	10.6	10.3
Sweden	13.0	13.3	12.4	12.8	12.2	13.5	13.0	13.0	13.0	12.9	13.0	12.9
Switzerland	5.7	5.6	5.4	5.4	5.4	6.2	6.2	6.2	6.4	6.9	7.0	7.1
Turkey	5.6	6.1	6.7	7.2	8.3	8.5	9.7	10.3	10.2	11.2	13.6	14.1
United Kingdom	11.2	11.6	12.1	11.8	12.0	12.3	12.2	12.3	12.0	11.6	12.0	11.7
United States	4.6	4.7	4.8	4.9	4.9	4.9	4.8	4.7	4.7	4.7	4.7	4.6
EU15	12.1	12.2	12.4	12.2	12.5	12.3	12.5	12.5	12.3	12.5	12.4	12.2
OECD total	10.8	11.0	11.2	11.4	11.5	11.5	11.6	11.5	11.4	11.6	11.6	11.4

StatLink: http://dx.doi.org/10.1787/160677855785

Taxes on goods and services
As a percentage of GDP, 2001

StatLink: http://dx.doi.org/10.1787/841333048406

OECD FACTBOOK 2005 – ISBN 92-64-01869-7 – © OECD 2005

PUBLIC POLICIES • TAXES

TAXES ON THE AVERAGE PRODUCTION WORKER

This series, taxes on a single production worker, measures the difference between the salary cost of a single average production worker to their employer and the amount of disposable income (net wage) that they receive. This "tax wedge" represents the extent to which the tax system discourages employment.

Definition

The taxes included in the measure are personal income taxes, employees' social security contributions and employers' social security contributions. For the few countries that have them, it also includes payroll taxes. The amount of these taxes paid in relation to employing one average production worker is expressed as a percentage of their labour cost (gross wage plus employers' social security contributions and payroll tax).

An average production worker (APW) is defined as somebody who earns the average income of full-time production workers in the manufacturing sector of the country concerned. The average production worker is single, meaning that he does not receive any tax relief in respect of a spouse, unmarried partner or child.

Comparability

The types of taxes included in the measure are fully comparable across countries, as they are based on common definitions agreed by all OECD countries and published in *Revenue Statistics*.

The income levels of the production workers are different in each country, but they are each equal to the average income of full-time production workers in the manufacturing sector. Thus, they can be regarded as income levels that correspond to comparable types of work in each country.

The information on the APW income level is supplied by the ministries of finance in all OECD countries and is based on national statistical surveys. The amount of taxes paid by the single production worker is calculated by applying the tax laws of the country concerned. Thus, the tax rates are the result of a modelling exercise rather than direct observation of taxes actually paid.

Long-term trends

On average, the taxes on a production worker increased until 1997 and have since declined, in both the European Union and the OECD as a whole. However, there are important differences between countries. Those that have experienced an overall increase in the taxes on a production worker include Australia, Austria, Germany, Japan and Korea. Countries that have experienced an overall decline include Denmark, France, Ireland and Mexico.

Source

OECD (2004), *Taxing Wages 2002-2003*, OECD, Paris.

Further information
• **Analytical publications**

Immervoll, H. (2004), "Average and Marginal Effective Tax Rates Facing Workers in the EU: A Micro-Level Analysis of Levels, Distributions and Driving Factors", *OECD Social, Employment and Migration Working Paper*, No. 19, www.oecd.org/els/workingpapers.

OECD (2004), *Benefits and Wages*, OECD, Paris.

• **Statistical publications**

OECD (2004), *Revenue Statistics*, OECD, Paris.

• **Web sites**

OECD Centre for Tax Policy and Administration: *www.oecd.org/ctp*.

Tax Policy Analysis: *www.oecd.org/ctp/tpa*.

Benefits and Wages: *www.oecd.org/els/social/workingincentives*.

PUBLIC POLICIES • TAXES

TAXES ON THE AVERAGE PRODUCTION WORKER

Taxes on the average production worker
As a percentage of labour cost

	1991	1993	1994	1995	1996	1997	1998	1999	2000	2001	2002	2003
Australia	22.8	23.0	23.5	24.0	24.4	24.8	25.4	25.9	22.8	23.3	28.3	28.3
Austria	39.1	40.0	39.7	41.2	41.5	45.6	45.8	45.9	44.9	44.5	44.7	45.0
Belgium	53.7	54.6	54.6	56.3	56.4	56.6	56.8	56.9	56.2	55.6	55.1	54.5
Canada	29.0	30.8	31.4	31.5	32.1	32.3	31.7	31.1	31.3	30.4	32.2	32.4
Czech Republic	..	42.6	42.8	43.2	42.6	42.9	42.8	42.7	43.1	43.1	43.5	43.8
Denmark	46.7	47.0	45.2	45.2	44.8	45.2	43.7	44.5	44.4	43.6	42.7	42.7
Finland	44.5	49.3	50.5	51.2	50.3	48.9	48.8	47.4	47.3	45.9	45.2	44.5
France			51.6	49.1	49.7	48.7	47.6	48.1	48.2	48.3	48.2	48.3
Germany	46.4	46.4	48.3	50.2	51.2	52.3	52.2	51.9	51.8	50.8	51.1	52.0
Greece	33.0	35.3	35.1	35.6	35.8	35.8	36.1	35.7	36.0	35.7	34.6	34.3
Hungary	..	..	..	51.4	52.0	52.0	51.6	50.7	49.6	49.0	49.0	45.7
Iceland	20.1	22.0	22.9	23.1	24.5	24.4	25.9	26.0	26.7	27.5	28.8	29.3
Ireland	39.8	40.0	38.4	36.9	36.1	33.9	33.0	32.4	28.9	25.8	24.5	24.5
Italy	48.8	49.2	49.9	50.3	50.8	51.5	47.5	47.2	46.7	46.1	46.0	45.3
Japan	21.5	21.2	21.6	19.5	19.4	20.7	19.6	24.0	24.1	24.2	29.8	27.0
Korea	..	..	..	6.9	6.3	12.4	14.7	16.1	16.5	16.6	14.1	14.1
Luxembourg	33.9	34.9	35.1	34.3	34.5	35.2	33.8	34.6	35.5	33.9	31.3	31.7
Mexico	24.4	26.6	26.5	27.2	25.4	20.8	21.9	14.1	15.4	14.4	16.1	17.3
Netherlands	46.5	45.7	45.6	44.8	43.8	43.6	43.5	44.3	45.1	42.3	42.5	43.0
New Zealand	23.8	24.0	24.3	24.5	22.3	21.6	20.0	19.4	19.5	19.5	20.1	20.6
Norway	41.2	36.8	36.9	37.5	37.6	37.4	37.5	37.3	37.2	36.9	36.9	36.8
Poland		44.1		44.7	44.7	43.9	43.2	43.0	43.0	42.7	42.8	42.9
Portugal	33.2	33.3	34.1	33.7	33.8	33.9	33.8	33.4	33.5	32.5	32.6	32.6
Slovak Republic	..	..	..	..	..	..	..	..	41.2	41.7	41.1	41.4
Spain	36.5	38.0	38.8	38.5	38.8	39.0	39.0	37.5	37.6	37.9	38.2	37.6
Sweden	46.0	45.6	46.8	49.3	50.2	50.7	50.7	50.5	49.5	48.5	47.6	46.6
Switzerland	27.3	28.7	28.7	30.6	30.4	30.0	30.0	29.8	29.5	29.5	29.6	29.2
Turkey	41.2	40.0	36.1	35.3	38.3	40.7	39.8	30.3	40.4	43.6	42.4	42.1
United Kingdom	33.2	32.6	33.3	33.4	32.6	32.0	32.0	30.8	30.1	29.5	29.5	31.1
United States	31.3	31.2	31.2	31.0	31.1	31.1	31.0	31.1	30.8	29.8	29.7	29.5
EU15	41.5	42.3	43.1	43.3	43.4	43.5	43.0	42.7	42.4	41.4	40.9	40.9
OECD total	36.0	37.0	37.4	37.3	37.3	37.5	37.2	36.7	36.9	36.4	36.6	36.5

StatLink: http://dx.doi.org/10.1787/624067136205

Income tax plus employee and employer contributions
As a percentage of labour cost

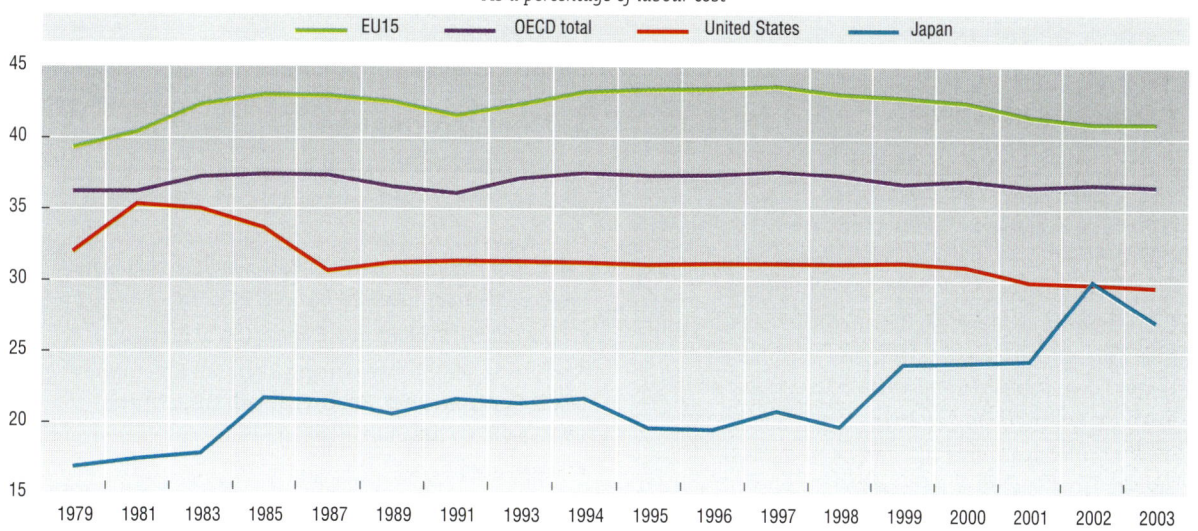

StatLink: http://dx.doi.org/10.1787/171422313142

REGIONAL GDP

Most governments of OECD countries try to ensure that the benefits of economic development and higher living standards are evenly spread between different regions within their country. This section presents the first of two measures of how well this objective is being achieved – differences between regions in per capita GDP.

Definition

Regional GDP is measured according to the definitions of the 1993 System of National Accounts.

The chart shows values of a modified Gini Index. The Gini Index is widely used to measure disparities in some aspect of a population – most commonly being used to measure inequalities in the distribution of income among households. The Gini Index takes values from one – indicating maximum disparity – to zero – indicating minimal disparity. The standard Gini Index is not suitable for measuring disparities between regions and has been modified to the *OECD Adjusted Territorial Gini Index*. See the "Further information" selection below for sources explaining how it has been constructed.

Comparability

The main problem with economic analysis at the sub-national level is the very unit of analysis, i.e. the region. The word "region" can mean very different things both within and between countries with significant differences in area and population (see box on page 185). A second issue concerns the different "geography" of each region where different communities are urban or rural (see box on page 187).

Regional GDP is measured by adding up the value added of producers located within each region. The main problem is in allocating among regions the value added of headquarter offices of enterprises that operate in more than one region of the country and the value added of "network enterprises" such as airlines, railways, and of utilities companies that operate in all regions. There are no OECD-wide standards for dealing with these issues.

Long-term trends

Differences between countries in regional disparities appear to be significant. For the OECD average, the Gini Index for per capita GDP is equal to 0.10 but varies between a high of 0.20 (large disparity) and 0.03 (low disparity). Germany, Italy, Hungary, the United States and Mexico appear to be the countries with the largest disparities while Sweden, Czech Republic, Norway, Australia and Denmark lie at the bottom of the ranking.

Source
OECD Territorial Database:
www.oecd.org/gov/territorialindicators.

Further Information
• *Analytical publications*

OECD (2001), *OECD Territorial Outlook*, OECD, Paris.

OECD (2003), *Geographic Concentration and Territorial Disparity in OECD Countries*, OECD, Paris, *www.oecd.org/dataoecd/43/1/15179757.DOC*.

OECD (2005), *Regions at a Glance*, OECD, Paris.

Spiezia, V. (2003), "Measuring Regional Economies", *OECD Statistics Brief*, No. 6, October, OECD, Paris, *www.oecd.org/std/statisticsbrief*.

• *Web sites*

OECD Territorial Indicators:
www.oecd.org/gov/territorialindicators.

PUBLIC POLICIES • REGIONAL DISPARITIES

REGIONAL GDP

Classification of regions

The smallest OECD region (*Concepcion de Buenos Aires*, Mexico) has an area of less than 10 square kilometres whereas the largest region (Nunavut, Canada) is over 2 million square kilometres. Similarly, population in OECD regions ranges from about 400 inhabitants in Balance (Australia) to more than 47 million in Kanto (Japan).

To address this issue, the OECD has established a classification of regions within each member country (see "OECD Territorial Outlook"), based on two territorial levels. The higher level (Territorial Level 2) consists of about 300 macro regions while the lower level (Territorial Level 3) is composed of more than 2 300 micro regions. Territorial Level 0 indicates the territory of the whole country while Level 1 denotes groups of macro regions. This classification – which, for European countries, is largely consistent with the Eurostat Classification 3 – facilitates greater comparability between regions at the same territorial level. Indeed, these two levels, which are officially established and relatively stable in all member countries, are used by many as a framework for implementing regional policies.

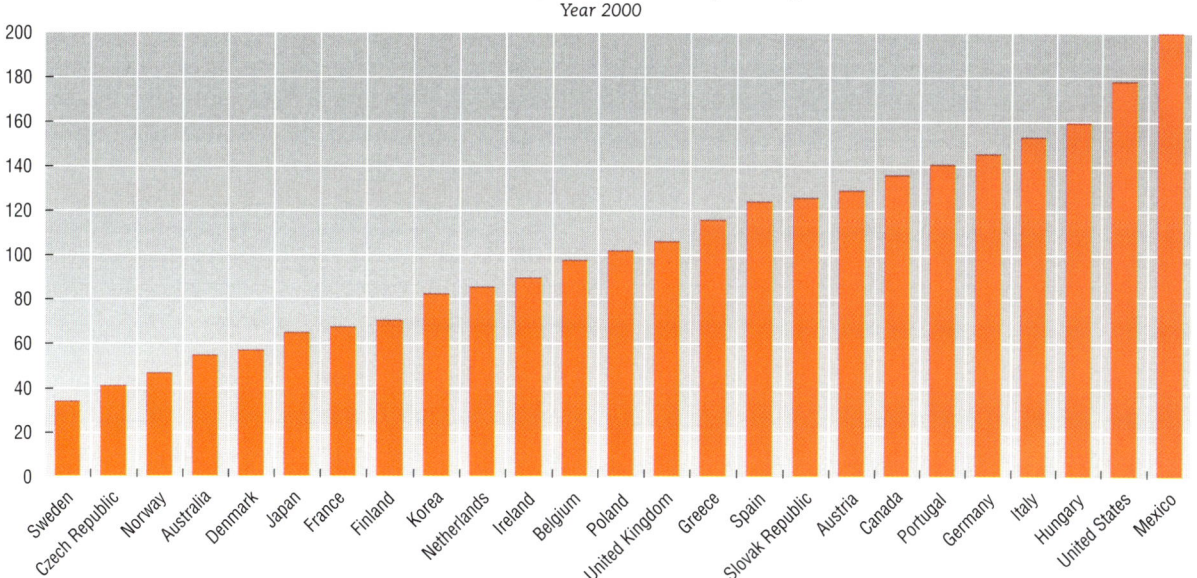

Territorial disparity in GDP per capita
Year 2000

StatLink: http://dx.doi.org/10.1787/741217582131

PUBLIC POLICIES • REGIONAL DISPARITIES

REGIONAL UNEMPLOYMENT

Most governments of OECD countries try to ensure that the benefits of economic development and higher living standards are evenly spread between different regions within their country. This section presents the second of two measures of how well this objective is being achieved – differences between regions in unemployment.

Definition

Unemployed persons are defined as those who report that they are without work, that they are available for work and that they have taken active steps to find work in the last four weeks. The unemployment rate is defined as the number of unemployed persons as a percentage of the civilian labour force, where the latter consists of the unemployed plus those in civilian employment. The latter are defined as persons who have worked for one hour or more in the last week.

Comparability

As is the case for disparities in GDP, the comparability of regional unemployment is affected by differences in the meaning of the word "region" (see box on page 185) and the different "geography" of rural and urban communities (see box on page 187) both within and between countries.

The chart shows values of a modified Gini Index. The Gini Index is widely used to measure disparities in some aspect of a population – most commonly being used to measure inequalities in the distribution of income among households. The Gini Index takes values from one – indicating maximum disparity – to zero – indicating minimal disparity. The standard Gini Index is not suitable for measuring disparities between regions and has been modified to the OECD *Adjusted Territorial Gini Index*. See the "Further information" section below for sources explaining how it has been constructed.

Regional unemployment is almost always measured by household labour force surveys. These provide measures of unemployment in the regions where the households are situated and are appropriate for the disparity indices shown here.

To interpret regional disparities correctly, it is necessary to look at the different "geography" of regions. The causes of unemployment in rural regions are not the same as in urban ones and the OECD Regional Typology has been developed to take these differences into account.

Long-term trends

Differences between countries are even larger when one looks at regional disparities in unemployment rates. For the OECD average, the Gini coefficient is equal to 0.19 (higher than for GDP per capita) and ranges from 0.39 in Italy to 0.08 in Australia. Germany, Belgium, Portugal and Spain are the other countries with large disparities; Denmark, Japan and Ireland lie at the bottom of the ranking.

Source
OECD Territorial Database:
www.oecd.org/gov/territorialindicators.

Further Information

• **Analytical publications**

OECD (2001), *OECD Territorial Outlook*, OECD, Paris.

OECD (2003), *Geographic Concentration and Territorial Disparity in OECD Countries*, OECD, Paris, *www.oecd.org/dataoecd/43/1/15179757.DOC*.

OECD (2005), *Regions at a Glance*, OECD, Paris.

Spiezia, V. (2003), "Measuring Regional Economies", *OECD Statistics Brief*, No. 6, October, OECD, Paris, *www.oecd.org/std/statisticsbrief*.

• **Web sites**

OECD Territorial Indicators:
www.oecd.org/gov/territorialindicators.

PUBLIC POLICIES • REGIONAL DISPARITIES

REGIONAL UNEMPLOYMENT

OECD Regional Typology

A second issue concerns the different "geography" of each region. For instance, in the United Kingdom one could question the relevance of comparing the highly urbanised area of London to the rural region of the Shetland Islands, despite the fact that both regions belong to the same territorial level. To take account of these differences, the OECD has established a Regional Typology according to which regions have been classified as *predominantly urban, predominantly rural* and *intermediate*. This typology, based on the percentage of regional population living in rural or urban communities, enables meaningful comparisons between regions belonging to the same type.

The OECD Regional Typology is based on two criteria. The first identifies rural communities according to their population density. A community is defined as rural if its population density is below 150 inhabitants per square kilometre (500 inhabitants for Japan because its national population density exceeds 300 inhabitants per square kilometre). The second classifies regions according to the percentage of population living in rural communities. Thus, a region is classified as:

- *Predominantly rural*, if more than 50% of its population lives in rural communities.
- *Predominantly urban*, if less than 15% of the population lives in rural communities.
- *Intermediate*, if the percentage of population living in rural communities is between 15 and 50%.

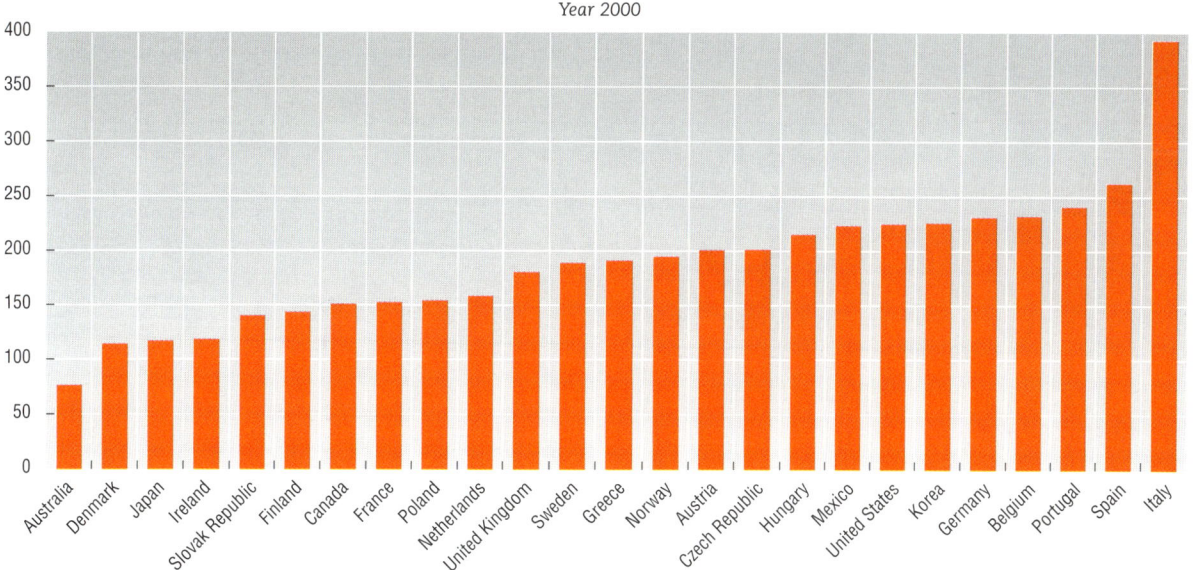

Territorial disparity in unemployment rates
Year 2000

StatLink: http://dx.doi.org/10.1787/246556646826

QUALITY OF LIFE

HEALTH
LIFE EXPECTANCY
INFANT MORTALITY
OBESITY
PUBLIC AND PRIVATE HEALTH EXPENDITURE

WORK AND LEISURE
HOURS WORKED
TOURISM: HOTEL NIGHTS

CRIME
PRISON POPULATION
VICTIMISATION RATES

TRANSPORT
ROAD MOTOR VEHICLES AND ROAD FATALITIES
PASSENGER TRANSPORT BY ROAD AND RAIL

QUALITY OF LIFE • HEALTH

LIFE EXPECTANCY

Life expectancy at birth remains one of the most frequently quoted indicators of a population's health status.

Gains in life expectancy in OECD countries in recent decades have come as a result of a number of important factors, including improvements in living conditions, public health interventions and progress in medical care. Although it is not easy to assess the relative contribution of each of these factors, recent research estimated that medical care may have accounted for around 17-18% of the increases in life expectancy seen in the United Kingdom and United States over the last century. Analysis of statistics on health care resources available in *OECD Health Data 2004* has found some correlation between variations in life expectancy and numbers of doctors per capita.

Long-term trends

Over the past 40 years or so, there have been huge gains in life expectancy at birth in OECD countries. On average, life expectancy at birth across OECD countries increased by 8.4 years, to reach 77.4 years in 2001, up from 69.0 years in 1960. The gains in life expectancy have been relatively steady over the past four decades across countries, averaging 1.5 years from 1960 to 1970 and around 2.2 years per decade since then.

Increases in life expectancy have been particularly pronounced in those countries starting out with a relatively low level in 1960. For instance, in Korea, life expectancy for men and women has increased by a remarkable 24 years between 1960 and 2001, and in Turkey, life expectancy at birth has increased by more than 20 years over the past four decades. In a number of countries, such significant gains in life expectancy at birth over the past decades have been driven by a continuous reduction in infant mortality rates together with rapidly falling death rates from circulatory diseases.

The gender gap in life expectancy stood at 5.9 years on average across OECD countries in 2001, with life expectancy reaching 80.3 years for women and 74.4 years for men. This gender gap has increased by almost one year on average since 1960. But this result hides different trends between earlier and later decades. While the gender gap in life expectancy increased substantially in many countries during the 1960s and the 1970s, it has narrowed during the past two decades. From 1980 to 2000, gains in life expectancy were on average higher for men than for women. This narrowing of the male-female gap in life expectancy since 1980 has been attributed partly to the convergence in risk factor behaviours (such as smoking) between men and women.

Definition

Life expectancy is the average number of years of life remaining to a person at a particular age, based on a given set of age-specific mortality rates. The rates shown here refer to life expectancy at birth.

Comparability

Each country calculates its life expectancy according to somewhat varying methodologies. Such differences in methodology can affect the comparability of life expectancy estimates but only change a country's life expectancy estimates by a fraction of a year.

Source

OECD (2004), *OECD Health Data 2004: A Comparative Analysis of 30 Countries*, OECD, Paris.

Further information
• *Analytical publications*

OECD (2002), *Measuring Up: Improving Health System Performance in OECD Countries*, OECD, Paris.

OECD (2003), *A Disease-based Comparison of Health Systems: What is Best and at What Cost?*, OECD, Paris.

OECD (2004), *Towards High-Performing Health Systems*, OECD Health Project, OECD, Paris.

OECD (2005), *Society at a Glance*, OECD, Paris.

• *Statistical publications*

OECD (2003), *Health at a Glance: OECD Indicators 2003*, OECD, Paris.

OECD (2004), *OECD Health Data 2004: A Comparative Analysis of 30 Countries*, also available on CD-ROM, OECD, Paris.

• *Online databases*

SourceOECD Health Data.

• *Web sites*

OECD Health Data: *www.oecd.org/health/healthdata*.

QUALITY OF LIFE • HEALTH

LIFE EXPECTANCY

Life expectancy at birth: total
Number of years

	1960	1970	1980	1990	1995	1996	1997	1998	1999	2000	2001	2002
Australia	70.9	70.8	74.6	77.0	77.9	78.2	78.5	78.7	79.0	79.3	79.7	80.0
Austria	68.7	70.0	72.6	75.5	76.6	76.9	77.3	77.7	77.8	78.1	78.6	78.8
Belgium	70.6	71.0	73.4	76.1	76.8	77.2	77.4	77.4	77.6	77.7	78.0	78.1
Canada	..	..	75.3	77.6	78.1	78.4	78.6	78.8	79.0	79.4	79.7	..
Czech Republic	70.7	69.6	70.3	71.5	73.2	73.9	74.0	74.6	74.8	75.1	75.3	75.4
Denmark	72.4	73.3	74.3	74.9	75.3	75.7	76.0	76.4	76.6	76.9	77.0	77.2
Finland	69.0	70.8	73.4	74.9	76.5	76.8	77.0	77.2	77.4	77.6	78.1	78.2
France	70.3	72.2	74.3	76.9	77.9	78.1	78.5	78.6	78.8	79.0	79.2	79.4
Germany	69.6	70.4	72.9	75.2	76.5	76.8	77.2	77.6	77.7	78.0	78.5	..
Greece	69.9	72.0	74.5	77.1	77.7	77.8	78.2	77.9	78.1	78.1	78.1	78.1
Hungary	68.0	69.2	69.1	69.4	69.9	70.4	70.8	70.7	70.8	71.7	72.3	72.6
Iceland	72.9	74.3	76.7	78.0	78.0	78.9	78.9	79.6	79.6	79.7	80.3	80.4
Ireland	70.0	71.2	72.9	74.9	75.7	75.9	76.0	76.2	76.1	76.5	77.2	77.8
Italy	..	..	74.0	76.9	78.1	78.4	78.7	78.8	79.2	79.6	79.8	79.9
Japan	67.8	72.0	76.1	78.9	79.6	80.3	80.5	80.6	80.5	81.2	81.5	81.8
Korea	52.4	..	..	..	73.5	..	74.4	..	75.5	..	76.4	..
Luxembourg	69.4	70.3	72.5	75.4	76.6	76.6	77.0	77.1	77.9	78.0	78.0	78.2
Mexico	57.5	60.9	67.2	71.2	72.7	72.9	73.2	73.4	73.7	74.1	74.4	74.6
Netherlands	73.5	73.7	75.9	77.4	77.5	77.5	77.9	77.9	77.9	78.0	78.3	78.4
New Zealand	71.3	71.5	73.2	75.4	76.9	77.0	77.5	77.8	78.5	78.5	78.5	..
Norway	73.6	74.2	75.8	76.6	77.8	78.2	78.3	78.5	78.4	78.7	78.9	79.0
Poland	67.8	70.0	70.2	71.5	72.0	72.4	72.8	73.1	72.7	73.8	74.3	74.6
Portugal	64.0	67.5	71.5	73.9	75.2	75.1	75.5	75.8	76.1	76.6	76.9	77.2
Slovak Republic	70.6	69.8	70.6	71.0	72.4	72.9	72.8	72.7	73.1	73.3	73.7	73.9
Spain	69.8	72.0	75.6	76.8	77.9	78.1	78.5	78.6	78.6	79.1	79.3	79.4
Sweden	73.1	74.7	75.8	77.6	78.8	79.0	79.3	79.4	79.5	79.7	79.9	79.9
Switzerland	71.6	73.8	76.2	77.4	78.5	79.0	79.2	79.4	79.7	79.8	80.2	80.4
Turkey	48.3	54.2	58.1	66.5	67.2	67.3	67.5	67.7	67.9	68.1	68.3	68.6
United Kingdom	70.8	71.9	73.2	75.7	76.6	76.9	77.2	77.3	77.4	77.9	78.1	..
United States	69.9	70.9	73.7	75.3	75.7	76.1	76.5	76.7	76.7	76.8	77.1	..
OECD average (unweighted and excluding Canada, Italy and Korea)	69.0	70.5	72.8	74.9	75.8	76.1	76.4	76.6	76.8	77.1	77.4	..

StatLink: http://dx.doi.org/10.1787/482736281066

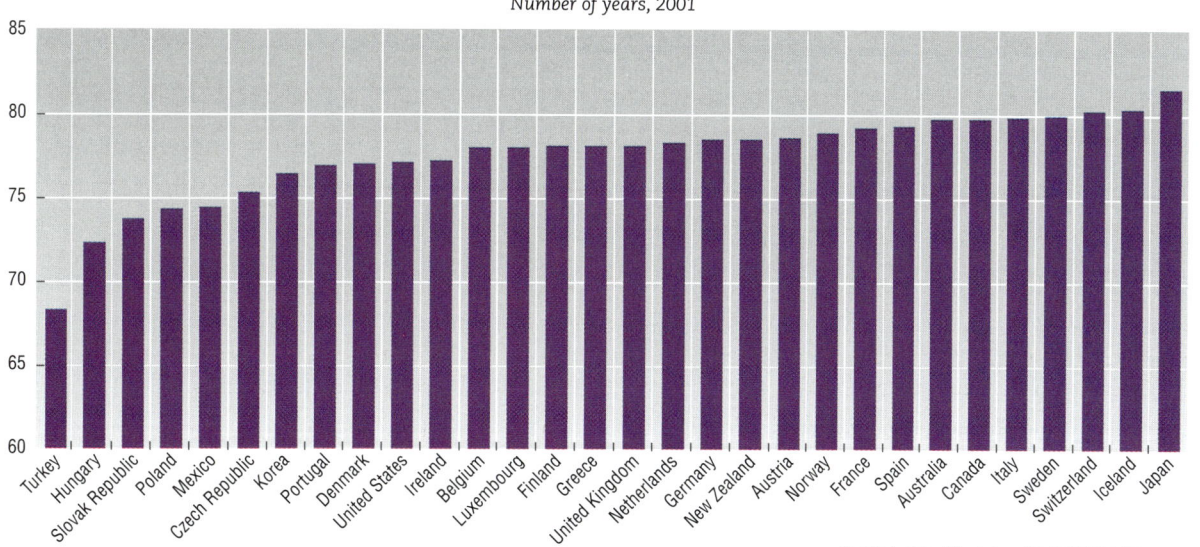

Life expectancy at birth: total
Number of years, 2001

StatLink: http://dx.doi.org/10.1787/434786127286

QUALITY OF LIFE • HEALTH

LIFE EXPECTANCY

Life expectancy at birth: men
Number of years

	1960	1970	1980	1990	1995	1996	1997	1998	1999	2000	2001	2002
Australia	67.9	67.4	71.0	73.9	75.0	75.2	75.6	75.9	76.2	76.6	77.0	77.4
Austria	65.4	66.5	69.0	72.2	73.3	73.7	74.1	74.5	74.8	75.1	75.6	75.8
Belgium	67.7	67.8	70.0	72.7	73.4	73.8	74.1	74.3	74.4	74.6	74.9	75.1
Canada	..	..	71.7	74.4	75.1	75.5	75.8	76.0	76.3	76.7	77.1	..
Czech Republic	67.9	66.1	66.8	67.6	69.7	70.4	70.5	71.1	71.4	71.7	72.1	72.1
Denmark	70.4	70.7	71.2	72.0	72.7	73.1	73.6	73.9	74.2	74.5	74.7	74.8
Finland	65.5	66.5	69.2	70.9	72.8	73.0	73.4	73.5	73.8	74.2	74.6	74.9
France	67.0	68.4	70.2	72.8	73.9	74.1	74.6	74.8	75.0	75.2	75.5	75.8
Germany	66.9	67.2	69.6	72.0	73.3	73.6	74.0	74.5	74.7	75.0	75.6	..
Greece	67.3	70.1	72.2	74.6	75.0	75.1	75.6	75.4	75.5	75.5	75.4	75.4
Hungary	65.9	66.3	65.5	65.1	65.3	66.1	66.4	66.1	66.4	67.4	68.1	68.4
Iceland	70.7	71.2	73.7	75.4	75.9	76.5	76.3	77.7	77.7	78.0	78.3	78.5
Ireland	68.1	68.8	70.1	72.1	72.9	73.1	73.3	73.4	73.4	73.9	74.7	75.2
Italy	..	..	70.6	73.6	74.9	75.3	75.7	75.7	76.1	76.6	76.7	76.8
Japan	65.3	69.3	73.4	75.9	76.4	77.0	77.2	77.2	77.1	77.7	78.1	78.3
Korea	51.1	..	..	..	69.6	..	70.6	..	71.7	..	72.8	..
Luxembourg	66.5	67.1	69.1	72.3	73.0	73.3	74.1	73.7	74.6	74.8	75.2	74.9
Mexico	55.8	58.5	64.1	68.3	70.0	70.3	70.6	70.8	71.2	71.6	71.9	72.1
Netherlands	71.5	70.8	72.5	73.8	74.6	74.7	75.2	75.2	75.3	75.5	75.8	76.0
New Zealand	68.7	68.3	70.0	72.4	74.2	74.3	74.9	75.2	76.0	76.0	76.0	..
Norway	71.3	71.0	72.3	73.4	74.8	75.4	75.5	75.6	75.6	76.0	76.2	76.4
Poland	64.9	66.6	66.0	66.7	67.6	68.1	68.5	68.9	68.2	69.7	70.2	70.4
Portugal	61.2	64.2	67.7	70.4	71.6	71.4	72.0	72.2	72.6	73.2	73.5	73.8
Slovak Republic	68.4	66.7	66.8	66.6	68.4	68.9	68.9	68.6	69.0	69.2	69.6	69.9
Spain	67.4	69.2	72.5	73.3	74.3	74.4	75.0	75.1	75.1	75.7	75.6	75.7
Sweden	71.2	72.2	72.8	74.8	76.2	76.5	76.7	76.9	77.1	77.4	77.6	77.7
Switzerland	68.7	70.7	72.8	74.0	75.3	75.9	76.3	76.3	76.8	76.9	77.4	77.8
Turkey	46.3	52.0	55.8	64.2	64.9	65.0	65.2	65.4	65.6	65.8	66.0	66.2
United Kingdom	67.9	68.7	70.2	72.9	74.0	74.3	74.7	74.8	75.0	75.5	75.7	..
United States	66.6	67.1	70.0	71.8	72.5	73.1	73.6	73.8	73.9	74.1	74.4	..
OECD average (unweighted and excluding Canada, Italy and Korea)	66.4	67.4	69.4	71.6	72.6	73.0	73.3	73.5	73.7	74.1	74.4	..

StatLink: http://dx.doi.org/10.1787/368123328437

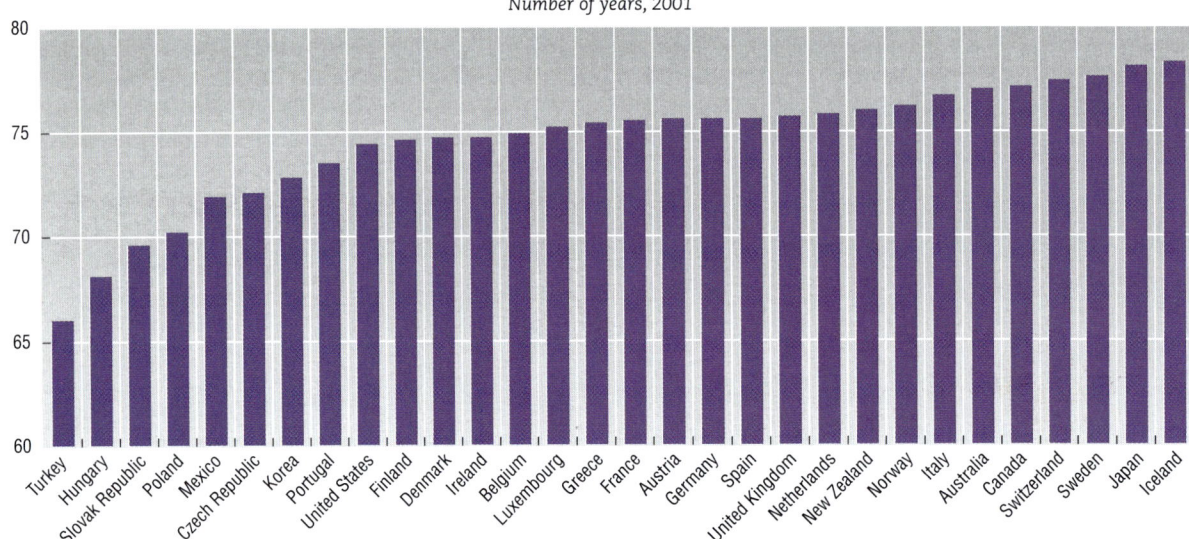

Life expectancy at birth: men
Number of years, 2001

StatLink: http://dx.doi.org/10.1787/567411222204

QUALITY OF LIFE • HEALTH

LIFE EXPECTANCY

Life expectancy at birth: women
Number of years

	1960	1970	1980	1990	1995	1996	1997	1998	1999	2000	2001	2002
Australia	73.9	74.2	78.1	80.1	80.8	81.1	81.3	81.5	81.8	82.0	82.4	82.6
Austria	71.9	73.4	76.1	78.8	79.9	80.1	80.5	80.8	80.8	81.1	81.5	81.7
Belgium	73.5	74.2	76.8	79.4	80.2	80.5	80.6	80.5	80.8	80.8	81.1	81.1
Canada	..	..	78.9	80.8	81.1	81.2	81.3	81.5	81.7	82.0	82.2	..
Czech Republic	73.4	73.0	73.9	75.4	76.6	77.3	77.5	78.1	78.2	78.4	78.5	78.7
Denmark	74.4	75.9	77.3	77.7	77.8	78.2	78.4	78.8	79.0	79.3	79.3	79.5
Finland	72.5	75.0	77.6	78.9	80.2	80.5	80.5	80.8	81.0	81.0	81.5	81.5
France	73.6	75.9	78.4	80.9	81.8	82.0	82.3	82.4	82.5	82.7	82.9	83.0
Germany	72.4	73.6	76.1	78.4	79.7	79.9	80.3	80.6	80.7	81.0	81.3	..
Greece	72.4	73.8	76.8	79.5	80.3	80.4	80.8	80.4	80.6	80.6	80.7	80.7
Hungary	70.1	72.1	72.7	73.7	74.5	74.7	75.1	75.2	75.2	75.9	76.4	76.7
Iceland	75.0	77.3	79.7	80.5	80.0	81.2	81.5	81.5	81.5	81.4	82.2	82.3
Ireland	71.9	73.5	75.6	77.6	78.4	78.7	78.6	79.0	78.8	79.1	79.7	80.3
Italy	..	..	77.4	80.1	81.3	81.4	81.6	81.8	82.2	82.5	82.8	82.9
Japan	70.2	74.7	78.8	81.9	82.9	83.6	83.8	84.0	84.0	84.6	84.9	85.2
Korea	53.7	..	..	..	77.4	..	78.1	..	79.2	..	80.0	..
Luxembourg	72.2	73.4	75.9	78.5	80.2	79.9	79.8	80.5	81.1	81.1	80.7	81.5
Mexico	59.2	63.2	70.2	74.1	75.3	75.4	75.7	75.9	76.1	76.5	76.8	77.1
Netherlands	75.4	76.5	79.2	80.9	80.4	80.3	80.5	80.6	80.5	80.5	80.7	80.7
New Zealand	73.9	74.6	76.3	78.3	79.5	79.6	80.1	80.4	80.9	80.9	80.9	..
Norway	75.8	77.3	79.2	79.8	80.8	81.0	81.0	81.3	81.1	81.4	81.5	81.5
Poland	70.6	73.3	74.4	76.3	76.4	76.6	77.0	77.3	77.2	77.9	78.3	78.7
Portugal	66.8	70.8	75.2	77.4	78.7	78.8	79.0	79.3	79.5	80.0	80.3	80.5
Slovak Republic	72.7	72.9	74.3	75.4	76.3	76.8	76.7	76.7	77.2	77.4	77.7	77.8
Spain	72.2	74.8	78.6	80.3	81.5	81.7	82.0	82.1	82.1	82.5	82.9	83.1
Sweden	74.9	77.1	78.8	80.4	81.4	81.5	81.8	81.9	81.9	82.0	82.1	82.1
Switzerland	74.5	76.9	79.6	80.7	81.7	82.0	82.1	82.4	82.5	82.6	83.0	83.0
Turkey	50.3	56.3	60.3	68.7	69.4	69.6	69.7	69.9	70.2	70.4	70.6	70.9
United Kingdom	73.7	75.0	76.2	78.5	79.2	79.5	79.6	79.7	79.8	80.2	80.4	..
United States	73.1	74.7	77.4	78.8	78.9	79.1	79.4	79.5	79.4	79.5	79.8	..
OECD average (unweighted and excluding Canada, Italy and Korea)	71.5	73.5	76.1	78.2	79.0	79.3	79.5	79.7	79.8	80.0	80.3	..

StatLink: http://dx.doi.org/10.1787/283834600722

Life expectancy at birth: women
Number of years, 2001

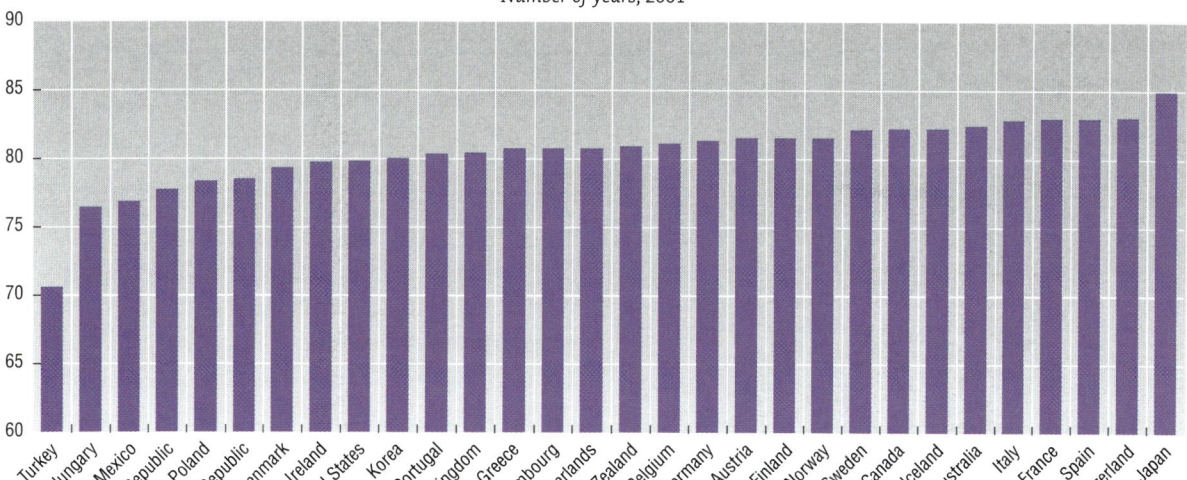

StatLink: http://dx.doi.org/10.1787/334856512734

QUALITY OF LIFE • HEALTH

INFANT MORTALITY

Infant mortality rates are an important indicator of the health of both pregnant women and newborns. They are also used in international comparisons to judge the effect of both economic and social policies on human health.

Definition

Infant mortality is the number of deaths of children under one year of age expressed per 1 000 live births.

Infant mortality rates are related to a number of social and economic factors, such as the average income level in a country, the income distribution and access to health services. Studies have found an association between cross-country variations in infant mortality rates and variations in the availability of health care resources such as the numbers of doctors and hospital beds. But a higher level of resources does not necessarily result in greater reductions in infant mortality. For instance, the United States has a significantly higher density per population of neonatologists and neonatal intensive care beds than Australia, Canada and the United Kingdom, yet the infant mortality rate in the United States remains higher than in these countries. Other factors such as the high level of teenage pregnancy and the lack of free prenatal and perinatal care in the United States have been put forward as contributory factors underlying the higher observed rates.

Comparability

Some of the international variation in infant mortality rates may be due to variations among countries in whether births of premature infants are reported as live births or not. In several countries, such as in the United States, Canada and the Nordic countries, very premature babies (with relatively low odds of survival) are registered as a live birth, which increases mortality rates compared with other countries that do not register them as live births.

Long-term trends

All OECD countries have achieved remarkable progress in reducing infant mortality rates since 1960. On average across OECD countries, infant mortality rates stood at 6.5 deaths per 1 000 live births in 2000 down from 36.4 in 1960. Portugal has made much progress, bringing its infant mortality rate down from 77.5 deaths per 1 000 live births in 1960 to 5.5 in 2000. Japan has also gone from a country previously in the bottom half of OECD countries in terms of its ranking on infant mortality in 1960 to currently being one of the countries with the lowest rates, along with historically low Nordic countries. Although infant mortality rates remain significantly higher than the OECD average in Mexico and Turkey, substantial reductions have also been achieved in these countries over the past decades. Neonatal deaths (deaths occurring in the first four weeks) can account for up to two-thirds of all infant mortality. Most neonatal deaths in developed countries are a result of congenital anomalies or premature birth. With the increasing age of motherhood and the rise in multiple pregnancies linked with fertility treatments, the number of premature births has tended to increase. For some countries with historically low infant mortality rates, such as in Nordic countries and western Europe, this has resulted in a levelling-off or reversal of the downward trend over the past few years.

Source

OECD (2004), *OECD Health Data 2004: A Comparative Analysis of 30 Countries*, OECD, Paris.

Further information
• *Analytical publications*

OECD (2002), *Measuring Up: Improving Health System Performance in OECD Countries*, OECD, Paris.

OECD (2003), *A Disease-based Comparison of Health Systems: What is Best and at What Cost?*, OECD, Paris.

OECD (2004), *Private Health Insurance in OECD Countries*, OECD Health Project, OECD, Paris.

OECD (2004), *Towards High-Performing Health Systems*, OECD Health Project, OECD, Paris.

OECD (2004), *Towards High-Performing Health Systems: Policy Studies*, OECD Health Project, OECD, Paris.

OECD (2005), *Long-term Care for Older People: Policy Issues for the 21st Century*, OECD, Paris.

OECD (2005), *Health Technology and Decision Making*, OECD Health Project, OECD, Paris.

• *Statistical publications*

OECD (2003), *Health at a Glance: OECD Indicators 2003*, OECD, Paris.

• *Methodological publications*

OECD (2000), *A System of Health Accounts*, OECD, Paris.

• *Online databases*

SourceOECD Health Data.

QUALITY OF LIFE • HEALTH

INFANT MORTALITY

Infant mortality
Deaths per 1 000 live births

	1960	1970	1980	1990	1995	1996	1997	1998	1999	2000	2001	2002
Australia	20.2	17.9	10.7	8.2	5.7	5.8	5.3	5.0	5.7	5.2	5.3	5.0
Austria	37.5	25.9	14.3	7.8	5.4	5.1	4.7	4.9	4.4	4.8	4.8	4.1
Belgium	31.2	21.1	12.1	8.0	6.1	5.6	6.1	5.6	4.9	4.8	4.5	4.9
Canada	27.3	18.8	10.4	6.8	6.0	5.6	5.5	5.3	5.3	5.3	5.2	..
Czech Republic	20.0	20.2	16.9	10.8	7.7	6.0	5.9	5.2	4.6	4.1	4.0	4.2
Denmark	21.5	14.2	8.4	7.5	5.1	5.6	5.2	4.7	4.2	5.3	4.9	4.4
Finland	21.0	13.2	7.6	5.6	3.9	4.0	3.9	4.2	3.6	3.8	3.2	3.0
France	27.5	18.2	10.0	7.3	4.9	4.8	4.7	4.6	4.3	4.6	4.5	4.1
Germany	35.0	22.5	12.4	7.0	5.3	5.0	4.9	4.7	4.5	4.4	4.3	4.3
Greece	40.1	29.6	17.9	9.7	8.1	7.2	6.4	6.7	6.2	6.1	5.1	5.9
Hungary	47.6	35.9	23.2	14.8	10.7	10.9	9.9	9.7	8.4	9.2	8.1	7.2
Iceland	13.0	13.2	7.7	5.9	6.1	3.7	5.5	2.6	2.4	3.0	2.7	2.2
Ireland	29.3	19.5	11.1	8.2	6.4	6.0	6.1	5.9	5.9	6.2	5.7	5.1
Italy	43.9	29.6	14.6	8.2	6.2	6.2	5.6	5.4	5.1	4.5	4.7	4.7
Japan	30.7	13.1	7.5	4.6	4.3	3.8	3.7	3.6	3.4	3.2	3.1	3.0
Korea	..	45.0	..	..	..	7.7	..	..	6.2	..	..	..
Luxembourg	31.5	24.9	11.5	7.3	5.5	4.9	4.2	5.0	4.6	5.1	5.9	5.1
Mexico	..	79.3	50.9	36.1	27.5	26.6	25.9	25.2	24.3	23.3	22.4	21.4
Netherlands	17.9	12.7	8.6	7.1	5.5	5.7	5.0	5.2	5.2	5.1	5.4	5.0
New Zealand	22.6	16.7	13.0	8.4	6.7	7.3	6.8	5.4	5.8	6.3	..	..
Norway	18.9	12.7	8.1	7.0	4.0	4.0	4.1	3.9	3.9	3.8	3.9	..
Poland	54.8	36.7	25.5	19.3	13.6	12.2	10.2	9.5	8.9	8.1	7.7	7.5
Portugal	77.5	55.5	24.3	11.0	7.5	6.9	6.4	6.0	5.6	5.5	5.0	5.0
Slovak Republic	28.6	25.7	20.9	12.0	11.0	10.2	8.7	8.8	8.3	8.6	6.2	7.6
Spain	43.7	28.1	12.3	7.6	5.5	5.5	5.0	4.9	4.5	3.9	3.5	3.4
Sweden	16.6	11.0	6.9	6.0	4.1	4.0	3.6	3.5	3.4	3.4	3.7	2.8
Switzerland	21.1	15.1	9.1	6.8	5.0	4.7	4.8	4.8	4.6	4.9	5.0	4.5
Turkey	189.5	145.0	117.5	57.6	45.6	44.0	42.4	42.7	43.3	41.9	40.6	39.4
United Kingdom	22.5	18.5	12.1	7.9	6.2	6.1	5.9	5.7	5.8	5.6	5.5	5.3
United States	26.0	20.0	12.6	9.2	7.6	7.3	7.2	7.2	7.1	6.9	6.8	..
OECD average (unweighted and excluding Korea)	36.8	26.6	16.8	10.3	7.9	7.4	7.1	6.9	6.6	6.6	6.3	..

StatLink: http://dx.doi.org/10.1787/054815728624

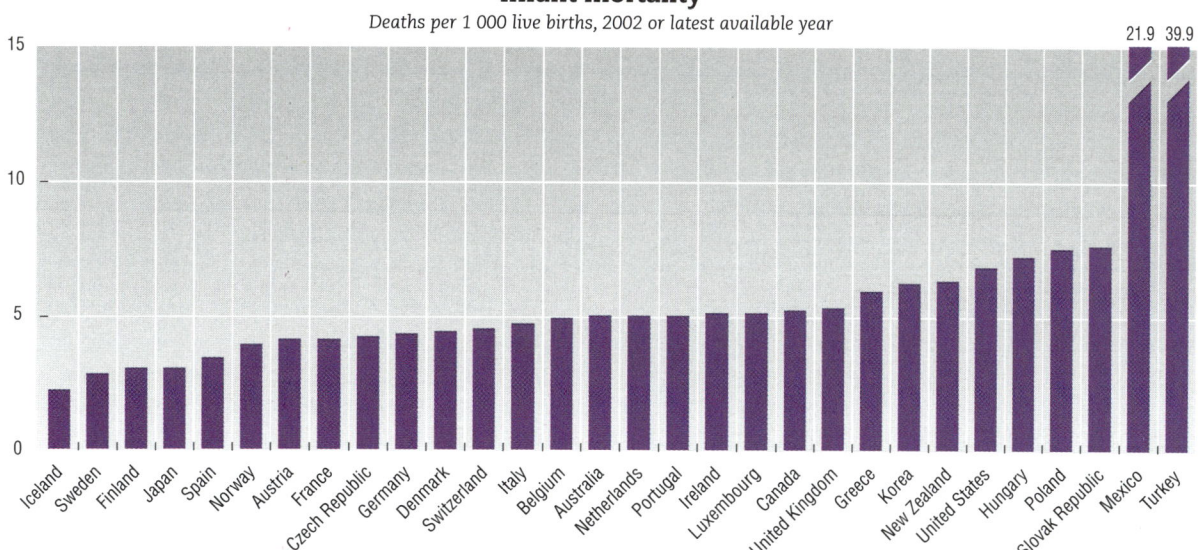

Infant mortality
Deaths per 1 000 live births, 2002 or latest available year

StatLink: http://dx.doi.org/10.1787/153212522571

QUALITY OF LIFE • HEALTH

OBESITY

Obesity is a known risk factor for several diseases such as diabetes, hypertension, cardiovascular disease, respiratory problems (asthma) and musculoskeletal diseases (arthritis). At an individual level, several factors can lead to obesity, including excessive calorie consumption, lack of physical activity, genetic predisposition and disorders of the endocrine system.

The economic and non-economic consequences of obesity are large. In the United States, a recent study looked at the relative consequences of obesity on various medical problems (such as diabetes and asthma) and related costs, in comparison with other risk factors such as smoking and alcohol consumption. The time lag between the onset of obesity and increases in chronic disease occurrence suggests that the large increase in obesity that has occurred in the United States and several other countries since 1980 will have substantial implications for future incidence of health problems and related spending.

Definition

Body mass index (BMI) is a single number that evaluates an individual's weight in relation to height (weight/height^2), with weight in kilograms and height in metres. Based on the WHO classification, individuals with a BMI over 30 are defined as obese.

Comparability

For most countries, data on obesity are self-reported and are collected in household surveys. The exceptions are Australia, the United Kingdom and the United States, where the data come from health examinations in which actual measures are taken of people's height and weight. These differences in data collection methodologies limit data comparability across countries. Estimates arising from health examinations are generally higher and more reliable than those coming from health interviews (because they preclude any misreporting), but health examination surveys are only conducted regularly in a few countries.

Long-term trends

Recent figures on the prevalence of obesity vary from lows of 3% and 4% in Korea and Japan, to a high of 31% in the United States. It should be noted however that this high estimate for the United States is based on health examinations whereby people's height and weight are measured (also the case for Australia and the United Kingdom), while data from other countries are based on self-reported information. For the United States, the adult obesity rate based on face-to-face interviews was 22% in 1999 (compared with 31% in that same year based on examinations), while the interview-based obesity rate in Australia was 18% in 2001 (compared with 21% in 1999 based on examinations).

Based on consistent measures of obesity over time (health examinations in the case of these three countries), the rate of obesity has more than doubled over the past 20 years in Australia and the United States, while it has tripled in the United Kingdom. As a result, more than 20% of the adult population in Australia and the United Kingdom are now defined as obese, the same rate as in the United States in the early 1990s. The obesity rate in Nordic countries and other European countries has also increased substantially over the past decade, but still remain lower than in English-speaking countries, even when differences in measurement methods are taken into account.

In most countries a higher percentage of women are obese than men.

Source

OECD (2004), *OECD Health Data 2004: A Comparative Analysis of 30 Countries*, OECD, Paris.

Further information
• *Analytical publications*

OECD (2002), *Measuring Up: Improving Health System Performance in OECD Countries*, OECD, Paris.

OECD (2003), *A Disease-based Comparison of Health Systems: What is Best and at What Cost?*, OECD, Paris.

OECD (2004), *Towards High-Performing Health Systems*, OECD Health Project, OECD, Paris.

• *Statistical publications*

OECD (2003), *Health at a Glance: OECD Indicators 2003*, OECD, Paris.

OECD (2004), *OECD Health Data 2004: A Comparative Analysis of 30 Countries*, also available on CD-ROM, OECD, Paris.

• *Web sites*

OECD Health Data: *www.oecd.org/health/healthdata*.

Session on Obesity and Health at the OECD Forum 2004: *www.oecd.org/forum2004*.

QUALITY OF LIFE • HEALTH

OBESITY

Obesity

Percentage of population aged 15 and above with a body mass index (BMI) greater than 30, 2003 or latest available year

		Females	Males	Total
Australia	1999	21.4	21.9	21.7
Austria	1999	9.1	9.1	9.1
Belgium	2001	12.2	11.1	11.7
Canada	2001	13.9	16.0	14.9
Czech Republic	2002	16.1	13.4	14.8
Denmark	2000	9.1	9.8	9.5
Finland	2003	11.7	14.0	12.8
France	2002	9.1	9.7	9.4
Germany	2003	12.3	13.6	12.9
Hungary	2000	18.5	18.0	18.2
Iceland	2002	12.4	12.4	12.4
Ireland	2002	12.0	14.0	13.0
Italy	2000	8.4	8.8	8.6
Japan	2002	3.8	3.4	3.6
Korea	2001	3.5	2.8	3.2
Luxembourg	2003	18.2	18.6	18.4
Mexico	2000	28.6	19.2	24.2
Netherlands	2002	11.0	9.0	10.0
New Zealand	1997	19.2	14.7	17.0
Norway	2002	8.2	8.4	8.3
Poland	1996	12.4	10.3	11.4
Portugal	1999	14.0	11.4	12.8
Slovak Republic	2002	25.4	18.8	22.4
Spain	2001	13.5	11.8	12.6
Sweden	2002	9.8	11.0	10.4
Switzerland	2002	7.5	7.9	7.7
United Kingdom	2002	22.8	22.1	22.4
United States	2002	33.3	27.8	30.6

StatLink: http://dx.doi.org/10.1787/710451128253

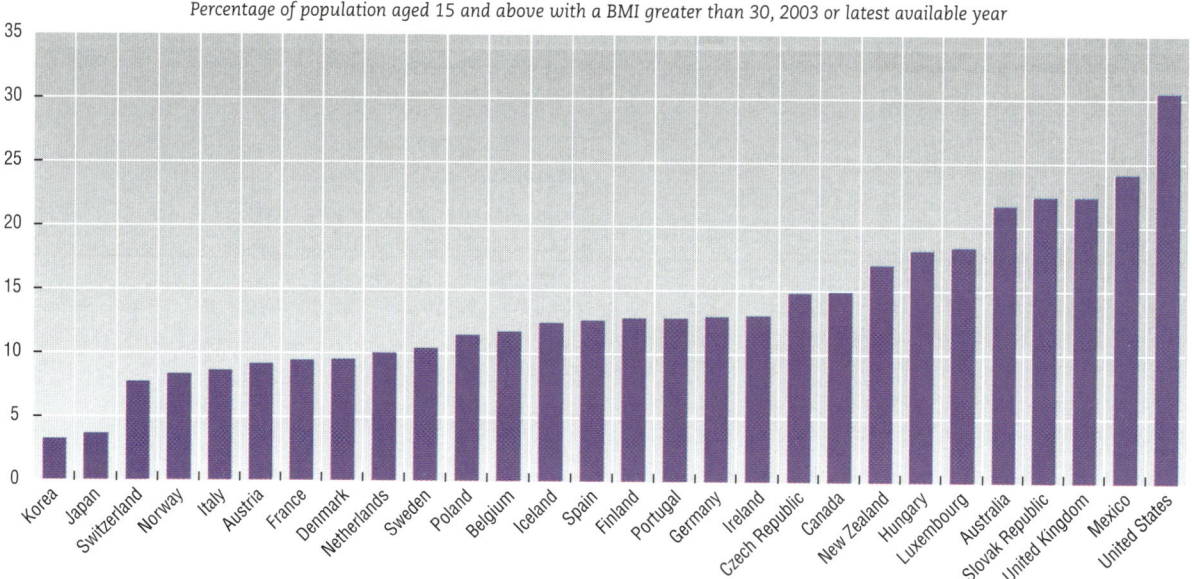

Obesity
Percentage of population aged 15 and above with a BMI greater than 30, 2003 or latest available year

StatLink: http://dx.doi.org/10.1787/501082745518

QUALITY OF LIFE • HEALTH

PUBLIC AND PRIVATE HEALTH EXPENDITURE

In most OECD countries, expenditures on health are large and are growing as a share of both public and private expenditure. The level of health spending varies considerably across countries, reflecting, among other factors, differences in price, volume and quality of medical goods and services consumed.

Definition

Total expenditure on health measures the final consumption of health care goods and services plus capital investment in health care infrastructure. This covers both public and private spending on medical services and goods, public health and prevention programmes and on the administration of medical faculties and programmes. Expenditures on training medical staff, on research and environmental health are excluded.

Comparability

The definition of total health expenditure can vary between countries: particular areas affecting the comparability are the treatment of long-term care, the degree of inclusion of expenditure of non-profit institutions and corporations, and the coverage of capital formation. For Australia and Japan, data shown for 2002 actually refer to 2001. For Turkey, data refer to 2000. The 1990 data for Germany refer to West Germany.

Health expenditure per capita, converted to US dollars using purchasing power parities (PPP), can be used to compare the overall level of consumption of health goods and services across countries. The economy-wide (GDP) PPPs are used as the most available and reliable conversion rates.

For Norway there is a change in methodology which affects the comparability between 1990 and 2002.

Long-term trends

In terms of total health spending per capita, the United States ranks way ahead of other OECD countries, spending over 50% more than the next highest spenders, Switzerland and Norway. At the other end of the scale, Turkey, Mexico, Poland, the Slovak Republic, Korea and Hungary all spent less than half the OECD average.

During the 1990s, there have been a number of changes in countries' positions relative to the OECD average in both total and public health spending per capita. For example, in 1990, Finland spent almost 20% more per capita than the OECD average, but by 2002 its spending level had dropped to less than 90% of the average. On the other hand, Ireland's public spending on health used to be 34% below the OECD average in 1990, but by 2002 it had surpassed the average by more than 10%. In general, many of the lower-income OECD countries have narrowed their gap from the OECD average, both in terms of total and public expenditure on health.

In many countries, the 1990s consisted of three different periods in terms of health expenditure growth rate. The first three years of the decade saw considerably higher growth than during the mid-1990s. Health expenditure started to rise again rapidly in many countries at the end of the 1990s and in the early part of this decade, reflecting deliberate policies in some countries to relieve pressures arising from cost containment in previous years.

In 2002, the public share of health spending stood at around 73% on average across OECD countries. It accounted for more than 80% of total health expenditure in several countries, including the Czech Republic, Norway, Sweden and the United Kingdom.

Source

OECD (2004), *OECD Health Data 2004: A Comparative Analysis of 30 Countries*, OECD, Paris.

Further information

• *Analytical publications*

OECD (2002), *Measuring Up: Improving Health System Performance in OECD Countries*, OECD, Paris.

OECD (2004), *Private Health Insurance in OECD Countries*, OECD Health Project, OECD, Paris.

OECD (2004), *Towards High-Performing Health Systems*, OECD Health Project, OECD, Paris.

OECD (2005), *Health Technology and Decision Making*, OECD Health Project, OECD, Paris.

• *Statistical publications*

OECD (2003), *Health at a Glance: OECD Indicators 2003*, OECD, Paris.

• *Methodological publications*

OECD (2000), *A System of Health Accounts*, OECD, Paris.

• *Online databases*

SourceOECD Health Data.

QUALITY OF LIFE • HEALTH

PUBLIC AND PRIVATE HEALTH EXPENDITURE

Total and public health expenditure
US dollars per capita, calculated using PPPs, 2002 or latest available year

	Total health expenditure per capita			Public expenditure on health per capita		
	US dollars	As a percentage of the OECD average		US dollars	As a percentage of the OECD average	
	2002	1990	2002	2002	1990	2002
Australia	2 504	109	119	1 708	94	113
Austria	2 220	112	100	1 551	114	98
Belgium	2 515	112	114	1 790	..	113
Canada	2 931	143	133	2 048	148	129
Czech Republic	1 118	46	51	1 022	62	64
Denmark	2 583	130	117	2 142	149	135
Finland	1 943	118	88	1 470	132	93
France	2 736	130	124	2 080	138	131
Germany	2 817	145	127	2 212	152	139
Greece	1 814	70	82	960	52	60
Hungary	1 079	..	49	757	..	48
Iceland	2 807	134	127	2 357	160	149
Ireland	2 367	66	107	1 779	66	112
Italy	2 166	117	98	1 639	128	103
Japan	2 077	92	99	1 696	99	112
Korea	996	28	45	519	15	33
Luxembourg	3 065	128	139	2 618	165	165
Mexico	553	24	25	249	14	16
Netherlands	2 643	119	120	..	110	..
New Zealand	1 857	83	84	1 447	94	91
Norway	3 409	116	154	2 845	133	179
Poland	654	25	30	474	32	30
Portugal	1 702	55	77	1 201	50	76
Slovak Republic	698	..	32	621	..	39
Spain	1 646	72	74	1 176	79	74
Sweden	2 517	131	114	2 148	163	135
Switzerland	3 446	171	156	1 995	123	126
Turkey	446	14	23	281	12	21
United Kingdom	2 160	82	98	1 801	94	113
United States	5 267	229	238	2 364	125	149

StatLink: http://dx.doi.org/10.1787/128754202605

Public and private expenditure on health
US dollars per capita, calculated using PPPs, 2002 or latest available year

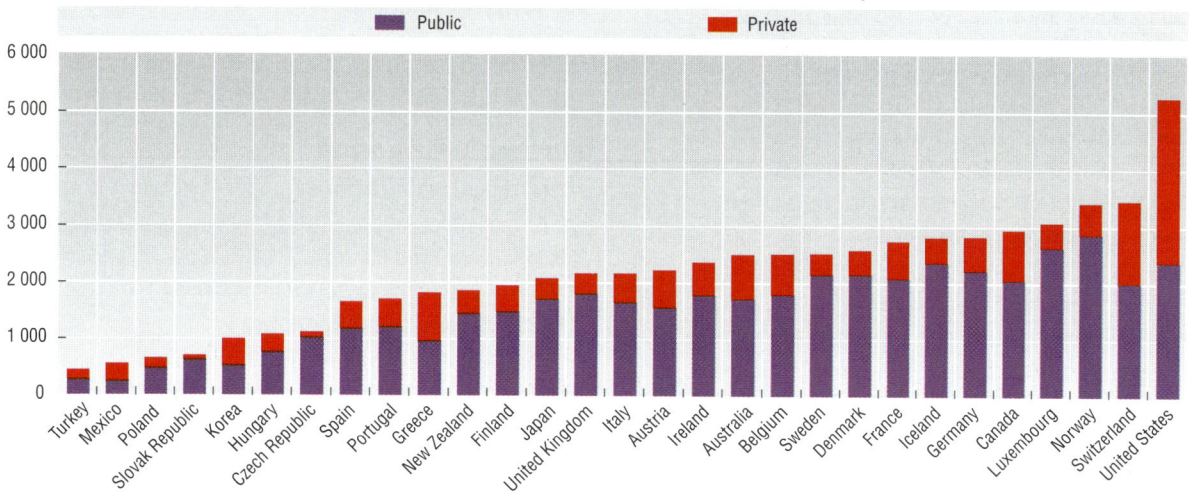

StatLink: http://dx.doi.org/10.1787/806145040581

HOURS WORKED

Governments of some OECD countries have pursued policies to make it easier for parents to reconcile work and family and some of these policies also tend to reduce working time. Examples include the extension of annual paid leave, maternity/parental leave and workers' options for working part-time schedules or, albeit less frequently, the reduction of the full-time workweek.

Definition

For this table, the total numbers of hours worked over the year are divided by the average numbers of people in employment. Data for Korea refer to hours worked by dependent employees only; data for other countries cover dependent and self-employed workers.

Employment is generally measured through household labour force surveys and, according to the *ILO Guidelines*, employed persons are defined as those aged 15 years or over who report that they have worked in gainful employment for at least one hour in the previous week.

Estimates of the hours actually worked are based on household labour force surveys in most countries, while the rest use establishment surveys, administrative sources or a combination of sources. They reflect regular work hours of full-time and part-time workers, over-time (paid and unpaid), hours worked in additional jobs and time not worked because of public holidays, annual paid leave, time spent on illness and maternity leave, strikes and labour disputes, bad weather, economic conditions and several other minor reasons.

Comparability

National statisticians and the OECD secretariat work to ensure that these data are as comparable as possible but they are based on a range of different sources of varying reliability. For example, for several EU countries the estimates are made by the secretariat using results from the Spring European Labour Force Survey. The results reflect a single observation in the year and the survey data have to be supplemented by information from other sources for hours not worked due to public holidays and annual paid leave. Annual working hours reported for the remaining countries are provided by national statistical offices and are estimated using the best available sources. The data are intended for comparisons of trends over time and are not yet suitable for inter-country comparisons because of differences in their sources and other uncertainties about their international comparability.

Long-term trends

In the large majority of OECD countries, hours worked have fallen over the period from 1990 to 2003. However, this decline was not particularly large in most countries, as compared to the decline in earlier decades and some of the decline in average hours between these two years may reflect transitory business cycle effects, since labour markets generally were more buoyant in 1990 (near the end of a long expansion in many OECD countries) than in 2003.

The average hours worked per year per employed person fell from 1 724 in 1990 to 1 649 in 2003; this is equivalent to a reduction in hours worked of nearly two 40-hour workweeks. The chart shows that working hours fell in a majority of countries; hours increased in only Denmark, Greece and Sweden (by a very small amount). Reductions in hours worked were most marked in France, Ireland, Japan and Portugal. With the exception of France, these were all countries that had rather high numbers of hours worked at the beginning of the period.

Although one should exercise caution when comparing between countries, it is clear from the table that actual hours worked in the Czech Republic, Greece, Korea, Mexico and Poland are above the average for OECD countries as a whole and that actual hours worked are relatively low in Denmark, France, Germany, Netherlands and Norway.

Source

OECD (2004), *OECD Employment Outlook*, OECD, Paris.

Further information

- *Analytical publications*

OECD (2004), "Clocking In and Clocking Out: Recent Trends in Working Hours", *OECD Policy Brief*, 19 October, www.oecd.org/dataoecd/42/49/33821328.pdf.

- *Methodological publications*

OECD (2004), "Clocking In (and Out): Several Facets of Working Time", *OECD Employment Outlook*, Chapter 1, see also Annex I.A1, OECD, Paris.

- *Web sites*

Labour Force Statistics database:
www.oecd.org/statistics/labour.

QUALITY OF LIFE • WORK AND LEISURE

HOURS WORKED

Actual hours worked
Hours per year per person in employment

	1990	1991	1992	1993	1994	1995	1996	1997	1998	1999	2000	2001	2002	2003
Australia	1 866	1 853	1 845	1 870	1 875	1 872	1 862	1 861	1 856	1 860	1 855	1 837	1 824	1 814
Austria	..	..	..	..	..	1 587	1 591	1 600	1 561	1 572	1 582	1 593	1 567	1 550
Belgium	1 690	1 656	1 640	1 601	1 603	1 627	1 602	1 614	1 618	1 546	1 524	1 548	1 547	1 542
Canada	1 743	1 722	1 715	1 718	1 735	1 730	1 739	1 751	1 753	1 759	1 752	1 749	1 731	1 718
Czech Republic	..	..	..	2 064	2 043	2 064	2 066	2 067	2 075	2 088	2 092	2 000	1 980	1 972
Denmark	1 452	1 442	1 463	1 430	1 495	1 459	1 463	1 476	1 467	1 496	1 467	1 495	1 462	1 475
Finland	1 771	1 749	1 755	1 756	1 777	1 776	1 775	1 771	1 761	1 765	1 750	1 734	1 727	1 713
France	1 610	1 600	1 600	1 588	1 582	1 558	1 562	1 556	1 545	1 540	1 496	1 475	1 437	1 431
Germany	..	1 541	1 557	1 537	1 536	1 520	1 502	1 496	1 489	1 479	1 463	1 450	1 443	1 446
Greece	1 919	1 920	1 947	1 965	1 935	1 926	1 944	1 928	1 933	1 947	1 921	1 928	1 928	1 938
Iceland	..	1 843	1 859	1 828	1 813	1 832	1 860	1 839	1 817	1 873	1 885	1 847	1 812	..
Ireland	1 911	1 882	1 843	1 823	1 824	1 823	1 826	1 783	1 713	1 692	1 687	1 680	1 666	1 613
Italy	1 655	1 649	1 636	1 622	1 619	1 620	1 623	1 623	1 620	1 617	1 613	1 601	1 599	1 591
Japan	2 031	1 998	1 965	1 905	1 898	1 884	1 892	1 864	1 842	1 810	1 821	1 809	1 798	1 801
Korea	2 514	2 498	2 478	2 477	2 471	2 484	2 467	2 436	2 390	2 497	2 474	2 447	2 410	2 390
Mexico	..	1 822	..	1 821	..	1 863	1 900	1 930	1 879	1 923	1 888	1 864	1 888	1 857
Netherlands	1 456	1 425	1 402	1 373	1 362	1 344	1 389	1 382	1 370	1 350	1 368	1 368	1 338	1 354
New Zealand	1 820	1 802	1 812	1 844	1 851	1 843	1 838	1 823	1 825	1 842	1 817	1 817	1 816	1 813
Norway	1 432	1 429	1 437	1 434	1 432	1 414	1 407	1 402	1 400	1 398	1 380	1 360	1 342	1 337
Poland	..	..	..	..	..	..	..	..	..	..	1 963	1 957	1 958	1 956
Portugal	1 858	1 787	1 768	1 756	1 744	1 799	1 753	1 723	1 720	1 734	1 691	1 696	1 697	1 676
Slovak Republic	..	..	..	..	1 975	2 003	2 023	2 055	2 034	2 022	2 017	2 026	1 979	1 814
Spain	1 824	1 833	1 825	1 816	1 816	1 815	1 810	1 813	1 834	1 816	1 814	1 816	1 813	1 800
Sweden	1 561	1 548	1 565	1 582	1 621	1 626	1 635	1 639	1 638	1 647	1 625	1 603	1 581	1 564
Switzerland	..	1 648	1 652	1 657	1 671	1 640	1 619	1 603	1 609	1 624	1 603	1 573	1 555	..
United Kingdom	1 767	1 768	1 729	1 723	1 737	1 739	1 738	1 737	1 731	1 719	1 708	1 711	1 692	1 673
United States	1 829	1 816	1 819	1 827	1 830	1 838	1 831	1 841	1 841	1 840	1 827	1 806	1 800	1 792

StatLink: http://dx.doi.org/10.1787/661822517874

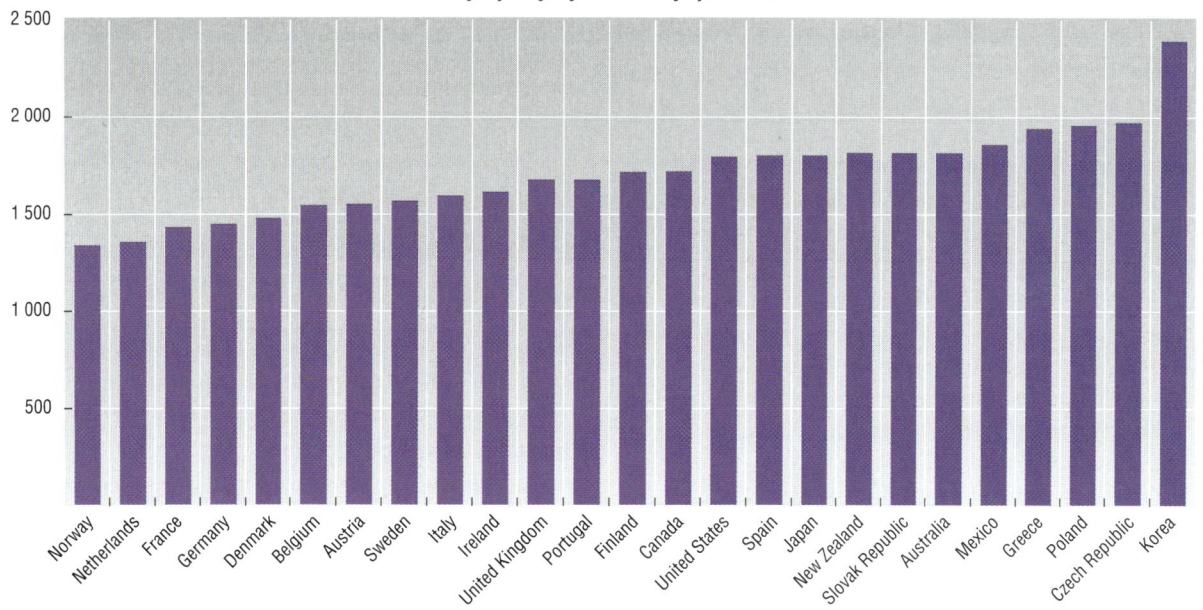

Actual hours worked
Hours per year per person in employment, 2003

StatLink: http://dx.doi.org/10.1787/342647085232

TOURISM: HOTEL NIGHTS

Arrivals of non-resident tourists is the standard measure of international tourism activity. It excludes tourists who take their holidays in their own country.

Definition

This statistic refers to the number of non-residents who arrive at the frontier and intend to stay at least one night in a hotel or similar establishment such as apartment-hotels, motels, roadside inns, beach hotels, residential clubs, boarding houses, and similar accommodation providing limited hotel services. Note that arrivals of non-resident tourists does not show the number of travellers. When a person visits the same country several times a year, each visit is counted as a separate arrival and if a person visits several countries during the course of a single trip, his/her arrival in each country is recorded as a separate arrival. Same day visitors are excluded as are tourists who stay with friends or relatives.

Comparability

Several OECD countries cannot provide statistics according to the standard definition given above. Australia, Canada, Japan and the United States report the number of non-residents arriving at their borders who intend to stay for at least one night, whether or not in a hotel or similar establishment. The figures for Korea and New Zealand are similar except that they also include same day visitors (very few in both countries).

Long-term trends

Over the period as a whole the United States recorded the largest number of arrivals followed by France, Italy and Spain. In general, the larger countries record the highest number of arrivals, although Austria and Greece are relatively small countries with a high number of arrivals, and Japan and Mexico are large countries but record relatively low numbers.

The 9/11 terrorist attacks resulted in sharp falls in arrivals in the United Kingdom and the United States but did not noticeably affect arrivals in most other countries. Countries in central and eastern Europe have recorded strong increases in arrivals since 1990.

Tourism 2020 Vision is the World Tourism Organization's (WTO-OMT) long-term forecast and assessment of the development of tourism up to the first 20 years of the new millennium. Although the evolution of tourism in the last few years has been irregular, WTO-OMT maintains its long-term forecast for the moment. The underlying structural trends of the forecast are believed not to have significantly changed. Experience shows that in the short term, periods of faster growth (1995, 1996, 2000) alternate with periods of slower growth (2001 and 2002).

WTO-OMT's *Tourism 2020 Vision* forecasts that international arrivals will reach over 1.56 billion by the year 2020. East Asia and the Pacific, south Asia, the Middle East and Africa are forecasted to record growth at rates of over 5% per year, compared to the world average of 4.1%. The more mature tourism regions, Europe and Americas, are expected to show lower than average growth rates. Europe will maintain the highest share of world arrivals, although there will be a decline from 60% in 1995 to 46% in 2020.

Sources

World Tourism Organization (WTO-OMT) and the Statistical Office of the European Communities (Eurostat).

Further information

• *Statistical publications*

Eurostat (2002), *Yearbook on Tourism Statistics*, Eurostat, Luxembourg.

WTO-OMT (2003), *Yearbook of Tourism Statistics 2003*, 55th edition, WTO Department of Statistics and Economic Measurement of Tourism, WTO-OMT, Madrid.

• *Methodological publications*

UN, Eurostat, OECD, WTO (2001), *Tourism Satellite Account: Recommended Methodological Framework*, OECD, Paris.

• *Web sites*

Eurostat: europa.eu.int/comm/eurostat

QUALITY OF LIFE • WORK AND LEISURE

TOURISM: HOTEL NIGHTS

Arrivals of non-resident tourists staying in hotels and similar establishments
Thousands

	1990	1991	1992	1993	1994	1995	1996	1997	1998	1999	2000	2001	2002	2003
Australia	2 215	2 370	2 603	2 996	3 362	3 726	4 165	4 318	3 825	4 109	4 530	4 435	4 420	..
Austria	13 827	13 616	13 664	13 032	12 878	12 464	12 533	12 329	12 803	12 755	13 240	13 279	13 487	13 748
Belgium	..	..	3 861	3 719	3 947	4 138	4 469	4 710	4 859	4 983	5 163	5 117	5 308	5 206
Canada	15 209	14 912	14 741	15 105	15 972	16 932	17 286	17 669	18 870	19 411	19 627	19 679	20 057	17 468
Czech Republic	..	..	..	..	2 448	2 891	3 696	4 013	4 067	4 141	3 863	4 439	4 314	4 485
Denmark	..	..	..	..	..	..	1 307	1 317	1 305	1 268	1 347	1 310	1 284	1 295
Finland	..	..	..	1 447	1 633	1 587	1 537	1 618	1 655	1 613	1 751	1 774	1 796	1 790
France	25 768	25 238	28 402	26 270	27 121	27 018	27 096	29 625	32 339	34 267	36 474	35 097	36 093	32 531
Germany	14 421	13 045	13 292	12 071	12 269	12 683	13 042	13 745	14 457	14 965	16 719	15 754	15 672	15 979
Greece	6 363	5 027	6 208	6 209	6 659	6 250	5 973	6 785	7 276	7 229	7 210	..	..	..
Hungary	..	..	..	..	2 122	2 116	2 202	2 188	2 472	2 401	2 604	2 669	2 659	..
Iceland	..	..	..	..	..	..	311	354	400	431	451	465	513	..
Ireland	1 652	1 673	1 598	1 643	1 901	..	..	..	3 077	3 343	5 491	3 577	..	..
Italy	17 924	17 061	17 366	17 919	21 074	23 467	24 929	25 133	25 927	26 530	28 797	29 138	29 340	..
Japan	3 236	3 533	3 582	3 410	3 468	3 345	3 837	4 218	4 106	4 438	4 757	4 772	5 239	..
Korea	2 959	3 196	3 231	3 331	3 580	3 753	3 684	3 908	4 250	4 660	5 322	5 147	5 347	4 754
Luxembourg	530	520	492	507	492	496	461	508	525	580	589	577	599	581
Mexico	4 882	5 032	4 805	5 174	5 159	6 718	7 491	8 155	8 157	9 501	9 867	9 410	7 869	..
Netherlands	3 903	3 687	3 900	3 778	4 456	4 797	4 999	6 163	7 432	7 550	7 738	7 445	7 433	..
New Zealand	976	963	1 056	1 157	1 323	1 409	1 529	1 497	1 485	1 607	1 787	1 909	2 045	2 104
Norway	1 955	2 114	2 375	2 556	2 830	2 880	2 746	2 702	3 256	3 223	3 104	3 073	3 107	..
Poland	..	1 939	2 210	2 315	2 540	2 792	3 020	2 919	2 695	1 982	2 505	2 488	2 536	..
Portugal	3 632	3 913	3 672	3 372	3 809	4 000	4 069	4 314	4 974	4 911	5 119	4 934	4 802	5 015
Slovak Republic	674	507	371	536	680	735	758	660	701	767	836	927	1 041	1 043
Spain	12 259	11 984	12 483	12 914	15 310	16 286	17 008	18 250	20 199	26 799	27 150	27 012	26 687	27 267
Sweden	1 697	1 580	1 572	1 629	1 830	1 995	2 091	2 143	2 304	2 320	2 465	2 586	2 577	2 557
Switzerland	7 963	7 400	7 528	7 225	7 358	6 946	6 730	7 039	7 185	7 154	7 821	7 455	6 868	..
Turkey	3 760	2 361	3 683	4 053	3 706	4 509	6 331	9 290	7 435	4 805	6 789	8 769	9 859	..
United Kingdom	12 931	12 293	13 306	14 259	14 927	17 118	16 890	17 110	16 304	17 019	17 019	17 019	14 176	13 542
United States	39 362	42 674	47 261	45 779	44 749	43 318	46 489	47 752	46 396	48 492	50 945	44 898	41 892	..

StatLink: http://dx.doi.org/10.1787/587055654400

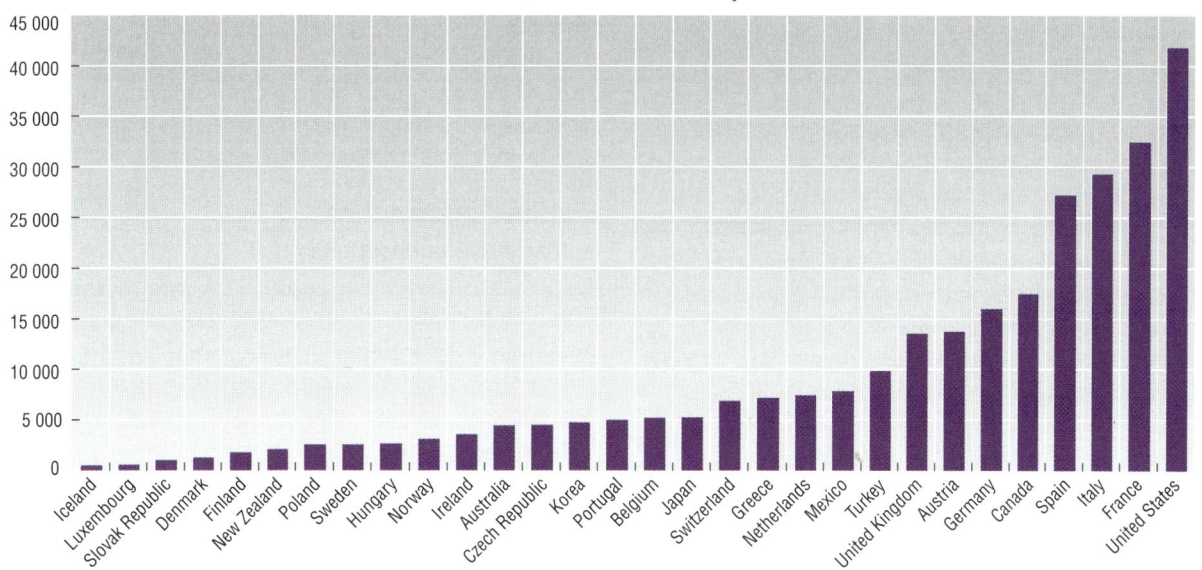

Arrivals of non-resident tourists staying in hotels and similar establishments
Thousands, 2003 or latest available year

StatLink: http://dx.doi.org/10.1787/052170373365

QUALITY OF LIFE • CRIME

PRISON POPULATION

Crime causes great suffering to victims and their families, but the costs associated with imprisonment can also be considerable. These costs are normally justified by reference to a combination of three societal "needs": to inflict retribution; to deter others from behaving in a similar way; and to prevent re-offending.

Definition

Not everyone in prison has been found guilty of a crime, especially those awaiting trial or adjudication. The indicator here considers only those sentenced to incarceration, excluding pre-trial and non-guilty offenders. The numbers of prisoners are shown per 100 000 population.

Comparability

The data are collected for a typical day that can be considered representative of the whole year. This information is collected by the United Nations as part of its work on the operation of criminal justice systems.

Long-term trends

Since the 1970s, OECD countries have experienced steady increases in prison population, with the exception of Finland where the rate has continued to decline. Over the last ten years, Portugal has recorded one of the largest increases together with Spain among European countries, though levels remain far below the United States. In this country, the prison population has witnessed a huge jump that bears no historical comparison, with a population in 2000 four times as high as in the early 1970s. Differences across countries have, surprisingly, only little to do with the prevalence and developments of crimes but more likely to do with political factors and responses to the increasing belief in certain countries that prison is preferable to other alternatives.

When comparing prison populations in 2000, again the United States stands far above the norm with an incarceration rates five times as high as the OECD average and three times larger than the Czech Republic, ranking second. More than 1.2 million convicted American adults are in gaol (a little less than 2 million when pre-trial and non-guilty offenders are included), which may have a significant distorting role on the labour market for young males. Rising prison populations, unless fully resourced, generally reduce the effectiveness of criminal re-education. Upward trends can pull down the staff-prisoner ratio, a key component for framing effective prevention of re-offending and promoting reintegration in the community. Moreover, prison overcrowding tends to exacerbate already high levels of tensions and violence, raising the risks of self-injury and suicide. Finally and unfortunately, overcrowded prisons are more likely to act as "universities of crime".

Source

United Nations (2002), "Seventh Survey on Crime Trends and the Operations of Criminal Justice Systems (1998-2000)", UN Office on Drugs and Crime, *www.unodc.org/unodc/crime_cicp_surveys.html*.

Further information
• Analytical publications

OECD (2003), *Society at a Glance: OECD Social Indicators*, OECD, Paris.

Walmsley, R. (2003), "Global Incarceration and Prison Trends", *Forum on Crime and Society*, Vol. 3, UNODC, Vienna.

• Web sites

OECD Social and Welfare Statistics: *www.oecd.org/statistics/social*.

United Nations Office on Drugs and Crime: *www.unodc.org*.

QUALITY OF LIFE • CRIME

PRISON POPULATION

Convicted adults admitted to prisons
Number per 100 000 population

	1990	1991	1992	1993	1994	1995	1996	1997	1998	1999	2000
Australia	133.5	149.6	160.6	148.0	133.2	85.4	86.8	89.3	91.1	96.5	93.4
Austria	56.1	52.6	58.0	55.6	62.0	..	..	..	..	..	..
Belgium	30.6	27.6	35.2	37.5	37.2	..	..	..	..	..	..
Czech Republic	38.2	69.1	75.7	82.8	94.6	109.6	124.4	132.5	143.5	155.3	150.1
Denmark	45.2	48.4	44.7	46.3	49.6	48.5	44.6	44.9	42.7	44.5	42.9
England and Wales	..	..	..	..	..	..	..	..	89.7	88.1	90.2
Finland	55.9	54.9	56.6	52.3	49.2	56.1	47.6	46.3	47.9	46.4	49.6
Germany	..	..	..	..	..	50.9	53.3	55.9	61.3	64.0	65.0
Greece	34.0	32.4	38.2	44.2	36.2	34.1	31.2	..	..	..	..
Hungary	80.9	94.1	105.8	87.1	83.3	..	85.2	91.6	97.7	103.7	109.0
Iceland	..	..	..	..	..	35.5	36.7	32.4	31.0	29.6	22.1
Ireland	51.2	52.8	52.2	52.0	..	51.9	52.9	59.1	..	..	..
Italy	19.4	24.6	34.6	39.2	44.4	45.2	46.5	46.6	46.3	49.0	50.8
Japan	32.3	30.5	30.0	29.9	30.0	30.8	32.1	33.1	34.3	35.7	39.3
Korea	67.7	70.6	72.1	75.6	75.8	71.1	69.8	71.7	75.9	79.7	78.6
Luxembourg	68.1	71.8	65.5	73.4	75.0	..	..	..	..	..	..
Mexico	44.4	47.7	50.4	51.3	50.2	..	..	..	78.3	84.2	92.9
Netherlands	..	..	..	..	..	43.0	48.0	46.6	39.4	38.5	34.8
New Zealand	..	..	..	..	..	115.0	..	131.2	128.0	128.0	132.3
Norway	..	..	..	..	..	36.1	35.2	32.0	29.8	..	..
Poland	81.6	104.1	114.9	114.6	113.3	..	..	..	..	..	..
Portugal	61.6	46.4	58.5	67.6	62.1	72.1	85.8	96.9	100.6	85.2	85.4
Slovak Republic	52.2	85.7	91.8	97.2	99.9	108.9	110.0	104.4	90.9	90.2	91.6
Spain	..	..	..	..	..	84.2	77.5	77.1	107.4	108.4	110.7
Sweden	49.3	49.0	50.7	53.8	58.5	50.5	48.0	41.3	..	..	..
Switzerland	55.4	56.3	56.5	60.5	63.4	60.1	59.1	58.5	45.4	45.7	48.4
Turkey	51.3	18.5	21.8	25.4	33.5	41.9	49.8	55.4	58.2	61.9	33.8
United States	143.2	..	160.0	..	..	..	..	..	452.9	469.1	468.5

StatLink: http://dx.doi.org/10.1787/785275234760

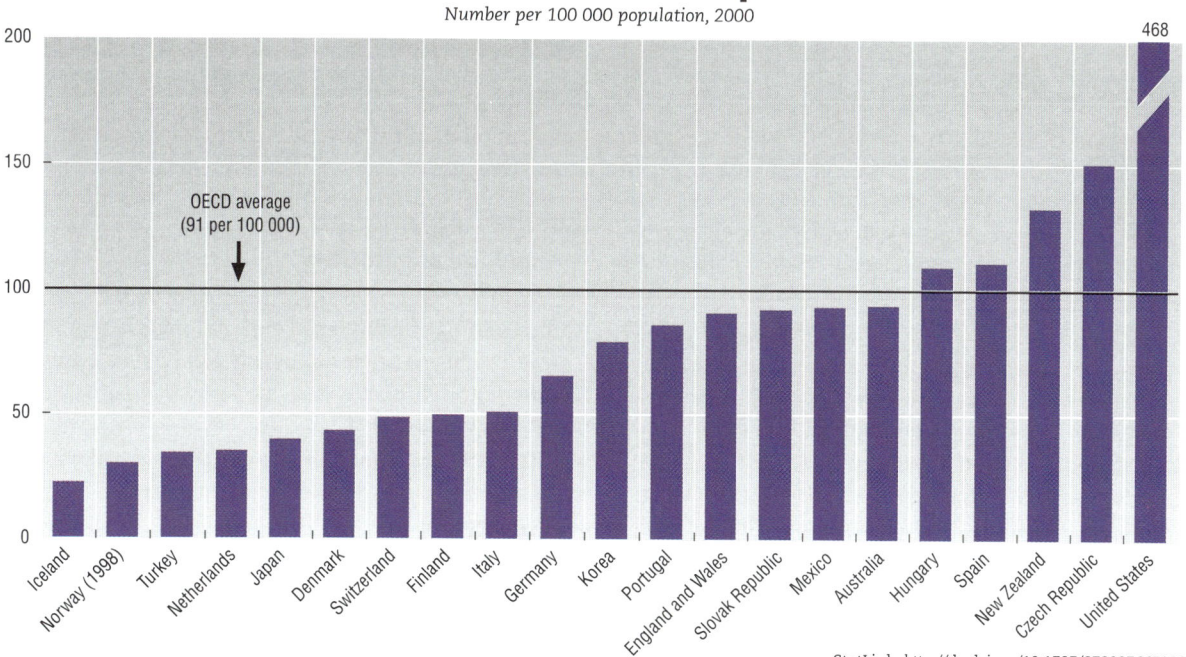

Convicted adults admitted to prisons
Number per 100 000 population, 2000

StatLink: http://dx.doi.org/10.1787/878027667088

QUALITY OF LIFE • CRIME

VICTIMISATION RATES

Definition

Using official records of crimes reported to the authorities may not be a very useful way of comparing crime rates across countries in view of the differences in policy on registering "trivial crime" between judicial systems and of individuals to report such incidences which they do not believe likely to be pursued. For crimes with an individual as opposed to a corporate victim, a more effective approach may be to ask people whether they have been victims of crime over a given period. A number of OECD countries participate in just such a study – the *International Crime Victims Survey*.

Comparability

Comparing the survey results with reported crime figures suggests that thefts of cars and burglaries both have about 80% reporting rates, on average. However, assault and especially sexual offences are heavily under-reported in most countries.

The *International Crime Victims Survey* uses standard questionnaires and survey methods in all participating countries. The results are broadly comparable.

Long-term trends

For those countries where comparable information is available, a majority have shown an increase in the proportion of people who were victims of a crime over the previous 12 months. Particularly large increases took place in England and Wales and Japan. However, there are a number of exceptions; most notably, four of the countries with particularly high crime rates in the late 1980s have experienced declines of some sort since then: Canada, the Netherlands, Poland and (especially) the United States. Across countries for which data are available, Australia, England and Wales and the Netherlands had the highest proportion (over 25%) of respondents that reported themselves as having been victims of crime over the preceding 12 months. Rates for Japan, Northern Ireland and Portugal barely exceeded 15% in 2000.

These high rates of people reporting being victims of crime reflect, in large part, high rates of vehicle-related crimes – particularly vandalism (more than 5% of the population in OECD countries experience car vandalism, other than those in Nordic countries, Japan and Switzerland). Thefts from cars are also very common in some countries.

People are particularly fearful of contact crime (robbery, assault and sexual assault). Such crimes are least common in Japan and Portugal. Over 6% of the population experience assaults and threats in Australia and the Great Britain. Indeed, Australia has one of the highest rates of all the different contact crimes. The incidence of sexual incidents is highest in Australia, Austria and the Netherlands.

Source

International Crime Victims Surveys, March 2002, *www.unicri.it/icvs*.

Further information

• *Analytical publications*

del Frate, A. Alvazzi (2003), "The Voice of Victims of Crime: Estimating the True Level of Conventional Crime"; *Forum on Crime and Society*, Vol. 3, Nos. 1 and 2, December, UNODC, Vienna, *www.unodc.org/pdf/crime/forum/forum3_note4.pdf*.

OECD (2003), *Society at a Glance: OECD Social Indicators*, OECD, Paris.*www.oecd.org/els/social/indicators*.

• *Web sites*

OECD Social and Welfare Statistics: *www.oecd.org/statistics/social*.

United Nations Office on Drugs and Crime: *www.unodc.org*.

QUALITY OF LIFE • CRIME

VICTIMISATION RATES

Population victimised at least once
As a percentage of total population, 2000 or latest available year

	Vehicle-related crimes					Contact crimes and burglaries			
	Car vandalism	Car theft	Theft from car	Motorcycle theft	Bicycle theft	Assaults and threats	Sexual incidents	Burglaries	Robberies
Australia	9.2	1.9	6.8	0.1	2.0	6.4	4.0	3.9	1.2
Austria	6.7	0.1	1.6	0.0	3.3	2.1	3.8	0.9	0.2
Belgium	6.1	0.7	3.6	0.3	3.5	3.2	1.1	2.0	1.0
Canada	5.5	1.4	5.4	0.1	3.5	5.3	2.1	2.3	0.9
Denmark	3.8	1.1	3.4	0.7	6.7	3.6	2.5	3.1	0.7
England and Wales	8.8	2.1	6.4	0.4	2.4	6.1	2.7	2.8	1.2
Finland	3.7	0.4	2.9	0.1	4.9	4.2	3.7	0.3	0.6
France	8.2	1.7	5.5	0.3	1.8	4.2	1.1	1.0	1.1
West Germany	8.7	0.4	4.7	0.2	3.3	3.1	2.8	1.3	0.8
Italy	7.6	2.7	7.0	1.5	2.3	0.8	1.7	2.4	1.3
Japan	4.4	0.1	1.6	1.0	6.6	0.4	1.2	1.1	0.1
Netherlands	8.9	0.4	3.9	0.6	7.0	3.4	3.0	1.9	0.8
New Zealand	7.9	2.7	6.9	0.3	4.4	5.7	2.7	4.3	0.7
Northern Ireland	4.5	1.2	2.7	0.0	1.4	3.0	0.6	1.7	0.1
Norway	4.6	1.1	2.8	0.3	2.8	3.0	2.2	0.7	0.5
Poland	7.0	1.0	5.5	0.1	3.6	2.8	0.5	2.0	1.8
Portugal	6.3	0.9	4.9	0.3	0.8	0.9	0.6	1.4	1.1
Scotland	9.0	0.7	4.2	0.1	2.0	6.1	1.1	1.5	0.7
Spain	6.6	1.4	9.6	0.8	1.1	3.1	2.3	1.6	3.1
Sweden	4.6	1.3	5.3	0.4	7.2	3.8	2.6	1.7	0.9
Switzerland	3.9	0.3	1.7	0.2	4.7	2.4	2.1	1.1	0.7
United States	7.2	0.5	6.4	0.3	2.1	3.4	1.5	1.8	0.6

StatLink: http://dx.doi.org/10.1787/718818238777

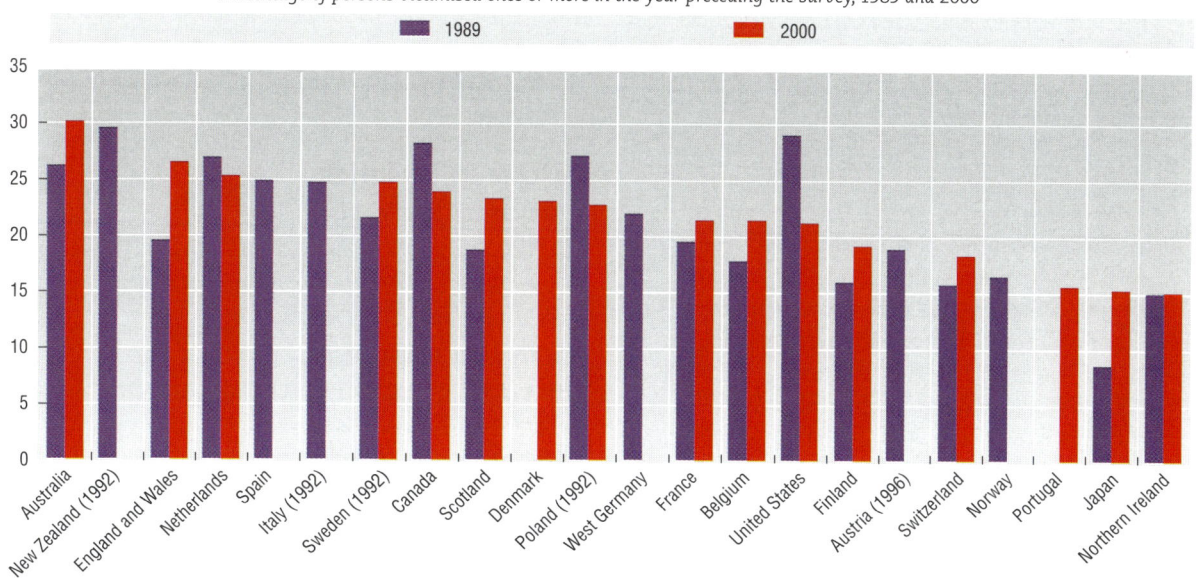

Variation in number of crimes reported across OECD countries
Percentage of persons victimised once or more in the year preceding the survey, 1989 and 2000

StatLink: http://dx.doi.org/10.1787/018106032634

ROAD MOTOR VEHICLES AND ROAD FATALITIES

The number of road motor vehicles is high and rising among OECD countries, and reducing road accidents is a concern in all countries. The tables in this section show the numbers of road motor vehicles per thousand inhabitants and two indicators of road safety – the number of road fatalities per million inhabitants and the number of road fatalities per million vehicles.

Long-term trends

Ratios of motor vehicles to population range from over 800 per thousand inhabitants in the United States to about 150 in Turkey. Over the periods shown in the table, ratios of vehicle to population increased in all countries except Canada, Korea and the United States. The ratios more than doubled in the Czech Republic, Portugal and Turkey and sharp increases also occurred in Greece and Poland.

In 2002, road fatalities per million inhabitants ranged from over 160 per million inhabitants in Portugal to less than 60 in Turkey. Over the periods shown in the table, rates have increased in the Czech Republic, Iceland, Italy and the Slovak Republic but have been falling in all other countries with particularly sharp falls in Germany, New Zealand, Switzerland and Turkey.

Accident rates per million inhabitants are an ambiguous indicator of road safety since the number of accidents depends to a great extent on the number of vehicles in each country. The last chart shows the number of fatalities per million vehicles together with fatalities per million inhabitants. Both ratios refer to 2002. Rates per million vehicles are affected by driving habits, traffic legislation and the effectiveness of its enforcement, road design and other factors over which governments may exercise control. In 2002, fatality rates per million vehicles were less than 130 in the United Kingdom, Norway, Netherlands, Japan, Sweden and Switzerland, but exceeded 400 in Poland, Hungary and Korea. Note that low fatality rates per million inhabitants may be associated with very high fatality rates per million vehicles. For example, a country with a small vehicle population could show a low fatality rate per million inhabitants and a high fatality rate per vehicle.

Definitions

A road motor vehicle is a vehicle running on wheels and intended for use on roads with an engine providing its sole means of propulsion and which is normally used for carrying persons or goods or for drawing, on the road, vehicles used for the carriage of persons or goods. Thus buses, coaches, freight vehicles and motor cycles are included as well as passenger motor cars. Road motor vehicles running on rails are excluded.

A fatality means any person killed immediately or dying within 30 days as a result of an accident.

Comparability

Road motor vehicles are attributed to the countries where they are registered while deaths are attributed to the countries in which they occur. As a result, ratios of fatalities to million inhabitants and of fatalities to million vehicles cannot strictly be interpreted as indicating the proportion of a country's population that is at risk of suffering a fatal road accident or the likelihood of a vehicle registered in a given country being involved in a fatal accident. In practice, however, this is not considered to be a serious problem because discrepancies between the numerators and denominators tend to cancel out.

The numbers of vehicles entering the existing stock is usually accurately but information on the numbers of vehicles withdrawn from use is less certain. This is believed to be especially a problem in countries of central and eastern Europe but statistics on the numbers of road motor vehicles in use can be considered reliable in most OECD countries.

Source

ECMT (2004), *Trends in the Transport Sector: 1970-2002*, ECMT, Paris.

Further information

• *Analytical publications*

ECMT (2004), *ECMT Annual Report 2003*, ECMT, Paris

ECMT (2004), *Road Safety Performance: National Peer Review: Lithuania*, ECMT, Paris.

• *Statistical publications*

ECMT (2003), *Statistical Report on Road Accidents in 1999-2000*, ECMT, Paris.

• *Methodological publications*

UNECE, ECMT, Eurostat (2003), *Glossary for Transport Statistics*, ECMT, Paris, www.oecd.org/cem/online/glossaries.

• *Web sites*

European Conference of Ministers of Transport: www.oecd.org/cem.

QUALITY OF LIFE • TRANSPORT

ROAD MOTOR VEHICLES AND ROAD FATALITIES

Road motor vehicles
Per thousand population

	1990	1991	1992	1993	1994	1995	1996	1997	1998	1999	2000	2001	2002
Australia	..	..	..	..	..	603	599	591	626	629	623	625	634
Austria	462	463	503	515	528	543	495	509	529	544	555	565	537
Belgium	432	442	441	454	464	487	494	482	490	500	511	517	520
Canada	600	619	627	595	569	565	565	564	580	566	569	572	581
Czech Republic	..	..	166	434	455	333	383	383	369	373	373	383	394
Denmark	371	367	370	373	374	386	398	406	411	420	421	425	428
France	503	504	505	509	518	520	526	532	548	559	573	583	587
Finland	447	441	445	425	422	427	434	436	451	465	476	481	488
Germany	527	527	427	478	523	540	547	551	556	564	570	582	589
Greece	248	246	257	271	283	298	313	328	351	378	406	428	450
Hungary	211	208	216	232	239	253	257	262	255	261	270	283	300
Iceland	484	..	..	..	433	453	467	554	574	609	636	629	645
Ireland	279	283	286	295	305	318	348	367	387	409	425	442	445
Italy	557	556	556	562	562	573	581	586	603	622	632	656	660
Japan	..	..	..	507	520	537	566	575	580	586	592	596	600
Korea	..	..	..	..	..	..	..	..	254	236	237	243	243
Luxembourg	532	549	542	580	580	625	669	675	671	666	693	719	728
Netherlands	411	412	414	419	426	430	443	450	464	461	478	496	504
New Zealand	..	..	..	645	649	658	654	636	643	659	679	684	688
Norway	460	457	458	461	465	474	467	491	498	503	511	516	516
Poland	..	..	204	210	222	231	250	285	296	309	333	349	368
Portugal	310	370	407	439	438	501	533	569	610	654	698	711	756
Slovak Republic	..	..	..	248	247	213	217	232	245	253	259	291	291
Spain	372	394	412	422	419	447	464	481	502	526	541	557	567
Sweden	457	456	452	444	442	447	450	456	468	481	494	497	500
Switzerland	489	494	494	487	492	498	504	511	518	528	536	545	551
Turkey	57	47	53	61	64	68	97	105	111	116	124	148	148
United Kingdom	443	433	453	441	439	428	448	458	474	486	493	516	533
United States	842	718	779	725	719	771	783	784	792	798	810	816	807

StatLink: http://dx.doi.org/10.1787/578605407765

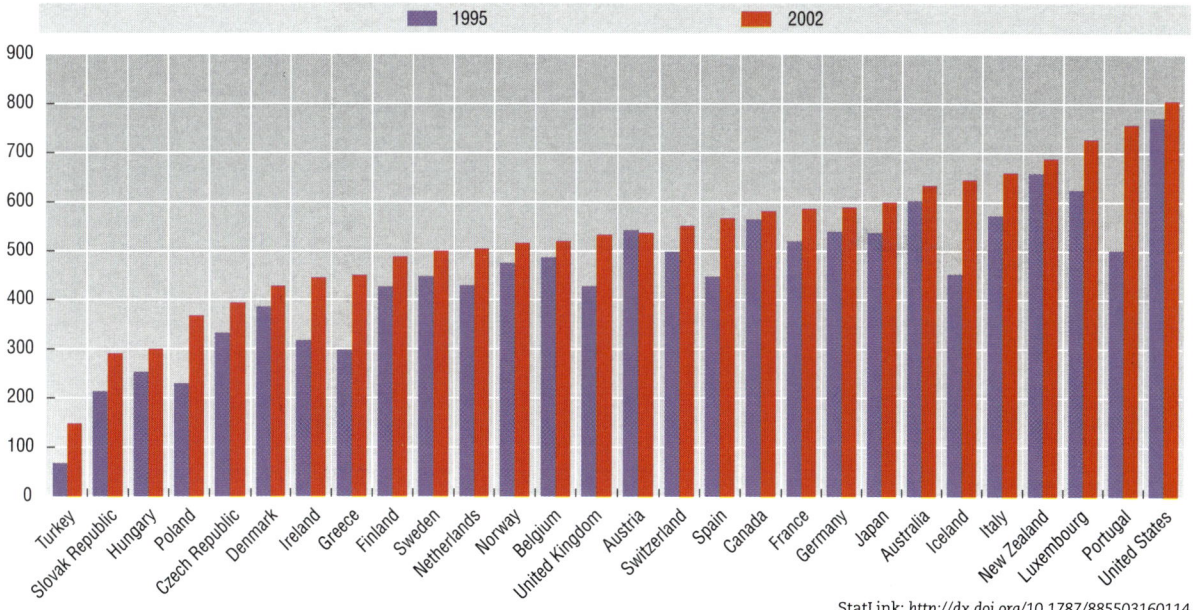

Road motor vehicles
Per thousand population

StatLink: http://dx.doi.org/10.1787/885503160114

QUALITY OF LIFE • TRANSPORT

ROAD MOTOR VEHICLES AND ROAD FATALITIES

Road fatalities
Per million population

	1990	1991	1992	1993	1994	1995	1996	1997	1998	1999	2000	2001	2002
Australia	137	123	113	111	109	111	108	95	94	93	95	90	88
Austria	200	199	177	161	167	150	127	137	121	135	122	119	119
Belgium	199	187	166	165	167	143	134	134	147	136	143	144	127
Canada	150	135	128	125	111	113	103	101	97	97	95	89	93
Czech Republic	125	129	150	147	158	154	155	155	132	141	145	130	140
Denmark	123	117	111	108	105	111	98	93	94	97	93	80	86
France	182	168	158	157	147	144	138	136	143	136	129	130	121
Finland	130	126	119	95	94	86	79	85	78	83	76	83	80
Germany	176	176	131	123	121	116	107	104	95	95	91	85	83
Greece	195	197	193	193	199	195	198	204	207	201	193	178	154
Hungary	235	195	193	163	152	155	135	137	136	130	118	122	141
Iceland	96	..	..	..	89	90	37	55	98	75	113	84	101
Ireland	139	126	118	122	113	123	125	129	124	110	110	107	96
Italy	115	130	129	116	115	114	108	108	110	116	115	117	117
Japan	..	..	..	106	102	100	93	89	85	82	82	79	75
Korea	..	..	..	..	..	..	..	..	226	232	218	171	149
Luxembourg	185	208	188	191	186	165	172	132	134	133	172	159	140
Netherlands	92	85	84	82	84	86	76	74	68	69	68	62	61
New Zealand	217	191	188	172	164	162	141	144	132	134	121	118	103
Norway	91	76	76	65	65	70	58	69	79	68	76	61	61
Poland	193	207	182	165	175	179	165	189	183	174	163	143	151
Portugal	234	251	240	210	195	210	241	222	213	200	186	161	165
Slovak Republic				109	118	123	115	146	152	122	120	116	116
Spain	179	174	154	163	146	147	139	142	150	144	143	135	129
Sweden	90	86	88	72	67	65	61	61	60	65	67	65	63
Switzerland	141	126	121	104	97	98	87	83	84	81	82	75	70
Turkey	125	109	106	108	97	97	86	81	76	69	58	58	58
United Kingdom	94	82	78	68	65	64	63	63	59	59	59	60	60
United States	188	165	154	156	156	159	158	158	155	153	152	148	148

StatLink: http://dx.doi.org/10.1787/554064521018

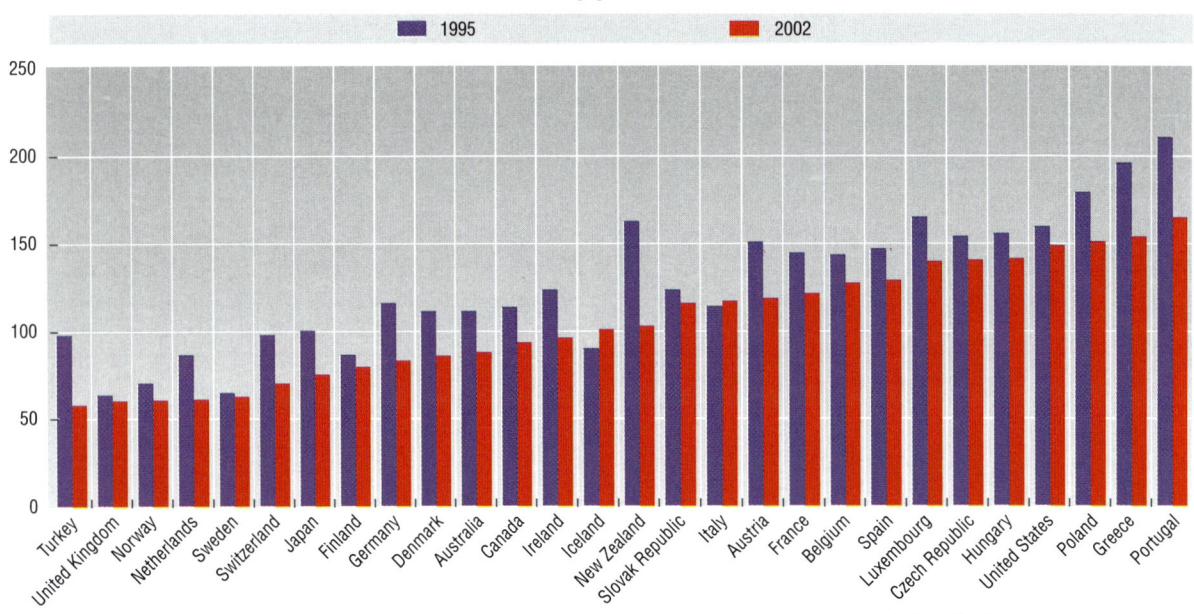

Road fatalities
Per million population, 2002

StatLink: http://dx.doi.org/10.1787/885503160114

QUALITY OF LIFE • TRANSPORT

ROAD MOTOR VEHICLES AND ROAD FATALITIES

Road fatalities
Per million vehicles

	1990	1991	1992	1993	1994	1995	1996	1997	1998	1999	2000	2001	2002
Australia	..	..	..	..	..	183.9	179.9	161.5	149.5	147.7	152.8	143.2	138.4
Austria	433.0	428.8	352.8	311.9	315.5	277.0	257.1	269.0	228.1	247.8	219.3	210.9	220.5
Belgium	459.3	423.0	376.5	362.2	359.8	293.6	270.2	278.0	299.9	272.7	280.5	279.0	244.0
Canada	250.1	218.8	205.0	209.5	195.8	200.1	182.1	178.9	166.9	172.2	167.1	156.4	160.4
Czech Republic	..	..	905.6	339.6	348.2	461.4	404.4	404.4	358.5	379.5	388.4	338.9	356.2
Denmark	332.1	320.1	300.7	288.6	280.6	287.1	245.6	228.2	228.0	230.5	221.0	189.1	201.1
France	361.5	333.6	312.6	307.4	284.1	277.7	262.7	255.5	261.1	242.6	226.0	223.1	206.1
Finland	290.6	284.9	267.0	224.5	223.2	202.2	181.2	195.4	171.7	179.4	160.6	173.2	163.4
Germany	334.6	335.1	307.3	257.1	230.6	214.1	195.5	188.9	170.9	167.7	159.9	145.5	140.8
Greece	787.2	798.3	753.1	715.1	704.4	656.3	630.7	622.4	591.3	531.7	476.0	414.4	341.7
Hungary	1114.1	936.4	895.2	702.7	635.7	613.5	523.9	523.3	532.8	498.5	436.5	430.1	469.4
Iceland	198.3	..	..	..	205.1	198.3	79.4	100.0	170.9	123.5	177.8	133.3	155.9
Ireland	495.9	445.9	411.7	414.8	371.0	387.0	359.5	350.9	319.7	269.5	258.0	242.3	215.8
Italy	206.4	233.7	231.7	207.2	205.1	198.5	185.5	184.7	182.6	186.6	181.9	178.8	177.0
Japan	186.5	185.9	186.2	209.7	196.4	186.3	163.9	155.0	147.2	139.6	138.4	132.5	125.2
Korea	..	..	..	..	..	..	..	..	891.8	983.4	919.5	702.9	612.7
Luxembourg	348.3	379.1	346.0	329.0	320.3	263.6	257.1	195.8	199.3	200.0	248.4	221.5	192.0
Netherlands	223.1	207.5	203.9	194.6	197.5	200.8	171.3	165.1	145.7	148.9	141.6	124.5	120.8
New Zealand	..	..	..	267.4	253.4	246.7	216.0	225.7	205.7	202.6	177.6	172.8	149.1
Norway	197.1	165.7	165.7	141.5	140.1	147.6	124.2	139.6	159.1	134.9	148.1	117.7	117.7
Poland	..	..	890.5	783.6	789.1	775.2	658.1	662.3	618.4	563.4	489.7	411.0	409.4
Portugal	757.5	677.0	590.9	479.1	444.3	419.5	452.1	390.7	349.7	305.3	265.7	226.9	217.6
Slovak Republic	..	..	588.7	441.4	477.7	577.9	527.9	629.9	620.0	481.3	463.2	396.8	396.8
Spain	480.4	442.7	373.7	385.8	347.8	327.8	300.7	295.6	298.7	273.1	264.5	242.3	227.1
Sweden	196.7	188.9	194.3	162.8	151.7	144.7	134.9	134.0	128.2	136.2	134.7	131.6	125.3
Switzerland	289.2	254.5	244.5	213.1	196.7	196.1	172.6	161.9	161.8	154.2	153.2	137.5	127.2
Turkey	2181.9	2293.3	2004.5	1775.4	1514.7	1441.2	886.6	770.8	680.5	596.4	469.4	391.0	391.0
United Kingdom	211.4	189.0	172.3	153.5	147.0	148.5	140.6	137.1	125.5	121.9	119.2	117.1	113.4
United States	223.1	229.4	197.5	214.7	217.3	206.1	202.2	201.0	196.1	191.5	187.5	181.3	184.0

StatLink: http://dx.doi.org/10.1787/371007666534

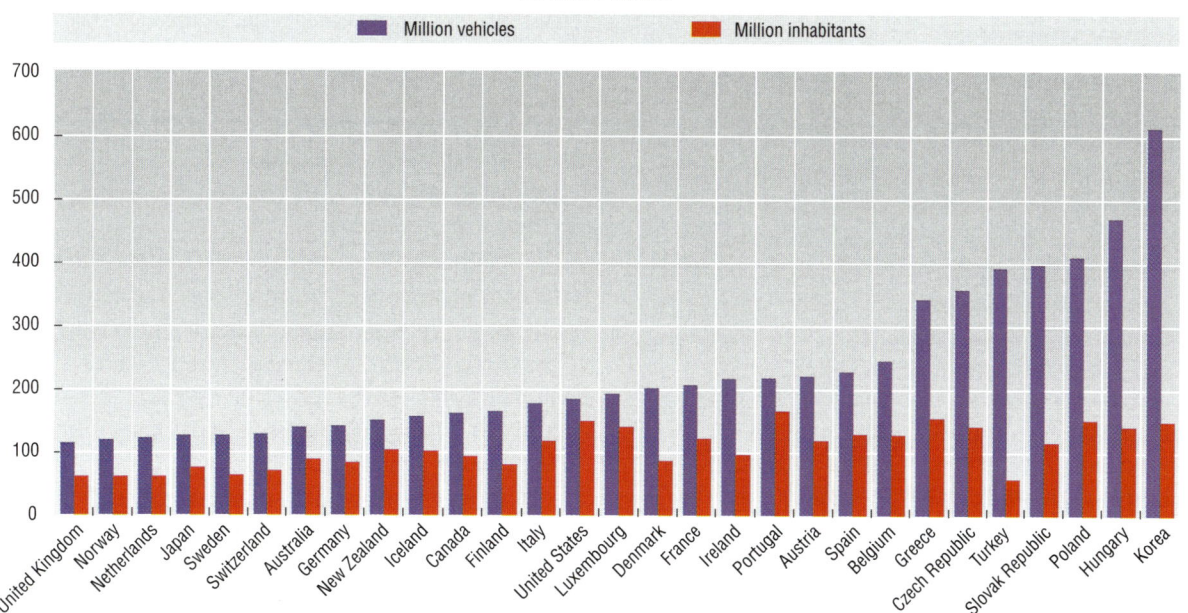

Road fatalities
Per million vehicles

StatLink: http://dx.doi.org/10.1787/525680333275

QUALITY OF LIFE • TRANSPORT

PASSENGER TRANSPORT BY ROAD AND RAIL

Over the past 50 years transport has seen phenomenal progress and change. Access opportunities and mobility have grown dramatically, supported by large investments and heavy spending from both the public and private sectors. Transport has facilitated globalisation of trade and contributed to conquering distance. It is, in general, faster, safer, cleaner and cheaper than it has ever been.

Definition
The table on passenger land transport presented here includes transport by rail, in private cars as well as in buses and coaches.

The data are presented in passenger-kilometres which is the total number of kilometers travelled by all passengers.

Comparability
The chart shows total passenger land transport by rail and road for ECMT member countries which are also members of OECD. Breaks occur in some series, notably for France.

Long-term trends
The number of passenger-kilometres travelled on the rail networks of Western Europe in 2003 shows an increase of over 50% since 1970. Since 1990, traffic has decreased three times, in 1993, 2002 and 2003. Passenger transport by bus and coach increased by over 56% from 1970 to 2003 and was able, in 2000, 2001, 2002 and 2003, to make up the decline in activity seen in 1999. As a result, 2003 was a record year, in contrast to rail passenger transport. Travel by private car in passenger-kilometres appears to have risen dramatically since 1970, increasing in overall volume by a factor of almost 2.6, despite the slight fall recorded for 2000. In contrast, growth was significant in all three of the following years, with practically 1.5% in 2003, on the heels of a 2.3% rise in 2002.

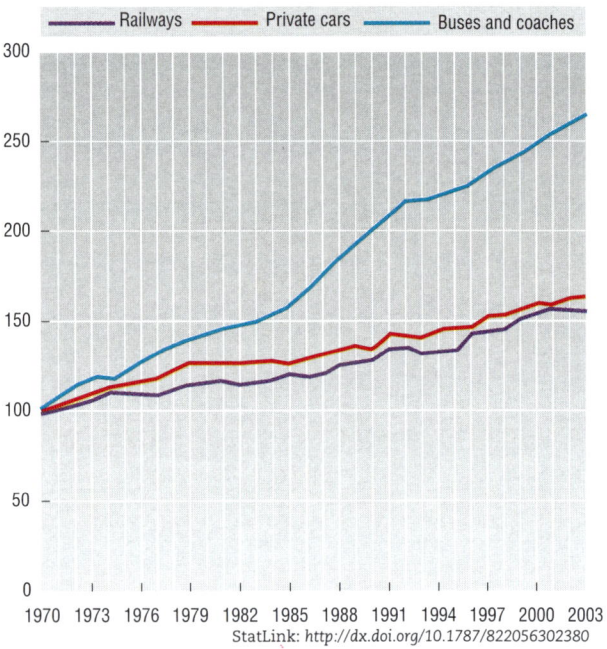

Passenger transport in Western Europe
Passenger-kilometres, year 1970 = 100

StatLink: http://dx.doi.org/10.1787/822056302380

Source
ECMT (2004), *Trends in the Transport Sector: 1970-2002*, ECMT, Paris.

Further information
• *Analytical publications*

ECMT (2002), *Crime in Road Freight Transport*, ECMT, Paris.

ECMT (2003), *Fifty Years of Transport Policy: Successes, Failures and New Challenges*, ECMT, Paris.

ECMT (2004), *Assessment and Decision Making for Sustainable Transport*, ECMT, Paris.

ECMT (2004), *Biofuels for Transport: An International Perspective*, ECMT, Paris.

ECMT (2004), *ECMT Annual Report 2003*, ECMT, Paris.

ECMT (2004), *Reforming Transport Taxes*, ECMT, Paris.

ECMT and UITP (International Association of Public Transport) (eds.) (2004), *Improving Access to Public Transport*, ECMT, Paris.

OECD (2003), *Delivering the Goods: 21st Century Challenges to Urban Goods Transport*, OECD, Paris.

OECD (2004), *Communicating Environmentally Sustainable Transport: The Role of Soft Measures*, OECD, Paris.

• *Web sites*

European Conference of Ministers of Transport: *www.oecd.org/cem*.

SPECIAL FOCUS

In close co-operation with the International Energy Agency

ENERGY

WORLD ENERGY SUPPLY
REGIONAL ENERGY SUPPLY
REGIONAL OIL PRODUCTION
REGIONAL NATURAL GAS PRODUCTION
REGIONAL HARD COAL PRODUCTION
RENEWABLES SUPPLY
WORLD ELECTRICITY GENERATION
FINAL CONSUMPTION BY SECTOR
SELECTED WORLD ENERGY INDICATORS
CRUDE OIL PRICES
IEA GOVERNMENT BUDGETS FOR ENERGY R&D
WORLD ENERGY PRODUCTION AND CONSUMPTION
WORLD PRIMARY ENERGY DEMAND OUTLOOK
REGIONAL PRIMARY DEMAND OUTLOOK
GLOBAL OIL IMPORT DEPENDENCY
CO_2 EMISSIONS OUTLOOK

WORLD ENERGY SUPPLY

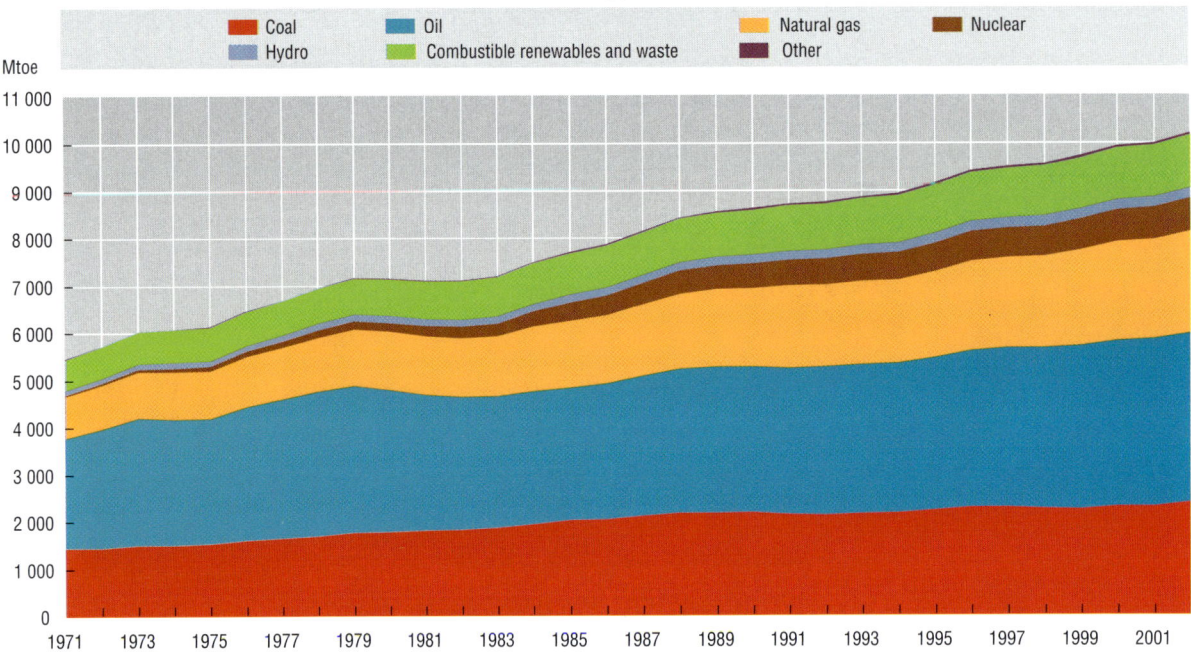

Note: Excludes international marine bunkers and electricity trade.

StatLink: http://dx.doi.org/10.1787/508217245068

- Over the 31-year period of 1971 to 2002, the world's total primary energy supply increased by 87%, reaching 10 230 Mtoe (million tonnes of oil equivalent). This equates to a compound growth rate of about 2.0% per annum. By comparison, world population grew by 1.6% and Gross Domestic Product by 2.9% over the same period.

- Energy supply growth was fairly constant over the period, except in 1974-1975 and in the early 1980s as a consequence of the first two oil shocks, and in the early 1990s following the dissolution of the Soviet Union.

- In 1971, oil was by far the largest component in total primary energy supply, with 42.8%. This share has fallen to only 34.9% in 2002.

- The share of coal dropped slightly, from around 26.4% to 23.5% in 2002. The share of combustible renewables and waste – mainly wood and charcoal, often referred to as traditional biomass, used for cooking in developing countries – has remained stable over the past 31 years, at around 11%.

- Natural gas and nuclear have experienced a significant increase from 16.4% and 0.5% respectively in 1971 to 21.2% and 6.8% in 2002.

Sources

IEA (2004), *Energy Balances of Non-OECD Countries*, IEA, Paris.

IEA (2004), *Energy Balances of OECD Countries*, IEA, Paris.

ENERGY

REGIONAL ENERGY SUPPLY

Regional energy supply
As a percentage of total supply

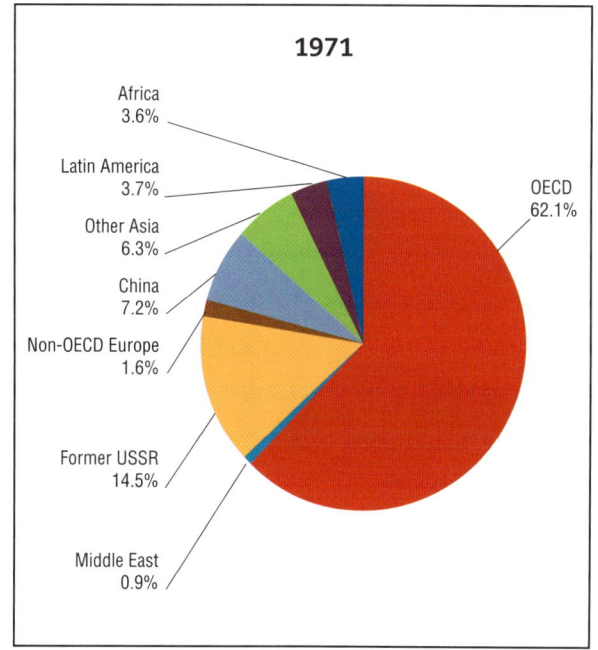
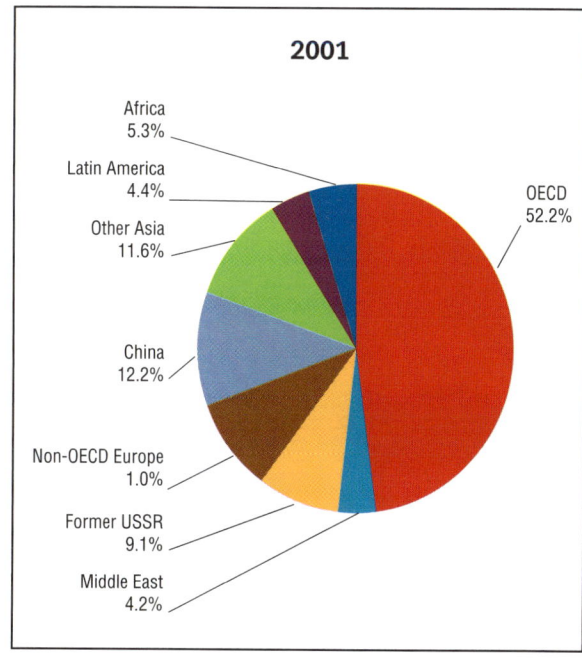

StatLink: http://dx.doi.org/10.1787/043821282610

- Although the OECD is still the largest energy user, its share of total primary energy supply declined significantly from 62.1% in 1971 to 52.2% in 2002.

- In absolute values, total primary energy supply in the OECD increased from 3 391 Mtoe in 1971 to 5 344 Mtoe in 2002. This corresponds to an annual growth rate of 1.5%, compared with a global rate of 2.0% for the same period.

- Strong economic development in Asia led to a large increase in the share of Asia (including China) in world energy supply, from 13.5% in 1971 to 23.8% in 2002.

- By contrast, the combined share of the former USSR and non-OECD Europe decreased significantly following the dissolution of the Soviet Union in the late 1980s.

Sources

IEA (2004), *Energy Balances of Non-OECD Countries*, IEA, Paris.

IEA (2004), *Energy Balances of OECD Countries*, IEA, Paris.

IEA (2004), *Energy Statistics of Non-OECD Countries*, IEA, Paris.

REGIONAL OIL PRODUCTION

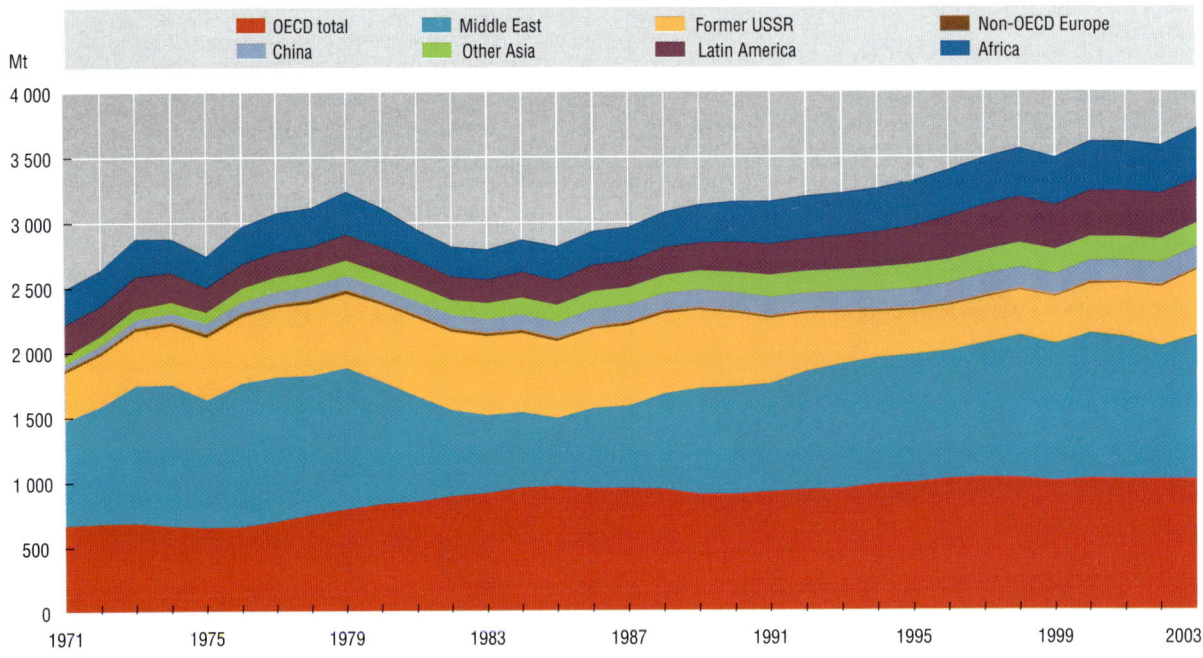

- World oil production increased by 49% over the 32-year period from 1971 to 2003. In 2003, the production reached 3 712 million tonnes or about 74 million barrels per day.

- Growth was not constant over the period as production declined in the aftermath of two oil shocks.

- In 2003, the Middle East region's share of supply was 29.7% of the world total. However, both production and share varied significantly over the period, with the Middle East representing 32.5% in 1971 falling to less than 19% in 1985.

- The OECD share increased from 26.6% in 1971 to 27.1% in 2003, on par with the Middle East as the largest oil-producing regions in the world. The development of oil production in both the North Sea and Mexico contributed to this increase.

- Meanwhile the share of the former Soviet Union fell from 15.2% in 1971 to 13.8% in 2003.

Source
IEA (2004), *Oil Information*, IEA, Paris.

ENERGY

REGIONAL NATURAL GAS PRODUCTION

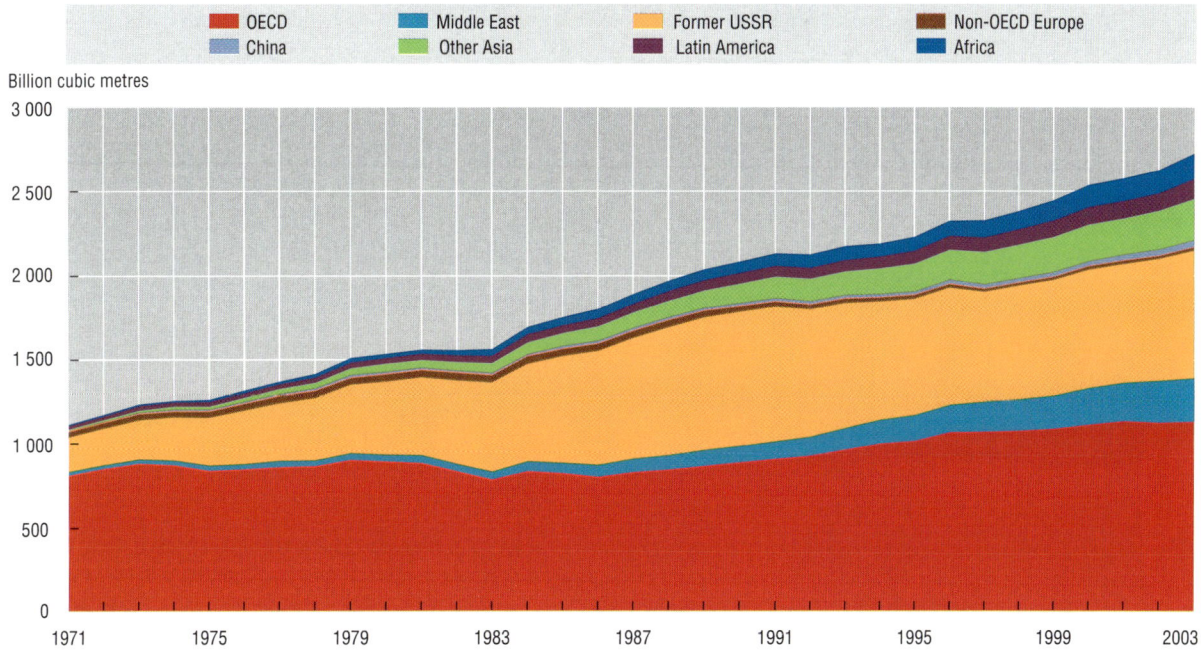

- World natural gas production in the 32 years from 1971 to 2003 increased at an annual average of 2.8%. In 2003, global production exceeded 2 700 billion cubic meters (BCM), representing an increase of 145% over the 1971 level.

- While OECD production over the period has risen in absolute terms, it's share of world production has decreased from nearly 73% in 1971 to just over 41% in 2003.

- The former USSR and non-OECD-Europe have provided the second largest share of global natural gas production over the entire period, accounting for 22% in the early 1970s and for 29% in 2003.

- The main increase in the use of natural gas has been for power generation, which with an average annual increase of 4.3% more than tripled over the period.

Source

IEA (2004), *Natural Gas Information*, IEA, Paris.

ENERGY

REGIONAL HARD COAL PRODUCTION

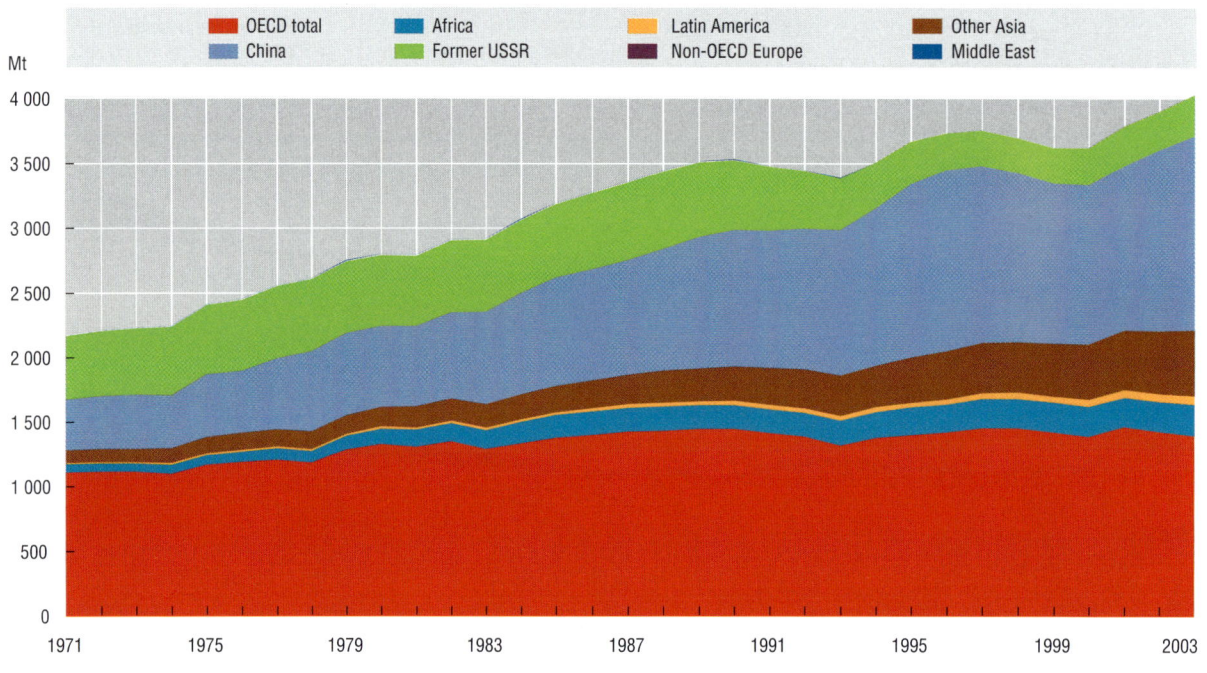

- World hard coal production increased annually by 2.0% over the 32-year period to 2003, and reached over 4.0 billion tonnes in 2003.

- The most dramatic driver of hard coal production in the past decade has been the restructuring and subsequent expansion of China's coal production.

- Rapid growth in Asia has been largely due to increased production in India for power generation and in Indonesia for export.

- Coal production in former USSR countries stabilized in early 2000, after declining throughout the 1980s and 1990s, and is now increasing.

- While OECD production over the past 32 years has risen in absolute terms, its share of world production has decreased from 51% in 1971 to 35% in 2003.

Source
IEA (2004), *Coal Information*, IEA, Paris.

ENERGY

RENEWABLES SUPPLY

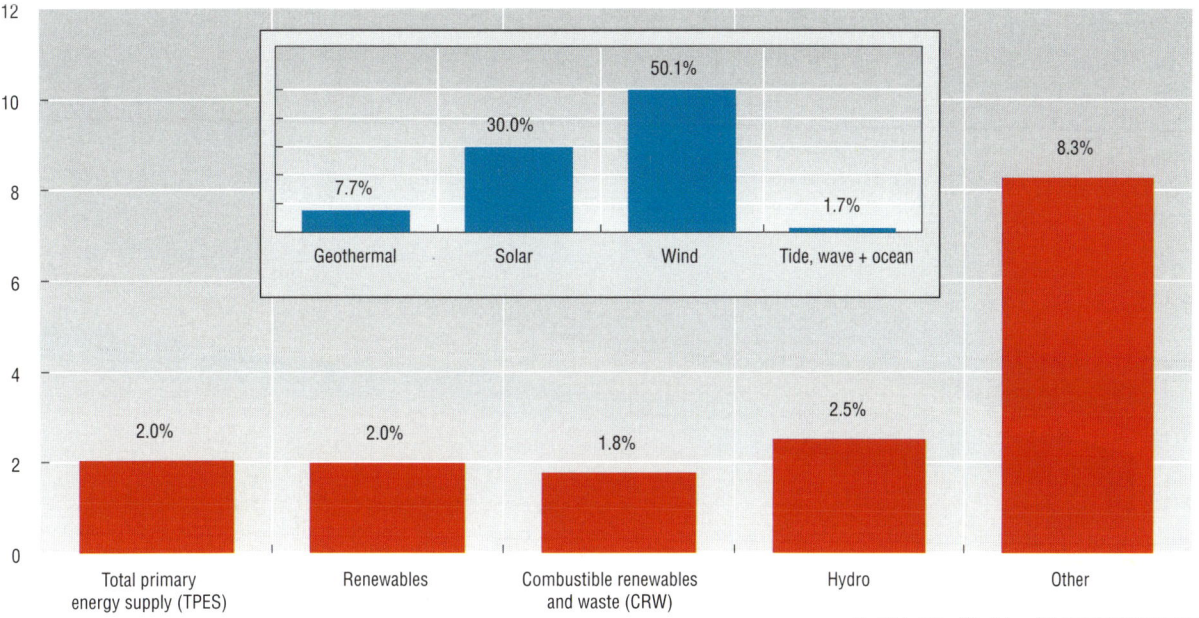

Annual growth of renewables supply
Annual average growth in percentage, 1971-2002

StatLink: http://dx.doi.org/10.1787/848241336587

- Total renewables supply experienced annual growth of 2.0% from 1971 to 2002, almost identical to the annual growth in TPES. However, the "other" category comprising geothermal, solar, wind and tide recorded a much higher annual growth of over 8%.

- The supply of combustible renewables is concentrated in non-OECD countries where extensive use of wood and other biomass for cooking, heating and small industry is common.

- Due to a very low 1971 base and to recent rapid development, wind energy generation experienced the highest increase, over 50% per year followed by solar at over 30%.

- The most rapid growth of non-combustible "Other" renewables like solar and wind energy has occurred in OECD member countries where government policies have stimulated expansion of these energy sources.

Source
IEA (2004), *Renewables Information*, IEA, Paris.

ENERGY

WORLD ELECTRICITY GENERATION

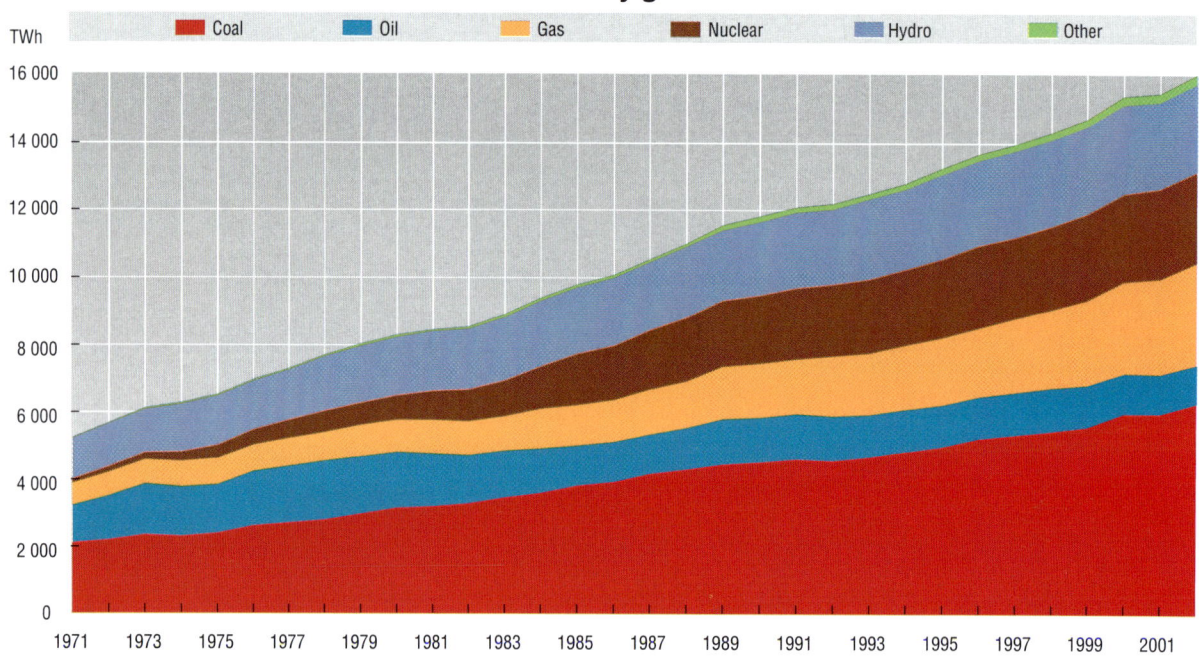

Note: Hydro-electricity excludes pumped storage.

StatLink: http://dx.doi.org/10.1787/650728222565

- World electricity generation rose at an average annual rate of 3.7% from 1971 to 2002, greater than the 2.0% growth in total primary energy supply. This increase was largely due to more electrical appliances, development of electrical heating in several developed countries and rural electrification programmes in developing countries.

- The share of thermal electricity production has gradually fallen, from just under 75% in 1971 to 65% in 2002. This decrease was due to a progressive move away from oil, which fell from 20.9% to 7.2%.

- Oil for power generation has been displaced in particular by dramatic growth in nuclear electricity generation, which rose from 2.1% in 1971 to 16.6% in 2002.

- The share of coal remained stable, near 38% while that of natural gas increased from 13.3% to 19.1%.

- The share of hydro-electricity decreased from 23.0% to 16.2%. The share of new and renewable energies, such as solar, wind and geothermal, grew but remains limited. In 2002, it accounted for only 1.9% of total electricity production.

Source

IEA (2004), *Electricity Information*, IEA, Paris.

ENERGY

FINAL CONSUMPTION BY SECTOR

Final consumption by sector
As a percentage of total consumption

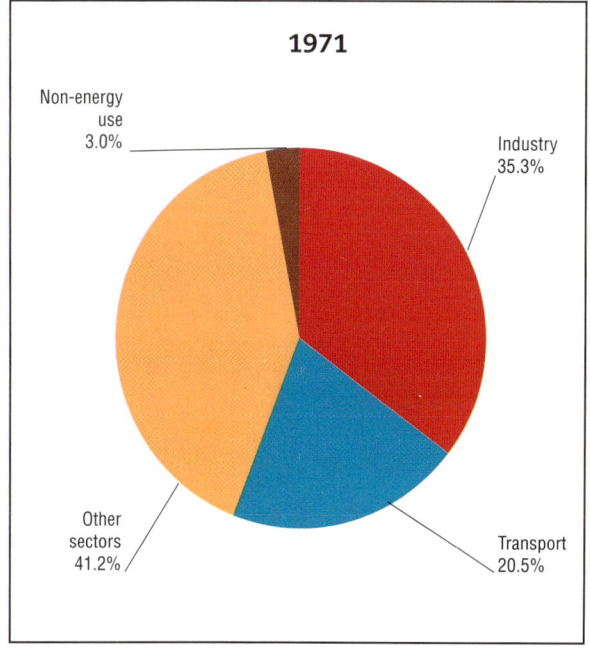

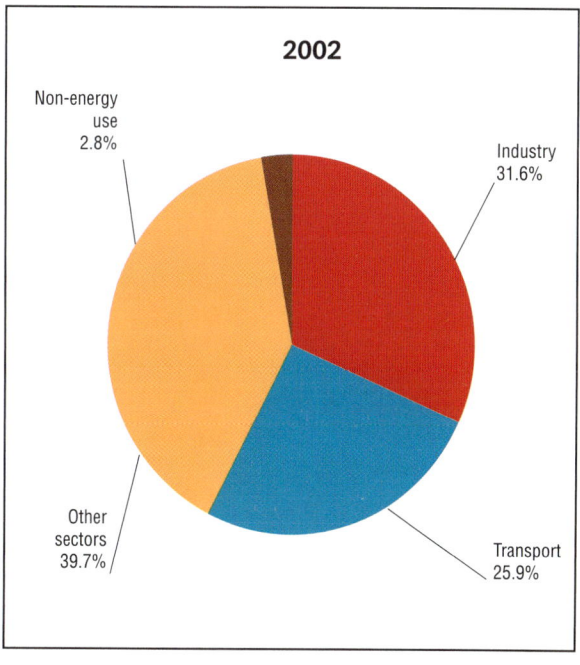

StatLink: http://dx.doi.org/10.1787/757076617162

- The overall breakdown of world total final consumption by sector did not vary greatly over the 31 years.

- Industry remains the main energy user. Its share fell, however, from 35.3% in 1971 to 31.6% in 2002.

- The share of transport rose from 20.5% in 1971 to 25.9% in 2002.

- Other sectors (residential, services and agriculture) represent roughly one-third of total consumption. Services are a growing component, especially in developed countries.

Sources

IEA (2004), *Energy Balances of Non-OECD Countries*, IEA, Paris.

IEA (2004), *Energy Balances of OECD Countries*, IEA, Paris.

SELECTED WORLD ENERGY INDICATORS

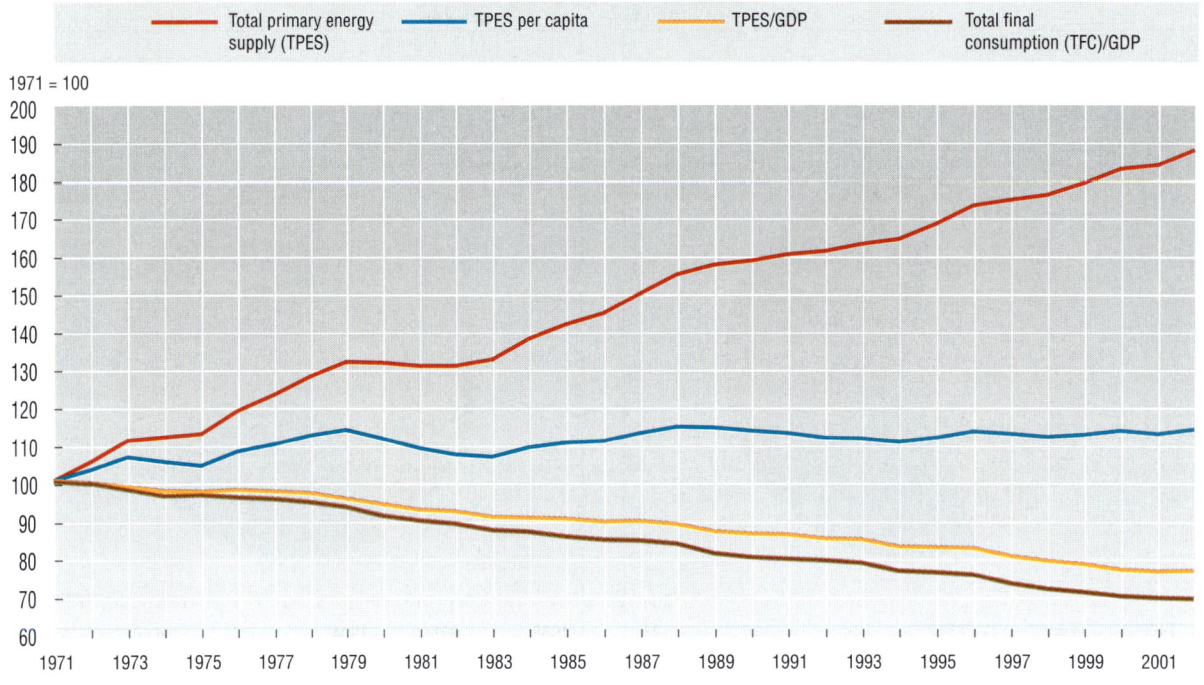

Selected world energy indicators

- World energy demand has continued to increase even while the efficiency of many vehicles and energy-using appliances have improved. Both developed and developing countries are responsible for the growth.

- Improvements in energy efficiency in developed countries over the recent past did not lead to decreases in energy demand, because higher living standards have resulted in higher consumer expectations. For example, vehicle efficiency improved but consumers chose to buy larger cars and drive more.

- In developing countries, rural and urban electrification programmes, together with the development of transport and industrialisation, led to a strong increase in energy demand. The increase in demand was often faster than the growth in population.

- Energy intensities across countries and regions vary dramatically according to factors such as geography and climate, population density and growth, economic situation and growth, the energy mix and the country specific factors.

Sources

IEA (2004), *Energy Balances of Non-OECD Countries*, IEA, Paris.

IEA (2004), *Energy Balances of OECD Countries*, IEA, Paris.

IEA (2004), *Energy Statistics of Non-OECD Countries*, IEA, Paris.

CRUDE OIL PRICES

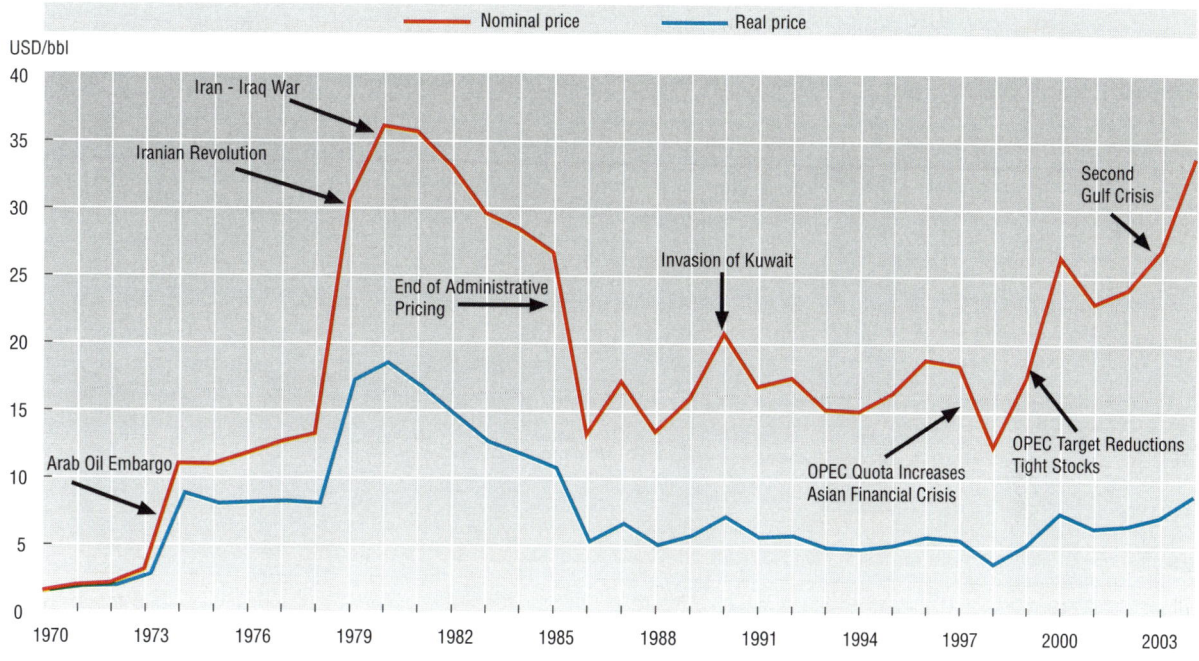

- The 1973 Arab oil embargo had a major price impact as Arabian Light prices surged from $1.84/bbl in 1972 to $10.77 in 1974. The only other experience of this kind of dramatic rise in prices was during the period of the Iranian revolution and the Iran-Iraq conflict.

- The first spike after 1973 came in 1981, in the wake of the Iranian revolution, when prices rose to an all-time high of nearly $40. Prices declined gradually after this crisis. They dropped considerably in 1986 when Saudi Arabia increased its oil production substantially.

- The first Gulf crisis in 1990 brought a new peak. In 1997, crude oil prices started to decline due to the impact of the Asian financial crisis.

- Prices started to increase again in 1999 with OPEC target reductions and tightening stocks. A dip occurred in 2001 and 2002, but the expectation of war in Iraq raised prices to over $30 in the first quarter of 2003. Prices remained high in the latter part of 2003 and in 2004.

- After the 1986 oil price decrease, the real price of crude oil has remained relatively stable.

Source

IEA (2004), *Energy Prices and Taxes*, IEA, Paris.

ENERGY

IEA GOVERNMENT BUDGETS FOR ENERGY R&D

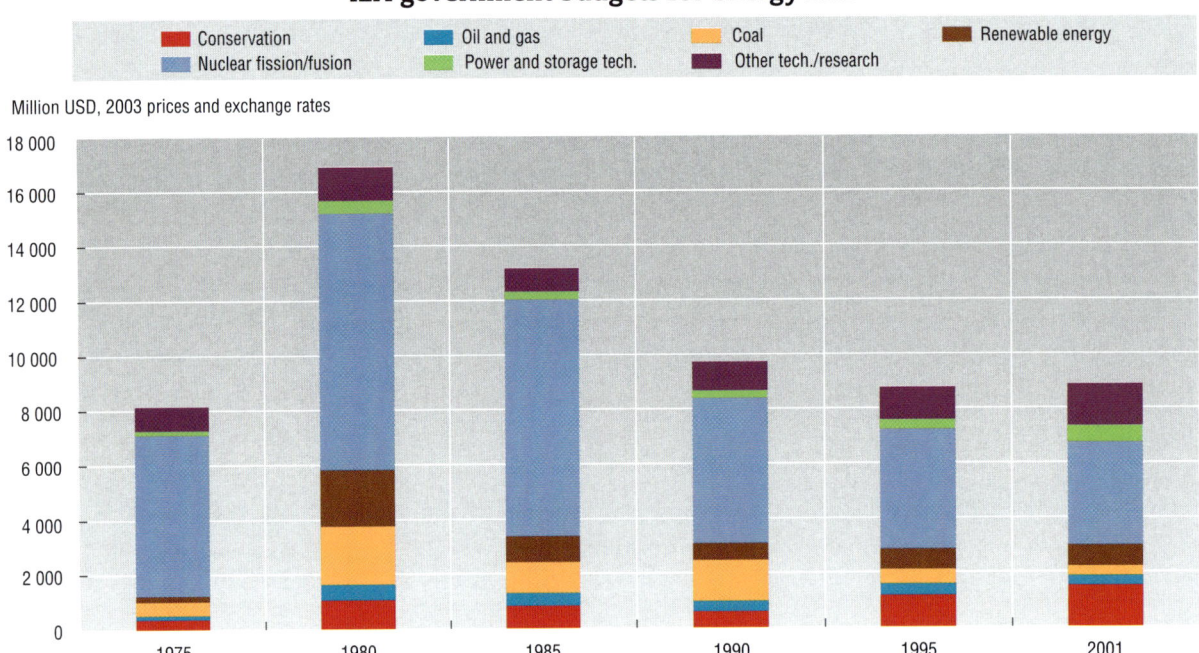

Note: Yearly totals are not always comparable due to unavailability of data for some countries.

StatLink: http://dx.doi.org/10.1787/758686207360

- The curve of IEA R&D budgets follows the general trend of crude oil prices, with a peak in the early 1980s, when the barrel of crude oil was at a high of nearly 40 US dollars, and a constant decline since then.

- In 1980, because of the search for alternatives to oil as a source of energy, R&D budgets reached 16 billion US dollars (2003 prices and exchange rates). By 1985, budgets had decreased 20% and by 1990 another 25%. The decrease continued through 1997. Budgets have been increasing since 1998, and in 2001 were about 10% higher than in 1997.

- Nuclear fission still accounts for the largest proportion of energy R&D expenditure, although its share (with the exception of coal) has declined most since 1985. Currently, about half of total IEA spending on R&D is committed to nuclear fission and fusion.

- Although the share of expenditure on energy conservation has increased over the last 15 years, investments in this area remain limited.

Source
IEA Energy Technology R&D Statistics.

ENERGY

WORLD ENERGY PRODUCTION AND CONSUMPTION

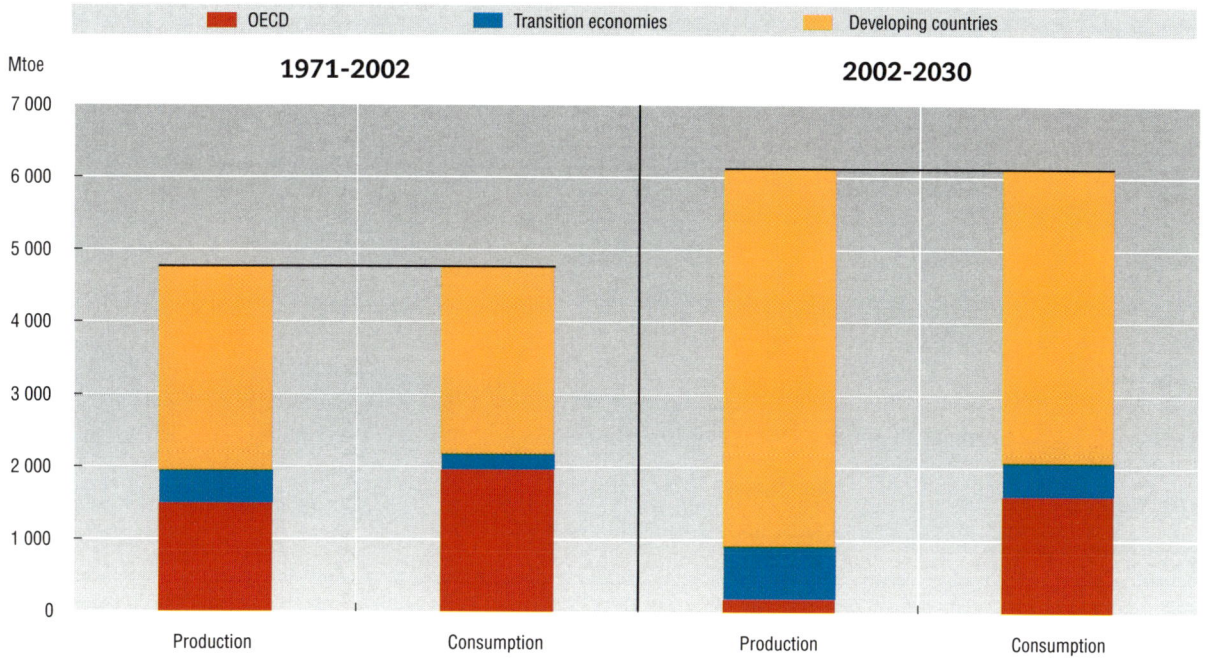

StatLink: http://dx.doi.org/10.1787/254630402252

- Growth in world energy production and consumption in the next three decades is projected expand by almost 60% between 2002 and 2030, reaching 16.5 billion tonnes of oil equivalent.

- There will be a pronounced shift in the geographical sources of incremental energy supplies over the next three decades in response to a combination of cost, geological and technical factors.

- Almost all growth in energy production over the next 30 years will come from non-OECD countries.

- More than 70% of energy demand growth over the next three decades will come from outside the OECD.

Source
IEA (2004), *World Energy Outlook*, IEA, Paris.

WORLD PRIMARY ENERGY DEMAND OUTLOOK

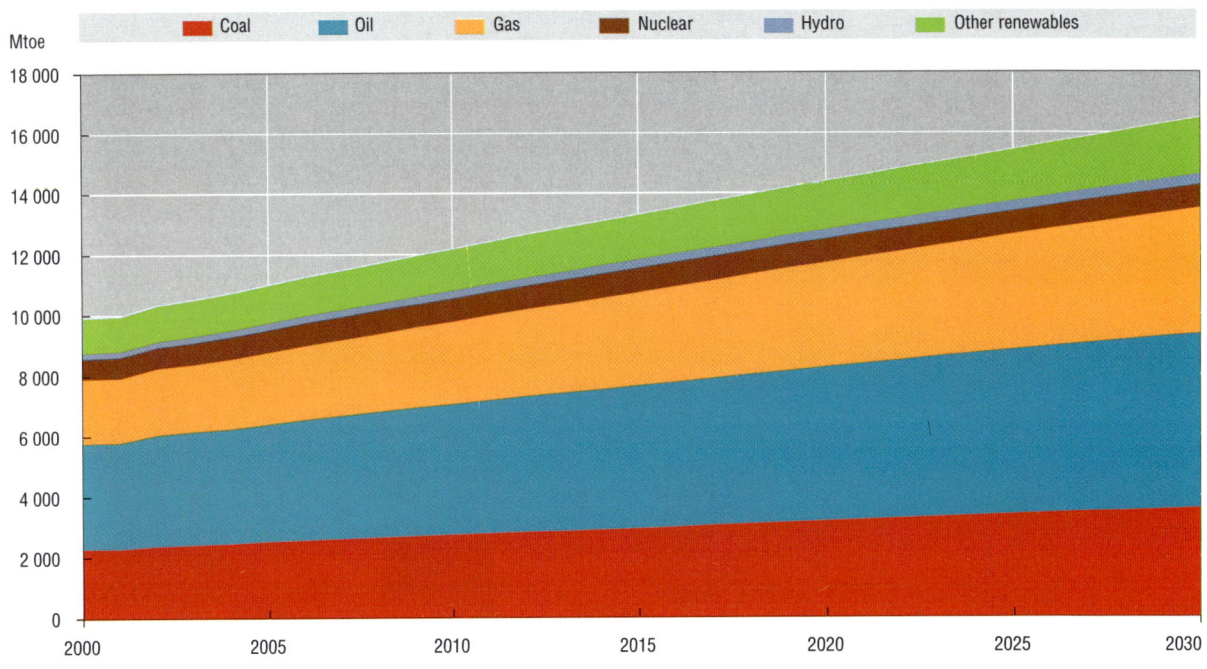

- Without policy changes, world energy demand is projected to increase steadily at 1.7% per year through 2030, less than the 2% annual growth over the past 30 years.

- In that event, fossil fuels will remain the primary sources of energy and will account for around 85% of the increase in demand between 2002 and 2030.

- Among fossil fuels, natural gas will grow fastest, but oil will remain the most important energy source. Oil demand will increase from 77 mb/d in 2002 to 121 mb/d in 2030. Coal, which remains important in power generation because of its low cost, will still account for 22% of TPES.

- Renewables will grow in importance, while the share of nuclear power in world energy supply will drop.

Source

IEA (2004), *World Energy Outlook*, IEA, Paris.

REGIONAL PRIMARY ENERGY DEMAND OUTLOOK

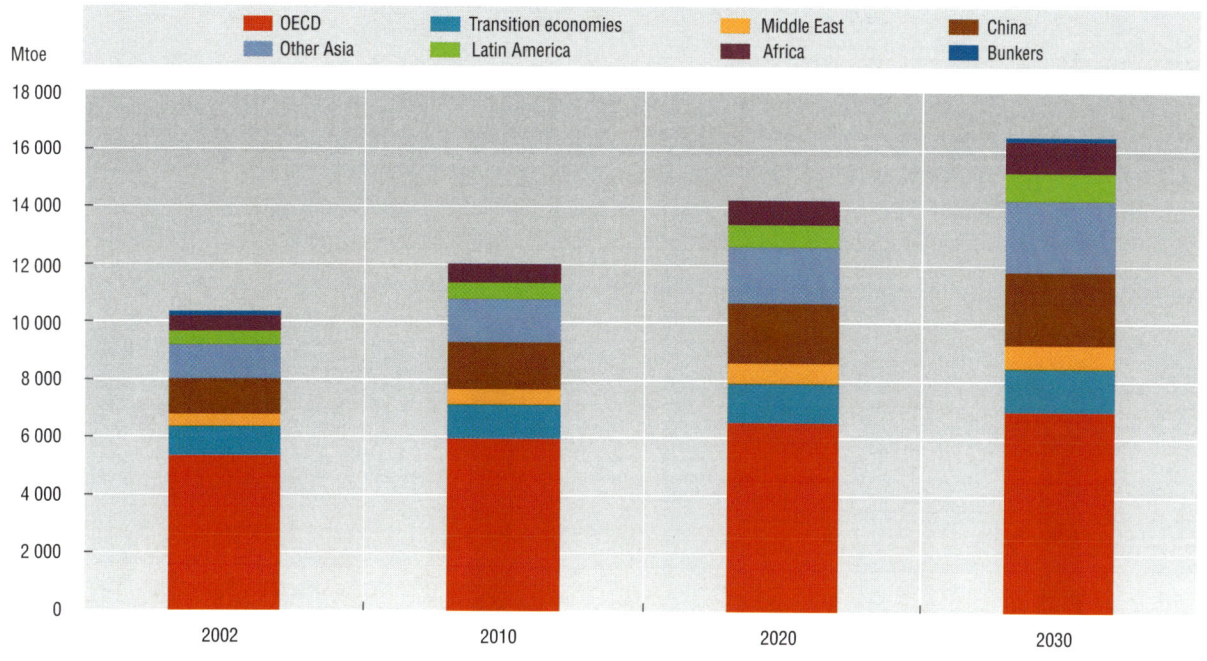

- A structural shift in the shares of different regions in world energy demand is likely to occur between now and 2030 with the OECD share of world energy demand falling from 52% in 2002 to 42% in 2030.

- More than 66% of the increase in world primary energy demand between 2002 and 2030 will come from the developing countries, particularly Asia.

- The increase in demand for China represents about a fifth of the total increase in worldwide demand from 2002 to 2030. As an example, demand for oil in China will be double that of Japan by 2030. The total share of Asia – including China – will amount to 30% in 2030.

- The increase in the share of the developing regions in world energy demand results from their rapid economic and population growth, industrialisation and urbanisation. The replacement of non-commercial biomass by commercial fuels will also help to boost demand.

Source
IEA (2004), *World Energy Outlook*, IEA, Paris.

ENERGY

GLOBAL OIL IMPORT DEPENDENCY

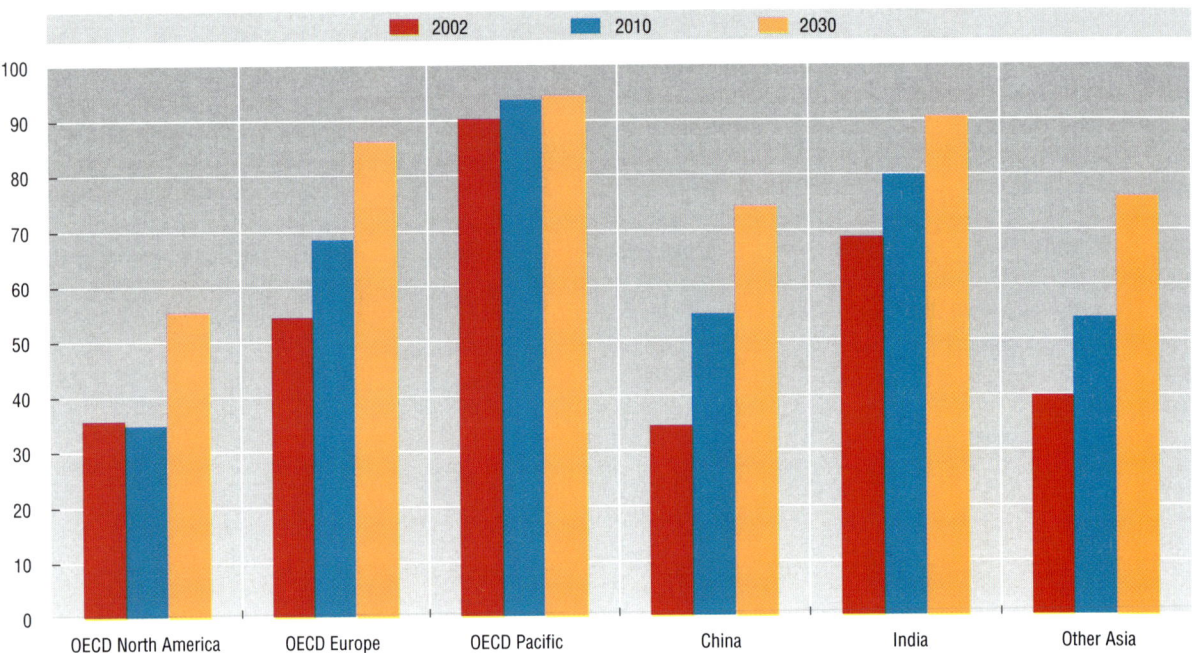

- Developing countries will account for almost two-thirds of the 43-mb/d increase in global oil consumption between 2002 and 2030. Developing Asian countries will contribute 18 mb/d, and China alone will account for nearly half of that.

- Oil import dependence is expected to increase in all major oil consuming regions. OECD increases will come from a combination of oil consumption growth and depletion of indigenous oil reserves in the United Kingdom, Norway and North America.

- Concerning natural gas import dependency, the biggest markets – particularly North America and Europe – will become much more dependent on imports between now and 2030.

- The increase in dependence will be most dramatic in China, which only became a net oil importer in 1993. By 2030 imports will meet 74% of China's oil demand. This is equal to 10 mb/d, the current volume of imports into the United States.

- Oil supply security is becoming an important political issue in Asia. Governments in both India and China have agreed to establish strategic oil reserves.

- OECD's share of global oil demand will decline significantly from 59% in 2002 to 47% in 2030.

Source
IEA (2004), *World Energy Outlook*, IEA, Paris.

ENERGY

CO_2 EMISSIONS OUTLOOK

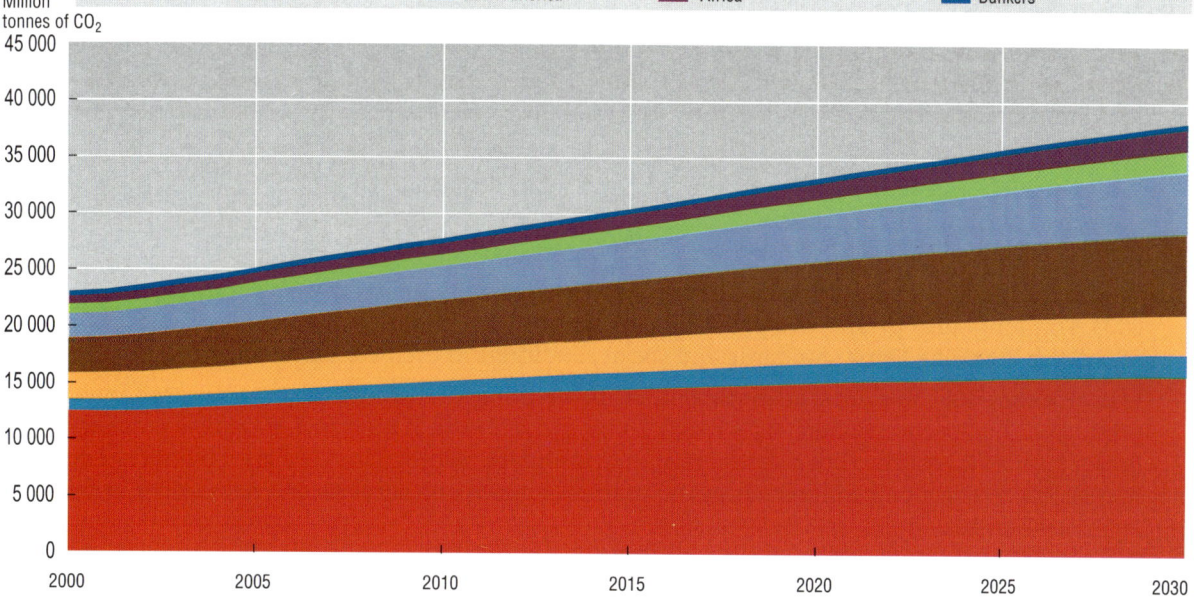

- Projections through the year 2030 show a continuing increase in global carbon dioxide emissions, if no new policies and measures are put in place. Under this scenario, between 2002 and 2030 emissions are projected to grow by 62%, slightly more than the growth of 59% in energy supply. The most rapid increases are seen as occurring in Non-OECD countries, where emissions will more than double over the period.

- The share of OECD emissions in total emissions will decrease from 53% in 2002 to 41% in 2030. Meanwhile China's share alone will increase from 13% to 19%.

- Power generation, which currently accounts for around 40% of the emissions will contribute half the increase (or 7.4 billion tonnes) in global emissions between 2002 and 2030. Transport will account for more than a quarter, residential, commercial and industrial sectors for the rest.

- The average carbon content of energy – CO_2 emissions per unit of aggregate primary energy consumption – will increase over the next 30 years. The main cause of this reversal will be the declining share of nuclear and hydro power in the global energy mix.

Source

IEA (2004), *World Energy Outlook*, IEA, Paris.

READER'S GUIDE

Main Features

Each of the ten themes of the *OECD Factbook* includes several indicators. For every indicator, the tables and graphs are preceded by a short text that explains how the statistics are defined (**Definition**) and identifies the main problems there may be in comparing the performance of one country with another (**Comparability**). It has thus been possible to dispense with footnotes although their absence does not in any way imply that perfect comparability has been achieved. To avoid misunderstandings, the tables must be read in conjunction with the texts that accompany them.

While general and media interest in statistics usually focuses on the short term – what has happened to employment, prices, GDP and so on in the last few months – the *OECD Factbook* takes a longer view.

The text and graphs mostly describe developments during the fourteen-year period from 1990 to 2003. This long-term perspective provides a good basis for comparing the successes and failures of policies in raising living standards and social conditions in their countries.

Many *Factbook* indicators have been standardised by relating them to each country's gross domestic product (GDP). In cases where GDP needs to be converted to a common currency, purchasing power parities (PPPs) have been used rather than exchange rates. When PPPs are used, differences in GDP levels reflect only differences in the volume of goods and services and differences in price levels are eliminated.

StatLinks

This book includes OECD's unique **StatLink** service, which enables you to download Excel™ versions of charts, tables and statistical annexes. Look for the **StatLink** at the foot of each table or chart. A **StatLink** behaves like an Internet address. Simply type the **StatLink** in your Internet browser to obtain the corresponding data in Excel™ format.

For more information about **StatLink**, please visit: *www.oecd.org/statistics/statlink*.

Glossary of Statistical Terms

The online *OECD Glossary of Statistical Terms* (available at *www.oecd.org/statistics/glossary*) is the perfect companion for the *OECD Factbook*. It contains close to 6 000 definitions of terms, acronyms and concepts in an easy to use format. These definitions are primarily drawn from existing international statistical guidelines and recommendations that have been prepared over the last two or three decades by organisations such as the United Nations, ILO, OECD, Eurostat, IMF and national statistical institutes.

Conventions

Unless otherwise specified, **OECD total** includes only those OECD member countries which are shown in the table. Data for the European Union (EU) always refer to the following 15 countries: Austria, Belgium, Denmark, Finland, France, Germany, Greece, Ireland, Italy, Luxembourg, The Netherlands, Portugal, Spain, Sweden and the United Kingdom.

OECD average refers to the unweighted average of the listed OECD member countries.

Period averages only take into account the years for which data are available.

The period covered is specified in each table and chart. The mention, XXXX or latest year available (where XXXX is a year) means that data for later years are not taken into account.

Unless otherwise specified, all values are in current prices and exchange rates.

National currency units for Turkey do not take into account the redenomination of the Turkish Lira on 1 January 2005 as the data cover a time period prior to that date.

Statistics presented in the Factbook have been derived from a wide range of OECD databases and publications. Due to the cut-off date, in some cases the data contained in the Factbook do not benefit from the latest updates. Therefore, some inconsistencies may appear between the data of the Factbook and those contained in other OECD publications and databases, or in national sources.

For OECD publications, the Source indicated in the Factbook is always the most recent one, even though the data can be derived from previous issues of the same publication.

Signs, abbreviations and acronyms

..	Missing value, not applicable or not available	Eurostat	Statistical Office of the European Communities
0	Nil or negligible	ILO	International Labor Organization
|	Break in series	IMF	International Monetary Fund
		UIS	Unesco Institute for Statistics
		UN	United Nations
		UNCTAD	United Nations Conference on Trade and Development
		UNECE	United Nations Economic Commission for Europe
		UNEP	United Nations Environment Programme
		UNODC	United Nations Office on Drugs and Crime
		WB	World Bank
		WHO	World Health Organisation
		WMO	World Meteorological Organisation
		WTO	World Trade Organisation
		WTO-OMT	World Tourism Organisation

Analytical index

A

Actual hours worked, *see*: Hours worked
Ageing societies, 14
Agricultural support estimates, 170
Agriculture, producer support, *see*: Agricultural support estimates
Agriculture, *see*: Agricultural support estimates
Agriculture, *see*: Evolution of GDP
Agriculture, *see*: Nutrient use in agriculture
Agriculture, *see*: Value added by activity
Aid, *see*: Official development assistance
Aquaculture, *see*: Fisheries
Aquaculture, *see*: Government support for fishing
Assistance, development, *see*: Official development assistance

B

Balance of payments, 66
Broadband access, *see*: Computer and Internet access by households

C

Carbon dioxide (CO_2), emission, *see*: Emissions of carbon dioxide (CO_2)
Child mortality, *see*: Infant mortality
Communications, *see*: Investment in ICT
Communications, *see*: Size of the ICT sector
Competiveness, *see*: International competitiveness
Computer and Internet access by households, 128
Consumer price indices (CPI), 76
Consumer price indices (CPI), *see*: International competitiveness
Crime, victims, *see*: Victimisation rates

D

Debt, government, *see*: Government debt
Deficit, government, *see*: Government deficits
Dependency ratio, *see*: Ageing societies
Development assistance, *see*: Official development assistance

E

Education, *see*: Expenditure by level of education
Education, *see*: International student assessment
Education, *see*: Public and private education expenditure
Education, *see*: Tertiary attainment
Education, tertiary, *see*: Tertiary attainment
Electricity generation, 44
Emissions of carbon dioxide (CO_2), 134
Employment rates by age group, 98
Employment rates by gender, 94
Employment rates, *see*: Employment rates by age group
Employment rates, *see*: Employment rates by gender
Energy supply, 42
Energy supply and economic growth, 142
Energy supply per capita, 144
Energy supply, *see*: Energy supply and economic growth
Energy supply, *see*: Energy supply per capita
Energy, *see*: Electricity generation
Energy, *see*: Emissions of carbon dioxide (CO_2)
Energy, *see*: Energy supply
Energy, *see*: Energy supply and economic growth
Energy, *see*: Energy supply per capita
Energy, *see*: Special chapter: energy
Evolution of GDP, 30
Evolution of the population, 10
Evolution of value added by activity, 32
Exchange rates, *see*: Rates of conversion
Expenditure by level of education, 156
Expenditure on R&D, 116
Exports of services, *see*: Trade in services
Exports, *see*: Trade in goods
Exports, *see*: Trade in services
Exports, *see*: Trading partners

F

FDI and employment, 72
FDI flows and stocks, 68
Fertility, *see*: Evolution of the population
Fisheries, 48
Fishing, government transfers, *see*: Government support for fishing
Foreign population, 16
Foreigners, foreign born, *see*: Foreign population

G

GDP, *see*: Evolution of GDP
GDP, *see*: Evolution of value added by activity
GDP, *see*: Regional GDP
GDP, *see*: Size of GDP
GDP, *see*: Value added by activity
Government debt, 164
Government deficits, 162
Government support for fishing, 172
Greenhouse gases, emission, *see*: Emissions of carbon dioxide (CO_2)

H

Health expenditure, 168
Health expenditure, *see*: Public and private health expenditure
High-technology exports, 130
Hours worked, 200
Household saving, 36

I

ICT Sector, *see*: Computer and Internet access by households
ICT Sector, *see*: High-technology exports
ICT Sector, *see*: Investment in ICT
ICT Sector, *see*: Size of the ICT sector
Immigration, *see*: Foreign population
Imports of services, *see*: Trade in services
Imports, *see*: Trade in goods
Imports, *see*: Trade in services
Imports, *see*: Trading partners
Industry, *see*: Evolution of value added by activity
Industry, *see*: Value added by activity
Infant mortality, 194
Information and communications technology, *see*: Computer and Internet access by households
Information and communications technology, *see*: High-technology exports
Information and communications technology, *see*: Investment in ICT
Information and communications technology, *see*: Size of the ICT sector
Interest rates, *see*: Long-term interest rates
International competitiveness, 88
International student assessment, 150
International migration, 18
Internet access, *see*: Computer and Internet access by households
Investment in ICT, 126
Investment in knowledge, 118
Investment, foreign, *see*: FDI and employment
Investment, foreign, *see*: FDI flows and stocks
Investment, foreign, *see*: Investment in ICT

K

Knowledge, *see*: Investment in knowledge

L

Labour costs, *see*: International competitiveness
Labour productivity, 38
Life expectancy, 190
Literacy, *see*: International student assessment
Long-term interest rates, 82
Long-term unemployment, 112

M

Mortality, *see*: Infant mortality
Multi-factor productivity, 40
Municipal waste, 138

N

Nutrient use in agriculture, 140

O

Obesity, 196
Official development assistance, 174

P

Part-time employment, 102
Passenger transport by road and rail, 212
Patents, 122
PISA, *see*: International student assessment
Population, *see*: Ageing societies
Population, *see*: Evolution of the population
Population, *see*: Foreign population
Population, *see*: International migration
PPP, *see*: Rates of conversion
Price indices, *see*: Consumer price indices (CPI)
Price indices, *see*: International competitiveness
Price indices, *see*: Producer price indices (PPI)
Prices, *see*: Consumer price indices (CPI)
Prices, *see*: International competitiveness
Prices, *see*: Producer price indices (PPI)
Prison population, 204
Producer price indices (PPI), 80
Productivity, *see*: Labour productivity
Productivity, *see*: Multi-factor productivity
Public and private education expenditure, 158
Public and private health expenditure, 198

R

R&D, *see*: Expenditure on R&D
R&D, *see*: Investment in knowledge
R&D, *see*: Patents
R&D, *see*: Researchers
Rates of conversion, 84
Regional GDP, 184
Regional unemployment, 186
Renewable energy, 146
Renewables, *see*: Renewable energy
Renewables, *see*: Special chapter: energy
Researchers, 120
Road motor vehicles and road fatalities, 208

S

Savings, *see*: Government debt
Savings, *see*: Household saving
Science scores, *see*: International student assessment
Self-employment, 104
Services, exports of, *see*: Trade in services
Services, imports of, *see*: Trade in services
Services, *see*: Trade in services
Services, trade balance, *see*: Trade in services
Services, trade, *see*: Trade in services
Share of trade in GDP, 52
Size of GDP, 22
Size of the ICT sector, 124
Social expenditure, 166
Special chapter, 213
Standardised unemployment rates, 108
Steel production, 46

T

Taxes on the average production worker, 182
Tertiary attainment, 152
Total tax revenue, 178
Tourism: hotel nights, 202
Tourists, *see*: Tourism: hotel nights
Trade in goods, 54
Trade in services, 58
Trade, *see*: Trade in goods
Trade, *see*: Trade in services
Trade, *see*: Trading partners
Trading partners, 62

U

Unemployment, *see*: Long-term unemployment
Unemployment, *see*: Regional unemployment
Unemployment, *see*: Standardised unemployment rates
Unit labour costs, *see*: International competitiveness

V

Value added by activity, 26
Value added, *see*: Evolution of value added by activity
Value added, *see*: Value added by activity
Victimisation rates, 206

W

Waste, *see*: Municipal waste
Water consumption, 136

OECD PUBLICATIONS, 2, rue André-Pascal, 75775 PARIS CEDEX 16
PRINTED IN FRANCE
(30 2005 04 1 P) – No. 53837